Myth and the American Experience

Volume One

THIRD EDITION

Edited and with an Introduction by
Nicholas Cords and Patrick Gerster

Lakewood Community College

HarperCollins*Publishers*

Sponsoring Editor: Lauren Silverman/Bruce Borland
Project Editor: Susan Goldfarb
Art Direction: Lucy Krikorian
Text Design Adaptation and Cover Design: Graphnick
Cover Coordinator: Lucy Krikorian
Photo Research: Mira Schachne/Liza Caldwell
Production: Willie Lane/Sunaina Sehwani
Compositor: David Seham Associates
Printer and Binder: R. R. Donnelley & Sons Company
Cover Printer: Lynn Art Offset Corporation

Myth and the American Experience (Volume One), Third Edition

Copyright © 1991 by Nicholas Cords and Patrick Gerster

Library of Congress Cataloging-in-Publication Data

Myth and the American experience / edited and with an introduction by
   Nicholas Cords and Patrick Gerster.—3rd ed.
      p. cm.
   ISBN 0-06-041379-4 (v. 1). —ISBN 0-06-041380-8 (v. 2)
      1. United States—History. 2. United States—Historiography.
   I. Cords, Nicholas. II. Gerster, Patrick.
   E178.6.M94   1991   90-5004
   973—dc20   CIP

90   91   92   93   9 8 7 6 5 4 3 2 1

To
Maggie and Carole

Mundus vult decipi
[The world wants to be deceived.]

All America lies at the end of the wilderness road,
and our past is not a dead past, but still lives in
us. Our forefathers had civilization inside them,
the wild outside. We live in the civilization they
created, but within us the wilderness still lingers.
What they dreamed, we live, and what they lived,
we dream.

T. K. Whipple, *Study Out the Land*

Contents

Preface

The enthusiastic response to previous editions of *Myth and the American Experience* has made this new edition possible. In receiving both words of praise and suggestions for improvement from users of earlier editions, our conviction about the viability of a mythic perspective on American history has, if anything, become more firm. The mythological approach to American history continues to be both relevant and exciting. It most assuredly has come of age, or at least it has assumed its proper place alongside more traditional contemporary perspectives on the American past.

Since the publication of the first edition of *Myth and the American Experience*, we have had occasion to comment further—in classroom lectures, during the presentation of professional papers, and with the publication of articles, books, and reviews—on the elusive relationship between myth and American history. Those experiences have led us to an even deeper awareness of myth's reality. We continue to see myth and reality as complementary elements of the historical record.

The selected historical myths discussed and analyzed in this work can best be understood as a series of *false beliefs* about America's past. They are false beliefs, however, which have been accepted as true and acted upon as real. Thus, one comes to see that myths remain both true and false simultaneously. They are false in the sense that they often enjoy only a remote relationship to what most informed historians consider to have actually happened; they are true in the sense that people believe them and that they form bases for action. It is well to remember that there is a point at which myth and reality intersect; at that given point, they become one and the same. A myth becomes reality precisely when people base their beliefs upon it and act as if the myth were true. In fact, the making of myths is a twofold process by which a culture structures its world and by which it perpetuates its grandest dreams.

The idea for *Myth and the American Experience* grew out of our own teaching experiences. In continually dealing with students who for the most part were beginning their collegiate study of American history, we found that a thematic approach to the nation's past was useful, even stimulating, for those intent on understanding the past of which they were a continuing part. More specifically, the theme of "myth"—a thread by which to trace the diverse tapestry of our cultural experience—proved to be especially engaging.

In creating a third edition of *Myth and the American Experience*, we are necessarily reminded of the history of the book itself—for without its own successful history, this new edition would never have come to pass. We have sought to retain the vitality and integrity of earlier editions, while remaining sensitive to recent scholarly trends. More specifically, while offering an especially strong foundation of "classic" historical writing and interpretation, we have sought to better reflect those habitually underrepresented, both in American society and in history texts. Thus, we have included several new selections on Indians and women; new material on the Great Awakening, the Chicano experience, and the social realities of the Jacksonian era; new studies of Andrew Jackson, Abraham Lincoln, Reconstruction, and the two Roosevelts; and fresh perspectives on such topics as workers, Victorian sexuality, the melting pot, Japanese Americans, John F. Kennedy, and the very nature of myth itself. We have found good reason to retain the basic organization of the previous edition and have been guided in our final selections by a desire to offer articles that voice our mythic theme in a scholarly way: articles that offer students readability and current interest without sacrificing the demands of thorough historical scholarship. Our emphasis on historiography remains, for historians continue to maintain their seemingly contradictory roles as mythmakers and, at the same time, myth-debunkers.

As the historical past itself is a collaborative enterprise, so too is this book. While we claim the mythic theme applied across the entire landscape of American history to be uniquely ours, we gratefully acknowledge those whose efforts came in various ways to be reflected in the final product. Our greatest thanks must be extended to our professional colleagues; the results of their many years of scholarly effort comprise the very heart of this work. Without their intellectual skills and narrative talents, this book would not have been possible. Students have helped us both to hone our ideas and to gauge better the critical reception of individual selections. Our families have granted us both support and a sounding board for the joys and problems that cumulatively accrue to such a project. The reviewers of this edition—Carol Jensen, University of Wisconsin at La Crosse; Charles Wilson, University of Mississippi; Tom Jones, Metropolitan State University; Bruce Dierenfield, Canisius College; and Marlette Rebhorn, Austin Community College—by their constructive criticism, also have made this a better project. The publishing support system of HarperCollins was most helpful in bringing our ideas from mind to printed page. Lauren Silverman, our original sponsoring editor, in particular showed early enthusiasm and added consistent strategic support to our efforts. Bruce Borland, sponsoring editor, and Susan Goldfarb, project editor, guided the work through its editorial journey. To all of these we offer thanks.

NICHOLAS CORDS
PATRICK GERSTER

Introduction: Myth and History

"Human Being is a featherless, storytelling animal. . . ." We tell stories—myths—about who we are, where we come from, where we are going and how we should live. And the myths we tell become who we are and what we believe—as individuals, families, whole cultures.[1]

The appearance of this third edition of *Myth and the American Experience* strongly suggests that many readers of our earlier editions have found myth an especially useful perspective from which to view the nation's past. In the interest of making this mythic perspective more explicit, we address these questions: What is myth? What is myth's relationship to history? Why study American history in terms of myth? And how does this third edition aid in answering these questions?

Myth and history always have enjoyed a close relationship. In preliterate societies, a sense of origins and traditions was preserved in cultural memory through stories told by elders whose task it was to be custodians of the past and the past's interpreters to the present. In ancient societies, myths were thus the "storied" explanations in both oral and, later, written form of the past order of things and how the culture had come through time to its current circumstance. While not always—or even often—completely "true" renditions of the culture's past, myths' power lay more with their capacity to provide a sense of cultural continuity. In brief, myths always have been the traditional stories a culture tells itself about itself.

Today the fashion regarding myth is to associate it with the ancient world—as Greek myths, for example, told fantastic tales of gods and heroes and collective cultural accomplishments. Also dating to classical times is the common historic usage of *myth* as a pejorative term, a synonym for "lie," "fabrication," or "false belief." Plato often emphasized this highly negative view towards myths, declaring them to be little more than silly beliefs on false parade. Aristotle, on the other hand, thought of myths as more serious—even useful—as a treasury of cultural stories about the past that provide meaning for the present. Myths function, he concluded, as a kind of cultural glue that holds a people together—however great their diversity. Aristotle's view was that a mythic tale may well be factually suspect even as it conveys the under-

1

lying realities of the culture. A myth could then be factually false and psychologically true simultaneously. Those who associate myth with falsehood wish
to invalidate it historically; but as Aristotle and others began to recognize,
such attacks are powerless against myth's psychological potency within the
context of the culture that chooses to believe it. Since Greek times, then, the
understanding and use of myth have been ambivalent—implying both falsehood and truth. To the degree that a uniform opinion had formed in the Greek
world regarding myth, it was simply that myth was a traditional story—perhaps false, perhaps true.

Throughout subsequent history, the view continued to be voiced that
myth was a mutation of historical fact, and thus more false than true. Just
as creditable over time, however, has been the view that myth is allegorical,
discussing cultural values under other images containing a special brand of
truth. Thus, as with so many other features of Western culture, the shaping of
opinion and attitude about myths bears a distinct Hellenic imprint. Armed
with these countervailing approaches to myth begun by the Greeks, the West
has since sat Janus-faced, viewing myth as both negative and positive, as both
profane and sacred.

So it has been, too, that a dialectical use of the term *myth* in American
historical studies mirrors this ambivalence with which Western culture has
long contended. Reflecting this tradition, the term *myth*, as presented in this
set of readings, is utilized in two ways. In many instances the material, at least
implicitly, reflects what one might call a Platonic tradition. This tradition has
been rearticulated by the American historian Thomas A. Bailey, who over two
decades ago wrote, "A historical myth is . . . an account or belief which is
demonstrably untrue in whole or substantial part."[2] Historians reflecting this
definition choose to emphasize the negative aspects of myth, to isolate and
debunk what they regard as erroneous belief and misguided scholarship. The
goal of historical study, as those of the Plato/Bailey tradition would have it,
lies especially with recording history "as it actually happened." The historian,
they insist, must stand as a transparent witness to the occurrences of the past.
The truth, if diligently sought and recorded, will out.

Other American historians, however, deal with myth in a way fundamentally sympathetic to Aristotelian thinking, as did Henry Nash Smith in his
famous study *Virgin Land: The American West as Symbol and Myth*. For
Smith, a cultural or social myth, even while often factually false, needs to
be sympathetically reckoned with, in that it contains an internal treasure—a
culture's ideological foundations. Thus are myths useful fictions for a culture.
When sensitively deconstructed, they can be shown to embody American culture's basic beliefs and highest aspirations—honesty, unpretentiousness, optimism, tolerance, hard work, sympathy for the underdog, dedication to God
and country, an abiding concern for all, and a special esteem for freedom.
Myths are especially powerful, rich, and revealing for students and scholars to
study because they are inspiring tales ripe with culturally received wisdom.
Myth, says Smith, is culturally significant in that it is "an intellectual construction that fuses concept and emotion into an image."[3] Myth is, so to speak,
a mental movie, with accompanying script, which Americans carry around in

their heads regarding their heritage and sense of special destiny. The American past is therefore scarcely a dead past; the past effects a presiding influence over the present. It continues to live within us. Myth lays claim to preserving, repeating, and defending the treasury of wisdom our forebears entrusted to us.

In summary, then, one school of thought on American historical myth seeks to emphasize historical inaccuracies, while the other approaches myth from the vantage point of social psychology. One sees myth as the by-product of historical scholarship (or lack of it), while the other demonstrates a marked concern for the ways in which myth serves the decidedly positive function of unifying cultural experience, providing, in the words of the literary scholar Mark Schorer, "a large controlling image that gives philosophical meaning to the facts of ordinary life. . . ."[4] Certainly at times both senses of myth are present; on occasion they tend to blend to the point of becoming nearly indistinguishable. Both notions of myth are germane to the study of American history.

University of Chicago historian William H. McNeill further observes that "myth and history are close kin inasmuch as both explain how things got to be the way they are by telling some sort of story."[5] In this way, history is "mythic" in Aristotle's and Henry Nash Smith's sense of the word, for history offers by its very nature a narrative reconstruction, a *story* of the past. This clear linkage of *story* and *history* is rather clearly recognized in some cultures. In the Italian and Spanish languages, for example, the words *history* and *story* are interchangeable. Historians are essentially the storytellers of the "tribe," functioning as purveyors of cultural stories. In this sense, surely, historians are mythmakers.

Historians also function as mythmakers in that, being human, they reflect their personal backgrounds, their times, their methodologies, their current interests—including biases and prejudices, and sometimes even their whims. All historical interpretation, in other words, is both personally contemporary and ideological—such is the nature of what has been called "the politics of interpretation." Moreover, historians constantly revise each other's work and sometimes even their own. This process of mythmaking by professional historians—myths as a critical by-product of what historians do—is given major emphasis in this work.

In addition to formal, academic study of American history, a sense of the past is frequently derived from a vast array of informational sources constantly assaulting the average citizen with a barrage of historical "facts" with implicit interpretations. These, too, structure and sustain the illusions and traditional stories—the myths—about America's past. Television and film especially, two of American culture's favorite recreations, transmit images and "re-creations" of the past in appealing sight and sound to eager audiences, most often with an eye to drama rather than solid research and scholarly validity. Similarly, "historical" novels, poetry, political rhetoric, children's literature, paintings, ballads, oral traditions, folklore, political cartoons, tourist shrines, and culturally induced sexist and racist stereotypes contribute in their own ways to our collective impression of the past. In the aggregate, they probably represent as consistent and enduring a fund of "historical" information as what we learn in more formalized educational settings. As Americans "make up their mind" about their cultural traditions, they fashion a colorful mental mosaic of their history. Song, story, nostalgia, and the ever-present media reinforce the picture. Such "mythic" history works its way to a level of operational reality when people act as if the myths are true. Policies—even laws—are based on them. In this way, the making of myths is a process by which a culture perpetuates its grandest illusions as it gives substance, order, and stability to its world.

Taking all of the above considerations into account, this new edition of *Myth and the American Experience* views myth on two levels—as a matter of correcting what is false or at least highly suspect about one's sense of the past, even while realizing myth to be highly emblematic of the nation's desires, dreams, and values. As the mathematician-turned-philosopher Alfred North Whitehead succinctly put the matter to a Virginia audience over half a century ago:

> The art of a free society consists first in the maintenance of the symbolic code; and secondly in a fearlessness of revision, to secure that the code serves those purposes which satisfy an enlightened reason. Those societies which cannot combine reverence to their symbols with freedom of revision, must ultimately decay either from anarchy, or from the slow atrophy of a life stifled by useless shadows.[6]

Seeking to offer cautionary comment as to American culture's many "useless shadows" while still cultivating a decent respect for "the symbolic code," this new edition offers much fresh material: on American Indians, the Great Awakening, colonial women, the American Revolution, Andrew Jackson, the Chicano experience, southern women, slavery, Abraham Lincoln, Reconstruction, the Gilded Age, Victorian sexuality, the American working class, the two Roosevelts, women's suffrage and feminism, immigration and minorities, the Great Depression, Pearl Harbor and Japanese Americans, the Eisenhower presidency, and the contemporary American scene—among other topics. Together with the many classic essays from earlier editions of this work, these new readings ought to contribute to a clearer yet critical vision of the nation's past. It is hoped that this selective study of myth and the American experience will launch the reader on an especially rewarding journey through America's storied mythic past.

Notes

1. Sam Keen, "Personal Myths Guide Daily Life: The Stories We Live By," *Psychology Today* (December 1989), p. 44.
2. Thomas A. Bailey, "The Mythmakers of American History," *The Journal of American History*, 55 (June 1968), p. 5.
3. Henry Nash Smith, *Virgin Land: The American West as Symbol and Myth* (New York, 1950), p. v.
4 Mark Schorer, "The Necessity of Myth," in Henry A. Murray (ed.), *Myth and Mythmaking* (New York, 1960), p. 355.
5. William H. McNeill, "Mythistory, or Truth, Myth, History, and Historians," *The American Historical Review*, 91 (February 1986), p. 1.
6. Alfred North Whitehead, *Symbolism: Its Meaning and Effect* (New York, 1959), p. 88.

Myths of Early America

For we must consider that we shall be as a City upon a hill, the eyes of all people are upon us.
John Winthrop *(1630)*

But how do they spend their time, think you? Faith, in imagining and framing fictions to themselves of things never done nor never likely to be done, in believing these their fictions, and in following these beliefs. This is the reason why they . . . hate to be interrupted in their airy castle-buildings.
Joseph Hall, *The Discovery of the New World* *(1605)*

Myth of the Bloodthirsty Savage. [John Vanderlyn, *The Murder of Jane McCrea* (1804). Courtesy of Wadsworth Atheneum, Hartford, Connecticut.]

Æ tatis suæ 21. Aº. 1616.

Matoaks als Rebecka daughter to the mighty Prince
Powhatan Emperour of Attanoughkomouck als Virginia
converted and baptized in the Christian faith, and
Wife to the Worll Mr Tho: Rolff.

Pocahontas: Myth of the Noble Savage. [Unknown artist, after 1616 engraving by Simon van de Passe. Courtesy of National Portrait Gallery, Smithsonian Institution;
transfer from the National Gallery of Art, gift of Andrew W. Mellon, 1942.]

*A*ccording to some reports, Sir Humphrey Gilbert was sitting on the deck of his ship reading a copy of Sir Thomas More's *Utopia* just prior to his demise in 1583 somewhere in the North Atlantic. Whether he was reading *Utopia* or (as some suggest) the Bible, or whether the account is sheer fabrication, is unimportant. The point is that Gilbert, rough-hewn as he might have been, was representative of the breed of Englishmen who early dreamed of New World possibilities and then attempted to realize them. Many of this group, including Gilbert, the Hakluyts, and Sir Walter Raleigh, indeed had read *Utopia* (published in Latin, 1516; English translation, 1551), as they were generally well educated, as well as being soldiers and courtiers (and, in the younger Hakluyt's case, clergyman and publicist). These men reflected the English Renaissance, one of the most stimulating, productive, and expansive eras in all of English history—the age of Jonson, Marlowe, Shakespeare, Byrd, Morley, and Bacon. Thomas More, a precursor of the English Renaissance, is supposed to have been enough influenced by some of Amerigo Vespucci's crewmen to set his *Utopia* somewhere in the New World.

Thus, inspiration for England's colonial beginnings, while in many respects similar to that of Portugal, Spain, and France, differed in that it generally reflected a broader utopian vision of the New World. This vision as it was practically worked out in English settlement of North America in the seventeenth and eighteenth centuries would indeed provide fertile ground for the development of myth as contemporaries and later historians attempted to tell the story of early America.

This story—a mixture of aspirations and the hard realities of actual settlement in the New World—many times resulted in frustration, whether that of the "gentlemen" of early Jamestown, or of John Winthrop. Another book could be written about frustrated utopias, but their development and many of their results have contributed heavily to the building of myth in American history.

Historians bring their own age to bear on the history they write—myths included. It should come as no surprise that faced with a two-front attack, early American history has succumbed to the onslaught of mythmaking—its own and that of future historians.

The readings in this section scan the American colonial experience as they introduce and demonstrate the viability of a myth-oriented approach to the study of American history generally, and to early American history in particular. This perspective can direct readers to new and exciting encounters in American history—perhaps involve them in a total revision of their ideas on the subject.

Colonial America Without the Indians: A Counterfactual Scenario

James Axtell

In the beginning were the Native Americans, and they enjoyed a civilized presence in North America for many centuries before the arrival of Europeans. Yet only recently has American society become sufficiently aware of the glaring omission of these peoples from American history; rather, the tendency habitually has been to regard them as a kind of historical antiquity—as "Vanishing Americans." Up to the present, any measure of understanding—if any recognition was accorded at all—seldom transcended the dual mythology of Bloodthirsty Savage versus Noble Red Man. As a result, American Indians have been the victims of both neglect and distortion. James Axtell—William R. Kenan, Jr., Professor of Humanities at the College of William and Mary—here creatively corrects the historical record. Apparently agreeing with the belief that one grand mythology deserves another, Axtell contemplates early American history totally without an Indian presence and Indian contributions. He thus jars one's historical sensibility toward an appreciation of Indians as principal determinants of American history.

More than thirty years ago, Bernard DeVoto lambasted students of American history, especially the academic kind, for having made "shockingly little effort to understand the life, the societies, the cultures, the thinking, and the feeling of Indians, and disastrously little effort to understand how all these affected white men and their societies. . . . Most American history," he chided, "has been written as if history were a function solely of white culture—in spite of the fact that till well into the nineteenth century the Indians were one of the principal determinants of historical events."

Three decades later, it behooves us to ask whether we should be tarred with the same brush. Have we done any more or any better to understand the American natives and especially to integrate them into the main course of American history, not as an exotic if melancholy footnote but as one of its principal *determinants?* In answer to the first part of the question, it can be argued that the history of America's Indian peoples has grown tremendously

From *Indians in American History: An Introduction,* ed. Frederick E. Hoxie. Published for the D'Arcy McNickle Center for the History of the American Indian, The Newberry Library, by Harlan Davidson, Inc., 1988.

in volume and sophistication since 1952, thanks less to traditional American historians than to historically minded ethnologists and those hybrid progeny of history and anthropology known as ethnohistorians. As for the second part, it must be confessed that the current generation, no less than DeVoto's, has made "disastrously little effort to understand how [the Indians] affected white men and their societies."

Where historians have not deigned to tread, others have rushed in. Since the last quarter of the nineteenth century, several articles and chapters have treated "The Contributions of the American Indian to Civilization" or "Americanizing the White Man." But most of them are either derivative, unhistorical, or downright foolish. They all suffer from at least one of four major problems. First, with one antiquated exception, they take as their subject all of American history and culture, with no differentiation of sections, classes, demography, or chronology. Second, "Indian" culture is similarly overgeneralized; no allowance is made for tribal, culture area, or chronological differences. Third, they focus on isolated *materials* and *traits* rather than on cultural *complexes* (how they were used, perceived, and adapted by the colonists). And, finally, the conclusions of some and the implications of all lack common sense. To suggest, even indirectly, that "what is distinctive about America is Indian, through and through" or that Americans are simply Europeans with "Indian souls" is blithely to ignore the "wholly other" nature of English colonial society—its aggressive capitalism; exploitative attitudes toward natural resources; social hierarchy; nuclear kinship system; religious intolerance; literacy and print communications; linear sense of time; imperialism based on conquest; superiority complex based on religion, technology, social evolution and, ultimately, race; and desire to replicate the major features of the mother society as completely and quickly as possible.

One predictable reaction to the well-meaning fatuity of such efforts to plug the Indian into American culture (if not history) was that of Wilbur Zelinsky, who surveyed *The Cultural Geography of the United States* in 1973. After scanning the colonial period, Zelinsky concluded that "the sum of the lasting aboriginal contribution to the North American extension of British culture was distinctly meager. . . . Had the European colonists found an utterly unpopulated continent, contemporary American life would not have differed in any major respect from its actual pattern."

Who's right—DeVoto or Zelinsky? Were the Indians a temporary and irrelevant backdrop to the realization of Anglo-American destiny or were they "one of the principal determinants" of American history? The answer is not without importance. If Professor Zelinsky is correct, colonial history can remain a monochromatic study of Puritan preaching, merchant adventure, and imperial legislation; and textbook publishers can—when the political "heat" from the Indian Movement cools—cut the now-mandatory opening chapter on America's "prehistory" and adventitious references to the familiar cast of kamikaze warriors, noble collaborators, and patriot chiefs.

In a brief essay it is impossible to describe all the ways in which the Indians determined American history in the colonial period. However, it might be possible to suggest the outlines of such a description by following Professor Zelinsky's lead and imagining what early American history might have looked like in the utter *absence* of Indians in the New World. This kind of counterfactual discussion has its pitfalls as history, but for heuristic purposes it has few rivals if handled with care. When the main issue is the indispensability or irrelevance of a people to a complex course of historical events, the shortest way to resolve it is to reconstruct those events without the disputed variable. "Had the European colonists found an utterly unpopulated continent," we should ask, "would colonial American life have differed in any major respect from its actual pattern?"

To begin at the beginning, in the period of European discovery and exploration, we can say with confidence that if Columbus had not discovered *los Indios* (and they him), the history of Spanish America would have been extremely short and uneventful. Since Columbus was looking for the Far East, not America or its native inhabitants, he personally would have not been surprised to find no Indians in the Caribbean—the new continent was surprise enough. But he would have been disappointed, not only because the islands of the Orient were known to be inhabited but also because there would have been little or no reason to spend time exploring and settling the New World in lieu of his larger goal. America would have been regarded simply as a huge impediment to his holy plan to mount an old-fashioned crusade to liberate Jerusalem with profits derived from his short-cut to Cathay.

If the Caribbean and Central and South America had been unpopulated, the placer mines of the islands and the deep mines of gold and silver on the mainland in all likelihood would not have been discovered and certainly not exploited quickly without Indian knowledge and labor. It is simply inconceivable that the Spanish would have stumbled on the silver deposits of Potosí or Zacatecas if the Incas and Aztecs had not set Spanish mouths to watering with their sumptuous gold jewelry and ornaments. Indeed, without the attraction of that enormous wealth to be commandeered from the natives, it is likely that the Spanish would not have colonized New Spain at all except with a few supply bases from which to continue the search for the Southwest Passage.

It is equally possible that without the immediate booty of Indian gold and silver, the Spanish would have dismissed Columbus as a crackbrained Italian after one voyage and redirected their economic energies eastward in the wake of the Portuguese, toward the certifiable wealth of Africa, India, and the East Indies. Eventually, sugar cane might have induced the Iberians to colonize their American discoveries, as it did the Cape Verdes, Madeiras, and Canaries, but black laborers would have had to be imported to mount production. Without Indian labor and discovery, however, saltwater pearls and the bright red dye made from the cochineal beetle—the second largest export in the colonial period—would not have contributed to Spain's bulging balance sheets, with all that meant for the political and economic history of Europe in the sixteenth and early seventeenth century.

Perhaps most important, without the millions of Native Americans who inhabited New Spain, our textbooks would be silent on the Spanish conquest—no "Black Legend," no Cortés or Montezuma, no brown-robed friars baptizing thousands daily or ferreting out "idolatry" with whip and fagot, no legalized plunder under the encomienda system, no cruelty to those who extracted the mines' treasures and rebuilt Spanish cities on the rubble of their own, no mastiffs mangling runaways. And without the fabulous lure of Aztec gold and Incan silver bound for Seville on the annual bullion fleets, it is difficult to imagine Spain's European rivals beating an ocean path to America to establish colonies of their own, certainly not as early as they did.

Take the French, for example. The teeming cod on the Grand Banks off Newfoundland would have drawn and supported a small seasonal population of fishermen, as it did early in the sixteenth century. But without the Indian presence, that would have been the extent of French colonial penetration. Verrazzano's 1524 reconnaissance of the Atlantic seaboard would have been an even bigger bust than it was, having found no promising Northwest Passage to the Orient; and Jacques Cartier probably would have made two voyages at most, the second to explore the St. Lawrence far enough to learn that *La Chine* did not lie on the western end of Montreal Island. He would have reported to Francis I that "the land God gave to Cain" had no redeeming features whatever, such as the greasy furs of Indian fishermen and the promise of gold and diamonds in the fabled Kingdom of the Saguenay, of which the Indians seemed to speak with such conviction.

If by chance Champlain had renewed the French search for the Northwest Passage in the seventeenth century, he quickly would have lost his backers without the lure of an established fur trade with the natives of Acadia and Canada, who hunted, processed, and transported the pelts in native-designed, -built, and -manned canoes or on native snowshoes and toboggans. And without the "pagan" souls of the Indians as a goad and challenge, the French religious orders, male and female, would not have cast their lot with Champlain and the trading companies that governed and settled New France before 1663. Without the Indian fur trade, in short, no seigneuries would have been granted along the St. Lawrence, no *habitants, engagés* or "King's girls" shipped out to Canada. Quebec and Montreal would not have been founded even as crude *comptoirs,* and no Jesuit missionaries would have craved martyrdom at an Iroquois stake. Needless to say, no "French and Indian" wars would mar our textbooks with their ethnocentric denomination. North America would belong solely to settlements of English farmers. For without the Indians and their fur trade, the Swedish and the Dutch would have followed the French lead by staying home or turning to the East for economic inspiration.

Without the lure of American gold and the Elizabethan contest with Spain that grew partly from its advent, the English, too, probably would have financed fewer ocean searches for the Northwest Passage. Unless Indian chamberpots were thought to have been made of gold, far fewer gentle-born investors and low-born sailors would have risked their lives and fortunes on the coasts of America. Unless the Spanish had reaped fabulous riches from the natives and then subjected the latter to cruel and unnatural bondage, Sir Walter Raleigh would not have sponsored his voyages of liberation to Guiana and

"Virginia." If the Spanish flotas had not sailed regularly through the Straits of Florida, English privateers would not have preyed on the West Indies nor captured the booty that helped to launch permanent colonies in Ireland and North America. Arthur Barlowe's 1584 voyage to North Carolina would probably not have been followed up so soon without the discovery of friendly natives capable of securing a fledgling colony from Spanish incursions. If settlers had come the following year, fewer need have been soldiers, they need not have been deposited on Roanoke Island for security reasons, and they probably would never have been lost without an Armada scare to detain supplies or the freelance privateering of rescuers.

Sooner or later, the English would have established colonies in America to provide a safety valve for the felt pressures of population growth and economic reorganization and as a sanctuary for religious dissenters. But without the Indians, our textbooks would assume a very different appearance in the chapters beyond the first; and the first, of course, would not be about the Indian "prehistory" of the continent but a much truncated treatment of exploration that barely mentioned the Spanish, Portuguese, French, Swedish, and Dutch.

Once English settlement was under way, the absence of native villages, tribes, and war parties would have altered rather drastically the timing and chronology of American history. In general, events would have accelerated because in reality the Indian presence acted as a major check on colonial development. Without a native barrier (which in the colonial period was much more daunting than the Appalachians), the most significant drag on colonial enterprise would have been the lack of Indian labor in a few minor economies, such as the domestic economy of southern New England (supplied by Indian captives in the Pequot and King Philip's wars) and the whale fisheries of Cape Cod, Long Island, and Nantucket. Indians were not crucial to wheat farming, lumbering, or rice and tobacco culture and would not have been missed by English entrepreneurs.

Without Indians to contest the land, English colonists would have encountered no opposition to their choice of prime locations for settlement except from English competitors. They would not have had to challenge Indian farmers for the fertile river valleys and coastal plains the natives had cultivated for centuries. Without potential Indian or European enemies, sites could have been located almost entirely for economic rather than military considerations, thus removing Jamestown, Plymouth, and St. Mary's City from the litany of American place-names. Boston, New York, Philadelphia, and Charleston would probably have developed where they are, either because Indian opposition to their founding was minimal or because they were situated for optimal access to inland markets and Atlantic shipping lanes.

In an empty land, English leaders would also have had fewer strategic and ideological reasons for communal settlements of the classic New England type. Without the military and moral threat of Indian war parties, on the one hand, and the puzzling seduction of native life, on the other, English colonists would have had to be persuaded by other arguments to cast their lots together.

One predictable result is that New England "Puritans" would have become unbridled "Yankees" even faster than they did, and other colonies would have spread across the American map with equal speed. In other words, by 1776, Anglo-American farmers in large numbers would have spilled over the Appalachians, headed toward their "Manifest Destiny" in the West. Without Indians, Frenchmen, or Spaniards in the Mississippi Valley and beyond to stop them, only the technology of transportation, the supply of investment capital, and the organization of markets en route would have regulated the speed of their advance.

Another consequence of an Indian-less America would be that we could not speak with any accuracy of "the American frontier" because there would be no people on the other side; only where two peoples and cultures intersect do we have a bona fide frontier. The movement of one people into uninhabited land is merely *exploration* or *settlement,* and does not constitute a frontier situation. In fact, without viable Indian societies, colonial America would more nearly resemble Frederick Jackson Turner's famous frontier in which Indians are treated more like geographical features than sociological teachers. In Turner's scenario, the European dandy fresh from his railroad car is "Americanized" less by contact with palpably attractive human societies than by the "wilderness" or Nature itself. Moreover, the distinctively "American" character traits in Turner's catalogue produced by living on the fore edge of westering "civilization" would have been exaggerated by the existence of *truly* limitless cheap land and much less control from the Old World and the eastern "Establishment."

Not only would Turner's mythopoeic frontier really have existed in a non-Indian America, but three other common misunderstandings in our teaching of colonial history would have been realities. First, America would indeed have been a "virgin land," a barren "wilderness" that was not home or well-known to perhaps 4 million native people north of Mexico. If those people had not existed, we would not have to explain their catastrophic decline—by as much as 90 percent—through epidemics of imported diseases, warfare, injustice, and forced migrations—the "widowing" of the once-virgin land.

Second, colonial history would be confined to the political boundaries of the future United States, much like the weather map on the six o'clock news. Without Indians, we could continue to ignore French Canada and Louisiana, the Spanish Southwest, the Russian Northwest (which would not exist without the Indian seal trade), and the borderless histories of Indian-white contact that determined so much of the shape and texture of colonial life.

And third, we would not have to step up from the largely black-and-white pageant of American history we are offered in our textbooks and courses to a richer polychromatic treatment if the Indians had no role in the past. We would not have to pay lip service to the roll call of exclusively male Indian leaders who have been squeezed into the corners of our histories by modern American Indian activists. Still less would we have to try to integrate into our texts an understanding of the various native peoples who were here first, remained against staggering odds, and are still here to mold our collective past and future.

To get a sharper perspective on an Indian-free scenario of colonial history, we should increase our focal magnification and analyze briefly four distinguishable yet obviously related aspects of colonial life—economics, religion, politics, and acculturation.

If Professor Zelinsky's thesis has any merits at all, they lie on the economic side of the ledger. The economy of Anglo-America without the Indians would have resembled in general outline the historical economy but with several significant exceptions. Farming would certainly have been the mainstay of colonial life, whether for family subsistence or for capitalist marketing and accumulation. But the initial task of establishing farms would have required far more grubbing and clearing without the meadows and "park-like" woods produced by seasonal Indian burning, and especially without the cleared expanses of Indian cornfields and village sites. Many colonists found that they could acquire cleared Indian lands with a few fathoms of trading cloth, some unfenced cows, or a well-aimed barrel of buckshot.

A more serious deficiency would have been the absence of maize or Indian corn, the staple crop grown by the colonists throughout the colonial period to feed their families and sometimes to fatten their livestock for export. If Indians had not adapted wild Mexican corn to the colder, moist climates of North America and developed the agricultural techniques of hilling, fertilizing by annual burning, and co-planting with nitrogen-fixing beans to reduce soil depletion, the colonists would have lacked a secure livelihood in both the long and the short run, particularly in the early years before traditional European cereal crops could be adapted to the American climate and soils. Even if traditional crops could have been transplanted with ease, colonial productivity would not have benefited from the efficiency and labor savings of native techniques, which were found taught by Indian prisoners (as at Jamestown) or by allies such as Squanto at Plymouth. So central was maize to the colonial economy that it is possible that its absence would have acted as a severe brake on westward settlement, thereby counteracting to some degree the magnetic pull of free land.

The colonial economy would also have been affected by the lack of Indian trade, the profits from which were used to fuel the nascent economies of several colonies, including Massachusetts, Rhode Island, New York, Pennsylvania, Virginia, and South Carolina. Without early fortunes made from Indian furs, some of the "first families" of America—the Byrds, Penns, Logans, Winthrops, Schuylers—would not have been launched so solidly or so soon in shipping, slaves, rice, tobacco, or real estate. Nor would the mature economies of a few major colonies have rested on the fur trade well into the eighteenth century. New York's and Pennsylvania's balance of payments with the mother country would have been badly skewed if Indian-generated furs had not accounted for 30–50 percent of their annual exports between 1700 and 1750. By the same token, a substantial portion of English exports to the colonies would not have been sent to colonial traders for Indian customers, whose historical appetites for English cloth and West Indian rum were appreciated even by those who realized that furs accounted for only 0.5 percent of England's colonial imports, far behind tobacco and sugar.

The lack of Indians and Indian property rights in America would have further complicated the colonial economy by greatly narrowing another classic American road to wealth. If the new land had been literally inexhaustible and "dirt cheap," the range of legal and extralegal means to acquire relatively scarce land for hoarding and speculation would have been markedly reduced. Within the unknown confines of the royal response to a huge, open continent, every man, great and small, would have been for himself. If the law condoned or fostered the selective aggrandizement of colonial elites, as it tended to do historically, unfavored farmers and entrepreneurs could simply move out of the effective jurisdiction of the government or find more congenial leaders to do their bidding. The proliferation of new colonies seeking economic and political "independence" from the "tyranny" of the Eastern Establishment would have been one certain result.

Finally, America without Indians would entail the rewriting of the history of black slavery in the colonies. It is likely that, in the absence of Indians, the colonial demand for and use of African slaves would have begun earlier and accelerated faster. For although the historical natives were found to be poor workers and poorer slaves, the discovery took some time. Not only would the rapid westward spread of settlements have called for black labor, perhaps more of it indentured, but the rice and tobacco plantations of the Southeast probably would have been larger than they were historically, if scarce land and high prices had not restricted them. In a virgin-land economy, agricultural entrepreneurs who wanted to increase their acreage could easily buy out their smaller neighbors, who lacked no access to new lands in the west. Of course, greater numbers of black laborers would have been needed to do the work because white indentured servants would have been extremely hard to get when so much land and opportunity beckoned over the horizon. By the same token, the slaves themselves would have been harder to keep to the task without surrounding tribes of Indians who could be taught to fear and hate the African strangers and to serve the English planters as slave-catchers.

While most colonists came to the New World to better their material condition, not a few came to ameliorate the spiritual condition of the "godless" natives. Without the challenge of native "paganism" in America, the charters of most English colonies would have been frankly materialistic documents with pride of motive going to the extension of His (or Her) Majesty's Eminent Domain. Thus American history would have lost much of its distinctively evangelical tone, though few of its millenarian, utopian strains. Without the long, frustrated history of Christian missions to the Indians, we would lack a sensitive barometer of the cultural values that the European colonists sought to transplant in the New World and one source of denominational competition in the eighteenth century.

Without Indian targets and foils, the colonists even of New England might not have retained their "Chosen People" conceit so long or so obdurately. On the other hand, without the steady native reminder of their evangelical mission in America, the colonists' early descent into ecclesiastical "tribalism" and spiritual exclusiveness might have accelerated with time. The jeremiads of New England would certainly have been less shrill in the absence of the Pequot War and King Philip's War, when the hostile natives seemed to be scourges sent by God to punish a sinful people. Without the military and psychological threat of Indians within and without New England's borders, the colonial fear of limitless and unpredictable social behavior would have been reduced, thereby diminishing the harsh treatment of religious deviants such as Roger Williams, Anne Hutchinson, Quakers, and the Salem witches. Finally, the French "Catholic menace" to the north would have been no threat to English Protestant sensibilities without hundreds of Indian converts, led by "deviously" effective Jesuit missionaries, ringing New England's borders. The French secular clergy who would have ministered to the handful of fishermen and farmers in Canada would have had no interest whatever in converting heretics hundreds of miles away and no extra manpower to attempt it.

The appearance of the "French menace" introduces the political realm of colonial life, which also would take on a new complexion in the absence of American natives. Even if the French had settled the St. Lawrence Valley without a sustaining Indian fur trade, the proliferating English population and European power politics would have made short work of the tiny Canadian population, now bereft of Indian allies and converts in the thousands. In all likelihood, we would write about only one short intercolonial war, beginning much earlier than 1689. Perhaps the Kirkes would never have given Quebec back to the French in 1632. Without the Catholic Indian *reserves* of Lorette, Caughnawaga, and St. François, Canada would quickly have become English, at least as far north as arable land and lumber-rich forests extended.

Without a formidable French and Indian threat, early Americans would not have developed—in conjunction with their conceit as God's "Chosen People"—such a pronounced "garrison mentality" as innocent and holy victims of heavily armed satanic forces. If the English had not been virtually surrounded by French-allied Indian nations and an arc of French trading forts and villages from Louisiana to Maine, the Anglo-American tendencies toward persecuted isolationism would have been greatly sublimated.

As the colonies matured, the absence of an Indian military threat would have greatly lightened the taxpayers' burden for colonial defense, thereby placing much less strain on the political relations between governors and representative assemblies. Indeed, the assemblies would not have risen to political parity with the royal administrators in the absence of financial crises generated by war debts and defense needs. Intercolonial cooperation would have been even less conspicuous than it was historically. Royal forces would not have been called in during the eighteenth century to bolster sagging colonial defenses, and no imperial debts would have been incurred which the colonies would be asked to help amortize. Consequently, the colonies would have had few grievances against the mother country serious enough to ignite an American Revolution, at least not in 1776. And without the concentration of Indian allies on the British side, the colonists might have achieved independence sooner than they did.

Another reason why the colonists would probably not have been ready for revolution in 1776 is that, without the steady impress of Indian culture, they would not have been or felt sufficiently "Americanized" to stand before the world as an independent nation. Without Indian societies to form our colonial frontiers, Anglo-American culture would have been transformed only by internal developments and the evolving influence of the mother country and of the black and other ethnic groups that shared the New World with the English. Black culture probably would have done the most to change the shape and texture of colonial life, especially in the South. But English masters saw little reason to emulate their black slaves in any positive way, to make any *adaptive* changes in their own cultural practices or attitudes to accommodate perceived superiorities in black culture. English colonial culture changed in response to the imported Africans largely in *reaction* to their oppositional being, and pervasive and often virulent racism was the primary result. Other changes followed, of course, from the adoption of staple economies largely but not necessarily dependent on black labor.

English reactions to the Indians, on the other hand, were far more mixed; the "savages" were noble as well as ignoble, depending on English needs and circumstances. Particularly on the frontier, colonists were not afraid or loath to borrow and adapt pieces of native culture if they found them advantageous or necessary for beating the American environment or besting the Indians in the contest for the continent. Contrary to metropolitan colonial opinion, this cultural exchange did not turn the frontiersmen into Indians. Indian means were simply borrowed and adapted to English ends. The frontiersmen did not regard themselves as Indians nor did they appreciably alter their basic attitudes toward the native means they employed. But they also knew that their American encounters with the Indians made them very different from their English cousins at home.

While the colonists borrowed consciously and directly from Indian culture only on the frontier, English colonial culture as a whole received a substantial but indirect impress from the Indians by being forced to confront the novel "otherness" of native culture and to cope with its unpredictability, pride, and retaliatory violence. Having the Indians as sometime adversaries and full-time contraries helped not only to reinforce the continuity of vital English traits and institutions but to Americanize all levels of colonial society more fully than the material adaptations of the frontiersmen. These *reactive* changes were, in large measure, responsible for transforming colonial Englishmen into native Americans in feeling, allegiance, and identity, a change without which, John Adams reminded us, the American Revolution would have been impossible. The whole colonial experience of trying to solve a related series of "Indian problems" had much to do with giving the colonists an identity indissolubly linked to America and their apprenticeship in political and military cooperation.

What are some of these changes that would *not* have taken place in colonial culture had the continent been devoid of Indians? The adaptive changes are the easiest to describe. Without native precedent, the names of twenty-eight states and myriad other place-names would carry a greater load of Anglophonic freight. The euphonious Shenandoah and Monongahela might well be known as the St. George and the Dudley Rivers. We might still be searching for suitable names for the *moose, skunk,* and *raccoon,* the *muskelunge* and *quahog,* the *hickory* tree and marshy *muskeg.* It would be impossible, no doubt, to find *moccasins* in an L. L. Bean catalogue, or canned *succotash* in the supermarket. We would never refer to our children playfully as *papooses* or to political bigshots as *mugwumps.* Southerners could not start their day with *hominy* grits.

Without Indian guides to the New World, the English colonists upon arrival would have lacked temporary housing in bark-covered wigwams and longhouses. Not only would their diet have depended largely on imported foods, but their techniques for hunting American game and fowl and coping in the woods would have been decidedly meager. Without native medicines, many colonists would have perished and the *U.S. Pharmacopeia* would be short some 170 entries. Without Indian snowshoes and toboggans, winter hunting and travel would have been sharply curtailed. Without the lightweight bark canoe, northern colonists would have penetrated the country on foot, and not in comfortable moccasins and Indian leggings. English hunters probably would have careened around the woods in gaudy colors and torn English garments much longer, oblivious that the unsmoked glint of their musket barrels frightened the game. One can only imagine what Virginia's patriotic rifle companies would have worn in 1775 as an alternative to moccasins, leggings, fringed hunting shirts, scalping knives, and tomahawks.

Without native opponents and instructors in the art of guerrilla warfare, the colonists would have fought their American wars—primarily with the British—in traditional military style. In fact, without the constant need to suppress hostile natives and aggressive Europeans, they might have lost most of their martial spirit and prowess, making their victory in the now-postponed Revolution less than certain. Beating the British regulars at their own game without some of the stratagems and equipment gained from the Indians would have been nearly impossible, particularly when the British in the eighteenth century had gained experience in counterinsurgent warfare in Scotland and on the Continent.

Although the absence of adaptive changes such as these would have done much to maintain the Anglicized tone and texture of colonial life, the absence of Indians would have preserved a number of more fundamental cultural values that were altered historically. The generalized European fear of barbarism that worried colonial planners and leaders would have dissipated without the Indian embodiment of the "heathenism" that seemed so contagious to English frontiersmen or the greater danger of Englishmen converting to an Indian way of life in captivity or, worse still, voluntarily as "apostates" and "'renegades." Without the seduction of an alternative life-style within easy reach, hundreds of colonists would not have become "white Indians."

Second, and more generally, the English definition of themselves in America would have lacked a crucial point of reference because the Indians would no longer symbolize the "savage" baseness that would dominate human nature if man did not—paradoxically—"reduce" it to "civility" through government, religion, and the capitalist work ethic. Only imported Africans, not American natives, could have shown "civilized men [what] they were not and must not be." Because the historical settlers were "especially inclined to discover attributes in savages which they found first but could not speak of in themselves," they defined themselves "less by the vitality of their affirmations than by the violence of their abjurations." While all peoples to some extent define themselves by contrast with other peoples, the English colonists forged their particular American identity more on an Indian anvil than upon other European colonists or Africans. If America had been vacant upon discovery, the Anglo-American character would have been very different from that which we inherited.

For the whole spectrum of colonial society, urban and rural, the Indians as cultural contraries were not as frustrating, alarming, or influential as the Indian enemy. As masters of an unconventional warfare of terror, they seared the collective memory, imagination, and even subconscious of the colonists, leaving a deep but blurred intaglio of fear and envy, hatred and respect. Having the American natives as frequent and deadly adversaries—and even as allies—did more not to "Indianize" but to "Americanize" the English colonists than any other human factor and had two contradictory results. When native warfare frustrated and humbled the English military machine, its successes cast into serious doubt the colonists' sense of superiority, especially when the only resource seemed to be the hiring of equally "savage" mercenaries. At the same time, victorious Indians seemed so insufferably insolent—a projection of the Christians' original sin—that the colonists redoubled their efforts to claim divine grace and achieve spiritual and social regeneration through violence. One of the pathetic ironies of early America is that in attempting to exterminate the wounding pride of their Indian enemies the colonists inflated their own pride to sinful proportions.

The Indians' brand of guerrilla warfare, which involved the "indiscriminate slaughter of all ranks, ages and sexes," torture, and captivity for adoption, gave rise to several colonial reactions. The first reaction to the offensive war of the natives (which was in reality retaliation for previous wrongs, real or perceived) was a well-founded increase in fear and paranoia. The second reaction, as we have already suggested, was the development of a defensive "garrison mentality," which in turn reinforced the colonists' sense of being a chosen if momentarily abandoned people. And the colonists' third response to being forced to confront such an enemy was that they were frequently torn from their own "civilized" moorings and swept into the kind of "savage" conduct they deplored in their enemies, motivated conspicuously by cold-blooded vengeance. Without Indian enemies, it is doubtful if the colonists would have fallen to the slaughter and torture of military prisoners, including women and children, taken scalps from friends and enemies to collect government bounties, encouraged the Spanish-style use of dogs, or made boot tops and tobacco pouches from the skins of fallen foes. It is a certainty that non-Indian enemies would not have been the target of frequent if unrealized campaigns of literal genocide; it is difficult to imagine English settlers coining an aphorism to the effect that "the only good Dutchman is a dead one."

It is both fitting and ironic that the symbol chosen by Revolutionary cartoonists to represent the American colonies was the Indian, whose love of liberty and fierce independence had done so much to Americanize the shape and content of English colonial culture. It is fitting because the Indians, by their long and determined opposition, helped to meld thirteen disparate colonies into one (albeit fragile) nation, different from England largely by virtue of having shared that common history of conflict on and over Indian soil. It is ironic because after nearly two centuries of trying to take the Indians' lives and lands, the colonists appropriated not only the native identity but the very characteristics that thwarted the colonists' ultimate arrogations.

If such a scenario seems plausible, we should be able to agree with De-Voto that, without the Indians, America would not be America as we know it. The sooner we acknowledge that fact, the sooner we can get down to the serious business of assessing the Indians' decisive place in American history.

Slavery and the Meaning of America

David Brion Davis

Early American history strongly reflects a European climate of opinion that for centuries had been nurtured by mythic predispositions toward a New World. It was within a utopian and mythic atmosphere that the transoceanic expeditions and geographic discoveries of Christopher Columbus and others took place. Long before settlement, America served as a useful fiction, providing Europeans an imaginative escape into a dreamworld of social, political, and religious alternatives. It seems plausible to argue, then, that this broadly based European utopian climate of opinion spawned the ideas and sentiments necessary to the development of an American mythology. Born in the romantic dreams of Europeans, reared in a tradition of glory and heroism, America soon became a land at ease with myth and legend. Contemporaneous with these utopian-mythic visions of and for America, however, were the beginnings of what a later scholar would see as the core of an American dilemma—black slavery. According to David Brion Davis of Yale University, the simultaneous development of utopianism and slavery has given the nation a paradoxical heritage. The presence of slavery in the Promised Land of the New World suggests many important questions about the ultimate meaning of America.

From the time of first discoveries Europeans had projected ancient visions of liberation and perfection into the vacant spaces of the New World. Explorers approached the uncharted coasts with vague preconceptions of mythical Atlantis, Antillia, and the Saint Brendan Isles. The naked savages, living in apparent freedom and innocence, awakened memories of terrestrial paradise and the Golden Age described by the ancients. Even the practical-minded Columbus fell under the spell of the gentle natives on the Gulf of Paria, who wore golden ornaments and lived in a land of lush vegetation and delicious fruits. He concluded in August, 1498, that he had arrived on the "nipple" of the earth, which reached closer to Heaven than the rest of the globe, and that the original Garden of Eden was nearby. Seventeen years later, when Sir Thomas More began writing *Utopia*, he naturally chose the Western Hemisphere as his setting.

Columbus's successors pursued elusive visions of golden cities and fountains of youth; their narratives revived and nourished the utopian dreams of Europe. From antiquity Western thought had been predisposed to look to nature for the universal norms of human life. Since "nature" carried connotations of origin and birth as well as of intrinsic character, philosophers often associated valid norms with what was original in man's primeval state. They contrasted the restraints, prejudices, and corrupting tastes of civilized life with either a former age of virtue or a simpler, more primitive state of society. Many of the explorers and early commentators on America drew upon this philosophic tradition; in the New World they found an Elysium to serve as a standard for criticizing the perverted manners of Europe. Catholic missionaries, being dedicated to ideals of renunciation and asceticism, saw much to admire in the simple contentment of the Indians, whose mode of living seemed to resemble that of the first Christians. As Gilbert Chinard has pointed out, the *voyageurs* and Jesuit priests who compared the evils of Europe with the freedom, equality, and felicitous life of the American savages, contributed unwittingly to the revolutionary philosophy of the eighteenth century.

Some writers, to be sure, described the Indians as inferior degenerates or as Satan's children, and presented a contrary image of America as an insalubrious desert. Antonello Gerbi has documented the long dispute over the nature of the New World—"mondo nascente o neonato, mondo deserto e misero." Howard Mumford Jones has recently shown that America was conceived at once as an idyllic Arcadia and as a land of cannibalism, torture, and brutality, where extremities of human greed and cruelty were matched by the unexpected terrors and monstrosities of the wilderness. But in Hebrew and Christian thought the idea of wilderness had long been linked with rebirth and fulfillment. After being delivered from slavery in Egypt, the children of Israel had crossed the Red Sea and had wandered in the wilderness for forty years before finding the Promised Land. The desert was a place of refuge and purification, of suffering and perseverance; and no matter what hardships it offered, there was the assurance that a fertile paradise would ultimately emerge from its desolate wastes. Thanks to the researches of George H. Williams, we know what an important part such imagery played in Christian ideas of redemption. The wilderness might be thought of as a purely spiritual state, or as the abode of monks, hermits, or persecuted sects. But early American colonists could hardly escape the symbolic implications of a baptismal crossing of the Atlantic, or of dwelling in a land which could be seen as either desert or primeval garden. The New World, like the wilderness in both the Old and New Testaments, was a place of extraordinary temptation, obligation, and promise.

While a growing literature celebrated America as a symbol of nature, free from the avarice, luxury, and materialism of Europe, promoters and colonizers saw the virgin land as a place for solving problems and satisfying desires. This was true of the conquistadores who tried to recreate the age of chivalric romance; it was true of the Jesuits who followed Manuel da Nóbrega to Brazil, determined to purify morals and spread the faith; it was true of the English Puritans who sought to build a New Jerusalem as a model of piety for the rest of the world; it was true of the drifters and ne'er-do-wells, the bankrupts and sleazy gentlemen, who fluttered to the New World like moths drawn to a light. In America things would be better, for America was the Promised Land. It could be said, of course, that America was an asylum for scoundrels, adventurers, and religious fanatics. But in time much of the magic of the virgin continent seemed to rub off on its conquerors. French humanitarians, for example, found it easy to shift their enthusiasm from noble savage to peace-loving Quaker. In Saint-John de Crèvecoeur's *Letters from an American Farmer* we see perhaps the clearest picture of the American idyll, a skillful weaving together of primitivist, pastoral, and democratic themes, the portrayal of a land in which individual opportunity and social progress are somehow merged with the simple, self-denying virtues of Seneca and Vergil.

This long tradition, based on a mixture of Biblical and classical sources, helped to shape the American's image of himself as the new Adam of the West, a being unencumbered by the fears and superstitions of a moldering civilization, a wise innocent dwelling in a terrestrial paradise. He was at once the Happy Husbandman, content to enjoy the serene blessings of a simple, rural life, and an adventurous pioneer, expansive and supremely confident of his ability to improve the world. Such an image contained an intrinsic contradiction which contributed to severe tensions in the face of rapid social and economic change. But if Americans were often inclined to see Satan fast at work corrupting their new Eden, this only enhanced the moral importance of their mission. And by the time of the Revolution many European liberals looked to America as the hope of mankind, for it was there that institutions seemed most clearly modeled on nature's simple plan. By reconciling nature and human progress, the newly independent states appeared to have fulfilled the ancient dream of a more perfect society.

. . . Yet slavery had been linked from the very beginning with what Edmundo O'Gorman had called "the invention of America." The African voyages promoted by Prince Henry of Portugal prepared the way for the first crossing of the Atlantic; and when Columbus arrived in Lisbon in 1477 the trade in Negro slaves was a flourishing enterprise. The same Columbus who identified the Gulf of Paria as the gateway to the Garden of Eden had no compunction about sending hundreds of Indians to be sold in the slave marts of Seville, although some two hundred died on the first voyage and had to be thrown into the sea. It was thus the discoverer of America who initiated the transatlantic slave trade, which moved originally from west to east.

It was soon apparent, however, as the Spanish came close to exterminating the native inhabitants of Hispaniola, that successful colonization would require a fresh supply of laborers. Negro slaves arrived in the New World at least as early as 1502, and by 1513 the sale of licenses for importing Negroes was a source of profit for the Spanish government. Following the Guinea current and trade winds, Portuguese ships provided the colonists with a mounting supply of slaves, but seldom with enough to meet the insatiable demand. As Negro labor became indispensable for Spanish and then Portuguese colonization, European traders and African chieftains slowly built a vast commerical system which brought a profound transformation in African culture and stunted the growth of other commerce between Europe and the Dark Continent.

For three centuries the principal maritime powers competed with one another in the lucrative slave trade, and carried at least fifteen million Africans to the New World. Historians have long been inclined to regard this vast movement of population as an unfortunate but relatively minor incident in American history. Interest in national and sectional history has often obscured the significance of Negro slavery in the overall development of the Americas. But if the institution was of little economic importance in Massachusetts or Nova Scotia, it nevertheless extended from Rio de la Plata to the Saint Lawrence, and was the basic system of labor in the colonies most valued by Europe. In the most profitable colonies Negro slaves were employed in mines and in clearing virgin land, or on the great plantations which provided Europe with sugar, rice, tobacco, cotton, and indigo. The northern colonies that were unsuited for the production of staple crops became dependent, early in their history, on supplying the slave colonies with goods and provisions of various kinds. As a stimulus to shipbuilding, insurance, investment, and banking, the slave trade expanded employment in a diversity of occupations and encouraged the growth of seaports on both sides of the Atlantic. Africa became a prized market for iron, textiles, firearms, rum, and brandy. Investments in the triangular trade brought dazzling rewards, since profits could be made in exporting consumer goods to Africa, in selling slaves to planters, and especially in transporting sugar and other staples to Europe. By the 1760s a large number of the wealthy merchants in Britain and France were connected in some way with the West Indian trade; and capital accumulated from investment in slaves and their produce helped to finance the building of canals, factories, and railroads. Even after the United States had achieved independence and a more diversified economy, her principal export was slave-grown cotton, which was the chief raw material for the industrial revolution.

Without exaggerating the economic significance of Negro slavery, we may safely conclude that it played a major role in the early development of the New World and in the growth of commercial capitalism. Given the lack of an alternative labor supply, it is difficult to see how European nations could have settled America and exploited its resources without the aid of African slaves. Yet slavery had always been more than an economic institution; in Western culture it had long represented the ultimate limit of dehumanization, of treating and regarding a man as a thing. How was one to reconcile the brute fact that slavery was an intrinsic part of the American experience with the image of the New World as uncorrupted nature, as a source of redemption from the burdens of history, as a paradise which promised fulfillment of man's highest aspirations? . . .

The European thinkers . . . had somewhat ambivalent views on the moral influence of the New World. George Bancroft, the most popular and nationalistic of early American historians, had not the slightest doubt that the influence had been all for the good. Limiting himself to the area included in the United States, he set out to explain how in only two centuries the happiest and most enlightened civilization in history had arisen from the wilderness to become a model for the rest of the world. But when he grappled with the problem of slavery—how it was related to the American mission, whether it was integral to American development, and whether its extension to the New World was a retrogression from the course of progress—he resorted to a curious mixture of assumptions which reflected inconsistencies prevalent in American thought from late colonial times to the twentieth century.

As a loyal Democrat and patriotic American, writing at a time when his party supported the expansion of slave territory, Bancroft went out of his way to emphasize the antiquity and universality of an institution which, one might conclude, was not so "peculiar" after all. . . . He found no continuing contest between liberty and bondage in the ancient world: "In every Grecian republic, slavery was an indispensable element." Nor was the practice wholly incompatible with virtue and religion, for "the light that broke from Sinai scattered the corrupting illusions of polytheism: but slavery planted itself even in the promised land, on the banks of Siloa, near the oracles of God." It was true that the extreme harshness of the Roman slave law had hastened the Empire's fall; but Bancroft's picture of the ancient world suggested that slavery might be planted in other promised lands without blighting their mission.

He adopted, however, the conventional view of Christianity slowly sapping the foundations of bondage in Europe. If slavery had not detracted from the splendor of Grecian republics, it was still incompatible with human progress, and would have disappeared entirely among civilized nations had not an outside force intervened. In Bancroft's eyes this outside force was not America, but the continuing wars between Islam and Christianity, which had nourished bigotry and revenge. Angered by the raids of Saracen corsairs, Christians had felt justified in capturing any Moor they could lay hands upon, and they had classified all Africans as Moors. In any event, the Negroes themselves had always accepted slavery, and when the Portuguese had commenced trading along the western coast of Africa, they had simply appropriated a commercial system which the Moors of the north had established centuries before. Bancroft admitted that the Portuguese were guilty of "mercantile cupidity," but in a certain sense it was Africa that had corrupted Europe.

The Spanish, who had also been brutalized by wars with the Moslems, had endeavored to enslave the Indians, or, as Bancroft called them, the "freemen of the wilderness." Even Columbus had participated in this unnatural act, though such a lapse was presumably redeemed by his contribution to the advance of liberty; and, as Washington Irving had said, "the customs of the times . . . must be pleaded in his apology." Slavery, however, was totally alien to American soil, and in order to rivet the system on their colonies, the Spanish had been forced to import a more docile and submissive race. The significant point about Bancroft's interpretation is that he considered slavery basically extraneous to the New World and contrary to the natural development of Europe. It was thus a kind of abnormal excrescence which had been fastened on America by Europeans whose avarice and brutality had been stimulated by their contact with Africa.

When Bancroft turned to the founding of the North American colonies, he underscored the fundamental conflict between slavery and the very meaning of the New World. "While Virginia," he wrote, "by the concession of a republican government, was constituted the asylum of liberty, by one of the strange contradictions in human affairs, it became the abode of hereditary bondsmen." Monarchy, aristocracy, and priestcraft had no motive to cross the Atlantic—"Nothing came from Europe but a free people. The people, separating itself from all other elements of previous civilization; the people, self-confiding and industrious; the people, wise by all traditions that favored popular happiness—the people alone broke away from European influence, and in the New World laid the foundations of our republic." As part of this classic picture of American innocence and separateness, Bancroft stressed the original and deep antipathy that the people felt for slavery. His argument that slavery was essentially foreign to America appeared to stumble a bit when, discussing South Carolina, he seemed to adopt Montesquieu's belief in the primacy of climate; he even asserted that the contrast between Carolina and New York was due to climate and not to the superior humanity of the original Dutch colonists. Yet he thought that the people and legislation of every colony had favored freedom, and that Massachusetts, especially, had opposed the introduction of slaves from the beginning. In Rhode Island, if Providence and Warwick had failed to enforce their law of 1652 against slavery, "the principle lived among the people."

How, then, could one account for the survival and growth of an institution so repugnant to the desires of a free people? Bancroft's answer was one which Americans had long resorted to; it was founded on a sharp moral distinction between the original cause of American slavery—the selfish greed of European merchants and governments—and the conditions which led to its perpetuation. If the type of servitude fastened on America had been the same as that which Europeans had long endured, the problem would soon have been solved "by the benevolent spirit of colonial legislation." But from the beginning, America had been plagued with racial incompatibility: "The negro race, from the first, was regarded with disgust, and its union with the whites forbidden under ignominious penalties."

Thus racial dissimilarity could be offered as an excuse for laws and practices which simply made the best of an unfortunate situation. And when Bancroft took a larger perspective, he had to admit that America's burden was not, after all, without its rewards. In his native continent the African would have remained in "unproductive servitude"; in America at least his labor contributed greatly to the wealth of nations. Adopting for the moment one of the favorite theories of Southern apologists, Bancroft concluded that "in the midst of the horrors of slavery and the slave trade, the masters had, in part at least, performed the office of advancing and civilizing the negro."

While Bancroft saw a basic contradiction between slavery and America's mission, he resolved the dilemma in a manner that was apparently satisfactory to most of his countrymen. The institution was alien to the true nature of the New World; it had been imposed on the people against their will, and the guilt thus fell upon an already guilt-sickened Europe. Yet in a larger view, even slavery appeared as part of the providential plan for the redemption of the human race. In Bancroft's eyes the first ship that brought Negroes to America was a "sure pledge" that in due time ships from the New World would carry the blessings of Christianity to Africa. Even selfishness and injustice had a role to play in the historical unfolding of truth and liberty. Americans could comfort themselves with the thought that Negro slavery, a vestige of Old World corruption, was only a temporary irritant which would gradually disappear under the beneficent pressure of democratic institutions. The history of the slavery controversy in the United States well testifies that Bancroft was not alone in this optimistic belief.

We have suggested that Negro slavery, a product of innumerable decisions of self-interest made by traders and princes in Europe and Africa, was an intrinsic part of American development from the first discoveries. The evolution of the institution was also coeval with the creation of the idea of America as a new beginning, a land of promise where men's hopes and aspirations would find fulfillment. The dreams and ideals embodied in various images of the New World would not necessarily conflict with the enslavement of a foreign people unless there were already tensions over slavery in the system of values which Europeans applied to America. That there were such tensions remains to be shown. For the moment it will suffice if we note that the problem of slavery in the New World could be conceptualized as part of a general conflict between ideals and reality in the course of human history. Thus the Abbé Raynal hinted that the discrepancy between natural law and colonial slavery was so great that revolution might be necessary to bring the ideal and reality of America into harmony. For Henri Wallon and Auguste Comte, America itself was something of an anomaly, since it represented a disturbing retrogression from the course of historical progress. Yet Wallon's faith in the power of Christianity and Comte's confidence in the inexorable laws of history led them to expect the imminent triumph of freedom. To some extent all three of these thinkers associated the paradox of modern slavery with America itself, but to George Bancroft servitude was fundamentally extrinsic to the New World, whose very meaning lay in the emancipation of mankind. Although Bancroft recognized that the Negro had played a vital part in the founding of certain colonies, he felt that slavery was so contrary to America's destiny that it would evaporate from the sheer heat of triumphant democracy.

Captain John Smith's Image of America

Edwin C. Rozwenc

Many early American historians and their works fell victim to the onslaught of the late-nineteenth-century "scientific" historians, who felt it necessary not only to expose their exaggerations and errors but also to discredit them completely as useful contributors to American history—they had not written history "as it actually happened." John Smith was one of these discredited historians. In this article, Edwin Rozwenc, late Professor of History at Amherst College, attacks the myth that Smith was not a credible historian. If Smith did elaborate, expand, and exhibit egotism, he was also one of the first to see the real promise and vision of America as well as to write much very solid history. Smith personified the era's utopian sensibility.

Nearly a hundred years ago, John Gorham Palfrey, a devoted student of New England's antiquities, remarked to Henry Adams that he had certain historic doubts as to the story of Captain John Smith and Pocahontas. An article in the *North American Review* on that subject, he suggested, "would attract as much attention, and probably break as much glass, as any other stone that could be thrown by a beginner." Adams' essay on Captain John Smith in the *North American Review* was a full-scale attack on Smith's veracity as a historian. He centered his attack on the Pocahontas story as it appears in *The Generall Historie of Virginia, New England and the Summer Isles* published more than a decade after Smith had written his first brief account of his adventures in the New World. Adams frankly stated that his purpose was "nothing less than the entire erasure of one of the more attractive portions of American history."

For a generation or more after Henry Adams' famous essay, Smith became the subject of one of the most celebrated controversies in American history. To a certain extent, the quarrel over Smith's reputation as a historian became a sectional battle in which Southern writers, particularly Virginians, sought to defend Smith against a Yankee conspiracy to defame him. More recent scholarship, however, demonstrates that there is substantial truth in Smith's historical writings, even in the fantastic European adventures recorded in *The True Travels, Adventures, and Observations of Captain John Smith.*

From "Captain John Smith's Image of America," by Edwin C. Rozwenc, in *William and Mary Quarterly*, Ser. 3, XVI (January 1959). Reprinted by permission of the publisher.

The interminable debate as to whether the dramatic Pocahontas story can be preserved as part of a true record of the American historical experience has diverted attention from important questions about Captain John Smith. Those we raise must be concerned with more than the truthfulness of his historical accounts, important—and fascinating—as such questions may be. The redoubtable Captain's accounts of the settlement of Virginia lie athwart the starting point of our history and in one way or another we must come to terms with them. His writings, indeed, are one of the first attempts to make an imaginative reconstruction of the origins and meaning of the American experience.

Every man's vision is directed by the metaphors which rule his mind. We must, therefore, seek to discover how Captain Smith chose to give order and meaning to his experiences in the New World: what models of historical reporting were available to him and what resources could he draw upon out of the imaginative experience of Europeans to construct his own narrative? In the light of these questions, we begin to see how a spirit of knight-errantry and the yearnings of a self-made man are interwoven in his conception of America and its possibilities.

The *Generall Historie*, which contains the fullest account of Smith's experiences in America, adds new dimensions to the literary conventions of the chivalric romance. The third and fourth books, particularly, have a dramatic rhythm and an exciting vividness that charmed Americans for generations until Henry Adams began to throw his stones. Excitement and suspense are at high pitch throughout the *Generall Historie*; surprise attacks and ambuscades, spectacular Indian fights in boats and canoes as well as in the forest, colorful Indian feasts, dances and ceremonies fill its pages. The creation of tension prior to the deliverance by Pocahontas is a little masterpiece of dramatic preparation. Our hero is tied to a tree, and Indian braves dance around him, painted in a fearful manner, shaking rattles and shouting; there are orations, with the chief priest speaking in a "hellish voyce," and the pitting of white man's magic against Indian magic. Throughout the narrative, Captain Smith looms above all other men, matching wits with a wily and resourceful Powhatan, issuing commands, performing acts of individual heroism when personal bravery was the last resource.

The *Generall Historie*, indeed, breathes a spirit that we associate with the popular romances of the Elizabethan Age. As Smith grew to manhood on a Lincolnshire farm, the vogue of the medieval chivalric romance was at its height in England. Popular versions of the knightly deeds of Guy of Warwick, Tom of Lincoln, and Palmerin of England fell from the presses like autumn leaves and fed the imaginations of middle-class readers for generations.

Although little is known of Smith's reading habits, Bradford Smith has reminded us that the captain's imagination was fired by the heroic models of the knightly romance. In the autobiographical *True Travels* written a few years after the *Generall Historie*, Smith chooses to recall that, when a young man, he left his home for a time and retired to a wooded area. "Here by a faire brook he built a Pavillon of boughes, where only in his cloaths he lay. His study was *Machiavills* Art of warre and *Marcus Aurelius*; his exercise a good horse, with his lance and Ring; his food was thought to be more of venison than anything else. . . ." His life as a knightly hermit attracted notice and he was soon invited to Tattersall Castle, the seat of Henry, Earl of Lincoln, where he was taught the finer arts of horsemanship by an Italian riding master. Afterwards, he went to the Low Countries to begin his series of "brave adventures" across Europe.

The romantic hermitage in the forest by "a faire brook" smacks of a Robin Hood without followers. There are resemblances, too, to certain familiar patterns in the Arthurian romances. Tom of Lincoln and Bevis of Hampton lived in fields and forests as shepherd boys until their true nobility could be put to the test before the princes and ladies of the world.

As for Smith's later adventures in Europe, we are reminded of Guy of Warwick who "enjoyed" his ladylove to watch and wait while he proved himself by "deeds." He then set sail for Normandy and fought his way through Flanders, Spain, and Lombardy, eventually to fight the Saracens at Constantinople. Smith followed a similar pattern of great deeds from the Low Countries across Europe to the Hungarian plains. There, in single combats before the eyes of the two armies, "the Rampiers all beset with fair Dames," Smith slew three Turkish champions with lance, pistol, and battle-ax. Their decapitated heads were mounted on lances at the subsequent ceremony, and the General of the army bestowed on Smith a promotion, "a faire Horse richly furnished," and a "Semitere and belt worth three hundred ducats."

Like many a knight of old, Smith was rescued by a fair lady at the moment of direst peril—not once, but three times. The beauteous Lady Tragabigzanda aided him when he was a captive of the Turks; the Lady Callamata give him succor after he arrived half dead from his fearful flight from Turkish captivity across the Russian steppes to the Don; and Pocahontas saved his life in the New World whence he had gone to add new deeds to the brave adventures already accomplished in the Old. Unlike the heroes of knightly romances however, Smith never had affairs of love with his rescuers. They were stage deities who intervened at the proper moments, and always women of high rank—an aid no doubt to Smith's pretensions to being a gentleman, coat of arms and all.

The fantastic adventures recorded in the *True Travels* were regarded by Henry Adams as partly fictitious and as a further reason for impugning the reliability of Smith's writings. More recent investigations have shown us that the inconsistencies and seeming inventions in Smith's writings are greatly outnumbered by reports and observations that have successfully passed the critical scrutiny of geographers, anthropologists, and historians. Henry Adams' generation was enthralled by the possibilities of scientific history, and Adams himself sought to discover whether history could be written "by the severest process of stating, with the least possible comment, such facts as seemed sure." Nevertheless the artist and the scientist are as inseparably connected in all of his historical writing as the two opposite faces of an ancient deity. Perhaps if Henry Adams had not been a mere "beginner" when he wrote his essay on Captain John Smith, he might have been able to appreciate that Smith's historical writing was affected by the popular literary attitudes of Elizabethan and Jacobean England.

Yet the influence of popular literary taste alone cannot account for the character of Smith's historical writing. We must remember also that the conceptions of the nature of history and of the office of the historian as it was held in Smith's day differ greatly from our own. When Smith's *Generall Historie* was written, one of the most widely read historians in England was Sir Walter Raleigh. In a panegyric on history prefixed to his own *History of the World*, Raleigh wrote:

> True it is, that among other benefits, for which History hath been honoured, in this one it triumpheth over all human knowledge—that it hath given us life in our understanding. Since the world itself and life and beginning, even to this day: yea it hath triumphed over time, which besides it, nothing but eternity hath triumphed over. . . . And it is not the least debt we owe to History, that it hath made us acquainted with our dead ancestors and out of the depth and darkness of the earth, delivered us of their memory and fame.

The end and scope of history, Raleigh wrote, was to "teach by example of times past such wisdom as may guide our desires and actions"; the memory and the fame of the great deeds of men were the best examples.

No less was Captain John Smith a child of the Elizabethan Age. In 1630, he wrote, "Seeing honour is our lives ambition, and our ambition after death, to have an honourable memory of our life: and seeing by no meanes we would be abated of the dignitie and glory of our predecessors, let us imitate their vertues to be worthily their successors. . . ." His opening lines in the third book of the *Generall Historie,* which relates the dramatic story of the founding of Virginia, express his desire for the "eternizing of the memory of those that effected it."

Smith's concept of history and his literary imagination gave him the proper dress with which to clothe his image of America. The deeds of Englishmen in Virginia were as worthy of being eternized as those of the Spaniards in Peru and Mexico. Although no gold and silver were discovered in Virginia, Smith saw much that was wondrous in the accomplishments of "those that the three first yeares began this Plantation; notwithstanding all their factions, mutinies, and miseries, so gently corrected, and well prevented. . . ." He challenged his readers to "peruse the *Spanish Decades*, the Relations of Master *Hackluit,* and tell me how many ever with such small meanes as a Barge of 22 *(or rather two)* tuns, sometimes with seaven, eight, or nine, or but at most, twelve or sixteene men, did ever so discover so many fayre and navigable Rivers, subject so many severall Kings, people, and Nations, to obedience and contribution, with so little bloudshed."

We can understand, therefore, why so much is related about Smith's explorations and Indian fights, and so little is told us of the day-by-day events at Jamestown. Whatever his motives to puff up his personal reputation, history was a matter of the glories and great deeds of men—not their prosaic daily affairs.

Yet we must not be led into a mistaken idea of John Smith's conception of America by the romantic glitter of many of the narrative passages in the *Generall Historie.* America was not simply another field of action for a bold knight. America was a land of opportunity—where men of enterprise might create a flourishing social order. The idea of America that is revealed in other portions of Smith's writing is filled with expectations of great opportunity for the individual even if the society of the New World does not change all of the distinctions of the English social order. John Smith was a self-made gentleman and the impulses that made for social mobility in Elizabethan England are writ large in his estimate of the New World's possibilities.

In the sixth book of the *Generall Historie* dealing with the prospects of New England, Smith asks:

> Who can desire more content that hath small meanes, or but onely his merit to advance his fortunes, than to tread and plant that ground he hath purchased by the hazard of his life; if hee have but the taste of vertue and magnanimity, what to such a minde can bee more pleasant than planting and building a foundation for his posterity, got from rude earth by Gods blessing and his owne industry without prejudice to any. . . .

America is not primarily a place for the soldier-knight; it beckons to the industrious who are willing to build a fortune for themselves and their posterity. But America offers more than a good chance for fortune hunters; it presents the opportunity for creating a happier and more enlightened society. In the same passage, he asks further:

> What so truly sutes with honour and honesty, as the discovering things unknowne, erecting Townes, peopling Countries, informing the ignorant, reforming things unjust, teaching vertue . . . finde imploiment for those that are idle, because they know not what to do: so farre from wronging any, as to cause posterity to remember thee; and remembering thee, ever honour that remembrance with praise.

This is a magnificent dream of America's possibilities, one which drew thousands of Englishmen to America's shores and is still with us in many respects. But we must remember that this vision of social opportunity is not one of a society of yeoman farmers each relatively equal to the other in his station in life. Much has been made of Captain Smith's effort to organize the labor of the Jamestown settlers when he was president by laying down the rule that "he that will not worke, shall not eate." Yet we must not assume that he was responding to the wilderness environment by instituting a rough-and-ready frontier equalitarianism. This was the order of a military captain seeking to maintain discipline, not that of a social visionary seeking to create a new social order in which manual labor was to have the highest value. Elsewhere, when Smith recounts the story of how he made "two gallants . . . both proper Gentlemen" cut down trees till their tender fingers were blistered, he hastens to add: "By this, let no man thinke that the President, and these Gentlemen spent their times as common Woodhaggers at felling of trees, or such other like labours; or that they were pressed to it as hirelings, or common slaves; for what they did, after they were but once a little inured, it seemed, and some conceited it, onely as a pleasure and recreation." Smith was too proud of his coat of arms acquired by valorous exploits in Transylvania to war upon a social system based on honor and distinction.

Nevertheless, something in Captain Smith, perhaps the hard core of common sense of a man who makes his own way, made him realize that the destiny of North America would not lie with gold and silver treasure. One cause of his quarrels with other leaders in Jamestown had been his opposition to vain searches after fool's gold; he preferred to direct the energies of the men at Jamestown into hacking trees, cutting clapboards, and making pitch and potash for shipment to England. Smith's vision of America is closer to that of Richard Hakluyt and Sir Humphrey Gilbert who thought of America as a place where a balanced English society would grow, producing commodities of use to the mother country and serving as a market for the profit of English merchants and manufacturers.

America was more than a land of profit and contentment, even more than a land of honour and virtue; it was a presence of great natural beauty. A tireless explorer and map-maker whose observations in Virginia and New England contributed much to the geographical knowledge of the time, Smith was also a man who felt the power and the charm of Nature in the New World. Often his descriptions have the obvious purpose of advertising the New World to prospective immigrants—the climate is temperate, the soil fertile, the woods abound with wild fruits and game, the waters swim with fish in plenty—but there are also frequent flashes of subjective responses to "glistering tinctures" of water rushing over the rocks in a mountain stream, "sweet brookes and christall springs," the awesome, craggy "clifty rocks" of the Maine coast near Penobscot, the "high sandy clifts" and "large long ledges" along the coast of Massachusetts Bay. By 1616, Smith had become a convinced "northern man" among those in England who were seeking to promote other colonial ventures in America. He speaks of Massachusetts as the "Paradice of all those parts" and declares "of all the foure parts of the world that I have yet seene not inhabited . . . I would rather live here than any where." To be sure, any honest New Englander will grant that Smith often exaggerates the fertility of the soil in New England and the moderateness of the climate, but no one can doubt that the natural beauty of the land had cast a spell on the Captain that exceeded the requirements of seventeenth-century advertising!

Aside from short voyages made to New England, Smith's experience with America was limited to the two years he lived in Virginia; yet to the end of his days his heart and mind were bewitched by America, as it was and as he dreamed it; and Americans in turn have been bewitched by him ever since. In the words of the poet [Stephen Vincent Benet]:

> He is one of the first Americans we know,
> And we can claim him, though not by bond of birth,
> For we've always bred chimeras.

In a very compelling sense, John Smith is an American historian—one who tried to express the meaning of events in the origins of American experience. By the modern canons of history, a man who writes of events in which he is a participant is already suspect, but, when he does so with zestful attention to his personal exploits, we are tempted to dismiss him as a braggart and a liar. Nevertheless, there is an intractable worth in John Smith's historical writings that will not allow us to cast them aside. Wesley Frank Craven says of him: "Allowing for the exaggeration of his own importance, it must be recognized that his works contain much reliable information and that he himself was a man of real courage and strength. . . . His judgment of the conditions of the colony and their causes in the maladministration of the company through the years immediately preceding its fall are supported in the main by a careful study of the sources now at hand."

By and large, the discrepancies of fact in his historical writing, involving as they often do such questions as the number of Indians who guarded him or the quantities of food served to him, are really trivial matters—the peccadillos of an amateur historian over which we need not blush any more than we do for the peccadillos of a historian of any age. The great amount of data in Smith's historical writings has survived tests of credibility in every generation since they were published. The Pocahontas story may be an invention of Smith's mind, or of many minds in the taverns of seventeenth-century London, but on the basis of recent reexaminations of the evidence, the critical historian can admit the likelihood of Smith's deliverance by "the Indian princess" with fewer doubts than he might have had a generation ago.

Smith's historical imagination is one key to our understanding of the approach of Englishmen to the New World. He wrote of a brief moment only in the minuscule beginnings of Anglo-Saxon culture in North America. But he brought to his relation of events in Virginia the spirit of knight-errantry which still had a hold upon the imaginations of men in Elizabethan and Jacobean England and gave to Englishmen a vision of America as a place in which to achieve personal honor and glory. When we remember W. J. Cash's penetrating analysis of the aristocratic ideals of the South, we can understand readily that the chivalric spirit of the *Generall Historie* makes the defense of John Smith's reputation by Southerners something of an automatic reflex. The *Generall Historie* points to social attitudes and styles of life that actually became fundamental social traits in Virginia and much of the South.

But Captain John Smith is more than a totem in the Southern tradition of chivalry. After his brief trials and encounters in Virginia, he understood well that America was destiny and possibility—that America's history lay in the future. He saw that destiny in terms of opportunity for improvement. America would be a place where men might find economic betterment, not by plunderings of gold and other treasure, but in a balanced society of husbandmen, tradesmen, and merchants. The New World, withal, would be a place where men might teach virtue and establish a morality free of the encumbrances of the Old. John Smith's *Generall Historie* is an important part of the deeper cultural consciousness which has sustained this perennial faith in the promise of American life.

Were the Puritans "Puritanical"?

Carl. N. Degler

Few groups in history have suffered more from a "bad press" than have the seventeenth-century Puritans of the Massachusetts Bay Colony. The word *Puritan* immediately evokes images of a dour and drab society populated by prigs and "moral athletes." This popular image of the Puritans as premature Victorians needs readjustment. In the essay that follows, Carl Degler, formerly of Vassar and now Professor of History at Stanford, challenges many of the stock notions so long associated with Puritan New England. He concludes that the Puritans were both more humane and more complex than formerly imagined.

To most Americans—and to most Europeans, for that matter—the core of the Puritan social heritage has been summed up in Macaulay's well-known witticism that the Puritans prohibited bearbaiting not because of torture to the bear, but because of the pleasure it afforded the spectators. And as late as 1925, H. L. Mencken defined Puritanism as "the haunting fear that someone, somewhere, may be happy." Before this chapter is out, much will be said about the somber and even grim nature of the Puritan view of life, but quips like those of Macaulay and Mencken distort rather than illumine the essential character of the Puritans. Simply because the word "Puritan" has become encrusted with a good many barnacles, it is worthwhile to try to scrape them off if we wish to gain an understanding of the Puritan heritage. Though this process is essentially a negative one, sometimes it is clarifying to set forth what an influence is *not* as well as what it is.

Fundamental to any appreciation of the Puritan mind on matters of pleasure must be the recognition that the typical, godly Puritan was a worker in the world. Puritanism, like Protestantism in general, resolutely and definitely rejected the ascetic and monastic ideals of medieval Catholicism. Pleasures of the body were not to be eschewed by the Puritan, for, as Calvin reasoned, God "intended to provide not only for our necessity, but likewise for our pleasure and delight." It is obvious, he wrote in his famous *Institutes*, that "the Lord hath endowed flowers with such beauty . . . with such sweetness of smell" in order to impress our senses; therefore, to enjoy them is not contrary to God's intentions. "In a word," he concluded, "hath He not made many things worthy of our estimation independent of any necessary use?"

It was against excess of enjoyment that the Puritans cautioned and legislated. "The wine is from God," Increase Mather warned, "but the Drunkard is from the Devil." The Cambridge Platform of the Church of 1680 prohibited games of cards or dice because of the amount of time they consumed and the encouragement they offered to idleness, but the ministers of Boston in 1699 found no difficulty in condoning public lotteries. They were like a public tax, the ministers said, since they took only what the "government might have demanded, with a more *general imposition* . . . and it employes for the welfare of the publick, all that is raised by the *lottery*." Though Cotton Mather at the end of the century condemned mixed dancing, he did not object to dancing as such; and his grandfather, John Cotton, at the beginning saw little to object to in dancing between the sexes so long as it did not become lascivious. It was this same John Cotton, incidentally, who successfully contended against Roger Williams' argument that women should wear veils in church.

In matters of dress, it is true that the Massachusetts colony endeavored to restrict the wearing of "some new and immodest fashions" that were coming in from England, but often these efforts were frustrated by the pillars of the church themselves. Winthrop reported in his *History,* for example, that though the General Court instructed the elders of the various churches to reduce the ostentation in dress by "urging it upon the consciences of their people," little change was effected, "for divers of the elders' wives, etc., were in some measure partners in this general disorder."

We also know now that Puritan dress—not that made "historical" by Saint-Gaudens' celebrated statue—was the opposite of severe, being rather in the English Renaissance style. Most restrictions on dress which were imposed were for purposes of class differentiation rather than for ascetic reasons. Thus long hair was acceptable on an upper-class Puritan like Cromwell or Winthrop, but it was a sign of vanity on the head of a person of lower social status. In 1651 the legislature of Massachusetts called attention to that "excess in Apparell" which has "crept in upon us, and especially amongst people of mean condition, to the dishonor of God, the scandall of our profession, the consumption of Estates, and altogether unsuitable to our poverty." The law declared "our utter detestation and dislike, that men or women of mean condition, should take upon them the garb of Gentlemen, by wearing Gold or Silver Lace, or Buttons, or Points at their knees, or to walk in great Boots; or Women of the same rank to wear Silk or Tiffany hoods, or Scarfes, which tho allowable to persons of great Estates, or more liberal education, is intolerable in people of low conditions." By implication, this law affords a clear description of what the well-dressed Puritan of good estate would wear.

If the Puritans are to be saved from the canard of severity of dress, it is also worth while to soften the charge that they were opposed to music and art. It is perfectly true that the Puritans insisted that organs be removed from the churches and that in England some church organs were smashed by zealots. But it was not music or organs as such which they opposed, only music in the meetinghouse. Well-known American and English Puritans, like Samuel

Sewell, John Milton, and Cromwell, were sincere lovers of music. Moreover, it should be remembered that it was under Puritan rule that opera was introduced into England—and without protest, either. The first English dramatic production entirely in music—*The Siege of Rhodes*—was presented in 1656, four years before the Restoration. Just before the end of Puritan rule, John Evelyn noted in his diary that he went "to see a new opera, after the Italian way, in recitative music and scenes. . . ." Furthermore, as Percy Scholes points out, in all the voluminous contemporary literature attacking the Puritans for every conceivable narrow-mindedness, none asserts that they opposed music, so long as it was performed outside the church.

The weight of the evidence is much the same in the realm of art. Though King Charles' art collection was dispersed by the incoming Commonwealth, it is significant that Cromwell and other Puritans bought several of the items. We also know that the Protector's garden at Hampton Court was beautified by nude statues. Furthermore, it is now possible to say that the Puritan closing of the theaters was as much a matter of objection to their degenerate lewdness by the 1640's as an objection to the drama as such. As far as American Puritans are concerned, it is not possible to say very much about their interest in art since there was so little in the seventeenth century. At least it can be said that the Puritans, unlike the Quakers, had no objection to portrait painting.

Some modern writers have professed to find in Puritanism, particularly the New England brand, evidence of sexual repression and inhibition. Though it would certainly be false to suggest that the Puritans did not subscribe to the canon of simple chastity, it is equally erroneous to think that their sexual lives were crabbed or that sex was abhorrent to them. Marriage to the Puritan was something more than an alternative to "burning," as the Pauline doctrine of the Catholic Church would have it. Marriage was enjoined upon the righteous Christian; celibacy was not a sign of merit. With unconcealed disapprobation, John Cotton told a recently married couple the story of a pair "who immediately upon marriage, without ever approaching the *Nuptial* Bed," agreed to live apart from the rest of the world, "and afterwards from one another, too. . . ." But, Cotton advised, such behavior was "no other than an effort of blind zeal, for they are the dictates of a blind mind they follow therein and not of the Holy Spirit which saith, *It is not good that man should be alone.*" Cotton set himself against not only Catholic asceticism but also the view that women were the "unclean vessel," the tempters of men. Women, rather than being "a necessary Evil are a necessary Good," he wrote. "Without them there is no comfortable Living for Man. . . ."

Because, as another divine said, "the Use of the Marriage Bed" is "founded in man's Nature," the realistic Puritans required that married men unaccompanied by wives should leave the colony or bring their wives over forthwith. The Puritan settlements encouraged marriages satisfactory to the participants by permitting divorces for those whose spouses were impotent, too long absent, or cruel. Indeed, the divorce laws of New England were the easiest in Christendom at a time when the eloquence of a Milton was unable to loosen the bonds of matrimony in England.

Samuel Eliot Morison in his history of Harvard has collected a number of examples of the healthy interest of Puritan boys in the opposite sex. Commonplace books, for example, indicate that Herrick's poem beginning "Gather ye rosebuds while ye may" and amorous lines from Shakespeare, as well as more erotic and even scatological verse, were esteemed by young Puritan men. For a gentleman to present his affianced with a pair of garters, one letter of a Harvard graduate tells us, was considered neither immoral nor improper.

It is also difficult to reconcile the usual view of the stuffiness of Puritans with the literally hundreds of confessions to premarital sexual relations in the extant church records. It should be understood, moreover, that these confessions were made by the saints or saints-to-be, not by the unregenerate. That the common practice of the congregation was to accept such sinners into church membership without further punishment is in itself revealing. The civil law, it is true, punished such transgressions when detected among the regenerate or among the nonchurch members, but this was also true of contemporary non-Puritan Virginia. "It will be seen," writes historian Philip A. Bruce regarding Virginia, "from the various instances given relating to the profanation of Sunday, drunkenness, swearing, defamation, and sexual immorality, that, not only were the grand juries and vestries extremely vigilant in reporting these offenses, but the courts were equally prompt in inflicting punishment; and that the penalty ranged from a heavy fine to a shameful exposure in the stocks . . . and from such an exposure to a very severe flogging at the county whipping post." In short, strict moral surveillance by the public authorities was a seventeenth-century rather than a Puritan attitude.

Relations between the sexes in Puritan society were often much more loving and tender than the mythmakers would have us believe. Since it was the Puritan view that marriage was eminently desirable in the sight of God and man, it is not difficult to find evidence of deep and abiding love between a husband and wife. John Cotton, it is true, sometimes used the Biblical phrase "comfortable yoke mate" in addressing his wife, but other Puritan husbands come closer to our romantic conventions. Certainly John Winthrop's letters to his beloved Margaret indicate the depth of attachment of which the good Puritan was capable. "My good wife . . . My sweet wife," he called her. Anticipating his return home, he writes, "So . . . we shall now enjoy each other again, as we desire. . . . It is now bed time; but I must lie alone; therefore I make less haste. Yet I must kiss my sweet wife; and so, with my blessing to our children . . . I commend thee to the grace and blessing of the Lord, and rest. . . ."

Anne Bradstreet wrote a number of poems devoted to her love for her husband in which the sentiments and figures are distinctly romantic.

> To my Dear and loving Husband
> I prize thy love more than whole Mines of gold
> Or all the riches that the East doth hold.
> My love is such that Rivers cannot quench,
> Nor aught but love from thee give recompense.

In another poem her spouse is apostrophized as

> My head, my heart, mine Eyes, my life, nay more
> My joy, my Magazine of earthly store

and she asks:

> If two be one, as surely thou and I,
> How stayest thou there, whilst I at Ipswich lye?

Addressing John as "my most sweet Husband," Margaret Winthrop perhaps epitomized the Puritan marital ideal when she wrote, "I have many reasons to make me love thee, whereof I will name two: First, because thou lovest God and, secondly, because thou lovest me. If these two were wanting," she added, "all the rest would be eclipsed."

It would be a mistake, however, to try to make these serious, dedicated men and women into rakes of the Renaissance. They were sober if human folk, deeply concerned about their ultimate salvation and intent upon living up to God's commands as they understood them, despite their acknowledgment of complete depravity and unworthiness. "God sent you not into this world as a Play-House, but as a Work-House," one minister told his congregation. To the Puritan this was a world drenched in evil, and, because it truly is, they were essentially realistic in their judgments. Because the Puritan expected nothing, Perry Miller has remarked, a disillusioned one was almost impossible to find. This is probably an exaggeration, for they were also human beings; when the Commonwealth fell, it was a Puritan, after all, who said, "God has spit in our faces." But Professor Miller's generalization has much truth in it. Only a man convinced of the inevitable and eternal character of evil could fight it so hard and so unceasingly.

The Puritan at his best, Ralph Barton Perry has said, was a "moral athlete." More than most men, the Puritan strove with himself and with his fellow man to attain a moral standard higher than was rightfully to be expected of so depraved a creature. Hence the diaries and autobiographies of Puritans are filled with the most torturous probing of the soul and inward seeking. Convinced of the utter desirability of salvation on the one hand, and equally cognizant of the total depravity of man's nature on the other, the Puritan was caught in an impossible dilemma which permitted him no rest short of the grave. Yet with such a spring coiled within him, the Puritan drove himself and his society to tremendous heights of achievement both material and spiritual.

Such intense concern for the actualization of the will of God had a less pleasant side to it, also. If the belief that "I am my brother's keeper" is the breeding ground of heightened social conscience and expresses itself in the reform movements so indigenous to Boston and its environs, it also could and did lead to self-righteousness, intolerance and narrow-mindedness, as exemplified in another product of Boston: Anthony Comstock. But this fruit of the loins of Puritanism is less typical of the earthy seventeenth-century New Englander than H. L. Mencken would have us think. The Sabbatarian, antiliquor, and antisex attitudes usually attributed to the Puritans are a nineteenth-century addition to the much more moderate and essentially wholesome view of life's evils held by the early settlers of New England.

To realize how different Puritans could be, one needs only to contrast

Roger Williams and his unwearying opponent John Cotton. But despite the range of differences among Puritans, they all were linked by at least one characteristic. That was their belief in themselves, in their morality and in their mission to the world. For this reason, Puritanism was intellectual and social dynamite in the seventeenth century; its power could behead kings, overthrow governments, defy tyrants, and disrupt churches.

The Reformation laid an awesome burden on the souls of those who broke with the Roman Church. Proclaiming the priesthood of all believers, Protestantism made each man's relationship to God his own terrifying responsibility. No one else could save him; therefore no one must presume to try. More concerned about his salvation than about any mundane matter, the Puritan was compelled, for the sake of his immortal soul, to be a fearless individualist.

It was the force of this conviction which produced the Great Migration of 1630–40 and made Massachusetts a flourishing colony in the span of a decade. It was also, ironically, the force which impelled Roger Williams to threaten the very legal and social foundations of the Puritan Commonwealth in Massachusetts because he thought the oligarchy wrong and himself right. And so it would always be. For try as the rulers of Massachusetts might to make men conform to their dogma, their own rebellious example always stood as a guide to those who felt the truth was being denied. Such individualism, we would call it today, was flesh and bone of the religion which the Puritans passed on. Though the theocracy soon withered and died, its harsh voice softened down to the balmy breath of Unitarianism, the belief in self and the dogged resistance to suppression or untruth which Puritanism taught never died. Insofar as Americans today can be said to be individualistic, it is to the Puritan heritage that we must look for one of the principal sources.

In his ceaseless striving for signs of salvation and knowledge of God's intentions for man, the Puritan placed great reliance upon the human intellect, even though for him, as for all Christians, faith was the bedrock of his belief. "Faith doth not relinquish or cast out reason," wrote the American Puritan Samuel Willard, "for there is nothing in Religion contrary to it, tho' there are many things that do transcend and must captivate it." Richard Baxter, the English Puritan, insisted that *"the most Religious, are the most truly, and nobly rational."* Religion and reason were complementary to the Puritan, not antithetical as they were to many evangelical sects of the time.

Always the mere emotion of religion was to be controlled by reason. Because of this, the university-trained Puritan clergy prided themselves on the lucidity and rationality of their sermons. Almost rigorously their sermons followed the logical sequence of "doctrine," "reasons," and "uses." Conscientiously they shunned the meandering and rhetorical flourishes so beloved by Laudian preachers like John Donne, and in the process facilitated the taking of notes by their eager listeners. One of the unforgivable crimes of Mistress Anne Hutchinson was her assertion that one could "feel" one's salvation, that one was "filled with God" after conversion, that it was unnecessary, in order to be saved, to be learned in the Bible or in the Puritan writers. It was not that the Puritans were cold to the Word—far from it. A saint was required to testify to an intense religious experience—almost by definition emotional in character—before he could attain full membership in the Church. But it was always important to the Puritans that mere emotion—whether it be the anarchistic activities of the Anabaptists or the quaking of the Friends—should not be mistaken for righteousness or proper religious conduct. Here, as in so many things, the Puritans attempted to walk the middle path—in this instance, between the excessive legalism and formalism of the Catholics and Episcopalians and the flaming, intuitive evangelism of the Baptists and Quakers.

Convinced of reason's great worth, it was natural that the Puritans should also value education. "Ignorance is the mother (not of Devotion but) of Heresy," one Puritan divine declared. And a remarkably well-educated ministry testified to the Puritan belief that learning and scholarship were necessary for a proper understanding of the Word of God. More than a hundred graduates of Cambridge and Oxford Universities settled in New England before 1640, most of them ministers. At the same date not five men in all of Virginia could lay claim to such an educational background. Since Cambridge University, situated on the edge of Puritan East Anglia, supplied most of the graduates in America, it was natural that Newtown, the site of New England's own college, would soon be renamed in honor of the Alma Mater. "After God had carried us safe to New-England," said a well-known tract, some of its words now immortalized in metal in Harvard Yard, "one of the next things we longed and looked after, was to advance learning, and perpetuate it to posterity; dreading to leave an illiterate ministry to the churches, when the present ministers shall lie in the dust." "The College," founded in 1636, soon to be named Harvard, was destined to remain the only institution of higher learning in America during almost all the years of the seventeenth century. Though it attracted students from as far away as Virginia, it remained, as it began, the fountainhead of Puritan learning in the New World.

Doubt as one may Samuel Eliot Morison's claims for the secular origins of Harvard, his evidence of the typically Renaissance secular education which was available at the Puritan college in New England is both impressive and convincing. The Latin and Greek secular writers of antiquity dominated the curriculum, for this was a liberal arts training such as the leaders had received at Cambridge in England. To the Puritans the education of ministers could be nothing less than the best learning of the day. So important did education at Harvard seem to the New Haven colony in 1644 that the legislature ordered each town to appoint two men to be responsible for the collection of contributions from each family for "the mayntenaunce of scolars at Cambridge. . . ."

If there was to be a college, preparatory schools had to be provided for the training of those who were expected to enter the university. Furthermore, in a society dedicated to the reading of the Bible, elementary education was indispensable. "It being one chief project of that old deluder Satan to keep men from the knowledge of the Scriptures" began the first school laws of Massachusetts (1647) and Connecticut (1650). But the Puritans supported education for secular as well as religious reasons. The Massachusetts Code of 1648, for instance, required children to be taught to read inasmuch "as the good education of children is of singular behoof and benefit to any Commonwealth."

The early New England school laws provided that each town of fifty families or more was to hire a teacher for the instruction of its young; towns of one hundred families or more were also directed to provide grammar schools, "the master thereof being able to instruct youths so far as they may be fitted for the University." Though parents were not obliged to send their children to these schools, if they did not they were required to teach their children to read. From the evidence of court cases and the high level of literacy in seventeenth-century New England, it would appear that these first attempts at public-supported and public-controlled education were both enforced and fruitful.

No other colony in the seventeenth century imposed such a high educational standard upon its simple farming people as the Puritans did. It is true, of course, that Old England in this period could boast of grammar schools, some of which were free. But primary schools were almost nonexistent there, and toward the end of the seventeenth century the free schools in England became increasingly tuition schools. Moreover, it was not until well into the nineteenth century that the English government did anything to support schools. Primary and secondary education in England, in contrast with the New England example, was a private or church affair.

Unlike the Puritans, the Quakers exhibited little impulse toward popular education in the seventeenth and early eighteenth centuries. Because of their accent on the Inner Light and the doctrine of universal salvation, the religious motivation of the Puritans for learning was wanting. Furthermore, the Quakers did not look to education, as such, with the same reverence as the Puritans. William Penn, for example, advised his children that "reading many books is but a taking off the mind too much from meditation." No Puritan would have said that.

Virginia in the seventeenth century, it should be said, was also interested in education. Several times in the course of the century, plans were well advanced for establishing a university in the colony. Free schools also existed in Virginia during the seventeenth century, though the lack of village communities made them inaccessible for any great numbers of children. But, in contrast with New England, there were no publicly supported schools in Virginia; the funds for the field schools of Virginia, like those for free schools in contemporary England, came from private or ecclesiastical endowment. Nor was Virginia able to bring its several plans for a college into reality until William and Mary was founded at the very end of the century.

Though the line which runs from the early New England schools to the distinctly American system of free public schools today is not always progressively upward or uniformly clear, the connection is undeniable. The Puritan innovation of public support and control on a local level was the American prototype of a proper system of popular education.

American higher education in particular owes much to religion, for out of the various churches' concern for their faiths sprang a number of colleges, after the example of the Puritans' founding of Harvard. At the time of the

Revolution, there were eight colleges besides Harvard in the English colonies, of which all but one were founded under the auspices of a church. William and Mary (1693) and King's College, later Columbia (1754), were the work of the Episcopalians; Yale (1701) and Dartmouth (1769) were set up by Congregationalists not comforted by Harvard; the College of New Jersey, later Princeton (1747), was founded by the Presbyterians; Queens College, later Rutgers (1766), by the Dutch Reformed Church; the College of Rhode Island, later Brown (1764), by the Baptists. Only the Academy of Philadelphia, later the University of Pennsylvania (1749), was secular in origin.

The overwhelming importance of the churches in the expansion of American higher education during the colonial period set a pattern which continued well into the nineteenth century and to a limited extent is still followed. Well-known colleges like Oberlin, Wesleyan, Haverford, Wittenberg, Moravian, Muhlenberg, and Notre Dame were all founded by churches in the years before the Civil War. By providing a large number of colleges (recall that England did not enjoy a third university until the nineteenth century), the religious impulses and diversity of the American people very early encouraged that peculiarly American faith in the efficacy and desirability of education for all.

When dwelling on the seminal qualities of the seventeenth century, it is tempting to locate the source of the later American doctrine of the separation of Church and State and religious freedom in the writings of Roger Williams and in the practices of provinces like New York, Maryland and Pennsylvania. Actually, however, such a line of development is illusory. At the time of the Revolution all the colonies, including Rhode Island, imposed restrictions and disabilities upon some sects, thus practicing at best only a limited form of toleration, not freedom of religion—much less separation of Church and State. Moreover, Roger Williams' cogent and prophetic arguments in behalf of religious freedom were forgotten in the eighteenth century; they could not exert any influence on those who finally worked out the doctrine of religious freedom enshrined in the national Constitution. In any case, it would have been exceedingly difficult for Williams to have spoken to Jefferson and the other Virginians who fought for religious freedom. To Williams the Puritan, the great justification for freedom of religion was the preservation of the purity of the Church; to the deistic Virginians, the important goal was the removal of a religious threat to the purity and freedom of the State.

The Great Awakening as Interpretive Fiction

Jon Butler

The "Great Awakening"—the era of religious revivalism that spread waves of religious enthusiasm across colonial America in the mid-eighteenth century—has been a convenient historiographical watershed used by historians to help explain the growing ideology of independence that eventually coalesced into full-scale revolution against England later in the century. Historian Jon Butler of Yale University finds the alleged unified and central significance traditionally accorded the Great Awakening in many ways problematic. While offering an enticing rubric under which to explain the shaping and character of prerevolutionary American society, it ought to be—says Butler—a matter treated with greater scholarly suspicion. The "event" is difficult to date, exhibits highly regionalized and provincial manifestations, and proved less than emotionally enduring. Revivalism was never the critical element in the expansion of colonial churches, much less the key to explaining in any thoroughgoing sense the gradual move toward independence and democracy.

In the last half-century, the Great Awakening has assumed a major role in explaining the political and social evolution of prerevolutionary American society. Historians have argued, variously, that the Awakening severed intellectual and philosophical connections between America and Europe (Perry Miller), that it was a major vehicle of early lower-class protest (John C. Miller, Rhys Isaac, and Gary B. Nash), that it was a means by which New England Puritans became Yankees (Richard L. Bushman), that it was the first "intercolonial movement" to stir "the people of several colonies on a matter of common emotional concern" (Richard Hofstadter following William Warren Sweet), or that it involved "a rebirth of the localistic impulse" (Kenneth Lockridge). . . .

These claims for the significance of the Great Awakening come from more than specialists in the colonial period. They are a ubiquitous feature of American history survey texts, where the increased emphasis on social history had made these claims especially useful in interpreting early American society to twentieth-century students. Virtually all texts treat the Great Awakening as a major watershed in the maturation of prerevolutionary American society.

From "Enthusiasm Described and Decried: The Great Awakening as Interpretive Fiction," by Jon Butler, in *Journal of American History*, 69 (September 1982), pp. 305–325. Copyright © 1982 Organization of American Historians. Reprinted by permission.

The Great Republic terms the Awakening "the greatest event in the history of religion in eighteenth-century America." *The National Experience* argues that the Awakening brought "religious experiences to thousands of people in every rank of society" and in every region. *The Essentials of American History* stresses how the Awakening "aroused a spirit of humanitarianism," "encouraged the notion of equal rights," and "stimulated feelings of democracy" even if its gains in church membership proved episodic. These texts and others describe the weakened position of the clergy produced by the Awakening as symptomatic of growing disrespect for all forms of authority in the colonies and as an important catalyst, even cause, of the American Revolution. The effect of these claims is astonishing. Buttressed by the standard lecture on the Awakening tucked into most survey courses, American undergraduates have been well trained to remember the Great Awakening because their instructors and texts have invested it with such significance.

Does the Great Awakening warrant such enthusiasm? Its puzzling historiography suggests one caution. The Awakening has received surprisingly little systematic study and lacks even one comprehensive general history. The two studies . . . that might qualify as general histories actually are deeply centered in New England. They venture into the middle and southern colonies only occasionally and concentrate on intellectual themes to the exclusion of social history. . . . The result is that the general character of the Great Awakening lacks sustained, comprehensive study even while it benefits from thorough local examinations. The relationship between the Revolution and the Awakening is described in an equally peculiar manner. Alan Heimert's seminal 1966 study, *Religion and the American Mind from the Great Awakening to the Revolution*, despite fair and unfair criticism, has become that kind of influential work whose awesome reputation apparently discourages further pursuit of its subject. Instead, historians frequently allude to the positive relationship between the Awakening and the Revolution without probing the matter in a fresh, systematic way.

The gap between the enthusiasm of historians for the social and political significance of the Great Awakening and its slim, peculiar historiography raises two important issues. First, contemporaries never homogenized the eighteenth-century colonial religious revivals by labeling them "the Great Awakening." Although such words appear in Edwards' *Faithful Narrative of the Surprising Work of God*, Edwards used them alternately with other phrases, such as "general awakening," "great alteration," and "flourishing of religion," only to describe the Northampton revivals of 1734–35. He never capitalized them or gave them other special emphasis and never used the phrase "the Great Awakening" to evaluate all the prerevolutionary revivals. Rather, the first person to do so was the nineteenth-century historian and antiquarian Joseph Tracy, who used Edwards' otherwise unexceptional words as the title of his famous 1842 book, *The Great Awakening*. Tellingly, however, Tracy's creation did not find immediate favor among American historians. Charles Hodge discussed the Presbyterian revivals in his *Constitutional History of the Presbyterian Church* without describing them as part of a "Great

Awakening," while the influential Robert Baird refused even to treat the eighteenth-century revivals as discrete and important events, much less label them "the Great Awakening." Baird all but ignored these revivals in the chronological segments of his *Religion in America* and mentioned them elsewhere only by way of explaining the intellectual origins of the Unitarian movement, whose early leaders opposed revivals. Thus, not until the last half of the nineteenth century did "the Great Awakening" become a familiar feature of the American historical landscape.

Second, this particular label ought to be viewed with suspicion, not because a historian created it—historians legitimately make sense of the minutiae of the past by utilizing such devices—but because the label itself does serious injustice to the minutiae it orders. The label "the Great Awakening" distorts the extent, nature, and cohesion of the revivals that did exist in the eighteenth-century colonies; encourages unwarranted claims for their effects on colonial society; and exaggerates their influence on the coming and character of the American Revolution. If "the Great Awakening" is not quite an American Donation of Constantine, its appeal to historians seeking to explain the shaping and character of prerevolutionary American society gives it a political and intellectual power whose very subtlety requires a close inspection of its claims to truth.

How do historians describe "the Great Awakening"? Three points seem especially common. First, all but a few describe it as a Calvinist religious revival in which converts acknowledged their sinfulness without expecting salvation. These colonial converts thereby distinguished themselves from Englishmen caught up in contemporary Methodist revivals and from Americans involved in the so-called Second Great Awakening of the early national period, both of which imbibed Arminian principles that allowed humans to believe they might effect their own salvation in ways that John Calvin discounted.

*   *   *

"The Great Awakening" also is difficult to date. Seldom has an "event" of such magnitude had such amorphous beginnings and endings. In New England, historians agree, the revivals flourished principally between 1740 and 1743 and had largely ended by 1745, although a few scattered outbreaks of revivalism occurred there in the next decades. Establishing the beginning of the revivals has proved more difficult, however. Most historians settle for the year 1740 because it marks British itinerant George Whitefield's first appearance in New England. But everyone acknowledges that earlier revivals underwrote Whitefield's enthusiastic reception there and involved remarkable numbers of colonists. Edwards counted thirty-two towns caught up in revivals in 1734–35 and noted that his own grandfather, Stoddard, had conducted no less than five "harvests" in Northampton before that, the earliest in the 1690s. Yet revivals in Virginia, the site of the most sustained such events in the southern colonies, did not emerge in significant numbers until the 1750s and did not peak until the 1760s. At the same time, they also continued into the revolutionary and early national periods in ways that make them difficult to separate from their predecessors.

Yet even if one were to argue that "the Great Awakening" persisted through most of the eighteenth century, it is obvious that revivals "swept" only some of the mainland colonies. They occurred in Massachusetts, Connecticut, Rhode Island, Pennsylvania, New Jersey, and Virginia with some frequency at least at some points between 1740 and 1770. But New Hampshire, Maryland, and Georgia witnessed few revivals in the same years, and revivals were only occasionally important in New York, Delaware, North Carolina, and South Carolina. The revivals also touched only certain segments of the population in the colonies where they occurred. The best example of the phenomenon is Pennsylvania. The revivals there had a sustained effect among English settlers only in Presbyterian churches where many of the laity and clergy also opposed them. The Baptists, who were so important to the New England revivals, paid little attention to them until the 1760s, and the colony's taciturn Quakers watched them in perplexed silence. Not even Germans imbibed them universally. At the same time that Benjamin Franklin was emptying his pockets in response to the preaching of Whitefield in Philadelphia—or at least claiming to do so—the residents of Germantown were steadily leaving their churches. . . .

Whitefield's revivals also exchanged notoriety for substance. Colonists responded to him as a charismatic performer, and he actually fell victim to the Billy Graham syndrome of modern times: his visits, however exciting, produced few permanent changes in local religious patterns. For example, his appearances in Charleston led to his well-known confrontation with Anglican Commissary Alexander Garden and to the suicide two years later of a distraught follower named Anne LeBrasseur. Yet they produced no new congregations in Charleston and had no documented effect on the general patterns of religious adherence elsewhere in the colony. The same was true in Philadelphia and New York City, despite the fact that Whitefield preached to enormous crowds in both places. Only Bostonians responded differently. Supporters organized in the late 1740s a new "awakened" congregation that reputedly met with considerable initial success, and opponents adopted a defensive posture exemplified in the writings of Charles Chauncy that profoundly affected New England intellectual life for two decades.

Historians also exaggerate the cohesion of leadership in the revivals. They have accomplished this, in part, by overstressing the importance of Whitefield and Edwards. Whitefield's early charismatic influence later faded so that his appearances in the 1750s and 1760s had less impact even among evangelicals than they had in the 1740s. In addition, Whitefield's "leadership" was ethereal, at best, even before 1750. His principal early importance was to serve as a personal model of evangelical enterprise for ministers wishing to promote their own revivals of religion. Because he did little to organize and coordinate integrated colonial revivals, he also failed to exercise significant authority over the ministers he inspired.

The case against Edwards' leadership of the revivals is even clearer. Edwards defended the New England revivals from attack. But, like Whitefield, he never organized and coordinated revivals throughout the colonies or even throughout New England. Since most of his major works were not printed in his lifetime, even his intellectual leadership in American theology occurred in the century after his death. Whitefield's lack of knowledge about Edwards on his first tour of America in 1739–40 is especially telling on this point. Edwards' name does not appear in Whitefield's journal prior to the latter's visit to Northampton in 1740, and Whitefield did not make the visit until Edwards had invited him to do so. Whitefield certainly knew of Edwards and the 1734–35 Northampton revival but associated the town mainly with the pastorate of Edwards' grandfather Stoddard. As Whitefield described the visit in his journal: "After a little refreshment, we crossed the ferry to Northampton, where no less than three hundred souls were saved about five years ago. Their pastor's name is Edwards, successor and grandson to the great Stoddard, whose memory will be always precious to my soul, and whose books entitled 'A Guide to Christ,' and 'Safety of Appearing in Christ's Righteousness,' I would recommend to all."

What were the effects of the prerevolutionary revivals of religion? The claims for their religious and secular impact need pruning too. One area of concern involves the relationship between the revivals and the rise of the Dissenting denominations in the colonies. Denomination building was intimately linked to the revivals in New England. There, as C. C. Goen has demonstrated, the revivals of the 1740s stimulated formation of over two hundred new congregations and several new denominations. This was accomplished mainly through a negative process called "Separatism," which split existing Congregationalist and Baptist churches along prorevival and antirevival lines. But Separatism was of no special consequence in increasing the number of Dissenters farther south. Presbyterians, Baptists, and, later, Methodists gained strength from former Anglicans who left their state-supported churches, but they won far more recruits among colonists who claimed no previous congregational membership.

Still, two points are important in assessing the importance of revivals to the expansion of the Dissenting denominations in the colonies. First, revivalism never was the key to the expansion of the colonial churches. Presbyterianism expanded as rapidly in the middle colonies between 1710 and 1740 as between 1740 and 1770. Revivalism scarcely produced the remarkable growth that the Church of England experienced in the eighteenth century unless, of course, it won the favor of colonists who opposed revivals as fiercely as did its leaders. . . .

Second, the expansion of the leading evangelical denominations, Presbyterians and Baptists, can be traced to many causes, not just revivalism or "the Great Awakening." The growth of the colonial population from fewer than three hundred thousand in 1700 to over two million in 1770 made the expansion of even the most modestly active denominations highly likely. This was especially true because so many new colonists did not settle in established communities but in new communities that lacked religious institutions. As Timothy L. Smith has written of seventeenth-century settlements, the new eighteenth-century settlements welcomed congregations as much for the social functions they performed as for their religious functions. Some of the denominations reaped the legacy of Old World religious ties among new colonists, and others benefited from local anti-Anglican sentiment, especially in the Virginia and Carolina backcountry. As a result, evangelical organizers formed many congregations in the middle and southern colonies without resorting to revivals at all. The first Presbyterian congregation in Hanover County, Virginia, organized by Samuel Blair and William Tennent, Jr., in 1746, rested on an indigenous lay critique of Anglican theology that had turned residents to the works of Martin Luther, and after the campaign by Blair and Tennent, the congregation allied itself with the Presbyterian denomination rather than with simple revivalism.

The revivals democratized relations between ministers and the laity only in minimal ways. A significant number of New England ministers changed their preaching styles as a result of the 1740 revivals. Heimert quotes Isaac Backus on the willingness of evangelicals to use sermons to "insinuate themselves into the affections of the people" and notes how opponents of the revivals like Chauncy nonetheless struggled to incorporate emotion and "sentiment" into their sermons after 1740. Yet revivalists and evangelicals continued to draw sharp distinctions between rights of ministers and the duties of the laity. Edwards did so in a careful, sophisticated way in *Some Thoughts concerning the Present Revival of Religion in New England*. Although he noted that "disputing, jangling, and contention" surrounded "lay exhorting," he agreed that "some exhorting is a Christian duty." But he quickly moved to a strong defense of ministerial prerogatives, which he introduced with the proposition that "the Common people in exhorting one another ought not to clothe themselves with the like authority, with that which is proper for ministers." Gilbert Tennent was less cautious. In his 1740 sermon *The Danger of an Unconverted Ministry*, he bitterly attacked "Pharisee-shepherds" and "Pharisee-teachers" whose preaching was frequently as "unedifying" as their personal lives. But Gilbert Tennent never attacked the ministry itself. Rather, he argued, for the necessity of a *converted* ministry precisely because he believed that only preaching brought men and women to Christ and that only ordained ministers could preach. Thus, in both 1742 and 1757, he thundered against lay preachers. They were "of dreadful consequence to the Church's peace and soundness in principle. . . . [F]or Ignorant Young Converts to take upon them authoritatively to Instruct and Exhort publickly tends to introduce the greatest Errors and the greatest anarchy and confusion."

*   *   *

Did itinerants challenge this ministerial hegemony?

Actually, itinerancy produced few changes in colonial American society and religion and is frequently misunderstood. Although some itinerants lacked institutionally based formal educations, none are known to have been illiterate. The most famous itinerant of the century, Whitefield, took an Oxford degree in 1736, and the most infamous, Davenport, stood at the top of his class at Yale in 1732. Itinerants usually bypassed the local church only when its minister opposed them; when the minister was hospitable, the itinerants preached in the church building. One reason itinerants eschewed the coercive instruments of the state was that they never possessed them before the Revolution. But after the Revolution the denominations they represented sought and received special favors from the new state governments, especially concerning incorporation, and won the passage of coercive legislation regarding morality and outlawing blasphemy. Finally, itinerants seldom ventured into the colonial countryside "clothed only with spiritual authority." Instead, itinerants acknowledged the continuing importance of deference and hierarchy in colonial society by stressing denominational approbation for their work. Virtually all of them wore the protective shield of ordination—the major exceptions are a few laymen who itinerated in New England in the early 1740s and about whom virtually nothing is known—and nearly all of them could point to denominational sponsorship. Even Virginia's aggressive Samuel Davies defended himself to the Bishop of London, Gov. William Gooch, and the sometimes suspicious backcountry settlers to whom he preached by pointing to his ordination and sponsorship by the Presbytery of New Castle. Only Davenport ventured into the countryside with little more than the spirit (and his Yale degree) to protect him. But only Davenport was judged by a court to have been mentally unstable.

In this context, it is not surprising that the eighteenth-century revivals of religion failed to bring significant new power—democracy—to the laity in the congregations. Although Gilbert Tennent argued that the laity had an obligation to abandon unconverted, unedifying ministers in favor of converted ones, it is not possible to demonstrate that the revivals increased the traditional powers that laymen previously possessed or brought them new ones. Congregations throughout the colonies had long exercised considerable power over their ministers through their effective control of church spending and fund raising as well as through the laity's ability simply to stop attending church services at all. As examples, witness alone the well-known seventeenth-century disputes between ministers and their listeners in Sudbury and Salem Village in Massachusetts and the complaints against ministers brought by the laity to the Presbytery of Philadelphia between 1706 and 1740. Yet, although the revivals should have increased this lay willingness to complain about ministerial failings, no historian ever has demonstrated systematically that this ever happened.

Nor did the revivals change the structure of authority within the denominations. New England Congregationalists retained the right of individual congregations to fire ministers, as when Northampton dismissed Edwards in 1750. But in both the seventeenth and eighteenth centuries, these congregations seldom acted alone. Instead, they nearly always consulted extensively with committees of ordained ministers when firing as well as when hiring ministers. In the middle colonies, however, neither the prorevival Synod of New York nor the antirevival Synod of Philadelphia tolerated such independence in congregations whether in theory or in practice. In both synods, unhappy congregations had to convince special committees appointed by the synods and composed exclusively of ministers that the performance of a fellow cleric was sufficiently dismal to warrant his dismissal. Congregations that acted independently in such matters quickly found themselves censured, and they usually lost the aid of both synods in finding and installing new ministers.

Did the revivals stir lower-class discontent, increase participation in politics, and promote democracy in society generally if not in the congregation? Even in New England the answer is, at best, equivocal. Historians have laid to rest John C. Miller's powerfully stated argument of the 1930s that the revivals were, in good part, lower-class protests against dominant town elites. The revivals indeed complicated local politics because they introduced new sources of potential and real conflict into the towns. New England towns accustomed to containing tensions inside a single congregation before 1730 sometimes had to deal with tensions within and between as many as three or four congregations after 1730. Of course, not all of these religious groups were produced by the revivals, and . . . some towns never tolerated the new dissidents and used the "warning out" system to eject them. Still, even where it existed, tumult should not be confused with democracy. Social class, education, and wealth remained as important after 1730 in choosing town and church officers as they had been before 1730. . . .

Recently, however, the specter of lower-class political agitation rampaging through other colonies disguised as revivals of religion has been raised in Nash's massive study of the northern colonial port cities and in Isaac's work on prerevolutionary Virginia. But in direct if quite different ways, both historians demonstrate the numerous difficulties of linking lower-class protest and political radicalism with "the Great Awakening." Nash notes that the link between lower-class political protest and revivalism was strongest in Boston. There, a popular party closely associated with the revivals attacked the city's propertied elite through the election process while the revivals prospered in the early 1740s. But the unfortunate lack of even a single tax list for the period and the lack of records from either the political dissidents or the revival congregations make it impossible to describe the social composition of either group with precision, much less establish firm patterns of interrelatedness. As a result, historians are forced to accept the nightmares of the antirevivalist Chauncy and the fulminations of the *Boston Evening Post* as accurate descriptions of all the agitators' religious and political principles. . . .

Isaac's recent work on Virginia demonstrates that the Baptist revival movement there in the 1760s and 1770s shattered the old Anglican-aristocratic alliance so thoroughly that its political importance hardly can be questioned. But two points are especially significant in assessing the relationship of Isaac's work to the problem of "the Great Awakening." First, Isaac nowhere argues that the Virginia revivals demonstrate either the power or even the existence of a broadly based revival movement in the prerevolutionary colonies. Indeed, as he describes the process, Virginia's Baptists succeeded out of a nearly unique ability to confront a political and religious aristocracy that also was virtually unique in the colonies. Second, we do not yet know how democratic and egalitarian these Baptists were within their own ranks. For example, we do not know if poor, uneducated Baptists became elders and preachers as frequently as did richer, better-educated Baptists. Nor do we know how judiciously Baptists governed non-Baptists in the southside and backcountry counties where they were strong but where many settlers eschewed any denominational affiliation.

*   *   *

What, then, of the relationship between the revivals and the American Revolution? Obviously, the revivals provided little focus for intercolonial unity in the way some historians have described. They appeared too erratically in too few colonies under too many different auspices to make such generalizations appropriate. The eighteenth-century colonial wars are more appropriate candidates for the honor. They raised significant legislative opposition to the crown in many colonies and cost many colonists their lives, especially in the last and most "successful" contest, the French and Indian War. Nor is it possible to demonstrate that specific congregations and denominations associated with the revivals originated anti-British protest that became uniquely important to the Revolution. . . . The connection is equally difficult to make with denominations. Connecticut New Lights and Pennsylvania Presbyterians played important roles in the colonial protests, but their activity does not, in itself, link revivals to the Revolution in any important way. First, the revivals in both places occurred a quarter of a century before the Revolution began. Second, neither group expanded in the 1740s or sustained its membership later exclusively because of the revivals. Third, the British probably angered laymen of both groups because the latter were important politicians rather than because they were New Lights and Presbyterians. Or, put another way, they were political leaders who happened to be New Lights and Presbyterians rather than Presbyterians and New Lights who happened to be politicians.

*   *   *

What, then, ought we to say about the revivals of religion in prerevolutionary America? The most important suggestion is the most drastic. Historians should abandon the term "the Great Awakening" because it distorts the character of eighteenth-century American religious life and misinterprets its relationship to prerevolutionary American society and politics. In religion it is a deus ex machina that falsely homogenizes the heterogeneous; in politics it falsely unites the colonies in slick preparation for the Revolution. Instead, a four-part model of the eighteenth-century colonial revivals will highlight their common features, underscore important differences, and help us assess their real significance.

First, with one exception, the prerevolutionary revivals should be understood primarily as regional events that occurred in only half the colonies. Revivals occurred intermittently in New England between 1690 and 1745 but became especially common between 1735 and 1745. They were uniformly Calvinist and produced more significant local political ramifications—even if they did not democratize New England—than other colonial revivals except those in Virginia. Revivals in the middle colonies occurred primarily between 1740 and 1760. They had remarkably eclectic theological origins, bypassed large numbers of settlers, were especially weak in New York, and produced few demonstrable political and social changes. Revivals in the southern colonies did not occur in significant numbers until the 1750s, when they were limited largely to Virginia, missed Maryland almost entirely, and did not occur with any regularity in the Carolinas until well after 1760. Virginia's Baptist revivalists stimulated major political and social changes in the colony, but the secular importance of the other revivals has been exaggerated. A fourth set of revivals, and the exception to the regional pattern outlined here, accompanied the preaching tours of the Anglican itinerant Whitefield. These tours frequently intersected with the regional revivals in progress at different times in New England, the middle colonies, and some parts of the southern colonies, but even then the fit was imperfect. Whitefield's tours produced some changes in ministerial speaking styles but few permanent alterations in institutional patterns of religion, although his personal charisma supported no less than seven tours of the colonies between 1740 and his death in Newburyport, Massachusetts, in 1770.

Second, the prerevolutionary revivals occurred in the colonial backwaters of western society where they were part of a long-term pattern of erratic movements for spiritual renewal and revival that had long characterized western Christianity and Protestantism since its birth two centuries earlier. Thus, their theological origins were international and diverse rather than narrowly Calvinist and uniquely American. Calvinism was important in some revivals, but Arminianism and Pietism supported others. This theological heterogeneity also makes it impossible to isolate a single overwhelmingly important cause of the revivals. Instead, they appear to have arisen when three circumstances were present—internal demands for renewal in different international Christian communities, charismatic preachers, and special, often unique, local circumstances that made communities receptive to elevated religious rhetoric.

Third, the revivals had modest effects on colonial religion. This is not to say that they were "conservative" because they did not always uphold the traditional religious order. But they were never radical, whatever their critics claimed. For example, the revivals reinforced ministerial rather than lay authority even as they altered some clergymen's perceptions of their tasks and methods. They also stimulated the demand for organization, order, and authority in the evangelical denominations. Presbyterian New Lights repudiated the conservative Synod of Philadelphia because its discipline was too weak, not too strong, and demanded tougher standards for ordination and subsequent service. After 1760, when Presbyterians and Baptists utilized revivalism as part of their campaigns for denominational expansion, they only increased their stress on central denominational organization and authority.

Indeed, the best test of the benign character of the revivals is to take up the challenge of contemporaries who linked them to outbreaks of "enthusiasm" in Europe. In making these charges, the two leading antirevivalists in the colonies, Garden of Charleston and Chauncy of Boston, specifically compared the colonial revivals with those of the infamous "French Prophets" of London, exiled Huguenots who were active in the city between 1706 and about 1730. The French Prophets predicted the downfall of English politicians, raised followers from the dead, and used women extensively as leaders to prophesy and preach. By comparison, the American revivalists were indeed "conservative." They prophesied only about the millennium, not about local politicans, and described only the necessity, not the certainty, of Salvation. What is most important is that they eschewed radical change in the position of women in the churches. True, women experienced dramatic conversions, some of the earliest being described vividly by Edwards. But, they preached only irregularly, rarely prophesied, and certainly never led congregations, denominations, or sects in a way that could remotely approach their status among the French Prophets.

Fourth, the link between the revivals and the American Revolution is virtually nonexistent. The relationship between prerevolutionary political change and the revivals is weak everywhere except in Virginia, where the Baptist revivals indeed shattered the exclusive, century-old Anglican hold on organized religious activity and politics in the colony. But, their importance to the Revolution is weakened by the fact that so many members of Virginia's Anglican aristocracy also led the Revolution. In other colonies the revivals furnished little revolutionary rhetoric, including even millennialist thought, that was not available from other sources, and provided no unique organizational mechanisms for anti-British protest activity. They may have been of some importance in helping colonists make moral judgments about eighteenth-century English politics, though colonists unconnected to the revivals made these judgments as well.

In the main, then, the revivals of religion in eighteenth-century America emerge as nearly perfect mirrors of a regionalized, provincial society. They arose erratically in different times and places across a century from the 1690s down to the time of the Revolution. Calvinism underlay some of them, Pietism and Arminianism others. Their leadership was local and, at best, regional, and they helped reinforce—but were not the key to—the proliferation and expansion of still-regional Protestant denominations in the colonies. As such, they created no intercolonial religious institutions and fostered no significant experiential unity in the colonies. Their social and political effects were minimal and usually local, although they could traumatize communities in which they upset, if only temporarily, familiar patterns of worship and social behavior. But the congregations they occasionally produced usually blended into the traditional social system, and the revivals abated without shattering its structure. Thus, the revivals of religion in prerevolutionary America seldom became proto-revolutionary, and they failed to change the timing, causes, or effects of the Revolution in any significant way.

Of course, it is awkward to write about the eighteenth-century revivals of religion in America as erratic, heterogeneous, and politically benign. All of us have walked too long in the company of Tracy's "Great Awakening" to make our journey into the colonial past without it anything but frightening. But as Chauncy wrote of the Whitefield revivals, perhaps now it is time for historians "to see that Things have been carried too far, and that the Hazard is great . . . lest we should be over-run with *Enthusiasm.*"

The Myth of the Golden Age
Mary Beth Norton

In ways often paralleling the experience of Indians and blacks, women in American history—and in its accompanying mythology—have often suffered neglect, as if they played no substantive role on history's stage. Ironically, however, a contrary interpretation is habitually offered regarding the colonial period. Colonial women, it is too often assumed, enjoyed a "golden age" of significance, status, involvement, and achievement—at least in comparison to the women of the revolutionary and later eras when, despite Abigail Adams's admonition, the Founding Fathers did "forget the Ladies." The lives of colonial women, it is correspondingly assumed, were more central to the workings of American society, however limited that society was. It was later, during the nineteenth-century Victorian period, that women lost status. To Professor Mary Beth Norton of Cornell University, however, the reality of colonial women's lives—whether Native American, African, or white—was patterned by the household. Women's lives outside the home were severely limited. Sex roles, and their accompanying social, economic, and political options, were much less fluid than myth presumes. During colonial times, women never achieved a status later to be lost. The colonial period, even comparatively speaking, was not a golden age for women.

When discussing colonial women, we must focus on the household, for that was where most of their lives were spent. As daughters as well as wives and mothers, white women were expected to devote their chief energies to housekeeping and to the care of children, just as their husbands were expected to support them by raising crops or working for wages. Household tasks were not easily or lightly accomplished, although their exact nature varied according to the wealth and size of the family and its place of residence. In addition to the common chores still done today—cooking, cleaning, and washing—colonial women had the primary responsibility for food preservation and cloth production.

On farms women raised chickens, tended vegetable gardens, and ran the dairy, making cheese and butter for family use. When hogs and cattle were butchered in the fall, women supervised the salting and smoking of the meat so that the family would have an adequate supply for the winter. They also gathered and dried fruits, vegetables, and berries and occasionally oversaw the making of hard cider, the standard drink in the colonies. In towns and cities women also performed many of these chores, though on a lesser scale: They

raised a few chickens and a cow or two, cultivated a kitchen garden, and preserved the beef and pork purchased at the local market. Only the wealthiest
women with numerous servants could escape tiring physical labor, and as mistresses of the household they too had to understand the processes involved,
for otherwise they could not ensure that the jobs were done correctly.

The task of making cloth by hand was tedious and time consuming. If
women lived in towns and could afford to do so, they would usually purchase
English cloth rather than manufacture their own. On remote farms or in poorer
households, however, females had no choice: If the family was to have clothes,
they had to spin the wool or flax threads, then weave those threads into material that could be used for dresses, shirts, and trousers. Usually girls were
taught to spin at the early age of 7 or 8 so that they could relieve their mothers
of that chore. Weaving demanded more technical skill, not to mention a large,
bulky loom, and so not all women in an area would learn to weave. Instead
neighbors would cooperate, "changing work," and the woman who wove the
cloth for her friends would be paid in cash or by barter.

Native American women had similar work roles. They did not spin or
weave, but they did make clothing for the family by tanning and processing
the hides of animals killed by their husbands and fathers. They had greater
responsibilities for the cultivation of plants than did their white counterparts;
the men of many tribes devoted most of their time to hunting, leaving their
wives with the major share of the burden of raising the corn, squash, and beans
that formed the staples of their diet. But like the whites, Native American
cultures drew a division between the domestic labors of women and the public
realm of men. Only in rare instances—as when the older women of the matrilineal Iroquois society named the chief of the tribe—did Indian women intrude
upon that male realm.

The patterns for African women were somewhat more complex, but their
lives too were largely determined by the type of household in which they lived.
A female slave in a northern urban home—and there were many such by the
mid-eighteenth century—would probably have been a cook or a maid. On
small farms slave women would have been expected to work in both field and
house. On large southern tobacco or rice plantations, however, black women
might specialize in certain tasks, devoting themselves exclusively to spinning,
cooking, childcare, dairy work, or poultry keeping, or they might be assigned
to the fields. Black women were therefore more likely than whites to engage
in labor out of doors. Significantly, the household in which they lived was not
theirs: Their interests and wishes, and those of their husbands and children,
always had to be subordinated to the interests of their white masters and mistresses. White women's lives, we might say, were governed by the whims of
men, legally and in reality; but black women's lives were governed by white
men and white women, and perhaps even by white children.

Women's Lives Outside the Home

For female whites or blacks living on isolated farms or plantations, opportunities for contacts with persons outside their immediate families were extremely

rare. Thus, farm and plantation women took advantage of every excuse they could to see friends and neighbors: Quilting bees and spinning frolics were common in the North, barbecues were prevalent in the South. Church attendance provided a rural woman not only with the solace of religion, but also with a chance to greet acquaintances and exchange news. Literate women kept in touch with each other by writing letters, many of them carried not by the rudimentary colonial mail service but by passing travelers, usually men.

Because there were few colonial newspapers, and those were published exclusively in cities like Boston or Philadelphia, most farm areas were a part of what has been termed an *oral culture.* Much of the important information about local and regional developments were passed on by person-to-person contact, which generally occurred at the local tavern or the county courthouse, both of which were male bastions. As a result, white farm women tended to be excluded from men's communication networks and to rely for news on exchanges with each other or with their husbands.

Urban women were not nearly so isolated. Close to their friends, they could visit every day. Their attendance at church was not limited to infrequent occasions, and so they could become more active in religious affairs than their rural sisters. They had greater opportunities to receive an education, since the few girls' schools were located in or near colonial cities. For the most part their education consisted of elementary reading, writing, and arithmetic, with perhaps some needlework or musical training thrown in for good measure. Once women knew how to read, they had newspapers and books at their disposal. Moreover, because their household tasks were less demanding than those of their rural counterparts, they had more time to take advantage of all these amenities of the urban setting.

If this account makes it seem as though colonial women's lives lacked variety, that impression is correct. Their environment was both limited and limiting: limited, because of the small sphere of activity open to them; limiting, because they could not realistically aspire to leave that sphere. Faced with a paucity of alternatives, colonial women made the best of their situation. What evidence is available suggests that both white and black women often married for love, and that they cared a great deal for their children. Their female friends provided support in moments of crisis—such as childbirth or the death of a family member—and women could take some satisfaction from knowing that they were active contributors to their families' well-being.

The Myth Analyzed

Historians of American women have traditionally regarded the seventeenth and eighteenth centuries as a "golden age" in which women were better off than their English female contemporaries or their descendants of the succeeding Victorian era. Elisabeth Anthony Dexter explicitly asserted as much; other authors have accepted the same argument implicitly by contending that female Americans "lost status" in the nineteenth century. But even leaving aside the troublesome (and infrequently addressed) issue of how status is measured, there are a number of difficulties with the standard interpretation. Evaluation of women's position depends on what aspects of their experience are relevant to an understanding of their social and economic position, for no one would claim that colonial females exerted much political power.

Three basic assertions support the traditional interpretation. First, historians have noted the imbalanced sex ratio in all the colonies before 1700 and in some parts thereof during later years. Hypothesizing that the absence of sufficient numbers of women to provide wives for all male colonists would lead men to compete vigorously for mates, they have concluded that women could wield a good deal of power through their choice of a spouse. Second, scholars have commonly pointed to the economic contributions women made to the colonial household through their work in food processing and cloth production. They have correctly noted that it was practically impossible for a man to run a colonial household properly without a wife, for a woman's labor was essential to the survival of the family. They presume, then, that husbands recognized their wives' vital contributions to the household by according them a voice in decision making, and that a woman's economic role translated itself into a position of power within the home. Third and finally, historians argue that sex roles in early America were far more fluid and less well defined than they were in the nineteenth and twentieth centuries. They quote both foreign travelers' accounts and newspaper advertisements to show that in many instances women labored at tasks later considered masculine and frequently ran their own businesses.

In assessing these common contentions, we must look closely at their component parts in light of recent scholarship. When we do so, all are rendered suspect. The first argument asserts that a scarcity of women works to their advantage in the marriage market and assumes that the choice of a husband was entirely within a seventeenth-century colonial woman's discretion. Yet demographic studies have clearly demonstrated that, when women are scarce, the average female age at first marriage drops, sometimes precipitously. Even in New England, where the sex ratio was closer to being balanced than anywhere else in the early settlements, the average marriage age for women seems to have fallen into the high teens during the first years of colonization, in sharp contrast to England, where the nuptial age for women remained near the mid-20s.

These figures have several implications. Initially, they suggest that first marriages were not long delayed by women's searches for spouses who met exacting criteria. Furthermore, since seventeenth-century brides were often teenagers, even more frequently so in the Chesapeake Bay area than in New England, one wonders just how much power they could have wielded. Immature themselves, legally the wards of their parents, it is highly unlikely that they had much to say about the choice of a spouse.

A possible counter-argument might assert that the advantages of the imbalanced sex ratio are more applicable to a woman's second or third marriage than to her first, because then she would be older and in addition would have control of her first husband's property. Although studies of remarriage patterns in the early years of the colonies are not completely satisfactory, they nevertheless appear to challenge even this claim. In New England, life expectancy in the seventeenth century was sufficiently great that few marriages seem to have been broken early by death. Therefore, relatively few persons married more than once. In the Chesapeake area, where mortality was much higher, the frequency of remarriage was similarly high, but analyses of wills demonstrate that widows were rarely given much control over their dead husbands' estates. The property was usually held in trust for the decedent's minor children, with the widow receiving only a life interest in part of it. Sometimes even that income was to cease upon her remarriage.

Taken as a whole, then, the evidence indicates that seventeenth-century English women transported to American shores might not find the imbalanced sex ratio to be beneficial. After all, a scarce resource can be easily exploited as it is cherished, an observation dramatically proved in the third section of this book [*Women of America*] by Lucie Hirata's examination of the exploitation of scarce Chinese women in sexually imbalanced nineteenth-century California. Also, by approximately 1720 the sex ratio had evened out in the Chesapeake, having already reached that point to the northward, so that whatever advantages women may have derived from the situation were negated and cannot be used to characterize the entire colonial period.

Turning next to the assertion that women's economic role gave them a powerful position in the household, we can discern problems with both the evidence and the reasoning that support it. Historians have not systematically examined the conditions under which women wield familial power, assuming instead that an essential economic contribution would almost automatically lead to such a result. Anthropologists who have investigated the question, however, have discovered that the mere fact that a woman's economic contribution to the household is significant is not sufficient to give her a voice in matters that might otherwise be deemed to fall within the masculine sphere. Rather, what is important is a woman's ability to control the distribution of familial resources. Thus, African women who not only cultivate crops but also sell that produce to others are more likely to wield power in their households than are their counterparts in other tribes whose husbands take on the trading role, or who live in a subsistence economy that does not allow for the sale of surplus goods.

That this analogy is indeed appropriate, despite the wide difference in time and space between twentieth-century Africa and colonial America, is suggested by a recent study of female Loyalist exiles in England after the American Revolution. In order to win compensation from the British government for the losses their families suffered as a result of their political sympathies, the women had to submit descriptions of the property confiscated from them by the rebels. In the process, they revealed their basic ignorance of family landholdings and income, in turn demonstrating that their husbands had not regularly discussed financial affairs with them. If the Loyalist women refugees, who were drawn from all ranks of society, had actively participated in economic decision making, then they would have been far better able to estimate their losses than they proved to be. Thus, the second foundation of the traditional interpretation is shown to be questionable.

The third standard contention, that colonial sex roles were relatively fluid, is rendered at least partially doubtful by other aspects of the same study of Loyalist exiles. The wide variations in the contents of men's and women's Loyalist claims, and the inability or the unwillingness of men to describe household furnishings in the same detail adopted by women, appear to indicate that a fairly rigid line separated masculine and feminine spheres in the colonies. Indeed, the fact that men did not talk about finances with their wives suggests that both sexes had a strong sense of the proper roles of women and men; women did not meddle with politics or economics, which were their husbands' provinces, and men did not interfere with their wives' overseeing of domestic affairs, excluding child rearing, where they did take an active role. Moreover, even though the claims show that some women did engage in business activities, their number was relatively small (fewer than 10 percent of the claimants), and most of them worked in their husbands' enterprises rather than running their own.

That the number of Loyalist women working in masculine areas was not uniquely limited has been suggested by a recent study of Baltimore women in the 1790s, which concludes that only about 5 percent of the female urban population worked outside the home. Thus, it seems likely that eighteenth-century Americans made quite distinct divisions between male and female roles, as reflected in the small numbers of women engaging in masculine occupations and in the fact that men did not normally interfere in the female sphere.

New Issues

Recent scholarship has considered a number of issues not even raised by earlier authors. Interest in these different areas of inquiry owes a great deal to current trends in the study of the history of the American family, of minority groups, and of ordinary people. Although this work has just begun, it is nevertheless already casting innovative light on the subject of colonial women's role in society.

In the first place, it is important to point out that published studies of the lives of colonial women have, with but one or two exceptions, centered wholly on whites. Even though at the time of the Revolution blacks constituted almost 20 percent of the American population, a higher percentage than at any time thereafter, historians have completely neglected the study of female slaves in the colonial era. Therefore, all the statements that women had a relatively good position in the colonies must be immediately qualified to exclude blacks. No one could seriously argue that enslavement was preferable to freedom, especially since female slaves were highly vulnerable to sexual as well as economic exploitation by their masters. Intriguingly, recent work has shown that the sexual imbalance among the earliest African slaves in the South was just as pronounced as that among whites, so that female blacks probably found themselves in a demographic situation comparable to that of their white mistresses. The sex-role definitions applied to whites, though, were never used with respect to blacks. The labor of slave women was too valuable for their masters to pay attention to the niceties of sex; thus, many of them spent their lives laboring in tobacco fields or on sugar plantations alongside their husbands, although others were indeed used as house servants performing typically feminine tasks.

The one concession wise colonial masters made to the sex of female slaves was a recognition of their importance as childbearers. Since under the law any child of a slave woman was also a slave, masters could greatly increase their human property simply by encouraging their female slaves' fertility. For example, Thomas Jefferson, whose solvency for some years depended on the discreet sale of young blacks, ordered his overseers to allow pregnant and nursing women special privileges, including lighter work loads and separate houses. Since colonial slave women normally bore their first children at the age of 17 or 18, they would experience perhaps 10 to 11 pregnancies (not all of which would result in live births) during their fertile years, which may be contrasted to the standard pattern among white eighteenth-century women, who married perhaps 4 to 6 years later and thus bore fewer children (the average being 6 offspring who lived).

This attention to childbearing patterns has led to a major challenge to the "golden age" theory. As Robert V. Wells pointed out in the first article in this book [*Women of America*], colonial women were either pregnant or nursing during most of their mature years. Such a pattern of constant childbearing was debilitating, even if it was not fatal to as many women as we once thought; the diaries of white female colonists are filled with references to their continued poor health, and the records of planters show similar consequences among female slaves. Furthermore, the care of so many children must have been exhausting, especially when combined with the extraordinary household demands made on women: production of clothing and time-consuming attention to food preservation and preparation, not to mention candle- and soap-making and doing laundry in heavy iron pots over open fires, with all the water carried by hand from the nearest well or stream. It is questionable how much household power could have been wielded by a woman constantly occupied with such work, even if she was in good health.

It is instructive to stress once again the lack of options in colonial women's lives. Until late in the eighteenth century, marriage was a near-universal experience for women; in an overwhelmingly agricultural society, most female whites ended up as farm wives and most female blacks were farm laborers. For black women burdened with small children, running away was not even the remote chance it was for young unattached male slaves. (In any case, until the Revolution there was no safe place to go, except Spanish Florida, because all the colonies, north and south, allowed slaveholding.)

It might be contended that since most white men were farmers, white women's lack of opportunities was not unique to them. But boys like John Adams, Richard Cranch, and John Shaw had opportunities to gain an education that were closed to their wives, the sisters Abigail, Mary, and Elizabeth Smith. All were exceptionally intelligent and well-informed women, but none received other than a rudimentary formal education, despite the fact that their father was a minister. Since the ability to write a good letter—defined as one that was neat, intelligently constructed, properly grammatical, and carefully spelled—was the mark of a person of substance and standing in colonial America, it is easy to discern the source of the distress Abigail Adams constantly expressed about her inability to write and spell well.

If a white woman did not want to be a farm wife, assuming she had a choice in the matter, then she had only a narrow range of alternatives. In order to take advantage of those alternatives she had to be located in an urban area, where she could support herself in one of three ways: by running a small school in her home; by opening a shop, usually but not always one that sold dry goods; or by in some manner using the household skills she had learned from her mother as a means of making money. This might involve hiring out as a servant, doing sewing, spinning, or weaving for wealthy families, or, if she had some capital, setting up a boardinghouse or inn. There were no other choices, and women who selected one of these occupations—or were compelled by adverse economic circumstances to do so—were frequently regarded as anomalous by their contemporaries.

A major component of the traditional view of American women's history is the assertion that the 40-year period centering on 1800 was a time of retrogression. Joan Hoff Wilson, the most recent proponent of this interpretation, links the setbacks she discerns in women's position explicitly to consequences of the American Revolution. But other work published in the last few years points to an exactly opposite conclusion: It has been suggested (if not yet fully proved) by a number of scholars that the late eighteenth century witnessed a series of advances for women, in some respects at least.

An examination of all extant Massachusetts divorce records seems to indicate, for example, that at the end of the century women seeking divorces were more likely to have their complaints judged fairly and were less likely to be oppressed by application of a sexual double standard than their predecessors had been. In a different area, it has been noted that women's educational opportunities improved dramatically after the mid-1780s, an observation that is supported by evidence presented in the essays by Ann Gordon and Kathryn Kish Sklar [in *Women of America*]. Finally, extensive research into the patterns of first marriage in one New England town has uncovered changes in marital alliances that can be interpreted as evidence of a greater exercise of independent judgment by girls. Analysis of the records of Hingham, Massachusetts, has shown that in the latter years of the century more daughters married out of birth order and chose spouses whose economic status differed from that of their own parents than had previously been the case. If we assume that both sorts of actions would be contrary to parents' wishes, and couple that assumption with the knowledge that in the same town the premarital conception rate (judged by a comparison of wedding dates with the timing of births of first children) simultaneously jumped to more than 30 percent, we receive the clear impression that parental control of sons and daughters was at a low ebb.

Paradoxically, that last piece of evidence can also be read as suggesting a greater exploitation of women by men. The rise in premarital conception rates, which stretched over the entire eighteenth century and peaked in its last two decades, does not necessarily mean that all the women involved were willing participants seeking what would today be termed sexual fulfillment. On this issue, as on others discussed in this essay, a great deal more research is needed in order to allow historians to gain a fuller picture of the female experience in colonial America.

The Virginia Gentry and the Democratic Myth

D. Alan Williams

One of the thrusts of post–World War II "consensus" conservative historians has been to demonstrate that democracy was indeed widespread and deep during the colonial period, particularly during the eighteenth century. In the case of Virginia it was argued that political, economic, and social democracy existed for all. According to this view, a political minority, the gentry, had to defer to the wishes of the majority—the owners of small and middle-sized farms. D. Alan Williams, Professor of History at the University of Virginia, calls that view fallacious. He demonstrates here that it was in fact the landed gentry—a tight-knit group—that dominated Virginia's political, economic, and social life, with the support and good wishes of the lesser groups. Important positions of power were controlled and filled by the gentry; the "people" could only vote for members of the House of Burgesses, but even then their choices came from among the privileged classes.

Colonial Virginia invariably provides the model for the typical southern colony—an aristocratic, staple-producing, agrarian society, divided geographically, economically, and socially into a coastal tidewater and an upcountry piedmont and valley. Originally conceived as a home for free laborers, craftsmen, and small farmers, Virginia by the eighteenth century exploited slave labor, nearly destroyed its yeoman farmer class, and turned over its government to a planter gentry. Landownership was a prerequisite for voting and essential for political advancement and social prestige, and though many were landowners, government remained a monopoly of the wealthy and wellborn. The Anglican church was more firmly established in law than New England Congregationalism. All political officials were appointed, except members of the House of Burgesses. In sum, Virginia possessed most of the classic ingredients for social and political conflict.

Yet, in fact, sectional and social controversy were at a minimum in eighteenth-century Virginia. Some historians have even proclaimed the colony a democratic society with power in the hands of the people rather than the gentry. They have duly noted the presence of such Virginia revolutionaries, repub-

From *Main Problems in American History*, Vol. I, Fifth Edition, ed. Howard H. Quint, Milton Cantor, and Dean Albertson. Copyright © 1964, 1968, 1972, 1978, 1988 by the Dorsey Press. Reprinted by permission of Wadsworth, Inc.

licans, and libertarians as George Washington, Patrick Henry, George Mason, Thomas Jefferson, and James Madison. Indeed, they have seen in Virginia's golden age (1720–70) the symbol of the ideal agrarian society whose monuments have been preserved in Williamsburg, Mount Vernon, Monticello, and the great James River plantations.

Clearly, Virginia presents us with contradictions. How do we explain them? Are historical appearances deceiving? Or is it a matter of semantics? Does government led by the wealthy necessarily mean aristocracy? Does democracy exist just because a majority of the populace has the right to vote?

Essentially, seventeeth-century Virginia society was a small-farmer society. Although some large landholders existed, most settlers themselves cultivated the fields with the aid of an occasional indentured servant. Even the large farmers were self-made men who had attained their positions by hard work. Small farmer and large planter sat together on the county courts, the vestries, and in the assembly. Class distinctions were blurred in a society made up entirely of struggling farmers, most of whom found life crude and precarious.

Three major developments between 1660 and 1720 changed the kind of society and government Virginia would have: (1) establishment of the English imperial system, (2) Bacon's Rebellion, (3) introduction of slavery and the large plantation.

The great test of whether Virginia would manage her own affairs came between 1660 and 1720. From the collapse of the London Company until the restoration of Charles II in 1660, Virginia, an isolated and insignificant royal colony, had been virtually free from English control. After 1660, the English formulated a uniform policy for their expanding empire. Political economists, royal officials, merchants, and parliamentary leaders were confident they could construct a thoroughly planned and integrated economy by fitting all parts into the whole and enforcing mercantilistic principles through the navigation acts. The Crown would manage the operation. Charles II and James II appointed governors loyal to them, and issued orders making the royal colonies responsive to their wishes. No longer could Virginia act without recourse to the motherland; the colony must fit the pattern.

In Virginia, it fell to popular Governor William Berkeley (1642–52, 1660–77) to reconstitute royal government after the Civil War and to enforce imperial policies with which he frequently disagreed. These were years of poverty, turmoil, and upheaval. The navigation acts, naval wars with the Dutch, and overproduction almost ruined the tobacco trade and plunged Virginia into a prolonged depression. King Charles not only granted the Carolinas, the Jerseys, and Pennsylvania to his favorites, but also gave away valuable Virginia lands. All colonists suffered, but none more than the small farmers and the older colonial leaders. The result was Bacon's Rebellion.

Bacon's Rebellion of 1676 has been called the forerunner of the American Revolution, a class war between small farmers and planter aristocrats, a struggle for self-government against a despotic governor, and a typical encounter between irresponsible frontiersmen and ill-treated Indians. Some have contended that the revolutionary generation, eager to find precedents for its own rebellion, created a myth out of a minor incident little different from numerous rural disturbances in North Carolina, New Jersey, Maryland, and in England itself.

An Indian war was the immediate cause of the rebellion. The obvious sources of upheaval were economic—depression, high taxes, war, and the destruction of the Dutch tobacco trade by the navigation acts. The underlying source was social—the old leaders' loss of status to new migrants coming into the colony after 1650.

For several years, both large landholders and small farmers had been gradually moving westward in search of rich tobacco land. They paid scant attention to Indian treaty rights or possible reprisals. Although settlement had reached only fifty miles beyond Jamestown and had barely penetrated inland from the rivers, incidents along the frontier mounted, with both whites and Indians committing raids and atrocities. The frontiersmen were no more restrained than the half-savage Indians. Though undeclared war raged, by early 1676 Governor Berkeley vacillated. He feared to touch off a general Indian war, which would bring needless bloodshed, as in King Philip's War in New England, and would upset the Indian trade that several of his friends were engaged in. The harassed settlers, some large landholders among them, rallied behind Nathaniel Bacon, a financially embarrassed young councilor whose overseer had been killed by roving Indians. Against Berkeley's express orders, Bacon attacked and slaughtered two tribes allied with Virginia. He contended that they were hostile Indians, but some cynics noted that these same Indians also held choice lands and large caches of furs. The governor promptly proclaimed the attackers in rebellion.

Bacon's forces, fully aroused and armed, turned from Indian problems to redress their political grievances, thereby revealing the social facet of the conflict. During the English Civil War, Virginians had had a taste of the independent local government they long savored. In the early part of the war, Berkeley set up efficient county and parish governments. After Cromwell triumphed in England, he abolished royal government in the colony and replaced Berkeley with powerless governors elected by the assembly. In the absence of effective central leadership, county justices of the peace, parish vestrymen, and local burgesses became Virginia's political leaders.

However, when the Restoration came in 1660, Berkeley regained his office and attempted to reestablish the central government in Jamestown. In the spirit of Stuart politics, he appointed favorites to the county courts and supported local cliques, which established property qualifications for voting and replaced popularly elected vestries with self-perpetuating vestries.

Berkeley consolidated his position by keeping the same loyal assembly in session for fifteen years. To the chagrin of the early colonial leaders, his favorites were new men who had come to Virginia during and after the Civil War. They were frequently well trained, and had political and economic connections in England. Bacon's chief lieutenants were older, established planters, disgruntled at losing their former power and prestige. These frustrated colonists seized on the unsettled Indian conditions to voice political protests. At a hastily called assembly in June, 1676, they passed laws, "democratical" in nature, aimed at breaking the power of Berkeley's county oligarchies and reasserting the position of the old settlers. What ultimately was intended is unknown. Bacon died; the rebellion collapsed; and Berkeley, going berserk, executed twenty men in what was the only political blood purge in American history.

Bacon's Rebellion produced no great Virginia victory over royal authority. Crown restraints in Virginia and other colonies grew greater in the 1680's. Governor Thomas Lord Culpeper (1677–83) and Lord Howard of Effingham (1684–88) both were selected representatives of Stuart imperial policies. Lord Howard, in particular, was a persistent, obedient servant of the Stuarts, a confirmed believer in the divine right of kings, and completely unsympathetic toward representative government. The assembly, he asserted, should meet only when called by the king, should consider business previously approved by the Crown, and should execute only those laws that had been scrutinized by royal attorneys. Had such a policy been carried out, colonial self-government would have been squelched. But this did not happen, because bitter opponents of the 1670's joined forces to isolate and neutralize the governors, thereby depriving them of the loyalty of a proroyalist political faction in Virginia.

The Stuart threat to representative government ended with the Glorious Revolution of 1688. Englishmen thrust James II from the throne and called William and Mary to be their monarchs. This bloodless coup brought significant changes to Virginia. Howard left the colony, and his able successors, if they did not always appreciate the assembly, respected its right to speak for the colony and relied heavily on it for direction. The Virginia Assembly, sensitive to the growing powers of Parliament, sought the same for itself. From stubbornly resisting direct royal influence in the 1680's, Virginia after 1690 waged a subdued, unspectacular, and highly effective campaign to neutralize the governor's influence in domestic politics. By 1720, the campaign had succeeded.

Social and economic changes understandably paralleled and interacted with political change. By the early eighteenth century, the Indian threat had vanished, expansion without fear was possible, altered marketing conditions in Europe created new demands, and English and Scottish merchants turned to the Virginia market with new vigor. The colony was looked on as an economically underdeveloped area in need of credit. British merchants who controlled the tobacco trades extended credit with reasonable assurance of recovering their investment. Most of this credit went to the larger planters and their friends, who, in turn, acquired more land, expanded operations, upgraded their standard of living, and built the great plantations for which the colony became known.

The slave was the decisive difference between mid-seventeenth-century and mid-eighteenth-century Virginia. Before 1680, slavery on a large scale was rare, but it was commonplace thereafter. Slavery and mass-production methods characterized the tobacco plantation economy after 1720. Virginians condoned slavery as an established fact, though few defended it. The real sufferers, they thought, were not the slaves but the small planter and yeoman farmers who worked the fields with their families and with an occasional indentured servant. The yeoman might draw some satisfaction from knowing that the slave was permanently tied to the bottom rung of the social scale, but he also knew that his position was not much higher because of that same slave. While the small planter might buy a few slaves, he lacked the resources to match his more affluent neighbors, and he lost economic power and social position to the growing number of large slaveholding, landed gentry.

One major change came after 1720, when thousands of Scots-Irish and German immigrants pushed down from Pennsylvania into the fertile Shenandoah Valley and into the western piedmont. Socially and religiously, these new settlers differed from those to the east. They were Presbyterians, Lutherans, Quakers, and German pietists—all dissenters from the established Church of England. Highly individualistic, they were alien to eastern traditions. Tobacco was not their king, since it could not be grown in the hilly back country. Yet, there was no sectionalism in colonial Virginia, no regulator uprisings similar to those of the Carolinas, no Paxton boys marching on Williamsburg as they did on Philadelphia, no tenant riots like those in New York and New Jersey. Unlike the Carolina frontier, the Virginia frontier was an overlay of new immigrants and old Virginians. At the same time that Germans and Scots-Irish were drifting south into the valley, settlers from eastern Virginia were moving west onto the piedmont, and speculators were making bold plans to sell their western lands. Acting with dispatch, the Virginia General Assembly wisely established counties and extended representation to the new areas, leaving the settlers with none of the complaints about governmental inequities that upset inhabitants in the Carolinas and Pennsylvania. In an earlier day, the influx of dissenters might have caused serious problems, but religious fanaticism (never strong in Virginia) was on the wane by the eighteenth century, and toleration was on the rise. Some dissenters were harassed, but most were left free to worship as they pleased, provided they paid their tithes to the Anglican church. Moreover, the colony's political leaders were also its leading land speculators. To sell land, they had to have settlers; to get settlers, they had to provide attractions. Their attractions were cheap land, available government, religious toleration, and a minimum of interference by spiritual and secular authorities. Most immigrants wanted no more than that. There was no sectionalism, for there were no sectional grievances. Sectionalism as a divisive force was not apparent until after the Revolution.

The golden age of the Virginia plantation society ran from about 1720 to the eve of the Revolution. The populace—free and slave, native and immigrant—doubled, tripled, and then quadrupled in number. Tobacco was king, land was wealth. With the widest coastal plain in the colonies and fertile valleys just beyond the first mountain ridge, Virginians, unlike South Carolinians, had little difficulty in acquiring land. Dominating this society were the planter gentry—the first aristocracy of the rural south, the counterparts of

Charleston's planter-merchants, the equals of Philadelphia and Boston merchants.

The first planter gentry of Virginia had been a score or so of men, primarily members of the council—the Carters, Randolphs, Byrds, Lees, Custises, Pages, and Ludwells—whose families in Virginia had found positions denied them in England, and who had risen to the top through shrewd business practices and the accumulation of vast tracts of land. They had helped carve a civilization out of the wilderness with little help from the Crown; consequently, they often thought royal governors were interlopers gathering spoils after the labor had been done. By intermarriage, they had created a tight coterie of leaders that no governor could break. Sensitive to insult and quick to anger, they zealously guarded their interests through the distribution of Crown land, a function of the council. Generous in parceling land to themselves and their friends, they were equally generous in granting the king's land to all Virginians.

By the mid-eighteenth century, as the colony grew and tobacco trading flourished, the number of affluent planter families reached several hundred. The council could no longer contain all the gentry families. Many burgesses not only were as wealthy as councilors but also were their social equals. As the lower house gained ascendancy over the upper house, the new generation of Randolphs, Harrisons, Lees, and Pages preferred to sit in the House of Burgesses alongside other rising gentry. No longer did small planters gain election to this "tobacco club." Neither did small farmers serve as justices or vestrymen, for offices at all levels were taken up by the gentry and their sons. Distinctions between classes, blurred in the seventeenth century, were much clearer in the eighteenth.

Even though well-defined class lines existed in colonial Virginia, government by the gentry was not necessarily detrimental to the popular interests or so difficult to perform objectively as it would be in a more diverse and complex social order. First, the common bond of land and farming gave the large and small cultivators similar economic interests and made the society homogeneous, at least east of the Blue Ridge Mountains. Second, the lesser farmer naturally elected his more affluent neighbors to the House of Burgesses, since the poorly run plantation was no recommendation for a public office whose main trust was promoting agricultural prosperity. Third, the hard-working small farmers lacked the time to serve in political offices. Finally, since social mobility was fairly fluid in a fast-growing society, the independent farmers and small shareholders saw no reason to oust or destroy the larger planters. They wanted to join them.

The liberal humanism of the planter gentry did much to assure the people that they had little to fear from planter leadership. The gentry willingly served in government because they believed in noblesse oblige—with power and privilege went responsibility. Honor, duty, and devotion to class interest had called them to office, and they took the call seriously. Not without a certain amount of condescension, they thought that government would be run by those less qualified if they refused to serve. They alone had the time, the financial resources, and the education necessary for public office. Moreover, they were the social leaders, and were therefore expected to set an example in manners and morals, to uphold the church, to be generous with benevolences, to serve the government with enlightened self-interest, and in general to be paragons of duty and dignity.

Not surprisingly, they enjoyed the prestige that came with office. To be in a position of authority, to control government, to enact laws, to have the power of life and death over men are intangibles for which there can be no financial compensation. Not that such compensations were omitted from the scheme of things. The real advantage of political service to most officeholders came from the opportunity to acquire land and to extend their business acquaintances. It would not be remiss to say that the gentry had a split personality—one side governed by duty, the other side by lust for land. Perhaps this is what is meant by "enlightened self-interest."

Trained for public duties on their self-contained plantations, the gentry brought to office well-developed talents and tastes for wielding power. Though they remembered their own interests, they nevertheless believed that they were bound to respect and protect those of others. They held that sovereignty was vested in the people, who delegated certain powers to government. They extolled republicanism and willingly enfranchised the people. Their humanism was a product of experience, common sense, and the common law. Liberal humanism not only seemed the right and just attitude; equally important, it worked. Of course, the Virginia gentry were in a position to be charitable. They trusted the people because the people trusted them. One may speculate whether their view of individual liberties would have been so liberal had Virginia been less homogeneous in character or had the lower classes challenged their leadership.

The small farmers and slaveholders had one protection against gentry oligarchy: they were in the majority and they had the right to vote. True, they elected only the burgesses, but that single choice was an important guarantee of their rights, since the House of Burgesses was the strongest political body in Virginia. Thomas Jefferson once remarked that the election process itself tended to eliminate class conflicts and extremism; the aristocrat with no concern for the small farmer was not apt to be elected, and the man who demagogically courted the popular vote was ostracized by the gentry. Therefore, the House of Burgesses became, at the same time, the center of planter rule and of popular government. It operated as a restraint on oligarchy.

Recently, historians Robert and B. Kathryn Brown have gone one step further and argued that Virginia, like Massachusetts, was a democratic society. Economic, social, and political opportunity, they say, existed for all. Far from the gentry's dominating the society, while the small- and middle-sized farmers and slaveholders deferred to their judgment, the reverse was actually the case. Since the gentry were in a minority, they had to defer to the wishes of the majority—the small landholders—if they wanted to retain the reins of office. So say the Browns.

A comparison of the relative positions of the small landowners in the seventeenth and eighteenth centuries shows that without doubt they had immeasurably improved their economic lot at the same time they were being socially outstripped by their more affluent neighbors. Politically, they shifted from holders of office to a check on officeholders.

Yet, was this democracy? What good, indeed, was majority vote when the majority had so little to vote for? Choosing a burgess to sit at the occasional meetings of the General Assembly in Williamsburg was not nearly so important as having a voice in county affairs, where most matters affecting small farmers were decided. Could a society be democratic when every single official except one was appointed by self-perpetuating justices, vestrymen, councilors, and the royal governor, none of whom was responsible to the electorate? Could it be democratic when only men of means held office and when advancement seemed more dependent on wealth and birth than on talent? To a large extent, the small farmers were effectively separated from the power structure, with little means of uniting in a rural society.

The gentry, a minority, were a group of like-minded men working in close alliance, careful not to disturb the social equilibrium. When they contested each other for a seat in the assembly, they offered the electorate only a choice between planter A and planter B, between Tweedledum and Tweedledee. They were the perfect example of what has been consistently true in American society: a cohesive minority dominating an amorphous majority. Perhaps the question that ought to be asked about this planter gentry government is not whether it was democratic but whether it was effective. William Penn once wrote, "Governments depend on men rather than men upon governments, let them be good and government cannot be bad." If this is the primary question, then must not one say that the planter gentry, with their own type of consensus politics, provided eighteenth-century Virginia with enlightened and dynamic leadership?

Or is the half-century of the golden age a period too short to judge the gentry society? After the Revolution, Virginia declined as the soil lost its richness, tobacco lacked foreign markets, and the younger generations moved west and south to more promising opportunities. When the planter aristocracy ceased to be infused and refreshed with the rising gentry, it became inert, lacking in insight, inbred, and distrustful of progress elsewhere. In the place of a masculine Washington or a visionary Jefferson, nineteenth-century leadership could offer as its spokesmen only an effete Edmund Randolph and a myopic John Tyler. Equally significant, the lower class, having deferred so long to the excellent leadership of the eighteenth century, could not recapture what it had let atrophy—its political consciousness. Not until the 1960's did Virginia voters exercise their voting privileges in proportions equaling those of their colonial ancestors.

II

Myths of the Revolutionary Era

In the beginning all the world was America.
John Locke

We are now to detail the causes of events, the most interesting of any in the history of the world; the overthrow of tyranny and despotism in the United Colonies, and the erection there of an altar, sacred to liberty.
Egbert Guernsey, *History of the United States Designed for Schools* (1848)

THE STORY OF THE REVOLUTION.

"The Story of the Revolution": an oft-told myth. [Currier & Ives lithograph, 1876. Reproduced from the collections of the Library of Congress.]

JUDGMENT DAY of TORIES.

The Tories' Day of Judgment: neglected underside of the American Revolution. [Engraving by E. Tisdale, 1795. Reproduced from the collections of the Library of Congress.]

*C*olonial scholar Alan Simpson once counseled students of the past to be especially aware of what he called the "special character of American history"—its "deceptive resemblance to a short story with a simple plot." Although initially suggested within the context of our colonial past, Simpson's concerns have come to be shared by students and scholars of America's revolutionary era as well. Perhaps for too long, as the historiographical article contained in this section will suggest, the Whig interpretation of the revolutionary era was dominant. According to Whig historians, of whom George Bancroft was the most accomplished practitioner, American history was told rather simply as the "story of liberty." To Bancroft's mind, the great dynamic of the Revolution and its aftermath was clearly the engagement of the principle of freedom and the instrument of tyranny. Simply put, America symbolized the forces of liberty and progress—Great Britain, those of despotism and reaction.

Whig historians were perhaps the first to systematically construct a usable past from America's revolutionary experiences. And although the Whig interpretation has been largely modified if not preempted, the spirit of nationalism and patriotism that the Whig historians inspired continues. Ever since, the era of the American Revolution has served as the touchstone of American institutions and traditions. The rhetoric of this period has at various times served to justify the designs of social and political movements from the radical left to the reactionary right. Both Black Nationalists and the Daughters of the American Revolution have found the Revolution "as American as apple pie." Not surprisingly, because of some rather blatant disregard for historical accuracy, the revolutionary era has remained all things to all people—and a rather grand mythology has followed in its wake. This section seeks to isolate some of the cherished historical myths that have continued to surround leading personalities and events of the revolutionary period. Historians have taken us far beyond merely questioning the historical accuracy of Paul Revere's ride or Washington's crossing the Delaware. Myths reside here, but they are of little consequence. Rather, twentieth-century historians in particular have forced us to reexamine our standard emphasis upon the heroic qualities of America's revolutionary leadership, the tyrannical nature of the British empire in general and George III in particular, the unity of revolutionary sentiment amongst the colonists, the failures of the Confederation period, and the almost-divine qualities of the Founding Fathers, as well as the role of Indians and women in the revolutionary era. The following selections present some significant challenges to viewing the revolutionary era in such simplistic and mythic terms.

The American Revolution: The Critical Issues

Robert F. Berkhofer, Jr.

Much that might be construed as historical myth is the by-product of historical study itself. In their quest for certitude and "truth," historians have often overstated their argument and so created a biased or distorted image of the past. For this reason, it seems advisable to include historiographical selections, particularly when dealing with the major wars of American history. The discrepancies that can emerge between history as actuality and history as perceived seem to be most apparent in this area. The inherent complexity of the wartime environment seems to trigger the intellectual energy of its commentators so that myth constructing is more likely to occur. Robert F. Berkhofer, Jr., of the University of Michigan, provides this perspective as regards the critical issues of the American Revolution. By emphasizing the "mental climate" in vogue as historians forwarded their differing interpretations, Professor Berkhofer stresses the importance of theory, in addition to evidence, as a determinant in historical judgment. Mr. Berkhofer also suggests that historians seek a new level of historical understanding—one based more on evidence than theory, perhaps more on reality than myth.

Before a historian can explain the whys of the American Revolution, he must figure out what it was; and its nature is as perplexing and controversial a problem in historical circles as the explanation of its causes. To professional historians, the phrase "American Revolution" means more than the hostilities between England and thirteen of her colonies. It refers also to the social, economic, and political changes in the colonies that they presume caused, accompanied, or resulted from the conflict. Historians, therefore, usually have grouped their questions about the nature, causes, and consequences of the Revolution around three images:

1. *A war of independence between colonies and a mother country.* Who initiated the hostilities? When and where did the conflict start? What were the issues? Did the conflict result from the grievances voiced shortly before the war broke out, or did it result from long-term trends? Who were the individuals involved upon both sides and why? What was the rebels' aim? Was it independence or some accommodation within the empire? Why were just

thirteen of England's North American colonies involved? Why was it a war of rebellion rather than a guerrilla war or a palace revolution?

2. *A political revolution.* Did the colonies revolt to preserve the basic political system they had or to establish a new kind of government? Why? Were there political innovations despite the aims of the revolutionaries, and, if so, why? What was new about the political results of the Revolution? Was it a new type of revolution at the time? Can it be compared to other revolutions at the time, such as the French Revolution? Can it be compared to the revolutions to establish new nations today?

3. *A social revolution.* Was the American Revolution a social revolution as well as a political revolution? If so, why; if not, why not? What is the model for the meaning of the word "revolution"? How do we judge a set of events to be a revolution? Is the American Revolution comparable to other full-scale revolutions or not? What is the relationship between the social structure of a country and a revolution in general and the social structure of the American colonies and the American Revolution in particular?

These questions suggest the whole problem of comparability as an important way of describing what the American Revolution was and explaining why it was what it was. In other words, we must try to determine what was "American" about the American Revolution and what was revolutionary about it in order to discuss its nature, causes, and consequences.

Answers to all these questions depend as much upon the historian's theories about human behavior as upon the evidence he discovers about past human actions. In fact, he cannot interpret the evidence about the past without employing his theories about the nature of man and society to make sense of it. The credence the historian gives the multitude of pamphlets, newspapers, and letters written by the participants in the Revolution directly reflects his belief whether professed ideals or something else better explains why men did what they did. For example, should the rhetoric of the Declaration of Independence be taken at face value in explaining why the colonists went to war with England? In other words, is there a difference between rationale and motivation, and how do we differentiate between them? Are there deeper causes for human behavior than men of the time say or even understand fully? How do we know whether to trust words or deeds more in seeking to understand the American Revolution? How does the historian know the real reasons for such a complex occurrence as the Revolution? Ultimately each student of history must combine the evidence from the past with his theories of how men act and societies operate in order to derive the "facts" he says happened and that he calls history.

The historian must use his theories of man and society to interpret his evidence in another way also, for he asserts facts about a whole society upon the basis of documents produced by a few of its members. How representative of the people of their time were Thomas Jefferson, Patrick Henry, or John and Sam Adams? Were their aims also the goals of all segments of the population? Or, did they desire some end quite different from what they told the public?

What is the role of leaders in a revolution, and what relationship do they bear to the society of their day? Were some groups of people quite unrepresented by any of the spokesmen for the Revolution? Did most colonists support the war? Did they even care about it? How do we know when so little evidence about their thoughts remains? Should the analyst presume a societal consensus on Revolutionary goals, excepting Tories of course, in order to interpret his evidence? Or, should he assume agreement on goals was due to majority compromise, or public apathy, or coerced submission, or all of these in combination? Again the historian resorts as much to his theories of culture and society as he does to his evidence in constructing the synthesis of facts that he calls history.

So fundamental are these questions about theoretical orientations and so complex the set of events called the Revolution that historians today are no more in agreement upon the answers about the nature, causes, and consequences of the Revolution than were contemporary observers. Now as then some historians focus their attention on the battle of ideas and ideals expressed in the polemical literature of the period . For them the Revolution was fought for political and constitutional ends and the society as a whole subscribed to these aims. Still other observers, then as now, picture the Revolutionary leaders as seeking only selfish political and economic ends behind their propaganda of ideals. To these analysts, the Revolution was perpetrated by an elite which sought to retain or gain political office and social status denied to them by the British imperial system. To attain their economic and political goals, according to this view, the Revolutionary leaders not only challenged English sovereignty and control but also repressed the demands of the masses for the very rights and ideals the leaders proclaimed they were denied in their polemics against England.

Although these two interpretations have existed since the Revolution, their fullest formulation has come in the twentieth century. One group of historians, led by Charles McLean Andrews in the 1920s and Lawrence Henry Gipson more recently, sought to place the colonists' aims and activities in the larger context of the British Empire. Hence, they are called the imperial school. In looking at the colonial struggle in terms of the imperial system, they generally took at face value the importance of the debates over political representation and the constitutional issues of empire. Opposing this approach were such historians as Carl Becker, Charles Beard, Arthur Schlesinger, Sr., and, more recently, Merrill Jensen. They portrayed the Revolution as a struggle among different colonial classes for economic and political hegemony in addition to the fight for independence from England. Since this interpretation arose during the Progressive period and featured an economic interpretation of people's motives, it has been named the progressive or economic interpretation school.

According to the progressive school, the Revolution became an internal or class conflict as well as a rebellion against an external power. As one of the chief formulators of this approach, Carl Becker, stated in *History of Political Parties in the Province of New York, 1760–1776,*

The American Revolution was the result of two general movements; the contest for home-rule and independence, and the democratization of American politics and society. Of these movements, the latter was fundamental; it began before the contest for home-rule, and was not completed until after the achievement of independence. From 1765 to 1776, therefore, two questions, about equally prominent, determined party history. The first was whether essential colonial rights should be maintained; the second was by whom and by what methods they should be maintained. The first was the question of home-rule; the second was the question, if we may so put it, of who should rule at home.

Arthur M. Schlesinger, Sr., bolstered this view with *The Colonial Merchants and the American Revolution*, in which he found that merchants in all the colonies spearheaded the opposition at first against the Stamp and Trade Acts. When, however, they discovered their movement encouraged men lower in the social hierarchy to question their leadership, they drew back from such bold opposition to English control. Only the Tea and Coercive Acts, in Schlesinger's opinion, provided sufficient provocation to reunite the merchants with the more radical elements of society in favor of open rebellion against British rule. As the capstone of this interpretation, Charles Beard in *An Economic Interpretation of the Constitution* portrayed the foundation document of the federal union as the work of conservative upper-class men to foster their own economic welfare by inventing a system of government directly benefitting their own economic interests at the expense of the bulk of small farmers and tradesmen and by forcing this document through ratifying conventions before the majority of Americans understood what was happening.

According to these historians and others who followed their lead, the course of the Revolution moved from conservatives demanding colonial rights, to radicals seeking the rights of men as opposed to property in the Declaration of Independence, to a counter-revolution of the conservatives culminating in the adoption of the Constitution and the temporary repression of the lower classes. It remained for Merrill Jensen to finish this picture by showing in *Articles of Confederation and New Nation* that the history of the whole Revolutionary era resulted from the struggle for power between two continuous and consistently opposed groups based upon socioeconomic cleavages fundamental in the American society of the time. On one side were most members of the colonial upper classes and nouveau riche of the Revolution who favored stronger central government always as means to check lower-class democracy and to regulate trade and pass taxes in their interest. In opposition to these "nationalists" were the "federalists," or the democratic radicals, who favored decentralization of government in the interests of the agrarian democratic views of the majority of the population. For Jensen, as for the others of this school, the ideals expressed in the polemics of the period determined less the actual behavior of the Founding Fathers than their economic interests, and the significant story of the Revolution was found more in the internal conflict of social classes based upon economic power than in the external struggle with England.

After World War II, the progressive version of the causes, nature, and consequences of the Revolution was denied by such writers as Daniel Boorstin, Louis Hartz, Benjamin Wright, and most important, Edmund Morgan, who synthesized his research and their outlook in his influential little book, *Birth of the Republic, 1763–89.* As the title of Benjamin Wright's *Consensus and Continuity, 1776–1787* suggests, these men find neither class conflict nor swings between radical and conservative leadership during the course of the Revolution. Rather they see a consensus upon ideals and aims among the whole non-Tory population. For them, as for nineteenth-century interpreters, the fight was over constitutional principles expressed in the rhetoric of the period, and they minimize the internal divisions among the people. Robert E. Brown in *Middle-Class Democracy and the Revolution in Massachusetts, 1691–1780,* in fact, reversed the progressive or social conflict school by arguing that the colonists were primarily middle-class property owners, making conflict as unnecessary as it was absent. According to these historians, the revolutionaries went to war to conserve or preserve the rights and class structure they already possessed against England's efforts to change the system rather than to gain new rights and new institutions. As a result of their approach, these men have been denominated the conservative or the consensus school. Later observers think they reflect the conservative ideology of the post-war Eisenhower years.

The consensus school approach continued into the decade of the 1960s and formed the focus of much of the discussion upon the nature of the Revolution. The inclusive term, consensus school, hides the difference between those concerned about the ideas of the revolutionists and those interested in the nature of social stratification and political power. The former analyzed the ideology said to be shared by all, while the latter reconstructed the statistics of class and leadership. During the 1960s Robert E. Brown extended his research to Virginia as a crucial example of his thesis on middle-class democracy and found the Old Dominion relatively equalitarian in class structure and open in economic opportunity. Jackson Turner Main came to the same conclusion in *The Social Structure of Revolutionary America.* However, in a study of legislative membership he found a trend toward greater democratization during the course of the Revolution. The major contributor to the analysis of ideology during the 1960s was Bernard Bailyn. By taking all of the rhetoric of the revolutionaries seriously, he reconstructed their world-view of political ideals, history, and social hierarchy. He also converted the previous static view of Revolutionary ideals and principles into one that was dynamic and evolving. Thus, he calls his introduction to *Pamphlets of the American Revolution,* "The Transforming Radicalism of the American Revolution." In these ways, both he and Main subtly but nevertheless definitely shifted the emphasis upon ideas and class of the consensus school into a new path stressing change and new developments.

Although the consensus school dominated the interpretation of the Revolution during most of the 1960s, it never held the field uncontested. Not only did older men such as Merrill Jensen continue to write vigorously in refutation of the consensus view, but younger men once again found class conflict a key to Revolutionary history. Chief among these was Staughton Lynd, who employed New York State, just as Becker did, to study the effects of class division upon Revolutionary politics. Parallel to this reemphasis upon class conflict and the internal struggle for political power has been the attempt of the "New Left" school, as it is called, to determine the actual views of the inarticulate masses, or to produce the history of "The American Revolution Seen From the Bottom Up," as Jesse Lemisch, the most vociferous advocate of this approach, phrased it in Barton Bernstein, ed., *Towards a New Past: Dissenting Essays in American History.*

By the end of the 1960s, a new mood was evident among historians of the Revolution. Even younger historians trained by consensus or idealist historians questioned the exclusive stress upon ideas, no matter how dynamic. Bailyn's student, Gordon Wood . . . wonders whether attention to rhetoric alone answers the question why the colonists acted as they did as opposed to what they said. Though his book, *The Creation of the American Republic, 1776–1787,* mainly examines the public ideology of Revolutionary leaders in the tradition of his mentor, he asserts in passing that the leaders' words were motivated by reasons other than those that appeared in their public pronouncements—by anxieties grounded in changing social realities of the time. Bailyn himself in *The Origins of American Politics* moved to place the ideology he had uncovered into a political context. Other historians reassessed their own and newer work upon the nature of political factions and conflict before, during, and after the Revolution. In short, the conflict and consensus schools seem to be combining to create a new synthesis that acknowledges the existence of social classes but also points out that conflict, except in certain conspicuous cases, was confined to fights among the elites in the colonies. Similarly this emerging synthesis says the majority of the population shared the same ideology although Tories and certain radicals formed a strong minority. Thus, neither conflict nor consensus, neither ideas nor action is stressed to the exclusion of the other. Rather, further research is needed to determine the role of each element.

So far we have discussed only the ideological and other behavior of the American side of the Revolution without giving any attention to the conflict between Britain and her colonies. A discussion of when and who began the Revolution and why must include consideration of both sides in the controversy, leading directly to the problem of overall causation. Again the historian must resort to some theoretical framework of how he explains revolution, or "internal wars" in the words of one analyst. Some patriot historians, inspired by the indictment in Jefferson's Declaration of Independence, blamed the war on English selfishness in general and the stupidity of George III in particular. Some loyalist historians, on the other hand, condemned the stubborn colonists and the shrewd demagogues who duped the people into disloyalty to Crown and mother country. On the whole, however, observers then and historians of this century agree that the factors that produced the hostilities were diverse and the causes for independence extend beyond the battles of Lexington and Concord or even the Sugar and Stamp Acts. No matter which side the imperial school historians took on the constitutionality of the English and colonial views of the empire and sovereignty, they placed the perspective of causation where it belonged: on the changing relations between both sides in the conflict. Though many books have been published on this phase of the Revolution, the relationships were so complex that still more research is needed. The imperial school also questioned whether the imperial economic regulations were unfair to colonial capitalists. In other words, did the colonists have legitimate grievances against trade regulation, or was the English government only requesting the colonists to pay their fair share of the empire's expenses? Today we study this issue on two levels: (1) what the actors said and believed regardless of what the true balance of payments may have been, and (2) what the historian reconstructs that true balance of payments to have been using statistics and economic theory. In this debate, as in preceding ones, we see historians seeking resolution of issues through greater precision in specifying what questions the problem involves and what theories and evidence are needed to produce answers to these questions. . . .

From this hasty survey of the history of the history (called historiography) of the Revolution, the student can see the importance of theory as well as evidence in seeking to understand the nature, causes, and consequences of it. Equally obvious is the need for a good set of questions about what has to be known and what we seek to and can know from the evidence. The student should therefore compare the questions historians ask and the questions that he wants to ask. . . .

The American Revolution created American history by creating a new nation. Thus, Americans study the history surrounding the American Revolution for clues to American identity and character. At the same time their beliefs about themselves as a people influence what they perceive to be the nature, causes, and consequences of the Revolution. What the Revolution was, then, depends to a large extent upon what Americans think they are or ought to be. Thus, as the attitudes Americans hold about themselves change, so too does the history of the Revolution and especially the meaning of the Revolution for American history. . . .

As a result of this changing compound of morality, theory, and the search for national identity, each generation interprets and reinterprets the American Revolution. Is this the ultimate, and perhaps the only, truth about the Revolution, or can we determine the facts about it independently of the mental climate of our times?

George III: The Myth of a Tyrannical King

Darrett B. Rutman

The name of George III of England and the word *tyranny* have become synonymous in the American mind. With the accumulation of new evidence, however, many historians challenge the legendary war guilt of King George. Representative of those who have contributed to the rehabilitation of his tarnished image is Darrett B. Rutman of the University of Florida. One of the premier scholars of colonial America, Professor Rutman here speaks to the seminal importance of Thomas Paine in redirecting the colonists' revolutionary sentiment from Parliament to king. As Rutman argues the case, before the appearance of Paine's pamphlet *Common Sense* of January 1776, the colonists had sustained their loyalty to the Crown and sought "home rule under the king" and a redress of grievances from the British Parliament, not independence.

What the colonists considered an effort to change the governance of the empire by depriving their little parliaments of the exclusive right to legislate in local affairs—an effort increasingly discerned as a conspiracy of tyrants against man's innate liberty—had led to open war. Through all of this, however, the colonists had remained loyal subjects of George III. Stamp distributors, customs commissioners, lobsterbacks, the intolerable acts—all symbolized a confrontation with Parliament and ministers, not king. Indeed, during the early years of argument, the king's governors were obeyed, even to the extent of the Virginians going unrepresented in the Stamp Act Congress because their governor dissolved the House of Burgesses just as it was about to name representatives. As late as 1775 the same crowd which "huzzahed" for George Washington as he crossed Manhattan Island on his way to take command of the colonial forces around Boston rushed to the Battery to "huzzah" for a newly-arrived royal governor. Anglicans in the colonies prayed for the health of the king in conformity with the Book of Common Prayer, while in the taverns men drank the health of George and wished him the best of fortune.

> This bumper I crown for our sovereign's health,
> And this for Britannia's glory and wealth.

So went the last verse of "The Liberty Song," almost the national anthem of pre-independence days. Petitions and remonstrances directed to the king professed in all sincerity the loyalty of the colonists. And as the confrontation with Parliament and the king's ministers continued in time, as the colonists came to the position of denying Parliament any authority whatsoever over them, the king, to an ever increasing extent, symbolized the colonists' attachment to an empire which they had not yet considered leaving. "Allegiance to Parliament?" the Second Continental Congress asked rhetorically in 1775; "we never owed—we never owned it. Allegiance to our king? Our words have ever avowed it—our conduct has ever been consistent with it."

Allegiance could be stretched so far, however, before it would break. And colonial allegiance to king and empire was brought almost to the breaking point by Lexington and Concord. In New York and Georgia, militiamen seized control of the ports; in Williamsburg, militiamen (including students at William and Mary College) patrolled the streets to prevent the royal governor from seizing the arms in the public magazine. Extra-legal governments began making their appearance, in some cases extensions of the committees of correspondence, more usually the old lower houses of the legislatures sitting independently of the governor and council. Thus in Virginia, when the governor attempted to stop certain activities of the House of Burgesses by dissolving the House as had been done in Stamp Act days, the House, rather than meekly obeying him, trooped across the street to a tavern and went about its business, subsequently setting itself up as a supreme Virginia Convention. Soon after the governor fled to the safety of a British warship. By December 1775, royal governments had been swept away in all but New Jersey, although the proprietary governments of Pennsylvania and Maryland remained. By July 1776 these too were gone.

On an inter-colonial level, the Second Continental Congress met in May 1775 to remain in session throughout the remainder of the controversy and through the war years ahead. The delegates from the various colonies to the Congress immediately accepted the war situation which existed. In June an organization for war was created, the Congress assuming control of the forces besieging Boston and appointing Virginia's George Washington to command. To pay for the war effort, the Congress authorized the issuance of two million dollars in paper money. In July a "Declaration of the Reasons for Taking up Arms" was issued.

Yet war and independence were not synonymous, a fact which the members of the Congress pressed in their "Declaration." Their quarrel was still with corrupt ministers and a Parliament which had sought "all the easy emoluments of statutable plunder" by undertaking "to give and grant our money without our consent, though we have ever exercised an exclusive right to dispose of our own property." They were resisting only the "intemperate rage for unlimited domination" on the part of ministers and Parliament. This had led to war, but for their part military activities would cease "when hostilities shall cease on the part of the aggressors, and all danger of their being renewed shall be removed." They were not seeking to break with their "friends and fellow subjects in any part of the empire." "We assure them that we mean not to dissolve that union which has so long and so happily subsisted between us, and which we sincerely wish to see restored." In a petition to the king approved at the same time—the so-called "Olive Branch Petition"—their loyalty to George III was expressed in fervent terms, and that good monarch was humbly requested to intercede for them with Parliament and the ministry to obtain a repeal of the intolerable acts, the withdrawal of the troops, and a renunciation of Parliament's assertion of authority over the colonies. Some objected to what seemed a craven appeal. Massachusetts' John Adams, a delegate to the Congress, considered that the outbreak of war signified the end of such petitions and denounced the Olive Branch as putting "a silly cast on all our doings." But undoubtedly it represented the feelings of most of the colonial leaders. They were fighting to preserve their liberty within the empire as it had been prior to 1763 and as they had come to define it formally during the long controversy: Home rule under the king.

For over a year the Continental Congress remained in this anomalous position of leading a fight against the king's troops for liberty under the king. In July 1775, the Congress hinted at the possibility of looking for foreign aid against the king's army and shortly after set up a five-man "Committee of Secret Correspondence" for the purpose of corresponding with "friends in Great Britain, Ireland, and other parts of the world"—the last phrase ominously portending the future alliance with France. War supplies were purchased abroad and a navy provided under Commodore Esek Hopkins. To the north, Fort Ticonderoga was taken by "rebels" commanded by Ethan Allen and Benedict Arnold; the Battle of Bunker Hill (more accurately Breed's Hill) was fought June 17, 1775 and the siege of Boston went on; an unsuccessful march on Canada was set underway. All in the name of the king.

But the king would not accept the role assigned him by the colonists. He would not be their father and protector. Firm in his support of Parliament and his ministers, he curtly rejected the Olive Branch Petition in August 1775. Subsequently he proclaimed that the Americans were in a state of rebellion to his person.

In the situation the position of the colonists was somewhat unique and certainly difficult. The king was the only link to England and empire which they were prepared by this time to admit, yet the king refused to serve as such a link. As a consequence this last link had to be severed.

It was not easy to do. The colonial leaders were Englishmen. Their professions of loyalty to the monarch were and had always been sincere. If they discerned—and wrote of—a conspiracy to tyrannize in London, the king was no part of it, only his ministers and the Parliament they dominated. Moreover, the king over the years of argument had always been well presented. There was, in effect, little if any animosity toward him.

Still, the last link was severed. Gradually the person of the king began losing some of the sanctity attached to him. The action of the monarch in bluntly and personally refusing the Olive Branch tarnished his reputation, as did the hiring of German mercenary soldiers for the war in America. The various actions of royal officials "in the name of the king" rubbed off on the monarch—Falmouth, Maine, shelled; Norfolk, Virginia, shelled and burned. Then, in January 1776, an outright attack on the king appeared, the first of importance since the start of the troubles. This was *Common Sense*, a little pamphlet by Thomas Paine, an English radical newly arrived in Philadelphia.

Here the very institution of monarchy was attacked, and the English monarchy in particular:

> Government by kings was first introduced into the world by the heathens, from whom the children of Israel copied the custom. It was the most prosperous invention the devil ever set on foot for the promotion of idolatry. The heathens paid divine honors to their deceased kings, and the Christian world has improved on the plan by doing the same to their living ones. How impious is the title of sacred majesty applied to a worm, who in the midst of his splendor is crumbling into dust!
>
> England since the conquest hath known some few good monarchs but groaned beneath a much larger number of bad ones; yet no man in his senses can say that their claim under William the Conqueror is a very honorable one. A French bastard landing with an armed banditti and establishing himself king of England against the consent of the natives is in plain terms a very paltry rascally original. It certainly hath no divinity in it.
>
> In England a king hath little more to do than to make war and give away places, which in plain terms is to impoverish the nation and set it together by the ears. A pretty business indeed for a man to be allowed eight hundred thousand sterling a year for and worshipped into the bargain! Of more worth is one honest man to society, and in the sight of God, than all the crowned ruffians that ever lived.
>
> But the king, you'll say, has a negative in England; the people there can make no laws without his consent. In point of right and good order, it is something very ridiculous that a youth of twenty-one (which hath often happened) shall say to several millions of people older and wiser than himself, 'I forbid this or that act of yours to be law.'

George III himself was castigated as "the royal brute." Aristocracy was castigated for its continual exploitation of the people for the support of luxuries. All the difficulties of the last years were laid not merely to Parliament or the ministers, but to the king as the very leader of their conspiracy against liberty and the thought of reconciliation under the king was dismissed as ridiculous. Independence and a republican government were, to Paine, the common sense solution to the preservation of liberty in America. Sold in record numbers, passed from hand to hand and from tavern to tavern, the pamphlet was vital in creating a tyrant of George III.

The Glorious Fourth—or, Glorious Second? or Eighth?

Marshall Smelser

Revolutions have a basic appeal for all peoples. Because their events are seen, with hindsight, as so critical and their leading characters as so heroic, they have a way of impressing themselves on the human imagination. Americans naturally regard the events of 1776 as the touchstone of the nation's history, and it should be no surprise that their memory would be enforced by the legends and myths that have come to surround these events. Independence Day is a familiar and relevant example. It has come to have a mythical hold on the American mind. While one might expect that the critical events surrounding the occasion of American independence would be clearly known because of their fundamental importance to the beginnings of the nation, such is not the case. According to Professor Marshall Smelser, late of the University of Notre Dame, both the facts and the chronology of the swiftly developing political circumstances of early July 1776 have become widely misunderstood. This is true not only of succeeding generations of Americans who have come to romanticize the events and lionize the personalities of the nation's revolutionary era, but indeed also of many of the participants themselves. The "glorious fourth" has become a mythic combination of fact, patriotic distortion, and nostalgia wedded to the nation's aspirations, dreams, and ideals.

On Monday, July 1, 1776, the Continental Congress sat as Committee of the Whole and drudged through a good deal of paper work. On Tuesday, July 2, 1776, the Committee of the Whole reported to the Congress, which made six decisions: it settled some financial accounts, ordered the publication of a letter which had been lying on the table, referred some papers to the Board of War, and told the Marine Committee to look into complaints against its operations. And it resolved to declare the independence of the United States. That very evening the *Pennsylvania Evening Post* printed a brief notice: "This day the Continental Congress declared the United Colonies Free and Independent States." On July 3 the *Pennsylvania Gazette* picked it up word for word except to begin the sentence with the word "Yesterday."

A committee had been at work on a public statement of the reasons for declaring independence since early in the previous month so that Congress would have an explanation *if* it were decided to speak on the subject.

From *The History Teacher*, Vol. 3, No. 2 (January 1970). Reprinted by permission of *The History Teacher*.

Thomas Jefferson, a lanky loose-jointed young Congressman from Virginia who served as the chief writer of the committee, had previously noted down his "first ideas" on the Virginia Convention as a draft preamble to the proposed Constitution of Virginia. These "first ideas," much revised, served as his guide to that part of the declaration which denounced the behavior of King George III, but the rest he did from memory. He consulted nothing in print but drew on useful ethical aphorisms about resistance to tyranny, all of which had been intellectual currency since before 1492. When on June 28, 1776, he presented his text to his fellow committeemen, Benjamin Franklin, John Adams, Robert Livingston, and Roger Sherman, he handed it over as a draft to be revised. For example, he had laboriously pointed out that the British and Americans could together have become a great and free people, but the British were too proud to collaborate, hence the Americans would go that road alone out of regrettable necessity. As polemics, this was to Americans a penetrating glimpse of the obvious and disappeared in revision. Franklin also interjected his scientific turn of thought by changing Jefferson's "sacred and undeniable" principles to "self-evident" truths, an eighteenth-century scientist's phrase for axioms, and a rather happier wording.

Thus a statement of independence had been in preparation for many days; it remained to approve the wording, a task which absorbed most congressional attention on July 3. On that day the Congress changed the document for the better. The verbal changes of both the committee and the Congress uniformly improved the paper.

Thursday, July 4, was a pleasant day in Philadelphia. Jefferson, whose curiosity ranged far enough to include meteorology, noted that his thermometer registered 68° at six o'clock in the morning; it rose to a high of 76° at one o'clock. Such fine weather seems to have invigorated him and his colleagues, which was just as well because there was plenty of work to do. By the end of the day the Congress had made seventeen formal decisions, including an order to design a great seal of the United States and one to send a man searching at public expense for stone suitable for musket flints. One of the seventeen resolutions approved the final draft of the Declaration of Independence.

The thing was not done hastily. The Philadelphia printer John Dunlap printed the Declaration as a broadside, folio size, on July 5 or 6, and not until Saturday, July 6, did the *Pennsylvania Evening Post* publish the Declaration, as signed by John Hancock, President of the Congress, and attested by Charles Thomson, Secretary (no other signatures were published until the next year, by which time seven broadside printings had appeared). On July 8, the next Monday, the Congress and local Committee of Public Safety proclaimed the Declaration from a stage in the yard of the State House. Such troops as there were nearby paraded, and spent much of their perilously short supply of gunpowder in exuberantly firing salutes, while the bells of Philadelphia, including the Liberty Bell in the State House tower, clanged all that day and far into the night. The local rebels added a clownish touch to the parade by dressing a well-known streetwalker in unaccustomed finery topped by the kind of headdress then affected by the loyalist ladies of Philadelphia.

The Congress ordered General George Washington to have the Declaration read to the troops who were at the moment rather nervously preparing to defend New York City from the largest expeditionary force ever sent out of Britain, a great army which even then was debarking on Staten Island. The American officers read the Declaration to their men on July 9, and, as Washington soberly put it, "the measure seemed to have their most hearty assent, the Expressions and behavior both of Officers and Men testifying their warmest approbation of it." Although the harbor was a forest of enemy masts, some of the civilians of New York testified their own warm approbation by going to the Bowling Green and pulling the equestrian statue of George III from its fifteen foot pedestal. The figure was of gilded lead, which made it easy to decapitate and useful to melt down for bullets.

The news moved up and down the coast. In Newport the Declaration proved its psychological value by shocking the Reverend Mr. Ezra Stiles (a future President of Yale) into the realization, for the first time, that the United States, which had been behaving very independently for a year and a half, were actually independent. In Providence the ship masters celebrated by firing thirteen salvos of ships' guns, while local rebels tore the King's arms from a government office, and the identifying crown from the Crown Coffee House, and burned both. In Boston the Declaration sounded from pulpits as the trumpet of the Lord of Hosts. In Baltimore an effigy of George III rode through town and perished in flames. The word reached Savannah on August 10 and was greeted with mixed solemnity and joy. The Declaration was read aloud in three places and thrice saluted by muskets and field guns, after which Governor, Council, gentlemen, and militia (a nice distinction) "dined under the cedar trees, and cheerfully drank to the united, free, and independent states of America." That night the Savannah citizens illuminated the town for a cortege which marched to bury the effigy of George III in a grave dug in front of the court house.

London learned of the Declaration about a fortnight after Savannah had the news, and a French translation was printed on the continent on August 30. The King's friends might have been excused if they had confined themselves to the language of scorn, but at least one (in America) tried a rational criticism, to wit, the Declaration cut the ground from under the American sympathizers in the Parliament, and was a very poor tactical response to the pro-American speeches of such men as Chatham and Richmond.

Until July 2 it had not been absolutely certain that the Congress would declare independence. Delaware was absent. New York had denied its congressional delegation the authority to vote for independence. The internal tensions of Pennsylvania politics handicapped the Congress—for example, some members from Pennsylvania, including Robert Morris and Thomas Willing of the Philadelphia mercantile firm which had much of the business of supplying the Army, abstained from voting on the final passage of the resolution to declare independence. The arrival of the New Jersey delegation, elected on June 22, made independence probable, but only the coming of Caesar Rodney of Delaware clinched the vote. The ballot, on July 2, by states, was 12–0, as New

York delegates watched with approval although abstaining. The text of the Declaration used the word "unanimous" but this did not come true until the New York Convention approved of independence on July 9 when it accepted the Declaration, because, it said, the reasoning was "cogent and conclusive." The New York congressmen declared their vote on July 15, which finally made the line-up "unanimous."

Caesar Rodney and some forgotten, steaming horses ought to get very special credit. Rodney (uncle of the national leader of the same name in the next generation) was a tall, thin, pallid man of whom John Adams said "his face is not bigger than a large apple." He sweated eighty miles on horseback to arrive on July 2 to put Delaware on record. This brave, practical, clear-minded man then went out and bore arms in the Delaware militia before returning to the Congress in 1777. President John Witherspoon of Princeton, a Presbyterian minister who entered politics reluctantly and became the leading token-Scot of a rebel cause which was rather short of Scottish rebels, came to Philadelphia in time to exhort waverers effectively, and stayed to serve on more than a hundred committees, wherein he bore witness to the natural and Christian virtues of fortitude, prudence, resignation, and hope.

Fifteen days after approving the text of the Declaration of Independence the Congress resolved to give it its title and have it engrossed on parchment and signed by every member. In time, all signed except John Dickinson, who hid out for a while in Delaware, to escape the hurt look of his colleagues and the I-told-you-so's of some loyalist in-laws. From the viewpoint of every King's Counsel and most judges of English commonlaw courts the list of signatories was a tally of traitors; hence their names were secret until sometime between January 18 and 31, 1777, when the Congress, then at Baltimore, sent authenticated copies to all the states for their archives. These copies listed the signers, although not by states. Folklore says that scholarly William Ellery of Rhode Island (a man fond of reading Cicero, even on his death bed), watched the expressions on the faces of the signers as they took quill in hand, for, after all, they might be signing their own death warrant. He reported, it is said, that all signers showed "undaunted resolution." This is a regrettably impossible tale, because the signing went on for several months.

The Americans have chosen July 4 as their Independence Day. They could as well have chosen July 2 or 8. The choice of the day on which the Congress merely authenticated the phraseology of its statement is less logical than the choice of the day on which the Congress voted independence or the choice of the day it officially proclaimed independence. John Adams wrote to his Abigail that July 2 would be "the most memorable" American anniversary. In the next generation editors doctored Adams' dating to remind people that Adams had been on the Declaration drafting committee and that it was not solely Jefferson's work. The result was that some have been confused about what happened on July 4. What did the Congress do on July 4? The Congress voted only that the text of the Declaration be approved and authenticated. It did not order the clerks to have it engrossed until July 19. Thus the only deeds of July 4 were that President John Hancock bravely affixed his bold signature and Secretary Charles Thomson added his name to attest to the correctness of the text. Then why is July 4 Independence Day? On that day the document lay untitled and undated, nor was it yet engrossed on parchment, nor did any signer after Hancock and Thomson put his name to it before August 3. In fact, some of the signers were not even members of the Congress at the time the Congress approved the Declaration, and some who were members and later signed it had voted "no." Matthew Thornton of New Hampshire did not take his seat until November 4, whereupon he signed the Declaration, no doubt with "dauntless resolution." The reasons the Americans celebrate "the Fourth of July" is that the parchment text ordered to be engrossed by resolution of July 19 is dated July 4 and the Declaration of Independence appears in the Journals of the Continental Congress under the date July 4, complete with title and list of signers. The format has given posterity reason to believe the job was all done on that one day.

The actual chronology was this: The Continental Congress voted independence on July 2, which the local Philadelphia press duly noted on that and the next day. The Congress, with the local Committee of Safety, proclaimed independence in the Pennsylvania State House yard on July 8. A committee drafted the explanatory document intended to accompany and justify the decision, through late June. The Congress polished this Declaration on July 3 and approved it on July 4. A printer brought it out as a single sheet on July 5 or 6, and the newspaper press had it on July 6. Engrossing the document began on July 19, and signing commenced on August 2 and ran into November. Later in January, 1777, the names of the signers (other than President John Hancock and Secretary Charles Thomson, which were public from the first) became known when the Congress distributed copies of the Declaration of Independence for the archives of the thirteen states. The Declaration of Independence, with its Fourth-of-July date of authentication, has had the publicity, but, nevertheless, the Congress voted independence on July 2 and proclaimed it on July 8.

The Loyalists and the American Revolution

Wallace Brown

History is particularly harsh with losers. It tends to recall mainly the triumphs and achievements of the victors. In this sense, the Loyalists or Tories—those who remained faithful to England and king during the course of the American Revolution—represent the forgotten Americans of the revolutionary period. If for no other reason than their numbers, however, they bear closer attention. On the eve of the conflict with England, the great majority of Americans could be justly described as "reluctant revolutionaries," and by most estimates clearly one-third of colonial society harbored loyalist sentiments and thought the move to revolution ill-advised. In the following essay, Canadian scholar Wallace Brown, of the University of New Brunswick, explores the attitudes and motives of the Loyalists, an often forgotten dimension of the American Revolution.

In the numerous celebrations of the American Civil War centenary now taking place, Northerners usually honor and respect the Southern rebels. But the losers of an earlier civil war, the War for Independence, are practically forgotten outside academic circles, and even there the only general study of the Loyalists, or Tories, is sixty years old; hence this article must be rather tentative in its conclusions. The Loyalists, those American colonists who opposed independence and wished to remain in the Empire, although often condemned out of hand during the nineteenth century, have since been more fairly treated by historians; but the present neo-Bancroftian interpretations of the Revolution, which minimize social conflict within the colonies, apparently forget them.

In Great Britain the Loyalists, perhaps an embarrassment to the Whig school of historiography, have been snubbed, just as they often were as refugees at the time. In Canada, however, where many emigrated and were officially named the United Empire Loyalists, they are venerated as founding fathers, which helps to explain the surprising differences—to many Americans, at least—between the Dominion and the United States.

Any discussion of the American Revolution that neglects the Loyalists is distorted. For a start, there is their sheer number. In 1814 Thomas McKean, the Pennsylvanian Patriot and statesman, agreed with ex-President John

From "The Loyalists and the American Revolution," by Wallace Brown, in *History Today*, 12 (March 1962). Reprinted by permission of the author and publisher.

Adams that about one-third of the colonists had been opposed to the Revolution. The usual estimate of the number of Loyalist exiles is 100,000 out of a population of 2,500,000, and Professor R. R. Palmer has recently suggested, on the basis of a lower estimate, that the American Revolution produced twenty-four émigrés per thousand of the population compared with only five per thousand in the French Revolution. He also calculated that the American confiscation of property was proportionally almost as great as the French. Between 30,000 and 50,000 Loyalists fought on a regular basis for the King, and many more served in the militia or engaged in guerilla warfare. In 1780 8,000 Loyalists were in the regular army at a time when Washington's army numbered only about 9,000. All these figures represent only hard-core Loyalists. Most escaped exile and confiscation, or were quietist, biding their time, merely expressing their loyalty with a secret prayer for the King or a muted curse for the Congress.

The strength of the Loyalists varied from state to state. John Adams believed that New York and Pennsylvania would have joined the British if strongly patriotic Virginia and New England on either side "had not kept them in awe," and he agreed with Chief Justice Marshall that the Southern States were "nearly equally divided." Timothy Pickering referred to eastern Pennsylvania as "enemies' country," and in 1776 Washington, who had many harsh words for the Tories, considered them "our great danger." Modern scholarship agrees that the Loyalists were very strong in the Middle States, the Carolinas and Georgia, and weakest in New England, Virginia and Maryland. But they were a force to be reckoned with everywhere.

John Adams has left contradictory estimates of the number of Loyalists; not surprisingly, because they are impossible to count and difficult to define. Many changed sides, sometimes more than once, and usually according to variations in the fortunes of war. Before the Declaration of Independence numerous Loyalists, such as Joseph Galloway of Pennsylvania and William Smith, last royal Chief Justice of New York, took a Whig position. Also it must be remembered that up to one-third of the population probably remained neutral during the struggle. Contemporary definitions of the Loyalists include, "A Tory is a thing whose head is in England, and its body in America, and its neck ought to be stretched," and "Every fool is not a Tory, yet every Tory is a fool," but basically a Tory was simply someone who remained loyal to George III and opposed the Declaration of Independence.

There are, as yet, no statistics with which to answer the question, who were the Loyalists? As with Whigs, Loyalists can be found in every class, race, occupation, religion and geographical area in the colonies. But some very speculative classification can be made.

Office-holders, from royal Governors to humble customs officials, were usually loyal, even when descended from old colonial families. William Franklin, Governor of New Jersey and illegitimate son of Benjamin Franklin, is a representative of this group. It has been estimated that between one-half and two-thirds of the members of the colonial councils remained loyal. So did many lawyers, like Jonathan Sewall of Massachusetts or Peter Van Schaak of

New York, who often did well out of Crown fees. Professional people in general, particularly doctors and teachers, contributed heavily to the Loyalist ranks. The leading physician of Charleston, South Carolina, was the loyal Alexander Garden, while Myles Cooper and John Camm, respectively heads of King's College, New York, and the College of William and Mary, Virginia, shared this outlook.

Two classes usually loyal were the large land-owners, especially proprietors like the Penns, or the Granville heirs in North Carolina, and the merchants (a list of proscribed Boston Tories in 1778 included thirty-six merchants).

Religion was sometimes important. Dissent tended to be patriotic, identifying Anglicanism with the setting up of a dreaded bishopric, missionaries and foreign domination. Anglicanism was often the religion of the conservative classes, and a revolt against King George was a revolt against the head of the Church. Thus the whole congregation of Trinity Church, New York, and their minister went to Nova Scotia to escape the Republican government. In Virginia, on the other hand, where the Church of England was in many ways independent, Anglicanism was not particularly associated with loyalism. Jefferson and Washington were at least nominal Anglicans. The pacifist religious sects, mainly the Quakers, were usually branded as Tories, not always fairly because they opposed violence by *both* sides, and their refusal to take oaths of allegiance to the new states was not necessarily political.

Some special categories of Loyalists should be mentioned. Political expediency could be the deciding factor; in New York the De Lanceys took the Tory side against the Whig Livingstons. Some loyalist groups perchance saw Great Britain as an ally against their own more immediate enemies; the small farmers of New York who had rebelled under Prendergast against their Whig landlords; the Baptists of Ashfield, Massachusetts, who were struggling against the established patriotic Congregational Church; the back-country Regulators of North Carolina defeated at the battle of Alamance by the dominating Whiggish seaboard; the Highlanders, sent to the Carolinas after the '45, who had been leniently treated and feared a Whig attack on their land titles. A number of Indians and Negroes can be classed as Loyalists. Dunmore, Clinton and Cornwallis offered Negroes their freedom in return for military service, and Joseph Brant led what was left of the Six Nations for the British.

Most Loyalists had, or thought they had, something material or spiritual to lose by the break with Britain. This fear is the great unifying factor. Officials had their jobs to lose, lawyers their fees, merchants their trade, land-owners their proprietorship, Anglicans their dream of a bishop, King-worshippers their idol, Anglophiles their membership of the Empire, Regulators and Massachusetts Baptists their hope of royal help, Negroes their freedom, Indians the British alliance against the frontiersmen. Conservatives and the better-off in general had most to lose in a revolutionary upheaval; the timid became loyalist in areas occupied by British troops; some office-holders, and perhaps the Highlanders, were loath to break their oaths of allegiance.

It is a great mistake to imagine that the Loyalists were always or even usually of high social standing. Most of those who settled in modern Canada were of humble origins, many signing their names with a cross. A recent study of New Brunswick Loyalists by Esther Clark Wright reveals that ninety per cent were American born and that the majority were farmers, tradesmen and artisans. Canada attracted the poorer classes because it was much more cheaply reached than England. Every colony abounds with examples of humble Loyalists, and the conclusion must be that the Loyalists were a complete cross-section of the population.

The example of a single state will illustrate this. In June 1778 Delaware listed forty-six particularly obnoxious Tories excepted from a general pardon. The list included: two captains, three physicians, one lawyer, and seven described as assemblymen, office-holders and wealthy citizens; then lower down the social scale, nine husbandmen and two yeomen; lower still, two labourers, one weaver, three coopers, one cordwainer, one coppersmith, one tailor, one saddler, one bricklayer, one hatter, two innkeepers, two mariners, three shallopmen and three pilots.

The Whigs, of course, had few good words for the Tories. Thomas Mc-Kean called them "the timid and those who believed the colonies would be conquered . . . also the discontented and capricious of all grades," while Tom Paine added "Interested men, who are not to be trusted; weak men who *cannot* see; prejudiced men who *will not* see; and a certain set of moderate men who think better of the European world than it deserves."

No doubt many Loyalists were weak and timid, but it took courage to face social ostracism, mob violence and finally, in some cases, banishment and confiscation. Tenacity was required to start a new life in the frozen wastes of Canada. It was the Whigs who were "discontented and capricious" as they continually shifted their argument from one stand to another, disavowing independence until almost the last moment.

In 1775 the *Massachusetts Spy* described a Tory as "one who is a maintainer of the infernal doctrine of arbitrary power, and indefeasible right on the part of the sovereign, and of passive obedience and non-resistance on the part of the subject." This was true only of extremists. Many Loyalists such as Thomas Hutchinson, the distinguished descendant of the seventeenth-century heretic, Anne Hutchinson, Daniel Dulany, the native-born Maryland lawyer, and Samuel Seabury, the Connecticut-born future first Episcopalian American bishop, vigorously opposed the Stamp Act and most of the "new" legislation after 1760. For example, Dulany had vehemently denied the right of Parliament to tax the colonies. The Declaration of Independence precipitated the genuine Loyalists, and in Hobbesian terms, at least, they became the rebels while the Whigs became the loyalists. The quarrel continued to be not over colonial rights or "passive obedience," but rather over whether the colonies' future well-being could be best assured within the Empire or without. The Loyalists had a fundamental trust in Britain, the Whigs a fundamental distrust.

Sometimes only very subtle differences might separate a Loyalist from a Whig. John Jay and Peter Van Schaak, both successful New York lawyers, came from similar aristocratic backgrounds. Jay became a reluctant Patriot, bowing before the *fait accompli*; Van Schaak became a reluctant Tory by following his conscience; both had opposed British policy, and both remained firm friends even after Jay had served on the committee which exiled Van Schaak.

That personal reasons often determined a man's allegiance is shown by the number of split families. As in every revolution, brother fought brother. General Timothy Ruggles, a leading Massachusetts Loyalist, was opposed by his wife, brothers and some of his children. David Ogden, a Loyalist judge from New Jersey, had three sons of the same persuasion, but two others were Patriots. Two of the sons of John Lovell, the eminent Loyalist teacher at the Boston Latin School, followed their father while a third was a Patriot.

Usually the younger generation in split families was Whig, such as John Randolph of Virginia, the Loyalist father of patriotic Edmund Randolph, but the Loyalist Governor of New Hampshire, John Wentworth, had a Whig father, and the Franklins offer a similar example.

Some split families were even accused of keeping a foot in both camps in order to be on the winning side whatever happened. Benjamin Pickman fled from Salem, Massachusetts, in 1775, but left his wife behind to look after their property to which he returned ten years later. The Dulanys of Maryland were charged with a similar subterfuge.

But kinship and intermarriage were often potent forces in deciding allegiance. In Petersham, Massachusetts, the Whig schoolmaster, Ensign Man, opposed the Loyalist minister, Aaron Whitney, until he married Whitney's daughter and became a Tory. Elizabeth Gray was of sterner stuff. From a Tory background she married into the patriotic Otis family, which isolated her from her own relatives. Rightly, she remained with her husband, but her letters reveal her unhappiness and continuing loyalty.

It is now necessary to explain the comparative ineffectiveness of the Loyalists, in spite of their number and talent. They were at an initial disadvantage because so many were in basic agreement with the Whigs until the Declaration of Independence. Because they were conservatives, the Loyalists failed to organize themselves and had nothing to compare with the Sons of Liberty or Committees of Correspondence. It was thought that the revolt would soon peter out, and many agreed with Lord Dunmore, Governor of Virginia, that the Patriots should be given enough rope to hang themselves. This attitude, combined with a belief in British invincibility, produced apathy. Many Loyalists neglected to vote for delegates to the first Continental Congress where the Loyalist Joseph Galloway's plan for reconciliation was narrowly defeated. Meanwhile, the revolutionary Whigs perfected their machinery and the Loyalists were not able to control a single state government.

Unfortunately, the Loyalist faith in the power of the redcoats was shared, especially in the early stages of the war, by the British authorities who failed to use the Loyalist support effectively. The British officers, true to perennial form, looked down on the colonials. Thus Colonel Timothy Ruggles, who raised a Loyalist Massachusetts regiment, was very badly treated, and Edward Winslow, the Master-Muster-General of the Loyalist Provincial Forces, testified to British neglect and contempt.

As an additional discouragement, there were the activities of the British and Hessian troops which must have alienated many Loyalists and made Patriots of many more. The Reverend Leonard Cutting wrote from a strongly Loyalist area, Hempstead, Long Island, in 1781, complaining: "We have nothing we can call our own, and the door to redress is inacessible. The army has done more essential injury to the King's cause than the utmost efforts of his enemies." Even Judge Thomas Jones, a leading New York Loyalist, devoted a whole chapter in his partisan history of the state to the "Illegal and Cruel Treatment of Loyalists by the British Military during the War!" It was reported that the British army was even driving the Quakers to take up arms.

But, of course, the worst persecution, both legal and illegal, came from the Whigs. The states passed test acts and finally acts of banishment and confiscation. Many Loyalists lost their civil liberties and political rights. At the same time they faced ostracism and the danger of mob violence. A Newport toast of 1775, "A cobweb pair of breeches, a hedge-hog saddle, a hard-trotting horse, and a continual riding to all enemies of America," was only too easily translated into destruction of property, tarring and feathering, or the horrible riding on a rail. Deaths, however, were rare. Loyalists were frequently imprisoned; one famous prison, which housed such distinguished inmates as William Franklin, was the "Newgate of Connecticut," the Simsbury copper mines transformed into dungeons.

Too much sympathy must not be lavished on the persecuted Loyalists. Where they were able, they dealt with the Whigs in similar fashion and, in spite of the British shortcomings, they did contribute to the war effort which naturally led to the bitterness of civil war. Several famous Loyalist regiments fought with distinction, such as Robert Rogers' Queen's Rangers, Patrick Ferguson's American Riflemen, Cortlandt Skinner's New Jersey Volunteers and John Butler's Loyal Rangers whose activities in New York state made Butler, possibly unfairly, a sort of folk-villain. (D. W. Griffith cast him for this role in his last great spectacle, *America.*)

The Loyalists were also used as civilian workers at army camps, as spies and as counterfeiters of Continental currency. Jonathan Bush of Shrewsbury, Worcester County, Massachusetts, owned an hotel which was the center for making and distributing counterfeit, but the Continental currency needed little encouragement to depreciate!

If the Loyalists had much talent, the Patriots had more. The Loyalists had no great leaders to compare with Washington, Jefferson, Franklin, or John Adams. They had only one really effective newspaper, James Rivington's *New York Gazetteer*, and no propagandist to compare with Samuel Adams. There were some outstanding Loyalist writers such as Jonathan Odell, the Tory satirist, and Joseph Stansbury, the song-writer, but Moses Coit Tyler, the literary historian of the Revolution, concluded that they were generally inferior to the Patriots. In the field of propaganda another scholar has reached a similar conclusion.

The exodus of the Loyalists began in 1776, when over 1,000 left Boston with the retreating British, and it continued throughout the war. In 1783 the evacuation of New York and Charleston resulted in the departure of 9,000 Loyalists from each city. The final total was probably 100,000 scattered around Great Britain, modern Canada, Florida and the British West Indies.

In London, the haven of the wealthier, the émigrés stuck together. In 1775 Samuel Curwen, of Salem, Massachusetts, founded a New England Club, meeting at the Adelphi Tavern for a weekly dinner, which was attended by such prominent New Englanders as ex-Governor Hutchinson, John Singleton Copley, the artist, Robert Auchmuty, the Boston lawyer, and Samuel Quincy, another lawyer, related to John Adams by marriage. The New England Coffee House in Threadneedle Street and the Old Jewry meeting-house were also habitual gathering-places. For most of them, separated from their homeland and often from their families, it was an unhappy time and sometimes one of real poverty. Furthermore, the exiles were the victims of English snobbery and patronage. Curwen was stung to write in his Journal for December 1776, after having heard the colonists described as "cowards" and "poltroons":

> It is my earnest wish the despised Americans may convince these conceited islanders, that without regular standing armies our continent can furnish brave soldiers and judicious and expert commanders, by some knock-down, irrefragable argument; for then, and not till then, may we expect generous or fair treatment. It piques my pride, I confess, to hear us called *"our colonies, our plantations,"* in such terms and with such airs as if our property and persons were absolutely theirs, like the "villains" and their cottages in the old feudal system, so long since abolished, though the spirit or leaven is not totally gone, it seems.

Curwen, like so many American visitors since, complained of inadequate heating in London. On January 28th, 1776, he wrote: "Almost as cold as ever I felt in New England," and the next day, "The fires here not to be compared to our large American ones of oak and walnut, nor near so comfortable; would that I was away!" It is not surprising that Curwen returned home at the end of the war.

Thomas Hutchinson, the loving historian of Massachusetts, wrote, "I had rather die in a little county farm-house in New England than in the best nobleman's seat in old England." There was also disillusionment with Nova Scotia. One writer reported plaintively in 1784:

> All our golden promises are vanished in smoke. We were taught to believe this place was not barren and foggy as had been represented, but we find it ten times worse. We have nothing but his Majesty's rotten pork and unbaked flour to subsist on. . . . It is the most inhospitable clime that ever mortal set foot on.

This was the Loyalists' tragedy; they were Americans without a home.

The Loyalists felt betrayed by the Peace Treaty of 1783. The British negotiators, Oswald and Shelburne, had tried to get them a complete amnesty and return of all rights and property, but the only American concession was that Congress would "earnestly recommend" to the various states that the Loyalists be allowed to return for twelve months "unmolested in their endeavours to obtain the restitution of their estates, rights, and property." Further confiscation of property was to cease. In fact, confiscation continued and Loyalists found it practically impossible to regain their possessions, and active Loyalists often found it unfeasible even to visit their native states. The Loyalists were abandoned by the Treaty. But short of re-opening the war, the British were impotent, nor had Congress the power to enforce its pledge.

Some conservative elements in the United States deplored the loss of the Loyalists and wished to encourage the exiles to return. Alexander Hamilton complained, "We have already lost too large a number of valuable citizens." As early as May 1783, John Rutherford of New Jersey argued that wealthy Loyalist merchants would aid the state commercially if they returned; in 1784 a New Haven town meeting voted that the Loyalists be allowed to return for similar reasons; and this was typical of the attitude of the business community. It is common to find former Tories in positions of social and political trust in the decade following the end of the war. Hatred was reserved for active Loyalists who had helped the British. One such was a South Carolinian named Love, a participator in a massacre, who was lynched after a court had discharged him. Generally speaking, bitterness depended on the degree of civil war there had been in an area.

Although they felt betrayed by the Peace Treaty, the Loyalists were handled quite well by the British government. Throughout the war several pensions were paid out which reached an annual bill of £70,000 by 1782, and in July 1783, a Compensation Act was passed appointing a commission of five to enquire into the claims of the Loyalists for losses of property and income sustained during the war. Claims were heard in London and various Canadian locations, and after several years the final tally was: 5,072 claims presented for a total sum of £10,358,413. About one thousand of these were for various reasons not proceeded with; the remainder were paid over £3 million out of a total claim of £8,216,126. This represented property losses. In addition, about £26,000 was granted annually in pensions for losses of salaries, and a further sum in annual allowances to such people as widows and orphans. Beyond all this an equal amount was spent to help the Loyalists settle in Canada, while many received offices in the colonies or commissions in the British army. One interesting footnote is that certain humble Loyalists who had emigrated to America, made good, and then returned to England for political reasons, found that their treatment by the Claims Commission was unfair because of prejudice and class attitudes—a rather sad reward for loyalty.

Finally, what is the importance of the Loyalist exiles? By creating New Brunswick and Nova Scotia, and by injecting a large English-speaking element into French Quebec, they helped assure the future of Canada within the British Empire. The break-up and sale of large Loyalist estates probably had a democratizing effect. (This is a moot point that awaits further research.) In some places new men replaced the departed Loyalists, such as the Cabots and Lowells who moved into Boston from Essex County early in the war. In Rhode Island, the war helped to advance Providence and its leading commercial family, the Browns, over Newport which was occupied by the British for a time and became partly loyalist. There certainly were some changes of leadership in parts of the North, but in the South there seems to have been very little social change.

The loss of the Loyalists has been likened to the departure of the French Huguenots and the expulsion of the Moors from Spain. The list of Loyalists banned from Massachusetts has been said to read "almost like a bead-roll of the oldest and noblest families concerned in the founding and the upbuilding of New England civilization." The great ability represented by New England Loyalists in particular cannot be denied, nor can the general cultural mediocrity of the first years of the Republic. The loss of such Loyalists as J. S. Copley, the artist, and Benjamin Thompson (Count Rumford), the scientist, must have had an effect; but against this it must be remembered that, apart from the fact that the United States *gained* certain useful people like Joseph Priestley, the exiled Loyalists represented the removal of the crust of increasing aristocratic pretensions that was forming on colonial society before the Revolution. Had they won, some Loyalists envisaged the setting up of a permanent aristocracy, and a lessening of the power of the lower houses of the colonial Assemblies. Because émigrés did not normally return, the United States was spared the sort of problems that France met after 1815, and it seems credible that the growth of democracy was thus helped considerably.

Against this it has been argued that the youthful financial, diplomatic and political mistakes of the Republic might have been ameliorated if the experience of the Loyalists had not been lost, but the trend of recent research is that the Tory emigration was less of a loss than previously thought; at any rate, the whole question is essentially speculative.

That it is probably fortunate that hard-core Loyalists generally left the United States is illustrated by considering two who did not—Catherine and Mary Byles. These two game old ladies, descended from the famous New England families, the Mathers and the Cottons, are perhaps a fitting subject on which to end this essay. They dwelt on in their old Boston house until the mid-1830's, reliving such memories as walking arm-in-arm with General Howe during the siege of Boston, frigidly putting up with the new régime, writing incessantly to their far-flung Loyalist family as they sipped "loyal tea" and complained of the "Yankees" maintaining their quarters as a permanent Loyalist museum (with themselves as chief exhibits), celebrating George III's birthday each year, and finally (Catherine) writing to congratulate George IV on his accession (the King never replied). They ensured that on their deaths their property all left the United States for more congenial loyal resting places. In 1835 the Boston authorities pulled down part of the sisters' home to make way for a road. They were outraged, but hardly surprised—it was simply "one of the consequences of living in a Republic."

John Eardley-Wilmot, one of the Claims Commissioners, began his enquiry with no particular liking for the Loyalists, but long familiarity with their misfortunes produced in him considerable admiration so that his account of the Claims Commission proceedings, published in 1815, was prefaced, rather appropriately, with the following lines from Milton:

> Their Loyalty they kept, their love, their zeal,
> Nor number, nor example with them wrought
> To swerve from truth, or change their constant mind.

Images: The Indian in the Revolution

Bernard W. Sheehan

By the time of the American Revolution, the dialectical images of Indians as either noble or ignoble had already assumed mythic proportions—for the Americans and the British alike. If these countervailing images—either Noble Red Man or Bloodthirsty Savage—bore any significant resemblance to the activities and diversities of native life, it was, at best, purely coincidental. What mattered most, both emotionally and ideologically, was that the white experience vis-à-vis the Indians could conveniently be mentally reduced to almost a cartoon version of a very complex social reality. The emotional maelstrom of the Revolution, concludes Bernard W. Sheehan of Indiana University, dramatized even more forcefully the importance of these images to the practical conduct of the war itself, both for an emerging America and for the British. Sheehan cites the fanciful work of the painter John Vanderlyn, especially *The Murder of Jane McCrea* (a work reproduced at the beginning of the first section of this volume), as particularly revealing the prevalent ignoble image of Indians then being given currency. As both sides in an increasingly ideological revolutionary conflict attempted to paint the other as "savage" in intent and behavior, the matter of truth, as well as the noble image of Indian cultures, became increasingly lost in the passions of propaganda. Americans came to live by their symbols as they formulated the meaning of their Revolution. The symbolic Indian played a crucial role both during the Revolution and well beyond it. The cultural theme of civility versus savagery begun by earlier Indian captivity narratives would continue to be the fundamental plot of the story of white-Indian relations for many generations to come.

It can be argued plausibly that the American Indians played only a minor role in the American Revolution. Early in the war they threatened the southern frontier, and after 1777 they kept the Kentucky and Ohio settlements on edge. But it cannot be said that the activities of the native warriors, as inconvenient and damaging as these might have been, in any appreciable way affected the outcome of the conflict. The war was won on the battlegrounds of the East by an army constructed and trained according to European standards and was not won in the West against the irregular soldiers of the native tribes, who employed a mode of warfare that Europeans had long identified with the "savage"

From Philip Weeks, ed., *The American Indian Experience: A Profile*, pp. 66–68, 70–72, and 77–78. Reprinted by permission of Harlan Davidson, Inc./The Forum Press, Inc., and the author.

condition. Yet both sides in the conflict eventually sought out the tribes as allies, and the British especially made extensive use of them during the war. It might be contended that the experience of the imperial wars, waged between 1689 and 1763 and still a vivid memory for both Englishmen and Americans, led easily to the belief that the native tribes might be valued allies in the achievement of victory as they had been assumed to be in the long hostilities between Britain and France in the New World. If so, the conviction was more likely the consequence of habit than conscious decision since the native tribes, for all of their activity in the imperial wars, had not been critical for the outcome.

But if the native people did not play an extensive or vital role in the war itself, they were an important factor in the thinking of Englishmen and Americans about the war. The symbolic Indian was nothing new in the New World experience but seldom in the past had the native carried quite the weight and significance that he was required to bear during the Revolution. From the earliest period of discovery and settlement, Europeans had incorporated the Indians into an intellectual scheme that satisfied the white man's need but bore little resemblance to the actuality of native life.

Although the phrase "noble savage" was not used until John Dryden invented it in 1664, and the term ignoble savage until much later, the word savage was employed from the very beginning. The word associated the Indians with the wilderness. They were assumed to represent the antithesis to civility and its distinguishing social elements. Montaigne formulated the classic definition in the late sixteenth century. According to his view the native people lived without society, government, economy, mental pursuits, and virtually every other characteristic of humanity or social order. As a later social commentator put it, the "savage" lived at the zero of the human condition. Of course it must be stressed that we have here an exercise in the European imagination, or better an expression of a very important mythic formulation. The idea of the "savage" in no way reflects the way any group of human beings live or have lived. All human organisms form societies, have language, govern themselves by some system of law or custom, and engage in economic activity. In European thinking and later in the American conception of native life, the condition of the savage could take either of two forms, though sometimes the images became mixed and the savage figure contained contradictory qualities. The noble savage was a benign, passive figure, utterly innocent, and reminiscent of the inhabitants of the Garden of Eden. The ignoble savage represented the summation of human vice. He was infinitely violent, inconstant, treacherous, and degraded. For Europeans and eighteenth-century Americans the noble savage represented an ideal from which they had fallen and to which they wished to return. Conversely the ignoble savage posed a threat to civil order and human decency.

As this dual figure of mythic proportions, the Indian served the propaganda purposes of both the British and the Americans. Overtly the ignoble savage was much more significant. Both sides interpreted the merits of their own position in contrast to the image of the savage. They both claimed to represent virtue and resorted easily to the accusations that their enemies betrayed the nature of their cause by behaving in a savage manner or allying themselves with savage Indians. At the same time Americans tended to couch public expressions describing the objects of their Revolution in terms plainly paralleled of the virtues long attributed to the noble savage.

The issue of the Indian arose in virtually the first moments of fighting between the Americans and the British. On April 19, 1775, at the North Bridge in Concord, one of the wounded British soldiers left behind by his retreating comrades was struck over the head with an ax by one of the young men of the town. Soon after, a contingent of British troops that had proceeded beyond the town searching for military supplies recrossed the bridge and sighted the dead soldier. They concluded from the spectacle that the Americans had fallen to scalping the wounded and spread rumors to this effect when they joined their comrades.

The charge that Americans scalped enemies appeared in the reports of the encounter turned in by British officers and in the official account sent by the commanding general, Thomas Gage, to the government in London. Descriptions of the incident varied, but there could be little doubt that the British officers and men were convinced that something terrible had occurred at the Concord Bridge. A number of popular pamphleteers in England took up the issue, adding to their broader condemnation of the American cause the accusation that "the Americans fought like the savages of the country."

The Americans were no less sensitive than the British about this supposed descent into savagery. Touched by British propaganda the Massachusetts Provincial Congress took depositions, which were duly published, from the two townsmen who had buried the British bodies. There were no signs of scalping. Thomas Gordon, a Roxbury minister, arrived in Concord within days of the battle seeking authentic information. In a short account published soon after and later in his history of the Revolution he told the true story. But the issue went beyond truth or falsity; it concerned the very nature of the Revolutionary conflict. In a contest increasingly ideological, both sides could not but think the worst of the opposition.

On the return march from Concord, the British troops, exhausted from the long hours under arms, severely mauled by farmers who seemed to break all the rules of civilized war, and perhaps provoked by the rumors of American barbarism, made free use of the bayonet and killed many Americans. The Americans reacted to this bloodletting by accusing the British of abandoning all restraint, of behaving like savage Indians who subscribed to none of the limitations that moderated civilized conflict. Thus almost instinctively in this first clash of the revolutionary conflict, both sides invoked the image of the Indian to condemn the behavior of their opponents. . . .

. . . In a war of images and propaganda the actual activities of the Indians, the near constant raiding of small bands of warriors with British or loyalist aid, meant less than a number of spectacular incidents seized on by the Americans to make their case against the British. When General John Burgoyne moved south from Canada into New York in the early summer of 1777, he was accompanied not only by an elaborate and cumbersome train of wagons but by a contingent of warriors. Burgoyne needed the Indians to ease his way in the wilderness, a point he knew well enough, but he plainly had misgivings about their mode of war. Burgoyne was a bon vivant, raconteur, and a play-wright whose personal style fell easily into bombast. One would find it diffi-cult to conceive of a character less likely to gain insight into Indian culture or less likely to succeed in changing the native way of making war. But these were precisely the ends Burgoyne had in mind. He wished to employ Indians on his own terms, which meant that the warriors were to cease being savages and to fight according to the rules of war honored in Europe. Of course he failed utterly to convince the warriors that they should change their ways. As his army advanced south the Indians played their usual havoc in the surround-ing countryside. This aroused the ire of the frontier settlements and helped to gather the American militia who halted Burgoyne's advance and then forced his surrender.

In late July an incident occurred that deepened Burgoyne's dilemma (he needed the warriors but at the same time he found this behavior distasteful) and became the source of much controversy. Jane McCrea, a young woman from a loyalist family whose fiancé served with Burgoyne, had been captured by Indians in the British service and then murdered when the warriors argued over whose prisoner she would be. One Wyandot Panther appeared in camp with the scalp. News spread quickly, and Burgoyne was forced to take action. He found the act appalling; indeed, not only was the victim a loyal subject of the Crown but he had given explicit instructions against taking the scalps of noncombatants. Torn between the need to uphold what he saw as the stan-dards of civilized war and the fear of losing the Indians' aid Burgoyne closed the incident by merely reprimanding the warriors responsible.

For the Americans the incident would not be so easily forgotten. Jane McCrea's political affiliation receded behind the overwhelming fact that she had been wantonly murdered by savage Indians in alliance with the British. The American commander, Horatio Gates, chided Burgoyne for responsibility, and the instruments of American propaganda immediately made all they could of the event. Jane McCrea became a symbol of innocence and virtue much like the infant republic, the victim of a brutal and conscienceless murder. In the immediate situation the killing contributed to Burgoyne's defeat, but more significant Jane McCrea became one of those important images used by white men to explain the meaning of the Indian in relation to the Americans' strug-gle to preserve their liberty. Later John Vanderlyn's fanciful painting of the affair (two burly Indians, one poised with a tomahawk and the other prepared to take a scalp, stand over the kneeling, terrified Miss McCrea) impressed it on the American imagination and made it legendary.

Burgoyne's defeat in October 1777, because it precipitated open alliance with France, may have been a decisive event in the outcome of the war, but it did little to quiet the frontier. The following year the Americans suffered two notable, well-publicized defeats at the hands of British rangers and Indians. At Wyoming Valley in July and at Cherry Valley in November 1778 bands of warriors and irregulars proved more than a match for the American frontier fighters. At Cherry Valley some forty survivors were massacred after having surrendered. The villain in these two incidents was Joseph Brant, who actually had taken no part in the attack on Wyoming but had been at Cherry Valley. Brant seemed to the Americans the perfect symbol of the British complicity with savage war. In fact, he was one of those rare human beings who had managed by superior intelligence and stable personality to bridge two cultures. As a young Mohawk his family became associated with the household of Sir William Johnson. He attended a mission school in Connecticut, converted to Anglicanism, and visited England where he learned to make his way in polite society. Yet he soon returned to his people, where he assumed a position of leadership during the troubled times of the Revolution. His warriors, together with loyalist rangers led by John and Walter Butler, kept the frontier in turmoil. True to his European training he attempted to modify native practices in war, though he remained loyal to his people. The Americans could scarcely see it this way. As a consequence Brant seemed present at every battle, guilty of every atrocity, and forever the exemplar of the British policy of intermingling savagery with civilized conflict. . . .

Although the war had shifted the British and American conception of the native people toward the ignoble side of the dichotomy, the noble savage was far from dead in the revolutionary age. Some historians, especially in recent times, have attempted to interpret the Revolution and the later movement toward the establishment of a new government as a conscious attempt to imitate the native way of life. The principal problem with this explanation is that it attributes to native societies a number of traits that are plainly anachronistic—democracy and political unity, the two major characteristics. In fact what this interpretation must assume is that the American Indian was indeed a noble savage and that the Americans, perceiving the advantages of this mode of life, determined to adopt it and hence generated a revolution. One will not find this interpretation in any of the major works devoted directly to the Revolution. Here the sources of the breakup of the empire are located in a wrongheaded ministerial policy, internal social developments in the colonies, or the tradition of British oppositionist thought. The Indian hardly enters into the subject.

But if the Indian was not a noble savage and if the Americans paid little attention to real Indians as they formulated the meaning of their revolution, the symbolic Indian did play an important role. The principal question concerned the problem of self-identity. The Americans could not, after all, make a revolution or even establish their independence until they had managed to distinguish America from Europe. And many of the qualities that tended to set off the American—what Crèvecœur called "this new man"—from the European turned out to be precisely the qualities of noble savagery. The Indian in this sense possessed all the attributes that had been lost or forgotten in Europe. Thus Americans—and Indians—were pristine, simple, rustic, open, unaffected, honest, disciplined, equal, individualistic, and free. Europeans against whom the Americans made their revolution were burdened by the past, effete, devious, corrupt, sunk in luxury, and subjected to despotic authority. As this contrast became more apparent in the development of the revolutionary ideology, it was difficult for American commentators to resist an appeal to the qualities of noble savagery. Hence in the years after the Revolution one finds the increasing presence of the Indian in American public iconography. But it must be stressed that direct reference to the noble savage or explicit references to the need to imitate native societies are few during the Revolution. The image of the ignoble savage predominated during the years of conflict.

Because the noble savage functioned as an ideal that had been lost but might again be attained, the image had long served the purposes of propaganda and partisan controversy. That, after all, was how Montaigne had employed the conception in the late sixteenth century. The writer stressed the inadequacies of his own world by contrasting it invidiously with the noble world of pristine savagery. Long before the eighteenth century the method had become conventional. It did not necessarily connote any particular affection for the native people. In fact since the noble savage derived from the white man's mind and celebrated qualities singular to European modes of thought, it had little if anything to do with the Indian, though it must be admitted that many people through the ages have believed that the noble savage described the real Indian. The important point is that the image performed a propagandistic mission. That was how Benjamin Franklin invariably made use of the noble savage, and the same can be said for Jefferson. Neither of them held the real Indian in high regard, particularly during the Revolutionary War. When the time came to complete the Revolution in the formation of a new political order, very little was said directly about the Indians. Except for practical references to Indian affairs, the subject did not arise in either the Constitutional Convention or the ratifying conventions. Nor did the noble Indian appear extensively in the correspondence of the founding fathers in the critical years after the Revolution.

And yet it is difficult to conceive of the Revolution without reference to the Indians. During the war they remained an issue of immense significance. Both sides sought self-definition by reference to their conception of the native people. The Americans, in particular, could scarcely have defined the nature of their virtuous republic if they could not have pointed out that the British had fallen from virtue by allying themselves with ignoble savages. Conversely, the American conception of virtue, the meaning and intellectual substance of the Revolution, drew heavily from the noble savage convention. The Indian as symbol proved indispensable in the making of American independence.

The Myth of the Critical Period

Merrill Jensen

The 1780s witnessed the institution of the Articles of Confederation as the first instrument of government, the first constitution, for the new nation. Given the document's life span—the Articles prevailed from 1781 until the implementation of the Constitution in 1789—it has often been seen as an unfortunate interlude in the development of American democracy. Though the Articles were from a later perspective imperfect instruments of federal control, they were not, as has been argued, grotesquely inadequate. Merrill Jensen, the foremost historical scholar of the Confederation period and late Professor of History at the University of Wisconsin, has sought to mitigate the stereotypes and deal sympathetically with the 1780s. Taking issue with the fashionable argument that the Articles represented the "critical period of American history," Jensen contends that such a view is a "phantom of the imagination," and that "some semblance of reality" can be achieved if one attempts rather to see the period from the perspective of those who lived it. Though much discussed since the publication of this article, Jensen's statement remains the standard measure.

This book is an account of the first years of the new nation that was born of the American Revolution. Like every other segment of time, the history of the United States from 1781 to 1789 was an integral part of the past in which it was rooted and of the future into which it was growing. It was a time when men believed they could shape the future of the new nation, and since it was also a time in which they disagreed as to what that future should be, they discussed great issues with a forthrightness and realism seldom equalled in political debates. The history of the Confederation is therefore one of great inherent importance for the study of human society if for no other reason than that during it men debated publicly and even violently the question of whether or not people could govern themselves.

Aside from its inherent importance, the history of the Confederation has been of enormous significance to one generation of Americans after another in the years since then. Repeatedly Americans have turned to that history in the course of innumerable social and political struggles. They have done so because it was during those years that the Articles of Confederation were replaced by the Constitution of 1787. In order to explain their Constitution, Americans have appealed to the history of the period out of which it came. In the course of such appeals, sometimes honestly for light and guidance and sometimes only for support of partisan arguments, Americans have usually found what they sought. As a result the "history" has been obscured in a haze of ideas, quotations, and assumptions torn bodily from the context of fact that alone gives them meaning. Again and again political opponents have asserted that the founding fathers stood for this or that, while their writings have stood idly and helplessly in volumes on shelves or have lain buried in yellowed manuscripts and newspapers.

Since the founding fathers themselves disagreed as to the nature of the history of the period and as to the best kind of government for the new nation, it is possible to find arguments to support almost any interpretation one chooses. It is not surprising therefore that conflicting interpretations have filled thousands of pages and that all this effort has never produced any final answers and probably never will, for men have ever interpreted the two constitutions of the United States in terms of their hopes, interests, and beliefs rather than in terms of knowable facts.

The conflict of interpretation has been continuous ever since the first debates over the Articles of Confederation in the summer of 1776. Men then differed as to the kind of government which should be created for the new nation. They continued to debate the issue during the 1780's. The members of the Convention of 1787 differed as to the need for and the amount of constitutional change. When the Constitution was submitted to the public in October 1787 the controversy rose to new heights. Men talked in public meetings and wrote private letters and public essays in an effort to explain, justify, or denounce what the Convention had done. They disagreed as to what had happened since the war. Some said there had been chaos; others said there had been peace and prosperity. Some said there would be chaos without the new Constitution; others that there would be chaos if it were adopted.

Once it was adopted Thomas Jefferson and Alexander Hamilton, with two opposed ideals of what the United States should be, laid down two classic and contradictory opinions of the nature of the Constitution. These two basic interpretations may be simply stated. Jefferson held that the central government was sharply limited by the letter of the Constitution; that in effect the states retained their sovereign powers except where they were specifically delegated. Hamilton argued in effect that the central government was a national government which could not be restrained by a strict interpretation of the Constitution or by ideas of state sovereignty. These rival interpretations did not originate with Hamilton and Jefferson, for they had been the very core of constitutional debate ever since the Declaration of Independence, and even before it, for that matter.

Jefferson and his followers used the states rights idea to oppose the plans of the Federalists when they passed the Alien and Sedition Acts in 1798. But when Jefferson became President and purchased Louisiana, he justified his actions by constitutional theories that even Hamilton hardly dared use. Meanwhile Jefferson's opponents seized upon his earlier theories in a vain attempt to block the expansion of the United States. They did so again during the War of 1812 when the Federalists of New England became out-and-out exponents of "states rights" and threatened secession because they were opposed to the war.

In the decades before the Civil War, Daniel Webster and John C. Calhoun carried on the dispute, each having changed sides since his youthful years in politics. Webster, who had been a states rights spokesman during the War of 1812, became the high priest of nationalism, while Calhoun, a leading nationalist in 1812, became the high priest of the states rights idea which he elaborated to defend the slave-owning aristocracy of the South.

The Civil War itself was the bloody climax of a social conflict in which the ultimate nature of the Constitution was argued again and again in seeking support for and arguments against antagonistic programs. But even the Civil War did not finally settle the constitutional issue. The stresses and strains that came with the rise of industrial and finance capitalism produced demands for social and regulatory legislation. The passage of such legislation by the states involved the interpretation of the nature of the Constitution, for business interests regulated by state governments denied their authority and appealed to the national courts. Those courts soon denied the power of regulation to state legislatures. Then, when regulatory laws were passed by the national government, the regulated interests evolved a "states rights" theory that limited the power of the central government, and the national courts once more agreed.

Throughout American history the courts have drawn boundary lines between state and national authority. The pose of judicial impartiality and finality assumed by the courts cannot hide the fact that they have shifted those boundary lines with the shifting winds of politics, and always with sufficient precedents, if not with adequate grace. As a result they had created by 1900 a legal and constitutional no man's land in which all sorts of activity could be carried on without effective regulation by either state or national governments.

The crash of the American economy in 1929 once more posed in imperative terms the problem of the nature of the Constitution. How should it, how could it deal with the potentiality of chaos inherent in unemployment, starvation, and bankruptcy, and ultimately, the loss of faith in the utility of the economic and political foundation of the society itself?

As the national government began to act where, plainly, state and local governments had failed to or were unable to act, the question of constitutionality was raised. For a time the courts once more listened to and heeded states rights constitutional theories which were expounded by opponents of the New Deal. New Deal lawyers, in turn, adopted as weapons John Marshall's nationalistic interpretations of the Constitution for ends which Marshall himself would have fought to the death. President Roosevelt, in his fight on the Supreme Court, declared that the Constitution was not a lawyer's document; yet some of the ablest lawyers who ever lived in America wrote it. New Deal publicists wrote tracts in the guise of history to prove that there had been a "national sovereignty" in the United States from the beginning of the Revolution. Therefore, they argued, the courts could not stop the New Deal from doing what needed doing by following a strict interpretation of the Constitution. Both the New Dealers and the Republicans insisted that they were the sole heirs of the legacy of Thomas Jefferson, while Alexander Hamilton went into an eclipse from which he has not yet emerged.

The most recent appeal to the history of the Confederation Period has come from those who support some form of world government. Adequate arguments for such a government can be found in twentieth-century experience, but, like most men, its backers turn to history for analogies and lessons.

When the League of Nations was set up at the end of the First World War men turned to American history after the American Revolution as a parallel experience. At that time books were written to show the "chaos" of the Confederation Period and the happy solution that came with the Constitution of 1787. Among them was a book by a great authority on international law with the title *James Madison's Notes of Debates in the Federal Convention of 1787 and their Relation to a More Perfect Society of Nations.* The book was widely distributed by the Carnegie Endowment for International Peace. This and other books like it had little relation to the realities of world politics in the 1920's and 1930's, but despite this supporters of the United Nations and of various plans of world government have again turned to the history of the American states after the American Revolution.

The most notable appeal has been that of Clarence Streit. In his book *Union Now* he analyzes the history of our past as he sees it. He calls the Articles of Confederation a "league of friendship." He says, paraphrasing John Fiske, that by 1786 there was universal depression, trade had wellnigh stopped, and political quackery with cheap and dirty remedies had full control of the field. Trade disputes promised to end in war between states. Territorial disputes led to bloodshed. War with Spain threatened. The "league" could not coerce its members. Secession was threatened by some states. Congress had no money and could borrow none. Courts were broken up by armed mobs. When Shays' Rebellion came, state sovereignty was so strong that Massachusetts would not allow "league" troops to enter the state, even to guard the "league's" own arsenal. Streit goes on to say that the idea of turning a league into a union was not even seriously proposed until the Convention opened in May 1787. And then, he says, within two years the freedom-loving American democracies decided to try out this invention for themselves. Streit goes on to argue that it would be just as easy to secure union of the democracies now as it was for the American democracies to achieve a union then. Some things made it difficult then; some make it so now. Some made it easy then; some make it easy now. . . .

Even if it can be granted that most appeals to the history of the Confederation have been sincere, let it also be said that they have seldom been infused with any knowledge of the period or its problems. The result has been the drawing of lessons the past does not have to teach. This is a luxury too expensive in an age when men have discovered how to unhinge the very force that holds matter itself together but have advanced very little beyond cavemen in their notions of how to live peacefully with one another.

Yet it is little wonder that such false lessons have been drawn in the twentieth century because most of them have come from John Fiske's *The Critical Period of American History*, a book of vast influence but of no value as either history or example. Fiske, a philosopher and popular lecturer, wrote the book "without fear and without research," to use the words of Charles A. Beard. As long ago as 1905, Andrew C. McLaughlin, an impeccably conservative historian of the Constitution who wrote a far better book on the same period, said that Fiske's book was "altogether without scientific standing, because it is little more than a remarkably skilful adaptation of a very few secondary authorities showing almost no evidence of first hand acquaintance with the sources."

The story told by Fiske and repeated by publicists and scholars who have not worked in the field—and some who have, for that matter—is based on the assumption that this was *the* "critical period" of American history during which unselfish patriots rescued the new nation from impending anarchy, if not from chaos itself. The picture is one of stagnation, ineptitude, bankruptcy, corruption, and disintegration. Such a picture is at worst false and at best grossly distorted. It is therefore important to attempt a history which makes an effort to examine the sources, which is concerned with the nature of political and economic problems rather than with proving that one side or another in the innumerable political battles of the period was "right" or "wrong." Nothing is to be gained by following a "chaos and patriots to the rescue" interpretation. We have too long ignored the fact that thoroughly patriotic Americans during the 1780's did not believe there was chaos and emphatically denied that their supposed rescuers were patriotic. The point is that there were patriots on both sides of the issue, but that they differed as to desirable goals for the new nation. At the same time, of course, there were men as narrow and selfish on both sides as their political enemies said they were.

If one approaches the history of the Confederation in this way, if one tries to see it as men who lived in it saw it and to write of it in their terms, one may achieve some semblance of reality. It is not the task of the historian to defend or attack the various groups of men whose conflicts were the essence of the period, but to set forth what they believed and what they tried to achieve. This can be illustrated no better than in the definition of terms. Throughout this book the words "federalist" and "nationalist" are used to describe two opposed bodies of opinion as to the best kind of central government for the United States. In so doing I have followed the members of the Convention of 1787. Those men believed that the Articles of Confederation provided for a "federal" government and the majority of them wanted to replace it with a "national" government. The fact that the men who wanted a national government called themselves Federalists after their work was submitted to the public is relevant to the history of politics after 1787, not to the discussion of the nature of the central government prior to and during the Convention of 1787.

Whatever the confusion since then, there was none at the time. Gouverneur Morris stated the issue concisely in the Convention when he "explained the distinction between a federal and a national, supreme government; the former being a mere compact resting on the good faith of the parties; the latter having a complete and compulsive operation." This explanation was in answer to those members of the Convention who wanted to know what Edmund Randolph meant in his opening speech when he spoke of the "defects of the federal system, the necessity of transforming it into a national efficient government. . . ."

The issue was not, as has been argued from time to time, whether there was a "nation" before the adoption of the Constitution of 1787. That was not the question at all during the 1780's. There was a new nation, as the men of the time agreed; they disagreed as to whether the new nation should have a federal or a national government. They did so from the outset of the Revolution and men have continued to do so ever since. The Constitution of 1787 was, as Madison said, both national and federal. And while this fact has led to innumerable conflicts of interpretation, it has also been a source of strength; for as one political group after another has gotten control of the central government it has been able to shape the Constitution to its needs and desires. Thus with the single exception of the Civil War, peaceful change has always been possible, and as long as Americans are willing to accept the decisions of ballot boxes, legislatures, and courts, the Constitution will continue to change with changing needs and pressures. . . .

The foregoing pages indicate that the Confederation Period was one of great significance, but not of the kind that tradition has led us to believe. The "critical period" idea was the result of an uncritical acceptance of the arguments of the victorious party in a long political battle, of a failure to face the fact that partisan propaganda is not history but only historical evidence. What emerges instead is a much more complex and important story in which several themes are interwoven. It was a period of what we would call post-war demobilization, of sudden economic change, dislocation, and expansion, and of fundamental conflict over the nature of the Constitution of the United States. Each of these themes is so interwoven with the others that any separation is arbitrary but, taken separately or together, they are better keys to an understanding of the period than the traditional one.

At the end of the war Americans faced innumerable problems arising from it. What should be done with war veterans? Should the Loyalists return to their homes? What should be our relations with foreign friends and foes? Should commerce be free or should there be discrimination, and if so, against whom and for whose benefit? How would peace affect the economy? How should the war debt be paid? What kind of taxes should be levied to pay it, and who should pay them? When the war-boom collapsed, why did it? What should the state or central governments, or both, do about it? Should government encourage one form of economic enterprise over another or should it keep hands off? What about discontented groups: should government ignore them, cater to them, or forcibly suppress those who might revolt?

Such questions or others like them have probably been asked after every great war in history. They were asked, debated, and given various solutions during the 1780's. The significance of those debates and solutions has often been misunderstood. This is no better illustrated than in the case of the national debt during the 1780's which is usually discussed only in terms of depreciation and nonpayment of interest. Actually much more was involved than this. The debt was fantastically low compared with the national debt of today—about twelve dollars per capita as compared with seventeen hundred—and the nation had vast untouched natural resources with which to pay it. Multitudes of accounts had to be reduced to simple forms so that they could be paid, and this the Confederation government managed to do. But even more important than the economics of the national debt was its politics: should it be paid by the states or the central government? A fundamental assumption of every political leader was that the political agency which paid the debt would hold the balance of power in the new nation. Hence, the supporters of a strong central government insisted that the national debt must be paid by Congress while their opponents insisted that it should be divided among the states and paid by them. The latter group was on the way to victory by the end of the 1780's, for they were supported by clamoring creditors. The result was that one state after another assumed portions of the national debt owing to its citizens. Thus the traditional story is so out of context as to be virtually meaningless. This is true of other traditions as well. Most of the ports of the world were open, not closed, to American citizens. Reciprocity and equal treatment of all United States citizens was the rule in the tonnage and tariff acts of the states, not trade barriers.

To say that many of the pessimistic traditions are false is not to say that all Americans were peaceful and satisfied. The holders of national and state debts wanted bigger payments than they got. The merchants wanted more government aid than was given them. The farmers, hit by high taxes and rigid collection of both taxes and private debts, demanded relief in the form of lower taxes and government loans from state legislatures. Such demands kept state politics in an uproar during the 1780's. However, the often violent expression of such discontents in politics should not blind us to the fact that the period was one of extraordinary economic growth. Merchants owned more ships at the end of the 1780's than they had at the beginning of the Revolution, and they carried a greater share of American produce. By 1790 the export of agriculture produce was double what it had been before the war. American cities grew rapidly, with the result that housing was scarce and building booms produced a labor shortage. Tens of thousands of farmers spread outwards to the frontiers. There can be no question but that freedom from the British Empire resulted in a surge of activity in all phases of American life. Of course not all the problems of the new nation were solved by 1789—all have not yet been solved—but there is no evidence of stagnation and decay in the 1780's. Instead the story is one of a newly free people who seized upon every means to improve and enrich themselves in a nation which they believed had a golden destiny.

Politically the dominating fact of the Confederation Period was the struggle between two groups of leaders to shape the character of the state and central governments. The revolutionary constitutions of the states placed final power in the legislatures and made the executive and judicial branches subservient to them. The members of the colonial aristocracy who became Patriots and new men who gained economic power during the Revolution deplored this fact, but they were unable to alter the state constitutions during the 1780's. Meanwhile they tried persistently to strengthen the central government. These men were the nationalists of the 1780's.

On the other hand the men who were the true federalists believed that the greatest gain of the Revolution was the independence of the several states and the creation of a central government subservient to them. The leaders of this group from the Declaration of Independence to the Convention of 1787 were Samuel Adams, Patrick Henry, Richard Henry Lee, George Clinton, James Warren, Samuel Bryan, George Bryan, Elbridge Gerry, George Mason and a host of less well known but no less important men in each of the states. Most of these men believed, as a result of their experience with Great Britain before 1776 and of their reading of history, that the states could be best governed without the intervention of a powerful central government. Some of them had programs of political and social reform; others had none at all. Some had a vision of democracy; others had no desire except to control their states for whatever satisfactions such control might offer. Some were in fact as narrow and provincial as their opponents said they were. However, the best of them agreed that the central government needed more power, but they wanted that power given so as not to alter the basic character of the Articles of Confederation. Here is where they were in fundamental disagreement with the nationalists who wanted to remove the central government from the control of the state legislatures.

The nationalist leaders from the Declaration of Independence to the Philadelphia convention were men like Robert Morris, John Jay, Gouverneur Morris, James Wilson, Alexander Hamilton, Henry Knox, James Duane, George Washington, James Madison, and many lesser men. Most of these men were by temperament or economic interest believers in executive and judicial rather than legislative control of state and central governments, in the rigorous collection of taxes, and, as creditors, in strict payment of public and private debts. They declared that national honor and prestige could be maintained only by a powerful central government. Naturally, not all men who used such language used it sincerely, for some were as selfish and greedy as their opponents said they were. The nationalists frankly disliked the political heritage of the Revolution. They deplored the fact there was no check upon the actions of majorities in state legislatures; that there was no central government to which minorities could appeal from the decisions of such majorities, as they had done before the Revolution.

There were men who veered from side to side, but their number is relatively small and their veering is of little significance as compared with the fact that from the outset of the Revolution there were two consistently opposed bodies of opinion as to the nature of the central government. There was, of course, a wide variation of belief among adherents of both points of view.

There were extremists who wanted no central government at all and others who wanted to wipe out the states entirely. There were some who wanted a monarchy and others who would have welcomed dictatorship. But such extremists are not representative of the two great bodies of men whose conflict was the essence of the years both before and after 1789.

While the federalist leaders gradually moved to a position where they were willing to add specific powers to the Articles of Confederation, the nationalist leaders campaigned steadily for the kind of government they wanted. During the war they argued that it could not be won without creating a powerful central government. After the war they insisted that such a government was necessary to do justice to public creditors, solve the problems of post-war trade, bring about recovery from depression, and win the respect of the world for the new nation. Meanwhile their experience with majorities in state legislatures merely intensified their desire. They became desperate as state after state in 1785 and 1786 adopted some form of paper money that could be loaned on farm mortgages and be used to pay taxes, and in some cases private debts as well. When they were able to hold off such demands and farmers revolted, as in Massachusetts, they were thoroughly frightened.

They looked upon such events as evidence of the horrors of unchecked democracy and they said so in poetry, private letters, newspaper essays, and public speeches. The problem, they said, was to find some refuge from democracy. They worked hard to control state legislatures and they were often successful, but such control was uncertain at best, for annual elections meant a constant threat of overturn and the threat was realized repeatedly.

We may not call it democracy, but they did. Edmund Randolph put their case bluntly in his opening speech in the Convention of 1787. He said, "Our chief danger arises from the democratic parts of our constitutions. . . . None of the [state] constitutions have provided a sufficient check against the democracy. The feeble senate of Virginia is a phantom. Maryland has a more powerful senate, but the late distractions in that state, have discovered that it is not powerful enough. The check established in the constitutions of New York and Massachusetts is yet a stronger barrier against democracy, but they all seem insufficient." Outside the Convention General Knox was saying that a "mad democracy sweeps away every moral trait from the human character" and that the Convention would "clip the wings of a mad democracy." James Madison in the *Federalist Papers* argued that the new Constitution should be adopted because a "republican" form of government was better than a "democracy."

The debate was white-hot and was carried on with utter frankness. It was white-hot because for a moment in history self-government by majorities within particular political boundaries was possible. Those majorities could do what they wanted, and some of them knew what they wanted. Democracy was no vague ideal, but a concrete program: it meant definite things in politics, economics, and religion. Whatever side of the controversy we take, whether we think the majorities in state legislatures governed badly or well—the fact to face is that men of the 1780's believed that the issue was democracy as a way of government for the United States of those days.

They faced the issue squarely. They thought hard and realistically about the problems of government. They understood that society is complex and that the truth about it is multifold rather than simple. James Madison summed it up as well as it has ever been done. There are, he said, many passions and interests in society and these will ever clash for control of government and will ever interpret their own desires as the good of the whole. Men like Madison and John Adams believed, as Madison said, that the "great desideratum which has not yet been found for Republican governments seems to be some disinterested and dispassionate umpire in disputes between different passions and interests in the state." In the tenth number of *The Federalist,* after citing various origins of political parties, Madison said that "the most durable source of factions [parties] has been the various and unequal distribution of property. Those who hold and those who are without property have ever formed distinct interests in society. Those who are creditors and those who are debtors, fall under a like discrimination. A landed interest, a manufacturing interest, a mercantile interest, a monied interest, with many lesser interests, grow up of necessity in civilized nations, and divide them into different classes, actuated by different sentiments and views. The regulation of these various and interfering interests forms the principal task of modern legislation, and involves the spirit of party and faction in the necessary and ordinary operations of the government."

The constitutional debate of the 1780's was thus carried on by men with a realistic appreciation of the social forces lying behind constitutional forms and theories, by men who were aware of the relationship between economic and political power. This realistic approach was lost sight of in the nineteenth century by romantic democrats who believed that once every man had the right to vote the problems of society could be solved. It was lost sight of too by those who came to believe in an oversimplified economic interpretation of history. In a sense they were as romantic as the democrats, for they assumed a rationality in the historic process that is not always supported by the evidence.

If the history of the Confederation has anything to offer us it is the realistic approach to politics so widely held by the political leaders of the time, however much they might differ as to forms of government and desirable goals for the new nation. Throughout the Confederation men with rival goals pushed two programs simultaneously. The federalists tried to strengthen the Articles of Confederation; the nationalists tried to create a new constitution by means of a convention, and thus avoid the method of change prescribed by the Articles of Confederation. The movement to strengthen the Articles failed on the verge of success; the movement to call a convention succeeded on the verge of failure. The failure of one movement and the success of the other, however we may interpret them, is one of the dramatic stories in the history of politics.

The Founding Fathers: Young Men of the Revolution

Stanley Elkins and Eric McKitrick

According to Stanley Elkins, Professor of History at Smith College in Northampton, Massachusetts, and Eric McKitrick, Professor of History at Columbia University, the American Constitution operated as "the central myth" of our political culture during the nineteenth century. The reverence accorded both the document and its formulators—the Founding Fathers—was pervasive indeed. In the twentieth century, the motives of those who met at Philadelphia in May of 1787 have come in for questioning and reexamination. As the ensuing article suggests, this reevaluation has developed in three rather distinct stages. According to Elkins and McKitrick, new perspectives on "the central myth" of the Constitution have resulted from changing definitions of historical "reality." Though the Constitutional bicentennial in 1989 prompted much publication on the topic, Constitutional historiography has been nearly at a standstill since this essay first appeared, at least in the sense that most of the important subsequent research has—in fact—confirmed its thesis.

The intelligent American of today may know a great deal about his history, but the chances are that he feels none too secure about the Founding Fathers and the framing and ratification of the Federal Constitution. He is no longer certain what the "enlightened" version of that story is, or even whether there is one. This is because, in the century and three quarters since the Constitution was written, our best thinking on that subject has gone through two dramatically different phases and is at this moment about to enter a third.

Americans in the nineteenth century, whenever they reviewed the events of the founding, made reference to an Olympian gathering of wise and virtuous men who stood splendidly above all faction, ignored petty self-interest, and concerned themselves only with the freedom and well-being of their fellow-countrymen. This attitude toward the Fathers has actually never died out; it still tends to prevail in American history curricula right up through most of the secondary schools. But bright young people arriving at college have been regularly discovering, for nearly the last fifty years, that in the innermost circle

From "The Founding Fathers: Young Men of the Revolution," by Stanley Elkins and Eric McKitrick, in *Political Science Quarterly*, Vol. LXXVI, No. 1 (June 1961). Reprinted by permission of the authors.

this was regarded as an old-fashioned, immensely oversimplified, and rather dewy-eyed view of the Founding Fathers and their work. Ever since J. Allen Smith and Charles Beard wrote in the early years of the twentieth century, the "educated" picture of the Fathers has been that of a group not of disinterested patriots but of hard-fisted conservatives who were looking out for their own interests and those of their class. According to this worldlier view, the document which they wrote—and in which they embodied these interests—was hardly intended as a thrust toward popular and democratic government. On the contrary, its centralizing tendencies all reflected the Fathers' distrust of the local and popular rule which had been too little restrained under the Articles of Confederation. The authors of the Constitution represented the privileged part of society. Naturally, then, their desire for a strong central government was, among other things, an effort to achieve solid national guarantees for the rights of property—rights not adequately protected under the Articles—and to obtain for the propertied class (their own) a favored position under the new government.

This "revisionist" point of view—that of the Founding Fathers as self-interested conservatives—has had immeasurable influence in the upper reaches of American historical thought. Much of what at first seemed audacious to the point of *lèse majesté* came ultimately to be taken as commonplace. The Tory-like, almost backward-turning quality which this approach has imparted to the picture of constitution-making even renders it plausible to think of the Philadelphia Convention of 1787 as a counter-revolutionary conspiracy, which is just the way a number of writers have actually described it. That is, since the Articles of Confederation were the product of the Revolution, to overthrow the Articles was—at least symbolically—to repudiate the Revolution. The Declaration of Independence and the Constitution represented two very different, and in some ways opposing, sets of aspirations; and (so the reasoning goes) the Philadelphia Convention was thus a significant turning-away from, rather than an adherence to, the spirit of the Declaration.

In very recent years, however, a whole new cycle of writing and thinking and research has been under way; the revisionists of the previous generation are themselves being revised. The economic ideas of the late Professor Beard, which dominated this field for so long, have been partially if not wholly discredited. And yet many of the old impressions, intermingled with still older ones, persist. Much of the new work, moreover, though excellent and systematic, is still in progress. Consequently the entire subject of the Constitution and its creation has become a little murky; new notions having the clarity and assuredness of the old have not as yet fully emerged; and meanwhile one is not altogether certain what to think.

Before the significance of all this new work can be justly assessed, and before consistent themes in it may be identified with any assurance, an effort should be made to retrace somewhat the psychology of previous conceptions. At the same time, it should be recognized that any amount of fresh writing on this subject will continue to lack something until it can present us with a clear new symbolic image of the Fathers themselves. The importance of this

point lies in the function that symbols have for organizing the historical imagination, and the old ones are a little tired. The "father" image is well and good,
and so also in certain respects is the "conservative" one. But we may suppose
that these men saw themselves at the time as playing other rôles too, rôles
that did not partake so much of retrospection, age, and restraint as those which
would come to be assigned to them in after years. The Republic is now very
old, as republics go, yet it *was* young once, and so were its founders. With
youth goes energy, and the "energy" principle may be more suggestive now,
in reviewing the experience of the founding, than the principle of paternal conservatism.

I

Charles A. Beard, who in 1913 published *An Economic Interpretation of the
Constitution of the United States,* did more than any single figure to make of
the Constitution something other than a topic for ceremonial praise. By calling
it a product of economic forces, Beard established an alternative position and
enabled the entire subject to become one for serious historical debate. He thus
created the first real dialectic on the Constitution and Founding Fathers, and
for that reason Beard's work must still be taken as the point of departure for
any historical treatment of that subject.

For Beard, the reality behind the movement for a constitution in the
1780's was economic interest. The animating surge came from holders of depreciated Continental securities who were demanding that their bonds be paid
at par, and from conservative elements throughout the Confederation who
wanted a national bulwark against agrarian-debtor radicalism. Beard thus identified the Federalists as those who wanted protection for property, especially
personal property. The Anti-Federalists, on the other hand, were the great
mass of agrarian debtors agitating for schemes of confiscation and paper money
inflation in the state legislatures. Their hard-earned taxes would go to support
any new bonds that a stronger United States government might issue; conversely, further fiscal experimentation on their part would be checked by national power. The Anti-Federalists, those who opposed a new constitution,
were therefore the radicals; the Federalists, who favored it, were the conservatives.

Beard's argument was immediately challenged and kept on being challenged, which helped it to retain the fresh attractiveness of an *avant-garde*
position for many years. But the man's influence grew, and his work played a
vital part in historical thinking until well after the Second World War. Historical thinking, however, has its own historical setting. Why should such a statement as Beard's not have been made until the twentieth century, more than
125 years after the event?

In the nineteenth century the American Constitution had operated as the
central myth of an entire political culture. While that culture was still in the
tentative stages of its growth, still subject to all manner of unforeseen men-
aces, and with very little that was nationally sacred, there reigned everywhere
the tacit understanding that here was the one unifying abstraction, the one

symbol that might command all loyalties and survive all strife. The Constitution thus served multiple functions for a society that lacked tradition, folk-memory, a sovereign, and a body of legend. The need to keep the symbol inviolate seems to have been felt more instinctively during its earlier history than later on. Public controversy of the bitterest kind might occur over the charter's true meaning; enemies might accuse each other of misconstruing the document; but one did not challenge the myth itself. Americans even fought a civil war with both sides claiming to be the true upholders of the Constitution. Thus it was natural that when the historians of the nineteenth century—Bancroft, Hildreth, Frothingham, Fiske, McMaster—came to describe the origins of the Constitution, they should reach for the noncontroversial idiom and imagery of a Golden Age. The Supreme Law had been fashioned and given to the people by a race of classic heroes.

America's veneration for its Constitution became steadily more intense in the years that followed the Civil War. Now it was the symbol not only of the Union, for which that generation had made such heavy sacrifices, but also of the unfettered capitalism which was turning the United States into one of the richest and most powerful nations in the world. The new material order—wasteful, disorderly, already acquainted with labor disturbances, yet immensely productive—was watched over by the benevolent and solicitous eye of the Constitution.

In 1888, in a setting darkened by portents of industrial warfare, John Fiske published *The Critical Period of American History*, an account of the events leading to the Philadelphia Convention of 1787. It was an instant success; the notion of the Confederation interlude as a "critical period" was dramatically perfect. A time of trouble, political drift, threatening disunity, and irresponsible agitation provided the occasion at Philadelphia for a supreme act of disinterested statesmanship. There, an intrepid conclave of Old Romans rose above personal and local concerns and presented their countrymen with an instrument of vigorous and effective government.

By the opening of the twentieth century, the state of mind in which men could uncritically ascribe a sort of immaculateness to their political and legal arrangements had altered sharply. By then a profound economic and social crisis had been met and overcome, but with remnants of psychological crisis left unresolved in its wake. The ending of the depression and hard times of the 1890's, the defeat of Populism and Bryanism, the election of McKinley and return of Republican rule—these things were not enough to restore the old complacent innocence. The American public, now full of guilty misgivings, had begun to ask itself searching questions about the evils of the existing order and about the price it had allowed itself to pay for material progress. The answer which was hit upon by publicists and civic spokesmen was *vested interest*. The formula was not exactly new, but after the experience of the 1890's, when public rhetoric had abounded in sinister allusions to "Wall Street" and "the monopolies," it was no more than natural that the "vested interest" concept should have taken on an immensely new and widened range of application. The "interests" were the shadowy powers that manipulated things and made them run the way they did. Thus vested interest came to be seen in the Progressive Era—those years roughly from the turn of the century through the First World War—as the ultimate reality behind the life of affairs.

It was in that era, moreover, that "reality" itself first came to be a synonym for all the equivocal, seamy, and downright evil facts of life from which innocent and respectable people are normally sheltered. Few periods in American history have been so strikingly noted for civic awareness and the reforming spirit—and reform meant getting to the bottom of things. The most efficacious step in exorcising an evil was exposing it. Thus the literature of exposure, which claimed an enormous amount of journalistic and literary energy, did much to whet and sustain that generation's relish for reform. "Muckraking" meant dredging up heaps of grubby "reality" for all to behold. "Reality," as Richard Hofstadter has said,

> was the bribe, the rebate, the bought franchise, the sale of adulterated food. It was what one found in *The Jungle, The Octopus, Wealth against Commonwealth,* or *The Shame of the Cities.* . . . Reality was a series of unspeakable plots, personal iniquities, moral failures, which, in their totality, had come to govern American society. . . .

The sheer excitement of discovery tended to leave people's perceptions of appearance and reality somewhat unbalanced. It is perhaps too much to say that anything hidden was taken as bad (though there were certainly strong presumptions); yet one of the great unspoken dogmas of American thought, implanted in this period, was that the "facts of life" had to be hidden in order to qualify as "real."

In academic precincts, meanwhile, such thinkers as Roscoe Pound, John Dewey, Thorstein Veblen, Arthur Bentley, and J. Allen Smith had begun to challenge the older static and formalist theories of law, philosophy, economics, and government. They were no longer so interested in the formal outlines which enclosed, say, government or the law; they were much more concerned to locate the dynamic forces inside these realms—to identify the powers that made them really work. Thus "economic interest" as a kind of *élan vital*, a basic prime mover, came to be given greater and greater emphasis. "Wherever we turn," wrote E. R. A. Seligman as early as 1902, ". . . we are confronted by the overwhelming importance attached by the younger and abler scholars to the economic factor in political and social progress." Here was "reality" being given an intellectual and scholarly sanction.

In view of this mounting preoccupation with "interests," one might be led to conclude that significant numbers of intelligent people were approaching a "class" theory of society not unlike that of Marx—a theory in which classes and class interests contended more or less frankly with each other for advantage. Yet by and large this did not happen; these were not the terms in which most people thought about society. For one reason, there was very little evidence to support such a theory. But a more important reason was that, to a people saturated in democratic prejudices, "class" habits of thought were fantastically difficult to understand, let alone imitate. To the Progressive mind, the way vested interest worked was not so much through class as through *conspiracy*.

Vested interest and conspiracy were concepts so closely related that they were almost synonymous. The interests worked in secret; their power rested on stealthy understandings and was exercised through the pulling of invisible strings. Hidden from view, they might freely circumvent the law and gain their ends by corrupting and manipulating the agencies of government. . . . Such a mode of conceiving reality would even be brought to bear upon the origins of the United States Constitution.

Two of Charles Beard's immediate precursors in that realm were J. Allen Smith and Algie Simons. They were, for their own purposes, innovators; yet in a broader sense their minds followed a typical Progressive pattern. [For example] in J. Allen Smith's *Spirit of American Government, A Study of the Constitution* (1907), the myth of the Philadelphia convention as a forum of disinterested statesmen came under sharp attack. . . .

But it was Charles A. Beard, taking up the "class interest" formula in his famous *Economic Interpretation* the following year, who succeeded to all intents and purposes in making it stick. Whereas neither Smith nor Simons had made any secret of their reforming passions (they denied that the Constitution was a sacred document, so their fellow-citizens should feel free to change it if they wished), Beard disclaimed any intention of writing a political tract. He would simply be the observer of historical events, impassively examining the facts. All he wanted to do was discover whether in fact economic forces had played a significant part in the drafting and ratification of the Constitution. Early in his book Beard insisted that it was not his purpose "to show that the Constitution was made for the personal benefit of the members of the Convention," but merely to determine whether the Fathers represented "distinct groups whose economic interests they understood and felt in concrete, definite form, through their own personal experience with identical property rights. . . ." Then, setting in motion an impressive system of scholarly apparatus, he proceeded to answer his own questions.

. . . At any rate, the reason he was able to create his sensation was that the things he showed the Fathers doing were of exactly the sort that the muckraking magazines had, in other connections, made all too familiar.

Beard's basic research materials were a batch of old Treasury records which had never previously been opened ("reality"), and in them he found the names of a number of the Federalist leaders, members of the Philadelphia Convention as well as delegates to ratifying conventions in the various states. These men held substantial amounts of Continental securities which—Beard reasoned from later developments—would rise sharply in value with the establishment of a strong central government. This seemed to explain the energy with which they worked to bring such a government into being, and this was just the sort of evidence that impressed Beard's contemporaries most. Beard himself, for all his disclaimers, sums up his argument in language whose dominant theme is *direct personal interest*. Here, three of his thirteen conclusions are quite explicit:

(1) The first firm steps toward the formation of the Constitution were taken by a small and active group of men immediately interested through their personal possessions in the outcome of their labors.

(2) The members of the Philadelphia Convention who drafted the Constitution were, with a few exceptions, immediately, directly, and personally interested in, and derived economic advantages from, the establishment of the new system.

(3) The leaders who supported the Constitution in the ratifying conventions represented the same economic groups as the members of the Philadelphia Convention; and in a large number of instances they were also directly and personally interested in the outcome of their efforts.

Accompanying the principal theme of personal interest were several sub-themes:

(1) The Constitution was essentially an economic document based upon the concept that the fundamental private rights of property are anterior to government and morally beyond the reach of popular majorities.

(2) [The entire process, from the calling of the Philadelphia Convention to the ratifying of the Constitution, was unrepresentative and undemocratic; there was no popular vote on calling the convention; a large propertyless (and therefore disfranchised) mass was not represented at Philadelphia; and only a small minority in each state voted for delegates to the ratifying conventions.]

(3) [Where battles did occur over ratification], the line of cleavage . . . was between substantial personalty [personal] interests on the one hand and the small farmers' and debtors' interests on the other.

. . . Beard himself was nothing if not a Progressive, fully immersed in his times. It was the interests and their inside doings that caught the Progressive imagination; it was this that the Progressives longed to befool and discomfit by public exposure. If Beard was to show that the Federal Constitution was not a product of abstract political theory but of concrete economic drives, there was no happier way of doing it than to paint the Founding Fathers in the familiar image of the vested interests—the small group of wealthy conspirators hostile to, even contemptuous of, the majority will, and acting for clear, "practical" reasons such as rigging the value of public securities.

Despite the bursts of pained protests which *An Economic Interpretation* initially drew from many older academics (who either thought that Beard could comprehend no motives other than base ones, or else concluded that he must be a socialist), it also drew plenty of praise from academic as well as non-academic quarters. Not only did the book do well for a scholarly monograph, it did better and better as time went on. . . .

At the same time Beard had bequeathed to American historical method something far more pervasive, a technique of explanation which could take "class" interpretations or leave them alone. This was the "reality" technique, which assumes that the most significant aspects of any event are those concealed from the eye. Men's true intentions are to be judged neither from the words we hear them speak nor the deeds we see them do, and the "real" forces behind historical change will turn out, more often than not, to be those of conspiracy.

II

In 1940 certain new and interesting corollaries were added to the mode of approach which, due so largely to Beard's example, had come to influence historical thinking on the formation of the Constitution. In that year Merrill Jensen published *The Articles of Confederation: An Interpretation of the Social-Constitutional History of the American Revolution, 1774–1781.* Jensen's own approach was consistent with most of the general principles which had been laid down by Beard. . . .

In a second book, *The New Nation* (1950), Jensen considered the accomplishments of the Confederation, together with the social and economic conditions of the period from 1781 to 1789. He concluded that the "critical period" was really not so critical after all. American ships were not excluded from many foreign ports; tariff wars between states were the exception rather than the rule; the Confederation government had solved the problem of western lands and was well on the way to settling the outstanding boundary disputes. By 1786 the economic depression which had struck the country in 1784 was coming to an end. Even the problem of national credit was not so serious as the Federalists wanted people to believe, since a number of the states had assumed responsibility for portions of the Continental debt held by their own citizens. Had the states been brought to accept a national impost—a tariff duty on incoming foreign goods levied solely and exclusively by Congress, the revenue of which would be reserved for the support of the government—the Confederation would have been fully capable of surviving and functioning as a true federal establishment.

The collapse of the Confederation, Jensen argued, was not the logical outcome of weakness or inefficiency. It was the result of a determined effort by a small but tightly-organized group of nationalists to impose a centralized government upon the entire country despite the contrary desires of great majorities everywhere:

> Most of these men were by temperament or economic interest believers in executive and judicial rather than legislative control of state and central governments, in the rigorous collection of taxes, and, as creditors, in strict payment of public and private debts.. . . . They deplored the fact that there was no check upon the actions of majorities in state legislatures; that there was no central government to which minorities could appeal from the decisions of such majorities, as they had done before the Revolution.

These were the men who conspired to overthrow the Confederation and who masterminded the triumph of the Constitution.

There were points at which Jensen had not seen eye to eye with Beard. He was more impressed, for instance, by the Fathers' general outlook and ideology than by their property holdings; unlike Beard, moreover, he denied that the Confederation era was a time of serious economic difficulty. Yet he had actually strengthened the Beardian logic at more than one point, and the differences were minor in the light of the convictions which united the two in spirit and intention. The work of Merrill Jensen, like that of Beard and Parrington and J. Allen Smith before him, still balanced on the assumption that the energy behind the American Constitution was conspiratorial energy, and that the Constitution came into being by means of a *coup d'état*—through the plotting of a well-disciplined Toryish few against the interests of an unvigilant democratic majority.

Indeed, Merrill Jensen's *The New Nation*—published two years after the death of Charles Beard—was the last major piece of Constitution scholarship to be done in the Progressive tradition, and represented the end of an era. By that time, 1950, Beard's own notions had begun to arouse not the admiration, but the suspicion, of a new generation of postwar intellectuals.

III

. . . By 1956, Beard's *Economic Interpretation* had been set up for the *coup de grâce*. The executioner was Robert E. Brown, a professor at Michigan State who had been at work for some time implacably compiling a catalogue of the Master's offenses. In his *Charles Beard and the Constitution*, published that year, Brown tracked Beard through every page of the latter's masterpiece and laid the ax to virtually every statement of importance that Beard had made in it. There was absolutely no correlation between the Philadelphia delegates' property holdings and the way they behaved on the question of a constitution. It was not true that large numbers of adult males were disfranchised; the suffrage was remarkably liberal everywhere. Farmers as a class were by no means chronically debtors; many were creditors and many others were both. The supporters of Shays' Rebellion (the debtors' uprising in western Massachusetts which occurred during the fall and winter of 1786–1787) were certainly not united against the Constitution; if they had been, it could never have been ratified, since the Shaysites had a clear majority at the time of the Massachusetts convention. . . .

Not only was Beard's evidence inconclusive at all points, Brown insisted, but there were even occasions when the Master had not been above doctoring it. He edited Madison's *Federalist* No. 10 to eliminate all but its economic emphasis; he quoted only those passages of the Philadelphia debates that made the Fathers look least democratic; he arranged his treatment of the ratification process in an order that violated chronology, centered unjustified attention on states where hard struggles did occur, overlooked the ease with which ratification was achieved in other states, and thus created a wildly exaggerated picture of the opposition at large.

Brown's book was respectfully received; there was little inclination to dispute his arguments; no champions arose to do serious battle for the departed Beard. Some of the reviewers were a little dismayed at Brown's tone; they thought it need not have been quite so ferocious. And the book did seem to bear out the principle that any work of destruction in the realm of discourse, however necessary, must be executed within restrictions that make for a certain stultification. Richard Hofstadter remarked in this connection that Brown was "locked in such intimate embrace with his adversary that his categories are entirely dictated by Beard's assertions." Even Brown, in his way, had toyed with the "reality" theme. He had exonerated the Fathers of conspiratorial intentions but convicted Charles Beard in their place: Beard had cooked the evidence, had conspired to hide the truth.

The first effort in recent years to view the Constitution all over again in a major way, shaking off the Beardian categories and starting as it were from scratch, has been undertaken by Forrest McDonald. *We The People*, published in 1958, was the first of a planned trilogy whose design was to survey anew the entire story of how the Constitution was brought into existence. Although McDonald, like Brown, felt it necessary to show the inadequacy of Beard's conclusions, his strategy was quite different from Brown's; it was undertaken less to discredit Beard than to clear the way for his own projected treatment of the great subject. In *An Economic Interpretation*, Beard had made a number of proposals for research which he himself had not performed—and never did perform—but which would, Beard felt, further corroborate his own "frankly fragmentary" work. McDonald began by undertaking the very research which Beard had suggested, and its results convinced him that Beard had simply asked all the wrong questions.

One of the things McDonald investigated in *We The People* was an assumption upon which Beard had put a great deal of stress, the notion of a fundamental antagonism between "personalty" and "realty" interests at the time of the Philadelphia Convention. ("Personalty" was wealth based on securities, money, commerce, or manufacturing; "realty" was landed property whose owners' outlook tended to be primarily agrarian.) He found that there was no such split in the Convention. The seven men who either walked out of the Convention or else refused to sign the completed document were among the heaviest security-holders there, and represented "an all-star team of personalty interests." In state after state, moreover, there was no appreciable difference between the property holdings of Federalists and Anti-Federalists. Finally, the three states that ratified the Constitution unanimously—Delaware, New Jersey, and Georgia—were overwhelmingly dominated by agrarian interests.

Unlike Brown, McDonald was quite unwilling to write off the possibility of an economic analysis (his book's subtitle was *The Economic Origins of the Constitution*); it was just that Beard's particular economic categories led nowhere. Beard's sweeping "personalty" and "realty" classifications were meaningless, and he had deceived himself profoundly in supposing that the Federalists' property interests "knew no state boundaries" but were "truly national in scope." On these two points of difference McDonald set up an entirely new and original research scheme, and in so doing effected a really impressive conceptual maneuver. He was quite ready, in the first place, to find "economic forces" behind the movement for a constitution, but these must be sought not in "classes" or in broad categories of property but rather in the specific business interests of specific groups in specific places. The other organizing category would be the individual states themselves. The political framework within which any group had to operate was still that imposed by the state; the states were, after all, still sovereign units, and the precise relationship between economic forces and political action depended almost entirely on the special conditions within those states, conditions which varied from one to the other.

By abandoning Beard's "national" framework and recasting the entire problem on a state-by-state basis, McDonald made it possible to see with a sudden clarity things which ought to have been obvious all along. The states where ratification was achieved most readily were those that were convinced, for one reason or another, that they could not survive and prosper as independent entities; those holding out the longest were the ones most convinced that they could go it alone. The reasons for supporting ratification might vary considerably from state to state. For Georgia, an impending Indian war and the need for military protection could transcend any possible economic issue; New York, at one time imagining for itself an independent political and economic future, would finally ratify for fear of being isolated from a system which already included ten states and which might soon be joined by a seceded New York City. . . .

Recognizing the importance of specific location made it also easier and more natural to appreciate the way in which particular interests in particular places might be affected by the question of a stronger national government. Boston shipping interests, for example, seem to have been less concerned in the 1780's over class ideology or general economic philosophy than over those conditions of the times which were especially bad for business. The British would not let them into the West Indies, the French were excluding their fish, and their large vessels were no longer profitable. A strong national government could create a navy whose very existence would reduce high insurance rates; it could guarantee an orderly tariff system that would remove all pressures for higher and higher state tariffs; and it could counter British and French discrimination by means of an effective navigation act. . . .

Forrest McDonald's work, according to him, has only just begun; years of it still lie ahead. But already a remarkable precision of detail has been brought to the subject, together with a degree of sophistication which makes the older economic approach—"tough-minded" as it once imagined itself— seem now a little wan and misty. The special internal conditions of the several states now seem fully valid as clues to the ratification policies of those states, each in its separate turn. And there is a credibility about the immediate needs and aspirations of particular groups, and the way they varied from place to place, that Beard's "interests" never quite possessed—or if they did, they had long since lost their hold on the modern mind.

And yet there are overtones in McDonald's work—for all its precise excellence, perhaps partly because of it—that have already succeeded in creating a new kind of "reality" spell. McDonald is very open-minded about all the manifold and complex and contradictory forces that converged upon the movement for a constitution. But somehow the ones he takes most seriously—the "real" forces behind the movement—were specific, particular, circumscribed, hard, and immediate. They were to be looked for mostly on the local level, because that is where one really finds things. A state—the largest permissible "reality" unit—was an agglomeration of specific, particular, immediate localities. There were interests to be served, political or economic, and they were *hard*. They were pursued rationally and without sentimentality; men came down where they did because their hard, immediate, specific interests brought them there. But are we prepared to say that the final result was just the sum— or extension—of these interests? . . .

The new approach is extremely enlightening and useful. But has it yet taken on life? When will it fully engage the question of initiative and energy? How do we account for the dedication, the force and *éclat*, of Federalist leadership? When all is said and done, we do not exactly refer to the "interests" of a James Madison. We wonder, instead, about the terms in which he conceives of personal fulfillment, which is not at all the same. What animates him? The nationalist movement *did* have a mystique that somehow transfigured a substantial number of its leaders. What was it like, what were its origins?

IV

The work of Merrill Jensen, done in the 1930's and 1940's, has suffered somewhat in reputation due to the sweep and vehemence of the anti-Beardian reaction. Yet that work contains perceptions which ought not to be written off in the general shuffle. They derive not so much from the overall Beardian traditions and influences amid which Jensen wrote, as from that particular sector of the subject which he marked off and preëmpted for his own. Simply by committing himself—alone among Beardians and non-Beardians—to presenting the Confederation era as a legitimate phase of American history, entitled to be taken seriously like any other and having a positive side as well as a negative one, he has forced upon us a peculiar point of view which, by the same token, yields its own special budget of insights. For example, Jensen has been profoundly impressed by the sheer force, determination, and drive of such nationalist leaders as Hamilton, Madison, Jay, Knox, and the Morrises. This energy, he feels, created the central problem of the Confederation and was the major cause of its collapse. He deplores this, seeing in the Confederation "democratic" virtues which it probably never had, finding in the Federalists an "aristocratic" character which in actual fact was as much or more to be found in the Anti-Federalists, smelling plots everywhere, and in general shaping his nomenclature to fit his own values and preferences. But if Professor Jensen seems to have called everything by the wrong name, it is well to remember that nomenclature is not everything. The important thing—what does ring true—is that this driving "nationalist" energy was, in all probability, central to the movement that gave the United States a new government.

The other side of the picture, which does not seem to have engaged Jensen's mind half so much, was the peculiar sloth and inertia of the Anti-Federalists. Cecelia Kenyon, in a brilliant essay on these men, has shown them as an amazingly reactionary lot. They were transfixed by the specter of power. It was not the power of the aristocracy that they feared, but power of any kind, democratic or otherwise, that they could not control for themselves. Their chief concern was to keep governments as limited and as closely tied to local interests as possible. Their minds could not embrace the concept of a national interest which they themselves might share and which could transcend their own parochial concerns. Republican government that went beyond the compass of state boundaries was something they could not imagine. Thus the chief difference between Federalists and Anti-Federalists had little to do with "democracy" (George Clinton and Patrick Henry were no more willing than Gouverneur Morris to trust the innate virtue of the people), but rather in the Federalists' conviction that there was such a thing as national interest and that a government could be established to care for it which was fully in keeping with republican principles. To the Federalists this was not only possible but absolutely necessary, if the nation was to avoid a future of political impotence, internal discord, and in the end foreign intervention. So far so good. But still, exactly how did such convictions get themselves generated?

Merrill Jensen has argued that the Federalists, by and large, were reluctant revolutionaries who had feared the consequences of a break with England and had joined the Revolution only when it was clear that independence was inevitable. The argument is plausible; few of the men most prominent later on as Federalists had been quite so hot for revolution in the very beginning as Patrick Henry and Samuel Adams. But this may not be altogether fair; Adams and Henry were already veteran political campaigners at the outbreak of hostilities, while the most vigorous of the future Federalists were still mere youngsters. The argument, indeed, could be turned entirely around: the source of Federalist, or nationalist, energy was not any "distaste" for the Revolution on these men's part, but rather their profound and growing involvement in it.

Much depends here on the way one pictures the Revolution. In the beginning it simply consisted of a number of state revolts loosely directed by the Continental Congress; and for many men, absorbed in their effort to preserve the independence of their own states, it never progressed much beyond that stage even in the face of invasion. But the Revolution has another aspect, one which developed with time and left a deep imprint on those connected with it, and this was its character as a continental war effort. If there is any one feature that most unites the future leading supporters of the Constitution, it was their close engagement with this continental aspect of the Revolution. A remarkably large number of those someday Federalists were in the Continental Army, served as diplomats or key administrative officers of the Confederation government, or, as members of Congress, played leading rôles on those committees primarily responsible for the conduct of the war.

Merrill Jensen has compiled two lists, with nine names in each, of the men whom he considers to have been the leading spirits of the Federalists and Anti-Federalists respectively. It would be well to have a good look at this sample. The Federalists—Jensen calls them "nationalists"—were Robert Morris, John Jay, James Wilson, Alexander Hamilton, Henry Knox, James Duane, George Washington, James Madison, and Gouverneur Morris. Washington, Knox, and Hamilton were deeply involved in Continental military affairs; Robert Morris was Superintendent of Finance; Jay was president of the Conti-

nental Congress and minister plenipotentiary to Spain (he would later be appointed Secretary for Foreign Affairs); Wilson, Duane, and Gouverneur Morris
were members of Congress, all three being active members of the war committees. The Anti-Federalist group presents a very different picture. It consisted
of Samuel Adams, Patrick Henry, Richard Henry Lee, George Clinton, James
Warren, Samuel Bryan, George Bryan, George Mason, and Elbridge Gerry. Only
three of these—Gerry, Lee, and Adams—served in Congress, and the latter two
fought consistently against any effort to give Congress executive powers. Their
constant preoccupation was state sovereignty rather than national efficiency.
Henry and Clinton were active war governors, concerned primarily with state
rather than national problems, while Warren, Mason, and the two Bryans were
essentially state politicians.

The age difference between the two groups is especially striking. The
Federalists were on the average ten to twelve years younger than Anti-Federal-
ists. At the outbreak of the Revolution George Washington, at 44, was the
oldest of the lot; six were under 35 and four were in their twenties. Of the
Anti-Federalists, only three were under 40 in 1776, and one of these, Samuel
Bryan, the son of George Bryan, was a boy of 16.

This age differential takes on a special significance when it is related to
the career profiles of the men concerned. Nearly half of the Federalist group—
Gouverneur Morris, Hamilton, and Knox—quite literally saw their careers
launched in the Revolution. The remaining five—Washington, Jay, Duane,
Wilson, and Robert Morris—though established in public affairs beforehand,
became nationally known after 1776 and the wide public recognition which
they subsequently achieved came first and foremost through their identification with the continental war effort. All of them had been united in an experience, and had formed commitments, which dissolved provincial boundaries;
they had come to full public maturity in a setting which enabled ambition,
public service, leadership, and self-fulfillment to be conceived, for each in his
way, with a grandeur of scope unknown to any previous generation. The careers of the Anti-Federalists, on the other hand, were not only state-centered
but—aside from those of Clinton, Gerry, and the young Bryan—rested heavily
on events that preceded rather than followed 1776. . . .

. . . A significant proportion of relative newcomers, with prospects initially
modest, happened to have their careers opened up at a particular time and in such
a way that their very public personalities came to be staked upon the national
quality of the experience which had formed them. In a number of outstanding
cases energy, initiative, talent, and ambition had combined with a conception
of affairs which had grown immense in scope and promise by the close of the
Revolution. There is every reason to think that a contraction of this scope, in the
years that immediately followed, operated as a powerful challenge.

V

The stages through which the constitutional movement proceeded in the
1780's add up to a fascinating story in political management, marked by no
little *élan* and dash. That movement, viewed in the light of the Federalist lead-

ers' commitment to the Revolution, raises some nice points as to who were the "conservatives" and who were the "radicals." The spirit of unity generated by the struggle for independence had, in the eyes of those most closely involved in coordinating the effort, lapsed; provincial factions were reverting to the old provincial ways. The impulse to arrest disorder and to revive the flame of revolutionary unity may be pictured in "conservative" terms, but this becomes quite awkward when we look for terms with which to picture the other impulse, so different in nature: the urge to rest, to drift, to turn back the clock. . . .

The revolutionary verve and ardor of the Federalists, their resources of will and energy, their willingness to scheme tirelessly, campaign everywhere, and sweat and agonize over every vote meant in effect that despite all the hairbreadth squeezes and rigors of the struggle, the Anti-Federalists would lose every crucial test. There was, to be sure, an Anti-Federalist effort. But with no program, no really viable commitments, and little purposeful organization, the Anti-Federalists somehow always managed to move too late and with too little. They would sit and watch their great stronghold, New York, being snatched away from them despite a two-to-one Anti-Federalist majority in a convention presided over by their chief, George Clinton. . . . By the time the New York convention was ready to act, ten others had ratified, and at the final moment Hamilton and his allies spread the chilling rumor that New York City was about to secede from the state. The Anti-Federalists, who had had enough, directed a chosen number of their delegates to cross over, and solemnly capitulated.

In the end, of course, everyone "crossed over." The speed with which this occurred once the continental revolutionists had made their point, and the ease with which the Constitution so soon became an object of universal veneration, still stands as one of the minor marvels of American history. But the document did contain certain implications, of a quasi-philosophical nature, that make the reasons for this ready consensus not so very difficult to find. It established a national government whose basic outlines were sufficiently congenial to the underlying commitments of the whole culture—republicanism and capitalism—that likelihood of its being the subject of a true ideological clash was never very real. That the Constitution should mount guard over the rights of property—"realty," "personalty," or any other kind—was questioned by nobody. There had certainly been a struggle, a long and exhausting one, but we should not be deceived as to its nature. It was not fought on economic grounds; it was not a matter of ideology; it was not, in the fullest and most fundamental sense, even a struggle between nationalism and localism. This key struggle was between inertia and energy; with inertia overcome, everything changed.

There were, of course, lingering objections and misgivings; many of the problems involved had been genuinely puzzling and difficult; and there remained doubters who had to be converted. But then the perfect bridge whereby all could become Federalists within a year was the addition of a Bill of Rights. After the French Revolution, anti-constitutionalism in France would be a burning issue for generations; in America, an anti-constitutional party was undreamed of after 1789. With the Bill of Rights, the remaining opponents of the new system could say that, ever watchful of tyranny, they had now got what they wanted. Moreover, the Young Men of the Revolution might at last imagine, after a dozen years of anxiety, that *their* Revolution had been a success.

The Illusion of Change: Women and the American Revolution

Joan Hoff-Wilson

Revolution has the effect of breaking the cake of custom. By definition, the trauma of revolution effects profound change in the very foundations of society. When the revolution in question is one predicated on an ideology of liberty and equality—as was America's—how could it have been otherwise than that the American Revolution *must* have resulted in greater liberty and equality for women? However, in the considered judgment of Joan Hoff-Wilson, former executive secretary of the Organization of American Historians and Professor of History at Indiana University, such an assumption is unwarranted. The American Revolution brought no significant benefits to women. Reflecting a division of labor based on sex-role stereotyping inherited from English custom, women's role was confined to the domestic sphere. In fact, so thoroughgoing was the mythic belief in "separate spheres" for men and women that it was conceptually difficult for women even to have contemplated the possibility of defining, much less realizing, liberty and equality in a political sense. Even assertive women such as Mercy Otis Warren and Abigail Adams were not "feminists"; they were not demanding—because they could not yet conceive of— equality in a legal sense. Even for the enlightened of the revolutionary generation, concludes Professor Hoff-Wilson, the mythic idea that men and women occupied two distinct spheres of worldly activity "was commonly accepted in the last half of the eighteenth century as one of the natural laws of the universe."

I will argue that certain types of female functions, leading either to the well-known exploitation of working women or to the ornamental middle-class housewife of the nineteenth century, were abetted by the American Revolution, although not caused by it.

This occurred because the functional opportunities open to women between 1700 and 1800 were too limited to allow them to make the transition in attitudes necessary to insure high status performance in the newly emerging nation. In other words, before 1776 women did not participate enough in conflicts over land, religion, taxes, local politics, or commercial transactions. They simply had not come into contact with enough worldly diversity to be prepared for a changing, pluralistic, modern society. Women of the postrevolutionary generation had little choice but to fill those low status functions prescribed by the small minority of American males who *were* prepared for modernization by enough diverse activities and experiences.

As a result, the American Revolution produced no significant benefits for American women. This same generalization can be made for other powerless groups in the colonies—native Americans, blacks, probably most propertyless white males, and indentured servants. Although these people together with women made up the vast majority of colonial population, they could not take advantage of the overthrow of British rule to better their own positions, as did the white, propertied males who controlled economics, politics, and culture. By no means did all members of these subordinate groups support the patriot cause, and those who did, even among whites, were not automatically accorded personal liberation when national liberation was won. This is a common phenomenon of revolution within subcultures which, because of sex, race, or other forms of discrimination or deprivation of the members, are not far enough along in the process toward modernization to express their dissatisfaction or frustration through effectively organized action.

Given the political and socioeconomic limitations of the American Revolution, this lack of positive societal change in the lives of women and other deprived colonials is to be expected. It is also surprising that until recently most historians of the period have been content to concentrate their research efforts on the increased benefits of Lockean liberalism that accrued to a relatively small percent of all Americans and to ignore the increased sexism and racism exhibited by this privileged group both during and after the Revolution. They have also tended to ignore the various ways in which the experience of the Revolution either hastened or retarded certain long-term eighteenth-century trends already affecting women.

What has been called in England and Europe "the transformation of the female in bourgeois culture" also took place in America between 1700 and 1800. This process would have occurred with or without a declaration of independence from England. It produced a class of American bourgeoises who clearly resembled the group of middle-class women evident in England a century earlier. However, the changing societal conditions leading up to this transformation in American women were much more complex than they had been for seventeenth-century British women because of the unique roles, that is, functions, that colonial women had originally played in the settlement and development of the New World. The American Revolution was simply one event among many in this century-long process of change. It was a process that ultimately produced two distinct classes of women in the United States—those who worked to varying degrees exclusively in their homes and those who worked both inside and outside of their homes. . . .

It is true, however, for most of the period up to 1750 that conditions *out of necessity* increased the functional independence and importance of all women. By this I mean that much of the alleged freedom from sexism of colonial women was due to their initial numerical scarcity and the critical labor shortage in the New World throughout the seventeenth and eighteenth centuries. Such increased reproductive roles (economic as well as biological) reflected the logic of necessity and *not any fundamental change* in the sexist, patriarchal attitudes that had been transplanted from Europe. Based on two types of scarcity (sex and labor), which were not to last, these enhanced functions of colonial women diminished as the commercial and agricultural economy became more specialized and the population grew.

A gradual "embourgeoisement" of colonial culture accompanied this preindustrial trend toward modern capitalism. It limited the number of high status roles for eighteenth-century American women just as it had for seventeenth-century English and European women. Alice Clark, Margaret George, Natalie Zemon Davis, and Jane Abray have all argued convincingly that as socioeconomic capitalist organization takes place, it closes many opportunities normally open to women both inside and outside of the family unit in precapitalist times. The decline in the status of women that accompanied the appearance of bourgeois modernity in England, according to Margaret George, "was not merely a relative decline. Precapitalist woman was not simply relatively eclipsed by the great leap foward of the male achiever; she suffered, rather, an absolute setback."

In the New World this process took longer but was no less debilitating. Before 1800 it was both complicated and hindered by the existence of a severe labor shortage and religious as well as secular exhortations against the sins of idleness and vanity. Thus, colonial conditions demanded that all able-bodied men, women, and children work, and so the ornamental, middle-class woman existed more in theory than in practice.

The labor shortage that plagued colonial America placed a premium on women's work inside and outside the home, particularly during the war-related periods of economic dislocation between 1750 and 1815. And there is no doubt that home industry was basic to American development both before and after 1776. It is also true that there was no sharp delineation between the economic needs of the community and the work carried on within the preindustrial family until after the middle of the eighteenth century. Woman's role as a household manager was a basic and integral part of the early political economy of the colonies. Hence she occupied a position of unprecedented importance and equality within the socioeconomic unit of the family.

As important as this function of women in the home was, from earliest colonial times, it nonetheless represented a division of labor based on sex-role stereotyping carried over from England. Men normally engaged in agricultural production; women engaged in domestic gardening and home manufacturing—only slave women worked in the fields. Even in those areas of Massachusetts and Pennsylvania that originally granted females allotments of land, the vestiges of this practice soon disappeared, and subsequent public divisions "simply denied the independent economic existence of women." While equality never extended outside the home in the colonial era, there was little likelihood that women felt useless or alienated because of the importance and demanding nature of their domestic responsibilities.

In the seventeenth and eighteenth centuries spinning and weaving were the primary types of home production for women and children (of both sexes). This economic function was considered so important that legal and moral sanctions were developed to insure it. For example, labor laws were passed, compulsory spinning schools were established "for the education of children of the poor," and women were told that their virtue could be measured in yards of yarn. So from the beginning there was a sex, and to a lesser degree a class and educational, bias built into colonial production of cloth, since no formal apprenticeship was required for learning the trade of spinning and weaving.

It has also been recognized that prerevolutionary boycotts of English goods after 1763 and later during the war increased the importance of female production of textiles both in the home and in the early piecework factory system. By mid-1776 in Philadelphia, for example, 4,000 women and children reportedly were spinning under the "putting out system" for local textile plants. . . .

American living standards fluctuated with the unequal prosperity that was especially related to wars. Those engaging in craft production and commerce were particularly hard hit after 1750, first by the deflation and depression following the French and Indian War (1754–1763), and then by the War for Independence. In fact, not only were the decades immediately preceding and following the American Revolution ones of economic dislocation, but the entire period between 1775 and 1815 has been characterized as one of "arrested social and economic development." These trends, combined with increased specialization, particularly with the appearance of a nascent factory system, "initiated a decline in the economic and social position of many sections of the artisan class." Thus with the exception of the innkeeping and tavern business, all of the other primary economic occupations of city women were negatively affected by the periodic fluctuations in the commercial economy between 1763 and 1812.

Women artisans and shopkeepers probably suffered most during times of economic crisis because of their greater difficulty in obtaining credit from merchants. Although research into their plight has been neglected, the documents are there—in the records of merchant houses showing women entrepreneurs paying their debts for goods and craft materials by transferring their own records of indebtedness, and in court records showing an increased number of single women, especially widows sued for their debts, or in public records of the increased number of bankrupt women who ended up on poor relief lists or in debtors' prisons or who were forced to become indentured servants or earn an independent living during hard times.

It was also a difficult time for household spinners and weavers, about whom a few more facts are known. First, this all-important economic function increasingly reflected class distinctions. In 1763 one British governor estimated that only the poor wore homespun clothes, while more affluent Americans bought English imports. Second, it was primarily poor women of the northern and middle colonies who engaged in spinning and weaving for pay (often in the form of credit rather than cash), while black slave women and white female indentured servants performed the same function in the South. Naturally women in full-frontier areas had no recourse but to make their own clothing. Beginning with the first boycotts of British goods in the 1760s, women of all classes were urged to make and wear homespun. Several additional "manufactory houses" were established as early as 1764 in major cities specifically for the employment of poor women. Direct appeals to patriotism and virtue were used very successfully to get wealthier women to engage in arduous home-spinning drives, but probably only for short periods of time.

Thus all classes of women were actively recruited into domestic textile production by male patriots with such pleas as, "In this time of public distress you have each of you an opportunity not only to help to sustain your families, but likewise to call your mite into the treasury of the public good." They were further urged to "cease trifling their time away [and] prudently employ it in learning the use of the spinning wheel." Beyond any doubt the most well-known appeal was the widely reprinted 9 November 1767 statement of advice to the "Daughters of Liberty" which first appeared in the *Massachusetts Gazette*. It read in part:

> First then throw aside your high top knots of pride
> Wear none but your own country linen.
> Of economy boast. Let your pride be the most
> To show cloaths of your make and spinning.

Peak periods in prerevolutionary spinning and weaving were reached during every major boycott from 1765 to 1777. But the war and inflation proved disruptive. For example, we know that the United Company of Philadelphia for Promoting American Manufactures, which employed 500 of the city's 4,000 women and children spinning at home, expired between 1777 and 1787, when it was revived. The record of similar organizations elsewhere was equally erratic.

It is common for developing countries with a labor shortage to utilize technological means to meet production demands. After the war, the new republic proved no exception, as the inefficiency and insufficiency of household spinners became apparent. Ultimately the "putting out" system was replaced entirely by the factory that employed the same women and children who had formerly been household spinners. It took the entire first half of the nineteenth century before this process was completed, and when it was, it turned out to be at the expense of the social and economic status of female workers. . . .

Why didn't the experiences of the Revolution result in changing the political consciousness of women? Part of the answer lies in the socialized attitudes among female members of the revolutionary generation that set them apart from their male contemporaries. Their attitudes had been molded by the modernization trends encountered by most women in the course of the eighteenth century. Out of the necessity wrought by the struggle with England, women performed certain tasks that appeared revolutionary in nature, just as they had performed nonfamilial tasks out of necessity throughout the colonial period. But this seemingly revolutionary behavior is not necessarily proof of the acceptance of abstract revolutionary principles.

Despite their participation in greater economic specialization, despite their experiences with a slightly smaller conjugal household where power relations were changing, despite a limited expansion of the legal rights and somewhat improved educational opportunities for free, white women, the revolutionary generation of females were less prepared than most men for the modern implications of independence. Their distinctly different experiential level, combined with the intellectually and psychologically limiting impact of the Great Awakening and the Enlightenment on women, literally made it impossible for even the best educated females to understand the political intent or principles behind the inflated rhetoric of the revolutionary era. Words like virtue, veracity, morality, tyranny, and corruption were ultimately given public political meanings by male revolutionary leaders that were incomprehensible or, more likely, misunderstood by most women.

As the rhetoric of the revolution began to assume dynamic, emotional proportions, its obsession with "virtue" versus "corruption" struck a particularly responsive chord among literate women, as evidenced, for example, in their patriotic statements as individuals and in groups when supporting the boycott of English goods between 1765 and 1774. While these statements are impressive both in number and intensity of feeling, it can be questioned whether the idea of taking "their country back on the path of virtue" and away from "the oppression of corrupt outside forces" was understood in the same way by female and male patriots, when even men of varying Whig persuasions could not agree on them. Virtue and morality for the vast majority of Americans, but particularly women, do not appear to have had the modernizing implications of pluralistic individualism, that is, of the "acceptance of diversity, the commitment to individual action in pursuit of individual goals, the conception of politics as an arena where these goals contest and the awareness of a national government which is at once the course of political power and the framework for an orderly clash of interest." These are characteristics of "modern man."

How does one prove such a generalization about attitudes behind the behavior of women during the Revolution? Few poor white or black women left records revealing how they felt about the war. Such women, whether Loyalists or patriots, conveyed their sentiments silently with their physical labor. Among the more articulate and educated women there is written testimony to at least an initial sense of pride and importance involved in their participation in the war effort. Thus a young Connecticut woman named Abigail Foote wrote in her diary in 1775 that carding two pounds of whole wool had made her feel "Nationly," while others recorded their contributions in similarly patriotic terms.

But the question remains: did their supportive actions prepare them to accept a vision of society anywhere near the version ultimately conveyed by James Madison's Federalist Number Ten in the fight over the Constitution of

1787? To date there is little evidence that this type of sophisticated political thought was present, either in the writings of women about the Revolution and its results or in the appeals made to them during or immediately following the war. From the popular 1767 statement of advice to the Daughters of Liberty to the 1787 one urging women to use "their influence over their husbands, brothers and sons to draw them from those dreams of liberty under a simple democratical form of government, which are so unfriendly to . . . order and decency," it is difficult to conclude that women were being prepared to understand the political ramifications of the Revolution.

The same lack of political astuteness appears to underlie even the least traditional and most overtly political activities of women, such as the fifty-one who signed the anti-tea declaration in Edenton, North Carolina, on 25 October 1774 (later immortalized in a London cartoon). The same could be said of the more than 500 Boston women who agreed on 31 January 1770 to support the radical male boycott of tea; of the Daughters of Liberty in general; and of the 1,600 Philadelphia women who raised 7,500 dollars in gold for the Continental Army. Even Mercy Otis Warren never perceived the modern political system that evolved from the Revolution. Instead she viewed the war and its aftermath as the "instrument of Providence that sparked a world movement, changing thought and habit of men to complete the divine plan for human happiness" largely through the practice of virtue.

Perhaps the most important aspect of the supportive activities among women for the patriot cause was the increase in class and social distinctions they symbolized. For example, it appears unlikely that poor white or black women joined Daughters of Liberty groups, actively boycotted English goods, or participated in any significant numbers in those associations of "Ladies of the highest rank and influence," who raised money and supplies for the Continental Army. On the contrary, it may well have been primarily "young female spinsters" from prominent families and well-to-do widows and wives who could afford the time or the luxury of such highly publicized activities. The vast majority, however, of middle-class female patriots (and, for that matter, Loyalists), whether single or married, performed such necessary volunteer roles as seamstresses, nurses, hostesses, and sometime spies, whenever the fighting shifted to their locales, without any undue fanfare or praise.

The same is true of poorer women, with one important difference: they had no choice. They had all they could do to survive, and although this did lead a few of them to become military heroines, they could not afford the luxury of either "disinterested patriotism" or the detached self-interest and indulgences that some of the richer women exhibited. The very poorest, particularly those in urban areas, had no resources to fall back on when confronted with the personal or economic traumas caused by the War for Independence. As noted above, this was especially evident in the case of women wage earners who, regardless of race or class, had apparently always received lower pay than free men or hired-out male slaves, and who had suffered severely from runaway inflation during the war. Women's services were more likely to be paid for in Continental currency than with specie. Fees for male "doctors," for example, according to one Maryland family account book, were made in specie payment after the middle of 1780, while midwives had to accept the depreciated Continental currency for a longer period of time. Thus, the American Revolution hastened the appearance of greater class-based activities among "daughters of the new republic," with poor women undertaking the least desirable tasks and suffering most from the inflationary spiral that plagued the whole country. It is easy to imagine the impact that inflation had on the rural and urban poor, but it even affected those middle- and upper middle-class women who were left at home to manage businesses, estates, plantations, or farms. Their activities often meant the difference between bankruptcy and solvency for male revolutionary leaders.

Probably the classic example of housewifely efficiency and economic shrewdness is found in Abigail's management of the Adams family and farm during John's long absences. But in this respect Abigail Adams stands in direct contrast to the women in the lives of other leading revolutionaries like Jefferson, Madison, and Monroe—all of whom were bankrupt by public service in part because their wives were not as capable at land management as she was. This even proved true of the most outspoken of all revolutionary wives, Mercy Otis Warren. Numerous less well-known women, however, proved equal to the increased domestic responsibilities placed upon them. Only the utterly impoverished could not resort to the traditional colonial task of household manager.

As the months of fighting lengthened into years, more and more poverty-stricken women left home to join their husbands, lovers, fathers, or other male relatives in the army encampments. Once there, distinctions between traditional male and female roles broke down. While a certain number of free white and black slave women were needed to mend, wash, and cook for officers and care for the sick and wounded, most enlisted men and their women took care of themselves and fought beside each other on many occasions. Moreover, unlike the English, German, and French commanders, American military leaders were often morally offended or embarrassed by the presence of these unfortunate and destitute women, "their hair flying, their brows beady with the heat, their belongings slung over one sholder [sic], chattering and yelling in sluttish shrills as they went and spitting in the gutters."

This puritanical, hostile attitude on the part of patriot army officers toward such a common military phenomenon insured that camp followers of the American forces were less systematically provided for than those of foreign troops. Aside from its class overtones (after all Martha Washington, Catherine Greene, and Lucy Knox were accepted as respectable camp followers), it is difficult to explain this American attitude, except that in the prevailing righteous rhetoric of the Revolution and of later historians these women were misrepresented as little better than prostitutes. In reality they were the inarticulate, invisible poor whose story remains to be told from existing pension records based on oral testimony. At any rate there is pathos and irony in the well-preserved image of Martha Washington, who visited her husband at Valley Forge during the disastrous winter of 1777–1778, copying routine military communiques and presiding over a sewing circle of other officers' wives, while the scores of combat-hardened women who died along with their enlisted men have been conveniently forgotten.

These camp followers, as well as the women who stayed at home, complained about their plight privately and publicly, and on occasion they rioted and looted for foodstuffs. Women rioting for bread or other staples never became a significant or even a particularly common revolutionary act in the New World as it did in Europe, largely because of the absence of any long-term, abject poverty on the part of even the poorest colonials. The most likely exception to this generalization came during the extreme inflation that accompanied the war. Then there is indeed some evidence of what can be called popular price control activity by groups of women who had a definite sense of what were fair or legitimate marketing practices. At the moment we have concrete evidence of only a half-dozen seemingly spontaneous instances of "a corps of female infantry" attacking merchants. Other examples will probably be discovered as more serious research into the "moral economy of the crowd" is undertaken by American historians.

What is interesting about the few known cases is that the women involved in some of them did not simply appear to be destitute camp followers passing through towns stripping the dead and looting at random for food. A few at least were women "with Silk gownes on," who were offering to buy sugar, salt, flour, or coffee for a reasonable price with Continental currency. When a certain merchant insisted on payment with specie or with an unreasonable amount of paper money, the women then, and only then, insisted on "taking" his goods at their price. These appear, therefore, to be isolated examples of collective behavior by women where there was, at the least, a very strongly held cultural notion of a moral economy.

Nevertheless, there is still no clear indication of an appreciable change in the political consciousness of such women. Perhaps it was because even the poorest who took part in popular price control actions primarily did so, like the Citoyennes Républicaines Révolutionnaires during the French Revolution, out of an immediate concern for feeding themselves and their children and not for feminist reasons growing out of their age-old economic plight as women in a patriarchal society. In addition, except for camp followers and female vagabonds, the principal concern of most members of this generation of primarily rural women remained the home and their functions there. During the home-spinning drives and during the war when their men were away, their domestic and agricultural duties became all the more demanding, but not consciousness-raising. . . .

Lastly, in explaining the failure of the equalitarian ideals of the Revolution to bear even limited fruit for women, one must analyze the narrow ideological parameters of even those few who advocated women's rights, persons such as Abigail Adams, Judith Sargent Murray, Elizabeth Southgate Bowne, Elizabeth Drinker, and Mercy Otis Warren.

These women . . . were not feminists. Like most of the better organized, but no less unsuccessful Républicaines of France, they seldom, if ever, aspired to complete equality with men except in terms of education. Moreover, none challenged the institution of marriage or defined themselves "as other than mothers and potential mothers." They simply could not conceive of a society whose standards were not set by male, patriarchal institutions, nor should they be expected to have done so. Instead of demanding equal rights, the most articulate and politically conscious American women of this generation asked at most for privileges and at least for favors—not for an absolute expansion of their legal or political functions, which they considered beyond their proper womanly sphere. Man was indeed the measure of equality to these women, and given their societal conditioning, such status was beyond their conception of themselves as individuals.

Ironically it is this same sense of their "proper sphere" that explains why the most educated female patriots did not feel obliged to organize to demand more from the Founding Fathers. It is usually overlooked that in the famous letter of 31 March 1776 where Abigail asks John Adams to "Remember the Ladies," she justified this mild request for "more generous and favourable" treatment on the grounds that married women were then subjected to the "un-limited power" of their husbands. She was not asking him for the right to vote, only for some legal protection of wives from abuses under common-law practices. "Regard us then," she pleaded with her husband, "as Beings placed by providence under your protection and in imitation of the Supreme Being make use of that power only for our happiness." Despite an earlier statement in this letter about the "Ladies" being "determined to foment a Rebelion" and refusing to be "bound by any Laws in which we have no voice, or Representation," Abigail Adams was not in any sense demanding legal, let alone political or individual, equality with men at the beginning of the American Revolution. If anything, her concept of the separateness of the two different spheres in which men and women operated was accentuated by the war and the subsequent trials of the new republic between 1776 and 1800.

This idea that men and women existed in two separate spheres or orbits was commonly accepted in the last half of the eighteenth century as one of the natural laws of the universe. While European Enlightenment theories adhered strictly to the inferiority of the natural sphere that women occupied, in colonial America they were tacitly challenged and modified by experience—as were so many other aspects of natural law doctrines. On the other hand, the degree to which educated, upper-class women in particular thought that their sphere of activity was in fact equal, and the degree to which it actually was accorded such status by the male-dominated culture, is all-important. Historians have tended to place greater emphasis on the former rather than the latter, with misleading results about the importance of the roles played by both colonial and revolutionary women.

It is true that Abigail Adams was an extremely independent-minded person who firmly criticized books by foreign authors who subordinated the female sphere to that of the male. Writing to her sister Elizabeth Shaw Peabody in 1799, she said that "I will never consent to have our sex considered in an inferior point of light. Let each planet shine in their own orbit, God and nature

designed it so—if man is Lord, woman is *Lordess*—that is what I contend for."
Thus, when her husband was away she deemed it was within her proper sphere
to act as head of the household on all matters, including the decision to have
her children inoculated against smallpox without his permission. At the same
time, however, she always deferred to his ambitions and his inherent superiority, because the equality of their two separate orbits did not make them equal
as individuals. In general Abigail Adams and other women of her class accepted the notion that while they were mentally equal to men their sphere of
activity was entirely private in nature, except on those occasions when they
substituted for their absent husbands. "Government of States and Kingdoms,
tho' God knows badly enough managed," she asserted in 1796, "I am willing
should be solely administered by the lords of creation. I should contend for
Domestic Government, and think that best administered by the female." Such
a strong belief in equal, but separate, spheres is indeed admirable for the times,
but it should not be confused with feminism. . . .

Only unusual male feminists like Thomas Paine asked that women be
accorded "the sweets of public esteem" and "an equal right to praise." It was
Paine—not the female patriots—who also took advantage of American revolutionary conditions to attack the institution of marriage. Later, in the 1790s,
only a few isolated women in the United States supported Mary Wollstonecraft's demand for the right to public as well as private fulfillment on the
grounds that "private duties are never properly fulfilled unless the understanding enlarges the heart and that public virtue is only an aggregate of
private. . . ." Her criticisms of marital bondage were never seriously considered by American women in this postrevolutionary decade.

The reasons for this unresponsiveness to the feminism of both Paine and
Wollstonecraft are complex, for this was not only opposed by the sexist Founding Fathers, but by most women. Again we must ask—why?

The physical and mental hardships that most women had endured during
the war continued to varying degrees in the economic dislocation that followed in its wake. Sheer personal survival, not rising social or material expectations, dominated the thinking and activities of lower- and even some mid-
dle- and upper-class women. Probably more important, the few well-educated
American women, fortunate to have the leisure to reflect, clearly realized the
discrepancy that had occurred between the theory and practice of virtue in the
course of the war and its aftermath. While it was discouraging for them to
view the corruption of morals of the society at large and particularly among
men in public life, they could take some satisfaction in the greater consistency
between the theory and practice of virtue in their own private lives. Such postrevolutionary women found their familial duties and homosocial relationships
untainted by the corruption of public life. They considered themselves most
fortunate and they *were*, compared to their nineteenth-century descendants,
who had to pay a much higher price for similar virtuous consistency and spiritual purity.

It was natural, therefore, for the educated among this generation to express disillusionment with politics, as they saw republican principles corrupted or distorted, and then to enter a stage of relative quiescence that marked the beginning of the transitional period between their war-related activities and a later generation of female reformers who emerged in the 1830s. They cannot be held responsible for not realizing the full extent of the potentially debilitating features of their withdrawal to the safety of modern domesticity—where virtue becomes its own punishment instead of reward.

A final factor that helps to explain the absence of feminism in the behavior of women during the Revolution and in their attitudes afterward is related to the demographic changes that were taking place within the family unit between 1760 and 1800. Middle- and upper-class women were increasingly subjected to foreign and domestic literature stressing standards of femininity that had not inhibited the conduct of their colonial ancestors. While the rhetoric of this new literature was that of the Enlightenment, its message was that of romantic love, glamorized dependence, idealized motherhood, and sentimentalized children within the ever-narrowing realm of family life. At poorer levels of society a new family pattern was emerging as parental control broke down, and ultimately these two trends would merge, leaving all women in lower status domestic roles than they had once occupied.

In general it appears that the American Revolution retarded those societal conditions that had given colonial women their unique function and status in society, while it promoted those that were leading toward the gradual "embourgeoisement" of late eighteenth-century women. By 1800 their economic and legal privileges were curtailed; their recent revolutionary activity minimized or simply ignored; their future interest in politics discouraged; and their domestic roles extolled, but increasingly limited.

Moreover, at the highest *and* lowest levels of society this revolutionary generation of women was left with misleading assumptions: certain educated women believing strongly in the hope that immediate improvement for themselves and their children would come with educational reform, and some lower-class women believing that improvement would come through work in the "manufactories." Both admitted, according to Mercy Otis Warren, that their "appointed subordination" to men was natural, if for no other reason than "for the sake of Order in Families." Neither could be expected to anticipate that this notion would limit their participation in, and understanding of, an emerging modern nation because the actual (as opposed to idealized) value accorded their postrevolutionary activities was not yet apparent.

A few, like Priscilla Mason, the valedictorian of the 1793 graduating class of the Young Ladies' Academy of Philadelphia, might demand an equal education with men and exhort women to break out of their traditional sphere, but most ended up agreeing with Eliza Southgate Bowne when she concluded her defense of education for women by saying: "I believe I must give up all pretension to *profundity*, for I am much more at home in my female character." And the dominate male leadership of the 1790s could not have agreed more.

For women, the American revolution was over before it ever began. Their "disinterested" patriotism (or disloyalty, as the case may be) was accorded identical treatment by male revolutionaries following the war: conscious neglect of female rights combined with subtle educational and economic exploitation. The end result was increased loss of function and authentic status for all women whether they were on or under the proverbial pedestal.

Myths of the National Period

Men are tormented by the opinions they have of things, rather than by the things themselves.
Old Stoic Proverb

This people is the hope of the human race. It may become the model. It ought to show the world, by facts, that men can be free and yet peaceful, and may dispense with the chains in which tyrants and knaves of every colour have presumed to bind them, under the pretext of the public good. The Americans should be an example of political, religious, commercial and industrial liberty. The asylum they offer to the oppressed of every nation, the avenue of escape they open, will compel governments to be just and enlightened; and the rest of the world in due time will see through the empty illusions in which policy is conceived. But to obtain these ends for us, America must secure them to herself; and must not become, as so many of your ministerial writers have predicted, a mass of divided powers, contending for territory and trade, cementing the slavery of peoples by their own blood.
Anne-Robert-Jacques Turgot   *(1778)*

Henry Steele Commager,
"The Search for a Usable Past"

Nicholas Cords,
"Parson Weems, the Cherry Tree and the Patriotic Tradition"

Alexander DeConde,
"Washington's Farewell, the French Alliance, and the Election of 1796"

Marshall Smelser,
"Mr. Jefferson in 1801"

Irving Brant,
"James Madison and His Times"

Wayne S. Cole,
"Myths Surrounding the Monroe Doctrine"

The legendary Washington: his apotheosis. [Chinese painting on glass, c. 1800, based on print by Simon Chaudron and John J. Barralet. Courtesy, The Henry Francis du Pont Winterthur Museum.]

GENERAL GEORGE WASHINGTON.
Reviewing the Western army at Fort Cumberland the 18th of Octobr 179—

The Father of His Country prepares to smite the people: the Whiskey Rebellion, 1794. [F. Kemmelmeyer, *General George Washington, Reviewing the Western Army at Fort Cumberland the 18th of October 1794* (1794). Courtesy, The Henry Francis du Pont Winterthur Museum.]

*A*s reflected in this section's opening quote from the French statesman Anne-Robert-Jacques Turgot, foreign expectations ran high as the United States launched a government in 1789 under the auspices of its new Constitution. America's own goals and aspirations, as manifested in the documents of the revolutionary era and the Constitution, matched those prevailing on the Continent. Throughout the National Period, as Americans strove to live up to the high standards set for them from both without and within, the temptation to mythologize proved insurmountable. Later historians would prove as susceptible as contemporaries to myth building. As Henry Steele Commager demonstrates in the first article in this section, Americans attempted to live up to this ideal image by displaying a tremendous urge to create a "usable past." The results only contributed further to the American propensity for mythmaking.

There was an abundance of material, and conditions were ripe for the hurried creation of a usable past as the National Period began to unfold. Getting the nation started under the new Constitution was important in itself, but to be led by the nation's most famous hero, George Washington, further heightened the level of excitement and expectation. If Washington's popularity waned during his second presidential term, his death in 1799 set him on the road to immortality, aided, of course, by the amiable Parson Weems.

The beginnings of American foreign policy formed another area of national concern rich with mythic possibilities. On the basis of Washington's "Neutrality Proclamation" and his "Farewell Address," contemporaries and later historians developed what can only be described as a paradox—a foreign policy of simultaneous involvement and noninvolvement. A closer look at some of the underlying assumptions of American foreign policy helps at least to neutralize some of the myths.

As the National Period progressed, America witnessed the early development of political parties from factions that had polarized around Alexander Hamilton and Thomas Jefferson. This led to the so-called Jeffersonian "Revolution of 1800." Perhaps a key to understanding the nature of this "revolution" is a demythologized picture of the central figure in the phenomenon—Thomas Jefferson.

The anomalous War of 1812, its causes dating back at least to the opening of the English-French hostilities in 1793, also demands attention from a myth-oriented approach to American history. The causes of the war and President Madison's role continue to be debated. No doubt myth has been generated, as historical consensus has tended to place blame on the president for our involvement and then to accuse him of a lack of wartime leadership. Does he deserve the rather harsh treatment that history has accorded him?

After the War of 1812, during the presidency of James Monroe, America's foreign policy had decided nationalistic overtones. For many, the Monroe Doctrine of 1823 epitomized this spirit of nationalism. Were they correct, or was the policy merely a measure that in the collective mythology of the nation, later conveniently fitted America's view of its foreign policy?

These are the topics drawn from the National Period to which a myth-oriented approach seems most viable and to which the articles in this section address themselves.

The Search for a Usable Past

Henry Steele Commager

It seems tenable that Americans have found the material for mythmaking more readily at hand than have Europeans. Henry Steele Commager, distinguished historian at Amherst College and a well-known public lecturer, explores the historical and psychological conditions that served to evoke a national consciousness in Americans during the period from the Revolution to the Civil War. Arguing that American self-consciousness was deliberately created and fostered, Commager sees that American nationalism, myths included, "was, to an extraordinary degree, a literary creation. . . ." It was poets and storytellers who "created" the fund of culture, tradition, and experience so necessary to bind national sentiments. As such, the growth of the American Republic has surely witnessed a merging of fact and fancy unique in modern history.

The United States was the first of the "new" nations. As the American colonies were the first to rebel against a European "mother country," so the American states were the first to create—we can use Lincoln's term, to bring forth—a new nation. Modern nationalism was inaugurated by the American, not the French, Revolution. But the new United States faced problems unknown to the new nations of nineteenth-century Europe—and twentieth. For in the Old World the nation came before the state; in America the state came before the nation. In the Old World nations grew out of well-prepared soil, built upon a foundation of history and traditions; in America the foundations were still to be laid, the seeds still to be planted, the traditions still to be formed.

    The problem which confronted the new United States then was radically different from that which confronted, let us say, Belgium, Italy, Greece, or Germany in the nineteenth century, or Norway, Finland, Iceland, and Israel in the twentieth. These "new" states were already amply equipped with history, tradition, and memory—as well as with many of the other essential ingredients of nationalism except political independence. Of them it can be said that the nation was a product of history. But with the United States, history was rather a creation of the nation, and it is suggestive that in the New World the self-made nation was as familiar as the self-made man.

    It is unnecessary to emphasize anything as familiar as the importance

From "The Search for a Usable Past," by Henry Steele Commager, in *American Heritage Magazine* (February 1965). Reprinted by permission from *American Heritage*, Vol. 16, No. 2. Copyright 1965 by American Heritage Publishing Co., Inc.

of history, tradition, and memory to successful nationalism. On this matter statesmen, historians, and philosophers of nationalism are all agreed. It was the very core of Edmund Burke's philosophy: the nation—society itsef—is a partnership of past, present, and future; we (the English) "derive all we possess as an inheritance from our forefathers." It is indeed not merely the course of history but of nature itself. Thus Friedrich von Schlegel, trying to quicken a sense of nationalism in the Germans, urged that "nothing is so important as that the Germans . . . return to the course of their own language and poetry, and liberate from the old documents of their ancestral past that power of old, that noble spirit which . . . is sleeping in them." And Mazzini, in his struggle for the unification of Italy, was ever conscious that "the most important inspiration for nationalism is the awareness of past glories and past sufferings."

So, too, with the philosophers of nationalism, and the historians as well. Listen to Ernest Renan. In that famous lecture "What Is a Nation?" he emphasized "the common memories, sacrifices, glories, afflictions, and regrets," and submitted that the worthiest of all cults was "the cult of ancestors." So, too, with the hard-headed John Stuart Mill, across the Channel. "The strongest cause [for the feeling of nationality] is identity of political antecedents, the possession of a national history, and consequent community of recollections, collective pride and humiliation, pleasure and regret."

But if a historical past and a historical memory are indeed essential ingredients for a viable nationalism, what was the new United States to do in 1776, or in 1789, or for that matter at almost any time before the Civil War? How does a country without a past of her own acquire one, or how does she provide a substitute for it? Where could such a nation find the stuff for patriotism, for sentiment, for pride, for memory, for collective character? It was a question that came up very early, for Americans have always been somewhat uncomfortable about their lack of history and of antiquity, somewhat embarrassed about being historical *nouveaux riches.*

It was Henry James who put the question in most memorable form. I refer to the famous passage about the historical and intellectual environment in which the young Nathaniel Hawthorne found himself in 1840. It takes a great deal of history to make a little literature, said James, and how could Hawthorne make literature with a history so meager and so thin: "No state, in the European sense of the word, and indeed barely a specific national name. No sovereign, no court, no personal loyalty, no aristocracy, no church, no clergy, no army, no diplomatic service, no country gentlemen, no palaces, no castles, nor manors, nor old country houses, nor parsonages, nor thatched cottages, nor ivied ruins; no cathedrals, nor abbeys, nor little Norman churches; no great Universities, nor public schools, no Oxford nor Eton nor Harrow; no literature, no novels, no museums, no pictures, no political society, no sporting class—no Epsom nor Ascot!"

There is almost too much here; the indictment, as James himself remarked, is a lurid one, and he noted, too, with some satisfaction, that Hawthorne had not been wholly frustrated by the thinness of his materials—how he managed was, said James wryly, our private joke. It is suggestive that James' famous outburst was inspired by Hawthorne himself; he had, so he wrote, delighted in a place—his own dear native land—which had "no shadow, no antiquity, no mystery, no picturesque and gloomy wrong, nor anything but a commonplace prosperity, in broad and simple daylight, as is happily the case with my dear native land." It is worth dwelling on this for a moment, for this is from the author of *The Scarlet Letter*, and of *The House of the Seven Gables*, and of a score of stories which did precisely dwell on shadows, antiquities, gloomy wrongs—witchcraft, for example. If a Hawthorne, who all his life felt it necessary to immerse himself in New England antiquities and inherited wrongs, could yet contrast his own dear native land with the Old World in these terms, think how unshadowed were the lives of most Americans—or how empty, if you want to adopt the James point of view.

A host of Americans had anticipated all this, but with different emphasis. Thus the poet Philip Freneau, introducing the abbé Robin's *New Travels in America:* "They who would saunter over half the Globe to copy the inscription on an antique column, to measure the altitude of a pyramid, or describe the ornaments on the Grand Seigneur's State Turban, will scarcely find anything in American Travels to gratify their taste. The works of art are there comparatively trivial and inconsiderable, the splendor of pageantry rather obscure, and consequently few or none but the admirers of simple Nature can either travel with pleasure themselves or read the travels of others with satisfaction, through this country." And half a century later James Fenimore Cooper, caught in that dilemma of New World innocence and Old World corruption so pervasive in the first century of our history, admitted that in America "there are no annals for the historian; no follies beyond the most vulgar and commonplace for the satirist; no manners for the dramatist; no obscure fictions for the writer of romance; no gross and hardy offenses against decorum for the moralist; nor any of the rich artificial auxiliaries of poetry."

But if there were "no annals for the historian," and if a historical past was necessary to nation-making, what were Americans to do?

Americans had, in fact, several courses open to them, and with characteristic self-confidence, took them all.

Over a century before the Revolution it had been observed of the Virginians that they had no need of ancestors, for they themselves were ancestors. The variations on this theme were infinite, but the theme was simple and familiar: that Americans had no need of a past because they were so sure of a future. Goethe had congratulated them on their good fortune in a famous but almost untranslatable poem: *Amerika, du hast es besser:* "no ruined castles, no venerable stones, no useless memories, no vain feuds [he said]. . . . May a kind providence preserve you from tales of knights and robber barons and ghosts."

Americans took up the refrain with enthusiasm. The romantic artist Thomas Cole observed that though American scenery was "destitute of the vestiges of antiquity" it had other features that were reassuring, for "American associations are not so much with the past as of the present and the future, and in looking over the uncultivated scene, the mind may travel far into futurity."

This theme runs like a red thread through early American literature and oratory, and finally connects itself triumphantly with Manifest Destiny. It began, appropriately enough, with Crèvecoeur: "I am sure I cannot be called a partial American when I say that the spectacle afforded by these pleasing scenes must be more entertaining and more philosophical than that which arises from beholding the musty ruins of Rome. Here everything would inspire the reflecting traveller with the most philanthropic ideas; his imagination, instead of submitting to the painful and useless retrospect of revolutions, desolations, and plagues, would, on the contrary, wisely spring forward to the anticipated fields of future cultivation and improvement, to the future extent of those generations which are to replenish and embellish this boundless continent." Washington Irving's friend and collaborator, James Paulding, entertained the same sentiment: "It is for the other nations to boast of what they have been, and, like garrulous age, muse over the history of their youthful exploits that only renders decrepitude more conspicuous. Ours is the more animating sentiment of hope, looking forward with prophetic eye."

Best of all is Cooper's John Cadwallader in *Notions of the Americans*, rebuking his travelling companion, the bachelor Count, for his unmanly longing for antiquity: "You complain of the absence of association to give its secret, and perhaps greatest charm which such a sight is capable of inspiring. You complain unjustly. The moral feeling with which a man of sentiment and knowledge looks upon the plains of your [Eastern] Hemisphere is connected with his recollections; here it should be mingled with his hopes. The same effort of the mind is as equal to the one as to the other."

The habit of looking forward instead of back blended readily enough with Manifest Destiny. Thus John Louis O'Sullivan, who all but invented Manifest Destiny, dismissed the past in favor of the future: "We have no interest in scenes of antiquity, only as lessons of avoidance of nearly all their examples. The expansive future is our arena. We are entering on its untrodden space with the truth of God in our minds, beneficent objects in our hearts, and with a clear conscience unsullied by the past. We are the nation of human progress, and who will, what can, set limits on our onward march? . . . The far-reaching, the boundless future will be the era of American greatness. . . ."

There was nothing surprising in Emerson's conclusion that America had no past. "All," he said, "has an outward and prospective look." For transcendentalism—the first genuine expression of the American temperament in philosophy, or New England's at least—was impatient with origins, put its confidence in inspiration, looked upon each day as a new epoch and each man as an Adam. It is difficult to exaggerate the impatience of the transcendentalists with the past. It was not so much that they were opposed to it as they found it irrelevant. And note that New England's major historians—Bancroft, Prescott, Ticknor, Motley, and Parkman—were all outside the mainstream of transcendentalism.

This was all very well, this confidence in the future. But it was, after all, pretty thin fare for nationalism to feed on at a time when other self-conscious nations were rejoicing in an ancient and romantic past. To be sure, the past became ancient and the future became present more rapidly in America than anywhere else: thus Thomas Jefferson could write from Paris in 1787 that much was to be said for keeping the "good, old, venerable, fabrick" of the six-year-old Articles of Confederation. And thus, too, John Randolph, in the Virginia ratifying convention, could "take farewell of the Confederation, with reverential respect, as an old benefactor."

Happily, there was a second formula to which Americans had recourse, and one no less convenient than the first: that America had, in fact, the most impressive of all pasts; *all* Europe was the American past. After all, we speak the tongue that Shakespeare spake—and for good measure, the tongues of Luther and Racine and Dante and Cervantes as well. Just because Americans had crossed the Atlantic Ocean did not mean that they had forfeited or repudiated their heritage. Americans enjoyed, in fact, the richest and most varied of all heritages. Other benighted peoples had only their past—the Danes a Danish, the Germans a German—but Americans had them all. Were we not in very truth a teeming nation of nations? Edward Everett asserted this as early as 1820: "We suppose that in proportion to our population Lord Byron and Walter Scott are more read in America than in England, nor do we see why we are not entitled to our full share of all that credit which does not rest . . . in the person of the author. . . ." Whitman made this the burden of "Thou Mother With Thy Equal Brood":

> Sail, sail thy best, ship of Democracy,
> Of value is thy freight, 'tis not the Present only,
> The Past is also stored in thee,
> Thou holdest not the venture of thyself alone, not of the Western Continent alone,
> Earth's résumé entire floats on thy keel O ship, is steadied by thy spars, . . .
> Steer then with good strong hand, and wary eye O helmsman, thou carriest great companions,
> Venerable priestly Asia sails this day with thee,
> And royal feudal Europe sails with thee.

All very well, but a risky business, this assimilation of the Old World past. For could the Old World be trusted? Could the past be trusted? We come here to one of the major themes of American intellectual history, and one of the most troublesome of all the problems in the creation of a usable past.

The theme of New World innocence and Old World corruption emerged early, and persisted all through the nineteenth century: it is a constant of American literature as of American politics, and if it no longer haunts our literature, it still bedevils our politics and diplomacy.

How deeply they were shocked, these innocent Americans, by the goings on in Europe! Benjamin Franklin, after a long residence in England, could deprecate the notion of a reconciliation between the Americans and the mother country on moral grounds: "I have not heard what Objections were made to the Plan in the Congress, nor would I make more than this one, that, when I consider the extreme Corruption prevalent among all Orders of Men in this old rotten State, and the glorious publick Virtue so predominant in our rising

Country, I cannot but apprehend more Mischief than Benefit from a closer Union." Dr. Benjamin Rush, who had studied in Edinburgh and in London, never ceased to preach the danger of contamination from abroad. With Jefferson—surely the most cosmopolitan American of his generation—New World innocence and Old World corruption was almost an *idée fixe*. How illuminating, that famous letter to John Banister about the education of his son. "Why send an American youth to Europe for education? ... Let us view the disadvantages. ... To enumerate them all, would require a volume. I will select a few. If he goes to England, he learns drinking, horse racing, and boxing. These are the peculiarities of English education. The following circumstances are common to education in that, and the other countries of Europe. He acquires a fondness of European luxury and dissipation, and a contempt for the simplicity of his own country; he is fascinated with the privileges of the European aristocrats and sees, with abhorrence, the lovely equality which the poor enjoy with the rich, in his own country; he contracts a partiality for aristocracy or monarchy; he forms foreign friendships which will never be useful to him ... he is led, by the strongest of all the human passions, into a spirit for female intrigue, destructive of his own and others' happiness, or a passion for whores, destructive of his health, and, in both cases, learns to consider fidelity to the marriage bed as an ungentlemanly practice. ... It appears to me, then, that an American coming to Europe for education, loses in his knowledge, in his morals, in his health, in his habits, and in his happiness. ...."

The theme, and the arguments, persisted. Hezekiah Niles wrote on the eve of the War of 1812 that "the War, dreadful as it is, will not be without its benefits in ... separating us from the *strumpet governments of Europe*." It is the most persistent theme in American literature from Crèvecoeur to Tocqueville, from Hawthorne's *Marble Faun* to James' *Daisy Miller* and *Portrait of a Lady*, from *Innocents Abroad* to *The Sun Also Rises*. Something of its complexity and difficulty can be seen in the position of the expatriate. Here Americans long maintained a double standard; it was taken for granted not only that European immigrants to the United States give up their nationality and identify themselves with their adopted country, but that they do so exuberantly. But for Americans to give up their nationality and identify themselves with a foreign country was another matter.

Needless to say, there are philosophical and psychological implications here which we ignore at our peril. For this concept of New World innocence and Old World corruption encouraged that sense of being a people apart which nature herself had already sufficiently dramatized. How characteristic that Jefferson should have combined nature and morality in his first inaugural: "Kindly separated by nature from one quarter of the globe; too high-minded to endure the degradations of the others ...." To this day Americans are inclined to think that they are outside the stream of history, exempt from its burden.

But quite aside from the theme of Old World corruption, the availability of the European past was not a simple matter of chronological assimilation or absorption. It was available, to be sure, but only on limited terms. It was there more for purposes of contrast than for enrichment; it pointed the moral of American superiority, and adorned the tale of American escape from contamination. It was there, too, as a museum, a curio shop, and a moral playground. But for practical purposes it contributed little to the juices of American Life.

Americans had a third choice: They could use what they had. "We have not, like England and France, centuries of achievements and calamities to look back on," wrote the indefatigable diarist George Templeton Strong, "but being without the eras that belong to older nationalities—Anglo-Saxon, Carolingian, Hohenstaufen, Ghibelline, and so forth—we dwell on the details of our little all of historic life and venerate every trivial fact about our first settlers and colonial governors and revolutionary heroes." Not all Americans struck so modest a pose. All their past lacked, after all, was antiquity, and antiquity was relative; in any event, this meant that the American past was better authenticated than the European.

Nothing in the history of American nationalism is more impressive than the speed and lavishness with which Americans provided themselves with a usable past: history, legends, symbols, paintings, sculpture, monuments, shrines, holy days, ballads, patriotic songs, heroes, and—with some difficulty—villains. Henry James speaks of Emerson dwelling for fifty years "within the undecorated walls of his youth." To Emerson they did not seem undecorated, for he embellished them with a profusion of historical association and of memory: the author of "Concord Hymn" was not unaware of the past.

Not every American, to be sure, was as deeply rooted as Emerson, but even to newcomers America soon ceased to be undecorated. Uncle Sam was quite as good as John Bull, and certainly more democratic. The bald eagle (Franklin sensibly preferred the turkey, but was overruled) did not compare badly with the British lion and was at least somewhat more at home in America than the lion in Britain. The Stars and Stripes, if it did not fall straight out of heaven like Denmark's *Dannebrog*, soon had its own mythology, and it had, besides, one inestimable advantage over all other flags, in that it provided an adjustable key to geography and a visible evidence of growth. Soon it provided the stuff for one of the greatest of all national songs—the tune difficult but the sentiments elevated—and one becoming to a free people. The Declaration of Independence was easier to understand than Magna Carta, and parts of it could be memorized and recited—as Magna Carta could not. In addition it had a Liberty Bell to toll its fame, which was something the British never thought of. There were no less than two national mottoes—*E pluribus unum*, selected, so appropriately, by Franklin, Jefferson, and John Adams, and *Novus ordo seclorum*, with their classical origins. There were no antiquities, but there were shrines: Plymouth Rock, of course, and Independence Hall and Bunker Hill and Mount Vernon and Monticello; eventually there was to be the Log Cabin in which Lincoln was born, as indestructible as the hull of the *Mayflower*.

These were some of the insignia, as it were, the ostentatious manifestations of the possession of a historical past. The stuff of that past was crowded and rich; it is still astonishing that Americans managed to fill their historical canvas so elaborately in so short a time. The colonial era provided a remote past: Pocahontas saving John Smith; the Pilgrims landing on the sandy coast of Plymouth, and celebrating the first Thanksgiving; Roger Williams fleeing through the wintry storms to Narragansett Bay; William Penn treating with the Indians; Deerfield going up in flames, its captives trekking though the snow to Canada; Franklin walking the streets of Philadelphia, munching those "three great puffy rolls" that came to be permanent props.

The Revolution proved a veritable cornucopia of heroic episodes and memories: Washington crossing the Delaware; Washington dwelling at Valley Forge; the signing of the Declaration; Captain Parker at Lexington Common: "If they mean to have a war, let it begin here!"; Prescott at Bunker Hill: "Don't fire until you see the whites of their eyes!"; John Paul Jones closing with the *Serapis*: "I have not yet begun to fight !"; Nathan Hale on the gallows: "I only regret that I have but one life to lose for my country"; Tom Paine writing the first *Crisis* on the flat of a drum, by the flickering light of campfires; George Rogers Clark wading through the flooded Wabash bottom lands to capture Vincennes; Washington at Yorktown: "The World Turned Upside Down "; Washington, again, fumbling for his glasses at Newburgh: "I have grown gray in your service, and now find myself growing blind"; Washington even in Heaven, not a pagan Valhalla but a Christian Heaven, doubly authenticated by a parson and a historian—one person to be sure—the incomparable Parson Weems.

The War of 1812, for all its humiliations, made its own contributions to national pride. Americans conveniently forgot the humiliations and recalled the glories: Captain Lawrence off Boston Harbor: "Don't give up the ship"; the *Constitution* riddling the *Guerrière*; Francis Scott Key peering through the night and the smoke to see if the flag was still there; Perry at Put-in-Bay: "We have met the enemy and they are ours"; the hunters of Kentucky repulsing Pakenham—

There stood John Bull in Martial pomp
But here was old Kentucky.

No wonder Old Hickory went straight to the White house.

The West, too—not one West but many—provided a continuous flow of memories and experiences and came to be, especially for immigrants, a great common denominator. There was the West of the Indian; of Washington at Fort Necessity; the West of Daniel Boone; of Lewis and Clark; of the Santa Fe Trail and the Oregon Trail and the California Gold Rush; the West of the miner and the cowboy; the West of the Union Pacific trail and the other transcontinentals. "If it be romance, if it be contrast, if it be heroism that we require," asked Robert Louis Stevenson, "what was Troytown to this?" What indeed?

And richest of all in its contribution to the storehouse of American memory was the Civil War, with its hero, Lincoln: it produced the best literature and the best songs of any modern war; it was packed with drama and with heroism. To one part of America it gave the common bond of defeat and tragedy, but a defeat that fed sentiment so powerful that it was metamorphosed into victory. It gave to the whole of America a dramatic sense of unity; to Negroes it associated national unity with freedom; and to all it gave the most appealing of national heroes, probably the only modern hero to rank with Alfred and Barbarossa and Joan of Arc. Certainly, of all modern heroes it is Lincoln who lends himself most readily to mythology; his birth humble and even mysterious; his youth gentle and simple; his speech pithy and wise; his wit homely and earthy; his counsels benign. He emerged briefly to save his nation and free the slaves, and died tragically as the lilacs bloomed; no wonder the poets and the mythmakers have exhausted themselves on this theme.

No less remarkable was the speed and comprehensiveness with which the new nation provided itself with an artistic record. From the beginning, to be sure, Americans had been fortunate in this realm; no other nation, it is safe to say, has had its entire history so abundantly recorded as the American, from the first contributions by Le Moyne and De Bry and John White to the realism of the Ash Can school of the early twentieth century. Never before in recorded history had anything excited the imagination like the discovery of the New World—O brave new world, O strange new world, new world that was Utopia and Paradise. Everything about it excited the explorers and conquerors: the Patagonian giants and the Amazons of Brazil and the pygmies of the Far North; the mountains that soared fifty miles into the clouds and lakes as vast as continents and the caves of solid gold; the natives who were descended from the Chinese or the Jews or the Norwegians or the Welsh; the flora and fauna so strange they all but defied description. How to make clear the wonder and the terror of it all?

All the explorers were historians, to be sure; almost all of them were artists as well, and soon all Europe could share the wonder of those who had seen what men had never seen before. It was as if cartographers had given us maps of the voyages of the Phoenicians or of the Vikings; it was as if artists had pictured Hector and Agamemnon before the walls of Troy or Romulus founding the city that would bear his name, or Hengist and Horsa on the shores of Ebbsfleet!

Political independence brought with it artistic freedom, and an ardent preoccupation with the birth of the nation created the stirring political drama; the scenes of battle, lurid and triumphant; the Founding Fathers, grave, as became men occupying a sure place in history. In a generation when Franklin doubted the possibility and John Adams the propriety of art, a host of artists emerged, as if in defiance of counsels too sober; if they were not Rembrandts or Turners, they were better than anyone had any right to expect. It is not, however, their artistic merits that interest us, but their historical function. John Singleton Copley gave us a rich and crowded portrait gallery of colonial society in the process of becoming American—the merchants, the statesmen, the captains, and their ladies as well. John Trumbull regarded himself as the official painter of the Revolution and covered that chapter of history systematically though not comprehensively. Scarcely less impressive was the contribution of the versatile Charles Willson Peale, who left us a whole gallery of Founding Fathers as well as an academy of artistic sons, while the achievement of Gilbert Stuart in impressing on future generations his image of the Father of His Country is almost without parallel in the history of art. This school of artistic historians came to an end when its work was done, when it had provided posterity with artistic archives and monuments of its birth and its youth. Then the new nation, secure in the possession of an artistic record, could afford to indulge the romanticism of an Allston or a Cole, of the Hudson River school, or of genre painters like the puckish John Quidor—worthy companion to Washington Irving—or William Sidney Mount.

The celebration of independence and the founding of the republic was but one chapter in the history of the creation of an artistic image of the American past. Another school seized, almost instinctively, on the inexhaustible theme of the Indian and the winning of the West. Thus, while scores of American artists sailed for the Italian Arcadia, others, untrained, or trained in the irrelevant school of Düsseldorf, moved quite as confidently across the Alleghenies and on to the prairies and the plains and the mountains of the West. What a romantic group they were: the Swiss Carl Bodmer, who went with Prince Maximilian of Wied up the Missouri River in the early 1830's, and who gave us a crowded gallery of Sioux, Crees, Assiniboins, and Mandans; the indefatigable George Catlin with his hundreds of Indian portraits—surely the fullest artistic re-creation of the West before photography; Alfred Jacob Miller, who was the artist for Captain Stewart's explorations in the Far West and who sketched not only Indians but the landscape—Chimney Rock and Independence Rock and the Tetons and the Wind River Mountains; the luckless John Mix Stanley, who was ubiquitous, from the lead mines of Galena to the Cherokee country, with Kearny on the Santa Fe Trail, one thousand miles by canoe up the Columbia, even to distant Hawaii—the work of a lifetime lost in the great Smithsonian fire of 1865.

Not all of these artists of the early West re-created the past for their own generation. Miller, for example, was not really known in his own day, nor was Stanley. Far more important in the creation of the popular image of America were two artist-ornithologists, Alexander Wilson and John James Audubon, who captured for all time the flora and fauna of America in its pastoral age. Wilson's nine-volume *American Ornithology* was perhaps the most ambitious work of science in the early republic. Soon came Audubon's *Birds of America*, less scientific than Wilson's *Ornithology* but more splendid, "the most magnificent monument" said Cuvier, "which art has ever raised to ornithology." And Audubon, of course, contributed more: his own extraordinary life and legend.

The sumptuous paintings of Wilson and Audubon reached the public only gradually, and in cheap reproductions. More effective was the impact of the almost forgotten school of panoramists. The hapless John Vanderlyn, who had dared display his nude *Ariadne* to an outraged public, introduced the panorama, in a specially built rotunda in New York's City Hall Park. But it was Versailles and Athens and Mexico which he chose to display; perhaps that is why he failed. His successors preferred to reveal America, and particularly the Father of Waters, which had the advantage of being almost the only object of nature longer than their paintings. One John Rowson Smith did a panorama of the Mississippi as early as 1844; when he displayed it at Saratoga Springs, New York, he took in twenty thousand dollars in six weeks. Soon there were a dozen rivals in the field: John Banvard, for example, who claimed that his Mississippi panorama was three miles long (actually it was only a quarter of a mile—a bad calculation, that). Poor John Stanley, who had so little luck with his Indian paintings, scored a tremendous success with a panorama of the *Western Wilds*, forty-two episodes, no less, requiring a minimum of two hours to view! Greatest of all the panoramists was Henry Lewis, who managed to cover almost three quarters of a mile of canvas with his paintings; his earnings from his great panorama enabled him to settle in Düsseldorf and learn to paint. Whatever their artistic merits, or demerits, the panoramas helped give a whole generation of Americans some feeling for the spaciousness and the beauty of the early West.

Writing in 1841, Emerson had lamented that "banks and tariffs, the newspaper and caucus, Methodism and Unitarianism, are flat and dull to dull people but rest on the same foundations of wonder as the town of Troy and the temple of Delphi. . . . Our logrolling, our stumps and their politics, our fisheries, our Negroes and Indians, our boasts and our repudiations . . . the northern trade, the southern planting, the western clearing, Oregon and Texas, are yet unsung. Yet America is a poem in our eyes; its ample geography dazzles the imagination." Poets and artists had responded, but none had quite encompassed American nature. Even Whitman and Winslow Homer could not quite do that. For nature played a special role in American history and in the process of creating a sense of history and a national consciousness. Since the seventeenth century, Europeans have not had to concern themselves energetically with the conquest of nature, for nature, like history, was given. For Americans, on the other hand, the relationship to nature was more personal, and more complex. They had an empty continent to settle and successive frontiers to conquer, and for them nature had always played a twofold role: her ruggedness was a challenge, and her richness a manifestation of divine favor. How suggestive it is that for over two hundred years Europeans could not make up their minds whether the New World was Paradise or an accursed place, whether its natives were Noble Savages or degenerate men without souls. But however nature was to be interpreted—and by the nineteenth century the paradisiacal interpretation had triumphed—it was, in a peculiar way, the great common denominator and the great common experience. Virginians, Pilgrims, and Quakers alike could rejoice in the abundance of nature, and generations of pioneers, even those who were not *Mayflower* descendants or FFV's, could cherish the common memory of hardship endured and overcome.

Because they had conquered nature, Americans came in time to think that they had created it and to display toward it a proprietary interest. The stupendous flow of Niagara, the luxuriance of the Bluegrass, the power and majesty of the Father of Waters, the limitless expanse of prairie and plain, the glory of the Rockies—all of these came to be regarded as national attributes, and failure to appreciate them, like failure to appreciate political attributes, an affront. How interesting that from "Swanee River" to "Ol' Man River" songs celebrating nature have usurped the place of formal patriotic music—"Dixie," for example, or "My Old Kentucky Home," or "On the Banks of the Wabash," or "Home on the Range," or best of all, "America, the Beautiful."

And how interesting, too, that where in other countries topography is local, in America it is national. In the Old World, plains, valleys, and mountains belong to the people who happen to inhabit them, but in America the whole country, "from sea to shining sea," belongs to the whole people. The Italians and Germans traditionally celebrate their own cities, their particular churches or bridges; the English write two-volume works on Fly-casting in the Dart, or Cricket in Lower Slaughter, but until recently there has been little of this local possessiveness about Americans. "We have so much country that we have no country at all," Hawthorne lamented back in 1837, but Hawthorne was far from typical, and newcomers who could find little satisfaction in the slums of New York or the coal mines of Pennsylvania or the steel mills of Gary might yet rejoice in the Great Lakes and Yosemite. Movement, especially westward movement, is an essential ingredient in the American memory. When John F. Kennedy hit on the slogan, "Get America moving," he touched a responsive chord.

The task of providing themselves with a historical past was peculiarly difficult for Americans because it was not something that could be taken for granted, as with most peoples, or arranged once and for all. It was something that had to be done over and over again, for each new wave of newcomers, and that had to be kept up to date, as it were, continually reinvigorated and modernized. Above all, it had to be a past which contained an ample supply of easily grasped common denominators for a heterogeneous people, English and German, Irish and Norse, white and black, gentile and Jew, Protestant, Mormon, and Catholic, old stock and newcomer. Almost inevitably the common denominators tended to be pictorial and symbolic: the Pilgrims and Valley Forge, Washington and Lincoln, cowboy and Indian, and along with them ideas and institutions like Democracy, Liberty, Equality, the American Dream, and the American Way of Life.

One consequence of this emphasis on the simple, the symbolic, and the ideological is that American patriotism tended to be more artificial, labored, and ostentatious than that of most Old World peoples. It was almost inevitably calculated and artificial: after all, the process of drawing the juices of tradition for a German boy newly arrived in America was very different from that for a French or an English lad at home, where everything could be taken for granted, or left to nature. Tradition in America had to be labored, for it was not born into the young; it did not fill the horizon, as the glory of Joan of Arc or the fame of Nelson filled the horizons of French and English boys and girls. The American past could not be absorbed from childhood on in the art and architecture of every town and village, in song and story and nursery rhyme, in novel and history, in the names of streets and squares and towns. Growing up in Pittsburgh or Chicago was a very different experience, historically, from growing up in London or Edinburgh, Paris or Rome. And patriotism probably had to be ostentatious; in any event, it is. Ostentation characterizes new wealth, and new loyalties as well. This is doubtless one reason there is so much emphasis on the overt observance of patriotism in America. Americans dedicate a large number of days to ceremonial patriotism: the Fourth of July, Memorial Day, Confederate Memorial Day, Veterans Day, Washington's Birthday, Lincoln's Birthday, Columbus Day, Loyalty Day, and many others, and for good measure many states have their own special holidays—Patriots' Day in Massachusetts or Texas Independence Day. Americans require children to "pledge allegiance to the flag," impose loyalty oaths for every conceivable occasion, and march in "I Am an American Day" parades, and there is no W. S. Gilbert to satirize what so many take with passionate seriousness. Perhaps nowhere else in the Western world is loyalty such a touchstone as in the United States, perhaps nowhere else are there so many organizations dedicated to fostering patriotism: the Daughters of the American Revolution, the Sons of the American Revolution, the Colonial Dames, the United Daughters of the Confederacy, the Americanism committees of the great veterans' organizations, and, more recently, the Minute Women.

The process of acquiring a usable past was immensely facilitated by two extraordinary circumstances. The first was the eagerness of almost all newcomers from every part of the globe to slough off their pasts and take on an American habit, an eagerness so avid and so pervasive that it made nonsense of the compunctions and fears of native Americans from Fisher Ames to Thomas Bailey Aldrich a century later. Perhaps no other society in the process of transforming itself into a nation had more co-operative material to work with. The American newcomer, as he told us over and over again, was under both moral and practical compulsions to achieve acceptance for himself and for his children by becoming completely American as rapidly and as thoroughly as possible. Crèvecoeur, who saw so much, saw this, and so too the magisterial Tocqueville, but it is a lesson that has had to be relearned in every generation.

That it was *possible* for newcomers to become American overnight was the second circumstance. The explanation here lies in large part in the high degree of literacy that obtained in America, even in the eighteenth century, and the tradition of literacy and of education that flourished in that and the next century. Schools proved, in the long run, the most effective agencies for the creation and the transmission of an American memory. If they did not deliberately inculcate Americanism, that was because they did not need to: Noah Webster's Spellers, McGuffey's many Readers, Jedidiah Morse's Geographies and Peter Parley's Histories—these and scores of books like them conjured up an American past and provided, for generations of children, the common denominators, the stories and songs and poems, the memories and symbols. And it was the children, in turn, who educated the parents, for America is the only country where, as a matter of course, it is assumed that each new generation is wiser and more sophisticated than the old, and where parents adopt the standards of their children rather than children adopting those of their parents. For newcomers too old for school, and too inflexible to learn from their children, the work of providing an American past was carried on by voluntary organizations which have always performed the most miscellaneous of social tasks: churches, political parties, labor unions, lyceums, fraternal and filiopietistic organizations, and so forth.

What this meant was that the sentiment of American nationalism was, to an extraordinary degree, a literary creation, and that the national memory was a literary and, in a sense, a contrived memory. The contrast here with the Old World is sharp. There the image of the past was conjured up and sustained by a thousand testimonials: folklore and folk song, the vernacular and the patois, church music and architecture, monuments, paintings and murals, the pageantry of the court and of popular feasts and holidays. To be sure, literature—poetry and drama and formal histories—came to play a role, but only when it was quarried from cultural foundations that went deep. In America the image of the past was largely the creation of the poets and the storytellers, and chiefly of the New England–New York group who flourished between the War of 1812 and the War for the Union, that group familiar to an earlier generation through the amiable game of Authors: Irving, Cooper, and Bryant; Longfellow, Hawthorne, and Whittier; Emerson, Lowell, and Holmes. These were the Founding Fathers of American literary nationalism, and their achievement was scarcely less remarkable than that of the Founding Fathers of political nationalism.

In a single generation these men of letters gave Americans the dramas, the characters, the settings, which were to instruct and delight succeeding generations: Uncas and Deerslayer and Long Tom Coffin; Rip Van Winkle and the Headless Horseman; Miles Standish, Paul Revere, Evangeline, and Hiawatha; Goodman Brown, the Grey Champion, and Hester Prynne, as well as the Salem Customs House, the House of the Seven Gables, the Old Manse, and the Great Stone Face; Skipper Ireson and Concord Bridge and Old Ironsides and the One-Hoss Shay and Hosea Biglow with all his Yankee company.

Note that this image of the past which the literary Founding Fathers created and imposed upon Americans was very largely a New England image, and much that was most distinctive about American nationalism was to be conditioned by this circumstance. It meant that Americans on Iowa prairies or the plains of Texas would sing *"I love thy rocks and rills, thy woods and templed hills"* with no sense of incongruity; that Plymouth would supplant Jamestown as the birthplace of America; that Thanksgiving Day would be a New England holiday; that Paul Revere would be the winged horseman of American history and Concord Bridge the American equivalent of the Rubicon; that Boston's Statehouse would vindicate its claim—or Holmes'—to be the "hub of the solar system." If all this was hard on the South, southerners had only themselves to blame for their indifference to their own men of letters. The most familiar of southern symbols came from the North: Harriet Beecher Stowe of New England gave us Uncle Tom and Little Eva and Topsy and Eliza, while it was Stephen Foster of Pittsburgh who sentimentalized the Old South, and even "Dixie" had northern origins.

The literary task of creating a usable past was largely performed by 1865; after that date perhaps only Mark Twain, Bret Harte, and Louisa May Alcott added anything substantial to the treasure house of historical memories. This was, in perspective, the most significant achievement of American literature and one almost without parallel in the literature of any other country in a comparable period. How interesting that a people supposed to be indifferent to literature—supposed by some to have no literature—should depend so largely upon literature for the nourishment of its historical self-consciousness. Certainly the speed and effectiveness with which Americans rallied their resources to supply themselves with a historical past cannot but excite astonishment. And what a past it was—splendid, varied, romantic, and all but blameless, in which there were heroes but no villains, victories but no defeats—a past that was all prologue to the Rising Glory of America.

Parson Weems, the Cherry Tree and the Patriotic Tradition

Nicholas Cords

Richard Hofstadter has argued that the Abraham Lincoln myth was self-made and self-perpetuated. While George Washington had some part in the creation of the myths concerning him (subjects usually do), one man, more than any other, was responsible for a vast proportion of his mythic monument. Mason Locke Weems was such a successful mythmaker that, as Marcus Cunliffe has suggested, he too has passed into folklore. This article by Nicholas Cords, one of this book's editors, briefly discusses Parson Weems, his times, the genesis and development of his *Life of Washington,* some of his techniques, and the strong emphasis on patriotism that was common throughout the National Period. No attempt is made to destroy either the Parson or his myths; late-nineteenth-century "scientific historians" attempted that, without much success. Indeed, the consensus now seems to be that, regardless of fabrication, one can learn a lot—even about Washington—from the "father" of the Father of Our Country.

American historical writing after the Revolution came to be dominated by the Federalist-Whig tradition. This tradition, while socially conservative, was consumed with liberal nationalism. Its proponents were of the upper-middle-class leisured group, and were highly selective in the materials they included in their histories. They accepted the view of the Revolution as put forth in the Whig publication, the *Annual Register,* and were anti-Jeffersonian. The providential approach to historical writing was on the wane, and this development continued as clergymen lost more and more of their influence. Local loyalties continued but were overshadowed by nationalistic fervor.

The new national spirit demanded of the historian that he express the ideals of the Republic and affirm its virtues and destiny. As the Revolution was the foundation stone of this new national spirit, its men and events provided the subject matter for most patriotic writing. Authors from Warren and Ramsay through Bancroft and Hildreth played heavily on the Whig-influenced patriotic theme. Even literary figures such as Barlow and Irving sang the refrain. The man who is the subject of this article, however, did more to enhance the patriotic tradition than any of the others. If he did not exactly fit into the Federalist-Whig mold, it was probably because he was the type of person who did not fit well into any fixed category. What he lacked in social conservatism and selectivity, he made up for in patriotism. Who was this figure? "I can't tell a lie"; it was Parson Weems.

Mason Locke Weems was born on October 11, 1759, at Marshes Seat, Herring Bay, Anne Arundel County, Maryland. His father was of a Scottish noble family (Wemyss) and had emigrated sometime before 1722. Little is known of Weems' early life, although legends abound. He is said to have made some voyages on his brothers' ships, and he studied medicine at Edinburgh or London.

By 1783 Weems was back in London where he studied for the Episcopal ministry. He was ordained in 1784 by the Archbishop of Canterbury, only after the oath of allegiance law had been abrogated (he had refused to take the oath). While in London he had correspondence with John Adams and Benjamin Franklin. On his return to Maryland he was rector of the All Hallows Parish (1785–89) and St. Margaret's (1791–94).

In 1794 Weems left the permanent ministry and pursued what was to become part of his life's work—bookselling. Striking up a relationship with Mathew Carey, a young Philadelphia publisher, Weems acted as his selling agent for practically the remainder of his life. His bookselling career was accompanied by one of editing and writing. He edited a series of improving books and wrote political pamphlets, biographies and tracts. He travelled between New York and Savannah, and became a well-known figure throughout the entire area.

It has already been stated that Mason Weems did not exactly belong to the Federalist-Whig historical tradition; this was mainly because of his attraction to, and constant dealings with, the common people. Although he got along well with people of all classes, he was more at home and more successful with those of the lower groups. The upper class tended to resent his crusading zeal, breadth of view in matters of dogma, outbursts of liberalism and lack of dignity. Also, his affinity for the Negro did not suit upper-class taste in the South. He conducted services for them every other Friday and once said concerning preaching to them, "Oh, it is sweet preaching, when people are desirous of hearing. Sweet feeding the flock of Christ, when they have so good an appetite." Bishop Meade referred to Weems as a "curious oddity," and to his family as "interesting and pious." What really irked Meade was the fact that Weems sold books in taverns on election and Court-House days, and extolled Tom Paine from the pulpit. Weems had once said concerning Paine, "Divinity, for this climate sh'd be very rational and liberal. . . ."

If Weems did not represent the socially conservative aspect of the Federalist-Whig tradition, he certainly had the patriotic line well in hand. His writings exude patriotism, embroidered with religion and morality. Concerning the Revolution, the Whig theory was easy for him to accept. The war had been cruelly made on the American people and its cause was simple to ascertain—"the king wanted money for his hungry relations and the ministers stakes for their gaming tables or diamond necklaces for their mistresses." Thus armed with these views, Weems, a merrily disposed white-haired individual, preached, prayed and sold his way back and forth across the southern half of the country. His saddlebags always contained a manuscript on which he was working, and he was constantly ready to dance or play the violin (Weems' family disclaimed that he ever played his violin on the road).

Weems' patriotic historical writing—as well as his talent for myth-building—is best typified by his biography of George Washington. The first known meeting between the two men occurred in 1787 and is recorded in Washington's diary for March 3rd of that year. Correspondence between them continued until Washington's death and Weems, always a businessman, used the acquaintanceship to his own advantage. Washington wrote a testimonial to an improving book edited by Weems, *The Immortal Mentor* (1796); the Parson immediately had it printed on the back of the title page. In 1799 Weems published *The Philanthropist; or A Good Twenty-five cents worth of Political Love Powder, for Honest Adamsites and Jeffersonians.* In this book Weems, brandishing his nationalism, pleaded for toleration in politics and recognition of what true equality meant. He defended John Adams and even Jefferson, of whom he was not particularly enamored. Washington's written praise of the effort appeared on the title page under the heading: "With the Following Recommendation by George Washington."

Upon Washington's death in 1799, the floodgates were released on the already swelling tide of legend concerning him. Here was an opportunity for Mason L. Weems and a torrent of other authors to expound the traditions, values and goals of the new nation in terms of the life and character of its most important citizen.

Parson Weems preached a eulogy at Pohick Church in Truro Parish, seven miles from Mount Vernon. This eulogy was expanded to eighty pages and published as a pamphlet under the title: *A History of the Life and Death, Virtues and Exploits of General George Washington.* The good Parson spent much of the remainder of his life expanding this work and bringing out new editions (twenty-nine before his death). The second edition added to the title: "faithfully taken from authentic documents." The fifth edition (1806) contained the cherry tree story and claimed that Weems was the "former rector of Mount Vernon Parish." Later the author went all out and called himself "former rector of General Washington's parish"—based on the fact that on a few occasions he had preached at the church Washington attended before the Revolution.

Weems is quite clear as to his purposes in the *Life of Washington.* The title of a later edition is helpful: *The Life of George Washington, with curious anecdotes equally honorable to himself and exemplary to his young countrymen....* In a letter to a publisher (1800) Weems said he wanted to bring out "his [Washington's] Great Virtues. 1 His Veneration for the Diety [sic], or Religious Principles. 2 His Patriotism. 3d His Magninimity [sic]. 4 his Industry. 5 his Temperance and Sobriety. 6 his Justice, &ᶜ &ᶜ." Another goal of Weems, interesting in light of criticism levelled at him for creating much of the Washington myth, was to get at the real Washington. He stated: "In most of the elegant orations pronounced to his praise, you see nothing of Washington below *the clouds* ... 'tis only Washington the HERO, and the

Demigod . . . Washington the *sun beam* in council, or the *storm* in war." The actual result of his effort, of course, was that Weems created a Washington which all research scholars have been unable to erase and with whom they must come to grips—"a figure of truly terrifying piosities and incredible perfections." According to Senator Albert Beveridge, at times this Washington was an "impossible and intolerable prig."

Washington's characteristics and accomplishments, as put forth by the Parson, are exhausting just to contemplate. He had the old-fashioned virtues, loved his parents, loved and feared God, was a leader, a good student, and was born to be a soldier. He proved that duty leads to advantage, he did not drink or gamble, he was talented and a case of smallpox marked him agreeably. He had a great sense of patriotism and duty combined with religiosity, he had intuitive perception, was a good writer, was benevolent, industrious and a gentleman. After all this—and more—Weems' readers were probably not surprised to find Washington, upon his death, ascending to heaven amidst choirs of angels to meet, among others, Benjamin Franklin and General Wolfe.

Reading two hundred and twenty-five pages of such material would not be too rewarding if it were not for Parson Weems' racy style, vivid descriptions and ever-present sense of humor. Throughout it all his delightful ability to adorn a tale keeps the narrative alive and interesting. One is tempted to agree with Sidney Fisher, who said: "Reckless in statement, indifferent to facts and research, his books are full of popular heroism, religion and morality, which you at first call trash and cant and then, finding it extremely entertaining, you declare with a laugh, as you lay down the book, what a clever rogue."

Weems used the anecdotal method extensively. Considering the general literacy level of the day and the fact that his reading public consisted mainly of lower-class southern people, this seems a wise choice. Besides, the anecdotal method gave Weems a better chance to moralize and inspire; it also sold more books. The *Life of Washington* was laden with these anecdotes, the most famous of which is the one concerning the cherry tree incident.

George was blessed with a kindly old homily-laden father who, although not intellectually endowed, was a wonderful man and a great teacher. He early had told little George that he would rather see him dead than to see him become a liar:

> Hard, indeed, would it be to me to give up my son, whose little feet are always so ready to run about with me, and whose fondly looking eyes, and sweet prattle make so large a part of my happiness. But still I would give him up, rather than see him a common liar.

When George was six years old, he was given a hatchet with which he blithely tripped around chopping everything that came in his way—including his mother's pea-sticks. One day, in Weems' words, "he unluckily tried the edge of his hatchet on the body of a beautiful young English cherry tree, which he barked so terribly, that I don't believe the tree ever got the better of it." When asked by his father if he knew who had done it, George gave the reply every schoolchild knows:

> "I can't tell a lie, Pa; you know I can't tell a lie. I did cut it with my hatchet."—

"Run to my arms, you dearest boy," cried his father in transports, "run to my arms; glad am I, George, that you killed my tree; for you have paid me for it a thousand fold. Such an act of heroism in my son is more worth than a thousand trees, though blossomed with silver, and their fruits of purest gold."

The documentation for this and other of the anecdotes was "an aged lady, who was a distant relative, and, when a girl, spent much of her time in the family." Although the consensus of opinion seems to be that the incident originated with Weems in 1806, Emily Ford Skeel, in her work on the Parson, shows an illustration of a pottery mug with the incident depicted on it; the mug is dated 1776 and is believed to have been made in Germany. Irrespective of this, certainly it was Weems who popularized the tale.

As to Washington's patriotism, Weems left no doubt. He quotes the general on his deathbed:

Your government claims your utmost confidence and support. Respect for its authority, compliance with its laws, acquiescence in its measures, are duties enjoined by the fundamental maxims of true liberty. The basis of our political system is the right of the people to make and alter their constitution of government. But the constitution, which at any time exists, until changed by an explicit and authentic act of the whole people, is sacredly obligatory upon all.

Again Washington is quoted upon hearing that his plantation manager had given supplies to a British frigate commander in order to avert the destruction of Mount Vernon:

Sir—It gives me extreme concern to hear that you furnished the enemy with refreshments. It would have been a less painful circumstance to me, to have heard that, in consequence of your non-compliance with their request, they had laid my plantation in ruins.

Weems was also concerned with the relationship of patriotism and religion, and thus Washington was. The book informed the reader that in the "Farewell to the People of the United States," Washington dwelled chiefly on the union and brotherly love. For Washington, in Weems' words, this combination appeared as "the one thing needful, the spring of political life, and bond of perfection."

The author outdid himself when it came to discussing the death of Washington. No normal death for the father of the country; after the rest of the book this would have been an anticlimax. After seeking the face of God (like Moses) and hesitating to quit the earth, Washington humbled himself (like Christ) and submitted to his fate. After death the following came to pass:

Swift on angels' wings the brightening saint ascended; while voices more than human were warbling through the happy regions, and hymning the great procession towards the gates of heaven. His glorious coming was seen afar off; and myriads of mighty angels hastened forth, with golden harps, to welcome the honoured stranger.

Weems' second biography was of General Francis Marion, the Swamp Fox. This work, although not as popular as the Washington biography, sold well and again shows Weems' ability to expound patriotism through his writing. The Parson got the material from General P. Horry, an old fighting mate and friend of Marion's. Horry wanted to write the book himself but lack of prose ability forced him to seek another author. Weems extracted the material from him on the promise that it would in no way be embellished or changed. In a statement of fact, Weems wrote to Horry on August 3, 1808: "I beg you to indulge no fears that Marion will ever die; while I can say or write anything to immortalize him. . . ." General Horry began to worry. Ten months later Weems wrote:

> It gives me great pleasure to inform you, by our mutual friend Dr. Blythe, that your ever honored and beloved Marion lives in History. . . . I have endeavored to throw your ideas and facts about General Marion into the garb and dress of a military romance.

Horry panicked. After taking to his sickbed he wrote a rather apt critique to Weems:

> You have carved and mutilated it [the book] with so many erroneous statements, that your embellishments, observations and remarks must necessarily be erroneous as proceeding from false grounds. Most certainly 'tis not my history, but your romance.

Perhaps an example of this "romance" is in order. Marion and his men surprised several score of Tory partisans who had been feasting, dancing and playing cards; the fight virtually ended with the first volley. Weems describes the post-battle scene thus:

> Even their fiddles and fiddle bows, and playing cards, were all left strewed around their fires. One of the gamblers (it is a serious truth) though shot dead, still held the cards hard griped [sic] in his hands. Led by curiosity to inspect this sight, a dead gambler, we found that the cards which he held were ace, deuce and jack. Clubs were trumps. Holding high, low, jack and the game in his own hand, he seemed in a fair way to do well; but Marion came down on him with a trump that spoiled his sport, and non-suited him forever.

Weems also wrote tracts. These were against a variety of things—bachelorhood, adultery, gambling, infidelity. They fit into the patriotic theme because of Weems' connection of good government with religion and morality. An uplifted and improved people would be more patriotic. Lack of time and space do not permit a discussion of the tracts here; however, the full title of one tells a great deal about this aspect of the Parson's literary efforts.

> The Drunkard's Looking Glass—Reflecting a faithful likeness of the drunkard, in sundry very interesting attitudes, with lively representations of the many strange capers which he cuts at different stages of his disease:
>> At first, when he has only "a drop in his eye;" second, when he is "half shaved;" third, when he is getting "a little on the staggers or so;" and fourth and fifth, and so on, till he is quite capsized;" or "snug under the table with the dogs," and can "stick to the floor without holding on."
>>   By Mason L. Weems

Mason Locke Weems has escaped relatively unscathed from over a century and a half of criticism. His acceptance by writers during the past fifty years has usually run the range from apathy to captivation.

Marcus Cunliffe refers to Weems as a Victorian before the Victorian era because he fitted Washington into the nineteenth-century mold. Thus Washington had all the nineteenth-century virtues from courage to punctuality, from modesty to thrift.

Lawrence C. Wroth claims that Weems was successful because Americans wanted an exciting vagabond writer—an American Marlowe or Villon. Wroth goes on to say that the Parson's influence on American youth has been good, citing the influence on Lincoln as an example. Besides, the anecdotes are good and are the only ones extant about Washington.

Harold Kellock sees Weems as the first American salesman, combining an indefatigable pushing ability with the instinct for giving the public what it wants. Weems did once say: "God knows there is nothing I so dread as Dead stock, dull sales, back loads, and blank looks. But the Joy of my soul is quick & clear sales—Heavy pockets, and light hearts."

Sidney Fisher claimed that Weems was a mixture of Scriptures, Homer, Virgil and backwoods. His history was all wrong but then so were all the other histories of the Revolutionary period. They were incorrect because they were based on the *Annual Register* and ignored the true documents. Bancroft was nothing more than a scholarly Weems. The Parson at least helped religion and youth.

Walter B. Norris evidently, or hopefully, has come under the influence of Weems' sense of humor. He wrote of a hypothetical S.P.P.C.T. (Society for the Protection and Preservation of *Cherished* Traditions) with Weems as chief *preserver*. He went on to say that the cherry tree incident could have taken place, offering as proof the known colonial regard for fruit trees and the fact that Virginia passed laws to protect them. He also suggested that, if the incident were false, the people living in Washington's home area would have disclaimed it.

There are other ways to judge the importance of an historian than to study his critics. Assuming success in sales and number of readers are valid criteria, perhaps we must agree with Sidney Fisher who viewed Weems as "a writer of the highest order of popularity, and in that sense and influence the ablest historian we have ever produced. Prescott, Motley and Parkman are mere children when compared with him."

Weems' contribution to American historical mythology is considerable; on the subject of George Washington he is without peer. Attempts to destroy his credibility generally have proved to be exercises in futility—perhaps they are even superfluous; ignoring him is impossible. This article has discussed the Parson, his times, some of his works, his "creative" techniques and his strong concern for patriotism, religion and morality, in the belief that, particularly in this case, understanding is the most viable approach to the subject; certainly it is the most enjoyable.

Washington's Farewell, the French Alliance, and the Election of 1796

Alexander DeConde

Largely because of services rendered during the war of the Revolution, American enthusiasm for France found friendly expression in the foreign policy of the postwar decades. Thus, the military marriage of France and the United States, itself the subject of considerable myth, bears strategic importance to the presidential administrations of George Washington—most particularly to his famous "Farewell" and the election of 1796. In addition to the fact that the "Farewell Address" was not an address at all but rather a position paper disseminated by Washington through the press, it was not the "wise, timeless, and unbiased warning to the nation" that it has traditionally been thought to be. As argued by Alexander DeConde, of the University of California at Santa Barbara, the "Farewell Address" was rather an important political manifesto critical to the election of 1796. It was only "posterity" that gave the piece a meaning it neither deserved nor intended.

When in 1789 George Washington became the nation's first president the French alliance was the cornerstone of American foreign policy. It largely had made possible American independence and had established American foreign policy orientation. At the end of Washington's second term, in fact as he prepared his farewell to public life, the life-giving alliance was practically dead and the United States was virtually at war with France. Why, in eight formative years, did such a drastic reversal in foreign policy take place? A full answer to this question would be long and complex; yet by looking closely at the election of 1796 and by reviewing the Farewell Address in its political context we may find a partial answer as to how the alliance received its mortal wound. We may also find additional reason for revising the traditional interpretation of the Farewell Address as a wise, timeless, and unbiased warning to the nation.

The blow from which the alliance never recovered was the Jay Treaty of 1794. While this Federalist-negotiated treaty averted a war with England, a war which Federalists feared, the major objectives which John Jay had been

From "Washington's Farewell, the French Alliance, and the Election of 1796," by Alexander De-Conde, in *Mississippi Valley Historical Review*, XLIII (March 1957), pp. 641–658. Reprinted by permission of *The Journal of American History*.

expected to win were not realized. Because it failed to obtain specific concessions on impressments, ship seizures, and Indian raids on the frontier, the treaty infuriated Republicans and others who still nurtured a Revolution-bred hatred of England. At the same time it blighted Franco-American relations. Successive French revolutionary governments were convinced that the Jay Treaty violated the Franco-American treaties of 1778 and that the American government had accepted it against the will of an overwhelming public sentiment. Believing that the bulk of the American people were pro-French even though Washington's Federalist government was pro-English, the French sought to arouse their allies, the American people, to their true interest. This true interest was alliance with France and disassociation with England, America's natural enemy and France's major antagonist in war since February, 1793.

To arouse the American people in defense of the 1778 alliance the French Directory in June, 1795, sent to the United States a new minister, a young man in his early thirties, Pierre Auguste Adet. To the French the Jay Treaty created an intimate alliance between the United States and France's worst enemy. In Adet's instructions, therefore, the idea that the treaty violated the French alliance stood out as the foremost grievance against the Washington administration.

Despite French anger, and despite Adet's attempts to prevent ratification, the Senate approved the Jay Treaty eleven days after Adet had landed in Philadelphia. Two months later, while Adet continued his efforts to kill it, Washington ratified the treaty. England accepted the ratified treaty and in April, 1796, after a long, last-ditch battle in which Adet used all the influence he could muster against the treaty, the House of Representatives voted funds to implement it. To Adet as to other Frenchmen this meant the end of the 1778 alliance and another triumph for England and English gold.

Not knowing that Washington already had decided to retire from the presidency, Adet now saw the overthrow of Washington and his Federalist administration as the only salvation for the 1778 alliance. Adet and the French Directory viewed the Washington administration as the captive of English policy; to save the alliance it had to be replaced by a pro-French Republican administration. Charles Delacroix, French foreign minister, advocated inciting an uprising against Washington to break the Jay Treaty and to invigorate the alliance. Thomas Jefferson, he believed, would replace Washington and thus France would command the influence in the United States which she deserved. Prospects for the defeat of Washington were good, he believed, since the President, once the idol of the American people, had become to some an object of scorn and even hatred as the result of the Jay Treaty; already the journals attacked him, his principles, and his conduct.

Taking into account what it conceived to be the temper of American popular opinion, and with the objective of destroying English influence in the United States and salvaging the 1778 alliance, the French government intervened actively in the presidential election of 1796. Through Adet and other French officials in the United States the Directory openly supported the Republican party and wherever possible attacked the Federalist party. French intervention in the election became, therefore, one of the main issues in the campaign of 1796. The fate of the alliance hung on the outcome of the election.

The decision of the Directory to intervene in the 1796 election, while a decisive factor, contributed but one element to the complex politics of the election. Domestic issues and the Jay Treaty itself contributed others. Final acceptance of the treaty plunged Franco-American relations to their lowest depths since independence and marked a great political triumph for Federalists. Yet to Republicans all hope of ultimately defeating the treaty did not appear lost. Seeing the extent of the Jay Treaty's unpopularity, Republican leaders believed that it would make an excellent campaign issue in the 1796 election as an unrivaled party rallying point for national sentiment. Thomas Jefferson, James Madison, and other party leaders believed that popular opinion remained still largely pro-French and anti-British. Being politicians they reacted logically. Their party had ready-made national issues; they had only to exploit them properly and victory would be theirs. Republicans, consequently, carried over into the election of 1796 their campaign against the Jay Treaty and the pro-British "system" of Alexander Hamilton.

Granted the logic and appeal of the Republican campaign plan, a towering obstacle—the person and prestige of George Washington—stood in the way of success, as was clear to the French. So deep was the impression Washington had made on fellow Americans that to attack him would be to risk injuring the attacker. Twice he had been chosen president without a dissenting vote. Had he so desired he could undoubtedly have held office for a third term, for, as a foreign observer remarked, "there is a Magic in his name more powerful in this Country than the Abilities of any other man." No man, moreover, was better aware of this than Jefferson. "Republicanism," he advised, "must lie on it's [sic] oars, resign the vessel to it's pilot [Washington], and themselves to the course he thinks best for them."

Despite Washington's great political strength the situation in 1796 was far different from 1789 and 1792; Washington probably could have had a third term, but not by unanimous choice. In political battles over neutrality, the Jay Treaty, and other issues, he had divested himself of nonpartisanship. To Republicans and Francophiles the guise of being above party and of working for the welfare of the nation as a whole, in view of his intimate connections with his Federalist subordinates and his consistent practice of acting in accord with their principles, appeared the sheerest hypocrisy. In town and country some men now spat at the mention of his name, denounced him as a monocrat and an Anglomaniac, and prayed for his removal from office. Washington in 1796 had become a central figure in emerging party politics; he was a principal target for the violent personal politics of the time; and to the French he was the main barrier to reactivation of the 1778 alliance.

So bitter was feeling between English and French partisans that domestic issues drifted into relative insignificance. In their conviction that the Federalist administration did not truly represent the American people, the French were encouraged by pro-French partisans among Republicans who indicated that the Federalist government would topple if only France were to take a strong hand. As the election year of 1796 opened, Republicans intensified their attacks against the Federalist administration. The Jay Treaty and the loud cry of aristocracy, monarchy, and plutocracy aroused deep popular emotions. Mutual hatred characterized the two large political segments of the American public.

With his government under fire on both domestic and foreign policy and with himself the target of unrestrained scurrility, Washington found the demands of his office increasingly difficult to endure. Publicly he maintained a dignified silence, but privately he revealed the strain. Even he had come to see that the myth of nonpartisanship was shattered, and that his concept of an administration above party and the tumult of politics had been illusory. Foreign relations had exploded the myth while serving as a catalyst in the formation of national political parties. This was an issue capable of transforming the opposing local alliances of Federalist and anti-Federalist into integrated national parties—an emotional foreign policy issue capable of capturing public imagination in a way which abstruse problems of finance could not.

Despite his increasing distaste for the office and the increasing speculation about his not wishing to be a candidate for a third term, the President remained silent as to future plans. Leaders of both political parties, however, had little doubt that he would not run. "He gave me intimations enough," asserted John Adams, "that his reign would be very short." Early in 1796, and even before, both parties had laid tentative plans which did not include Washington as a candidate.

The attacks on Washington grew increasingly bitter during the year. Opponents charged that he had betrayed a solemn pledge to France by destroying the French alliance. Personal attacks accused him of taking more salary than was allotted him. His mail was tampered with for political advantage, and forged letters of 1777 were refurbished and printed as genuine. Particularly cutting was Tom Paine's bitter attack from Paris, which city was the source, Federalists were convinced, of the anti-Washington campaign. Jefferson, too, had lost patience with the exalted role of Washington. The President, he wrote, like Samson had had his head "shorn by the harlot England."

Despite pressures to stay and ride out the storm, Washington disclosed in May, 1796, that he intended definitely to retire. If he had nurtured at all the desire to seek a third term it was killed by the acid criticism to which he had been subjected. The President decided not to seek a third term not only because he sought retirement in his old age but also because he was disgusted with the abuse from political opponents. "The true cause of the general's retiring," declared one of his staunchest supporters, "was . . . *the loss of popularity* which he had experienced, and the further loss which he apprehended from the rupture with France, which he looked upon as inevitable."

Once the decision to retire was made, Washington turned to Hamilton, as usual, for advice. When, he asked, would be the best time for publication of his farewell to the nation? Hamilton, with his eye on the coming election, advised that the public announcement be held off as long as possible. "The proper period now for your declaration," wrote Hamilton, "seems to be *Two months* before the time for the Meeting of the Electors. This will be sufficient. The parties will in the meantime electioneer conditionally, that is to say, *if you decline*; for a serious opposition to you will I think hardly be risked."

Three months before the gathering of electors Washington announced to the nation his intention to retire. Although in 1792 he had planned a valedictory to the nation and James Madison had drafted one, the September, 1796, version, in which Hamilton's hand was prominent, became a piece of partisan politics directed specifically against Republicans and Francophiles who had made Washington's last years miserable. At the time, it was recognized for what it was: a political manifesto, a campaign document. The 1792 version, drawn up before popular passions had been stirred by the war in Europe, did not, for example, stress politics nor did it touch on foreign affairs. In the 1796 version partisan politics and foreign affairs were central.

Washington's specific target in foreign affairs, heartily seconded by Hamilton, was the alliance with France. He struck at Adet's partisan activities, at French meddling in American politics (while passing over British meddling), and at the allegedly dangerous implications of the French alliance. Washington told Hamilton that had it not been for the status of "party disputes" and of foreign affairs he would not have considered it necessary to revise his valedictory. He was convinced that a warning to the nation was necessary to combat foreign (French) intrigue "in the internal concerns of our country." It is indeed easy "to foresee," he warned, "that it may involve us in disputes and finally in War, to fulfill political alliances." This was the crux of the matter; Washington believed that the French alliance was no longer an asset to the country.

Washington's valedictory trumpeted the Federalist answer to Republican accusations that the administration had sold the country to the British; it countered the anti-administration furor over the Jay Treaty; it was a justification and defense of his policies. As such it was designed and as such it became the opening blast in the presidential campaign, contrived to prevent the election of Thomas Jefferson. The Farewell laid the basis for Federalist strategy of using Washington's great prestige to appeal to patriotism, as against the evil of foreign machinations, to make "Federalist" and "patriot" synonyms in the minds of the electorate. Under the banner of patriotism the Farewell spearheaded the attack on the opposition party and on French diplomacy.

In the address Washington opened with the announcement that he would not be a candidate for a third term and then stressed the advantages of union and the evils of political parties. Having in mind, undoubtedly, the French Republic, he advised against "a passionate attachment of one Nation for another." Such "sympathy for the favorite nation," he warned, leads to wars and quarrels "without adequate inducement or justification." Then followed the oft-quoted "Great rule of conduct" that with foreign nations we should have "as little *political* connection as possible." While stressing fidelity to "already formed engagements," he announced that " 'tis our true policy to steer clear of permanent Alliances with any portion of the foreign world." Washington deplored the growth of political opposition, chastised the public for its attachment to France, and concluded with a defense of his foreign policy, particularly his much criticized policy of neutrality which was based on the Proclamation of April 22, 1793. He called this the "index" to his plan or policy.

Although cloaked in phrases of universal or timeless application, the objectives of the address were practical, immediate, and partisan. Men often attempt to rationalize their partisan political views in pronouncements studded with timeless patriotic appeals; so it was with Washington and Hamilton. The valedictory bore directly on the coming election, on the French alliance, and on the status of Franco-American relations in general.

While expressed cogently and linked forever with Washington's name, the main ideas and foreign policy principles of the Farewell were not unique with either Hamilton or Washington. They were prevalent Federalist ideas on current foreign policy and politics, and can be found expressed in various ways in the polemical literature of the time. The concept of no entanglement with Europe, for instance, was a common one among Federalists and others. More often than not it was a universalized reaction against a specific annoyance—the French alliance. Stated as non-involvement with Europe an attack against the alliance had great psychological appeal. In time this specific meaning was lost and only the generalization remained.

As partisans had expected, Washington's words stoked an already hot political situation. "It will serve as a signal," exclaimed New England Federalist Fisher Ames, "like dropping a hat, for the party racers to start." The Farewell was indeed soon under partisan attack. Washington's advice for the future, taunted William Duane, "is but a defence for the past." Referring to the warning against "permanent alliances," he exclaimed, "this extraordinary advice is fully exemplified in your departure from the spirit and principle of the treaty with France, which was declared to be permanent, and exhibits this very infidelity you reprobate in a most striking and lamentable light." The President had not, Duane continued, "adhered to that rigid and neutral justice which you profess—every concession to Britain in prejudice of France was a deviation from neutrality." Much of the evil which Washington attributed to faction, he claimed, came from the Federalist party. "Your examples of party influence are uniformly drawn from occasions wherein your personal opinions, your pride and passions, have been involved." As to Washington's advice to steer clear of permanent alliances, why, critics asked, was it unwise to extend the nation's political engagements? Was not the Jay Treaty a political connection, practically an alliance with England?

To James Madison—who earlier had feared that under Hamilton's influence the address would become a campaign document—the valedictory confirmed his assumptions; it was all politics. Under the complete influence of the British faction, Madison wrote, Washington obviously sought to destroy the French alliance. "It has been known," he continued, "that every channel has been latterly opened that could convey to his mind a rancor against that country [France] and suspicion of all who are thought to sympathize with its revolution and who support the policy of extending our commerce and in general of standing well with it. But it was not easy to suppose his mind wrought up to the tone that could dictate or rather adopt some parts of the performance."

Minister Adet believed wrongly that the address would arouse the indignation of pro-French "patriots" and would not have the effect on the people that the British faction hoped it would. He consequently plunged into the campaign to see to it that the address would not have its intended effect. Looking upon John Adams as an enemy of France and a friend of England, he electioneered brazenly for Jefferson. The future conduct of France toward America, he made clear to Americans, would be governed by the election's outcome.

Beginning at the end of October and timing himself carefully, Adet began publication of a series of public manifestoes designed to influence the electorate. He conjured up the prospect of war with France, stressing that Jefferson's election would eliminate such a possibility. With the Quakers of Pennsylvania, Federalists lamented, Adet's strategy of fear worked. Fearing a Federalist-sponsored war against France, Quakers cast their votes for Republicans. "French influence never appeared so open and unmasked as at this city [Philadelphia] election," cried William Loughton Smith, Hamilton's congressional mouthpiece. "French flags, French cockades were displayed by the Jefferson party and there is no doubt that French money was not spared. . . . In short there never was so barefaced and disgraceful an interference of a foreign power in any free country."

Adet's procedure was to write an official note to the Secretary of State and then to send a copy for publication to Benjamin Bache's Philadelphia *Aurora*. In his note of October 27, for example, he protested against American foreign policy and appealed to the people to renew their friendship with France by disavowing the Jay Treaty and honoring the French alliance. A few days later (November 5) the pages of the *Aurora* carried Adet's second manifesto, dubbed by Federalists the "cockade proclamation." In the name of the Directory it called on all Frenchmen in the United States—in the land of an ally—to mount the tricolored cockade, symbol of liberty. Those who did not so give public evidence of their support of the French Republic were to be denied the services of French consuls and the protection of the French flag. Immediately the tricolored cockade blossomed in the streets. Americans as well as Frenchmen wore it as a badge of devotion to the French cause. It became, in short, a symbol of Republicanism.

Ten days later Adet followed the "cockade proclamation" with his last and most florid note, which he again sent simultaneously to the Secretary of State and to Bache's *Aurora*. In it he announced that as a result of the Jay Treaty his function as minister had been suspended and that he was returning to France. Adet had timed his announcement so that it might have a maximum political influence, particularly on the electors who were soon to meet to choose Washington's successor.

Adet's notes and Secretary of State Timothy Pickering's replies were used as campaign ammunition by both sides. Federalists, of course, were furious. They denounced Adet's pronouncements for what they were—brazen electioneering maneuvers by a foreign agent. John Adams, against whom the last note was directed, found it "an instrument well calculated to reconcile me to private life. It will purify me from all envy of Mr. Jefferson, or Mr. Pinckney, or Mr. Burr, or Mr. any body who may be chosen President or Vice President."

William Cobbett, violent Francophobe and anti-Jeffersonian, published Adet's note under the title of *The Gros Mousqueton Diplomatique; or Diplomatic Blunderbuss.* He ran with it, of course, an adverse commentary.

Friends of France, according to Adet, were delighted. Republican leaders were willing and even eager to use the issue of the French alliance to gain votes. But, contrary to Adet's opinion, they were not happy with the French minister's personal interference. Madison, for instance, maintained that Adet's note announcing his return to France worked "all the evil with which it is pregnant." Its indiscretions, he added, gave comfort to Federalists who had the "impudence" to point out that it was "an electioneering maneuver," and that "the French government had been led into it by the opponents of the British treaty."

Adet did not realize that his activities worked mainly to injure the cause he sought to aid. French popularity, according to competent observers, decreased as a result. Disgusted by Adet's conduct, Washington drew even closer to the British. One piqued New England writer went so far as to declare that since Adet's electioneering on behalf of Jefferson "there is not an elector on this side of the Delaware that would not be sooner shot than vote for him." And Philip Key maintained that Adet's meddling "irretrievably diminished that good will felt for his Government & the people of France by most people here."

Unaware of any adverse reaction, Adet and his intimates believed that his actions and the Directory's measures would influence the presidential electors decisively in favor of Jefferson. What Adet and the Directory had not taken into account was that invariably when a foreign diplomat takes sides openly in the domestic politics of the nation to which he is accredited he makes the party leader he seeks to aid appear to be the pawn of a foreign government. Such a charge, whether or not true, gives the opposition the opportunity of patriotically denouncing foreign interference and of posing as the defender of national honor against foreign subversives. So it was with the Adet case. His activities seemed to confirm the very warnings of foreign interference that were stressed in Washington's Farewell Address.

Sensing the opportunity, Federalists attacked the French alliance, denounced French domestic interference, and pitted the patriotism of Washington and Adams against the Jacobin-tainted Republican campaign. Voters were importuned to beware of foreign influence; to "decide between the address of the President and the [French]"; to follow Washington's counsel. Adet and the Directory, they were told, wished to draw the nation into war and to sever the western from the Atlantic states. No doubt clouded the Federalist mind; the Union was in danger.

Federalist warnings, persistent though they were, did not stop French interference in American politics; nor did the interference end with the choosing of electors in November. Few of the electors were pledged to a specific candidate, so the campaign continued with increasing tumult until December 7, when the electors cast their ballots. Adet, having suspended his diplomatic functions, remained in Philadelphia to continue his anti-administration campaign. He and the Republicans hammered at similar themes, stressing that if Adams were elected the errors of the Washington administration would be continued, since Adams was committed to Washington's tragic policies; and that such policies would lead to war with France.

Candidate Adams, on the other hand, believed that only time would tell whether "the French Directory have only been drawn in to favor the election of a favorite, or whether in their trances and delirium of victory they think to terrify America, or whether in their sallies they may not venture on hostilities." He advised that under the circumstances "Americans must be cool and steady if they can."

But Americans were not cool and steady. In newspapers and elsewhere they debated the French alliance, the mounting crisis with France, and the possibility of war. Hamilton, as was his practice in time of crisis, wrote articles for the press to reply to Adet's manifestoes, to defend administration foreign policy, and to attack the French alliance. Another prominent Federalist, Noah Webster, editor of the *American Minerva*, wrote a series of articles in which he also attacked the alliance. His articles were reprinted and widely circulated. In the Federalist press, in fact, attacks on the alliance now became common. Webster in his article stressed that France had equated the term ally with that of vassal; "an *open* enemy," he declared, "is less dangerous than an *insidious friend*." Although the British, too, had injured the United States, Webster maintained that the American connection with Great Britain was stronger than the French alliance because "our connection with her is solely *an alliance of interest*. This is the true basis of all national connections. We are therefore in no danger from Great Britain."

In the first week of February, 1797, the American people finally learned the results of the election. Although the Federalist victory was narrow, it was enough to sink French hopes for a revived alliance. By "three votes" John Adams, who wisely had perceived that he was "not enough of an Englishman, nor little enough of a Frenchman, for some people," was elected second president of the United States.

Jefferson, however, captured the second highest electoral total and became vice-president. America's first contested presidential election therefore, although a clear-cut Federalist victory, gave some comfort to Republicans and struck fear into Federalist ranks. But Republican strength had not been sufficient to overturn the government and hence to reverse the course of Franco-American relations. To staunch Hamiltonian Federalists this aspect of the election was indeed sweet. In various election post-mortems, in New England in particular, such Federalists rejoiced that the "French party is fallen," and that the French alliance was at last valueless. Even Adet, one of them pointed out, "avows, and it is rather a tough point to avow, that our treaty is disadvantageous." Now he might inform the Directory that it has "been deceived by the revolutionary Americans in Paris; that we (at least the Yankees) have not been traitors, and have ceased to be dupes."

With the Federalist victory, narrow though it was, the Farewell Address had done its work. The French alliance which had been drawn to last "forever" and which had been the core of American foreign policy when Washington launched the federal government was practically dead as he prepared to leave office. Despite French and Republican efforts to the contrary, and in large part because of the impact of Washington's Farewell, the basic foreign policy orientation of the United States remained pro-British. The Farewell Address now belonged to posterity and posterity has given it meanings to fit its own problems.

Mr. Jefferson in 1801

Marshall Smelser

Thomas Jefferson—author of the Virginia statute on religious freedom, founder of the University of Virginia, and architect of the Declaration of Independence—was in many ways a political philosopher without a doctrine. Despite what the late Marshall Smelser of the University of Notre Dame calls "a monumental Jeffersonian mythology which makes him out a doctrinaire democrat," the essential Jefferson was of adaptable thought and character. As Mr. Smelser would have it, our understanding of Mr. Jefferson has been too much drawn in terms of Alexander Hamilton. Jefferson has traditionally served as a convenient "liberal" foil for the "conservative" dogmas of Hamilton. Thomas Jefferson was more moderate than radical, and he was motivated more by what he saw as the public good than by any set of political ideas.

At least we know what he looked like. He was tall and slender, framed of large, loosely shackled bones. His clothes, including a cherished scarlet vest and a pair of run-over slippers, never seemed quite to fit. He struck one observer as a man who was all ends and angles. A Federalist senator, William Plumer of New Hampshire, on calling at the White House, mistook him for "a servant" and carefully noted that he wore a dirty shirt. The senator was fair-minded enough to record the wearing of a clean shirt at a dinner some time later.

Mr. Jefferson's usual manner was good-humored, even sunny, although occasionally abstracted or cynical. His disposition fitted a country squire whose excellent health and enviable digestion gave him a lifelong euphoria, interrupted only by periodic headaches and occasional rheumatic twinges. He had the typical complexion of the freckled gray-eyed Celt. His hair was cut short and powdered. Its color we know, because a correspondent saluted him in a letter, carefully preserved by the recipient, as "You red-headed son of a bitch."

His small talk was built as loosely as his lounging body. Although often brilliant, his conversation was usually rambling and diffuse. It might range from weather and crops to the ingenuity of the Senate in finding excuses to recess during the local race meetings. Following the ponies was a lesser vice than dice; it gave the gentlemen "time for reflection," as he put it, between investments of their risk capital.

That was the exterior Jefferson as seen by the casual caller, but his personality had layers like an onion. His intimate friends knew the next layer, his family knew the third, but no one except God and Thomas Jefferson knew what lay farther inside this sensitive, unsentimental violinist, bird-watcher, and horticulturist. We do know that forgiveness of his enemies did not come to him easily.

He broke the precedent of delivering messages orally to the Congress, which was set by George Washington and carried on by John Adams. Jefferson sent his messages to Capitol Hill to be read by a clerk. He said it was to save time, but we know he hated to speak in public, and he was only entirely at ease in the company of kinfolk, artists, savants, and a few Republican leaders. Margaret Bayard Smith, daughter of a warm Federalist and wife of the Republican editor of the new *National Intelligencer*, expected to meet a fanatical boor. To her surprise he was "so meek and mild, yet dignified in his manners, with a voice so soft and low, with a countenance so benignant and intelligent. . . ." But Anthony Merry, the British minister, and his wife did not think the President so dignified and benignant. When Jefferson, lacking a hostess, disregarded all protocol at state dinners, saying "pele-mele is our law," they felt literally degraded and quit coming to the White House. The Spanish minister joined the banquet boycott.

The absence of the diplomatic corps was not of first importance. To Jefferson the dinner party—particularly the stag dinner party—was a principal domestic political tool. Inviting not more than a dozen legislators at a time, he managed to get through the whole list more than once a session. The groups were chosen for compatibility. He seated them at a round table where he would be only first among equals and where private conversations would be difficult. He served his guests himself from a dumb-waiter to preclude the presence of eavesdropping servants. His French chef has been rated highly and his cellar must have been superb. Never dominating the conversation, he guided it away from the shoptalk in which congressmen found themselves already too much immersed, and planted the seeds of his political philosophy by indirection, letting his charm and his menu carry things along. The diplomatic corps knew well enough what he was doing, since it was the customary procedure of European courts, but to the political community in the raw new capital it seems to have been dazzling, and it showed Thomas Jefferson at his guileful best in the tactics of politics.

The contrast between his manner with Mrs. Smith across a tea table and his treatment of the diplomatic corps makes clear the split between his private life and his public bearing as the chief of state of a democratic republic. In private, the gentle introvert; in public matters, the incarnation of a stormy nation of freemen, willing to provoke contention, even though he found controversy painful. When relaxed with friends or family, his simple carriage was obviously not the way of a clod, but was more the manner of a negligent, self-assured nobleman, correctly confident of his status and of his own good taste. Yet, in a conference on the public's business, a senator could notice his "stiff gentility or lofty gravity."

It seems very unlikely that such an undramatic and diffident man, whose charm was felt only in private, could have reached the White House in any later generation. His merits were publicized only by his friends. Not for him was the alley fighting of ballot politics. Once he warned his grandson to avoid two kinds of disputants: self-assured young intellectuals with more confidence than knowledge, and bad-tempered, passionate politicians—these latter needed "medical more than moral counsel."

Now peel down to the third layer. There one sees a homesick widower with chronic money troubles, yearning for his children and his grandchildren. His was a great career but rarely a happy life. Between 1772 and 1782, four of his six children died. In 1781 a British army devastated his farm, and the difficulties of his term as governor of Virginia left a faint smear on his reputation. Then in 1782 Mrs. Jefferson died. At the age of forty his life had become a vacuum. It is almost enough to explain his later career to say that political, scientific, and intellectual projects rushed into his vacant soul to fill that vacuum and to make him the man we remember instead of the reclusive squire he wished to be. His two surviving daughters married young. One, Polly Jefferson Eppes, died in childbirth. He had a brief hope of something approaching normal family life when both of his sons-in-law were elected to the House of Representatives, but each of the girls was advanced in pregnancy and dared not risk the rigors of travel to Washington.

After assuming the debts of his father-in-law, his personal finances were forever out of control. In old age he owed $107,000. When his daughters married, there was nothing left for him to take pleasure in except the talk of his intellectual friends, and the forty years of building and rebuilding Palladian Monticello. What he liked about Washington was that it lay between Monticello and "The American Philosophical Society Held at Philadelphia for the Diffusion of Useful Knowledge."

II

All men claim to be Jeffersonians today. It is doubtful whether the study of any other public man in our national story has been equally absorbing to so many minds. Jefferson's popularity has reached its zenith since 1920. The published evaluations differ so widely that they tell us more about their writers than about Jefferson. There is so much to see, so much to understand about this man of many flashing facets that it requires more self-discipline than most students have been willing to exercise in order to get the emphases in the right places. He would, perhaps, be easier to understand except for the monument of literary evidence he left us—fifty thousand items, dated from 1760 to 1826, one of the richest left by any man. It has not yet been completely mastered.

Thomas Jefferson's work has been scrutinized and searched not so much for understanding as to justify positions which often contradict each other. As the pendulum of public favor swings from generation to generation, he and Alexander Hamilton exchange the roles of Saint Michael and Lucifer. Laissez faire, states' rights, isolationism, agrarianism, rationalism, civil liberty, and constitutional democracy have all been fiercely defended by the use of quotations from Jefferson's writings, regardless of context. On a more sophisticated level of scholarship, professors drub each other with Jeffersonian tags to prove mutually exclusive generalizations. To get all of the academic theorizers under Jefferson's roof, we must label him the Agrarian Commercial Industrial Democratic Federalist. Fortunately for the history of the republic, the Jeffersonian administration, because of its optimistic evaluation of the public's common sense, was keen on explaining everything to the people. The wholly public business, despite the inner personal subtleties and complexities of the leaders, was very well documented, although one must read the public statements with the usual disciplined skepticism.

III

Nothing that promised the ultimate physical or moral improvement of mankind was alien to the polygonal mind of Thomas Jefferson. With the Adamses and Woodrow Wilson he was one of the four most intellectual of the Presidents of the United States, and he and Wilson are still the objects of hero worship by some Americans. His own heroes were Francis Bacon, Isaac Newton, and John Locke, a "trinity of the three greatest men the world had ever produced." His nominal occupations were farmer and lawyer. He was close to being a true scientist of agriculture, and he was a much more active and successful lawyer, at least up to 1771, when public affairs began to take more and more of his time, than has been generally known.

He mastered Greek and Latin before he was eighteen. Thereafter his reading revolved around the classical authors like a wheel around its hub. Because so few of us nowadays know the classics, we miss much in his mind. He not only knew Greek but he tried to reform its pronunciation by an essay in which he leaned more toward eighteenth-century Greek pronunciation than toward the Italian style then in vogue. He spoke French and Italian, although not fluently, and he had looked into, and had some acquaintance with, forty Indian languages. He also tried to reform the spelling of English. Although he was surely a first-rate writer of his own language, he thought of himself only as a discriminating reader. Omnivorous would be as good an adjective as discriminating. By 1794 he could honestly say he had the best library in the United States. Its 6,500 volumes, all of them collected since a fire destroyed his first library in 1770, formed the nucleus of the Library of Congress.

He must have been a pretty fair violinist or he could not have endured to practice as much as he did, and he certainly has won praise as an architect, but his attitude toward the arts was the attitude of his age. Artists were craftsmen who succeeded if their works pleasantly filled the leisure of the connoisseur by giving him something animating, interesting, attractive to contemplate. Jefferson would not have understood the phrase "art for art's sake," nor could he have approved of the self-appointed Great Tormented Souls who floridly dominated the next generation's lush romanticism.

Thomas Jefferson was more inclined toward science than toward politics. He knew more of applied science, and he knew more scientists, than any of his American contemporaries. He was *the* American agricultural student of his day. For forty-seven years he belonged to the American Philosophical Society; for nearly twenty years he was its president and may have contributed more to its greatness than Benjamin Franklin. Not only was his *Notes on the State of Virginia* (1784–85) a respectable contribution, but his stimulation of the researches of other men, for example, Lewis and Clark, is an influence still felt. His scientific methods will still pass close scrutiny. If the Revolution had failed, and if he had escaped the gallows, he would probably have been barred from public life; in the seclusion of Albemarle County, Virginia, he likely would have become the father of American agricultural chemistry.

Early in life he lost his faith, but not his morals; nevertheless, he had his children baptized in the Anglican Church, attended Anglican services, and had all of his relatives buried according to the Anglican rites. In Pennsylvania, he was Unitarian; in Virginia, Episcopalian; and in the District of Columbia, who-knows-what. He ended as a deist after enduring a lifetime of fierce, intemperate, even slanderous attacks on his infidelity from many who became Unitarians, that is, deists, themselves. According to his home-made theology, Saint Paul corrupted Christianity to prove Christ divine. Better, he said, that men should apply reason to the Book of Nature in order to discover the laws of God.

This remarkable virtuoso, nationally honored for the virtues of the intellect before the time of the establishment of the federal government, was a talented connoisseur of all the arts. In some he had a taste and dexterity which approached professional standards. He was neither pure scientist nor pure philosopher.

IV

Thomas Jefferson's prefederal political career was the career of a man who hated contention, who was better at counsel than at execution, who was better in committee than on the floor. As the scribe of Independence he had drawn together the feelings of his fellow countrymen into superb but prudently circumscribed prose. He gained no glory as revolutionary governor of Virginia and, indeed, barely escaped the censure of the Virginia legislature at the end of his term. The famous legislative reforms in Virginia, which were enacted under his leadership, were merely reforms of the squirearchy.

His mild and conversationally uncontentious liberalism, and his diplomatic experience as minister to France, made him seem the natural choice for Secretary of State in President George Washington's new administration. Jefferson accepted the appointment reluctantly and assumed the office in March, 1790. At that moment in the story, the President and the Secretary were cordial friends, but their relations chilled in the late 1790's. When the new Secretary of State came to New York, he was walking on to a political battlefield. He did not take a place in the array immediately. Indeed, as late as 1792, he still recoiled from direct political action.

An opposition had emerged in the Congress, led by Representative James Madison of Virginia. It was hotly opposed to the Treasury policies of Alexander Hamilton. Madison and John Beckley, the Clerk of the House, carried the anti-administration banner. From early 1791 they had Jefferson's sympathy, but he did not create their faction. It recognized and claimed him as its leader. Not until 1796, during the fierce wrangle over the Jay Treaty, did Jefferson become the public partisan head of anti-Federalism. The notion that Jefferson founded the opposition was an invention of the Hamiltonians, to suit their short-range vote-getting purposes.

True, Jefferson disapproved of Hamilton's policies because Hamilton influenced the Congress to favor finance and commerce over farming. By late 1792 he was so stirred that he could describe Hamilton's career to the uneasy Washington as "a tissue of machinations against the liberty of the country," but the explanation of the history of the Federalist period as a struggle between Jefferson and Hamilton is useful only as what Broadus Mitchell called "a sociological shorthand." It was Madison and Beckley who organized the group that later made Jefferson its idol. The squire of Monticello has been sketched as a shadowy *provocateur* from 1790 to 1795, holding other men's coats while they smote the enemy in the public prints, but this picture too is a Hamiltonian caricature. Only twice did Jefferson urge men to take up their quills and stab Hamilton, and in each instance it was in a public debate on a question of deep importance. Jefferson was always available at the elbows of the front-rank anti-Hamiltonians, but he did not march in public. The famous liberal sentiments which are so venerated by modern democrats were—after 1776—all written in private letters, not for publication. Even during the campaign of 1800 he stayed at Monticello to supervise the baking of bricks, while letting his political views filter out to the public through letters to his friends.

Thomas Jefferson was never a flaming radical. His environment made it impossible, although there is a monumental Jeffersonian mythology which makes him out a doctrinaire democrat. In truth, he believed in getting what seemed best for the public good with as little painful acrimony and criticism as possible. He had no oratorical talent as a crowd pleaser and he never made a speech that brought cheers. The energy and admiration of his friends, not his own qualities of leadership, put him in the White House.

If the French Revolution had not caused a recanvass of fundamental libertarian principles, he and his supporters probably could not have pulled off the electoral coup of 1800. Nor was his election a victory for infidel rationalism. It was the counterattack of theologically conservative farmers against the Federalists' aristocratic contempt for America's sunburned agricultural drudges. They thought they were voting for electors, or assemblymen who would choose electors, who would favor Thomas Jefferson, a Whiggish moderate, whose only controversial publications had been the Declaration of Independence and the Virginia Statute for Religious Freedom long, long before. And they were right.

James Madison and His Times

Irving Brant

Americans are prone to see history from Jefferson's presidency to that of Andrew Jackson as an obscure interlude in American political development, filled only by vague images of the continuing "Virginia Dynasty"—the presidencies of Jefferson, Madison, and Monroe. Despite its indistinct flavor, however, the period produced its share of myths. Specifically, the late Irving Brant, biographer of James Madison and free-lance historian, proposes that myths surround James Madison and his times. Positing a favorable interpretation of the "Father of the Constitution," Mr. Brant seeks to temper former preconceptions generated both by historians and by what he sees as "the distorting shadows of political prejudice." Long overshadowed by the imposing figure of Thomas Jefferson, James Madison emerges as a significant governmental administrator in his own right. Rather than the "errand boy" of Jefferson, Madison was more often a positive force well-attuned to developing political realities.

In a recently published magazine article on the life portraits of James Madison, the following statement is quoted from the biographer of Charles Wilson Peale: "Peale painted Jefferson in December, 1791. He tried to paint 'coming men' for his gallery, and in selecting them relied mostly on the advice of those whose judgment he trusted. It is a fairly safe supposition that Jefferson recommended Madison for this honor."[1]

Why should it be assumed that Jefferson was the one who recommended Madison? The Philadelphia painter had many contacts with Frenchmen. Might he not have heard that French Minister Luzerne, seven years earlier, had described Madison as the foremost member of the Continental Congress?[2] Could he not have heard, from almost anybody in public life, that Madison was at least the godfather of the new Constitution? As a Philadelphian, Peale might have heard the complaint of Senator Maclay of Pennsylvania in 1789 that Madison "already affects to govern" President Washington.[3] The recommendation might even have come from Madison's principal adversary in Congress, Fisher Ames, who wrote of him in that same year: "He is our first man."[4]

From "James Madison and His Times," by Irving Brant, in *American Historical Review*, Vol. 57 (July 1952), pp. 853–870. Reprinted by permission of the American Historical Association.

In rejecting the supposition that Madison needed sponsorship in 1791, I do not mean to disparage Mr. Sellers, the author of the very excellent life of Peale. The biographer of an artist, when he deals with statesmen, naturally relies on the verdicts of historians and political biographers. Why should he not suppose that Jefferson was responsible for Madison's inclusion in the portrait gallery, when everything else in his life—his education, his political and constitutional opinions, his career in public office; everything you can think of, except, perhaps, his birth—has been placed to Jefferson's credit? In making this comment, I should at once point out some conspicuous exceptions. There is nothing like this in Dumas Malone's life of Jefferson, nor in Miss Koch's studies of the philosophy and letters of Jefferson and Madison. I might add that according to some reports, Douglass Adair's doctoral thesis at Yale was so favorable to Madison that it almost paralyzed some of the examining professors.

Pick out at random a dozen histories of the double decade ending in 1800. In how many of them will you find a factual basis for the statements of Luzerne and Fisher Ames? In how many will you find that Madison laid the foundations of the Democratic party, by his opposition to Hamilton's funding system, while Jefferson was still on his way from the American legation in France to the cabinet of President Washington? In how many will you learn that, as late as 1795, Federalists in Congress were calling their opponents "the Madisonians"?[5]

For an example of the way history has been perverted to support a preconception, consider this extract from Beveridge's *Life of Marshall*, dealing with events of 1793: "Jefferson was keeping pace with the anti-Nationalist sentiment of the masses—drilling his followers into a sternly ordered political force. 'The discipline of the [Republican] party,' wrote Ames, 'is as severe as the Prussian.' "[6]

Compare that with what Ames actually wrote: ". . . the discipline of the party is as severe as the Prussian. Deserters are not spared. Madison is become a desperate party leader, and I am not sure of his stopping at any ordinary point of extremity."[7]

Beveridge, I am sure, did not intend to distort. He merely reshaped the material to fit the distortions of earlier writers. These he brought to a magnificent climax of his own, brilliantly epitomizing a hundred years of error, in the statement that Madison was the valley between the mountain peaks of Jefferson and Hamilton.[8]

To a great extent this impression reflects the interplay of hero and devil worship. Until the American people subscribe to Confucianism, there is no possibility that they will deify James Madison. As long as half of them look upon Jefferson as a god and Hamilton as a devil, while the other half sees them in opposite roles, there is little likelihood of building a really commodious American Pantheon. What has actually happened is that a fairly level Jefferson-Madison-Hamilton plateau has been converted into two mountains and a valley by the unremitting activities of cairn-builders and rock-throwers. Some political geologists are beginning to suspect that this plateau, instead of being depressed in the middle, may originally have had a few bulges upward there.

Disparagement of Madison as a supposed satellite did not begin with historians. It began as a defense mechanism of Federalist politicians. During the formation of the new government, Madison and Hamilton were linked in the public mind. They were the outstanding advocates of the Constitution, and a few close friends knew them as joint authors of the *Federalist.*

When the great political cleavage came, in 1790, it was a direct break between Madison and Hamilton. Madison delivered his opening speech against Hamilton's financial system on February 11, 1790. On that day, in that speech, the wheels of Hamiltonian federalism and Jeffersonian democracy started rolling down the political highway.

Jefferson did not even know this was going on. The debate was over, the vote was taken, the fundamental cleavage in American politics was indelibly recorded, four weeks before he arrived at the capital to enter Washington's cabinet. Now that implied no defect in Jefferson's principles or in his perception. It was no reflection on him that a letter telling him of Hamilton's report on public credit took nineteen days to reach Monticello.[9] But there were reasons, deep in human nature, why neither Federalists nor Jeffersonians could admit that Madison laid the cornerstone of the Democratic party and continued to be an independent, creative force in its development.

During the ensuing years, it became apparent that between Jefferson and Madison there existed perfect harmony of feeling and a close correspondence of political views. Each time the basic issue arose in some new form, Madison took the lead in Congress, Jefferson in the cabinet, both working to the same end. The Federalists, tied up with rich speculators, were under constant compulsion to deny the moral flaws in their own position. They must see themselves, they must be seen, as the representatives of morality, intelligence, and respectability. On that score, Madison's opposition was far more distressing than Jefferson's. It was easy to endow Jefferson with diabolical traits, especially after the six years he had spent in Paris, the devil's paradise. But Madison was beyond the reach of ordinary attack. The principal architect of the new Constitution could not be suspected of a malicious desire to tear it down or to ruin the national credit which he had been working for ten years to establish. How could it be explained to the public that a man of his acknowledged wisdom, stability, and integrity was on the wrong side? That proved quite easy. He had gone over to please Jefferson. A good man had been seduced by Satan.

So said Hamilton, though he knew it was not true. So said a hundred others, and believed it.[10] But that was just the beginning. Once this explanation was given, Madison's character had to be reshaped to make it credible. A little earlier, he had been accused of twisting George Washington around his fingers. Jefferson was still in transit when Madison's challenge of the money power inspired a Massachusetts newspaper writer to exclaim: "Happy there is a Madison who fearless of the bloodsuckers will step forward and boldly vindicate the rights of the widows and orphans, the original creditors and the war worn soldier."[11]

Bold? Fearless? That did not fit the new story. What sort of man would change his political convictions to please a friend? Only a soft-willed man, a weak and timid man. So Madison was pictured as the submissive errand boy of Thomas Jefferson, perverting his intellectual genius to political purposes alien to his mind. Federalists dared not admit that Madison had sacrificed his dominant position in Congress, sacrificed his influence over President Washington, for the sake of principle. So they made a double assault—an assault on Jefferson for political immorality and on Madison for weakness and timidity.

The technique of the big lie, the big smear, was not invented in our day. It was brought to perfection against Jefferson and Madison, but with differing results. Madison was admired, for his mental endowments, by friends and foes alike, and he made warm friendships. But he had no political glamour. Jefferson, a symbol as well as a leader of democracy, had personal qualities which made people either worship or hate him. His admirers threw back the slanders against him. Did they likewise reject the perverted picture of Madison? On the contrary they made it their own, and thereby placed Jefferson on a still higher pedestal. So there you had both Federalists and Democrats, for totally different reasons, agreeing on a characterization of Madison which was not only unsupported by the record but was refuted by it at every turn.

At this point historians and biographers took over from the politicians. The big lie became the lasting misconception. The historians had testimony from both sides that Madison drew his ideas from the master of Monticello and did what he was told to do. If everybody said it, it must be true.

Let us see how this operated in the fight over federal assumption of state war debts. The conventional story is that about June 20, 1790, Hamilton and Jefferson made a trade. Jefferson agreed to assumption in exchange for the national capital on the Potomac, and induced Madison, his henchman, to help it through Congress. Apply the chronological test to that story of events in 1790, and what do you get?

March, 1783—Madison, in the Continental Congress, proposed federal assumption of state debts.[12]

July, 1783—Madison proposed a national capital on the Potomac.[13]

February, 1790—Madison spoke against *unqualified* assumption.

March 2—Madison proposed a qualified assumption, which the Hamiltonians rejected.

March 20—Jefferson returned from his diplomatic exile.

June 17—Madison wrote to a friend that to save the whole funding bill from defeat and national credit from destruction, assumption probably would have to be admitted in some form, and the Potomac might show up in the business.

June 20—Hamilton and Madison, brought together by Jefferson on Hamilton's initiative, agreed to a compromise—the national capital on the Potomac, in exchange for qualified assumption, which Madison had offered three months before without a *quid pro quo*.[14]

In other words, both of the basic policies originated with Madison. Both features of the compromise came from him and so did the idea of linking them. All he got out of it was a reputation for weakness and timidity. The valley travailed and brought forth two mountains.

Next came the great conflict over the power to create a national bank. I quote from Beveridge: "Jefferson was already opposing, through the timid but resourceful Madison and the fearless and aggressive Giles, the Nationalist statesmanship of Hamilton. Thus it came about that when Washington asked his cabinet's opinion upon the bill to incorporate the Bank of the United States, Jefferson promptly expressed with all his power the constitutional theory of the Virginia legislature." To this Beveridge affixed a footnote: "and see Madison's argument against the constitutionality of the Bank Act in Annals, 1st Congress, February 2, 1791."[15]

What would have been the effect if Beveridge had omitted the Virginia legislature, which had no more to do with it than the parliament of Timbuktu, and had stated the simple, chronological truth? This was that Madison launched the attack against the national bank on February 2, and Jefferson, thirteen days later, paraphrased Madison's speech in a report to the President. That couldn't be told. It would have ruined a preconception.[16]

Madison was Secretary of State throughout the two Jefferson administrations. You can imagine how contemporary politicians and many historians have treated these eight years. The prevalent practice has been to credit Jefferson with every policy, every action, every document of any importance that came from the State Department. If Madison is mentioned at all, he is the errand boy, the amanuensis, obeying implicitly every order handed to him. One of our standard diplomatic histories does not even mention that Jefferson had a Secretary of State. Another mentions him only once.

Now it happens that a very different appraisal of Madison was recorded in 1806 by a Federalist senator, along with his own conventional one. Senator Plumer of New Hampshire, in his diary, quoted Senator Adair of Kentucky, a Democrat, as saying: "The President [Jefferson] wants nerve—he has not even confidence in himself. For more than a year he has been in the habit of trusting almost implicitly in Mr. Madison. Madison has acquired a complete ascendancy over him." To this the New Hampshire Federalist replied: "I observed that I considered Mr. Madison as an honest man—but that he was too cautious—too fearful and too timid to direct the affairs of the nation."[17]

Here, it would seem, was a sharp challenge to historians, especially to those equipped with the instruments of modern scholarship—in this instance, the writings of Jefferson and Madison and their associates and the diplomatic archives of the United States, Great Britain, France, and Spain. That brings us to Henry Adams, the first historian who tapped these rich sources of information. Adams wrote nine volumes whose effect is to sustain the negative side of both appraisals. His history sustains Senator Adair's conclusion that Jefferson lacked nerve and confidence in himself, and Plumer's opinion that Madison was fearful and timid. Henry Adams leaves it uncertain which of these two weaklings ruled the other, but, employing endless condemnation and an irony far more deadly, he created the impression that between them, in their successive presidencies, they reduced the United States to the depths of national degradation. And what shape was the country in at the end of this period of humiliation? Its area and population, Adams noted, had doubled, and it was on a tidal wave of prosperity and confidence. I quote from his ninth volume:

> These sixteen years set at rest the natural doubts that had attended the nation's birth. . . . Every serious difficulty which seemed alarming to the people of the Union in 1800 had been removed or had sunk from notice in 1816. . . . Not only had the people during these sixteen years escaped from dangers, they had also found the means of supplying their chief needs. . . . The continent lay before them, like an uncovered ore-bed.

That was the economic picture. And the national character? I quote once more from Adams:

> In 1815 for the first time Americans ceased to doubt the path they were to follow. Not only was the unity of the nation established, but its probable divergence from older societies was also well defined. . . . The public seemed obstinate only in believing that all was for the best, as far as the United States were concerned, in the affairs of mankind.[18]

This mighty material and spiritual advance had been brought about, if we may believe Adams, not with the aid of Jefferson and Madison but in spite of their blundering and cowardice. It was the communal product of Mother Nature and the Goddess of Luck, with a little timely assistance from Albert Gallatin, John Armstrong, and John Quincy Adams, Henry's grandfather.

One would suppose that the grotesque inconsistency between Adams' premises and his conclusions would raise suspicion in the minds of his more critical readers. But the magnitude of his research was enough in itself to discourage skeptical inquiry. His conclusions as to Jefferson and Madison were in line with contemporary Federalist verdicts, while the historian himself, though plainly a Federalist in his sympathies, drove away the thought of bias by damning the Essex Junto with a violence he never employed upon the chiefs of administration. So the Adams history has become the accepted classic, virtually unchallenged by historians, biographers, journalists, or statesmen, except in the emotional resentment of admirers of Jefferson. That emotional rebellion, plus the Louisiana Purchase, was enough to lift Jefferson into the lists of great Presidents. Madison was left buried under 750,000 disparaging words, marked with the same stamp of goodness, weakness, timidity, and blundering that was originally placed on him by Federalist politicians to fortify their own self-esteem.

The Adams history, as most people know, is a compendium of documents as well as an interpretation. The factual material has been selected with very little bias, and the interpretations are honest. But isolate the documents from the interpretation and strange results ensue. The documents will support, nay they are likely to demand, a drastically different set of conclusions.

As I read Henry Adams, he was neither partial nor impartial. He was just a solid mass of conditioned reflexes. His Federalist leanings conditioned him against Jefferson and Madison. His family descent conditioned him against every President not named Adams, and against every enemy of President John Adams—against Hamilton and Wolcott, against Pickering and the whole traitorous gang who sabotaged the War of 1812. His life in his father's American embassy during the Civil War conditioned him against British diplomats—against Canning, Castlereagh, and Wellesley. He needed no conditioning against Napoleon and Talleyrand. Among these objects of his dislike, Henry Adams played no favorites. He hit them all whenever their heads came up, and thus achieved the air of magnificent impartiality, with devastating effect upon the capacity of many later historians for independent judgment.

I shall come back to Henry Adams, but first let us pursue a more basic inquiry. Was Madison weak and timid? To what extent was he Jefferson's errand boy, and to what extent did he direct policy, during his eight years as Secretary of State?

The errand-boy assumption runs up against some curious facts. In the summer of 1801, British Chargé d'Affaires Thornton complained to Madison that a certain action by French seamen violated the Anglo-American treaty of 1794. Madison and Jefferson were at their homes in Virginia, and the policy adopted would be put into effect by Gallatin. Madison wrote to Jefferson that the circumstances admitted an easy reply "that the case is not considered as within the purview of the treaty." Jefferson replied that he thought the vessel "must fairly be considered as a prize made on Great Britain to which no shelter is to be given in our ports according to our treaty." But he wanted Madison to feel free to revise this opinion and act as he thought best. Madison wrote at once to Gallatin: "It was readily decided that the treaty of '94 is inapplicable to the case." The President, he said, "has thought, as I do," that the ship should be sent away under a different sanction. And when Madison communicated the decision to Thornton, the British diplomat replied that he found himself "entirely at a loss to comprehend the ground on which the President is pleased to regard the case . . . as in no manner falling within the provisions of the treaty of 1794." Here you have not only an instantaneous reversal of Jefferson's judgment by Madison, but a total concealment from Gallatin and Thornton that there had been any difference of opinion.[19]

There was in fact no basic difference. Thornton was trying to give British prizes a preferred position over French prizes in American ports. Madison realized this. Jefferson did not, but Madison knew that the President would approve in retrospect. This was a minor incident, but consider what it means when applied to Madison's position, character and conduct. Was there weakness? Was there vacillation? Was there timidity? Was there subordination of intellect and will? Was there inferiority of judgment?

Turn now to the most important event and greatest achievement of the Jefferson administration—the Louisiana Purchase. Historians have tried for generations to decide how Louisiana was won. From Henry Adams we hear that Madison invited France to build an empire west of the Mississippi, and that Jefferson had no means of preventing it until the French military downfall in San Domingo made American hostility troublesome to France. "President Jefferson [I quote from Adams] had chiefly reckoned on this possibility as his hope of getting Louisiana; and slight as the chance seemed, he was right."[20] From various other commentators, we hear of the diplomatic skill and relentless pressure of Minister Robert Livingston or of the shrewd and forceful guidance of Jefferson. And we are told by Professor Channing that Napoleon "suddenly . . . threw the province" at the American government, with no credit to anybody else except for catching and holding it.[21] As to Madison, the only question raised would seem to be: Was he an absolute nonentity, or did he surrender to France, failing even to discern, as Jefferson did, that French defeat in San Domingo held the hope of American success?

There can be no doubt that the wiping out of General Leclerc's army, in the war with Toussaint L'Ouverture, was the crucial factor in the cession of Louisiana. It destroyed the fulcrum of French power in the Western Hemisphere. Now let us trace the American attitude toward Leclerc. His army reached San Domingo in February, 1802. He carried instructions which included this sentence: "Jefferson has promised that the instant the French army arrives, all measures will be taken to starve Toussaint and to aid the army."[22]

That promise was made to the French chargé d'affaires, Pichon, in the summer of 1801. Reporting this joyously to his government, Pichon said it relieved him of fears derived from a prior talk with Madison. The Secretary of State, he said, had seemed ready to support Toussaint, and in the same talk had given warning that collision between the United States and France would be inevitable if the latter should take possession of Louisiana from Spain. That, please observe, was in July, 1801, seven months before the French opened their campaign to reconquer San Domingo and nearly two years before Napoleon offered Louisiana to the United States. One month later, Pichon wrote that Madison's San Domingo policy still seemed to be in effect. Six months later he reported that he had complained once more to Jefferson about it, and "I found him very reserved and cold, while he talked to me, though less explicitly, in the same sense as Mr. Madison."[23]

Here we have a repetition of the Thornton incident, this time at the highest level of national policy. Madison realized instantly what San Domingo meant. Jefferson did not, but swung over to Madison's policy when the realities were placed before him. The result? The United States allowed American ships to go on trading with the Negro rebels while guerrilla warfare and yellow fever wiped out the army of occupation. That was tough power politics—brutal politics. It did not come from a weak and vacillating errand boy.

Let us jump a year or two. On April 10, 1803, Easter Sunday, Napoleon sent for his finance minister, Marbois. Before Marbois left the palace Napoleon said to him: "I renounce Louisiana. It is not only New Orleans that I mean to cede, it is the whole colony without reserving any of it." It is well known that Napoleon made this decision two days after he read the resolutions of Senator Ross of Pennsylvania authorizing military occupation of New Orleans. But that was not the latest news he had from America. In the course of the talk with Marbois, Napoleon remarked: "The London cabinet is informed of the *resolutions taken* at Washington."[24] That means that Napoleon had received the London diplomatic pouch of April 7. He sent for Marbois after reading, in the London *Times* of that date, that the United States Senate had passed a bill to construct fifteen gunboats for use at the mouth of the Mississippi and that Congress was about to authorize the raising of 80,000 men for invasion purposes. Napoleon renounced Louisiana a few hours after he read the following London summary of American policy:

> Whether Spain continues in possession of Louisiana, or possession is taken by France, it is no longer doubtful that the deliberations of Congress are in unison with the feelings of the people. . . . The government and people seem to be aware that a decisive blow must be struck before the arrival of the expedition now waiting in the ports of Holland.

This was no thunderclap out of a clear sky. For two years the French legation in Washington had been describing the clouds that were rolling up, and here was evidence that there was lightning in them. It was not merely the danger of British seizure of Louisiana that Napoleon faced—he could have sidestepped that by leaving the country in the hands of Spain. The prospect that confronted him was both a danger and an opportunity—the certain prospect that some day the United States would take the country away from either Spain or France, and the reassuring certainty that they would never let it pass into the hands of Great Britain. These considerations were decisive, provided they were enforced by evidence of American strength and determination. Did Livingston provide that evidence? I quote from his letter of January 18, 1803, to Talleyrand, urging the cession of Florida and part of Louisiana to the United States:

> Under any other plan, sir . . . the whole of this establishment must pass into the hands of Great Britain. . . . France, by grasping at a desert and an insignificant town, and thereby throwing the weight of the United States into the scale of Britain, will render her [Great Britain] mistress of the new world.[25]

Madison had instructed Livingston to assure France that American self-interest forbade either a "voluntary or compulsive transfer" of these provinces from Spain to Great Britain.[26] Instead, the minister pictured the United States as supinely submitting to encirclement and domination through a compulsive transfer from France to Britain.

Was it from Jefferson that Napoleon heard of American strength and determination? The President wrote many forceful letters which did not go to the First Consul, and at times made threats which did, but observe what he said at the moment of highest crisis. I quote Pichon's report of what Jefferson said to him on January 12, 1803, explaining the decision made two days earlier to send Monroe to France:

> That Mr. Monroe was so well known to be a friend of the Western people that his mission would contribute more than anything else to tranquillize them and prevent unfortunate incidents; that he will be authorized jointly with Messrs. Pinckney and Livingston to treat with France or Spain, according to the state of things, in order to bring the affairs of the Mississippi to a definite conclusion. That the administration would try peaceful means to the last moment and they hoped that France would be disposed to concur in their views for the preservation of harmony.[27]

Livingston described the effect of this conciliatory attitude upon a promise just given to him to confirm American treaty rights at New Orleans: "Unfortunately, dispatches arrived at that moment from Mr. Pichon, informing them that the appointment of Mr. Monroe had tranquillized everything . . . they determined to see whether the storm would not blow over."[28]

Six days later more dispatches arrived, giving Madison's far different account of the reasons for sending Monroe—reasons which "imperatively required that this mission should have a prompt conclusion." Instead of quoting from his veiled threats of war, I present Pichon's comments upon them:

> The implicit language of Mr. Madison . . . brings to light ideas too general to be neglected. . . . Louisiana in the first moment of war will answer for the behavior of our administration. . . . The crisis grows greater every day, and we cannot push it into the distant future. . . . I should fail in my duty if I did not tell you that these feelings of concern which Mr. Madison expressed to me are generally felt and that public opinion in the latest circumstances expresses itself at least as strongly and energetically as the government.[29]

That was the last diplomatic word from Washington before Napoleon read about the fifteen gunboats and 80,000 men. Who put the heat on Bonaparte?

Now let us come back to Henry Adams. I spoke of his charge that Madison invited France to build an empire west of the Mississippi. That amounted to nothing. Adams merely failed to recognize a threat of war in thirteen-letter words like "circumstances" and "eventualities."[30] But he was well aware that for two years Madison had been working incessantly against French occupation of the trans-Mississippi country. Ignoring all that, he relied on one cryptic passage in one letter to brand the Secretary of State as a blundering nincompoop.

That was the way Adams operated. Without a particle of mental dishonesty in his makeup, he always searched for the worst and never failed to find it. A British diplomat wrote: "Madison is now as obstinate as a mule."[31] A man cannot be obstinate as a mule without having that trait show up again and again. It does not show up in Adams' history, even though he quoted that particular statement. There you find that Madison was fretful, he was irritable, he had "a feminine faculty for pressing a sensitive point."[32] Always the adjectives imply weakness. There is nothing to account for the fact that, as one foreign diplomat after another took him on, those who were hostile went home in discomfiture. Consider, as the most extreme case, the man who described Madison's obstinacy. Francis James Jackson—"Copenhagen Jackson"—was the hatchet man of the British Foreign Office. On his arrival at Washington he wrote to Canning that his predecessor had told him "of the most violent things said to him" by President Madison. Erskine, he observed, had turned the other cheek, but "I shall give blow for blow."[33] Jackson delivered one blow and was ordered out of the country.

Let us examine the most damning characterization of Madison to be found in the Adams history—an account by French Minister Turreau of his protest to Madison against the filibustering expedition of General Miranda.

General Turreau was a tough guy. He hammered his wife with a club while his secretary played on the French horn to drown her screams[34] and he aspired to be just as brutal in diplomacy. "I have never yet beheld a face so cruel and sanguinary as his," wrote a United States senator. On the occasion told of by Adams, he was acting as the agent of Spanish Minister Yrujo, with whom Madison had refused to have any more dealings. I quote from Adams' translation of Turreau's letter to the Spaniard: "I was this morning with Madison. . . . He was in a state of extraordinary prostration while I was demanding" etc., etc.[35]

It is a vivid picture—Madison collapsing with weakness and fright before the terrible Turreau. Let us look now at the French text. Turreau wrote: *"Il était dans un abattement extraordinaire."*[36] I asked two Frenchmen on the Library of Congress staff to translate that. The first one said: "He was in very low spirits." The second: "He was very dejected." I showed the Adams translation to Ambassador Bonnet and he exclaimed: "How could anybody make a mistake like that?" It could be done, quite readily, by anybody who would also say that to hold a man in suspense means to hang him by the neck. For sixty years, this false picture of James Madison has blackened the canvas of history.

Adams' favorite technique against Madison was the left-hand, right-hand, left-hand punch—condemnation first, then quotation, then condemnation. In 1805, when England was at war with France and Spain, American Minister Armstrong in Paris sent home the "well-considered suggestion," as Henry Adams called it, that the United States take Texas away from Spain by force. Jefferson, Adams writes, "seized Armstrong's idea, and uniting it with his own, announced the result to Madison as the true solution." The United States should first obtain a promise from England not to make peace without American consent, then Congress should grant the President discretionary authority to make war on Spain. "Here at length," Adams commented, "was a plan—uncertain indeed because dependent on British help, but still a scheme of action." And then Madison knocked it on the head by observing that England was unlikely to bind herself positively not to make peace unless the United States bound itself positively to make war. Madison, Adams commented, "had nothing to propose except negotiation without end."

At this moment news reached America of William Pitt's second coalition against Napoleon. The whole continent of Europe was flaring into battle. International alignments were melting like wax. Madison's reaction opened the way for a one-two-three. Adams began with condemnation: "Upon Madison's mind this European convulsion acted as an additional reason for doing nothing."

The quotation to prove it. Madison to Jefferson: "I think it very questionable whether a little delay may not be expedient," but meanwhile the United States should order Morales, Casa Calvo, and Yrujo out of the country.

Then final condemnation based on the quotation: "Madison's measures and conduct toward Europe showed the habit of avoiding the heart of every issue, in order to fret its extremities."[37]

All this because Madison thought a little delay would be expedient before jumping into the Napoleonic wars. Adams' specific complaint was that Madison "disregarded Armstrong's idea of seizing Texas." But when Madison, as President, seized West Florida on the same theory advanced by Armstrong for Texas, that it had been paid for in the Louisiana Purchase, Adams described it as "filching a petty sandheap," an action imbued with force and fraud, and he quoted at length the protesting preachment of a British diplomat against "wresting a province from a friendly power . . . at the time of her adversity." In brief, Madison was damned if he did and damned if he didn't.[38]

All through the controversy over West Florida, Adams supported Spain with a zeal which cannot be accounted for by this conviction that there was no merit in the American position. The glee with which he upheld the foreign side of international disputes was in exact proportion to the opportunities they gave him to pillory Madison and condemn Jefferson. Early in 1804, Congress authorized the President to make Mobile Bay part of a customs district. The Spanish minister, Adams writes, sent Madison "a note so severe as to require punishment, and so able as to admit of none. . . . Madison could neither maintain the law nor annul it; he could not even explain it away. . . . The President came to Madison's relief. By a proclamation," he limited the district to places lying within the United States. The proclamation—which Adams condemned as a perversion of a perverse law—was based entirely on the reply Madison already had written to Yrujo, that Section II (on Mobile) was subordinate to Section 4, which set up a more inclusive customs district but contained the limiting words, "lying within the United States." If anybody came to anybody's relief, Madison came to the President's, and in doing so, did just what Adams said he could not do—explained away what Yrujo had objected to.[39]

My final impression is that Henry Adams did not understand the policies of Jefferson and Madison at all. He saw weakness and national humiliation in their failure to go to war over this or that outrage—to war with England over impressment, or to avenge the attack on the *Chesapeake;* to war with France because of the Berlin and Milan decrees. Jefferson and Madison saw three choices—war, submission, or economic pressure and negotiation while the fast-growing nation gathered basic strength. They chose this third course, well knowing that war was the ultimate and probable alternative. Adams and a host of other writers have construed this course as submission, and have treated the War of 1812 as evidence of its failure.

Go back ten years. Go back to July 7, 1802, and read what Pichon wrote to Talleyrand on that day about the purposes of Jefferson and Madison: "They fear exceedingly to be forced to war, as they go on the principle that they ought not to try their strength within ten years, by which time they count on diminution of debt, growth of population and riches."

This was said in telling of an interview in which "Mr. Madison talked to me with much coolness, much method, and as if he had been prepared." The subject was Louisiana. It should be recognized, said Madison, "that France cannot long preserve Louisiana against the United States." As for other colonies of the European powers—in South America, the West Indies—the United States had no desire to possess them. But, said Madison, by joining England in the next war, they could throw all these distant territories into her hands, and "could without difficulty, in ten years, divide with her . . . all the export and import trade of these colonies."[40]

He was saying, in effect, that England and the United States could handle France at any time, and that in ten years the United States by itself would be strong enough to compel England to abandon its system of colonial monopoly.

For two reasons, and two only, the compulsive system which Madison threatened against both France and England was put into operation against England alone. France escaped it by ceding Louisiana. England brought it on by the blundering obstinacy of Canning, Wellesley, and Castlereagh. And the war started just three weeks short of the ten years Madison allowed for postponement of a showdown.

There is plenty to criticize in the presidencies of Jefferson and Madison. But their weaknesses were in general the weaknesses of the American people. Their major difficulty was one that we can appreciate today—that of living and working in a power-mad world dominated by lunatics. Study the work of Madison in that light, without the distorting shadows of political prejudice, and you will find the clear-cut lines of greatness in it.

I began writing the life of Madison without the slightest suspicion that the prevailing estimates of him were incorrect. Not in the remotest fashion did I suspect that in their political symbiosis, Jefferson might owe as much to Madison as Madison to Jefferson. My interest was in Madison the political philosopher, the architect of the Constitution, the author of the Bill of Rights—fields in which his primacy was universally acknowledged. Everything after 1789 was expected to be anticlimax. That has not proved true. The ultimate verdict upon Madison depends in part upon the future of the American people—upon their continued devotion to liberty, self-government, and personal honor. But, granted this fidelity, I have no doubt of the final verdict. Madison the diplomatist, Madison the President, will be found to measure up to the father of the Constitution. Washington, Jefferson, Jackson, Lincoln, Wilson, Roosevelt. Move over a little, gentlemen.

Notes

1. Quoted by Theodore Bolton in "The Life Portraits of James Madison," *William and Mary Quarterly*, VIII (January, 1951), 28–29.
2. Chevalier de la Luzerne, "Liste des Membres du Congrès depuis 1779 jusqu'en 1784," Archives des Affaires Etrangères, Mémoires et Documents, Etats-Unis, vol. 1, ff. 253–87.
3. *The Journal of William Maclay*, ed. Edgar S. Maclay (New York, 1890), July 1, 1789, p. 97.
4. Fisher Ames to George R. Minot, May 3, 1789, *Works of Fisher Ames*, ed. Seth Ames (Boston, 1854), I, 36.
5. Ames to Minot, January 20, 1795, *ibid.*, I, 165.
6. Albert J. Beveridge, *The Life of John Marshall* (Boston, 1916–19), II, 81.
7. Ames to Thomas Dwight, January, 1793, *Ames*, I, 127.
8. "He [Madison] was easily influenced by such lordly wills as Hamilton, easily seduced by such subtle minds as Jefferson. Thus his public service was a series of

contradictions, compromises, doubts and fears. . . . Between those tremendous mountain peaks of power, Hamilton and Jefferson, standing over against each other, Madison was the valley." Albert J. Beveridge, quoted in the Madison volume of "Autographs of the Presidents," Morgan Library, New York.

9. Madison to Jefferson, January 24, 1790, *The Writings of James Madison*, ed. Gaillard Hunt (New York, 1900–10), V, 434; received February 12, Epistolary Record, Jefferson Papers, Library of Congress.

10. Alexander Hamilton to Edward Carrington, May 26, 1792, *The Works of Alexander Hamilton*, ed. Henry Cabot Lodge (New York, 1904), IX, 528–29.

11. *Columbian Centinel* (Boston), February 24, 1790.

12. Irving Brant, *James Madison, II: The Nationalist* (Indianapolis, 1948), 233; Papers of the Continental Congress, No. 26, pp. 438–40; Notes of Debates, March 7, 1783, *Writings of James Madison*, I, 399.

13. Brant, II, 300; Madison to Edmund Randolph, July 28, 1783, *Writings of James Madison*, II, 4.

14. Brant, *James Madison, III: Father of the Constitution* (Indianapolis, 1950), 306–18. The June 20 date is approximate.

15. Beveridge, *John Marshall*, II, 71, n. 2.

16. February 2, 8, 1791, *Annals of Congress* (Washington, 1834), II, cols. 1944–52, 2008–12; "Opinion against the Constitutionality of a National Bank," February 15, 1791, *The Writings of Thomas Jefferson*, ed. A. A. Lipscomb and A. E. Bergh (Washington, 1903–1904), III, 145. Jefferson enlarged Madison's argument by contending that the "necessary and proper" clause of the Constitution restricted Congress "to those means without which the grant of power would be nugatory"—a test which would invalidate any action to which there was a possible alternative.

17. William Plumer, diary, April 8, 1806 (Library of Congress), quoted by Charles E. Hill in *The American Secretaries of State and Their Diplomacy*, ed. Samuel F. Bemis (New York, 1927–29), III, 7.

18. Henry Adams, *History of the United States*, IX, 173, 220, 240.

19. Madison to Jefferson, August 12 (received), 18, 27, 1801, Jefferson Papers, Library of Congress. Jefferson to Madison, August 22, 1801, Madison Papers, Library of Congress. Madison to Gallatin (private), August 29, 1801, Gallatin Papers, New York Historical Society. Edward Thornton to Madison, July 23, November 11, 1801, National Archives, General Records of the Department of State, Notes from the British Legation, II (1796–1803).

20. Adams, II, 54–55.

21. Edward Channing, *History of the United States*, IV, 319n.

22. *Lettres du Général Leclerc*, Appendix I, 269: Carl L. Lokke, "Jefferson and the Leclerc Expedition," *American Historical Review*, XXXIII (January, 1928), 324, 327–28.

23. L. A. Pichon to Talleyrand, July 22, August 11, 1801, February 24, 1802, Arch. Aff. Etr., Correspondance politique, Etats-Unis, vol. 53, f. 179; vol. 54, f. 161.

24. François Barbé-Marbois, *Histoire de la Louisiane* (Paris, 1829), pp. 298, 301; R. R. Livingston to Madison, April 11, 1803, *American State Papers, Foreign Affairs*, II, 552 (hereafter cited as *State Papers*). The italics in the quotation are added.

25. Livingston to Talleyrand, January 18, 1803, *State Papers*, II, 531. This letter is dated January 10, 1803, in *State Papers* and "20 Nivose an XI (January 10, 1803)" in the State Department copy (National Archives, Diplomatic Dispatches, France, VIII, enclosure to Livingston dispatch of January 24, 1803) from which it was taken for publication. It is dated January 18 in Livingston's letterbook (New York Historical

Society) and January 18 in a copy in Monroe Papers, VII, Library of Congress. At the end of the original letter (Arch. Aff. Etr., Etats-Unis, Supp., vol. 7, ff. 310–13) is the date 20 Frimaire an XI (December 11, 1802). This cannot be correct because the letter opens with a reference to the closing of New Orleans to American commerce by Spain, news of which did not reach France until January. Arthur B. Darling (in *Our Rising Empire, 1763–1803* [London, 1940], p. 447), observing no signature to the letter, concluded that this was Livingston's December 11 memoir to Joseph Bonaparte, wrongly addressed to Talleyrand by somebody who transcribed it in the foreign ministry. The letter is actually in the handwriting of Livingston's usual copyist, and is signed "Robt. R. Livingston," but the faded ink of the signature is almost invisible in the photographic reproduction in the Library of Congress. News of the New Orleans closure reached Livingston on or just before January 7 (Livingston to Joseph Bonaparte, January 7, 1803, *State Papers*, II, 536). Talleyrand learned of it between January 10 and 14 (Talleyrand to General Bernadotte, January 10, 14, 1803, Arch. Aff. Etr., Etats-Unis, vol. 55, ff. 164, 170). The original letter is indorsed as received on 30 Nivose (January 20), which confirms the date of January 18 found on two manuscript copies of it. What happened, apparently, was that Livingston wrote a paragraph about New Orleans and directed his clerk to add the Bonaparte memoir of December 11 to it. The clerk copied it date and all, then noticed the error while preparing a copy for Madison and changed 20 Frimaire to 20 Nivose, both wrong. Minus the opening paragraph, it is, as Darling concluded, the only known text of the memoir to Joseph Bonaparte.

26. Madison to Livingston, September 28, 1801, National Archives, General Records of the Department of State, Instructions to Consular Representatives, I (1800–1806). In the published instructions (*State Papers*, II, 510), the words "from Spain to Great Britain" appear as "from Spain to France," making the whole sentence nonsensical.

27. Pichon to Talleyrand, January 21, 24, 1803, Arch. Aff. Etr., Etats-Unis, vol. 55, ff. 184v, 192.

28. Livingston to Madison, March 24, 1803, *State Papers*, II, 549; Talleyrand to Livingston, 1 Germinal an 11 (March 22, 1803, misdated March 21), *ibid.*, II, 550.

29. Pichon to Talleyrand, January 24, 1803, Arch. Aff. Etr., Etats-Unis, vol. 55, ff. 196–98v.

30. *Ibid.*; Adams, II, 54.

31. Francis James Jackson, October 26, 1809, quoted in Adams, V, 130.

32. Adams, II, 74; V, 187.

33. Francis J. Jackson to Canning, September 14, 1809, Foreign Office, 353, vol. 60.

34. Register, I, 181, William Plumer Papers, Library of Congress. Ordinarily, Turreau needed no provocation to beat his wife, but in this instance she had just hit him with a flatiron.

35. *Ibid.*, I, 105; Adams, III, 192–95.

36. General Turreau to the Marquis d'Yrujo, February 7, 1806, Archives Hist. Nac. Madrid, leg. 5544 pt. 1.

37. Adams, III, 69–74.

38. Adams, V, 309, 315. One's belief that Henry Adams did not distort intentionally is put to quite a strain at finding three distortions on one page (II, 69), all designed to prove that Minister Robert R. Livingston did not think that the portion of West Florida lying west of the Perdido River was included in the Louisiana Purchase until several weeks after the treaty negotiated by him and James Monroe had been signed. Adams wrote: (1) "In the preceding year one of the French ministers had

applied to Livingston 'to know what we understand in America by Louisiana'; and Livingston's answer was on record in the State Department at Washington: 'Since the possession of the Floridas by Britain and the treaty of 1762, I think there can be no doubt as to the precise meaning of the terms.' " This alleged answer was actually a comment by Livingston upon a letter from John Graham at Madrid, and concerned ancient French claims to the Ohio country as part of *Louisiane Orientale*. On the query of the French minister Livingston merely wrote: "You can readily conceive my answer." Where would Adams have been if he had quoted what Livingston wrote only two weeks later on the subject really at issue: "I find all the old French maps mark the river Perdido as the boundary between Florida and Louisiana." Livingston to Madison, July 30, August 16, 1802, *State Papers*, II, 519, 524. (2) "He had himself drafted an article which he tried to insert in Marbois' *projet*, pledging the First Consul to interpose his good offices with the King of Spain to obtain the country east of the Mississippi." The article actually covered all Spanish territory "on the continent of North America laying to the east of the river"—a description which did not make the Mississippi the boundary (Monroe Papers, VII, 1270v). Livingston and Monroe jointly asked aid in obtaining "so much of his [the king of Spain's] territories as lay *to the east of the ceded territory*. . . ." Livingston and Monroe to Marbois, May 2, 1803, Arch. Aff. Etr., Etats-Unis, vol. 55, f. 416. (3) "As late as May 12, Livingston wrote to Madison: 'I am satisfied that . . . if they [the French] could have concluded with Spain, we should also have had West Florida.' " This did not refer to the negotiations of Livingston and Monroe, nor to the treaty they signed on May 2, 1803, but was a speculation about what the French might have been willing to do in the previous year, when Livingston made a bid for West Florida and the country above the Arkansas River.

39. Adams, II, 257–63; the marquis of Casa Yrujo to Madison, March 7, 1804, National Archives, General Records of the Department of State, Notes from the Spanish Legation, II; Madison to Yrujo, March 19, 1804, Monroe Papers; *Annals of Congress*, XIII, col. 1253 (the "Mobile Act"). Adams' methods of creating adverse impressions find an illustration (II, 262) in the way he quoted from Madison's letter to Livingston, March 31, 1804, about the belatedness of Yrujo's protest: "The Act had been for many weeks depending in Congress with these sections, word for word, in it; . . . it must in all probability have been known to the Marquis d'Yrujo in an early stage of its progress." The statement would have sounded less like an unsupported conjecture if Adams had not omitted part of it: "as two copies are by a usage of politeness always allotted for each foreign minister here it must in all probability" etc.

40. Pichon to Talleyrand, July 7, 1802, Arch. Aff. Etr., Etats-Unis, vol. 54, f. 410.

Myths Surrounding the Monroe Doctrine

Wayne S. Cole

In this article, Wayne S. Cole, a diplomatic historian at the University of Maryland, takes issue with the stock textbook interpretation of the Monroe Doctrine. He focuses his attack on several myths, concluding that the doctrine "was not a treaty, not an executive agreement, not an act of Congress, not a multilateral inter-American policy, and not international law." He questions whether the principles of the doctrine originated with Monroe as well as challenging the myth of immediate effective United States enforcement. Professor Cole does warn, however, against depreciating the doctrine's place in history, reminding us that the *idea* of the Monroe Doctrine grew in influence and stature in the American mind following the Civil War. This development became particularly evident "as both the interests and the power of the United States grew in Latin America."

No policy statement in the history of American foreign affairs has captured such an enduring and revered hold on American thought as President James Monroe's statement in 1823. That Monroe Doctrine was not a treaty, not an executive agreement, not an act of Congress, not a multilateral inter-American policy, and not international law. Its principles were not original with Monroe. It was not effectively enforced by the United States for many years. And it was not even called the Monroe Doctrine until long after Monroe left the Presidency. It was simply a statement of policy included in the President's message to Congress on December 2, 1823.

In its original form it had three main premises. First, it warned the Quadruple Alliance against extending European political systems to the Western Hemisphere:

> The political system of the allied powers is essentially different . . . from that of America. . . . we should consider any attempt on their part to extend their system to any portion of this hemisphere as dangerous to our peace and safety. With the existing colonies or dependencies of any European power we have not interfered and shall not interfere. But with the Governments who have declared their independence and maintained it, and whose independence we have, on great consideration and on just principles, acknowledged, we could not view any interposition

for the purpose of oppressing them, or controlling in any other manner their destiny, by any European power in any other light than as the manifestation of an unfriendly disposition toward the United States.

Second, Monroe advanced the noncolonization principle:

... the occasion has been judged proper for asserting, as a principle in which the rights and interests of the United States are involved, that the American continents, by the free and independent condition which they have assumed and maintain, are henceforth not to be considered as subjects for future colonization by any European powers.

And third, Monroe endorsed the American policy of nonintervention in Europe:

In the wars of the European powers in matters relating to themselves we have never taken any part, nor does it comport with our policy so to do. . . . Our policy in regard to Europe . . . remains the same, which is, not to interfere in the internal concerns of any of its powers; to consider the government *de facto* as the legitimate government for us; to cultivate friendly relations with it, and to preserve those relations by a frank, firm, and manly policy, meeting in all instances the just claims of every power, submitting to injuries from none.

Monroe's statement was aimed against two apparent external threats to American interests in the Western Hemisphere and was triggered by a British proposal to the United States. First, the Monroe Doctrine was aimed against the danger that the Concert of Europe might use its power (as it had in Italy and Spain) to put down the Latin-American revolutions and reestablish monarchical governments there. Second, the Monroe Doctrine was aimed against Russian colonial expansion south into the Oregon Territory. In 1821, under Czar Alexander I, Russia issued a ukase that, in effect, extended the southern boundary of its Alaskan colony to the fifty-first parallel. The Ukase of 1821 gave Russians exclusive trading and navigation rights down to 51° north latitude. It also barred foreign ships from approaching within 115 miles of that coast on pain of seizure.

Like the United States, Great Britain preferred an independent Latin America and objected to efforts by the Quadruple Alliance (or one of its members) to reestablish European control there. In August, 1823, the British Foreign Secretary, George Canning, suggested to Richard Rush, the United States Minister in London, that Britain and the United States issue a joint declaration. That statement would have questioned Spain's ability to recover its colonies; it would have renounced any desire by the United States or Britain to seize Latin America; and it would have opposed the transfer of any part of Latin America to any other state. The idea appealed to Rush, who promptly transmitted it to his government in Washington. President Monroe, too, was favorably disposed, as were the two former Presidents, Jefferson and Madison, that he consulted. Secretary of State John Quincy Adams, however, objected. He did not believe the European powers would intervene in Latin America and, in any event, he opposed a joint statement with Britain. He believed it would be more dignified for the United States to act unilaterally rather "than to come in as a cock-boat in the wake of the British man-of-war." Consequently, the United States rejected Canning's proposal, but his suggestion led directly to Monroe's statement in his message to Congress.

Not only did external challenges and a foreign proposal lead to the Monroe Doctrine, but circumstances and developments abroad also prevented the threats from materializing. Contrary to American mythology, neither the Quadruple Alliance nor Russia actually endangered the Western Hemisphere at the time Monroe issued his message. So far as the Concert of Europe was concerned, neither Austria nor Prussia had any interest in Latin America or any plans to intervene. Russia had not formulated its policies on the matter by December, 1823, and ironically Czar Alexander I did not even toy with the possibility of intervention until after Monroe's message. Even then it was just a passing consideration unaffected by United States opposition. France had considered the possibility of establishing independent Bourbon monarchies in Latin America but had not acted on the idea. In October, Canning discussed the matter with the French Ambassador to Britain, the Prince de Polignac. As a result, in the so-called Polignac Memorandum of October 12, 1823, France "disclaimed . . . any intention or desire . . . to appropriate to Herself any part of the Spanish Possessions in America. . . . She adjured, in any case, any design of acting against the Colonies by force of arms." Thus British diplomacy and power checked the slight possibility of French intervention nearly two months before the Monroe Doctrine.

So far as Russian colonial expansion in the Northwest was concerned, Secretary of State Adams had protested against the Ukase of 1821 through regular diplomatic channels long before Monroe's message. Alexander I had no colonial ambitions in America. He was not impressed by the United States, but he did view America as a potential adversary of Britain and did not want to antagonize America. The Czar decided to yield on the boundary matter as early as July, 1822, a year and a half before the Monroe Doctrine. In 1824, in the first treaty between Russia and the United States, Russia accepted 54° 40' north latitude as the southern boundary of Alaska and agreed to freedom of seas in the North Pacific. That favorable treaty, however, was not due to the Monroe Doctrine. As Dexter Perkins, the leading scholar on the Monroe Doctrine, phrased it: "From the standpoint of its immediate results, it was close to futility."

In addition to external influences, the Monroe Doctrine was consistent with the dominant domestic ideological, political, and economic patterns within the United States. Its antiforeign, anti-European, and antimonarchical tenor reflected American chauvinism in the Era of Good Feelings. The Doctrine's unilateralism and noninterventionism (the central ingredients of isolationism) expressed American nationalism.

Furthermore, like political patterns in the Era of Good Feelings, the Monroe Doctrine was consistent with the desires of both the urban shipping-commercial interests on the one hand and the farmer-agrarian interests on the other. That was symbolized in its authorship. President Monroe of planter Virginia was responsible for the statement aimed against intervention by the Quadruple Alliance in Latin America. He was also responsible for presenting the policy in his message to Congress. Secretary of State Adams from commercial Massachusetts was responsible for the noncolonization principle, for emphasizing nonintervention in Europe, and for making it a unilateral policy rather than a joint statement with Britain. That dual authorship symbolized the temporary political alliance of planter and merchant during the Era of Good Feelings.

The Monroe Doctrine appealed to both wings of that political alliance by keeping the door open for continued expansion by both commercial and agrarian interests. American merchants wanted to increase trade in Latin America. They feared that reestablishment of Spanish control, intervention by the Quadruple Alliance, or any European colonial expansion in Latin America would conflict with their commercial ambitions there. The noncolonization principle did not apply to the United States (unlike Canning's original proposal). It opposed only European competitors of American territorial expansion. Thus the Monroe Doctrine was in tune with the expansionist ambitions of both agrarian and commercial groups within the United States.

The immediate impetus for the Monroe Doctrine came from external influences, but it was consistent with American emotions and sentiments in that nationalistic era. It was directed against European expansion, but it also left the door open for continued commercial and territorial expansion by the United States in the Western Hemisphere. It would have been difficult to formulate any foreign policy that appealed more neatly to the interests and ambitions of the two main economic groups in the United States than did the Monroe Doctrine.

It did not, however, get nearly so much attention in 1823 as it won subsequently. European and Latin-American leaders were not awed by it. Colombia in 1824 and Brazil in 1825 responded by seeking defensive alliances with the United States. The United States rebuffed their approaches, however, and for more than a century the Monroe Doctrine remained a unilateral United States policy, not a multilateral policy shared with other states in the Western Hemisphere.

Simon Bolivar organized a Pan-American Conference in Panama in 1826. He envisaged a confederation of Spanish-American states, but the United States was invited to the meeting. John Quincy Adams, then President, and his Secretary of State, Henry Clay, did not object to accepting the invitation. Many congressmen, however, feared entangling alliances and involvement in Latin-American affairs. The Senate finally approved the two delegates named by Adams, but one died on the way and the other arrived after the conference ended. Only Colombia, Mexico, Peru, and Central America were represented at Panama, though Britain and the Netherlands had observers on hand. The conference approved a treaty of confederation, but only Colombia ratified it.

Not only did the Monroe Doctrine win little attention or respect but European states frequently violated it with impunity. Britain seized the Falkland Islands off Argentina in 1833. In 1838 France blockaded Mexico at Vera Cruz and invaded and blockaded Argentina. Britain extended the boundaries of British Honduras and seized one of the Bay Islands off Honduras in 1838. From 1845 to 1849 Britain and France jointly intervened in Argentina. The United States government either ignored each of those episodes or made only token protests. In no case did the United States compel the European state to withdraw.

The failure to invoke the Monroe Doctrine effectively before the Civil War was the result of America's limited interests and limited power. The agrarians who controlled the government most of the time before 1861 were interested in those parts of Latin America adjoining the United States, including Florida, Texas, New Mexico, and California. Some were even attracted by Cuba and Central America. But they had no interest in South America. New England traders might be affected by developments in Argentina, but generally they did not control American foreign policies. Even America's security interests in South America were not so great as they became later. Argentina was farther from the United States than Great Britain was. With the relatively limited mobility of nineteenth-century military forces, and with no isthmian canal to defend, European intervention in Argentina did not seem to represent so much of a threat to American security as it would have in the twentieth century. United States relations with Latin-American states generally were not very close before the Civil War. The United States did not even maintain diplomatic relations with Argentina from 1830 to 1844.

In addition to America's limited interests in South America, the Untied States also lacked the power necessary to enforce the Monroe Doctrine effectively. In those parts of Latin America that adjoined the United States, American power was adequate. In South America, however, and in much of the Caribbean and Central America, the United States was not strong enough to make its will prevail, even if its interests there had been much greater than they were. In the nineteenth century, Great Britain, not the United States, was the most powerful outside state in South America. And in international affairs, principles (even good ones) cannot prevail if they are not backed with sufficient power.

Nevertheless, as Dexter Perkins wrote of the Monroe Doctrine, ". . . We must not . . . err on the side of too complete a depreciation of its place in the history of American foreign policy. . . . It became in later years an American shibboleth, powerful in its appeal, and far-reaching in its influence." It obtained that greater importance as both the interests and the power of the United States grew in Latin America.

IV

Myths from the "Age of the Common Man"

And we Americans are the peculiar chosen people—the Israel of time; we bear the ark of the liberties of the world.
Herman Melville, *White Jacket*

"Westward the star of empire takes its way." As a true patriot I should be ashamed to think that Adam in paradise was more favorably situated on the whole than the backwoodsman in this country.
Henry David Thoreau, *Walking*

The object of this history is to follow the steps by which a favoring Providence, calling our institutions into being, has conducted the country to its present happiness and glory. God himself, working through the course of history, was behind the common man.
George Bancroft, *The History of the United States of America from the Discovery of the Continent* (1879)

Robert V. Remini,
"The Jacksonian Revolution: Myth and Reality"

Thomas P. Abernethy,
"Andrew Jackson and the Rise of Southwestern Democracy"

William H. Goetzmann,
"The Mountain Man as Jacksonian Man"

Richard P. McCormick,
"New Perspectives on Jacksonian Politics"

Edward Pessen,
"The Egalitarian Myth and the American Social Reality"

C. Vann Woodward,
"The Antislavery Myth"

Rodolfo Acuña,
"Legacy of Hate: The Myth of a Peaceful Belligerent"

"The Verdict of the People": democratic upheaval in the Age of the Common Man? [George Caleb Bingham, *The Verdict of the People* (1855). From the art collection of The Boatman's National Bank of St. Louis.]

"The Dinner Party": persistent elitism in the Age of the Common Man? [Henry Sargent, *The Dinner Party* (1821). Gift of Mrs. Horatio A. Lamb in memory of Mr. and Mrs. Winthrop Sargent, Courtesy, Museum of Fine Arts, Boston.]

*A*fter Abraham Lincoln, Andrew Jackson ranks as perhaps the greatest of America's political folk heroes. A substantial mythology, along with a certain symbolism and mystique, surrounds our historical understanding of both these men. In the case of Andrew Jackson, historical judgment suffers most from the fact that Jackson was allegedly America's first "popular" president. Jackson's popularity stemmed not so much from the degree to which his countrymen came to admire him (for certainly George Washington before him was thus admired), but rather from the degree to which he is said to have represented the "common man." Indicative of Jackson's attunement to the political pulse of "the people," we are told, was the fact that he was the first "outsider" to become president. To many, Jackson personified the interests, the values, and the prejudices of newly emergent Frontier America. But in addition to his identification with expansive "upland democracy," Jackson was also viewed as challenging precedent, in that presidents before him had always risen from the ranks of cabinet service—a national apprenticeship that Jackson never served. Similarly, Andrew Jackson was the first president seemingly close enough to the people to be known by a nickname—"Old Hickory." So close an association between Old Hickory and the masses has been traditionally supposed that, in fact, the era of his presidency has long been affectionately labeled the "Age of the Common Man."

It is precisely the affinity between Andrew Jackson and the "common man" that recent historical scholarship has sought to reexamine. Legitimate questions have been raised as to the extent of democratization during Jackson's term as president, whether Jackson was a cause or consequence of his age, and whether Andrew Jackson himself was in fact a Jacksonian. "Jacksonian Democracy" eludes simple historical explanation, then, not only because of Old Hickory's personal and symbolic presence but also because of the complex developments in American society that were contemporary with his age, such as social and political reform, Manifest Destiny, and the Mexican War. As a result, neither the myth nor the reality of Jackson the man or the times in which he lived has as yet been finally determined.

The Jacksonian Revolution: Myth and Reality

Robert V. Remini

Historical legend holds that a coalition of circumstances following the War of 1812—the rise of the West as a political force, the growing democracy of the frontier, and a new style of American politics—brought one Andrew Jackson to the nation's center stage; from Tennessee to Washington, D.C., from the backwoods of the "throne" of national political leadership. Without doubt Jackson was a remarkable charismatic figure, but much of his image and the associated reputation of his time is due to a complex blend of sentimentalism, folklore, misinformation, and myth. Finding a clear historiographical path through the ensuing interpretive wilderness of Jacksonian scholarship is the task Robert V. Remini, Professor of History at the University of Illinois, Chicago Circle, sets for himself. Since Jackson's "career and personality stirred the imagination" both of his own time and of later historians (often in conflicting ways in both instances), the matter of temperate, truthful evaluation is an elusive one. Though none deny the significant presence of Jackson's "imperial," assertive presidency, scholarly judgment remains sharply divided both on Andrew Jackson the man and on the political and social culture that bears his name.

"What?" cried the outraged North Carolina lady when she heard the dreadful news. "Jackson up for president? *Jackson? Andrew* Jackson? The Jackson that used to live in Salisbury? Why, when he was here, he was such a rake that my husband would not bring him into the house! It is true, he *might* have taken him out to the stable to weigh horses for a race, and might drink a glass of whiskey with him *there*. Well, if Andrew Jackson can be president, anybody can!"

Indeed. After forty years of constitutional government headed by presidents George Washington, John Adams, Thomas Jefferson, James Madison, James Monroe, and John Quincy Adams, the thought of Gen. Andrew Jackson of Tennessee—"Old Hickory" to his devoted soldiers—succeeding such distinguished statesmen came as a shock to some Americans in 1828. And little did they know at the time that Old Hickory would be followed in succession by the little Magician, Tippecanoe and Tyler, too, Young Hickory, and then Old Rough and Ready.

This article appeared in the January 1988 issue and is reprinted with permission from *The World and I*, a publication of The Washington Times Corporation, © 1988.

What had happened to the American political process? How could it come about that the Washingtons, Jeffersons, and Madisons of the world could be replaced by the Van Burens, Harrisons, Tylers, and Taylors? What a mockery of the political system bequeathed by the Founding Fathers!

The years from roughly 1828 to 1848 are known today as the Age of Jackson or the Jacksonian era. To many contemporaries, they initiated a "revolution," a shocking overthrow of the noble republican standards of the founders by the "common people," who in 1828 preferred as president a crude frontiersman like Andrew Jackson to a statesman of proven ability with a record of outstanding public service like John Quincy Adams.

Over the forty years following the establishment of the American nation under the Constitution, the United States had experienced many profound changes in virtually all phases of life. Following the War of 1812, the industrial revolution took hold and within thirty years all the essential elements for the creation of an industrial society in America were solidly in place. At the same time, a transportation revolution got underway with the building of canals, bridges, and turnpikes, reaching a climax of sorts in the 1820s with the coming of the railroads. The standard of living was also improved by numerous new inventions. Finally, many of the older eastern states began to imitate newer western states by democratizing their institutions, for example, amending their constitutions to eliminate property qualifications for voting and holding office, thereby establishing universal white manhood suffrage.

The arrival of many thousands of new voters at the polls in the early nineteenth century radically changed American politics. In the past, only the wealthy and better educated were actively involved in government. Moreover, political parties were frowned upon by many of the Founding Fathers. Parties stood for factions or cliques by which greedy and ambitious men, who had no interest in serving the public good, could advance their private and selfish purposes. John Adams spoke for many when he declared that the "division of the republic into two great parties . . . is to be dreaded as the greatest political evil under our Constitution."

But times had changed. An entirely new generation of politicians appeared at the outbreak of the War of 1812, men like Henry Clay, John C. Calhoun, Martin Van Buren, and Daniel Webster, who regarded political parties more favorably. Indeed, the party structure that had emerged before the end of President Washington's administration had been their corridor to power, since none of them could offer to their constituents a public record to match what the founders had achieved. None had fought in the Revolution. None had signed the Declaration or participated in the debates leading to the writing and adoption of the Constitution. Some of them—Martin Van Buren is probably the best example—actually considered parties to be beneficial to the body politic, indeed essential to the proper working of a democratic society. Through the party system, Van Buren argued, the American people could more effectively express their will and take measures to ensure that that will was implemented by their representatives. "We must always have party distinctions," he wrote," "and the old ones are the best. . . . Political combinations between the inhabitants of the different states are unavoidable and the most natural and beneficial to the country is that between the planters of the South and the plain Republicans of the North."

In supporting Andrew Jackson for the presidency in 1828 and trying to win support from both planters and plain Republicans, Van Buren affirmed his belief in the American need for a two-party system. Jackson's election, he told Thomas Ritchie, editor of the Richmond *Enquirer*, "as the result of his military services without reference to party, and, as far as he alone is concerned, scarcely to principle, would be one thing. His election as the result of combined and concerted effort of a political party, holding in the main, to certain tenets and opposed to certain prevailing principles, might be another and far different thing."

Van Buren eventually formed an alliance with John C. Calhoun and a number of other southern politicians, and led the way in structuring a political organization around the presidential candidacy of Andrew Jackson. That organization ultimately came to be called the Democratic Party. Its leaders, including Jackson, Van Buren, Calhoun, and Thomas Hart Benton, claimed to follow the republican doctrines of Thomas Jefferson. Thus they opposed both a strong central government and a broad interpretation of the Constitution, and they regarded the states, whose rights must be defended by all who cared about preserving individual liberty, as a wholesome counterweight to the national government. Many of them opposed the idea of the federal government sponsoring public works, arguing that internal improvements dangerously inflated the power of the central government and jeopardized liberty. As president, Andrew Jackson vetoed the Maysville road bill and contended that the national government should avoid internal improvements as a general practice, except for those essential to the national defense.

The political philosophy these Democrats espoused was fundamentally conservative. It advocated economy in operating the government because a tight budget limited government activity, and Jackson swore that if ever elected president he would liquidate the national debt. True to his word, he labored throughout his administration to cut expenditures by vetoing several appropriations bills he tagged as exorbitant, and he finally succeeded in obliterating the national debt altogether in January 1835—a short-lived accomplishment.

The organization of the Democratic Party in its initial stages included a central committee, state committees, and a national newspaper located in Washington, D.C., the *United States Telegraph*, which could speak authoritatively to the party faithful. In time it was said that the Democratic organization included "a chain of newspaper posts, from the New England States to Louisiana, and branching off through Lexington to the Western States." The supporters of Jackson's election were accused by their opponents of attempting to regulate "the popular election by means of organized clubs in the States, and organized presses everywhere."

Democrats took particular delight in celebrating the candidacy of Andrew Jackson. They found that Old Hickory's personality and military accomplishments made him an attractive and viable candidate for the ordinary voter. Indeed his career and personality stirred the imagination of Democratic leaders around the country and they devised new methods, or improved old ones, to get across the message that Andrew Jackson was a "man of the people." "The Constitution and liberty of the country were in imminent peril, and he has preserved them both!" his supporters boasted. "We can sustain our republican principles . . . by calling to the presidential chair . . . ANDREW JACKSON."

Jackson became a symbol of the best in American life—a self-made man, among other things—and party leaders adopted the hickory leaf as their symbol. Hickory brooms, hickory canes, hickory sticks shot up everywhere—on steeples, poles, steamboats, and stage coaches, and in the hands of all who could wave them to salute the Old Hero of New Orleans. "In every village, as well as upon the corners of many city streets," hickory poles were erected. "Many of these poles were standing as late as 1845," recorded one contemporary, "rotten momentoes [sic] of the delirium of 1828." The opponents of the Democratic Party were outraged by this crude lowering of the political process. "Planting hickory trees!" snorted the Washington *National Journal* on May 24, 1828. "Odds nuts and drumsticks! What have hickory trees to do with republicanism and the great contest?"

The Democrats devised other gimmicks to generate excitement for their ticket. "Jackson meetings" were held in every county where a Democratic organization existed. Such meetings were not new, of course. What was new was their audience. "If we go into one of these meetings," declared one newspaper, "of whom do we find them composed? Do we see there the solid, substantial, moral and reflecting yeomanry of the country? No. . . . They comprise a large portion of the dissolute, the noisy, the discontented, and designing of society." The Democratic press retorted with the claim that these so-called dissolute were actually the "bone and muscle of American society. They are the People. The real People who understand that Gen. Jackson is one of them and will defend their interests and rights."

The Jacksonians were also very fond of parades and barbecues. In Baltimore a grand barbecue was scheduled to commemorate the successful defense of the city when the British attacked during the War of 1812. But the Democrats expropriated the occasion and converted it into a Jackson rally. One parade started with dozens of Democrats marching to the beat of a fife and drum corps and wearing no other insignia save "a twig of the sacred [hickory] tree in their hats." Trailing these faithful Jacksonians came "gigantic hickory poles," still live and crowned with green foliage, being carted in "on eight wheels for the purpose of being planted by the democracy on the eve of the election." These poles were drawn by eight horses, all decorated with "ribbons and mottoes." Perched in the branches of each tree were a dozen Democrats, waving flags and shouting, "Hurrah for Jackson!"

"Van Buren has learned you know that the *Hurra Boys* were for Jackson," commented one critic, "and to my regret they constitute a powerful host." Indeed they did. The number of voters in the election of 1828 rose to 1,155,340, a jump of more than 800,000 over the previous presidential election of 1824.

The Hurra Boys brought out the voters in 1828, but at considerable cost. The election set a low mark for vulgarity, gimmickry, and nonsensical hijinks.

Jackson's mother was accussed of being a prostitute brought to America to service British soldiers, and his wife was denounced as an "adulteress" and bigamist. "Ought a convicted adulteress and her paramour husband to be placed in the highest offices of this free and Christian land?" asked one editor. But the Democrats were no better, accusing John Quincy Adams of pimping for the czar of Russia.

The tone and style of this election outraged many voters who feared for the future of American politics. With so many fresh faces crowding to the polls, the old republican system was yielding to a new democratic style and that evolution seemed fraught with all the dangers warned against by the Founding Fathers. Jackson's subsequent victory at the polls gave some Americans nightmares of worse things to come

At his inauguration people came from five hundred miles away to see General Jackson, wrote Daniel Webster, "and they really seem to think that the country is rescued from some dreadful danger!" They nearly wrecked the White House in their exuberance. Their behavior shocked Joseph Story, an associate justice of the Supreme Court, and sent him scurrying home. "The region of KING MOB seemed triumphant," he wailed. But a western newspaper disagreed. "It was a proud day for the people," reported the *Argus of Western America*. "General Jackson is *their own* President."

Jackson himself was fiercely committed to democracy. And by democracy he meant majoritarian rule. "The people are the government," he wrote, "administering it by their agents; they are the Government, the sovereign power." In his first message to Congress as president, written in December 1829, Jackson announced: "The majority is to govern." To the people belonged the right of "electing their Chief Executive." He therefore asked Congress to adopt an amendment that would abolish the College of Electors. He wanted all "intermediary" agencies standing between the people and their government swept away, whether erected by the Founding Fathers or not. "The people are sovereign," he reiterated. "Their will is absolute."

So committed was Jackson to the principle of popular self-rule that he told historian-politician George Bancroft that "every officer should in his turn pass before the people, for their approval or rejection." And he included federal judges in this sweeping generalization, even justices of the Supreme Court. Accordingly, he introduced the principle of rotation, which limited government appointments to four years. Officeholders should be regularly rotated back home and replaced by new men, he said. "The duties of all public officers are . . . so plain and simple that men of intelligence may readily qualify themselves for their performance." Otherwise abuse may occur. Anyone who has held office "a few years, believes he has a life estate in it, a vested right, & if it has been held 20 years or upwards, not only a vested right, but that it ought to descend to his children, & if no children then the next of kin—This is not the principles of our government. It is rotation in office that will perpetuate our liberty." Unfortunately, hack politicians equated rotation with patronage and Jackson's enemies quickly dubbed his principle "the spoils system."

But it was never meant to be a spoils system. Jackson wanted *every* office of government, from the highest to the lowest, within the reach of the electorate, arguing that "where the people are everything . . . there and there only is liberty." Perhaps his position was best articulated by Alexis de Tocqueville, the French visitor in the 1830s whose *Democracy in America* remains one of the most profound observations about American life in print. "The people reign in the American political world," declared Tocqueville, "as the Deity does in the universe. They are the cause and aim of all things; everything comes from them, and everything is absorbed in them." The "constant celebration" of the people, therefore, is what Jackson and the Democratic Party provided the nation during his eight years in office. It is what Jacksonian Democracy was all about.

As president, Jackson inaugurated a number of important changes in the operation of government. For example, he vetoed congressional legislation more times than all his predecessors combined, and for reasons other than a bill's presumed lack of constitutionality. More importantly, by the creative use of his veto power he successfully claimed for the chief executive the right to participate in the legislative process. He put Congress on notice that they must consider his views on all issues *before* enacting them into law or run the risk of a veto. In effect he assumed the right to initiate legislation, and this essentially altered the relationship between the executive and the Congress. Instead of a separate and equal branch of the government, the president, according to Jackson, was the head of state, the first among equals.

Jackson also took a dim view of the claim that the Supreme Court exercised the final and absolute right to determine the meaning of the Constitution. When the court decided in *McCulloch vs. Maryland* that the law establishing a national bank was constitutional, Jackson disagreed. In his veto of a bill to recharter the Second National Bank in 1832, he claimed among other things that the bill lacked authority under the Constitution, despite what the high court had decided. Both the House and the Senate, as well as the president, he continued, must decide for themselves what is and what is not constitutional before taking action on any bill. The representatives of Congress ought not to vote for a bill, and the president ought not to sign it, if they, in their own good judgment, believe it unconstitutional. "It is as much the duty of the House of Representatives, of the Senate, and of the President to decide upon the constitutionality of any bill or resolution which may be presented to them for passage or approval as it is of the supreme judges when it may be brought before them for judicial decision." Jackson did not deny the right of the Supreme Court to judge the constitutionality of a bill. What he denied was the presumption that the Court was the final or exclusive interpreter of the Constitution. All three branches should rule on the question of constitutionality, Jackson argued. In this way the equality and independence of each branch of government is maintained. "The authority of the Supreme Court," he declared, "must not, therefore, be permitted to control the Congress, or the Exec-

utive when acting in their legislative capacities, but to have only such influence as the force of their reasoning may deserve." What bothered Jackson was
the presumption that four men could dictate what 15 million people may or
may not do under their constitutional form. To Jackson's mind that was not
democratic but oligarchic. But that was precisely the intention of the Founding
Fathers: to provide a balanced mix of democratic, oligarchic, and monarchical
forms in the Constitution.

Of course Jackson was merely expressing his own opinion about the right
of all three branches to pass on the constitutionality of all legislation, an opinion the American people ultimately rejected. The great fear in a democratic
system—one the Founding Fathers knew perfectly well—was the danger of the
majority tyrannizing the minority. Jackson would take his chances. He believed the American people were virtuous and would always act appropriately.
"I for one do not despair of the republic," he wrote. "I have great confidence
in the virtue of a great majority of the people, and I cannot fear the result. The
republic is safe, the main pillars [of] virtue, religion and morality will be fostered by a majority of the people." But not everyone shared Jackson's optimism
about the goodness of the electorate. And in time—particularly with the passage of the Fourteenth Amendment—it fell to the courts to guard and maintain
the rights of the minority.

Jackson summed up his assertion of presidential rights by declaring that
he alone—not Congress, as was usually assumed—was the sole representative
of the American people and responsible to them. After defeating Henry Clay
in the 1832 election, he decided to kill the Second National Bank by removing
federal deposits because, as he said, he had received a "mandate" from the
people to do so. The Senate objected and formally censured him, but Jackson,
in response, merely issued another statement on presidential rights and the
democratic system that had evolved over the last few years.

By law, only the secretary of the treasury was authorized to remove the
deposits, so Jackson informed his secretary, William Duane, to carry out his
order. Duane refused pointblank. And he also refused to resign as he had promised if he and the president could not agree upon a common course of action
with respect to the deposits. Thereupon, Jackson sacked him. This was the
first time a cabinet officer had been fired, and there was some question
whether the president had this authority. After all, the cabinet positions were
created by Congress and appointment required the consent of the Senate. Did
that not imply that removal also required senatorial consent—particularly the
treasury secretary, since he handled public funds that were controlled by Congress? The law creating the Treasury Department never called it an "executive" department, and it required its secretary to report to the Congress, not
the president. None of this made a particle of difference to Andrew Jackson.
All department heads were *his* appointees and they would obey *him* or pack
their bags. The summary dismissal of Duane was seen by Jackson's opponents

as a presidential grab for the purse strings of the nation. And in fact presidential control over all executive functions gave the chief executive increased authority over the collection and distribution of public funds.

The Jacksonian Revolution

By the close of 1833 many feared that Andrew Jackson was leading the country to disaster. Henry Clay regularly pilloried the president on the Senate floor. On one occasion he accused Jackson of "open, palpable and daring usurpation" of all the powers of government. "We are in the midst of a revolution," Clay thundered, "hitherto bloodless, but rapidly tending towards a total change of the pure republican character of the Government."

A "revolution"—that was how the opposition Whig Party characterized Jackson's presidency. Thenation was moving steadily away from its "pure republican character" into something approaching despotism. What the nation was witnessing, cried Clay, was "the concentration of all power in the hands of one man." Thereafter Whig newspapers reprinted a cartoon showing Jackson as "King Andrew the First." Clad in robes befitting an emperor, he was shown wearing a crown and holding a scepter in one hand and a scroll in the other on which was written the word "veto."

Democrats, naturally, read the "revolution" differently. They saw it as the steady progress of the country from the gentry republic originally established by the Founding Fathers to a more democratic system that mandated broader representation in government and a greater responsiveness to popular will.

Andrew Jackson did not take kindly to Clay's verbal mauling. "Oh, if I live to get these robes of office off me," he snorted at one point, "I will bring the rascal to a dear account." He later likened the senator to "a drunken man in a brothel," reckless, destructive, and "full of fury."

Other senators expressed their opposition to this "imperial" president and seconded Clay's complaints. John C. Calhoun, who by this time had deserted to the enemy camp, adopted the Kentuckian's "leading ideas of revolution" and charged that "a great effort is now making to choke and stifle the voice of American liberty." And he condemned Jackson's insistence on taking refuge in democratic claims. The president "tells us again and again with the greatest emphasis," he continued, "that he is the immediate representative of the American people! What effrontery! What boldness of assertion! Why, he never received a vote from the American people. He was elected by electors . . . who are elected by Legislatures chosen by the people."

Sen. Daniel Webster and other Whigs chimed in. "Again and again we hear it said," rumbled Webster, "that the President is responsible to the American people! . . . And this is thought enough for a limited, restrained, republican government! . . . I hold this, Sir, to be a mere assumption, and dangerous assumption." And connected with this "airy and unreal responsibility to the people", he continued, "is another sentiment . . . and that is, that the

President is the direct representative of the American people." The sweep of his language electrified the Senate. And "if he may be allowed to consider himself as the sole representative of all the American people," Webster concluded, "then I say, Sir, that the government . . . has already a master. I deny the sentiment, and therefore protest against the language; neither the sentiment nor the language is to be found in the Constitution of this Country."

Jackson's novel concept that the president served as the people's tribune found immediate acceptance by the electorate, despite the warnings of the Whigs. In effect, he altered the essential character of the presidency. He had become the head of government, the one person who would formulate national policy and direct public affairs. Sighed Senator Benjamin W. Leigh of Virginia: "Until the President developed the faculties of the Executive power, all men thought it inferior to the legislature—he manifestly thinks it superior: and in his hands [it] . . . has proved far stronger than the representatives of the States."

Jackson Interpreted

From Jackson's own time to the present, disagreement and controversy over the significance of his presidency have prevailed. In the twentieth century the disagreements intensified among historians. Confusion over the meaning of Jacksonian Democracy, varying regional support for democratic change, and the social and economic status of the Democrats and Whigs have clouded the efforts of scholars to reach reliable conclusions about the Old Hero and the era that bears his name.

Andrew Jackson himself will always remain a controversial figure among historians. That he can still generate such intense partisan feeling is evidence of his remarkable personality. He was an aggressive, dynamic, charismatic, and intimidating individual. And although modern scholars and students of history either admire or dislike him intensely, his rating as president in polls conducted among historians over the past thirty years varies from great to near great. He carries an enormous burden in winning any popularity contest because of his insistence on removing the eastern Indians west of the Mississippi River and on waging a long and vicious war against the Second National Bank of the United States.

His first biographer, James Parton, wrote a three-volume *Life of Andrew Jackson* (1859, 1860), and came away with mixed feelings about the man and his democracy. At times Parton railed against the mindless mob "who could be wheedled, and flattered, and drilled," but at other times he extolled democracy as the mark of an enlightened society. What troubled Parton particularly was the spoils system. Rotation, he wrote, is "an evil so great and so difficult to remedy, that if all his other public acts had been perfectly wise and right, this single feature of his administration would suffice to render it deplorable rather than amiable."

William Graham Sumner's *Andrew Jackson* (1882) was relentlessly critical of his subject, deploring in particular Jackson's flawed moral charter and emotional excesses. Sumner and other early historians, such as Herman von Holst and James Schouler, constituted what one student of the Jacksonian age called a "liberal patrician" or "Whig" school of history. These individuals came from European middle- or upper middle-class families with excellent backgrounds of education and public service. Because their class had been ousted from political power, these historians were biased against Jacksonian Democracy, and their books reflect their prejudice.

The interpretation of Old Hickory and his adherents took a sharp about-face with the appearance in 1893 of the vastly influential article by Frederick Jackson Turner, "The Significance of the Frontier in American History." Turner argued that American democracy emerged from the wilderness, noting that universal white manhood suffrage guaranteed by the new western states became something of a model for the older, eastern states. Naturally Jackson and his followers were seen as the personification of this frontier democracy. The thesis was advanced and sometimes amplified by Charles A. Beard, Vernon L. Parrington, and other western and southern historians of the early twentieth century who were caught up in the reform movement of the Progressive era. They dubbed the Jacksonian revolution an age of egalitarianism that produced the rise of the common man. Jackson himself was applauded as a man of the people. Thus the liberal patrician school of historiography gave way to the Progressive school.

This interpretation dovetailed rather well with the views of Tocqueville. During his visit, Tocqueville encountered a widespread belief in egalitarianism but worried that majoritarian rule could endanger minority rights. There are so many sharp and accurate insights into American society and institutions in *Democracy in America* that it ought to be the first book anyone reads in attempting to understand the antebellum period of American history. Among other things, he catches the American just as he is emerging from his European and colonial past and acquiring many of the characteristics [that] are generally regarded as typically American today.

Tocqueville's democratic liberalism, augmented by the works of the Progressive historians—especially Turner, Beard and Parrington—dominated historical thought about the American past for the next fifty years or more. Almost all the Progressive historians stressed the role of geographic sections in the nation, and Turner at one point even denied any class influence in the formation of frontier democracy. The only important negative voice concerning Jackson during this period came from Thomas. P. Abernethy, whose *From Frontier to Plantation in Tennessee: A Study in Frontier Democracy* (1932) insisted that Jackson himself was a frontier aristocrat, an opportunist, and a land speculator who strongly opposed the democratic forces in his own state of Tennessee.

The virtual shattering of the Progressive school's interpretation of Jacksonian Democracy came with the publication of one of the most important historical monographs ever written concerning American history: *The Age of*

Jackson (1945), by Arthur M. Schlesinger, Jr. This classic work virtually rivals in importance the frontier thesis of Frederick Jackson Turner. It is a landmark study and represents the beginning of modern scholarship on Jackson and his era.

Schlesinger argued that class distinctions rather than sectional differences best explain the phenomenon of Jacksonian Democracy. He interpreted Jackson's actions and those of his followers as an effort of the less fortunate in American society to combat the power and influence of the business community. The working classes in urban centers as well as the yeoman farmers, he argued, were the true wellsprings of the Jacksonian movement. Jacksonian Democracy evolved from the conflict between classes and best expressed its goals and purposes in the problems and needs facing urban laborers. Schlesinger singled out the bank war as the most telling example of the conflict and as the fundamental key to a fuller understanding of the meaning of Jacksonian Democracy. What attracted many historians to this path-breaking study, besides its graceful and majestic style, was Schlesinger's perceptive definition of Jacksonian Democracy and a precise explanation of its origins.

The reaction to Schlesinger's work was immediate and dramatic. It swept the historical profession like a tornado, eliciting both prodigious praise and, within a relatively short time, fierce denunciations. Bray Hammond, in a series of articles as well as his *Banks and Politics in America from the Revolution to the Civil War* (1957), and Richard Hofstadter, in his *The American Political Tradition and the Men Who Made It* (1948), contended that the Jacksonians were not the champions of urban workers or small farmers but rather ambitious and ruthless entrepreneurs principally concerned with advancing their own economic and political advantage. They were "men on the make" and frequently captains of great wealth. According to Hofstadter, the Jacksonians were not so much hostile to business as they were hostile to being excluded from entering the confined arena of capitalists. Where Schlesinger had emphasized conflict in explaining the Jacksonian era, Hofstadter insisted that consensus best characterized the period. The entrepreneurial thesis, as it was called, found strong support among many young scholars who constituted the Columbia University school of historians. In a series of articles and books produced by these critics, Jackson himself was described as an inconsistent opportunist, a strikebreaker, a shady land speculator, and a political fraud. Marvin Meyers, in his *The Jackson Persuasion* (1957), provides a slight variation on the entrepreneurial thesis by arguing that Jacksonians did indeed keep their eyes on the main chance but yearned for the virtues of a past agrarian republic. They hungered after the rewards of capitalism but looked back reverentially on the blessings of a simpler agrarian society.

A major redirection of Jacksonian scholarship came with the publication of Lee Benson's *The Concept of Jacksonian Democracy: New York as a Test Case* (1961). This work suggested a whole new approach to the investigation of the Jacksonian age by employing the techniques of quantification to uncover solid, factual data upon which to base an analysis. Moreover, Benson emphasized social questions and found that such things as ethnicity and religion were far more important than economics in determining how a person voted or which party won his allegiance. He dismissed Jacksonian rhetoric about democracy and the rights of the people as "claptrap" and contended that local issues in elections meant more to the voters than national issues. Andrew Jackson himself was dismissed as unimportant in understanding the structure and meaning of politics in this period. In time, some college textbooks virtually eliminated Jackson from any discussion of this period except to mention that he opposed social reforms and that his removal of the Indians was one of the most heinous acts in American history.

An ethnocultural school of historical writing soon emerged that rejected class difference as an important factor in political determinism. German and Irish Catholics, for example, were more likely to vote Democratic because of their ethnicity and religion than anything else. Besides, some argued, Whigs were not materially richer than Democrats. Edward Pessen, in a series of books and articles, took the argument one step further and insisted that Jacksonian America was not particularly egalitarian in terms of wealth, as Tocqueville had stated. He rejected the argument that the common man politically came into his own during the Jacksonian age. In a nice turn of phrase concluding his *Jacksonian America: Society, Personality, and Politics* (1969), Pessen declared that there was only "*seeming* deference to the common man by the uncommon men [the rich and powerful] who actually ran things."

By the end of the 1970s the ethnocultural approach had quieted down and was replaced by newer kinds of social analyses, most particularly by cultural Marxists who reemphasized class conflict in understanding voter preference. Other historians took a different approach and sought to describe what might be called a "political culture" for the period. However, many of the insights of Benson and the other students of the ethnocultural school have been incorporated into the whole to form a more sophisticated analysis. Joel Silbey, Sean Wilentz, Harry L. Watson, and others have shown that the electorate normally develops a wide set of values based on class, religion, nationality, family, residence, and several other factors and then invariably votes to safeguard those values as they perceive them. Watson particularly has demonstrated by his study of North Carolina politics that national issues did in fact matter in general elections. Even Jackson has been somewhat restored to his former importance, if not his former heroic stature. My own three-volume life of Old Hickory, *Andrew Jackson and the Course of American Empire, 1767–1821; Andrew Jackson and the Course of American Freedom, 1822–1832; Andrew Jackson and the Course of American Democracy, 1833–1845* (1977, 1981, 1984) highlights Schlesinger's findings and Jackson's faith and commitment to liberty and democracy. I contend that Jackson was in fact a man of the people, just as the Progressive historians had argued, and that he actively attempted to advance democracy by insisting that all branches of government, including the courts, reflect the popular will. I also tried to show that, for a number of reasons, the president's policy of Indian removal was initiated to spare the

Indian from certain extinction. And Francis Paul Prucha has argued persuasively that Indian removal was probably the only policy possible under the circumstances.

The study of the Jacksonian era is essential for any serious examination of the evolution of the American presidency. This has been widely recognized since the avalanche of articles and books triggered by the appearance of Schlesinger's monumental work. Jackson himself has never lost his ability to excite the most intense passions and interest among students of American history. No doubt scholars and popular writers will continue to debate his role as a national hero and as an architect of American political institutions.

Andrew Jackson and the Rise of Southwestern Democracy

Thomas. P. Abernethy

The association of Andrew Jackson with the emergent democracy of early nineteenth-century America is myth—or at least so says the late Thomas P. Abernethy of the University of Virginia in this now classic article. According to Abernethy, Jackson's political career was schizophrenic. The character of Jackson's political attitudes and behavior in the state of Tennessee bears little resemblance to that of the yet more famous Jackson of the national political arena. There is more to Jackson than his military exploits and his presence as symbolic president. Abernethy concludes that "the truth of the matter is that Jackson had little to do with the development of the democracy of the West." Jackson was much more the product than the champion of the democratic awakening we so readily associate with his name.

The name of Andrew Jackson is inseparably linked with the rise of Western democracy, but the biographers of the general have confined their attention largely to his military exploits and to his contest for and occupancy of the presidency. It is not these phases of his life, however, which connect him most intimately with the struggle of the pioneer and early Western farmer for political power. Before he was a general or a presidential possibility, he was a Tennessee politician. In this capacity he was closely associated with those events which constituted an integral part of the democratic movement of the West. A study of this phase of his career, and of the setting in which he worked, should give a better idea of the man and of the cause for which his name has come to stand.

In 1796 Tennessee adopted her first constitution. Jackson was a member of the committee which drafted it. For its day it was a liberal document, but among its provisions were two which later attracted much unfavorable attention. One provided that the justices of the peace should be chosen by the general assembly for life terms, and that the justices should choose, with a few exceptions, the other county officials; the second stipulated that all acreage should be taxed at the same rate, regardless of value.

From "Andrew Jackson and the Rise of Southwestern Democracy," by Thomas P. Abernethy, in *American Historical Review*, October 1927. Reprinted by permission of American Historical Association.

These provisions make it clear that the democracy of the West had not grown to full stature by 1796. The peculiarities of the early frontier go far toward explaining this fact. The familiar portraits of John Sevier show him in military costume of the Continental type, such as officers of the line wore during the Revolutionary War, but in his fighting days he wore a hunting shirt as did the men who followed him as he tracked the elusive Indian through the forest. Distinctions existed on the border, but they were not patent to the eye and the simple backwoodsman was not alive to them. The voters who elected delegates to the constitutional convention of 1796 did not realize to what extent they were smoothing the way for the self-aggrandizement of their leaders, the colonels, the legislators, and the land-grabbers—classifications which greatly overlapped.

The years which elapsed between 1796 and 1812 were years of relative peace and considerable growth for the Southwest, but frontier conditions persisted throughout the period. The settlers, whether in town or country, continued, in the main, to live in log cabins and wear homespun. The acquisition of Louisiana and the final opening of the Mississippi River to the trade of the West was a boon to the country. Such towns as Nashville began to emerge from the primitive and to take on the appearance of civilization. Yet it was only with great difficulty that the rivers could be ascended by keel boats, and the majority of the roads were mere trails through the woods. Money was scarce and the interchange of goods was difficult and hazardous. Barter was still commonly employed in conducting commercial transactions.

The War of 1812 ushered in a change. Tennessee troops saw considerable service in the campaigns against the Indians and the British, and the supplies necessary for their maintenance were secured largely in the West. This brought ready money into regions which had previously known little of its use, and money meant purchasing power, and luxuries, and trade. Moccasins gave place to shoes, and log cabins to brick and frame houses. The Indians caused less trouble after Jackson's conquest of the Creeks in 1813, and large tracts of land were wrested from the natives. The depression suffered by our infant industries as a result of the dumping of British goods on the American market at the end of the long European wars, and the depleted condition of the soils of the South Atlantic states were conditions tending to force population westward. The Cotton Kingdom of the Gulf region was planted in these years. The high price of the staple, which reached thirty-four cents a pound in 1817, hastened this movement, and the steamboat came just in time to facilitate the commercial side of the development.

Specie payments had been suspended by the banks south of New England in 1814, and cheap paper money had been one of the elements conducive to the rapid exploitation of the West which followed the war. In 1817 the Second Bank of the United States went into operation, and it was hoped that it would, by bringing pressure to bear upon doubtful state banks, be able to restore the currency of the country to a sound basis. This meant the retirement of much worthless paper money issued by the state banks, and a consequent restraint on speculative operations.

In order to offset this curtailment of currency and credit, Tennessee chartered a "litter" of state banks in 1817. Kentucky did likewise during the next year. At the same time, the legislature of Tennessee prevented the establishment of a branch of the Bank of the United States within her borders by levying a tax of $50,000 a year upon any such institution. This prohibitive measure was sponsored by Hugh Lawson White, while the opposition was led by Felix Grundy and supported by William Carroll and Andrew Jackson. Its passage seems to indicate the jealousy felt by local financial interests rather than the influence of constitutional scruples on the subject.

The period of speculation was followed by the panic of 1819. East Tennessee had largely escaped the financial excesses of the post-war boom, for her valleys were not suited to the culture of cotton, and transportation was so difficult as to make commercial expansion almost impossible. In Middle Tennessee, however, the growing of cotton was far more widespread during these years than it is at the present time. It was, for instance, Jackson's principal crop at the Hermitage, whereas one now has to travel many miles south of Nashville before reaching cotton country. The very high price which the staple commanded from 1815 to 1819 was the primary cause of this expansion, and the result was that thousands of farmers in this section were ruined when the price fell and the panic came on in 1819. Between five and six hundred suits for debt were entered at one term of the court of Davidson County—the county of which Nashville is the seat of justice.

The indications are that the panic of 1819 hit the small farmers of the Southwest harder than has any succeeding financial disaster. After settled conditions are established and farms are paid for, economic crises do their worst only among the trading and speculating classes, but in new country the farmers are the speculators. The result in this case was that the democracy, for the first time, rose up to demand legislative relief.

In Tennessee the agitation was led by Felix Grundy, who piloted through the assembly a bill providing for the establishment of a loan office. The state was to furnish the capital, the legislature was to elect the directors, and the loans were to be appointed among the counties according to the taxes paid in each. A "stay" law was also enacted which provided that any creditor who refused to receive the notes issued by the loan office, or state bank, as it was called, would be required to wait two years before he could enforce collection of his debt. These measures were passed by the votes of Middle Tennessee, East Tennessee being opposed. For the first and last time, the debtors of the state were clearly in the saddle.

Within a few months Kentucky established a loan office similar to that of Tennessee, and in 1823 Alabama launched a state-owned bank. Relief legislation was quite general throughout the states south of New England.

The only prominent men in Middle Tennessee who were conspicuous for their opposition to these measures were Edward Ward and Andrew Jackson. They addressed a memorial of protest to the assembly which that body refused to accept on the ground that its language was disrespectful to the law-makers. The memorial did, in fact, charge the members who voted for the loan office act with perjury since they had taken an oath to support the Constitution of the United States, and now assented to a law which made something beside gold and silver a tender in payment of debts.

In 1821 Tennessee experienced one of her most exciting gubernatorial elections. The candidates were Edward Ward and William Carroll. The former was he who had, together with Jackson, protested against the loan office; he was a native of Virginia, a man of education and wealth, and a neighbor to General Jackson. The latter was a merchant from Pennsylvania who had opened the first nail store in Nashville. He was a young man of energy and address, and Jackson had befriended him in his early days. As major-general of Tennessee militia he had served with signal distinction at the battle of New Orleans, but a break, the causes of which are obscure, developed between him and Jackson in 1816.

In the contest of 1821 Jackson used his influence in support of Ward, and looked upon Carroll and his friends as a group of demagogues. The press of the state entered heartily into the campaign and Carroll was touted as a man of the people—an unpretentious merchant, without wealth and without social prestige—whereas Ward's wealth, his slaves, and his education were held against him. He was pictured in the press as a snobbish representative of the aristocracy of the planters.

Both candidates were opposed to the loan office of 1820. Ward advocated a centralized state-banking system in place of it, whereas Carroll simply stressed a policy of retrenchment. The people appear to have discovered that the legislative relief was no panacea for their financial ills, and they were ready to accept Carroll's harsher doctrine of economy. They were beginning to understand that farmers, whose profits did not often run above five percent, could not afford to borrow from banks at six percent. Carroll carried every county in the state except two, and the mere magnitude of the victory indicates that his success was due to his reputation for democracy rather than to his merchant-class economic ideas.

With the exception of a one-term intermission made necessary by the state constitution, William Carroll presided over the government of Tennessee continuously until 1835. He was the most constructive governor who ever held office in the state, for, curiously enough, it was he who, staunchly opposed by Jackson, established "Jacksonian democracy" within her borders. He believed in government of, for, and by the people, but he also believed in a financial policy of specie payments and legislative non-interference between debtor and creditor. Under his leadership, Tennessee disavowed the kind of democracy which had mounted into the saddle on the heels of the panic of 1819, and of which Felix Grundy had been the protagonist.

In his first message to the general assembly, the new chief magistrate outlined his policy. He stuck tenaciously to his program throughout his twelve years in office, and, though it was slow work, nearly every item of his platform was finally carried into effect. In 1821 he advocated the erection of a penitentiary and the abolition of the use of the whipping post, the pillory, and the branding iron. These changes were finally brought about in 1831. Imprisonment for debt was abolished at the same time. In 1821 the "stay" law of 1820 was held unconstitutional by the supreme court of the state. In 1826 the law of 1817, which prevented the establishment of a branch of the Bank of the United States in Tennessee, was repealed with few dissenting votes in the lower house of the legislature, and accordingly that institution established an office in Nashville during the following year. In 1831 the loan office of 1820 was abolished upon Carroll's recommendation, and in 1832 and 1833 several important privately-owned banks of the usual commercial type were established. The sales of the public lands belonging to the state, which had been put upon a credit basis in 1819, were put upon a cash basis in 1823, and the prices were graduated according to the principle later advocated in Congress by Thomas H. Benton. Finally, after several unsuccessful attempts had been made in the legislature to bring the question before the people, a referendum was held and a constitutional convention assembled in 1834. The new instrument of government which was now drawn up and adopted provided for a revision of the judicial system which would facilitate the collection of debts, for popular election of county officials, and for the taxation of real estate according to its value. Thus democracy won its victory in Tennessee, and the guiding spirit was that of William Carroll.

Up to this time, the state had gone through three distinct political phases. The first, extending from 1796 until the panic of 1819, was a period during which the people gratefully and implicitly accepted the leadership of a group of outstanding citizens. The frontiersman was busy with his clearings and he gladly accepted the services of such energetic men as would organize governments and fight the Indians. The fact that these same men were usually land speculators did not disturb him even if he knew it. Land was cheap.

The second period was that of the panic of 1819 during which economic ills aroused the people to a consciousness of their political power. Felix Grundy was the first to see the possibilities of the situation and to organize the movement for his own advancement. He was the first, but by no means the last, demagogue of Tennessee. Carroll won the people away from him and inaugurated the third period, which was one of constructive social and conservative economic legislation. It is noteworthy that until 1829 both Carroll and the legislature favored federal as well as state banks, nor does anything in the history of the state indicate that there was any general feeling against such institutions before Jackson became President.

It was well for Tennessee that Carroll remained so long in office, for the demagogue was not dead. The people had been aroused and Grundy had taught a lesson to the politicians. Public office was eagerly sought by the young lawyers and others, and electioneering, unknown in the earlier days, grew rapidly in vogue during the period following 1819. Stump speaking came to be an art and cajolery a profession, while whiskey flowed freely at the hustings. The politicians could most easily attain their object by appealing to the prejudices of the masses. Colleges were said to exist for the rich, and the ignorant were asked to elect the ignorant because enlightenment and intelligence were not democratic. America, to say nothing of Tennessee, has not outlived this brand of democracy.

It was during the years of Carroll's supremacy that the Jackson presidential boom took shape and ran its course. The relation between this movement and the rise of Western democracy is of considerable interest for the reason that the two have ordinarily been considered as amounting to practically the same thing. The truth of the matter is that Jackson had little to do with the development of the democracy of the West. The movement made him President, but he contributed to it not one idea previous to his election in 1828. He rode into office upon a military reputation and the appeal which a self-made man can make so effectively to self-made men.

It did not take as astute a politician as Aaron Burr to see the possibility of making the Hero of New Orleans President of the United States. Not only Burr, but Edward Livingston and others saw it shortly after January 8, 1815. In fact, the general himself probably saw it, but did not admit it. He at least began taking a keen interest in national politics and set himself the agreeable task of helping Monroe keep [William H.] Crawford out of the chief magistracy, for the enmity between the general and the secretary dates from 1816. It arose as a result of an agreement which Crawford negotiated with the Cherokees during that year, according to the terms of which the Indians were allowed to retain three million acres of land which the Creeks had claimed and which had been ceded to the government by Jackson's treaty of 1813. The Cherokees were also allowed damages for depredations alleged to have been committed by Jackson's troops during the course of the Creek campaign. The general considered this a slur on his military reputation, and the author of it was duly condemned. It was also good political material, for Crawford was made to appear an enemy of the Western heroes and an opponent of westward expansion. It was only after the election of 1820, however, that the friends of Jackson could tactfully avow their intention to make him President, and the movement did not actually take shape until after his retirement from the governorship of Florida in 1821.

At the time when Jackson resigned this commission and returned to the Hermitage to spend his declining years "surrounded by the pleasures of domestic felicity," a little group of friends in Nashville was forming to make plans of campaign for their distinguished fellow-townsman. The leaders of this group were William B. Lewis, John Overton, and John H. Eaton.

The first-named was a planter and Jackson's neighbor. He was a close personal friend and adviser of long standing, but he was not a man of large affairs. Parton has overestimated his importance because he obtained much of his information on the campaign from Lewis himself. John Overton was a former member of the supreme court in Tennessee and one of the richest men in the state. At that time he and Jackson were partners in a large land deal: namely, the establishment of a trading-town on the Mississippi by the name of Memphis. They were closely associated in Jackson's political venture, too, and Overton later burned the papers relating thereto so that the curious might not pry into its details. In 1816 John H. Eaton, then comparatively unknown in Tennessee, undertook to complete a biography of Jackson. In 1818 he was appointed to the United States Senate, and in 1819 he defended the general when the Seminole campaign was before that body for investigation. From his vantage-point in Washington he served as field agent for the little group of Nashville managers.

Both Overton and Eaton were accused of having entertained Federalist opinions in their early days. There was certainly nothing in the background or the connections of the group to tie it up with the democratic movement which was in full tide about them. In 1823 a former judge who had sat with Overton in the supreme court of the state wrote to him: "True republicanism must supersede the Democracy of the present day before public employment will be suited to my taste. . . . There are too many who would prefer a directly contrary state of things." At about this time Jackson himself was keenly interested in a legal scheme to throw open to question the titles to about half the occupied lands in Tennessee. This, of course, was in the interest of speculators like himself. The legislature however set itself against the plan and it failed miserably.

The general had no personal dealings with either Grundy or Carroll during the early years of his candidacy, and though Grundy, with an eye to personal advancement, refused to break with him politically, and Carroll was later reconciled, it is significant that the latter is the only outstanding Tennessee Democrat who did not, sooner or later, receive federal recognition at the hands of Jackson's party.

Yet Jackson's political views were little known outside Tennessee at the time when he began to be looked upon as presidential timber. His strength lay in his military reputation, in his connection with the expansion of the West at the expense of the Spanish and Indians, and in the fact that he was not closely connected with the intrigue of Washington politics. A movement to turn out the "Virginia dynasty" and to forestall Crawford, the "heir apparent," was inevitable. The dissatisfied element in the Southern and Middle states instinctively turned to Jackson as the logical instrument for this purpose, and certainly no rôle could have been more congenial to the general than one which cast him in opposition to William H. Crawford.

The first statement that he was being definitely considered for the presidency came from Pennsylvania in 1821, where the leaders were said to have canvassed the situation and found that he was the logical man. North Carolina followed the lead of Pennsylvania, and word came from Virginia that the people were for Jackson, but that leadership was needed in order that the politicians be overthrown.

The movement in Tennessee was brought to the surface in 1822 when it was proposed that the general assembly present the general's name to the nation as a suitable candidate for the presidency. The proposition was carried by that body without a dissenting vote. This in the face of the fact that Jackson's candidate for the governorship had been defeated during the previous year by an overwhelming majority. This apparently conflicting vote merely shows that national and state politics were not closely related at that time. The general had been repudiated in no uncertain manner as a state politician, but as a national hero he was a success. Discredited because of his conservative stand in the state, he was chosen to lead the progressive movement in the nation.

A sidelight on the situation is afforded by an incident which occurred during the next year. Colonel John Williams, of Knoxville, had represented Tennessee in the United States Senate since 1815, and had attacked Jackson during the Seminole investigation of 1819. His term expired in 1823, and he was up for re-election with excellent prospects of success. Jackson's friends decided that his presidential prospects would be blighted by the election of one of his bitterest enemies to the Senate from his own state, and when no other candidate could develop sufficient strength to defeat Williams, the general himself was, at the last minute, induced to run. A number of the members of the legislature had already pledged their votes to Williams and could not change, but the ballot, when counted, stood twenty-five to thirty-five in favor of Jackson. The names of those voting were not recorded in the journal—a significant omission. Tennesseans would not permit Jackson to dictate to them, but his personal prestige was great, and there were few who dared stand against him face to face.

Jackson went to the Senate against his will. Back in 1798 he had resigned from that body after a year of uncongenial service. He was now returned to the national forum at the behest of friends who had previously devoted their best efforts to keeping him quiet. Yet it was not because he was afraid to speak his mind that he shrank from the Senate. Above all things, save perhaps a good fight, the general liked to speak his mind. That he gave in so often to his advisers shows that he was not devoid of political discretion. His real objection to Washington, as he so often stated, was its partisan intrigue. There was too much competition in the capital.

There was no doubt but that, before the presidential election, Jackson's hand would be revealed in regard to the important questions which were agitating the country. It was a brave stand for a general in politics to take, but he took it unequivocally. He voted consistently for internal improvements and for the tariff of 1824.

Jackson posed as a Jeffersonian, as did nearly all the Southern Republicans of his day, and in 1822 he had written to Monroe congratulating him upon the veto of the Cumberland Road bill. Yet Tennessee needed internal improvements and ardently desired them. As late as 1825 James K. Polk advocated federal aid for such purposes. In voting as he did in 1824, Jackson represented the interests of his constituents, but during the same year he expressed the opinion that the consent of the state should be secured before the national government should give assistance. During 1827 his supporters in the Tennessee legislature were said to have opposed a federal aid project because of the effect that the agitation of such a question by them might have upon the presidential election in Pennsylvania and Virginia. Finally, when the general became President, he vetoed the Maysville Road bill on the ground that the thoroughfare in question was one of only local importance. The fact was, however, that it was the main highway—an extension of the old Cumberland Road—along which the eastern mail was, at the very time, being carried to Nashville and the Southwest.

In his stand on the tariff question in 1824, Jackson stressed the military importance of domestic manufactures, and also argued for the development of a home market for agricultural products. In this matter he doubtless voiced his personal convictions. The home-market argument had an appeal for the grain farmers of the West, and there were more grain farmers in Tennessee than there were cotton planters, yet Jackson himself belonged to the latter group and protection was not popular with them as a class. Furthermore, despite the rise of democracy, the wealthy cotton planters still had a large share in the creation of public opinion, and there were, in Tennessee, few active advocates of a high tariff before 1840.

In regard to the Bank of the United States, Jackson's views were not developed until after the period of his senatorial services. He certainly did not take a stand against that institution before 1826. In 1827 he began making unfavorable comments on it, but public opposition did not develop until after his election to the presidency. This was clearly not a question of long-standing prejudice with him, and the evidence seems to point to Van Buren as the source of his opinions on the subject. In addition to this, Jackson knew that most of the branches of the bank were in the hands of his opponents and had good reason to believe that their influence was used against him during the election of 1828. It was entirely Jacksonian for him to form his opinion upon such grounds.

Jackson had once been a merchant and he was still a man of business affairs. He had long been a believer in a sound currency and the rights of the creditor. His early economic ideas were in accord with those of William Carroll, and there was nothing here to bring him into conflict with the Bank of the United States. The motives of his opposition were political, not economic.

No historian has ever accused Jackson, the great Democrat, of having had a political philosophy. It is hard to see that he even had any political principles. He was a man of action, and the man of action is likely to be an opportunist. Politically speaking, Jackson was certainly an opportunist. If he gave any real help or encouragement before 1828 to any of the movements which, under men like Carroll, aimed at the amelioration of the condition of the masses, the fact has not been recorded. He belonged to the moneyed aristocracy of Nashville, yet he was a self-made man and devoid of snobbishness. He thought he was sincere when he spoke to the people, yet he never really championed their cause. He merely encouraged them to champion his.

It seems clear that Jackson's political habits were formed in the period of the early settlement of the Southwest when a few leaders were able to shape the public mind and use their official positions as an aid to their exploitation of the land. He never failed, for instance, to use the patronage of office for the promotion of the interests of his friends. The democratic awakening which took such hold upon the people of Tennessee after the panic of 1819 failed to enlist his sympathy. He was called upon to lead the national phase of this movement, but played no part in the formulation or promotion of its constructive program. He did, however, in 1824, represent the needs of the West for improved commercial facilities, and he was a nationalist from early conviction. After 1824 he came under political influence—that of Van Buren, it seems, being paramount—which caused him to change his earlier opinions in several respects. This accounts for the fact that his presidential policy favored the seaboard staple growers rather than the grain producers of the West. Yet he failed, in the main, to capture the support of the cotton planters of the South, for many of them either sympathized with nullification or desired a United States bank and internal improvements. He was a political hybrid— too strong a nationalist for some, too strong a state-rights man for others. On the other hand, he held to the end the loyalty of the small farmers, for the Jacksonian tradition was deeply rooted in them, and Jackson's bank policy looked to them like democracy. Banks often worked to their disadvantage, and they could manage without commercial facilities. They constituted the rank and file of the Democratic party in the South until the Whig organization went to pieces and the planters were thereby forced to accept, at a late date, the bait which Jackson had proffered them in vain.

The Mountain Man as Jacksonian Man*

William H. Goetzmann

William H. Goetzmann, Professor of American Studies and History at the University of Texas at Austin, presents new information concerning the social and economic behavior of the Mountain Men during the Jacksonian period. Faced with the fact that "the Mountain Man exists as a figure of American mythology rather than history"—a romantic fixture on Americans' mental map, the West of the imagination—Goetzmann offers a vigorous and effective statement concerning this elusive hero of American folklore. The Mountain Men most often have been considered exemplars of a free and unrestrained existence; and the myths that surrounded them had enough validity to gain acceptance, as all lasting myths do. Yet in analyzing those who lived close to nature as they worked the Rocky Mountain fur trade, Goetzmann concludes that few were willing to remain "free agents of nature" if given the chance at other occupations. Most shared a distinct desire to return to civilized comforts. Most sought, and many attained, the respectability and success so valued by the society they had left behind. In the end, the Mountain Men fit the pattern of most "Jacksonian Men"—surprisingly, in their case, they were "venturous conservatives."

One of the most often studied and least understood figures in American history has been the Mountain Man. Remote, so it would seem, as Neanderthal, and according to some almost as inarticulate, the Mountain Man exists as a figure of American mythology rather than history. As such he has presented at least two vivid stereotypes to the public imagination. From the first he has been the very symbol for the romantic banditti of the forest, freed of the artificial restrictions of civilization—a picturesque wanderer in the wilderness whose very life is a constant and direct association with Nature.

---

*The term "Jacksonian Man" is used throughout this essay in a general rather than a particular sense. It is intended to describe a fictional composite, the average man of the period under consideration regardless of whether or not he was a follower of Andrew Jackson and his party. Those qualities which I take to be general enough to characterize the average man are defined in my quotations from Richard Hofstadter, Marvin Meyers and Alexis de Tocqueville. It should not be inferred from this that I seek to portray the Mountain Men as members of Andrew Jackson's political party nor that I mean to suggest that the particular objectives of the Democratic Party were necessarily those described by Hofstadter, Meyers and Tocqueville. Rather their terms seem

From "The Mountain Man as Jacksonian Man," by William H. Goetzmann, in *American Quarterly*, XV, No. 3 (Fall 1963), pp. 402–415. Copyright 1963, Trustees of the University of Pennsylvania. Reprinted by permission.

"There is perhaps, no class of men on the face of the earth," said Captain Bonneville [and through him Washington Irving], "who lead a life of more continued exertion, peril, and excitement, and who are more enamoured of their occupations, than the free trappers of the west. No toil, no danger, no privation can turn the trapper from his pursuit. His passionate excitement at times resembles a mania. In vain may the most vigilant and cruel savages beset his path; in vain may rocks, and precipices, and wintry torrents oppose his progress; let but a single track of a beaver meet his eye, and he forgets all dangers and defies all difficulties. At times, he may be seen with his traps on his shoulder, buffeting his way across rapid streams amidst floating blocks of ice: at other times, he is to be found with his traps on his back clambering the most rugged mountains, scaling or descending the most frightening precipices, searching by routes inaccessible to the horse, and never before trodden by white man, for springs and lakes unknown to his comrades, and where he may meet with his favorite game. Such is the mountaineer, the hardy trapper of the west; and such as we have slightly sketched it, is the wild, Robin Hood kind of life, with all its strange and motley populace, now existing in full vigor among the Rocky mountains."

To Irving in the nineteenth century the Mountain Man was Robin Hood, a European literary convention. By the twentieth century the image was still literary and romantic but somewhat less precise. According to Bernard DeVoto, "For a few years Odysseus Jed Smith and Siegfried Carson and the wing-shod Fitzpatrick actually drew breath in this province of fable," and Jim Beckwourth "went among the Rockies as Theseus dared the wine-dark seas. Skirting the rise of a hill, he saw the willows stirring; he charged down upon them, while despairing Blackfeet sang the death-song—and lo, to the clear music of a horn, Roland had met the pagan hordes. . . ."

On the other hand, to perhaps more discerning eyes in his own day and down through the years, the Mountain Man presented another image—one that was far less exalted. Set off from the ordinary man by his costume of greasy buckskins, coonskin cap and Indian finery, not to mention the distinctive odor that went with bear grease and the habitual failure to bathe between one yearly rendezvous and the next, the Mountain Man seemed a forlorn and pathetic primitive out of the past. "They are stared at as though they were bears," wrote Rudolph F. Kurz, a Swiss artist who traveled the Upper Missouri.

The Mountain Man, so it was said, was out of touch with conventional

---

to characterize to some extent men of all political persuasions in this period. Lee Benson, in his recent book, *The Concept of Jacksonian Democracy,* has shown that in New York State, at least, the Jackson party had no particular monopoly on such terms as "egalitarianism" and "democracy," and that indeed most parties in the state, including the Whigs, actually preceded the Jackson men in their advocacy of these views. He thus demonstrates that there were certain values and goals common to all men of the day. Benson then concludes that instead of calling the period "The Age of Jackson," it should properly be called "The Age of Egalitarianism." His evidence indicates to me, however, that a still more precise term for the period might well be "The Age of Expectant Capitalism," and following Hofstadter and Meyers, and before them Frederick Jackson Turner, I have seen this as the most generally applicable descriptive concept for the period. Thus it forms the basis for my definition of "Jacksonian Man," or *Genus Homo Americanus* during the years of the presidency of Andrew Jackson and his successor Martin Van Buren.

civilization and hence not quite acceptable. Instead in his own time and even more today he has been viewed as a purely hedonistic character who lived for the year's end rendezvous where he got gloriously drunk on diluted rot-gut company alcohol, gave his beaver away for wildly inflated company trade goods and crawled off into the underbrush for a delirious orgy with some unenthusiastic Indian squaw. In this view the romantic rendezvous was nothing more than a modern company picnic, the object of which was to keep the employees docile, happy and ready for the coming year's task.

Pacified, satisfied, cheated, impoverished, and probably mortified the next day, the Mountain Man, be he free trapper or not, went back to his dangerous work when the rendezvous was over. He was thus to many shrewd observers not a hero at all but a docile and obedient slave of the company. By a stretch of the imagination he might have seemed heroic, but because of the contrast between his daring deeds and his degraded status he seemed one of the saddest heroes in all history. Out of date before his time was up, he was a wild free spirit who after all was not free. He was instead an adventurer who was bringing about his own destruction even as he succeeded in his quest to search out the beaver in all of the secret places of the mountain West. A dependent of the London dandy and his foppish taste in hats, the Mountain Man was Caliban. He was a member of a picturesque lower class fast vanishing from the face of America. Like the Mohican Indian and quaint old Leatherstocking he was a vanishing breed, forlorn and permanently class-bound in spite of all his heroics.

Both of these stereotypes embody, as do most effective stereotypes, more than a measure of reality. The Mountain Man traveled far out ahead of the march of conventional civilization, and the job he did required him to be as tough, primitive and close to nature as an Indian. Moreover, it was an out-of-doors life of the hunt and the chase that he often grew to like. By the same token because he spent much of his time in primitive isolation in the mountains, he very often proved to be a poor businessman ignorant of current prices and sharp company practices. Even if aware of his disadvantageous position he could do nothing to free himself until he had made his stake.

The fact is, however, that many Mountain Men lived for the chance to exchange their dangerous mountain careers for an advantageous start in civilized life. If one examines their lives and their stated aspirations one discovers that the Mountain Men, for all their apparent eccentricities, were astonishingly similar to the common men of their time—plain republican citizens of the Jacksonian era.

Jacksonian Man, according to Richard Hofstadter, "was an expectant capitalist, a hardworking ambitious person for whom enterprise was a kind of religion." He was "the master mechanic who aspired to open his own shop, the planter or farmer who speculated in land, the lawyer who hoped to be a judge, the local politician who wanted to go to Congress, the grocer who would be a merchant. . . ." To this list one might well add, the trapper who hoped some day, if he hit it lucky and avoided the scalping knife, to be one or all of these, or perhaps better still, a landed gentleman of wealth and prestige.

"Everywhere," writes Hofstadter, the Jacksonian expectant capitalist "found conditions that encouraged him to extend himself." And there were many like William Ashley or Thomas James who out of encouragement or desperation looked away to the Rocky Mountains, teeming with beaver and other hidden resources, and saw a path to economic success and rapid upward mobility. In short, when he went out West and became a Mountain Man the Jacksonian Man did so as a prospector. He too was an expectant capitalist.

Marvin Meyers has added a further characterization of Jacksonian Man. He was, according to Meyers, the "venturous conservative, the man who desired relative freedom from restraint so that he might risk his life and his fortune, if not his sacred honor, on what appeared to be a long-term, continent-wide boom. Yet at the same time he wished to pyramid his fortune within the limits of the familiar American social and economic system, and likewise to derive his status therefrom. Wherever he went, and especially on the frontier, Jacksonian Man did not wish to change the system. He merely wished to throw it open as much as possible to opportunity, with the hope that by so doing he could place himself at the top instead of at the bottom of the conventional social and economic ladder. "They love change," wrote Tocqueville, "but they dread revolutions." Instead of a new world the Jacksonian Man wished to restore the old where the greatest man was the independent man— yeoman or mechanic, trader or ranchero—the man who basked in comfort and sturdy security under his own "vine and fig tree."

The structure of the Rocky Mountain fur trade itself, the life stories of the trappers and on rare occasions their stated or implied aspirations all make it clear that if he was not precisely the Meyers-Hofstadter Jacksonian Man, the Mountain Man was most certainly his cousin once removed, and a clearly recognizable member of the family.

It is a truism, of course, to state that the Rocky Mountain fur trade was a business, though writers in the Mountain Man's day and since have sometimes made it seem more like a sporting event. The Mountain Man himself often put such an ambiguous face on what he was doing.

> "Westward! Ho!" wrote Warren Ferris, an American Fur Company trapper. "It is the sixteenth of the second month A.D. 1830, and I have joined a trapping, trading, hunting expedition to the Rocky Mountains. Why, I scarcely know, for the motives that induced me to this step were of a mixed complexion,—something like the pepper and salt population of this city of St. Louis. Curiosity, a love of wild adventure, and perhaps also a hope of profit,—for times *are* hard, and my best coat has a sort of sheepish hang-dog hesitation to encounter fashionable folk— combined to make me look upon the project with an eye of favor. The party consists of some thirty men, mostly Canadian; but a few there are, like myself, from various parts of the Union. Each has some plausible excuse for joining, and the aggregate of disinterestedness would delight the most ghostly saint in the Roman calendar. Engage for money! no, not they;—health, and the strong desire of seeing strange lands, of beholding nature in the savage grandeur of her primeval state,—these are the only arguments that *could* have persuaded such independent and high-minded young fellows to adventure with the American Fur Company in a trip to the mountain wilds of the great west."

Ambiguous though the Mountain Man's approach to it may have been, it is abundantly clear that the Rocky Mountain fur trade was indeed a *busi-*

ness, and not an invariably individualistic enterprise at that. The unit of operation was the company, usually a partnership for the sake of capital, risk and
year-round efficiency. Examples of the company are The Missouri Fur Company, Gantt and Blackwell, Stone and Bostwick, Bean and Sinclair, and most
famous of all, the Rocky Mountain Fur Company and its successors, Smith,
Jackson, and Sublette, Sublette & Campbell, and Sublette, Fitzpatrick, Bridger,
Gervais and Fraeb. These were the average company units in the Rocky Mountain trade and much of the story of their existence is analogous to Jackson's
war on the "Monster Bank" for they were all forced to contend against John
Jacob Astor's "Monster Monopoly," the American Fur Company, which was
controlled and financed by eastern capitalists.

Perhaps the most interesting aspect of the independent fur companies
was their fluid structure of leadership. There was indeed "a baton in every
knapsack" or more accurately, perhaps, in every "possibles" bag. William Ashley, owner of a gunpowder factory and Andrew Henry, a former Lisa lieutenant, and lead miner, founded the Rocky Mountain Fur Company. After a few
years of overwhelming success, first Henry, and then Ashley, retired, and they
were succeeded by their lieutenants, Jedediah Smith, David Jackson and William Sublette, three of the "enterprising young men" who had answered Ashley's advertisement in the St. Louis *Gazette and Public Advertiser* in 1823.
When Smith and Jackson moved on to more attractive endeavors, first William
Sublette and Robert Campbell, then Tom "Broken Hand" Fitzpatrick, James
"Old Gabe" Bridger, Henry Fraeb, Milton "Thunderbolt" Sublette and Jean
Baptiste Gervais moved up to fill their entrepreneurial role.

In another example Etienne Provost was successively an employee of
Auguste Chouteau, partner with LeClair and leader of his own Green River
brigade, and servant of American Fur. Sylvestre Pattie became a Santa Fe
trader, then an independent trapper, then manager of the Santa Rita (New
Mexico) Copper Mines and ultimately leader of an independent trapping
venture into the Gila River country of the far Southwest—a venture that
ended in disaster when he was thrown into a Mexican prison in California
and there left to die. Most significant is the fact that few of the trappers declined the responsibility of entrepreneurial leadership when it was offered
them. On the contrary, the usual practice was to indenture oneself to an established company for a period of time, during which it was possible to acquire the limited capital in the way of traps, rifles, trade goods, etc., that was
needed to become independent and a potential brigade leader. Referring to
his arrangement with the old Missouri Fur Company in 1809, Thomas James
wrote,

> We Americans were all private adventurers, each on his own hook, and were led
> into the enterprise by the promise of the Company, who agreed to subsist us to
> the trapping grounds, we helping to navigate the boats, and on our arrival there
> they were to furnish us each with a rifle and sufficient ammunition, six good
> beaver traps and also four men of their hired French, to be under our individual
> commands for a period of three years.

By the terms of the contract each of us was to divide one-fourth of the profits of our joint labor with the four men thus to be appointed to us.

James himself retired when he could from the upper Missouri trade and eventually became an unsuccessful storekeeper in Harrisonville, Illinois.

In addition to the fact of rapid entrepreneurial succession within the structure of the independent fur companies, a study of 446 Mountain Men (perhaps 45 percent of the total engaged in this pursuit between 1805 and 1845) indicates that their life-patterns could be extremely varied. One hundred seventeen Mountain Men definitely turned to occupations other than trapping subsequent to their entering the mountain trade. Of this number 39 followed more than one pursuit. As such they often worked at as many as four or five different callings.

Moreover beyond the 117 definite cases of alternative callings, 32 others were found to have indeterminate occupations that were almost certainly not connected with the fur trade, making a total of 149 out of 154 men for whom some occupational data exists who had turned away from the trapping fraternity before 1845. Of the remaining men in the study, 110 men yielded nothing to investigation beyond the fact that they had once been trappers, 182 can be listed as killed in the line of duty and only five men out of the total stayed with the great out-of-doors life of the free trapper that according to the myth they were all supposed to love.

The list of alternative callings pursued by the trappers is also revealing. Twenty-one became ranchers, fifteen farmers, seventeen traders (at stationary trading posts), eight miners, seven politicians, six distillers, five each storekeepers and army scouts, four United States Indian agents, three carpenters, two each bankers, drovers and hatters and at least one pursued each of the following occupations: sheepherder, postman, miller, medium, ice dealer, vintner, fancy fruit grower, baker, saloon keeper, clockmaker, cattle buyer, real estate speculator, newspaper editor, lawyer, lumberman, superintendent of schools, tailor, blacksmith, and supercargo of a trading schooner. Moreover many of these same individuals pursued secondary occupations such as that of hotel keeper, gambler, soldier, health resort proprietor, coal mine owner, tanner, sea captain, horse thief and opera house impresario.

From this it seems clear that, statistically at least, the Mountain Man

Table 1

Total number of cases	446
Persons whose other occupations are known	117
Persons whose other occupations are probable	32
Persons with more than one other occupation	39
Persons who stayed on as trappers	5
Persons whose status is unknown	110
Persons killed in the fur trade	182

Table 2 LIST OF OCCUPATIONS

A. *Primary*

1.	Farmer	15	17.	Blacksmith	1
2.	Rancher	21	18.	Tailor	1
3.	Politician	7	19.	Supercargo	1
4.	Sheepherder	1	20.	Superintendent of Schools	1
5.	Scout [for Govt.]	5	21.	Lumberman	2
6.	Trader	17	22.	Newspaper Editor	1
7.	Miner	8	23.	Carpenter	3
8.	Postman	1	24.	Cattle Buyer	1
9.	Distiller	6	25.	Clockmaker	1
10.	Miller	1	26.	Saloon Keeper	1
11.	Storekeeper	5	27.	Baker	1
12.	Medium	1	28.	Fruit Grower	1
13.	Banker	2	29.	Vintner	1
14.	Drover	2	30.	Ice Dealer	1
15.	Hatter	2	31.	Real Estate Speculator	1
16.	Indian Agent	4	32.	Lawyer	1

B. *Secondary*

1.	Trader	4	12.	Lumberman	2
2.	Transportation	2	13.	Gambler	3
3.	Scout	5	14.	Blacksmith	1
4.	Hotel Keeper	1	15.	Soldier	1
5.	Miner	2	16.	Spa Keeper	1
6.	Farmer	5	17.	Coal Mine Operator	1
7.	Politician	3	18.	Tanner	1
8.	Rancher	5	19.	Opera House Impresario	1
9.	Storekeeper	4	20.	Sea Captain	1
10.	Miller	3	21.	Carpenter	1
11.	Real Estate	3	22.	Horse Thief	1

was hardly the simple-minded primitive that mythology has made him out to be. Indeed it appears that whenever he had the chance, he exchanged the joys of the rendezvous and the wilderness life for the more civilized excitement of "getting ahead." In many cases he achieved this aim, and on a frontier where able men were scarce he very often became a pillar of the community, and even of the nation. From the beginning, as Ashley's famous advertisement implied, the Mountain Men were men of "enterprise" who risked their lives for something more than pure romance and a misanthropic desire to evade civilization. The picturesqueness and the quaintness were largely the creation of what was the literary mentality of an age of artistic romanticism. For every "Cannibal Phil" or Robert Meldrum or "Peg-Leg" Smith there was a Sarchel Wolfskill (vintner), a George Yount (rancher) and a William Sublette (banker-politician).

Two further facts emerge in part from this data. First, it is clear that though the Jeffersonian agrarian dream of "Arcadia" bulked large in the Mountain Man's choice of occupations, it by no means obscured the whole range of "mechanical" or mercantile pursuits that offered the chance for success on the frontier. Indeed, if it suggests anything, a statistical view of the Mountain Man's "other life" suggests that almost from the beginning the Far Western frontier took on the decided aspect of an urban or semi-urban "industrial" civilization. Secondly, though it is not immediately apparent from the above statistics, a closer look indicates that a surprising number of the Mountain Men succeeded at their "other" tasks to the extent that they became regionally and even nationally prominent.

William H. Ashley became Congressman from Missouri and a spokesman for the West, Charles Bent an ill-fated though famed governor of New Mexico. "Doc" Newell was a prominent figure in the organization of Oregon Territory. Elbridge Gerry, William McGaa and John Simpson Smith were the founders and incorporators of Denver. Lucien Maxwell held the largest land grant in the whole history of the United States.

Joshua Pilcher was a famous superintendent of Indian Affairs. William Sublette, pursuing a hard money policy, saved the Bank of Missouri in the panic of 1837 and went on to be a Democratic elector for "young hickory" James K. Polk in 1844. Benjamin Wilson was elected first mayor of Los Angeles. James Clyman and his Napa Valley estate were famous in California as were the ranches of George Yount and J. J. Warner, while Sarchel Wolfskill was a co-founder of the modern California wine industry. James Waters built the first opera house in Southern California, and Kit Carson, in his later years a silver miner, received the supreme tribute of finding a dime novel dedicated to his exploits in plunder captured from marauding Apache Indians who had recently attacked and massacred a wagon train.

Many of the Mountain Men achieved fame and national status through works that they published themselves, or, as in the case of Carson, through works that immortalized correctly, or as was more usual, incorrectly, their exploits. Here one need only mention Kit Carson's *Autobiography* and his favorable treatment at the hands of Jessie Benton Frémont, T. D. Bonner's *Life and Adventures of James Beckwourth*, Francis Fuller Victor's *River of the West* (about Joe Meek), James Ohio Pattie's *Personal Narrative*, Thomas James' *Three Years Among the Indians and Mexicans*, H. L. Conard's *Uncle Dick Wooton*, David Coyner's *The Lost Trappers* (about Ezekial Williams), Irving's portrait of Joseph Reddeford Walker in *The Adventures of Captain Bonneville*, Zenas Leonard's *Narrative*, Peg-Leg Smith's "as told to" exploits in *Hutchings' California Magazine*, Stephen Meek's *Autobiography*, Warren Ferris' letters to the Buffalo, New York, *Western Literary Messenger*, John Hatcher's yarns in Lewis H. Garrard's *Wah To Yah and The Taos Trail* and perhaps most interesting of all, trapper John Brown's pseudo-scientific *Mediumistic Experiences*, to realize the extent and range of the Mountain Man's communication with the outside world in his own day. Not only was he a typical man of his time, he was often a conspicuous success and not bashful about communicating the fact in somewhat exaggerated terms to his fellow countrymen.

Direct evidence of the Mountain Men's motives is scarce, but it is clear their intentions were complex.

"Tell them that I have no heirs and that I hope to make a fortune," wrote Louis Vasquez ("Old Vaskiss" to Bernard DeVoto) in 1834 from "Fort Convenience" somewhere in the Rockies. Later as he set out on one last expedition in 1842 he added somewhat melodramatically, "I leave to make money or die." And finally Colonel A. G. Brackett, who visited Fort Bridger (jointly owned by Bridger and Vasquez), described him as "a Mexican, who put on a great deal of style, and used to ride about the country in a coach and four."

"It is, that I may be able to help those who stand in need, that I face every danger," wrote Jedediah Smith from the Wind River Mountains in 1829, "most of all, it is for this, that I deprive myself of the privilege of Society and the satisfaction of the Converse of My Friends! but I shall count all this pleasure, if I am allowed by the Alwise Ruler the privilege of Joining my Friends. . . ." And he added "Let it be the greatest pleasure that we can enjoy, the height of our ambition, now, when our Parents are in the decline of Life, to smooth the Pillow of their age, and as much as in us lies, take from them all cause of Trouble." So spoke Jedediah Smith of his hopes and ambitions upon pursuing the fur trade. No sooner had he left the mountains, however, than he was killed by Plains Indians before he could settle down in business with his brothers as he had intended. Noble and ignoble were the motives of the Mountain Men. Colonel John Shaw, starting across the southern plains and into the Rockies in search of gold; Thomas James, desperate to recoup his failing fortunes; the Little Rock *Gazette* of 1829 "confidently" believing "that this enterprise affords a prospect of great profit to all who may engage in it"; the St. Louis *Enquirer* in 1822 labeling the Rocky Mountains "the Shining Mountains," and innocently declaring, "A hunter pursuing his game found the silver mines of Potosi, and many others have been discovered by the like accidents, and there is no reason to suppose that other valuable discoveries may not be made"; Ashley calling clearly and unmistakably for men of "enterprise," all added up to the fact that the Mountain Man when he went West was a complex character. But in his complexity was a clearly discernible pattern—the pattern of Jacksonian Man in search of respectability and success in terms recognized by the society he had left behind. His goal was, of course, the pursuit of happiness. But happiness, contrary to Rousseauistic expectations, was not found in the wilderness; it was an integral product of society and civilization.

If the Mountain Man was indeed Jacksonian Man, then there are at least three senses in which this concept has importance. First, more clearly than anything else a statistical and occupational view of the various callings of the Mountain Man tentatively indicates the incredible rate and the surprising *nature* of social and economic change in the West. In little more than two decades most of the surviving enterprising men had left the fur trade for more lucrative and presumably more useful occupations. And by their choice of occupations it is clear that in the Far West a whole step in the settlement process had been virtually skipped. They may have dreamed of "Arcadia," but when they turned to the task of settling the West as fast as possible, the former Mountain Men and perhaps others like them brought with them all the aspects of an "industrial," mercantile and quasi-urban society. The opera house went up almost simultaneously with the ranch, and the Bank of Missouri was secured before the land was properly put into hay.

Secondly, as explorers—men who searched out the hidden places in the western wilderness—the Mountain Men as Jacksonian Men looked with a flexible eye upon the new land. Unlike the Hudson's Bay explorer who looked only for beaver and immediate profit, the Mountain Man looked to the future and the development of the West, not as a vast game preserve, but as a land like the one he had known back home.

> "Much of this vast waste of territory belongs to the Republic of the United States," wrote Zenas Leonard from San Francisco Bay in 1833. "What a theme to contemplate its settlement and civilization. Will the jurisdiction of the federal government ever succeed in civilizing the thousands of savages now roaming over these plains, and her hardy freeborn population here plant their homes, build their towns and cities, and say here shall the arts and sciences of civilization take root and flourish? Yes, here, even in this remote part of the Great West before many years will these hills and valleys be greeted with the enlivening sound of the workman's hammer, and the merry whistle of the ploughboy ... we have good reason to suppose that the territory *west* of the mountains will some day be equally as important to the nation as that on the east."

In 1830 in a famous letter to John H. Eaton, the Secretary of War, Jedediah S. Smith, David E. Jackson and William L. Sublette aired their views on the possibilities of the West. Smith made clear that a wagon road route suitable for settlers existed all the way to Oregon, and Sublette dramatized the point when he brought ten wagons and two dearborns and even a milch cow over the mountains as far as the Wind River rendezvous. Their report made abundantly clear that in their opinion the future of the West lay with settlers rather than trappers. Indeed they were worried that the English at Fort Vancouver might grasp this fact before the American government. In short, as explorers and trappers theirs was a broad-ranging, flexible, settler-oriented, public view of the Far West.

Tied in with this and of the greatest significance is a third and final point. Not only did they *see* a settler's future in the West, but at least some of the Mountain Men were most eager to see to it that such a future was *guaranteed* by the institutions of the United States Government which must be brought West and extended over all the wild new land to protect the settler in the enjoyment of his own "vine and fig tree." The Mexican Government, unstable, and blown by whim or caprice, could not secure the future, and the British Government, at least in North America, was under the heel of monopoly. France was frivolous and decadent. Russia was a sinister and backward despotism. Only the free institutions of Jacksonian America would make the West safe for enterprise. So strongly did he feel about this that in 1841 the Mountain Man Moses "Black" Harris sent a letter to one Thornton Grimsley offering him the command of 700 men, of which he was one, who were eager to "join the standard of their country, and make a clean sweep of what is called the

Origon [*sic*] Territory; that is clear it of British and Indians." Outraged not only at British encroachments, he was also prepared to "march through to California" as well. It may well have been this spirit that settled the Oregon question and brought on the Mexican War.

Settlement, security, stability, enterprise, free enterprise, a government of laws which, in the words of Jackson himself, confines "itself to equal *protection*, and as Heaven does its rains, showers its favors alike on the high and the low, the rich and the poor," all of these shaped the Mountain Man's vision of the West and his role in its development. It was called Manifest Destiny. But long before John L. O'Sullivan nicely turned the phrase in the *Democratic Review*, the Mountain Man as Jacksonian Man—a "venturous conservative"— was out in the West doing his utmost to lend the Almighty a helping hand. James Clyman perhaps put it most simply:

> Here lies the bones of old Black Harris
> who often traveled beyond the far west
> and for the freedom of Equal rights
> He crossed the snowy mountain Hights
> was free and easy kind of soul
> Especially with a Belly full.

New Perspectives on Jacksonian Politics

Richard P. McCormick

Questions as to the political character of Jacksonian Democracy have precipitated
considerable intellectual debate among historians. The controversy has revolved
around one central issue: What was the extent of voter participation in the American
political process during the age of Andrew Jackson? Related to this issue is the
following question: Was Andrew Jackson a cause or a consequence of his age?
Richard P. McCormick, Emeritus Professor of History at Rutgers University, offers
insight into this continuing debate. Through his statistical analysis of voter
participation in presidential elections during the early-to-mid-nineteenth century,
McCormick demonstrates conclusively that the so-called "mighty democratic
uprising" long associated with Jackson's ascendancy did not occur until 1840; in the
process he destroys the myth that Jackson was swept into the presidency on a wave
of popular voter sentiment.

The historical phenomenon that we have come to call Jacksonian democracy
has long engaged the attention of American political historians, and never
more insistently than in the past decade. From the time of Parton and Bancroft
to the present day scholars have recognized that a profoundly significant
change took place in the climate of politics simultaneously with the appearance of Andrew Jackson on the presidential scene. They have sensed that a full
understanding of the nature of that change might enable them to dissolve
some of the mysteries that envelop the operation of the American democratic
process. With such a challenging goal before them, they have pursued their
investigations with uncommon intensity and with a keen awareness of the
contemporary relevance of their findings.

A cursory view of the vast body of historical writing on this subject suggests that scholars in the field have been largely preoccupied with attempts to
define the content of Jacksonian democracy and identify the influences that
shaped it. What did Jacksonian democracy represent, and what groups, classes,
or sections gave it its distinctive character? The answers that have been given
to these central questions have been—to put it succinctly—bewildering in
their variety. The discriminating student, seeking the essential core of Jackso-

From "New Perspectives on Jacksonian Politics," by Richard P. McCormick, in *American Historical Review* (January 1960). Reprinted by permission of the author.

nianism, may make a choice among urban workingmen, southern planters, venturous conservatives, farm-bred *nouveaux riches,* western frontiersmen, frustrated entrepreneurs, or yeoman farmers. Various as are these interpretations of the motivating elements that constituted the true Jacksonians, the characterizations of the programmatic features of Jacksonian democracy are correspondingly diverse. Probably the reasonable observer will content himself with the conclusion that many influences were at work and that latitudinarianism prevailed among the Jacksonian faithful.

In contrast with the controversy that persists over these aspects of Jacksonian democracy, there has been little dissent from the judgment that "the 1830's saw the triumph in American politics of that democracy which has remained pre-eminently the distinguishing feature of our society." The consensus would seem to be that with the emergence of Jackson, the political pulse of the nation quickened. The electorate, long dormant or excluded from the polls by suffrage barriers, now became fired with unprecedented political excitement. The result was a bursting forth of democratic energies, evidenced by a marked upward surge in voting. Beard in his colorful fashion gave expression to the common viewpoint when he asserted that "the roaring flood of the new democracy was . . . [by 1824] foaming perilously near the crest. . . ." Schlesinger, with his allusion to the "immense popular vote" received by Jackson in 1824, creates a similar image. The Old Hero's victory in 1828 has been hailed as the consequence of a "mighty democratic uprising."

That a "new democracy, ignorant, impulsive, irrational" entered the arena of politics in the Jackson era has become one of the few unchallenged "facts" in an otherwise controversial field. Differences of opinion occur only when attempts are made to account for the remarkable increase in the size of the active electorate. The commonest explanations have emphasized the assertion by the common man of his newly won political privileges, the democratic influences that arose out of the western frontier, or the magnetic attractiveness of Jackson as a candidate capable of appealing with singular effectiveness to the backwoods hunter, the plain farmer, the urban workingman, and the southern planter.

Probably because the image of a "mighty democratic uprising" has been so universally agreed upon, there has been virtually no effort made to describe precisely the dimensions of the "uprising." Inquiry into this aspect of Jacksonian democracy has been discouraged by a common misconception regarding voter behavior before 1824. As the authors of one of our most recent and best textbooks put it: "In the years from the beginning of the government to 1824, a period for which we have no reliable election statistics, only small numbers of citizens seemed to have bothered to go to the polls." Actually, abundant data on pre-1824 elections is available, and it indicates a far higher rate of voting than has been realized. Only by taking this data into consideration can voting behavior after 1824 be placed in proper perspective.

The question of whether there was indeed a "mighty democratic uprising" during the Jackson era is certainly crucial in any analysis of the political character of Jacksonian democracy. More broadly, however, we need to know the degree to which potential voters participated in elections before, during, and after the period of Jackson's presidency as well as the conditions that apparently influenced the rate of voting. Only when such factors have been analyzed can we arrive at firm conclusions with respect to the dimensions of the political changes that we associate with Jacksonian democracy. Obviously in studying voter participation we are dealing with but one aspect of a large problem, and the limitations imposed by such a restrictive focus should be apparent.

In measuring the magnitude of the vote in the Jackson elections it is hardly significant to use the total popular vote cast throughout the nation. A comparison of the total vote cast in 1812, for example, when in eight of the seventeen states electors were chosen by the legislature, with the vote in 1832, when every state except South Carolina chose its electors by popular vote, has limited meaning. Neither is it revealing to compare the total vote in 1824 with that in 1832 without taking into consideration the population increase during the interval. The shift from the legislative choice of electors to their election by popular vote, together with the steady population growth, obviously swelled the presidential vote. But the problem to be investigated is whether the Jackson elections brought voters to the polls in such enlarged or unprecedented proportions as to indicate that a "new democracy" had burst upon the political scene.

The most practicable method for measuring the degree to which voters participated in elections over a period of time is to relate the number of votes cast to the number of potential voters. Although there is no way of calculating precisely how many eligible voters there were in any state at a given time, the evidence at hand demonstrates that with the exception of Rhode Island, Virginia, and Louisiana the potential electorate after 1824 was roughly equivalent to the adult white male population. A meaningful way of expressing the rate of voter participation, then, is to state it in terms of the percentage of the adult white males actually voting. This index can be employed to measure the variations that occurred in voter participation over a period of time and in both national and state elections. Consequently a basis is provided for comparing the rate of voting in the Jackson elections with other presidential elections before and after his regime as well as with state elections.

Using this approach it is possible, first of all, to ascertain whether or not voter participation rose markedly in the three presidential elections in which Jackson was a candidate. Did voter participation in these elections so far exceed the peak participation in the pre-1824 election as to suggest that a mighty democratic uprising was taking place? The accompanying data (Table 1) provides an answer to this basic question.

In the 1824 election not a single one of the eighteen states in which the electors were chosen by popular vote attained the percentage of voter participation that had been reached before 1824. Prior to that critical election, fifteen of those eighteen states had recorded votes in excess of 50 percent of their adult white male population, but in 1824 only two states—Maryland and Alabama—exceeded this modest mark. The average rate of voter participation in

Table 1 PERCENTAGES OF ADULT WHITE MALES VOTING IN ELECTIONS

State	Highest known % AWM voting before 1824		Presidential elections					
	Year	% AWM	1824	1828	1832	1836	1840	1844
Maine	1812ᵍ	62.0	18.9	42.7	66.2*	37.4	82.2	67.5
New Hampshire	1814ᵍ	80.8	16.8	76.5	74.2	38.2	86.4*	65.6
Vermont	1812ᵍ	79.9	—	55.8	50.0	52.5	74.0	65.7
Massachusetts	1812ᵍ	67.4	29.1	25.7	39.3	45.1	66.4	59.3
Rhode Island	1812ᵍ	49.4	12.4	18.0	22.4	24.1	33.2	39.8
Connecticut	1819¹	54.5	14.9	27.1	45.9	52.3	75.7*	76.1
New York	1810ᵍ	41.5	—	70.4*	72.1	60.2	77.7	73.6
New Jersey	1808ᵖ	71.8	31.1	70.9	69.0	69.3	80.4*	81.6
Pennsylvania	1808ᵍ	71.5	19.6	56.6	52.7	53.1	77.4*	75.5
Delaware	1804ᵍ	81.9	—	—	67.0	69.4	82.8*	85.0
Maryland	1820¹	69.0	53.7	76.2*	55.6	67.5	84.6	80.3
Virginia	1800ᵖ	25.9	11.5	27.6*	30.8	35.1	54.6	54.5
North Carolina	1823ᶜ	70.0#	42.2	56.8	31.7	52.9	83.1*	79.1
Georgia	1812ᶜ	62.3	—	35.9	33.0	64.9*	88.9	94.0
Kentucky	1820ᵍ	74.4	25.3	70.7	73.9	61.1	74.3	80.3*
Tennessee	1817ᵍ	80.0	26.8	49.8	28.8	55.2	89.6*	89.6
Louisiana	1812ᵍ	34.2	—	36.3*	24.4	19.2	39.4	44.7
Alabama	1819ᵍ	96.7	52.1	53.6	33.3	65.0	89.8	82.7
Mississippi	1823ᵍ	79.8	41.6	56.6	32.8	62.8	88.2*	89.7
Ohio	1822ᵍ	46.5	34.8	75.8*	73.8	75.5	84.5	83.6
Indiana	1822ᵍ	52.4	37.5	68.3*	61.8	70.1	86.0	84.9
Illinois	1822ᵍ	55.8	24.2	51.9	45.6	43.7	85.9*	76.3
Missouri	1820ᵍ	71.9	20.1	54.3	40.8	35.6	74.0*	74.7
Arkansas	—	—	—	—	—	35.0	86.4	68.8
Michigan	—	—	—	—	—	35.7	84.9	79.3
National average			26.5	56.3	54.9	55.2	78.0	74.9

*Exceeded pre-1824 high
ᵍGubernatorial election
ᵖPresidential election

#Estimate based on incomplete returns
ᶜCongressional election
¹Election of legislature

the election was 26.5 percent. This hardly fits the image of the "roaring flood of the new democracy . . . foaming perilously near the crest. . . ."

There would seem to be persuasive evidence that in 1828 the common man flocked to the polls in unprecedented numbers, for the proportion of adult white males voting soared to 56.3 percent, more than double the 1824 figure. But this outpouring shrinks in magnitude when we observe that in only six of the twenty-two states involved were new highs in voter participation established. In three of these—Maryland, Virginia, and Louisiana—the recorded gain was inconsiderable, and in a fourth—New York—the bulk of the increase might be attributed to changes that had been made in suffrage qualifications as recently as 1821 and 1826. Six states went over the 70 percent mark, whereas ten had bettered that performance before 1824. Instead of a "mighty democratic uprising" there was in 1828 a voter turnout that approached—but in only a few instances matched or exceeded—the maximum levels that had been attained before the Jackson era.

The advance that was registered in 1828 did not carry forward to 1832. Despite the fact that Jackson was probably at the peak of his personal popularity, that he was engaged in a campaign that was presumably to decide issues of great magnitude, and that in the opinion of some authorities a "well-developed two party system on a national scale" had been established, there was a slight decline in voter participation. The average for the twenty-three states participating in the presidential contest was 54.9 percent. In fifteen states a smaller percentage of the adult white males went to the polls in 1832 than in 1828. Only five states bettered their pre-1824 highs. Again the conclusion would be that it was essentially the pre-1824 electorate—diminished in most states and augmented in a few—that voted in 1832. Thus, after three Jackson elections, sixteen states had not achieved the proportions of voter participation that they had reached before 1824. The "new democracy" had not yet made its appearance.

A comparison of the Jackson elections with earlier presidential contests is of some interest. Such comparisons have little validity before 1808 because few states chose electors by popular vote, and for certain of those states the complete returns are not available. In 1816 and 1820 there was so little opposition to Monroe that the voter interest was negligible. The most relevant elections, therefore, are those of 1808 and 1812. The accompanying table (Table 2) gives the percentages of adult white males voting in 1808 and 1812 in those states for which full returns could be found, together with the comparable percentages for the elections of 1824 and 1828. In 1824 only one state—Ohio—surpassed the highs established in either 1808 or 1812. Four more joined this list in 1828—Virginia, Maryland, Pennsylvania, and New Hampshire—although the margin in the last case was so small as to be inconsequential.

Table 2 PERCENTAGES OF ADULT WHITE MALES
VOTING IN PRESIDENTIAL ELECTIONS

State	1808	1812	1824	1828
Maine	Legis.	50.0	18.9	42.7
New Hampshire	62.1	75.4	16.8	76.5
Massachusetts	Legis.	51.4	29.1	25.7
Rhode Island	37.4	37.7	12.4	18.0
New Jersey	71.8	Legis.	31.1	70.9
Pennsylvania	34.7	45.5	19.6	56.6
Maryland	48.4	56.5	53.7	76.2
Virginia	17.7	17.8	11.5	27.6
Ohio	12.8	20.0	34.8	75.8

Note: No complete returns of the popular vote cast for electors in Kentucky or Tennessee in 1808 and 1812 and in North Carolina in 1808 could be located.

The most significant conclusion to be drawn from this admittedly limited and unrepresentative data is that in those states where there was a vigorous two-party contest in 1808 and 1812 the vote was relatively high. Conversely, where there was little or no contest in 1824 or 1828, the vote was low.

When an examination is made of voting in other than presidential elections prior to 1824, the inaccuracy of the impression that "only small numbers of citizens" went to the polls becomes apparent. Because of the almost automatic succession of the members of the "Virginia dynasty" and the early deterioration of the national two-party system that had seemed to be developing around 1800, presidential elections did not arouse voter interest as much as did those for governor, state legislators, or even members of Congress. In such elections at the state level the "common man" was stimulated by local factors to cast his vote, and he frequently responded in higher proportions than he did to the later stimulus provided by Jackson.

The average voter participation for all the states in 1828 was 56.3 percent. Before 1824 fifteen of the twenty-two states had surpassed that percentage. Among other things, this means that the 1828 election failed to bring to the polls the proportion of the electorate that had voted on occasion in previous elections. There was, in other words, a high potential vote that was frequently realized in state elections but which did not materialize in presidential elections. The unsupported assumption that the common man was either apathetic or debarred from voting by suffrage barriers before 1824 is untenable in the light of this evidence.

In state after state (see Table 1) gubernatorial elections attracted 70 percent or more of the adult white males to the polls. Among the notable highs recorded were Delaware with 81.9 percent in 1804, New Hampshire with 80.8 percent in 1814, Tennessee with 80.0 percent in 1817, Vermont with 79.9 percent in 1812, Mississippi with 79.8 percent in 1823, and Alabama with a highly improbable 96.7 percent in its first gubernatorial contest in 1819. There is reason to believe that in some states, at least, the voter participation in the election of state legislators was even higher than in gubernatorial elections. Because of the virtual impossibility of securing county-by-county or district-by-district returns for such elections, this hypothesis is difficult to verify.

Down to this point the voter turnout in the Jackson elections has been compared with that in elections held prior to 1824. Now it becomes appropriate to inquire whether during the period 1824 through 1832 voters turned out in greater proportions for the three presidential contests than they did for the contemporary state elections. If, indeed, this "new democracy" bore some special relationship to Andrew Jackson or to his policies, it might be anticipated that interest in the elections in which he was the central figure would stimulate greater voter participation than gubernatorial contests, in which he was at most a remote factor.

Actually, the election returns show fairly conclusively that throughout the eight-year period the electorate continued to participate more extensively in state elections than in those involving the presidency. Between 1824 and

1832 there were fifty regular gubernatorial elections in the states that chose their electors by popular vote. In only sixteen of these fifty instances did the vote for President surpass the corresponding vote for governor. In Rhode Island, Delaware, Tennessee, Kentucky, Illinois, Mississippi, Missouri, and Georgia the vote for governor consistently exceeded that for President. Only in Connecticut was the reverse true. Viewed from this perspective, too, the remarkable feature of the vote in the Jackson elections is not its immensity but rather its smallness.

Finally, the Jackson elections may be compared with subsequent presidential elections. Once Jackson had retired to the Hermitage, and figures of less dramatic proportions took up the contest for the presidency, did voter participation rise or fall? This question can be answered by observing the percentage of adult white males who voted in each state in the presidential elections of 1836 through 1844 (Table 1). Voter participation in the 1836 election remained near the level that had been established in 1828 and 1832, with 55.2 percent of the adult white males voting. Only five states registered percentages in excess of their pre-1824 highs. But in 1840 the "new democracy" made its appearance with explosive suddenness.

In a surge to the polls that has rarely, if ever, been exceeded in any presidential election, four out of five (78.0 percent) of the adult white males cast their votes for Harrison or Van Buren. This new electorate was greater than that of the Jackson period by more than 40 percent. In all but five states— Vermont, Massachusetts, Rhode Island, Kentucky, and Alabama—the peaks of voter participation reached before 1824 were passed. Fourteen of the twenty-five states involved set record highs for voting that were not to be broken throughout the remainder of the ante bellum period. Now, at last, the common man—or at least the man who previously had not been sufficiently aroused to vote in presidential elections—cast his weight into the political balance. This "Tippecanoe democracy," if such a label is permissible, was of a different order of magnitude from the Jacksonian democracy. The elections in which Jackson figured brought to the polls only those men who were accustomed to voting in state or national elections, except in a very few states. The Tippecanoe canvass witnessed an extraordinary expansion of the size of the presidential electorate far beyond previous dimensions. It was in 1840, then, that the "roaring flood of the new democracy" reached its crest. And it engulfed the Jacksonians.

The flood receded only slightly in 1844, when 74.9 percent of the estimated potential electorate went to the polls. Indeed, nine states attained their record highs for the period. In 1848 and 1852 there was a general downward trend in voter participation, followed by a modest upswing in 1856 and 1860. But the level of voter activity remained well above that of the Jackson elections. The conclusion to be drawn is that the "mighty democratic uprising" came after the period of Jackson's presidency.

Now that the quantitative dimensions of Jacksonian democracy as a political phenomenon have been delineated and brought into some appropriate perspective, certain questions still remain to be answered. Granted that the Jacksonian electorate—as revealed by the comparisons that have been set forth—was not really very large, how can we account for the fact that voter participation doubled between the elections of 1824 and 1828? It is true that the total vote soared from around 359,000 to 1,155,400 and that the percentage of voter participation more than doubled. Traditionally, students of the Jackson period have been impressed by this steep increase in voting and by way of explanation have identified the causal factors as the reduction of suffrage qualifications, the democratic influence of the West, or the personal magnetism of Jackson. The validity of each of these hypotheses needs to be reexamined.

In no one of the states in which electors were chosen by popular vote was any significant change made in suffrage qualifications between 1824 and 1828. Subsequently, severe restrictions were maintained in Rhode Island until 1842, when some liberalization was effected, and in Virginia down to 1850. In Louisiana, where the payment of a tax was a requirement, the character of the state tax system apparently operated to restrict the suffrage at least as late as 1845. Thus with the three exceptions noted, the elimination of suffrage barriers was hardly a factor in producing an enlarged electorate during the Jackson and post-Jackson periods. Furthermore, all but a few states had extended the privilege of voting either to all male taxpayers or to all adult male citizens by 1810. After Connecticut eliminated its property qualification in 1818, Massachusetts in 1821, and New York in 1821 and 1826, only Rhode Island, Virginia, and Louisiana were left on the list of "restrictionist" states. Neither Jackson's victory nor the increased vote in 1828 can be attributed to the presence at the polls of a newly enfranchised mass of voters.

Similarly, it does not appear that the western states led the way in voter participation. Prior to 1824, for example, Ohio, Indiana, and Illinois had never brought to the polls as much as 60 percent of their adult white males. Most of the eastern states had surpassed that level by considerable margins. In the election of 1828 six states registered votes in excess of 70 percent of their adult white male populations. They were in order of rank: New Hampshire, Maryland, Ohio, New Jersey, Kentucky, and New York. The six leaders in 1832 were: New Hampshire, Kentucky, Ohio, New York, New Jersey, and Delaware. It will be obvious that the West, however that region may be defined, was not leading the "mighty democratic uprising." Western influences, then, do not explain the increased vote in 1828.

There remains to be considered the factor of Jackson's personal popularity. Did Jackson, the popular hero, attract voters to the polls in unprecedented proportions? The comparisons that have already been made between the Jackson elections and other elections—state and national—before, during, and after his presidency would suggest a negative answer to the question. Granted that a majority of the voters in 1828 favored Jackson, it is not evident that his partisans stormed the polls any more enthusiastically than did the Adams men. Of the six highest states in voter participation in 1828, three favored Adams and three were for Jackson, which could be interpreted to mean that the convinced Adams supporters turned out no less zealously for their man than did the ardent Jacksonians. When Van Buren replaced Jackson in 1836, the voting average increased slightly over 1832. And, as has been demonstrated, the real manifestation of the "new democracy" came not in 1828 but in 1840.

The most satisfactory explanation for the increase in voter participation between 1824 and 1828 is a simple and obvious one. During the long reign of the Virginia dynasty, interest in presidential elections dwindled. In 1816 and 1820 there had been no contest. The somewhat fortuitous termination of the Virginia succession in 1824 and the failure of the congressional caucus to solve the problem of leadership succession threw the choice of a President upon the electorate. But popular interest was dampened by the confusion of choice presented by the multiplicity of candidates, by the disintegration of the old national parties, by the fact that in most states one or another of the candidates was so overwhelmingly popular as to forestall any semblance of a contest, and possibly by the realization that the election would ultimately be decided by the House of Representatives. By 1828 the situation had altered. There were but two candidates in the field, each of whom had substantial sectional backing. A clear-cut contest impended, and the voters became sufficiently aroused to go to the polls in moderate numbers.

One final question remains. Why was the vote in the Jackson elections relatively low when compared with previous and contemporary state elections and with presidential votes after 1840? The answer, in brief, is that in most states either Jackson or his opponent had such a one-sided advantage that the result was a foregone conclusion. Consequently there was little incentive for the voters to go to the polls.

This factor can be evaluated in fairly specific quantitative terms. If the percentage of the total vote secured by each candidate in each state in the election of 1828 is calculated, the difference between the percentages can be used as an index of the closeness, or one-sidedness, of the contest. In Illinois, for example, Jackson received 67 percent of the total vote and Adams, 33; the difference—thirty-four points—represents the margin between the candidates. The average difference between the candidates, taking all the states together, was thirty-six points. Expressed another way this would mean that in the average state the winning candidate received more than twice the vote of the loser. Actually, this was the case in thirteen of the twenty-two states (see Table 3). Such a wide margin virtually placed these states in the "no contest" category.

A remarkably close correlation existed between the size of the voter turnout and the relative closeness of the contest. The six states previously listed as having the greatest voter participation in 1828 were among the seven states with the smallest margin of difference between the candidates. The exception was Louisiana, where restrictions on the suffrage curtailed the vote. Even in this instance, however, it is significant that voter participation in Louisiana reached a record high. In those states, then, where there was a close balance of political forces the vote was large, and conversely, where the contest was very one-sided, the vote was low.

Most of the states in 1828 were so strongly partial to one or another of the candidates that they can best be characterized as one-party states. Adams

Table 3   DIFFERENTIAL BETWEEN PERCENTAGES OF TOTAL
VOTE OBTAINED BY MAJOR PRESIDENTIAL
CANDIDATES, 1828–1844

State	1828	1832	1836	1840	1844
Maine	20	10	20	1	13
New Hampshire	7	13	50	11	19
Vermont	50	10	20	29	18
Massachusetts	66	30	9	16	12
Rhode Island	50	14	6	23	20
Connecticut	50	20	1	11	5
New York	2	4	9	4	1
New Jersey	4	1	1	4	1
Pennsylvania	33	16	4	1	2
Delaware	—	2	6	10	3
Maryland	2	1	7	8	5
Virginia	38	50	13	1	6
North Carolina	47	70	6	15	5
Georgia	94	100	4	12	4
Kentucky	1	9	6	29	8
Tennessee	90	90	16	11	1
Louisiana	6	38	3	19	3
Alabama	80	100	11	9	18
Mississippi	60	77	2	7	13
Ohio	3	3	4	9	2
Indiana	13	34	12	12	2
Illinois	34	37	10	2	12
Missouri	41	32	21	14	17
Arkansas	—	—	28	13	9
Michigan	—	—	9	4	26
Average differential	36	36	11	11	6

encountered little opposition in New England, except in New Hampshire, and Jackson met with hardly any resistance in the South. It was chiefly in the middle states and the older West that the real battle was waged. With the removal of Adams from the scene after 1828, New England became less of a one-party section, but the South remained extremely one-sided. Consequently it is not surprising that voter participation in 1832 failed even to match that of 1828.

Here, certainly, is a factor of crucial importance in explaining the dimensions of the voter turnout in the Jackson elections. National parties were still in a rudimentary condition and were highly unbalanced from state to state. Indeed, a two-party system scarcely could be said to exist in more than half of the states until after 1832. Where opposing parties had been formed to contest the election, the vote was large, but where no parties, or only one, took the field, the vote was low. By 1840, fairly well-balanced parties had been organized in virtually every state. In only three states did the margin between Harrison and Van Buren exceed twenty points, and the average for all the states was only eleven points. The result was generally high voter participation.

When Jacksonian democracy is viewed from the perspectives employed in this analysis, its political dimensions in so far as they relate to the behavior of the electorate can be described with some precision. None of the Jackson elections involved a "mighty democratic uprising" in the sense that voters were drawn to the polls in unprecedented proportions. When compared with the peak participation recorded for each state before 1824, or with contemporaneous gubernatorial elections, or most particularly with the vast outpouring of the electorate in 1840, voter participation in the Jackson elections was unimpressive. The key to the relatively low presidential vote would seem to be the extreme political imbalance that existed in most states as between the Jacksonians and their opponents. Associated with this imbalance was the immature development of national political parties. Indeed, it can be highly misleading to think in terms of national parties in connection with the Jackson elections. As balanced, organized parties subsequently made their appearance from state to state, and voters were stimulated by the prospect of a genuine contest, a marked rise in voter participation occurred. Such conditions did not prevail generally across the nation until 1840, and then at last the "mighty democratic uprising" took place.

The Egalitarian Myth and the American Social Reality

Edward Pessen

The historical reputation of the Jacksonian era—and a consequent centerpiece of belief about it—has been that American society to a notable degree became far more egalitarian than it had been in earlier times. The Age of Jackson, it has been alleged, was an especially propitious time for upward social and economic mobility—a time, in short, when antebellum American society began to effect social practices commensurate with the American Dream of "making it." The resultant notion persists that common, ordinary folk (exclusive of women, blacks, and Indians, of course) were the dominant social type and that the proverbial "doors of opportunity" swung open ever more widely. The erasure of class barriers, in tandem with a broader distribution of wealth, brought an equality of condition to the great many. Whereas this may have been the generally accepted version of social reality even at the time, according to social historian Edward Pessen, Distinguished Professor of History at Baruch College and the City University of New York Graduate Center, American social reality on the basis of quantitative data evinces slim evidence indeed that equality reigned. At best, a "fictitious equality" prevailed. While a Jacksonian myth of economic and social equality was quick to become part of Americana, social and economic democracy in any thoroughgoing sense was more illusion than reality. According to Pessen, elitism persisted in the Age of the Common Man. It was "neither an age of egalitarianism nor of the Common Man."

The bedrock of the egalitarian theory is the belief that in Jacksonian America a rough equality prevailed. The very first words in Tocqueville's classic set forth this view: "Among the novel objects that attracted my attention during my stay in the United States, nothing struck me more forcibly than the general equality of condition among the people." This equality was not simply one among a number of equally important features of American life. Rather it was "the fundamental fact from which all others seem to be derived and the central point at which all ... [his] observations constantly terminated." Tocqueville was both too sophisticated and, for all his predilection for theorizing, too observant to believe that wants were satisfied equally here. He spoke, after all, of a general, not an absolute, equality. He allows for differences.

Any attempt, however, to dilute Tocqueville's observation, to water it down to a belief in mere equality of opportunity, flies in the face of his numerous assertions to the contrary. For the United States to him was not simply a manifestation of Benjamin Constant's liberal bourgeois ideal, a society whose "careers were open to talents." What made it a unique society, among other things, was its democratic distribution of life's good things. While riches and poverty existed here as elsewhere, America was marked by the relative absence of extremes. If the social ladder could be easily ascended here, it was due not only to the absence of both aristocratic restraints and a restrictive political order, but ultimately to an abundance that made all other benefits possible. Many of Tocqueville's contemporaries and later commentators alike, as I mentioned at the outset, shared his belief that an essential equality of condition was the norm.

A strong case can be made, however, that not equality but disparity of condition was the rule in Jacksonian America. It was manifested above all in the nation's cities which were becoming increasingly important in an era marked by a great urban expansion. Old cities grew at an unprecedented rate while new ones were built seemingly overnight. Rochester was not the only city in which tree stumps could be found in the cellars of the buildings that had been put up around them. In the West, too, cities became increasingly important, attracting large amounts of speculative capital, providing their classic economic functions for their hinterlands, and acting as a magnet to settlers, many of whom "came across the mountains in search of promising towns as well as good land." Turner's frontier, as Richard C. Wade has shown, also included Cincinnati, Lexington, Pittsburgh, St. Louis, and Louisville.

The housing of the urban rich, as a case in point, set them apart from the great majority of town dwellers. In western cities choice locations were preempted by the well-to-do; "other people moved to less desirable areas." In the East, observers commented on the "genteel dwelling houses [of the rich]," made of fine stone or brick, with white marble increasingly used for doorsteps, window sills, lintels, and entire first stories. Pure silver ornaments and "costly European importations [that] decorated the homes of the rich," led one almost abject admirer of this country to concede that there was something in such refinements "very unlike republican simplicity."

Working people lived very differently. According to Mathew Carey, the wealthy philanthropist, working-class families in Philadelphia were squeezed together, 55 families to a tenement, lacking "the accommodation of a privy for their use." Their houses, according to a recent study, "were strung along, side to side as boxcars . . . obscured from the street view. . . ." Their tenants typically had one room per family, living "huddled to the rear . . . victims of a parsimonious building policy which meant crowding, noise, inadequate sanitation, lack of facilities for rubbish removal." The fresh water newly pumped from the Schuylkill—and which was so admired by many European travelers—went into the homes of the wealthy but not to the working classes. According to the labor press, the major cities of the nation abounded with dismal alleys, "the abodes of the miserable objects of grinding poverty." Andrew Jackson and Nicholas Biddle, on the other hand, could repair to the "Hermitage," outside of Nashville, or "Andalusia," near Philadelphia, similar in their opulence for all the political differences of their owners.

Glaring disparities were not confined to housing alone. If beggars were not readily apparent on the streets, they could be discerned in less public places. Bell had seen "scores of destitute homeless wretches lying on bulks or under the sheds about the markets of New York and Philadelphia." Fellow travelers claimed they saw as much poverty here as elsewhere. Statistical studies confirmed the rising rates of pauperism and of those too poor to pay a minimal tax. Nor does the evidence indicate that membership in these forlorn groups was swelled by the dramatic failure of eminent men. Rather some poor men became poorer. Imprisonment for debt was also on the rise, in some cities evidently accounting for the majority of men in jail. This abuse was shortly to be outlawed, in large part because its negative effects were felt by businessmen as well as by the poor. In the Jacksonian era, however, its main victims were men who owed debts of $20 or less. Abject poverty was not the characteristic lot of Americans who were not wealthy, but neither was it a negligible problem. One labor newspaper edited by the respected George Henry Evans— who was to become "the heart and soul" of the land reform movement of the 1840's—estimated that in Boston in 1834 more than 5,000 persons were "aided annually as paupers." The reliable Edward Abdy reported that not only was pauperism increasing in the nation's major cities, but that "there . . . [was] little reason to hope it . . . [could] be checked by the judicious application of charity."

The great bulk of Americans living in towns and cities were neither paupers nor debtors facing imprisonment. They were for the most part artisans or mechanics, to a lesser extent small business people and less than wealthy professionals. If they did not live in penury, the nation's journeymen lived and worked under conditions of extreme difficulty, far removed indeed from the "general equality of condition" mentioned by visitors who merely glanced their way. For the better part of the period, artisans put in a working day that rivalled the farmers' sunup to sundown. The spectre of unemployment haunted them, particularly in the cold weather months of short working days. And when they did work, artisans were paid in a paper currency that invariably was not worth its face value. They had little to fall back on when their shops closed down. In the decade of inflation that preceded the Panic of 1837, workers discovered that their wages did not keep up with runaway prices. The depression that came on the heels of the Panic kept perhaps one third of the working classes unemployed for long periods in the early 1840's. Quite apart from the depression years, labor fared poorly during the Jacksonian era. Most modern studies indicate that real wages stood still during an otherwise exuberant economic surge in the 1830's, at best approximating what they had been at the turn of the century.

Most Americans during the era were farmers, an estimated two thirds or more of the American working population making its living in agriculture. The income of farmers is notoriously hard to come by. In the case of people who largely consume their own product, income is by no means the most relevant clue to standard of living. Nor is the relatively unrevealing census data for the years before 1840 particularly helpful. And of course there were farmers and farmers, with successful but atypical operators of huge farms and plantations at one extreme and a much larger number of slaves at the other. Wages of farm hands and farm labor were even lower than those earned by urban workers. Impressionistic evidence, in the form of diaries and journals left by moderately successful independent farm families in different sections of the country, suggests the monotony, the hard work and the generally poor quality of life enjoyed by the nation's yeomanry during the era. Thomas Coffin's family in New Hampshire worked hard, lived frugally and had little leisure. Ridding the farm of vermin constituted an amusement or form of recreation for the young. A large farm that was regarded as "fairly well improved," located on one of the "better developed farm communities" in Iredell County, North Carolina, characteristically eked out a living, its "produce yielding only a small return for the work involved, while prices of necessities bought were high." Living conditions were indeed discouraging to men who found that their incomes from sales frequently only balanced their purchases. American farmers in the antebellum period were also convinced that their status was low. The "agrarian myth" that romanticized rural life was either unknown to most farmers or disbelieved by them.

The leaders of the labor organizations that formed several years before the great depression spoke of the daily worsening of the American working man's condition. Most people, they said, would suffer hunger and ruin "if sickness or want of employment should intervene for any length of time." Such sources did not provide an objective study of American conditions, focusing as they did on the grimmer aspects of American life. Yet contemporary reports by government and private sources, accounts by visitors, and modern studies confirm not only the difficult situation faced by most skilled and semiskilled artisans, but the truly dismal lot of most factory operatives.

It was not only radical labor leaders who charged that real equality did not exist in the United States. The point was also made by conservative Americans of the highest standing. John Quincy Adams had told Tocqueville that while in the north there was "a great equality before the law, . . . it ceases absolutely in the habits of life. There are upper classes and working classes." In Philadelphia Tocqueville had been advised by an eminent attorney, "There is more social equality with you at home [in France] than with us. Here . . . wealth gives a decided pre-eminence." Peter Duponceau confirmed Adams' point "that equality exists only on the street. Money creates extreme inequalities in society." But such comments seem to have made little impression on a mind that was busy creating theories based on very different assumptions. Some years later James Fenimore Cooper would assert that in the United States "inequality . . . [existed] and in some respects, with stronger features than it is usual to meet with in the rest of christendom." Thomas Hamilton would not go so far: the United States was no worse than Britain in this regard. But it was nonsense to call this country the land of equality merely because it lacked a "privileged order." Chevalier, too, impressed as he was by the absence here of aristocratic titles or an idle rich, concluded that great inequalities in income were becoming more and more the rule, dividing society as forcefully as name and land did in Europe. Even Mrs. Trollope, who had been willing to concede an equality of condition for which she had no admiration, came to the conclusion that the American poor were "kept in a state of irritation by feeling that their boasted equality is a falsehood." For all the absence of aristocratic distinctions in this country, it enjoyed only a "fictitious equality."

The case for egalitarianism is a subtle one, depending on a number of propositions that have nothing to do with wealth as such. But its underlying axiom, alleging the slightness of disparities in material condition, does not come off too well. The American rich lived a most distinctive life of relative comfort and splendor that differed dramatically, not only from the lives of the poor, but from the experience of the great majority of ordinary citizens. True, the rich were few in number. Moses Beach's list of New York City's rich men, the Boston list of the most heavily taxed, Philadelphia's roster of wealthy citizens, contained closer to 2 percent than 5 of their cities' populations. But that is precisely the case in most societies marked by inequality. Were the rich more typical, yea-sayers could quite rightly make much of the great amount of room at the top available in the egalitarian society they admire.

The egalitarian theory is also based on certain assumptions concerning social class and its role. It does not deny the existence of classes but rather stresses the ease of movement between them. The term "class" has been variously defined, of course. Sociologists have come to no agreement: one school emphasizing wealth and income; another, occupation; another, family; another, such intangibles as prestige and standing; another, style of life; another, religion and nationality; Miss Nancy Mitford recently redirected attention to the importance of speech; while eclectics have combined some or all of these plus other attributes to fashion their concept of class. In this discussion, the term will assume a group that is distinguished from others mainly by its members' means of making a living, the costliness and quality of the life they command, and the comparative influence and prestige they enjoy.

E. Digby Baltzell has sensibly written that "leadership and some form of stratification are inherent in all human social organization." When we leave the drawing board or the realm of the purely theoretical, there are no classless societies, certainly not in the civilized world. The important questions concerning a society have to do not with whether classes exist, but with the extent of class differences, the relative ease of access to the most favored class, and the degree of power and influence wielded by the latter. Where differences are slight, upward mobility is great, and power is with the middling orders, the society can properly be adjudged socially democratic. Jacksonian society, of course, enjoys just such a reputation.

The case for social fluidity, as might have been expected, was put most forcefully by Tocqueville. "In America," he wrote, "most of the rich men were formerly poor." It is a striking idea, of profound importance, not least because for later periods in American history it does not seem to be true. Stephan Thernstrom's recent study of working people in the Massachusetts town of

Newburyport, for the period 1850 to 1880, shows that while parents were pleased at the rise to more prestigious working-class occupations that was made by some of their sons, no dramatic movement to the top took place. Earlier studies of the social backgrounds of rich men of the late 19th and 20th centuries disclosed that, for the most part, they were sons of men of unusual wealth, prestige, education, favored religious denomination and other attributes of high rank. If Tocqueville was right, then the Jacksonian era stands alone for the 19th century. He may yet turn out to be right, but unfortunately his assertions are based not on substantial evidence, but rather on his own deductions, largely from what one informant told him concerning the disappearance of the law of entail in this country.

Of course the egalitarian thesis does not depend on so exaggerated a statement as Tocqueville's. If a substantial minority of the rich were born poor, America would have been unusual enough. To date, however, claims to an amazing social fluidity have not been substantiated. As always, Tocqueville's logic was excellent, for certainly it followed that in a dynamic social democracy, "the conditions of life are very fluctuating, men have almost always recently acquired the advantages which they possess. . . . [A]t any moment the same advantages may be lost." The fact was, however, that the United States and his ideal democracy were two most unlike things. Buckingham may have been closer to the mark when he wrote that "the greater number [of America's social elite] . . . inherit land, or houses, or stock, from their parents."

Alexandra McCoy's recent study of Wayne County, Michigan, for the latter part of the Jacksonian era, defines mobility as "the achievement of wealth by men of lower class origins," and finds very little evidence of the phenomenon. The economic elite of that important area were not self-made men. Like the successful men of a half century later, shown by William Miller and his students to be fortunate sons of wealthy fathers, Wayne County's rich seem to have "enjoyed an advantaged early environment to enable them to start a business in the west." Plebeians could not afford the five or six thousand dollars required. If the wealthy were born of the rich, they also tended to remain in that closed circle. "Those [in Wayne County] who were at the top in 1844 tended to stay there. Only one took a fall." The eminent modern historian, Oscar Handlin, long ago disclosed that Boston in the 1830's and 1840's "offered few opportunities to those who lacked the twin advantages of birth and capital." Boston was not unique.

A wide gulf existed between the classes. At the top of the urban social structure was an upper crust, some of whose members came of old family and long-established wealth, others of whom were considered parvenu and shunned by their social betters. Both groups lived and moved in a world apart from the one inhabited by those below. One informant told Tocqueville that rich Americans might be democratic enough to receive a man of talent but they would make him aware that he was not rich and refuse to receive his wife and children. Large merchants scorned small, while in a number of cities merchants of any sort would receive neither mechanics nor their children.

Richard Wade has shown that even in the youthful cities of the West, at the beginning of the era, merchants made up a distinctively wealthy and socially prominent group. "Their wives belonged to the same clubs, their children went to the same schools, and they participated in the same amusements and recreations." They lived in their own districts, physically separated from others; "by 1830, social lines could be plotted on a map of the city." They went to great pains to match the lavish living of the older upper classes of the eastern cities, succeeding to a large degree. Many of them lived in "villas." Expensive furniture, overloaded tables, fancy dress for dinner, extravagant entertainment, elegant carriages, ornate cotillions led by dancing masters imported from the East, characterized merchant life in the "frontier towns." Wade notes dryly that in the first decades of the 19th century, "local boosters talked a great deal about egalitarianism in the West, but urban practice belied the theory. Social lines developed very quickly and although never drawn as tightly as in Eastern cities, they denoted meaningful distinctions." Vigne found "an aristocracy in every city of the Union; and perhaps as many as four or five different sects or circles, notwithstanding their boasted equality of condition." Logan would have reduced the number of elite strata to three.

The behavior of the eastern social elite was vividly, in some cases ludicrously, influenced by class bias. Grund found that it was not simply that the fashionable would not mingle with the vulgar. In Boston, good society would not permit itself to be seen publicly. Women of society, more expert than men in the finer points of snobbishness, curtsied according to their wealth or circumstances. Not only was seating in theatres arranged according to class, applause was given by class. Class distinction was worse here than in England, it was said, manifesting itself in exquisite attention to nuances. Thus the "second society" of Boston—itself unacceptable to the first—with a vulgarity peculiar to itself, in turn displayed contempt for its inferiors. The fine gradations within society were of a complexity that only a mathematician could analyze. Grund found such behavior repellent but he did not think it was confined to Boston. Other visitors, while conceding the pretentiousness of Boston and even of New York, gave the nod to Philadelphia as the most exclusive of American cities. Bell was told that there were "nine or ten distinct ranks in the city, beginning at the lower class of traders and ending in the dozen or so who keep . . . a large establishment; each of these circles, repelling and repelled, carefully keeps itself apart, and draws a line that no one of doubtful status may pass." Murray believed that these lines were drawn tighter than ever. Even Tocqueville made the uncharacteristic admission, at the close of his second chapter, that "the picture of American society has . . . a surface covering of democracy, beneath which the old aristocratic colors sometimes peep out."

Americans, too, were aware that class distinctions were important here. In *Home As Found*, Cooper wrote a biting satire directed in part against the varieties of class snobbishness practiced in American cities and villages. In western cities, "people felt them [distinctions] and contemporaries thought them important." Contemporaries, of course, thought a variety of things, their viewpoints about class running the gamut from denial of its existence to enthusiastic recognition of class division. A few would maintain, even try to widen, the existing cleavage. The era's workingmen's parties and trade unions were led by men who believed that America was torn by class conflict. According to the labor spokesmen, the capitalist's attempt to beguile workers into the false belief that social harmony prevailed here was only a stratagem in the unremitting, if subtle, class warfare waged by the rich. In view of upper class control of the major parties, the press, and all other influential institutions, workers had no alternative to recognizing the harsh fact of American life: that class conflict existed here. Labor's way out was not to deny the fact but to accept it and rely on its own efforts in order to change it. Since most of the labor radicals had earned leadership in their movement precisely because their views were well known, it would appear they spoke not for themselves alone but at least in part for their memberships.

That some persons evidently believed American society was under the tight control of a small upper class is more a sign of the proneness of zealots to exaggerate than of anything else. The charge was poorly documented, flies in the face of good sense, and cannot be taken seriously—except as a clue to the state of mind of those who believed it. In the latter sense, however, it was significant testimony that many of the nation's workingmen believed America to be a class society dominated by a powerful few. While extant evidence proves nothing so extreme, it does appear to show that wealthy men commanded an inordinate political influence over American society.

The egalitarian theory is in part based on the belief that the common man dominated Jacksonian politics. Popular suffrage meant to Tocqueville the "sovereignty of the people. . . . The people reign in the American political world," he wrote, "as the Deity does in the universe." Chevalier called America a "popular despotism." By this theory of politics, near oligarchies which regularly send 95 percent or better of their citizenry to the polls, are actually ruled by their voters. It is not necessary to subscribe to an ultrarealist view of politics to detect the naïveté in such an analysis.

In Jacksonian America, the common man's possession of the suffrage subjected him to much flattery by political leaders, for it is quite true that his votes decided whether this or that one would take office. (Tocqueville, who was no great admirer of the common man, hoped that direct elections would be increasingly replaced by indirect ones, thus minimizing the dangers of the manhood suffrage.) In his brilliant book of two decades ago, Arthur M. Schlesinger, Jr., synthesized, updated, and gave new life to a traditional interpretation which held that since the party battles of the era were fought over great social and economic principles, the common man's choice of Jackson over his enemies was fraught with crucial political significance and was as well a demonstration of popular power. That is not the view, however, of many of the excellent studies of the past 20 years. They tell a tale of major parties during the Jacksonian era, which, for all the difference in their political rhetoric, were more like than unlike, not least in the extent to which their basic structures and policymaking apparatus were controlled by unusually wealthy men.

How much power could the common man exercise when there was little real choice left open to him by the parties that counted? In the states, small groups of insiders had a tight control over nominations and policymaking, with popular influence more nominal than real. Whether in New York or Mississippi, Pennsylvania or South Carolina, Michigan or New Jersey, Massachusetts or Florida, Tennessee or Ohio, Democratic leaders, more often than not, were speculators, editors, lawyers, the "land office crowd," coming from the "wealthier elements in the society," typically of the same economic background as their Whig opponents. For that matter, Andrew Jackson himself, not to mention the men who launched him in presidential politics, were uncommonly wealthy. As Robert V. Remini has noted, "it cost a great deal of money to enter politics." Jackson may have spoken in ringing terms of the common man's right to high office, as well as his ability to perform its tasks, but in point of fact Jackson, like his "aristocratic" predecessors, filled Cabinet and high civil service posts with men who possessed unusual wealth and social eminence. This is not to say that the era's leaders dealt with political issues primarily in terms of class interest. Rich men no more than poor live by bread alone. It is not farfetched, however, to interpret the lack of real issues on the national level in the decade of the 1820's, or the ambiguity of issues in the subsequent decades of the Jacksonian era, as due in part to the backgrounds of the era's leaders.

Wealth exerted political power most directly on the local level. At a time when local boards of government typically received small salaries or none at all, wealthy merchants sat in the seats of municipal power, determining policies and expenditures. The way of life of the town dweller was significantly affected by upper class decisions to build wharves or expensive market houses rather than improve the night watch or drain pools. Robert Dahl's recent study of New Haven politics underscores these points. In that small eastern city, prior to 1842, "public office was almost the exclusive prerogative of the patrician families. . . . Wealth, social position and education" were the main determinants of patrician status. During this period, according to Dahl, control over such a factor as wealth enabled the individual who enjoyed it, to "be better off in almost every other resource"—such as "social standing and control over office." The prime beneficiaries of this "cumulative inequality" were the old merchant elite. A revolution of sorts was to take place in 1842 with the election of a wealthy manufacturer to the office of mayor, ushering "in a period during which wealthy entrepreneurs dominated public life almost without interruption for more than half a century." I am not sure whether the Jacksonian era was still in force when new wealth replaced older in the City Hall of New Haven, but in the one case as in the other, working people and so-called "ethnic groups" made up nothing better than a passive electorate. Until well after the middle of the 19th century, the city's aldermen continued to be composed almost entirely of wealthy professionals and businessmen in the entrepreneurial as during the patrician phase of their city's political evolution. Nor was New Haven atypical. Elite upper classes controlled mayors' offices and municipal councils or boards of aldermen in New York City and Boston as well as in Detroit and the cities of the South and West for most of the era.

The Jacksonian era witnessed no breakdown of a class society in America. If anything, class lines hardened, distinctions widened, tensions increased. Wade noted that while, with the passage of time, "new families entered the circle [of the merchant elite] and older ones fell out," there was also a "heightened . . . sense of separateness, . . . the circle itself becoming tighter and more distinct." Communities already stratified, "found lines sharpened, class division deepened," as they grew in size and as their economies became more specialized. The wealthiest merchants, according to the testimony of their own diaries and of travelers' accounts, became even more class conscious. Their children had absorbed so well the lesson of social exclusiveness that, if anything, they "moved in an even more insulated circle than their parents." In eastern cities it has also been noted that social stratification intensified during the Jacksonian era.

Has the time not come, then, to discard the label, the Era of the Common Man? Like its companion designation, the Age of Egalitarianism, it has rested on questionable assumptions. Struck by surface examples of popular influence or by the absence of aristocratic titles in America, we have jumped to unwarranted conclusions. The absence of a caste system has been interpreted as though it denoted the absence of a class system. It is true that, theoretically, individuals could move freely up the social ladder, actually doing so if they had the talent and good fortune. But these restless men on the make should not be confused with the bulk of the nation's workingmen or small farmers. An expanding capitalistic society everywhere dips into the less privileged strata to provide some of the manpower it requires for entrepreneurial leadership. There is no evidence, however, that during the Jacksonian era the poor made dramatic movement up the social ladder in greater numbers than they made the move westward to Turner's frontier and its alleged safety valve.*

The belief that the era was dominated by the common man has rested on political assumptions that have been pretty well demolished. That white men without property had won the right to vote, even before Andrew Jackson stood for the presidency, is something that every politician knew. Shrewd men in politics, therefore, paid lip service to the common man, managing to explain their own origins, their careers, and their political beliefs in terms that were highly flattering to Tom, Dick, and Harry. Though Jackson spoke of turning high office over to ordinary men, he did not do so. The men surrounding the Old General, like those who ran his party on the state level, were decidedly uncommon or wealthy. Common men there were in abundance. That pragmatists in high places addressed them artfully, however, is less proof that the common man held power than that skillful politicians knew how to delude him into believing that he did.

An age is not ordinarily named after its most typical members, regardless

---

*Although in recent years a number of students have written in praise of Turner on the subject, it is a fair conclusion that most scholars do not believe that eastern workingmen went west in great numbers. For an informed discussion that includes reference to the most recent work, see Ray A. Billington, ed., *The Frontier Thesis*, New York 1966.

of their real power. For if it were, almost every age would have to be known as the era of the ordinary man. Whatever it might have been, the era named after Andrew Jackson was neither an age of egalitarianism nor of the common man. . . .

The era that bears his name was not really the age of Jackson. The label has been attached too long for it to be torn off, however, and it continues to be most satisfactory to a people who like to think their history was made by mythic figures of heroic stature who imposed their will on their times. Were the name of an era determined by a scholarly process that assigned a proper weight to all the relevant factors that shaped it, it would be apparent that no individual, not even Andrew Jackson, dominated the period 1825 to 1845. Certainly he was not the typical man of the time. For all his towering personality, his own and his party's influence even on the politics of the period have been exaggerated. That in hundreds of places the name Jackson was invoked by men eager to win office bespeaks not real influence so much as the power of propaganda and popular hero worship. The notion that the era was his has also rested on a belief that an indissoluble bond connected the Hero and the common man, to whom Jacksonian Democracy ostensibly gave power. But in fact Jacksonian Democracy gave power not to Tom, Dick, and Harry but to the shrewd, ambitious, wealthy, and able politicians who knew best how to flatter them.

Nor was it the age of the common man. If talk alone determined the character of an era then there would be much reason to think that it was. Politicians who sought the common man's vote bombarded him with praise. Romantic artists, whether using pen or brush, extolled his simplicity and his innate wisdom. The American style of life, for all its unloveliness, seemed to be shaped by his mannerisms, his interests, his limitations. Scandalmongering journalism, coarse public manners, the frenzied pursuit of things, the indifference to learning and unconcern with quality, were only some of the characteristics of American civilization that bore the stamp of the ordinary man. Since it was primarily the surface aspect of things that he influenced most—precisely those phenomena that caught the eye of outsiders passing through—visitors understandably concluded that here the common man was sovereign. But he was not.

Political authority belonged not to him but to the uncommon men who typically controlled the major parties at every level. It goes without saying that unusual men will emerge as leaders, even in the most democratic society conceivable. The era's political leaders were distinctive, however, not only in their ability but also in the possession of status and wealth that were unrepresentative of the mass of men. The seats of power in society and the economy were also filled by men whose origins and outlook were not plebeian. Self-made men *were* in greater abundance here than in the Old World. The relative absence of a feudal tradition meant that in the 1830's as before, individual Americans of whatever origins might move to positions of eminence that in Europe were unattainable to men of like background. But their numbers were not legion. The weight of the evidence is that family ties and a form of nepotism played an important part in singling out fortune's favorites. Andrew Jackson's own political appointments were heavily influenced by such considerations.

The era's egalitarianism seems also to have been more apparent than real. American farmers and working men *were* better off than their European counterparts. Their material condition was superior, as were their opportunities, their status, and their influence. Yet this remained a class society. The small circles that dominated the life in the great cities of the East as well as the new towns of the West, lived lives of relative opulence, while socially during the Jacksonian era they became, if anything, more insulated against intrusion by the lower orders. Social lines were drawn even tighter in the slave states. For all the era's egalitarian reputation, evidence is lacking that movement up the social ladder was any more commonplace than it was in subsequent periods of American life; eras whose reputations for social fluidity have been largely deflated by modern empirical studies that characteristically reveal that the race was to the well born. Tocqueville's influential insight that the American rich man was typically born poor was not a conclusion drawn from evidence but an undocumented inference, characteristic of the brilliant French visitor's flair for generalizing from unproven assumptions. James Fenimore Cooper and Michel Chevalier were among the contemporaries who observed that money increasingly tended to be concentrated in relatively few hands, widening the gulf between classes for all the brave talk to the contrary.

It is impossible to know whether people believed that their chances for success were as great as some contemporaries claimed they were. Certainly most Americans seemed to throw themselves into the race for gain, undeterred by religious enthusiasms which cheerfully approved worldly success. Materialism and a love of money were perhaps their most noticeable traits. An ambivalence may be detected in the fact that while the notion participated in a speculative orgy whose goals were selfish and material, reform movements designed to enhance the quality of American life and end social injustice, also flourished. But the two "movements" had different memberships. The movements to uplift slaves, the poor, and the conditions of the weak have caught the eye of scholars—themselves relatively perfectionist when their values are compared to those of more unreflective men. The reform cause was not insignificant. But it was led and kept alive by unusual men whose values were outside the mainstream of American life. The mass of Americans seemed far more interested in personal enrichment than in moral uplift.

The depression that followed the great panic at the end of the 1830's temporarily halted the economic growth that had moved the young nation into a prominent place in the world economy. It also dampened if it did not completely suppress the exuberant mood that characterized the earlier period. Optimism had by no means been totally misplaced. The great enhancement of profit-making opportunities only reflected solid advances in the nation's technology, its agricultural and industrial capacity, and above all in the scope and quality of its internal transportation system. Currency was a problem to a country whose opportunities far outstripped its gold supply and whose urge to profit was so overwhelming. Americans, said by discerning observers to value quantity over quality, were content to use vast amounts of paper currency as though it were solid coin. In the absence of sufficient precious metals, the system was not without redeeming social value. Yet it was a precarious one. In a sense, the great Bank War represented the brushing aside of an agency that would restrain the flood of paper desired by the community of profit seekers, although Jackson had not intended such a result.

The nation's modern political system was born during the era, reflecting beautifully the traits of the people it served. Dominated by pragmatic parties which placed electoral success above principle while managing to remain distinctive from one another—in part because of differences in policy as well as in style—it was marked by extravagant campaign techniques, sordid manipulation, brilliant organization, marvelous rhetorical flourishes and a degree of popular participation that were unknown on the Continent. It was not as democratic a system as it seemed, however. Not only were large numbers denied the suffrage by virtue of sex or color, but astute party managers devised ways of confining real control to small cliques of insiders, just as corporate managers would later use widespread stock ownership as a means of tightening their control over business organizations. While the rhetorical excesses of demagogues had little relationship to their parties' actual achievements, real issues were not altogether avoided, in part because of the clamor of dissenters. Characteristically the great parties dealt with the great issues not by meeting them squarely but by indirection.

Tocqueville thought that the American people were essentially conservative. For all their restless temper, their hunger to change both their lot and their locales, they had no interest in drastic alteration of their society. They loved change (in their personal status) but dreaded revolution. The American exceptions to this rule were fascinating but in view of their small numbers and unrepresentativeness, their influence was slight. The dominant values, like the dominant political, economic, and social tendencies of the Jacksonian era, were essentially conservative. Moralistic dissenters, unhappy with the era's prevalent opportunism, like social radicals displeased with its inequality, got equally short shrift.

It is undoubtedly too late to try to change the name of the Jacksonian era. If it could be done, my idea of a new label would not be a catchy one. For one thing the era was too heterogeneous to be captured by any simple rubric. If the attempt were made nevertheless to capture its spirit in a phrase, there is something to be said for calling it an age of materialism and opportunism, reckless speculation and erratic growth, unabashed vulgarity, and a politic *seeming* deference to the common man by the uncommon men who actually ran things.

The Antislavery Myth

C. Vann Woodward

Layers of fantasy and romance have come to cloud the historical reality of the
Northern position on the slavery issue before the Civil War. Marshaling his facts with
sophistication and skill, C. Vann Woodward, former president of the American
Historical Association and Sterling Professor of History Emeritus at Yale, reviews
the status of historical study on the antislavery question. Noting that the antislavery
myth gained its greatest measure of vitality only after the Civil War was ended,
Woodward takes direct aim at the mythological trappings that still adhere to the
Underground Railroad and, more importantly, at the revered notion that racial
discrimination was a condition only to be found in the prewar South. Woodward's
thesis suggests that the antislavery myth was a Northern exercise in atonement for
social guilt. The Mason-Dixon Line did not successfully divide slavery from freedom
in antebellum America.

Slavery and the Civil War were prolific breeders of myth, and their fertility
would seem to wax rather than wane with the passage of time. Neither the
proslavery myths of the South nor the antislavery myths of the North ceased
to grow after the abolition of the Peculiar Institution. In fact they took on new
life, struck new roots and flourished more luxuriantly than ever. Both myths
continually found new sources of nourishment in the changing psychological
needs and regional policies of North and South. The South used the proslavery
myth to salve its wounds, lighten its burden of guilt and, most of all, to rationalize and defend the system of caste and segregation that was developed in
place of the old order. The North, as we shall see, had deeply felt needs of its
own to be served by an antislavery myth, needs that were sufficient at all times
to keep the legend vital and growing to meet altered demands.

In late years the proslavery myth and the plantation legend have been
subjected to heavy critical erosion from historians, sociologists and psycholo-
gists. So damaging has this attack been that little more is heard of the famous
school for civilizing savages, peopled with happy slaves and benevolent masters. Shreds and pieces of the myth are still invoked as props to the crumbling
defenses of segregation, but conviction has drained out of it, and it has been
all but relegated to the limbo of dead or obsolescent myths.

Nothing like this can be said of the antislavery myth. Its potency is at-

Reprinted from *The American Scholar*, Vol. 31, No. 2 (Spring 1962). Copyright © 1962 by the
United Chapters of Phi Beta Kappa. By permission of the author.

tested by a steady flow of historical works by journalists and reputable scholars. It is obvious that the myth can still dim the eye and quicken the pulse as well as warp the critical judgment. Apart from the fact that it is a creation of the victor rather than the vanquished, there are other reasons for the undiminished vitality of the antislavery myth. One is that it has not been subjected to as much critical study as has the proslavery myth.

Before turning to certain recent evidence of the exuberant vitality of the antislavery myth, however, it is interesting to note two penetrating critical studies of some of its components. Larry Gara, in *The Liberty Line: The Legend of the Underground Railroad*, addresses himself to a limited but substantial element of the myth. No aspect of the myth has so deeply engaged the American imagination and entrenched itself in the national heritage as the Underground Railroad, and no aspect so well reflects what we fondly believe to be the more generous impulses of national character. It is a relief to report that Mr. Gara is a temperate scholar and has avoided handling his subject with unnecessary rudeness. By the time he finishes patiently peeling away the layers of fantasy and romance, however, the factual substance is painfully reduced and the legend is revealed as melodrama. Following the assumptions that the better critics of the proslavery legend make about the slave, he assumes that "abolitionists, after all, were human," and that the "actual men and women of the abolition movement, like the slaves themselves, are far too complex to fit into a melodrama."

One very human thing the authors of the melodrama did was to seize the spotlight. They elected themselves the heroes. It was not that the abolitionists attempted to stage *Othello* without the princely Moor, but they did relegate the Moor to a subordinate role. The role assigned him was largely passive—that of the trembling, helpless fugitive completely dependent on his noble benefactors. The abolitionist was clearly the hero, and as Gerrit Smith, one of them, put it, the thing was brought off by the "Abolitionists and the Abolitionists only." As Mr. Gara points out, however, it took a brave, resourceful and rebellious slave to make good an escape, not one temperamentally adapted to subordinate roles—no Uncle Tom, as abolitionists often discovered. Moreover, by the time he reached the helping hands of the Underground Railroad conductors—if he ever did in fact—he had already completed the most perilous part of his journey, the southern part.

Another important actor in the drama of rescue who was crowded off-stage by the abolitionists was the free Negro. According to the antislavery leader James G. Birney, the assistance of the fugitives was "almost uniformly managed by the colored people. I know nothing of them generally till they are past." The fugitive slaves had good reason to mistrust any white man, and in the opinion of Mr. Gara the majority of those who completed their flight to freedom did so without a ride on the legendary U.G.R.R.

Still another human failing of the legend-makers was exaggeration, and in this the abolitionists were ably assisted by their adversaries, the slaveholders, who no more understood their pecuniary losses than the abolitionists underestimated their heroic exploits. Under analysis the "flood" of fugitives diminishes to a trickle. As few as were the manumissions, they were double the number of fugitives in 1860 according to the author, and by far the greater number of fugitives never got out of the slave states. Another and even more fascinating distortion is the legend of conspiracy and secrecy associated with the U.G.R.R. The obvious fact was that the rescue of fugitive slaves was the best possible propaganda for the antislavery cause. We are mildly admonished that the U.G.R.R was "not the well-organized and mysterious institution of the legend." "Far from being secret," we are told, "it was copiously and persistently publicized, and there is little valid evidence for the existence of a widespread underground conspiracy."

But there remains the haunting appeal and enchantment of the secret stations, the disguised "conductors," and the whole "underground" and conspiratorial aspect of the legend that is so hard to give up. "Stories are still repeated," patiently explains Mr. Gara, "about underground tunnels, mysterious signal lights in colored windows, peculiarly placed rows of colored bricks in houses or chimneys to identify the station, and secret rooms for hiding fugitives." These stories he finds to be without basis in fact. While we must continue to bear with our Midwestern friends and their family traditions, we are advised that "hearsay, rumor, and persistent stories handed down orally from generation to generation are not proof of anything."

The most valuable contribution this study makes is the revelation of how the legend grew. It was largely a postwar creation, and it sprang from a laudable impulse to be identified with noble deeds. Family pride, local pride and regional pride were fed by abolitionist reminiscences and floods of memoirs and stories. "Every barn that ever housed a fugitive, and some that hadn't," remarks Mr. Gara, "were listed as underground railroad depots." There were thousands of contributors to the legend, but the greatest was Professor Wilbur H. Siebert, whose first book, *The Underground Railroad from Slavery to Freedom*, appeared in 1898. In the nineties he painstakingly questioned hundreds of surviving antislavery workers, whose letters and responses to questionnaires Mr. Gara has reexamined. Mr. Siebert accepted their statements at face value "on the ground that the memories of the aged were more accurate than those of young people." The picture that emerged in his big book was that of "a vast network of secret routes," connecting hundreds of underground stations, operated by 3,200 "conductors"—the very minimum figure, he insisted. This work fathered many subsequent ones, which borrowed generously from it. There has been no lag in legend-building since. "The greater the distance," observes Mr. Gara, "the more enchantment seems to adhere to all aspects of the underground railroad, the legend that grew up around it, and its role in America's heritage."

A second and more elaborate aspect of the antislavery myth is the legend that the Mason and Dixon Line not only divided slavery from freedom in antebellum America, but that it also set apart racial inhumanity in the South from benevolence, liberality and tolerance in the North. Like the Underground Railroad Legend, the North Star Legend (for lack of another name) was a postwar creation. Looking back through a haze of passing years that obscured historical realities, the myth-makers credited the North with the realization in its own society of all the war aims for which it fought (or eventually proclaimed): not only Union and Freedom, but Equality as well. True, the North did not win the third war aim (or if it did, quickly forfeited it), but it nevertheless practiced what it preached, even if it failed to get the South to practice it, and had been practicing it in exemplary fashion for some time.

For a searching examination of the North Star Legend we are indebted to Leon F. Litwack, *North of Slavery: The Negro in the Free States, 1790–1860.* He starts with the assumption that, "The inherent cruelty and violence of southern slavery requires no further demonstration, but this does not prove northern humanity." On racial attitudes of the two regions he quotes with approval the observation of Tocqueville in 1831: "The prejudice of race appears to be stronger in the states that have abolished slavery than in those where it still exists." White supremacy was a national, not a regional credo, and politicians of the Democratic, the Whig and the Republican parties openly and repeatedly expressed their allegiance to the doctrine. To do otherwise was to risk political suicide. "We, the Republican party, are the white man's party," declared Senator Lyman Trumbull of Illinois. And, as Mr. Litwack observes, "Abraham Lincoln, in his vigorous support of both white supremacy and denial of equal rights for Negroes, simply gave expression to almost universal American convictions." These convictions were to be found among Free Soil adherents and were not unknown among antislavery and abolitionist people themselves.

One reason for the unrestrained expression of racial prejudice from politicians was that the Negro was almost entirely disfranchised in the North and was therefore politically helpless. Far from sharing the expansion of political democracy, the Negro often suffered disfranchisement as a consequence of white manhood suffrage. By 1840 about 93 percent of the free Negroes in the North were living in states that excluded them from the polls. By 1860 only 6 percent of the Northern Negro population lived in the five states that provided legally for their suffrage. In only three states were they allowed complete parity with whites in voting. Even in those New England states doubts lingered concerning the practical exercise of equal political rights. As late as 1869, the year before the ratification of the 15th Amendment, New York State voted against equal suffrage rights for Negroes. Four Western states legally excluded free Negroes from entry.

In Northern courtrooms as at Northern polls racial discrimination prevailed. Five states prohibited Negro testimony when a white man was a party to a case, and Oregon prohibited Negroes from holding real estate, making contracts or maintaining lawsuits. Only in Massachusetts were Negroes admitted as jurors, and that not until the eve of the Civil War. The absence of Negro judges, jurors, witnesses and lawyers helps to explain the heavily disproportionate number of Negroes in Northern prisons.

Custom, extralegal codes and sometimes mob law served to relegate the Negro to a position of social inferiority and impose a harsh rule of segregation in Northern states. According to Mr. Litwack:

In virtually every phase of existence, Negroes found themselves systematically separated from whites. They were either excluded from railway cars, omnibuses, stagecoaches, and steamboats or assigned to special "Jim Crow" sections; they sat, when permitted, in secluded and remote corners of theaters and lecture halls; they could not enter most hotels, restaurants, and resorts, except as servants; they prayed in "Negro pews" in white churches, and if partaking of the sacrament of the Lord's Supper, they waited until the whites had been served the bread and wine. Moreover, they were often educated in segregated schools, punished in segregated prisons, nursed in segregated hospitals, and buried in segregated cemeteries.

Housing and job opportunities were severely limited. A Boston Negro wrote in 1860 that "it is five times as hard to get a house in a good location in Boston as it is in Philadelphia; and it is ten times as difficult for a colored mechanic to get work here as it is in Charleston." The earlier verdict of Tocqueville continued to ring true. "Thus the Negro is free," he wrote, "but he can share neither the rights, nor the pleasures, nor the labor, nor the afflictions, nor the tomb of him whose equal he has been declared to be; and he cannot meet him upon fair terms in life or in death."

In Northern cities with large Negro populations, violent mob action occurred with appalling frequency. Between 1832 and 1849 mobs touched off five major anti-Negro riots in Philadelphia. Mobs destroyed homes, churches and meeting halls, and forced hundreds to flee the city. An English Quaker visiting Philadelphia in 1849 remarked that there was probably no city "where dislike, amounting to hatred of the coloured population, prevails more than in the city of brotherly love!"

The Southern historian will be struck with the remarkable degree to which the South recapitulated a generation later the tragic history of race relations in the North. Once slavery was destroyed as a means of social control and subordination of the Negro, and Reconstruction was overthrown, the South resorted to many of the devices originally developed in the North to keep the Negro in his "place." There was more delay in the resort to segregation than generally supposed, but once it came toward the end of the century it was harsh and thorough. One important difference was that in the antebellum North the Negro was sometimes free to organize, protest and join white sympathizers to advance his cause and improve his position. His success in these efforts was unimpressive, however, for by 1860, as Mr. Litwack says, "despite some notable advances, the Northern Negro remained largely disfranchised, segregated, and economically oppressed." The haven to which the North Star of the legend guided the fugitive from slavery was a Jim Crow haven.

While these two studies of the antislavery myth are valuable and significant, they are slight in scope and modest in aim when compared with the far more ambitious—and traditional—book of Dwight Lowell Dumond, *Antislavery: The Crusade for Freedom in America.* Elaborately documented, profusely illustrated and ornately bound, this massive volume is easily twice the bulk of an average-sized book. It covers the entire scope of the organized antislavery movement in this country, as well as preorganizational beginnings, and is the most extensive work on the subject in print. Represented as the result of "more than thirty years" of research by the Michigan historian, it is the outcome of a lifetime absorption in antislavery literature. It is doubtful that any other scholar has lavished such devoted study upon this vast corpus of writings.

The author's total absorption with his source materials is, indeed, the key to the theory of historiography upon which this remarkable work would appear to be based. That theory is that the purest history is to be derived from strict and undivided attention to source materials—in this case chiefly the writings, tracts and propaganda, running to millions upon millions of words, of the antislavery people themselves. If the author is aware of any of the scholarly studies of slavery and antislavery that have appeared in the last generation or more, he does not betray awareness by reference to the questions they have raised, by use of methods they have developed, or by incorporation of findings they have published. Neither the problems of slavery and antislavery that have been pressed upon the historian by new learning in psychology, anthropology, sociology and economics, nor the questions that have been raised by fresh encounters with Africa and Afro-Americans and by new experience with reformers and revolutionists and their motivation, receive any attention from the author. It is difficult to comment intelligently upon a work that so persistently and successfully avoids engagement with the contemporary mind, its assumptions, its preoccupations, its urgent questions, its whole frame of reference.

Mr. Dumond's treatment of slavery and the abolitionists admits of no complexities or ambiguities beyond the fixed categories of right and wrong. All of his abolitionists are engaged in a single-minded crusade wholly motivated by a humanitarian impulse to destroy an evil institution and succor its victims. They are moral giants among the pygmies who cross their will or fail to share their views. The single exception is William Lloyd Garrison, for whom he shares the strong distaste of his onetime collaborator Gilbert H. Barnes, the Midwestern historian. "In fact," writes Dumond (the italics are his), *"he was a man of distinctly narrow limitations among the giants of the antislavery movement."* Why Garrison falls so far short of the stature of the giants is not quite clear, but we are assured that he was "insufferably arrogant," given to "cheap cynicism" and withal "a timid soul except when safely behind the editorial desk."

Apart from Garrison, the antislavery leaders command Mr. Dumond's unqualified admiration, and his praise of them is unbounded. "What a combination of intellect, courage, and Christian faith!" he exclaims in describing the founders of the American Antislavery Society. The abolitionists are indeed due a redress of grievances at the hands of the historians, for they have had something less than justice from the craft. They are remembered more as pictured by caricatures such as Henry James drew in *The Bostonians* than for their good works and genuine merits. The wild eccentricities, the fierce comeouterism, the doctrinaire extravagancies and the armchair bloodlusts of some of the abolitionists have been stressed and repeated to the neglect of the dedicated and fearless work they did in the face of ridicule, mob violence and all

the pressures that wealth and established order can bring to bear upon dissenters. Their cause was just, and among their numbers were men and women
of courage, intelligence and moral force. They deserve their due and need a
sympathetic defender.

The trouble with Mr. Dumond as historian of the antislavery movement
is his total involvement. This involvement extends beyond hatred of slavery
and approval of abolition. It commits him as well to the style and tone and
temper, the immediacy of indignation, the very idiom and rhetoric of a movement of thought that took its shape from intellectual influences and social
conditions existing nearly a century and a half ago. The effect is startling. The
rhythm and color of his prose is in perfect keeping with the style and tone
of the scores of lithographs and prints from old abolitionist tracts that serve
appropriately to illustrate the book. The author paints just what he sees, but
he sees everything through the eyes of the 1830's. The result is more than an
anachronism. It gives the effect of a modern primitive, a Henri Rousseau of
historiography.

Any treatment of the antislavery movement necessarily involves some
treatment of the institution it opposed. Mr. Dumond's conception of slavery
would seem to have taken shape in considerable degree from the antislavery
literature he has so thoroughly mastered. At any rate, he quotes liberally from
this literature in characterizing slavery. Among other things, he quotes a poem
by Timothy Dwight, published in 1794, the year before he became president
of Yale. The last stanza of it reads as follows:

> Why shrinks yon slave, with horror, from his meat?/ Heavens! 'tis his flesh, the
> wretch is whipped to eat./ Why streams the life-blood from that female's throat?/
> She sprinkled gravy on a guest's new coat!

"Poetic license?" asks the historian. "Exaggeration? Fantasy? *Only half the
truth, if a thousand witnesses are to be believed.*" And they, he assures us,
are to be believed.

Mr. Dumond selects Theodore Dwight Weld's *American Slavery As It Is*,
published in 1839, as "the greatest of the antislavery pamphlets," and still the
best historical authority on slavery. "It is an encyclopedia of knowledge. It is
a book of horrors," he writes. Weld himself correctly described it as "a work
of incalculable value" to the abolitionist cause. "Facts and testimonies are
troops, weapons and victory, all in one," he wrote. The principles governing
its composition are suggested by a letter to Weld from two editorial advisors,
Sereno and Mary Streeter: "Under the head of personal cruelty [you] will be
obliged to reject much testimony; and this is not because the facts are not well
authenticated but because those which are merely *horrid* must give place to
those which are absolutely diabolical." Absolutely diabolical or not, in the
opinion of Professor Dumond, "It is as close as history can come to the facts."
According to his theory of historical evidence, "Diaries and plantation records
are largely worthless because slaveholders never kept a record of their own
evil ways."

The strong sexual theme that pervades antislavery literature often took a prurient turn, but in Mr. Dumond's hands the pruriency is transmuted by bold treatment. The presence of miscegenation is attested by the Census of 1860 and the proportion of the colored population of the South that was of mixed blood. But to Mr. Dumond, sexual exploitation becomes very nearly the basis of the institution of slavery. "Its prevalence leads to the inescapable conclusion," he writes, "that it was the basis—unspoken to be sure—of much of the defense of the institution." Ulrich B. Phillips, the Southern historian of slavery, doubtless betrayed a certain blindness when he reported that in all the records he studied he could find only one instance of deliberate "breeding" of slaves, and that an unsuccessful one in colonial Massachusetts. To Mr. Dumond, however, it is plain as day that the "breeding" was practiced by *all* slaveholders: "That is exactly what slave owners did with the slaves, and there were no exceptions." To the Georgia historian there were no instances, to the Michigan historian no exceptions! What is one to tell the children?

Mr. Dumond's main subject, of course, is not slavery but antislavery. In his treatment of this great theme the myth is slightly muted, but it nevertheless pulses powerfully through the whole narrative. The Underground Railroad is described as "a highly romantic enterprise" that became "well organized." In these pages it operates with all the enchanting conspiracy and secrecy of the legend, with fugitive slaves, "secreted in livery stables, in attics, in storerooms, under featherbeds, in secret passages, in all sorts of out of the way places." There was one hayloft in Detroit that "was always full of Negroes."

In Professor Dumond's history the North Star Legend is given very nearly full credence. In striking contrast with the account rendered in detail by Mr. Litwack, we are informed that Negroes "continued to vote without interruption in New Hampshire, Vermont, Rhode Island, and in the two slave states of New York and New Jersey," and that there were never "any distinctions whatever in criminal law, judicial procedure, and punishments" in any New England states. "Negroes were citizens in all of these [free?] states," he writes (leaving it unclear how many). "They were citizens by enjoyment of full political equality, by lack of any statements to the contrary in any constitution or law, by complete absence of legal distinctions based on color, and by specific legal and constitutional declaration, and any statements to the contrary by courts, federal or state, were contrary to historical fact and are worthless as historical evidence." There is no hint of the thoroughgoing system of Northern segregation described by Mr. Litwack. It is admitted that one might "find a less liberal attitude toward free Negroes" in the Midwestern states, but that is easily accounted for: "There was a preponderance of Southern immigrants in the populations." In spite of this, we learn that in Jackson's time, "the Northern people, freeing themselves of the last vestiges of slavery, moved forward in a vast liberal reform movement."

The theory Mr. Dumond applies to the antislavery movement colors and coerces his reading of the whole of American history from the Revolution through the Civil War. This reading amounts to a revival of the long discredited theory of the Slave Power Conspiracy, a dominant hypothesis two or three generations ago. Slavery, we are told, "gave clay feet to Patrick Henry . . . and

I suspect to Washington and Jefferson as well." Of the Revolutionary leaders he writes: "Those men were perfectly willing to spread carnage over the face of the earth to establish their own claim to freedom, but lacked the courage to live by their assertion of the natural rights of men." Of the Presidential contest of 1800 we are told: "This election enabled Jefferson to lay solidly the foundations of the party of agrarianism, slavery, and decentralization." Any mention of Jefferson is accompanied by a reminder that he owned slaves. The achievement of a group is discredited with the phrase, "slaveholders all." The Virginia Dynasty, its heirs and successors of the next three decades, and most of their acts and works including the Constitution, fare pretty harshly under this restricted historical criterion.

The whole sectional conflict that eventually erupted in the Civil War is construed, of course, in terms of right versus wrong, North against South. Civil War historians will be interested to learn that "there was complete coordination by the Congress, the President, and the field commanders of the Army" in their mutual determination to abolish slavery at the earliest possible moment. This revelation will require a good deal of revision in accepted views, which take into account a great lack of coordination among those distracted branches of the wartime government.

It is possible that Professor Dumond's interpretations of American history might be traced directly to an unfortunate theory of historical method. Neither this nor the extended criticism of his work already undertaken would be worth the effort, however, were it not for what the book reveals about the present vitality and amazing persistence of the antislavery myth. His book is the latest and fullest embodiment of the myth. Yet it comes with endorsements of unqualified praise from leading authorities in the field. The wide flaps of the dust jacket bear such recommendations from the three foremost present-day historians of the American Civil War, followed by the equally enthusiastic praise of prominent historians from four of our most respected universities. These are not men who share Mr. Dumond's restrictive concepts of historiography, nor are they given to bestowing praise lightly. They undoubtedly mean what they say. What two of them say is that this book is "definitive," and all agree that from their point of view it is wholly satisfying.

One would like to know more about their reasoning. Several of them refer directly or obliquely to present-day social problems that are a heritage of slavery, meaning segregation and the movement for Negro rights. But surely one can establish his position upon such clear-cut contemporary moral problems as these without compromising the standards of historical criticism. And by this time, one hopes, it is possible to register a stand on the slavery issue without feigning the apocalyptic rages of a John Brown. No, these are not adequate or convincing explanations, at least for the reactions of these particular historians.

In all probability the real reason why this ponderous, fierce and humorless book is handled with such piety and solemnity is the very fact that it does embody one of the great American myths. We have never faced up to the relationship between myth and history. Without tackling the semantic difficulties involved, we know that *myth* has more than pejorative usages and that it can be used to denote more than what one deems false about the other man's beliefs. In the non-pejorative sense myths are images, or collections of them, charged with values, aspirations, ideals and meanings. In the words of Mark Schorer, they are "the instruments by which we continually struggle to make our experience intelligible to ourselves." Myths *can* be, in short, "a good thing." No man in his right mind, and surely not a responsible historian, will knowingly and wantonly destroy a precious thing. And no doubt some would hesitate to lay hands on a book that, improperly though it may be, got itself identified as a repository of cherished values.

Serious history is the critique of myths, however, not the embodiment of them. Neither is it the destruction of myths. One of the great national myths is the equality of man, embodied in the Declaration of Independence. Tocqueville's study of equality in America is a valid critique of the myth, with neither the intention nor the effect of destroying it or doing it injury. Henry Nash Smith's *Virgin Land* provides a valid critique of the West's Myth of the Garden and symbols of the frontier without succumbing to impulses of iconoclasm. There is no comparable critique of the more elaborate myth—one might say mythology—of the South. What has been done in this respect has been mainly the work of imaginative writers rather than historians of the South. Historians have made a beginning, however, and a recent contribution by William R. Taylor, *Cavalier and Yankee,* which illuminates the legend of aristocratic grandeur, is an excellent illustration of what is needed.

As a result of such studies, intelligent, contemporary Americans can speak of the myth of equality without self-consciousness or cynicism, and embrace it without striking the pose of a defiant Jacksonian of the 1830's. Contemporary westerners are able to cherish and preserve frontier values without assuming the role of a Davy Crockett. And southerners can even salvage some of the aristocratic heritage without wallowing in the Plantation Legend.

As yet, however, the Yankee remains to be fully emancipated from his own legends of emancipation. Confront him with a given set of symbols and he will set his sense of humor aside, snap to attention and come to a full salute. In the ensuing rigidities of that situation, conversation tends to lag. The pertinent interjections by Mr. Gara on the U.G.R.R. and by Mr. Litwack on the North Star Legend, already noticed, may help to break the ice, but the thawing will probably be slow. The provocative suggestions of Stanley M. Elkins, in *Slavery: A Problem in American Institutional and Intellectual Life,* have been gravely rebuked for impropriety, if not impiety. The orthodox text is obviously still the gospel according to Mr. Dumond.

The big assignment on the Antislavery Myth still awaits a taker. The eventual taker, like any historian who would make myth the proper subject of his study, should be involved without running the risks of total involvement. It would help a great deal if he could contrive to bring detachment as well as sympathy to his task. It is also to be hoped that he might make legitimate use of irony as well as compassion. And, finally, no aspirant with inappropriate regional identifications need apply.

Legacy of Hate: The Myth of a Peaceful Belligerent

Rodolfo Acuña

American visions of a vast "Empire of Democracy" that would one day extend from the Atlantic Ocean to the western rim of the continent had been animating the national imagination at least since the Louisiana Purchase of 1803. It was during the presidency of James K. Polk some forty years later, however, that expansionist ideas, rationalized as Manifest Destiny, became most overt—and aggressive. In the judgment of Rodolfo Acuña of California State University at Northridge, perhaps nowhere are the illusions, distortions, and myths that supported the notion of Manifest Destiny more evident than in the events surrounding Texas independence, its annexation to the United States, and the ensuing Mexican War. Lapsing into a self-righteous rhetoric of peace, thereby working to sustain the myth of America as a nonviolent nation, American leaders nonetheless through their actions reflected their imperial ambitions. The "glorious" victory over Mexico did much to fulfill the mythical dreams of Manifest Destiny even as it left a significant "legacy of hate" among Mexicans and Chicanos toward their Anglo conquerors.

The tragedy of the Mexican cession is that most Anglo-Americans have not accepted the fact that the United States committed an act of violence against the Mexican people when it took Mexico's northwestern territory. Violence was not limited to the taking of the land; Mexico's territory was invaded, her people murdered, her land raped, and her possessions plundered. Memory of this destruction generated a distrust and dislike that is still vivid in the minds of many Mexicans, for the violence of the United States left deep scars. And for Chicanos—Mexicans remaining within the boundaries of the new United States territories—aggression was even more insidious, for the outcome of the Texas and Mexican-American wars made them a conquered people. Anglo-Americans were the conquerors, and they evinced all the arrogance of military victors.

Background to the Invasion of Texas

An integral part of Anglo rationalizations for the conquest has been either to ignore or to distort events that led up to the initial clash in 1836. To Anglo-

Americans, the Texas War resulted because of a tyrannical or, at best, an incompetent Mexican government that was antithetical to the ideals of democracy and justice. The truth is that the roots of the conflict extended back to as early as 1767 when Benjamin Franklin marked Mexico and Cuba for future expansion. Filibusters* from the United States planned expeditions into Texas in the 1790s. The Louisiana Purchase in 1803 stimulated U.S. ambitions in the Southwest and six years later Thomas Jefferson predicted that the Spanish borderlands "are ours the first moment war is forced upon us." The war with Great Britain in 1812 heightened Anglo-American designs on the Spanish territory.

The U.S. experience in Florida set the pattern for expansionist activities in Texas. In 1818 several posts in East Florida were seized in unauthorized, but never officially condemned U.S. military expeditions. Negotiations then in progress with Spain finally terminated in the Adams-Onis or Transcontinental Treaty (1819) whereby Spain ceded Florida to the United States and the United States renounced its claim to Texas. The treaty set the U.S. boundary at the Sabine River, thereby excluding Texas. When the treaty was ratified in February 1821 Texas was part of Coahuila, a state in the independent Republic of Mexico. Many North Americans claimed that Texas belonged to the United States, pointing to Jefferson's contention that Texas's boundary extended to the Rio Grande and that it was part of the Louisiana Purchase. They condemned the Adams-Onis Treaty. The expanded boundary would have "put several key Mexican posts, notably San Antonio, Albuquerque and Santa Fe inside the United States." Therefore, Anglo-Americans made forays into Texas similar to those they had made into Florida. In 1819 James Long led an abortive invasion to establish the "Republic of Texas." Long, like many Anglos, believed that Texas belonged to the United States and that "Congress had no right or power to sell, exchange, or relinquish an 'American possession.' "

The Mexican government opened Texas, provided settlers agreed to certain conditions, and for a time filibustering subsided. Moses Austin was given permission to settle in Texas. He died shortly afterwards and his son continued his venture. In December 1821 Stephen Austin founded the settlement of San Felipe de Austin. Large numbers followed, many coming to Texas in the 1820s as refugees from the depression of 1819 and in the 1830s as entrepreneurs seeking to profit from the availability of cheap land. By 1830 there were about 20,000 settlers, along with about 2,000 slaves.

Settlers agreed to obey the conditions set by the Mexican government—that all immigrants be Catholics and that they take an oath of allegiance to Mexico. However, Anglo-Americans became resentful when Mexico tried to enforce the agreements and Mexico became increasingly alarmed at the flood of immigrants from the United States, most of whom retained their Protestant religion.

It soon became apparent that the Anglo-Texans had no intention of obey-

---

*A *filibuster* is an adventurer who engages in insurrectionist or revolutionary activity in a foreign country.

ing Mexican laws. Many settlers considered the native Mexicans to be the intruders in the territory and encroached upon their lands. In a dispute with Mexicans and Indians, as well as Anglo-American settlers, Hayden Edwards arbitrarily attempted to evict settlers from the land before the conflicting claims could be sorted out by the Mexican authorities. As a result the authorities nullified his settlement contract and ordered him to leave the territory. He and his followers seized the town of Nacogdoches and on December 21, 1826, proclaimed the Republic of Fredonia. Mexican officials, who were supported by some Anglo-Americans (such as Stephen Austin), suffocated the Edwards revolt. However, many U.S. newspapers played up the rebellion as "200 Men Against a Nation!" and described Edwards and his followers as "apostles of democracy crushed by an alien civilization."

In 1824 President John Quincy Adams "began putting pressure on Mexico in the hope of persuading her to rectify the frontier. Any of the Texan rivers west of the Sabine—the Brazos, the Colorado, the Nueces—was preferable to the Sabine, though the Rio Grande was the one desired." In 1826 Adams offered to buy Texas for the sum of $1 million. Mexican authorities refused the offer. The United States launched an aggressive foreign policy, attempting to coerce Mexico into selling Texas.

Mexico tried to consolidate its control over Texas, but the number of Anglo-American settlers and the vastness of the territory made it an almost impossible task. Anglo-Americans in Texas had already created a privileged caste, which depended in great part on the economic advantage given to them by their slaves. When Mexico abolished slavery on September 15, 1829, Texans circumvented the law by "freeing" their slaves and then signing them to lifelong contracts as indentured servants. Anglos resented the Mexican order and considered it an invasion of their personal liberties. In 1830 Mexico prohibited further Anglo-American immigration to Texas. Anglos were outraged at the restrictions. Meanwhile, Andrew Jackson increased tensions by attempting to purchase Texas for as much as $5 million.

Mexican authorities grew more nervous as the Anglo-Americans' dominance of Texas increased; they resented the Anglo-Americans' refusal to submit to Mexican laws. Mexico moved reinforcements into Coahuila, and readied them in case of trouble. Anglos viewed this move as a Mexican invasion.

Anglo-Texan colonists grew more defiant and refused to pay customs and actively supported smuggling activities. Armed clashes broke out. When the "war party" rioted at Anahuac in December 1831 it had the popular support of Anglo-Texans. One of its leaders was Sam Houston, who "was a known protégé of Andrew Jackson, now president of the United States. . . . Houston's motivation was to bring Texas into the United States."

In the summer of 1832 a group of Anglos attacked a Mexican garrison and were routed. A state of insurrection existed and Mexican authorities were forced to defend the territory. Matters worsened when the Anglo settlers met at San Felipe in October 1832. At this convention Anglos drafted resolutions sent to the Mexican government and to the state of Coahuila which called for more autonomy for Texas. A second convention was held in January 1833. Significantly, not one Mexican pueblo in Texas participated in either convention, many clearly branding the act sedition. Increasingly it became evident that the war party under Sam Houston was winning out. Sam Houston was elected to direct the course of events and Austin was appointed to submit the grievances and resolutions to Mexico City.

Austin left for Mexico City to press for lifting of restrictions on Anglo-American immigration and separate statehood. The slave issue also burned in his mind. Austin, anything but conciliatory, wrote to a friend from Mexico City, "If our application is refused . . . I shall be in favor of organizing *without it*. I see no other way of saving the country from total anarchy and ruin. I am totally done with conciliatory measures and, for the future, shall be uncompromising as to Texas."

On October 2, 1833, he wrote a letter to the *ayuntamiento* at San Antonio encouraging it to declare Texas a separate state. He later stated that he had done so "in a moment of irritation and impatience"; nevertheless, his actions were not those of a moderate. Contents of the note fell into the hands of Mexican authorities, who had begun to question Austin's good faith. Subsequently, they imprisoned him, and much of what Austin had accomplished in the way of compromise was undone.

Contributing to the general distrust were actions of U.S. Minister to Mexico Anthony Butler, whose crude attempts to bribe Mexican officials to sell Texas infuriated Mexicans. He offered one official $200,000 to "play ball."

In the autumn of 1834 Henry Smith published a pamphlet entitled *Security for Texas* in which he advocated open defiance of Mexican authority. The agents of Anglo land companies added to the polarization by lobbying in Washington, D.C., and within Texas for a change in governments. The Galveston Bay and Texas Land Company of New York, acting to protect its investments, worked through its agent Anthony Butler, the U.S. Minister to Mexico, to bring about the cooperation of the United States.

According to Dr. Carlos Castañeda:

> The activities of the "Land Companies" after 1834 cannot be ignored. Their widespread advertisement and indiscriminate sale of "landscrip" sent hundreds, perhaps thousands, to Texas under the impression that they had legitimate title to lands equal to the amount of scrip bought. The Galveston Bay and Texas Land Company, which bought the contracts of David S. Burnet, Joseph Vahlein, and Lorenzo de Zavala, and the Nashville Company, which acquired the contract of Robert Leftwitch, are the two best known. They first sold scrip at from one to ten cents an acre, calling for a total of seven and one-half million acres. The company was selling only its permit to acquire a given amount of land in Texas, but since an empresario contract was nontransferable, the scrip was, in fact, worthless. . . .

The scrip would be worthless as long as Texas belonged to Mexico.

On July 13, 1835, a general amnesty released Austin from prison. While en route to Texas, he wrote a letter from New Orleans to a cousin expressing the view that Texas should be Americanized even though it was still a state of Mexico, and indicating that it should one day come under the American flag. In this letter he called for a massive immigration of Anglo-Americans, *"each man with his rifle,"* whom he hoped would come *"passports or no pass-ports, anyhow."* He continued: "For fourteen years I have had a hard time of it, but nothing shall daunt my courage or abate my . . . object . . . to *Americanize* Texans."

Anglos in Texas saw separation from Mexico and eventual union with the United States as the most profitable political arrangement. Texas-Mexican historian Castañeda notes:

> Trade with New Orleans and other American ports had increased steadily. This development was naturally distasteful to Mexico, for the colonists fostered strong economic ties with . . . the United States rather than with Mexico. Juan H. Almonte in his 1834 report, estimated the total foreign trade of Texas—chiefly with the United States—at more than 1,000,000 pesos, of which imports constituted 630,000 and exports, 500,000. He calculated the exportation of cotton by the settlers in 1833, as approximately 2,000 bales.

Colonel Almonte recognized the fundamental economic conflict reflected in these figures and his report recommended many concessions to the *Tejanos,* but also urged that "the province be well stocked with Mexican troops."

The Invasion of Texas

Not all the Anglo-Texan settlers favored the conflict. Austin belonged to the peace party, which at first opposed a confrontation with Mexicans. Ultimately, this faction joined the "hawks." Eugene C. Barker states that the immediate cause of the war was "the overthrow of the nominal republic [by Santa Anna] and the substitution of centralized oligarchy," which allegedly would have placed the Texans more strictly under the control of Mexico. Barker admits that "earnest patriots like Benjamin Lundy, William Ellery Channing, and John Quincy Adams saw in the Texas revolution a disgraceful affair promoted by the sordid slaveholders and land speculators."

Barker draws a parallel between the Texas revolt and the American Revolution, stating: "In each, the general cause of revolt was the same—a sudden effort to extend imperial authority at the expense of local privilege." In fact, in both instances the central governments attempted to enforce existing laws that conflicted with illegal activities of some very articulate men. Barker further attempts to justify the Anglo-Texans' actions by observing: "At the close of summer in 1835 the Texans saw themselves in danger of becoming the alien subjects of a people to whom they deliberately believed themselves morally, intellectually, and politically superior. The racial feeling, indeed, underlay and colored Texan-Mexican relations from the establishment of the first Anglo-American colony in 1821." Therefore, the conflict, according to Barker, was inevitable and, consequently, justified.

Texas history is elusive—a mixture of selected fact and generalized myth. Many historians admit that racism played a leading role in the causes for revolt, that smugglers were upset with Mexico's enforcement of her import laws, that Texans were upset about emancipation laws, and that an increasing number of the new arrivals from the United States actively agitated for independence. But despite these admissions, many historians like Barker refuse to assign guilt to their countrymen. Instead, Barker blamed it on the racial and cultural mistrust between Mexicans and the colonists.

The antipathies of the Texans escalated into a full-scale rebellion. Austin gave the call to arms on September 19, 1835, stating, "War is our only recourse. There is no remedy." Anglo-Americans enjoyed very real advantages in 1835. They were "defending" terrain with which they were familiar. The 5,000 Mexicans living in the territory did not join them, but the Anglo population had swelled to almost 30,000. The Mexican nation was divided, and the centers of power were thousands of miles away from Texas. From the interior of Mexico Santa Anna led an army of about 6,000 conscripts, many of whom had been forced into the army and then marched hundreds of miles over hot, arid desert land. Many were Mayan and did not speak Spanish. In February 1836 the majority arrived in San Antonio, Texas, sick and ill-prepared to fight. Although the Mexican army outnumbered the Anglo contingent, the latter were much better armed and enjoyed the position of being the defenders. (Until World War I, this was a decided advantage during wartime.) Santa Anna, on the other hand, had overextended his supply lines and was many miles from his base of power.

The defenders of San Antonio took refuge in a former mission, the Alamo. In the days that followed, Texans inflicted heavy casualties on the Mexican forces, but eventually the Mexicans' sheer superiority in numbers won out. Much has been written about Mexican cruelty in relation to the Alamo and about the heroics of the doomed men. The result was the creation of the Alamo myth. Within the broad framework of what actually happened— 187 Texans barricading themselves in the Alamo in defiance of Santa Anna's force and the eventual triumph of the Mexicans—there has been much distortion.

Walter Lord, in an article entitled "Myths and Realities of the Alamo," sets much of the record straight. Texas mythology portrays the Alamo heroes as freedom-loving defenders of their homes; they were supposedly all good Texans. Actually, two-thirds of the defenders had recently arrived from the United States, and only a half dozen had been in Texas for more than six years. The men in the Alamo were adventurers. William Barret Travis had fled to Texas after killing a man, abandoning his wife and two children. James Bowie, an infamous brawler, made a fortune running slaves and had wandered into Texas searching for lost mines and more money. The fading Davy Crockett, a legend in his own time, fought for the sake of fighting. Many others in the Alamo were men who had come to Texas for riches and glory. These defenders were hardly the sort of men who could be classified as peaceful settlers fighting for their homes.

The folklore of the Alamo goes beyond the legendary names of the defenders. According to Lord, it is riddled with dramatic half-truths that have been accepted as history. Defenders at the Alamo are portrayed as selfless heroes who sacrificed their lives to buy more time for their comrades-in-arms.

As the story is told, William Barret Travis told his men that they were doomed; he drew a line in the sand with his sword, saying that all who crossed it would elect to remain and fight to the last. Supposedly all the men there valiantly stepped across the line, with a man in a cot begging to be carried across it. The bravery of the defenders has been *dramatized* in countless Hollywood movies.

In reality the Alamo had little strategic value, it was the best fortified fort west of the Mississippi, and the men fully expected help. The defenders had twenty-one cannons to the Mexicans' eight or ten. They were expert marksmen equipped with rifles with a range of 200 yards, while the Mexicans were inadequately trained and armed with smooth-bore muskets with a range of only 70 yards. The Anglos were protected by the walls and had clear shots, while the Mexicans advanced in the open and fired at concealed targets. In short, ill-prepared, ill-equipped, and ill-fed Mexicans attacked well-armed and professional soldiers. In addition, from all reliable sources, it is doubtful whether Travis ever drew a line in the sand. San Antonio survivors, females and noncombatants, did not tell the story until many years later, when the tale had become well circulated and the myth was a legend. Probably the most widely circulated story was that of the last stand of the aging Davy Crockett who fell "fighting like a tiger," killing Mexicans with his bare hands. This is a myth; seven of the defenders surrendered, and Crockett was among them. They were executed. And, finally, one man, Louis Rose, did escape.

Travis's stand delayed Santa Anna's timetable by only four days, as the Mexicans took San Antonio on March 6, 1836. At first, the stand at the Alamo did not even have propaganda value. Afterwards, Houston's army dwindled, with many volunteers rushing home to help their families flee from the advancing Mexican army. Most Anglo-Texans realized that they had been badly beaten. It did, nevertheless, result in massive aid from the United States in the form of volunteers, arms, and money. The cry of "Remember the Alamo" became a call to arms for Anglo-Americans in both Texas and the United States.

After the Alamo and the defeat of another garrison at Goliad, southeast of San Antonio, Santa Anna was in full control. He ran Sam Houston out of the territory northwest of the San Jacinto River and then camped an army of about 1,100 men near San Jacinto. There, he skirmished with Houston on April 20, 1836, but did not follow up his advantage. Predicting that Houston would attack on April 22, Santa Anna and his men settled down and rested for the anticipated battle. Texans, however, attacked during the *siesta* hour on April 21. Santa Anna had made an incredible blunder. He knew that Houston had an army of 1,000, yet he was lax in his precautionary defenses. The surprise attack caught him totally off guard. Shouts of "Remember the Alamo! Remember Goliad!" filled the air. Houston's successful surprise attack ended the war. He captured Santa Anna, who had no choice and signed the territory away. Although the Mexican Congress repudiated the treaty, Houston was elected president of the Republic of Texas.

The battle of San Jacinto was literally a slaughter of the Mexican forces.

Few prisoners were taken. Those who surrendered "were clubbed and stabbed," some on their knees. The slaughter . . . became methodical: the Texan riflemen knelt and poured a steady fire into the packed, jostling ranks. . . . They shot the "Meskins" down as they fled. The final count showed 630 Mexicans dead versus 2 Texans.

It is commonly believed that after the surrender Texan authorities let Santa Anna off lightly, but, according to Dr. Castañeda, Santa Anna "was mercilessly dragged from the ship he had boarded, subjected to more than six months' mental torture and indignities in Texas prison camps."

The Texas victory paved the way for the Mexican-American War, feeding the growing nationalism of the young Anglo-American nation. Officially the United States had not taken sides, but men, money, and supplies poured in to aid fellow Anglo-Americans. U.S. citizens participated in the invasion of Texas with the open support of their government. Mexico's Minister to the United States, Manuel Eduardo Gorostiza, vehemently protested the "arming and shipment of troops and supplies to territory which was part of Mexico, and the dispatch of United States troops into territory clearly defined by treaty as Mexican territory." General Edmund P. Gaines, Southwest Commander, had been sent into Western Louisiana on January 23, 1836; shortly thereafter, he crossed into Texas in an action that was interpreted to be in support of the Anglo-American filibusters in Texas: "The Jackson Administration made it plain to the Mexican minister that it mattered little whether Mexico approved, that the important thing was to protect the border against Indians and Mexicans." U.S. citizens in and out of Texas loudly applauded Jackson's actions. The Mexican minister resigned his post in protest. "The success of the Texas Revolution thrust the Anglo-American frontier up against the Far Southwest, and the region came at once into the scope of Anglo ambition."

The Invasion of Mexico

The United States during the nineteenth century moved its boundaries westward. In the mid-1840s, Mexico was again the target. Expansion and capitalist development moved together. The two Mexican wars gave U.S. commerce, industry, mining, agriculture, and stockraising a tremendous stimulus. "The truth is that [by the 1840s] the Pacific Coast belonged to the commercial empire that the United States was already building in that ocean."

The United States's population of 17 million people of European extraction and 3 million slaves was considerably larger than Mexico's 7 million, of which 4 million were Indian, and 3 million Mestizo and European. The United States acted arrogantly in foreign affairs, partly because its citizens believed in their inherent cultural and racial superiority. Mexico was plagued with financial problems, internal ethnic conflicts, and poor leadership. General anarchy within the nation conspired against its cohesive development.

By 1844 war with Mexico over Texas and the Southwest was only a matter of time. James K. Polk, who strongly advocated the annexation of Texas and expansionism in general, won the presidency by only a small margin, but his election was interpreted as a mandate for national expansion. Outgoing President Tyler decided to act and called upon Congress to annex Texas by joint resolution; the measure was passed a few days before the inauguration of Polk, who accepted the arrangement. In December 1845, Texas became a state.

Mexico promptly broke off diplomatic relations with the United States, and Polk ordered General Zachary Taylor into Texas to "protect" the border. The location of the border was in doubt. Texas contended it was at the Rio Grande, but based on historical precedent, Mexico claimed it was 150 miles farther north, at the Nueces River. Taylor took his forces across the Nueces into the disputed territory, wanting to provoke an attack.

In November 1845, Polk sent John Slidell on a secret mission to Mexico to negotiate for the disputed area. The presence of Anglo-American troops between the Nueces and the Rio Grande and the annexation of Texas made negotiations an absurdity. They refused to accept Polk's minister's credentials, although they did offer to grant him an ad hoc status. Slidell refused anything less than full acceptance and returned to Washington in March 1846, convinced that Mexico would have to be "chastised" before it would negotiate. By March 28, Taylor had advanced to the Rio Grande with an army of 4,000.

Polk, incensed at Mexico's refusal to meet with Slidell on his terms and at General Mariano Paredes's reaffirmation of his country's claims to all of Texas, began to draft his declaration of war when he learned of a Mexican attack on U.S. troops in the disputed territory. He immediately declared that the United States had been provoked into war, that Mexico had "shed American blood upon the American soil." On May 13, 1846, Congress declared war and authorized the recruitment and supplying of 50,000 troops.

Years later, Ulysses S. Grant said that he believed Polk wanted and planned for war to be provoked and that the annexation of Texas was, in fact, an act of aggression. He added: "I had a horror of the Mexican War . . . only I had not moral courage enough to resign. . . . I considered my supreme duty was to my flag."

The poorly equipped and poorly led Mexican army stood little chance against the thrust of expansion-minded Anglos. Even before the war Polk planned a campaign of three stages: (1) Mexicans would be cleared out of Texas; (2) Anglos would occupy California and New Mexico; and (3) U.S. forces would march to Mexico City to force the beaten government to make peace on Polk's terms. And that was the way the campaign basically went. In the end, at a relatively small cost in men and money, the war netted the United States huge territorial gains. In all, the United States took over 1 million square miles of Mexican lands.

The Rationale for Conquest

In his *Origins of the War with Mexico: The Polk-Stockton Intrigue,* Glenn W. Price states: "Americans have found it rather more difficult than other peoples to deal rationally with their wars. We have thought of ourselves as unique, and of this society as specially planned and created to avoid the errors of all other nations." In this vein, many Anglo-American historians attempt to dismiss the Mexican-American War by simply stating that it was a "bad war," which took place during the U.S. era of Manifest Destiny.

Manifest Destiny had its roots in Puritan ideas, which continue to influence Anglo-American thought to this day. According to the Puritan ethic, salvation is determined by God. The establishment of the City of God on earth is not only the duty of those chosen people predestined for salvation, but is also the proof of their state of grace. This belief carried over to the Anglo-American conviction that God had made them custodians of democracy and that they had a mission, that is, that they were predestined to spread its principles. As the young nation survived its infancy, established its power in the defeat of the British in the War of 1812, expanded westward, and enjoyed both commercial and industrial success, its sense of destiny heightened. Many citizens believed that God had destined them to own and occupy all of the land from ocean to ocean and pole to pole. Their mission, their destiny made manifest, was to spread the principles of democracy and Christianity to the unfortunates of the hemisphere. By dismissing the war simply as part of the era of Manifest Destiny the apologists for the war ignore the consequences of the doctrine.

The Monroe Doctrine of the 1820s told the world that the Americas were no longer open for colonization or conquest; however, it did not say anything about that limitation applying to the United States. Uppermost in the minds of the U.S. government, the military, and much of the public was the acquisition of territory. No one ever intended to leave Mexico without extracting territory. Land was the main motivation.

Further obscuring the issue of planned Anglo-American aggression is what Professor Price exposes as the rhetoric of peace, which the United States has traditionally used to justify its aggressions. The Mexican-American War is a study in the use of this rhetoric.

Consider, for example, Polk's war message of May 11, 1846, in which he gave his reasons for going to war:

> The strong desire to establish peace with Mexico on liberal and honorable terms, and the readiness of this Government to regulate and adjust our boundary and other causes of difference with that power on such fair and equitable principles as would lead to permanent relations of the most friendly nature, induced me in September last to seek reopening of diplomatic relations between the two countries.

He went on to state that the United States had made every effort not to inflame Mexicans, but that the Mexican government had refused to receive an Anglo-American minister. Polk reviewed the events leading to the war and concluded:

> As war exists, and notwithstanding all our efforts to avoid it, exists by the act of Mexico herself, we are called upon by every consideration of duty and patriotism to indicate with decision the honor, the rights, and the interests of our country.

Historical distance from the events has not reduced the prevalence of this rhetoric. The need to justify has continued. In 1920 Justin F. Smith received a

Pulitzer prize in history for a work that blamed the war on Mexico. What is amazing is that Smith allegedly examined more than 100,000 manuscripts, 120,000 books and pamphlets, and 200 or more periodicals to come to this conclusion. It is fair to speculate that he was rewarded for relieving the Anglo-American conscience. His two-volume "study," entitled *The War with Mexico*, used analyses such as the following to support its thesis:

> At the beginning of her independent existence, our people felt earnestly and enthusiastically anxious to maintain cordial relations with our sister republic, and many crossed the line of absurd sentimentality in the cause. Friction was inevitable, however. The Americans were direct, positive, brusque, angular and pushing; and they would not understand their neighbors in the south. The Mexicans were equally unable to fathom our goodwill, sincerity, patriotism, resoluteness and courage; and certain features of their character and national condition made it far from easy to get on with them.

This attitude of righteousness on the part of government officials and historians toward their aggressions spills over to the relationships between the majority society and minority groups. Anglo-Americans believe that the war was advantageous to the Southwest and to the Mexicans who remained or later migrated there. They now had the benefits of democracy and were liberated from their tyrannical past. In other words, Mexicans should be grateful to the Anglo-Americans. If Mexicans and the Anglo-Americans clash, the rationale runs, naturally it is because Mexicans cannot understand or appreciate the merits of a free society, which must be defended against ingrates. Therefore, domestic war, or repression, is justified by the same kind of rhetoric that justifies international aggression.

Professor Gene M. Brack, in the most recent of these works, attacks those who base their research on Justin Smith's outdated work: "American historians have consistently praised Justin Smith's influential and outrageously ethnocentric account."

The Myth of a Nonviolent Nation

Most works on the Mexican-American War have dwelt on the causes and results of the war, sometimes dealing with war strategy. It is necessary, however, to go beyond this point, since the war left bitterness, and since Anglo-American actions in Mexico are vividly remembered. Mexicans' attitude toward Anglo-Americans has been influenced by the war just as the United States's easy victory conditioned Anglo-American behavior toward Mexicans. Fortunately, many Anglo-Americans condemned this aggression and flatly accused their leaders of being insolent, land hungry, and of having manufactured the war. Abiel Abbott Livermore in *The War with Mexico Reviewed* accused his country, writing:

> Again, the pride of race has swollen to still greater insolence the pride of country, always quite active enough for the due observance of the claims of universal brotherhood. The Anglo-Saxons have been apparently persuaded to think themselves the chosen people, annointed race of the Lord, commissioned to drive out

the heathen, and plant their religion and institutions in every Canaan they could subjugate. . . . Our treatment both of the red man and the black man has habituated us to feel our power and forget right. . . . The passion for land, also, is a leading characteristic of the American people. . . . The god Terminus is an unknown deity in America. Like the hunger of the pauper boy of fiction, the cry had been, 'more, more, give us more.'

Livermore's work, published in 1850, was awarded the American Peace Society prize for "the best review of the Mexican War and the principles of Christianity, and an enlightened statesmanship."

The United States provoked the war and then conducted it violently and brutally. Zachary Taylor's artillery leveled the Mexican city of Matamoros, killing hundreds of innocent civilians with *la bomba* (the bomb). Many Mexicans jumped into the Rio Grande, relieved of their pain by a watery grave. The occupation that followed was even more terrorizing. Taylor's regular army was kept in control, but the volunteers presented another matter:

The regulars regarded the volunteers, of whom about two thousand had reached Matamoros by the end of May, with impatience and contempt. . . . They robbed Mexicans of their cattle and corn, stole their fences for firewood, got drunk, and killed several inoffensive inhabitants of the town in the streets.

There were numerous eyewitnesses to these incidents. For example, on July 25, 1846, Grant wrote to Julia Dent:

Since we have been in Matamoros a great many murders have been committed, and what is strange there seemes [sic] to be very week [sic] means made use of to prevent frequent repetitions. Some of the volunteers and about all the Texans seem to think it perfectly right to impose on the people of a conquered city to any extent, and even to murder them where the act can be covered by dark. And how much they seem to enjoy acts of violence too! I would not pretend to guess the number of murders that have been committed upon the persons of poor Mexicans and our soldiers, since we have been here, but the number would startle you.

On July 9, 1846, George Gordon Meade, who like Grant later became a general during the U.S. Civil War, wrote:

They [the volunteers] have killed five or six innocent people walking in the street, for no other object than their own amusement. . . . They rob and steal the cattle and corn of the poor farmers, and in fact act more like a body of hostile Indians than civilized Whites. Their officers have no command or control over them. . . .

Taylor knew about the atrocities, but Grant observed that Taylor did not restrain his men. In a letter to his superiors, Taylor admitted that "there is scarcely a form of crime that has not been reported to me as committed by them." Taylor requested that they send no further troops from the state of Texas to him. These marauding acts were not limited to Taylor's men. The cannons from U.S. naval ships destroyed much of the civilian sector of Vera Cruz, leveling a hospital, churches, and homes. The bomb did not discriminate as to age or sex. Anglo-American troops destroyed almost every city they invaded; first it was put to the test of fire and then plundered. *Gringo* volunteers had little respect for anything, desecrating churches and abusing priests and nuns.

Military executions were common. Captured soldiers and civilians were hanged for cooperating with the guerillas. Many Irish immigrants, as well as some other Anglos, deserted to the Mexican side, forming the San Patricio Corps. Many of the Irish were Catholics, and they resented treatment of Catholic priests and nuns by the invading Protestants. As many as 260 Anglo-Americans fought with the Mexicans at Churubusco in 1847:

> Some eighty appear to have been captured. . . . A number were found not guilty of deserting and were released. About fifteen, who had deserted before the declaration of war, were merely branded with a "D," and fifty of those taken at Churubusco were executed.

Others received two hundred lashes and were forced to dig graves for their executed comrades.

These acts were similar to those in Monterey when George Meade wrote on December 2, 1846:

> They plunder the poor inhabitants of everything they can lay their hands on, and shoot them when they remonstrate; and if one of their number happens to get into a drunken brawl and is killed, they run over the country, killing all the poor innocent people they find in their way to avenge, as they say, the murder of their brother. . . .

As Scott's army left Monterey, they shot Mexican prisoners of war.

Memoirs, diaries, and news articles written by Anglo-Americans document the reign of terror. Samuel F. Chamberlain's *My Confessions* is a record of Anglo racism and destruction. He was only 17 when he enlisted in the army to fight the "greasers." At the Mexican city of Parras, he wrote:

> We found the patrol had been guilty of many outrages. . . . They had ridden into the church of San José during Mass, the place crowded with kneeling women and children, and with oaths and ribald jest had arrested soldiers who had permission to be present.

On another occasion, he described a massacre by volunteers, mostly from Yell's Cavalry, at a cave:

> On reaching the place we found a "greaser" shot and *scalped*, but still breathing; the poor fellow held in his hands a Rosary and a medal of the "Virgin of Guadalupe," only his feeble motions kept the fierce harpies from falling on him while yet alive. A Sabre thrust was given him in mercy, and on we went at a run. Soon shouts and curses, cries of women and children reached our ears, coming apparently from a cave at the end of the ravine. Climbing over the rocks we reached the entrance, and as soon as we could see in the comparative darkness a horrid sight was before us. The cave was full of our volunteers yelling like fiends, while on the rocky floor lay over twenty Mexicans, dead and dying in pools of blood. Women and children were clinging to the knees of the murderers shrieking for mercy. . . . Most of the butchered Mexicans had been scalped; only three men were found unharmed. A rough crucifix was fastened to a rock, and some irrever-

ent wretch had crowned the image with a bloody scalp. A sickening smell filled the place. The surviving women and children sent up loud screams on seeing us, thinking we had returned to finish the work! . . . No one was punished for this outrage.

Near Satillo, Chamberlain reported the actions of Texas Rangers. His descriptions were graphic:

[A drunken Anglo] entered the church and tore down a large wooden figure of our Saviour, and making his lariat fast around its neck, he mounted his horse and galloped up and down the *plazuela*, dragging the statue behind. The venerable white-haired Priest, in attempting to rescue it, was thrown down and trampled under the feet of the Ranger's horse.

Mexicans were enraged and attacked the Texan. Meanwhile, the Rangers returned:

As they charged into the square, they saw their miserable comrade hanging to his cross, his skin hanging in strips, surrounded by crowds of Mexicans. With yells of horror, the Rangers charged on the mass with Bowie Knife and revolver, sparing neither age or sex in their terrible fury.

Chamberlain blamed General Taylor not only for collecting over $1 million (from the Mexican people) by force of arms, but also for letting "loose on the country packs of human bloodhounds called Texas Rangers." He goes on to describe the Rangers' brutality at the Rancho de San Francisco on the Camargo road near Agua Fria:

The place was surrounded, the doors forced in, and all the males capable of bearing arms were dragged out, tied to a post and shot! . . . Thirty-six Mexicans were shot at this place, a half hour given for the horrified survivors, women and children, to remove their little household goods, then the torch was applied to the houses, and by the light of the conflagration the ferocious *Tejanos* rode off to fresh scenes of blood.

These wanton acts of cruelty, witnessed by one man, augmented by the reports of other chroniclers, add to the evidence that the United States, through the deeds of its soldiers, left a legacy of hate in Mexico.

The Treaty of Guadalupe Hidalgo

By late August 1847 the war was almost at an end. General Winfield Scott's defeat of Santa Anna in a hard-fought battle at Churubusco put Anglo-Americans at the gates of Mexico City. Santa Anna made overtures for an armistice, and for two weeks negotiations were conducted. Santa Anna reorganized his defenses and, in turn, the Anglo-Americans renewed their offensives. On September 13, 1847, Scott drove into the city. Although Mexicans fought valiantly, the battle left 4,000 of their men dead with another 3,000 taken prisoner. On September 13, before the occupation of Mexico City began, *Los Niños Héroes* (The Boy Heroes) fought off the conquerors and leapt to their deaths rather than surrender. These teenager cadets were Francisco Márquez, Agustin

Melgar, Juan Escutia, Fernando Montes Oca, Vicente Suárez, and Juan de la Berrera. They became "a symbol and image of this unrighteous war."

Although beaten, the Mexicans continued fighting. The presidency devolved to the presiding justice of the Supreme Court, Manuel de la Peña y Peña. He knew that Mexico had lost and that he had to salvage as much as possible. Pressure mounted, with U.S. troops in control of much of present-day Mexico.

Nicholas Trist, sent to Mexico to act as peace commissioner, had arrived in Vera Cruz on May 6, 1847, but controversy with Scott over Trist's authority and illness delayed arrangements for an armistice and hostilities continued. After the fall of Mexico City, Secretary of State James Buchanan wanted to revise Trist's instructions. He ordered Trist to break off negotiations and come home. Polk apparently wanted more territory from Mexico while paying less for it. Trist, however, with the support of Winfield Scott, decided to ignore Polk's order, and began negotiations on January 2, 1848, on the original terms. Mexico, badly beaten, her government in a state of turmoil, had no choice but to agree to the Anglo-Americans' proposals.

On February 2, 1848, the Mexicans agreed to the Treaty of Guadalupe Hidalgo, in which Mexico accepted the Rio Grande as the Texas border and ceded the Southwest (which incorporated the present-day states of California, New Mexico, Nevada, and parts of Colorado and Arizona) and accepted the Anglo-Americans' proposals.

Polk was furious about the treaty; he considered Trist "contemptibly base" for having ignored his orders. Yet he had no choice but to submit the treaty to the Senate. With the exception of article X, which concerned the rights of Mexicans in the ceded territory, the Senate ratified the treaty on March 10, 1848, by a vote of 28 to 14. To insist on more territory would have meant more fighting, and both Polk and the Senate realized that the war was already unpopular in many sections. The treaty was sent to the Mexican Congress for ratification; although the Congress had difficulty forming a quorum, the agreement was ratified on May 19 by a 52 to 35 vote. Hostilities between the two nations were now officially ended. Trist, however, was branded as a "scoundrel," because Polk was disappointed in the settlement. There was considerable support and fervor in the United States for acquisition of all Mexico.

During the treaty talks Mexican negotiators were concerned about Mexicans left behind and expressed great reservations about these people's being forced to "merge or blend" into Anglo-American culture. They protested the exclusion of provisions that protected Mexican citizens' rights, land titles, and religion. They wanted to know the Mexicans' status, and protect their rights by treaty.

Articles VIII, IX, and X specifically referred to the rights of Mexicans. Under the treaty Mexicans left behind had one year to choose whether to return to Mexico or remain in "occupied Mexico." About 2,000 elected to leave; most remained in what they considered *their* land.

Article IX of the treaty guaranteed Mexicans "the enjoyment of all the rights of citizens of the United States according to the principles of the Constitution; and in the meantime shall be maintained and protected in the free enjoyment of their liberty and property, and secured in the free exercise of their religion without restriction." While Anglo-Americans have respected the Chicanos' religion, their rights of cultural integrity and rights of citizenship have been constantly violated. Lynn I. Perrigo in *The American Southwest* summarizes the guarantees of articles VIII and IX: "In other words, besides the rights and duties of American citizenship, they [the Mexicans] would have some special privileges derived from their previous customs in language, law, and religion."

The omitted article X had comprehensive guarantees protecting "all prior and pending titles to property of every description." When this provision was deleted by the U.S. Senate, Mexican officials protested. Anglo-American emissaries reassured them by drafting a Statement of Protocol on May 26, 1848, which read:

> The American government by suppressing the Xth article of the Treaty of Guadalupe Hidalgo did not in any way intend to annul the grants of lands made by Mexico in the ceded territories. These grants . . . preserve the legal value which they may possess, and the grantees may cause their legitimate [titles] to be acknowledged before the American tribunals.
>
> Conformable to the law of the United States, legitimate titles to every description of property, personal and real, existing in the ceded territories, are those which were legitimate titles under the Mexican law of California and New Mexico up to the 13th of May, 1846, and in Texas up to the 2nd of March, 1836.

Considering the Mexican opposition to the treaty, it is doubtful whether the Mexican Congress would have ratified the treaty without this clarification. The vote was close.

The Statement of Protocol was reinforced by articles VIII and IX, which guaranteed Mexicans rights of property and protection under the law. In addition, court decisions have generally interpreted the treaty as protecting land titles and water rights. Generally, the treaty was ignored and during the nineteenth century most Mexicans in the United States were considered as a class apart from the dominant race. Nearly every one of the obligations discussed above was violated, confirming the prophecy of Mexican diplomat Manuel Crescion Rejón who, at the time the treaty was signed, commented:

> Our race, our unfortunate people will have to wander in search of hospitality in a strange land, only to be ejected later. Descendants of the Indians that we are, the North Americans hate us, their spokesmen depreciate us, even if they recognize the justice of our cause, and they consider us unworthy to form with them one nation and one society, they clearly manifest that their future expansion begins with the territory that they take from us and pushing [sic] aside our citizens who inhabit the land.

Conclusion

As a result of the Texas War and the Anglo-American aggressions of 1845–1848, the occupation of conquered territory began. The attitude of the Anglo,

during the period of subjugation following the wars, is reflected in the conclusions of the past-president of the American Historical Association, Walter
Prescott Webb:

> A homogenous European society adaptable to new conditions was necessary. This
> Spain did not have to offer in Arizona, New Mexico, and Texas. Its frontier, as it
> advanced, depended more and more on an Indian population. . . . This mixture of
> races meant in time that common soldiers in the Spanish service came largely
> from pueblo or sedentary Indian stock, whose blood, when compared to that of
> the plains Indians, was as ditch water. It took more than a little mixture of Span-
> ish blood and mantle of Spanish service to make valiant soldiers of the timid
> Pueblo Indians.

In material terms, in exchange for 12,000 lives and more than
$100,000,000 the United States acquired a colony two and a half times as large
as France, containing rich farm lands and natural resources such as gold, silver,
zinc, copper, oil, and uranium which would make possible its unprecedented
industrial boom. It acquired ports on the Pacific which generated further economic expansion across that ocean. Mexico was left with its shrunken resources to face the continued advances of the expanding capitalist force on its
border.

V

The Mythology of the South

The past is never dead. It's not even past.
William Faulkner

"Those are the Confederate dead," said Sally Carrol
simply.

They walked along and read the inscriptions,
always only a name and a date, sometimes quite
indecipherable.

"The last row is the saddest—see, way over there.
Every cross has just a date on it, and the word
'Unknown.'"

She looked at him and her eyes brimmed with tears.

"I can't tell you how real it is to me, darling—if you
don't know."

"How you feel about it is beautiful to me."

"No, no, it's not me, it's them—that old time that
I've tried to have live in me. These were just men,
unimportant evidently or they wouldn't have been
'unknown'; but they died for the most beautiful thing
in the world—the dead South. You see," she
continued, her voice still husky, her eyes glistening
with tears, "people have these dreams they fasten onto
things, and I've always grown up with that dream. It
was so easy because it was all dead and there weren't
any disillusions comin' to me. I've tried in a way to
live up to those past standards of noblesse oblige—
there's just the last remnants of it, you know, like the
roses of an old garden dying all round us—streaks of
strange courtliness and chivalry in some of these boys
an' stories I used to hear from a Confederate soldier
who lived next door, and a few old darkies. Oh, Harry,
there was something, there was something! I couldn't
ever make you understand, but it was there."

F. Scott Fitzgerald, "The Ice Palace" *(1920)*

A COTTON PLANTATION ON THE MISSISSIPPI.

The plantation legend: racial myth. [Currier & Ives lithograph, 1884. Reproduced from the collections of the Library of Congress.]

The New South: racial reality. [Reproduced from the collections of the Library of Congress.]

*T*he South" is more than a geographical expression; it is at once a way of life and a state of mind. It remains a region struck by a sense of its uniqueness and proud of its past, its traditions, and its ceremonial style. Burdened with a history of frustration, poverty, defeat, and prejudice, in the view of the noted southern historian C. Vann Woodward, the southern imagination has sought compensation through mythical images. The vision of a hospitable and mannered society populated by contented blacks, aristocratic cavaliers, and virtuous belles has come to supplant the South's true historical experience. In short, the South's collective consciousness has sought escape and isolation behind a boundary of sentiment. One of those who recognized the pervasiveness of the southern myth was the "progressive" historian Vernon Louis Parrington, who observed:

> *A golden light still lingers upon the old plantation. Memories are still too dear to the Virginian to suffer any lessening of the reputed splendors of antebellum days. The tragedy of a lost cause has woven itself into the older romance and endowed the tradition with an added sanction. It has long since spread beyond the confines of Virginia and become a national possession. North as well as South is so firmly convinced of its authenticy that realism has never had the temerity to meddle with it.*

Thus has the South's search for a usable past and a sectional image signaled a retreat from reality and the enforcement of rigid opinions concerning its history.

The prevailing mood of the South—its distinct regional identification and mystique—balanced against the complexity of its historical past, then, often has proved an enigma to historians. Forced to combat long-standing impressions, they have found doubly difficult the task of piecing together the dislocated and fragmentary evidence with which all history must deal. It is only of late that the interrelationships between the mythic and the historical South are becoming clear, as historians seek to reconsider southern history within the context of mythology.

Out of the process of reviewing hardening southern stereotypes—the collective products of southerners and northerners, abetted by historians themselves—has emerged yet another South. This new view suggests a region of complex social structure, populated not only by a white southern gentry but also by frontiersmen, small farmers, women, Indians, black slaves, and Unionists. The mythological approach to understanding the southern past has yielded significant new historical insight; and as the native southern historian George B. Tindall suggests, mythology has indeed become the "new frontier in Southern history." The way thus seems open to pursuing the theme of southern mythology more forcefully. In the interest of exploring this "new frontier" in some detail, and given the South's central place in the nation's history, a separate section deals with southern mythology exclusively.

Southern Indians and the Cult of True Womanhood

Theda Perdue

At least one useful means of dealing with American Indians in a more historically sensitive fashion is to transcend myth and stereotype by acknowledging significant cultural differences between and among distinct Indian groups. The study of southern Indians offers a case in point: Their cultural experience differs markedly from that of other Native Americans of, say, the Plains or the Southwest. Using the specific case of the Cherokee as the focus of her study, Professor Theda Perdue of the University of Kentucky examines the self-directed cultural transformation of the tribe from a matriarchy to a form that embraced the developing central white myth of "the cult of true womanhood." Cherokee culture was co-opted by this mythic cult being purveyed by Protestant missionaries and government officials precisely because it appeared to be to the Cherokees' practical advantage—cultural harmony with the majority white culture—to adopt it. The ideology of women's "separate sphere" was so powerful a cultural myth in nineteenth-century America as to encourage these Indians to refashion their culture in the image of another.

Southern Indians stand apart culturally and historically from other native Americans. Building of temple mounds, an elaborate ceremonial life, a complex belief system, riverine agriculture, and matrilineal descent characterized their aboriginal culture. Southern Indians embraced European culture with such enthusiasm and success that they came to be known as the "five civilized tribes." They acquired this sobriquet in the half-century after the ratification of the United States Constitution, a time when many southern Indians came to believe that their physical survival depended on adopting an Anglo-American lifestyle and value system. These Indians gradually abandoned hunting and subsistence agriculture, the practice of blood vengeance, their traditional religious beliefs and practices, and other aspects of their aboriginal way of life. Some individual Indians succeeded so well that they became culturally indistinguishable from their white neighbors. They owned large plantations, operated successful businesses, attended Christian churches, promoted formal legal and judicial systems, and wrote and conversed in the English language.

An integral part of this cultural transformation was redefinition of gender roles. Just as men could no longer follow their aboriginal pursuits of hunting and warfare, women could no longer behave in what was perceived to be a "savage" or "degraded" way. Instead, they had to attempt to conform to an Anglo-American ideal characterized by purity, piety, domesticity, and submissiveness. By the second quarter of the nineteenth century, the glorification of this ideal had become so pervasive in American society that the historian Barbara Welter has called it the "cult of true womanhood." A true woman was essentially spiritual rather than physical. She occupied a separate sphere apart from the ambition, selfishness, and materialism that permeated the man's world of business and politics. Her proper place was the home, and because of her spiritual nature, she imbued her home with piety, morality, and love. The home was a haven from the outside world, and in its operation a true woman should excel. Openly submissive to men, a true woman influenced them subtly through her purity and piety.

Traditionally southern Indians had a very different view of womanhood. Indian women occupied a separate sphere from that of men, but they had considerable economic, political, and social importance. While men hunted and went to war, women collected firewood, made pottery and baskets, sewed clothes, cared for children, and cooked the family's food. These tasks certainly fell within the nineteenth-century definition of domesticity, but the sphere of Indian women extended beyond home and hearth to encompass economic activities that seemed far less appropriate to their sex. In particular, women farmed in a society that depended primarily on agriculture for subsistence, and women performed most of the manual labor with men assisting only in clearing fields and planting corn. This inequitable division of labor elicited comments from most Euro-American observers. In 1775, Bernard Romans described the women he encountered on a journey through east and west Florida: "Their strength is great, and they labor hard, carrying very heavy burdens great distance." On his 1797 tour of the Cherokee country, Louis-Philippe, who later would become king of France, observed: "The Indians have all the work done by women. They are assigned not only household tasks; even the corn, peas, beans, and potatoes are planted, tended, and preserved by the women." In the economy of southern Indians, therefore, women did what Euro-Americans considered to be work—they farmed—while men did what was considered sport—they hunted.

This arrangement was amazing in that women did not seem to object to doing most of the work. In the early nineteenth century, a missionary commented on the willingness with which the women toiled: "Though custom attached the heaviest part of the labor of the women, yet they were cheerful and voluntary in performing it. What others have discovered among the Indians I cannot tell, but though I have been about nineteen years among the Cherokees, I have perceived nothing of that slavish, servile fear, on the part of women, so often spoke of." One reason women may have worked so gladly was that they received formal recognition for their economic contribution and they controlled the fruit of their labor. In the Green Corn Ceremony, the southern Indians' most important religious event, women ritually presented the new crop, which was sacrificed to the fire, and when Europeans occasionally purchased corn from Indians in the eighteenth century, they bought it from women. Women may also have labored without complaint because farming was one of the determinants of gender. Southern Indians distinguished between the sexes on other than merely biological grounds. Women were women not only because they could bear children but because they farmed, and men who farmed came to be regarded sexually as women. Men hunted, therefore, because hunting was intrinsically linked to male sexuality; women farmed because farming was one of the characteristics that made them women.

The matrilocal residence pattern of southern Indians probably contributed to the association of women and agriculture. A man lived in the household of his wife's lineage, and buildings, garden plots, and sections of the village's common field belonged to her lineage. A man had no proprietary interest in the homestead where he lived with his wife or in the land his wife farmed. Nor was a husband necessarily a permanent resident in the household of his wife's lineage. Polygamy was common, and he might divide his time between the lineages of his wives. Furthermore, southeastern Indians frequently terminated their marriages, and in the event of divorce, a man simply left his wife's household and returned to his mother's house and his own lineage. Because southeastern Indians were also matrilineal, that is, they traced kinship only through the female line, children belonged to the mother's lineage and clan rather than to the father's, and when divorce occurred, they invariably remained with their mothers. Men, therefore, had no claim on the houses they lived in or the children they fathered.

John Lawson tried to explain matrilineal lineage, which he considered an odd way of reckoning kin, by attributing it to "fear of Imposters; the Savages knowing well, how much Frailty possesses *Indian* women, betwixt the Garters and the Girdle." Women in southern Indian tribes did enjoy considerable sexual freedom. Except for restraints regarding incest and menstrual taboos, Indian women were relatively free in choosing sexual partners, engaging in intercourse, and dissolving relationships. All southern Indians condoned premarital sex and divorce, which were equally female or male prerogatives, but attitudes toward adultery varied from one tribe to another.

Indian women usually displayed a sense of humor and a lack of modesty regarding sexual matters. One member of Lawson's expedition took an Indian "wife" for a night. The couple consummated their marriage in a room occupied by other members of the company and guests at the wedding feast. In the morning the groom discovered that both his bride and his shoes were gone. So brazen and skilled were most Cherokee women that Louis-Philippe concluded that "no Frenchwomen could teach them a thing." When his guide made sexual advances to several Cherokee women in a house they visited, he recorded in his journal that "they were so little embarrassed that one of them who was lying on a bed put her hand on his trousers before my eyes and said scornfully, *Ah, sick.*"

Compared to the other southern Indians, Louis-Philippe decided, the Cherokees were "exceeding casual" about sex. Although all southern Indians had certain common characteristics—they were matrilineal and matrilocal, women farmed, and both sexes enjoyed some sexual freedom—Cherokee women had the highest degree of power and personal autonomy. The trader James Adair maintained that the Cherokees "have been a considerable while under a petticoat-government." In Cherokee society, women spoke in council and determined the fate of war captives. Some even went on the warpath and earned a special title, "War Woman." In fact, Cherokee women were probably as far from the "true women" of the early nineteenth-century ideal as any women Anglo-Americans encountered on the continent. When the United States government and Protestant missionaries undertook the "civilization" of native Americans in the late eighteenth century, however, the Cherokees proved to be the most adept at transforming their society. Because the Cherokees provide the greatest contrast between the aboriginal role of women and the role that emerged in the early nineteenth century as a consequence of civilization, I will examine the impact of the cult of true womanhood on the status of Cherokee women.

Until the late eighteenth century, Europeans had few relations with Cherokee women other than sexual ones. Europeans were primarily interested in Indian men as warriors and hunters and considered women to be of little economic or political significance. After the American Revolution, native alliances and the deerskin trade diminished in importance. All the Indians still had that Europeans valued was land. George Washington and his advisers devised a plan which they believed would help the Indians recover economically from the depletion of their hunting grounds and the destruction experienced during the Revolution while making large tracts of Indian land available for white settlement. They hoped to convert the Indians into farmers living on isolated homesteads much like white frontiersmen. With hunting no longer part of Indian economy, the excess land could be ceded to the United States and opened to whites.

The Cherokees traditionally had lived in large towns located along rivers. These towns were composed of many matrilineal households containing several generations. A woman was rarely alone: her mother, sisters, and daughters, with their husbands, lived under the same roof, and other households were nearby. Beyond the houses lay large fields which the women worked communally. Originally, these towns had served a defensive purpose, but in the warfare of the eighteenth century, they became targets of attack. In the French and Indian War and the American Revolution, soldiers invaded the Cherokee country and destroyed towns and fields. As a result, Cherokees began abandoning their towns even before the United States government inaugurated the civilization program. When a government agent toured the Cherokee Nation in 1796, he passed a number of deserted towns; at one site he found a "hut, some peach trees and the posts of a town house," and at another there was only a "small field of corn, some peach, plumb and locust trees."

Agents appointed to implement the civilization program encouraged this trend. They advised the Cherokee to "scatter from their towns and make individual improvements also of cultivating more land for grain, cotton &c. than they could while crowded up in towns." The Cherokees complied: "They dispersed from their large towns,—built convenient houses,—cleared and fenced farms, and soon possessed numerous flocks and herds." By 1818 missionaries complained that "there is no place near us where a large audience can be collected as the people do not live in villages, but scattered over the country from 2 to 10 miles apart." The breaking up of Cherokee towns resulted in a very isolated existence for women because new households often consisted of only one nuclear family. This isolation occurred just at the time when the work load of women was increasing.

In a letter of 1796, George Washington advised the Cherokees to raise cattle, hogs, and sheep. He pointed out that they could increase the amount of corn they produced by using plows and that they could also cultivate wheat and other grains. Apparently addressing the letter to the men, Washington continued: "To these you will easily add flax and cotton which you may dispose of to the White people, or have it made up by your own women into clothing for yourselves. Your wives and daughters can soon learn to spin and weave." Washington apparently knew nothing about traditional gender roles, and the agents he sent usually had little sympathy for the Indian division of labor. They provided plows to the men and instructed them in clearing fields, tilling soil, and building fences. Women received cotton cards, spinning wheels, and looms.

The women, politically ignored in the eighteenth century and bypassed in the earlier hunting economy, welcomed the opportunity to profit from contact with whites. In 1796, agent Benjamin Hawkins met with a group of Cherokee women and explained the government's plan. He reported to Washington that "they rejoiced much at what they had heard and hoped it would prove true, that they had made some cotton, and would make more and follow the instruction of the agent and the advice of the President." According to a Cherokee account, the women proved far more receptive to the civilization program than the men: "When Mr. Dinsmore, the Agent of the United States, spoke to us on the subject of raising livestock and cotton, about fifteen years ago, many of us thought it was only some refined scheme calculated to gain an influence over us, rather than to ameliorate our situation, and slighted his advice and proposals; he then addressed our women, and presented them with cotton seeds for planting; and afterwards with cards, wheels and looms to work it. They acquired the use of them with great facility, and now most of the clothes we wear are of their manufacture." Two censuses conducted in the early nineteenth century reveal the extent to which women accepted their new tasks. In 1810 there were 1,600 spinning wheels and 467 looms in the Cherokee Nation; by 1826 there were 2,488 wheels and 762 looms.

In 1810, one Cherokee man observed that the women had made more progress toward civilization than the men: "The females have however made much greater advances in industry than the males; they now manufacture a great quantity of cloth; but the latter have not made proportionate progress in agriculture; however, they raise great herds of cattle, which can be done with little exertion." At the same time, women continued to do most of the farming, and many even raised livestock for market. This extension of woman's work concerned government agents because many men were not acquiring the work habits considered essential to "civilized" existence. They had not been able to accomplish a shift in gender roles merely by introducing the tools and techniques of Western culture. Gender roles as well as many other aspects of Cherokee culture proved extremely difficult to change.

Cultural change came more easily, however, among Cherokees who already had adopted the acquisitive, materialistic value system of white Americans. Turning from an economy based on hunting, they took advantage of the government's program and invested in privately owned agricultural improvements and commercial enterprises. They quickly became an economic elite separated from the majority of Cherokees by their wealth and by their desire to emulate whites. In the early nineteenth century, members of this economic elite rose to positions of leadership in the Cherokee Nation because of the ease and effectiveness with which they dealt with United States officials. Gradually they transformed Cherokee political institutions into replicas of those of the United States. This elite expected Cherokee women to conform to the ideals of the cult of true womanhood, that is, to be sexually pure, submissive to fathers and husbands, concerned primarily with spiritual and domestic matters, and excluded from politics and economic activities outside the home. In 1818, Charles Hicks, who later would become principal chief, described the most prominent men in the nation as "those who have kept their women & children at home & in comfortable circumstances." Submissive, domestic wives were a mark of prominence.

Cherokees learned to be true women primarily through the work of Protestant missionaries whom tribal leaders welcomed to the nation. In 1800 the Moravians arrived to open a school, and in the second decade of the nineteenth century Congregationalists supported by the interdenominational American Board of Commissioners for Foreign Missions, Baptists, and Methodists joined them. Except for the Methodists, missionaries preferred to teach children in boarding schools, where they had "the influence of example as well as precept." In 1819 President James Monroe visited the American Board's Brainerd mission and approved "of the plan of instruction; particularly as the children were taken into the family, taught to work, &c." This was, the president believed, "the best, & perhaps the only way to civilize and Christianize the Indians." For female students, civilization meant becoming true women.

Mission schools provided an elementary education for girls as well as boys. Either single women or the wives of male missionaries usually taught the girls, but all students studied the same academic subjects, which included reading, writing, spelling, arithmetic, geography, and history. Examinations took place annually and were attended by parents. The teachers questioned students in their academic subjects as well as Bible history, catechism, and hymns, and "the girls showed specimens of knitting, spinning, mending, and fine needlework."

Mastery of the domestic arts was an essential part of the girls' education because, according to one missionary, "all the females need is a proper education to be qualified to fill any of the relations or stations of domestic life." The children at the mission schools performed a variety of tasks, and the division of labor approximated that in a typical Anglo-American farming family. The boys chopped wood and plowed fields, and the girls milked, set tables, cooked meals, washed dishes, sewed clothing, knitted, quilted, did laundry, and cleaned the houses. Because their fathers were wealthy, many students were not accustomed to such menial labor. Missionaries endeavored to convince them that "the charge of the kitchen and the mission table" was not degrading but was instead a "most important station," which taught them "industry and economy."

The great advantage of teaching Cherokee girls "industry and economy" was the influence they might exert in their own homes. One girl wrote: "We have the opportunity of learning to work and to make garments which will be useful to us in life." Another girl expressed gratitude that missionaries had taught the students "how to take care of families that when we go home we can take care of our mother's house." A missionary assessed the impact of their work: "We cannot expect that the influence of these girls will have any great immediate effect on their acquaintance—but I believe in each case it is calculated to elevate the families in some degree, with which they are connected." Although missionaries and students expected the domestic arts learned in the mission schools to improve the parental home, they believed that the primary benefit would be to the homes the girls themselves established. Missionary Sophia Sawyer specifically hoped to "raise the female character in the Nation" so that "Cherokee gentlemen" could find young women "sufficiently educated for companions." In 1832 missionaries could report with satisfaction that the girls who had married "make good housewives and useful members of society."

The marriages missionaries had in mind were not the Cherokees' traditional polygamous or serial marriages. Louis-Philippe had believed that such a marriage "renders women contemptible in men's eyes and deprives them of all influence." A monogamous marriage was supposedly liberating to women because these "serve exclusively to heighten the affections of a man." Although the Cherokee elite accepted most tenets of Western civilization, some balked at abandoning the practice of polygamy. The chief justice was one who had more than one wife, but these marriages differed from traditional ones in which a man lived with his wives in their houses. Polygamous members of the elite headed more than one patriarchal household. They recognized the desirability of monogamous unions, however, encouraged others to enter into them, and sent their children to mission schools where they were taught that polygamy was immoral.

In practice, religious denominations confronted the problem of polygamy in different ways. Moravians apparently allowed converts to keep more than one wife. The American Board required a man "to separate himself from all but the first." Perhaps because some of their chief supporters were polygamists, the governing body in Boston advised missionaries in the field to be "prudent and kind" when dealing with this "tender subject" and to instruct polygamous converts "in the nature and design of marriage, the original institution, and the law of Christ, that they may act with an enlightened conviction of duty." American Board ministers sometimes remarried in a Christian service couples who had lived for years in "a family capacity." Missionaries also rejoiced when they united in matrimony young couples of "industrious habits & reputable behavior" who were "very decent and respectable in their moral deportment."

Achieving "moral deportment" at the mission schools was no simple matter, but missionaries considered the teaching of New England sexual mores to be one of their chief responsibilities. According to some reports, they enjoyed success. In 1822, American Board missionaries reported: "Mr. Hall thinks the moral influence of the school has been considerable. . . . The intercourse between the young of both sexes was shamefully loose. Boys & girls in their teens would strip & go into bathe, or play ball together naked. They would also use the most disgustingly indecent language, without the least sense of shame. But, when better instructed, they became reserved and modest." To maintain decorum, the missionaries tried to make certain that girls and boys were never alone together: "When the girls walk out any distance from the house they will be accompanied by instructors." Male and female students normally attended separate classes. When Sophia Sawyer became ill in 1827 she reluctantly sent the small girls to the boys' school but taught the larger girls in her sickroom. Miss Sawyer so feared for the virtue of the older girls that she asked the governing board "could not the boys at Brainerd be at some other school." The Moravians did resort to separate schools. The American Board, however, simply put locks on the bedroom doors.

Even with these precautions, difficulties arose. In 1813 the Moravians recorded in their journal: "After prayer we directed our talk toward Nancy, indirectly admonishing her to abstain from the lust which had gripped her. She seemed not to have taken it to heart, for instead of mending her ways she continues to heap sin upon sin." Nancy Watie later moved to an American Board mission along with her cousin Sally Ridge. Their fathers were prominent in the Cherokee Nation, and they had left strict instructions that their daughters be supervised constantly and their purity preserved. A problem occurred when teenage boys in the neighborhood began calling on the girls at the mission. At first, the young people decorously sat in front of the fire under the watchful eyes of the missionaries, but soon the conversation shifted from English to Cherokee, which none of the chaperons understood. Suspecting the worst, the missionaries ordered the suitors to "spend their evenings in some other place." A year later, however, the missionaries reported that despite their care, the girls "had given themselves up to the common vices."

The missionaries did not, of course, intend to cloister the young women to the extent that they did not meet suitable young men. Sophia Sawyer observed: "Like all females they desire the admiration of men. They can easily be shown that the attention, or good opinion of men without education, taste, or judgment is not worth seeking, & to gain the affection or good opinion of the opposite character, their minds must be improved, their manner polished, their persons attended to, in a word they must be qualified for usefulness." Attracting the right young men was permissible and even desirable.

The girls' appearance was another concern of the missionaries. Ann Paine related an attempt to correct the daughter of a particularly prominent Cherokee: "Altho' her parents supplied her with good clothes, she was careless and indifferent about her appearance.—I often urged her attention to these things and offered as a motive her obligation to set a good example to her nation as the daughter of their chief. Told her how the young ladies of the North were taught to govern their manners and tempers and of their attention to personal appearance. She never appeared more mortified than in hearing of her superiority of birth, and of the attention she ought to pay to her personal appearance." Paine soon had "the satisfaction of witnessing her rapid improvement." Four years later, Sophia Sawyer complained about the female students in general: "I have had to punish several times to break bad habits respecting cleanliness in their clothes, books, & person—I found them in a deplorable situation in this respect. The largest girls I had in school were not capable of dressing themselves properly or of folding their clothes when taken off." Sometimes concern for the students' appearance went beyond clothing. One girl wrote a correspondent: "Mr. Ellsworth told me I had better alter my voice. He said I spoke like a man."

In addition to a neat, feminine appearance, respectable men presumably also admired piety in young women and probably expected them to be more pious than they themselves were. The missionaries clearly believed that the female students in mission schools were more serious about religion than the male students, and they encouraged this emotion. Nancy Reece wrote her northern correspondent that "after work at night the girls joined for singing a special hymn Mr. Walker wrote for them & then go to worship services." Many of the girls wrote about their spiritual lives. A ten-year-old confided in a letter that "some of the girls have been serious about their wicked hearts and have retired to their Chambers to pray to God. . . . I feel as though I am a great sinner and very wicked sinner."

The piety of the girls at the mission station was manifest in other ways. They organized a society to raise money to send missionaries into heathen lands. The American Board agreed to pay them for clothing they made, and they in turn donated the money to mission work. They also sold their handwork to local Cherokee women. The piety of the girls extended beyond the school and into the community. Once a month, neighboring women would gather at the mission for a prayer meeting "that missionary labors may be blessed." One missionary reported with satisfaction that "the females have a praying society which is well attended, and they begin to do something by way of benevolence."

Of the several hundred Cherokee girls who attended mission schools, the best example of "true womanhood" was Catharine Brown. She was sixteen or seventeen years old when she arrived at the Brainerd mission. She had some European ancestry, and although she had grown up in a fairly traditional Cherokee household, she spoke and read a little English. The missionaries reported that, despite the absence of a Christian influence in her childhood, "her moral character was ever good." Her biographer added: "This is remarkable, considering the looseness of manners then prevalent among the females of her nation, and the temptations to which she was exposed, when during the war with the Creek Indians, the army of the United States was stationed near her father's residence. . . . Once she even fled from her home into the wild forest to preserve her character unsullied." When she applied for admission to Brainerd, the missionaries hesitated because they feared that she would object to the domestic duties required of female students. They later recalled that she was "vain, and excessively fond of dress, wearing a profusion of ornaments in her ears." Catharine "had no objection" to work, however, and shortly after her admission, her jewelry disappeared "till only a single drop remains in each ear." After she became a part of the mission family, Catharine became extremely pious: "She spent much time in reading the Scriptures, singing, and prayer." She attended weekly prayer meetings and helped instruct the younger girls in the Lord's Prayer, hymns, and catechism. In 1819, Catharine received baptism. Her intellectual achievements were also remarkable, and soon the missionaries sent her to open a female school at the Creek Path Mission station. There she fulfilled not only her spiritual and educational responsibilities but also her domestic ones. Visitors reported: "We arrived after the family had dined, and she received us, and spread a table for our refreshment with the unaffected kindness of a sister." When her father proposed to take the family to Indian territory, Catharine was appropriately submissive. Although she did not want to go, she acquiesced to his wishes and prepared to leave for the West. Catharine's health, however, was fragile. She became ill, and "as she approached nearer to eternity her faith evidently grew stronger." In July 1823, "this lovely convert from heathenism died."

Few women in the Cherokee Nation could equal Catharine Brown, and perhaps the majority of Cherokee women had little desire to be "true women." The historical record contains little information about the Cherokee masses, but from the evidence that does exist, we can infer that many Cherokees maintained a relatively traditional way of life. Continuing to exist at the subsistence level, they rejected Christianity and mission schools and relied on local councils rather than the central government dominated by the elite. Borrowing selectively from the dominant white society, a large number of women also maintained a semblance of their aboriginal role. As late as 1817, a council of women petitioned the Cherokee National Council to refrain from further land cessions, and in 1835 at least one-third of the heads of households listed on the removal roll were women. Some probably were like Oo-dah-less who, according to her obituary, accumulated a sizable estate through agriculture and commerce. She was "the support of a large family" and bequeathed her property "to an only daughter and three grand children." Other women no doubt lived far more traditionally, farming, supervising an extended household, caring for children and kinsmen, and perhaps even exercising some power in local councils.

Although the feminine ideal of purity, piety, submissiveness, and domesticity did not immediately filter down to the mass of Cherokees, the nation's leaders came to expect these qualities in women. Therefore, the influence of the cult of true womanhood probably far exceeded the modest number of women trained in mission schools. The Cherokee leaders helped create a new sphere for women by passing legislation that undermined matrilineal kinship and excluded women from the political process. In the first recorded Cherokee law of 1808, the national council, which apparently included no women, established a police force "to give their protection to children as heirs to their father's property, and to the widow's share." Subsequent legislation gave further recognition to patrilineal descent and to the patriarchial family structure common among men of wealth. In 1825 the council extended citizenship to the children of white women who had married Cherokee men, another act that formally reordered descent. Legislation further isolated women by prohibiting polygamy and denied women the right to limit the size of their families by outlawing the traditional practice of infanticide. In 1826 the council decided to call a constitutional convention to draw up a governing document for the tribe. According to legislation that provided for the election of delegates to the convention, "No person but a free male citizen who is full grown shall be entitled to vote." Not surprisingly, when the convention met and drafted a constitution patterned after that of the United States, women could neither vote nor hold office. The only provisions in the Cherokee legal code reminiscent of the power and prestige enjoyed by aboriginal women were laws that protected the property rights of married women and prohibited their husbands from disposing of their property without consent.

The elite who governed the Cherokee Nation under the Constitution of 1827 regarded traditionalists with considerable disdain. Having profited from the government's civilization program, most truly believed in the superiority of Anglo-American culture. Some leaders and, to an even greater extent, United States officials tended to question the ability of traditionalists to make well-informed, rational decisions. This lack of faith provided a justification for those highly acculturated Cherokees who in 1835, without tribal authorization, ceded Cherokee land in the Southeast contrary to the wishes of the vast majority of Indians. The failure of many Indian women to conform to the ideals of womanhood may well have contributed to the treaty party's self-vindication. Perhaps they believed that the land could have little meaning for the Cherokees if women controlled it, that the Indians must still depend primarily on hunting if women farmed, and that the Indians had no notion of ownership if men had no proprietary interest in their wives.

Of all the southern tribes, the Cherokees provide the sharpest contrast between the traditional role of women and the role they were expected to assume in the early nineteenth century. In this period, the Cherokees excluded women, who originally had participated in tribal governance, from the political arena. Women in other tribes had been less active politically; consequently, their status did not change as dramatically. All southern nations, however, did move toward legally replacing matrilineal with patrilineal descent and restricting the autonomy of women. In 1824, for example, the

Creeks passed one law prohibiting infanticide and another specifying that upon a man's death, his children "shall have the property and his other relations shall not take the property to the injury of His children."

Men of wealth and power among the Creeks, Choctaws, and Chickasaws as well as the Cherokees readily accepted the technical assistance offered through the government's civilization program and gradually adopted the ideology it encompassed. Although these changes occurred at different rates among southern Indians, women began to fade from economic and political life in the early nineteenth century. Just as the traditional female occupation, farming, became commercially viable, men took over and women became only secondarily involved in subsistence. Women, of course, still had their homes and families, but their families soon became their husbands' families, and domesticity brought influence, not power. Similarly, purity and piety seemed almost anachronistic in a culture and age that tended to value the material above the spiritual. Perhaps all that remained for women was what historian Nancy Cott has called "bonds of womanhood," but Indian women did not even develop closer ties to other women. Living a far more isolated existence than ever before, they no longer shared labor and leisure with mothers, daughters, and sisters. Instead they spent most of their time on remote homesteads with only their husbands and children.

This separate sphere in which Indian women increasingly lived in the nineteenth century could hardly give rise to a women's rights movement, as some historians have suggested it did among white women, because true womanhood came to be associated with civilization and progress. Any challenge to the precepts of the cult of true womanhood could be interpreted as a reversion to savagery. Ironically, by the end of the century, some white Americans had come to view the traditional status of Indian women in a far more favorable light. In 1892 the author of an article in the *Albany Law Review* applauded the revision of property laws in the United States to protect the rights of married women and noted that such a progressive practice had long existed among the Choctaw and other southern Indians. This practice, however, was only a remnant of a female role that had been economically productive, politically powerful, and socially significant but had been sacrificed to the cult of true womanhood.

There Was Another South
Carl N. Degler

As a student of both individual and social behavior, the historian must constantly seek to establish the tenuous line between the truth of the particular and that of the general. In that the profiles of history have generally been drawn either in terms of its "great men" or in terms of its general "movements," the difficulty seems to lie in striking a balance of emphasis between the two. The historian's problem is to find generalizations that neither distort nor violate truth. Such a balance is offered by Carl Degler of Stanford University as he treats the subjects of secession and slavery in the antebellum South. As Degler suggests, contrary to popular mythology, the South before the Civil War did not represent a monolithic point of view on these issues. In the prewar South there was a scarcity neither of Unionists nor of abolitionists.

The stereotype of the South is as tenacious as it is familiar: a traditionally rebellious region which has made a dogma of states' rights and a religious order of the Democratic party. Here indeed is a monotonous and unchanging tapestry, with a pattern of magnolia blossoms, Spanish moss, and the inevitable old plantations running ceaselessly from border to border. To this depiction of almost willful backwardness, add the dark motif of the Negro problem, a few threads of poor white, and the picture is complete.

Such is the mythical image, and a highly inaccurate one it is, for the South is a region of immense variety. Its sprawling landscape ranges from the startlingly red soil of Virginia and North Carolina to the black, sticky clay of the Delta; from the wild and primitive mountain forests of eastern Kentucky to the lush, junglelike swamps of southern Louisiana; from the high, dry, wind-swept plains of the Texas Panhandle to the humid tidelands of the South Carolina coast. An environment so diverse can be expected to produce social and political differences to match, and in fact, it always has.

Today, with the South in ferment, we have come to recognize increasingly the wide variety of attitudes that exist in the region. But this denial of the southern stereotype is a relatively new development, even among historians. For too long the history of the region has been regarded as a kind of unbroken plain of uniform opinion. This is especially true of what has been written about the years before the Civil War; a belief in states' rights, the legality of secession, and the rightfulness of slavery has been accepted almost without question as typical of southern thought. In a sense, such catch phrases do represent what many southerners have believed; but at the same time there were many others who both denied the legality of secession and denounced slavery. It is time this "other South" was better known.

Let us begin with the story of those southerners who so cherished the Union that they refused to accept the doctrine of nullification and secession. They included not only humble farmers and remote mountain men, but some of the greatest names in the history of the South; their devotion to the Union was tested in several bitter clashes with states' righters during the antebellum decades. The first of these contests came over the question of the high protective tariffs which many southerners felt would hurt the cotton trade; the arguments advanced at the beginning set forth the basic lines of debate that were followed thereafter. South Carolina's *Exposition and Protest* of 1828, which John C. Calhoun wrote secretly in opposition to the tariff passed that year, embodied the classic defense of state sovereignty. In the *Exposition*, Calhoun contended that nullification of federal legislation by a state and even secession were constitutional—a doctrine rejected by many prominent southerners in 1828 and after.

Foremost among them was former President James Madison, the reputed "father of the Constitution." As a Jeffersonian in politics and a Virginian by birth and heritage, Madison was no friend of the protective tariff, and certainly not of the monstrous one of 1828, which had been promulgated by the Jacksonian faction in Congress in an effort to discredit the Adams administration. But he could not accept even that politically inspired tariff as sufficient reason for nullification. Indeed, he could not accept the constitutional doctrine of nullification on any grounds. It is worthwhile to consider briefly Madison's views on nullification, because virtually all subsequent southern defenses of the Union followed his line of thought; at the time, no man in the South carried more authority on the meaning and interpretation of the Constitution than the venerable Virginian, who celebrated his eightieth birthday in 1830, and was the last surviving signer of that document.

Many political leaders sought his views all through the tariff crisis of 1828–33, and to all of them Madison reiterated the same conclusions. The United States was a "mixed government" in which the states were supreme in some areas and the federal government in others. In the event of conflict between them, the Supreme Court was the intended arbiter under the Constitution; the Court, Madison wrote, was "so constituted as to be impartial as it could be made by the mode of appointment and responsibility of the judges."

If confidence were lacking in the objectivity of the judges, Madison continued, then there were further remedies: the impeachment of offending officials, election of a new government, or amendments to the Constitution. But neither nullification nor secession was legal, he tirelessly pointed out. Of course, if tyrannized sufficiently, a state could invoke its natural right to overthrow its oppressor; but that was a right of revolution, and not a constitutional right as Calhoun and his followers maintained.

As a southern Unionist, Madison did not stand alone, either at the time of the nullification crisis or later. In Calhoun's own state, in fact, the Unionists were a powerful and eloquent minority. Hugh S. Legaré (pronounced Legree, curiously enough), Charleston aristocrat, intellectual, and one-time editor of the *Southern Review*, distinguished himself in defense of the Union, vigorously opposing Calhoun during the heated debates in Charleston in 1832. (Eleven years later, as United States Attorney General, Legaré again differed with the majority of southerners when he offered the official opinion that free Negroes in the United States enjoyed the same civil rights as white men.)

James Petigru and Joel Poinsett (who, as minister to Mexico, gave his name to the Poinsettia) were two other prominent Charlestonians who would not accept the doctrine that a state could constitutionally withdraw from the Union. Unlike Legaré and Poinsett, Petigru lived long enough to fight nullification and secession in South Carolina until that state left the Union. (When asked by a stranger in December, 1860, where the insane asylum was, he contemptuously pointed to the building where the secession convention was meeting.)

Andrew Jackson is often ignored by those who conceive of the South as a monolith of states' rights and secession. A Carolinian by birth and a Tennessean by choice, Jackson acted as an outspoken advocate of the Union when he threatened South Carolina with overwhelming force in the crisis of 1832–33. Jackson's fervently nationalistic proclamation to the people of the dissident state was at once a closely reasoned restatement of the Madisonian view that the United States was a "mixed government," and a highly emotional panegyric to the Union. Though there can be no question of Jackson's wholehearted acceptance of every patriotic syllable in that proclamation, it comes as no surprise to those acquainted with the limited literary abilities of Old Hickory that its composition was the work of an adviser. That adviser, it is worth noting, was a southerner, Secretary of State Edward Livingston of Louisiana.

There were few things on which Henry Clay of Kentucky and Andrew Jackson could agree, but the indissolubility of the Union was one of them. Clay never concurred with those southern leaders who accepted Calhoun's position that a state could nullify national legislation or secede from the Union. As a matter of fact, Henry Clay's Whig party was probably the most important stronghold of pro-Union sentiment in the antebellum South. Unlike the Democratic party, the Whigs never succumbed, in defending slavery, to the all-encompassing states' rights doctrine. Instead, they identified themselves with the national bank, internal improvements, the tariff, and opposition to the "tyranny" of Andrew Jackson. Despite the "unsouthern" sound of these principles to modern ears, the Whig party was both powerful and popular, capable of winning elections in any southern state. In the heyday of the Whigs, a solidly Democratic South was still unimaginable.

In 1846, the attempt of antislavery forces to prohibit slavery in the vast areas about to be acquired as a result of the Mexican War precipitated another bitter sectional struggle. But as much as they might support the "peculiar institution," the southern Whigs stood firm against Calhoun's efforts to commit the whole South to a states' rights position that once more threatened the existence of the Union. When, in 1849, Calhoun invited southern Congressmen to join his Southern Rights movement in order to strengthen resistance against northern demands, forty of the eighty-eight he approached refused to sign the call. Almost all of them were Whigs.

Throughout the Deep South in the state elections of 1851, Unionist Democrats and Whigs combined to stop the incipient secessionist movement in its tracks. In Georgia, Howell Cobb, the Unionist candidate for governor, received 56,261 votes to 37,472 for his opponent, a prominent Southern Rights man; in the legislature the Unionists captured 101 of the 127 seats. After the same election the congressional delegation of Alabama consisted of two secessionists and five Union supporters. In the Calhoun stronghold of Mississippi, where Jefferson Davis was the best-known spokesman for the Southern Rights movement, Davis was defeated for the governorship, 28,738 to 27,729, by his Unionist opponent, Henry S. Foote. Even in fire-eating South Carolina itself, the anti-Calhoun forces won overwhelmingly, 25,045 to 17,710.

By the time of the Kansas-Nebraska Act of 1854, the Whig party had all but disappeared, the victim of a widening sectional schism. Bereft of its traditional political organization, southern Unionism was, for the time, almost voiceless, but it was not dead. In the election of 1860, it reappeared in the shape of the Constitutional Union party. Its candidate was John Bell of Tennessee, an old-line Whig and staunch Unionist who, in order to prevent disruption of the nation, made his platform the Union itself. That year, in a four-party race, the Constitutional Unionists were the effective second party to the southern Democrats; for Stephen A. Douglas, the candidate of the northern Democrats, received few votes outside the border states, and Lincoln was not even on a ballot in ten of the fifteen slave states.

The Constitutional Unionists gave the dominant Democratic party a hot fight in every southern state. Of the upper southern states, Virginia, Kentucky, and Tennessee went to Bell outright, while Maryland gave him forty-five per cent and North Carolina forty-seven per cent of their votes.

Bell's showing in the Deep South was not as strong as in the upper South, but it nonetheless demonstrated that those southerners still willing to be counted for the Union were a large minority in almost all of the states. From the whole South, Bell received forty percent of the popular vote to southern Democrat Breckinridge's forty-five.

A clear indication of the continuity of Unionism from the days of the Whigs to the election of 1860 is that Bell's support in the Deep South centered in the same general areas where the Whigs had been most powerful in the 1840's. Many of the delta counties along the Mississippi River—in Arkansas, Mississippi, and Louisiana—which were always strongholds of Whiggery, went for Bell. Whig votes had always been conspicuous in the black belt counties of central Alabama and Georgia, and so were Bell's in 1860.

Surprisingly enough, the wealthy, slaveholding counties of the South were more often Whig than Democratic in the years before the war. Ever since the days of Jackson, the Democracy had been predominantly the party of the small planter and non-slaveholder. Regardless of the serious threat to slavery posed by the Republican party in 1860, many slaveholders could still not bring themselves to violate their traditional political allegiances and vote for a Democratic candidate identified with states' rights.

A further test of southern Unionism was provided in the election of delegates to the state secession conventions in the winter of 1860–61. Unfortunately, the voting figures do not tell us as much as we would like to know. To most southerners at the time, the issue was not simply the Union versus the right of a state to secede; more often it was whether secession was expedient, with little thought about its constitutionality. Therefore, those delegates who favored a course other than immediate secession did not necessarily support the Union under all and every circumstance.

Nevertheless, these voting returns make clear that even on the verge of secession, tens of thousands in all the states of the Deep South were still opposed to a break with the Union. In Alabama, for example, 28,200 voted against immediate secession to 35,700 for; furthermore, one third of the delegates to the convention refused to sign the secession ordinance because it would not be submitted to the people. In Georgia, 37,123 were against secession to 50,243 in favor; in Louisiana the Unionists were an even larger minority: 17,296 against secession, 20,448 for. In Texas, despite much intimidation of Unionists, twenty-two percent of the voters still opposed secession.

Before Sumter was fired upon and Lincoln called for volunteers, the states of the upper South refused to join the seceding states. Early in 1861, the people of Tennessee voted against having a secession convention, 68,282 to 59,449; the vote of the people of Arkansas against secession in February, 1861, was 22,000 to 17,000. North Carolina, in a popular vote, also turned down a call for a secession convention. As late as April 4, the Virginia convention voted down a proposal to draw up an ordinance of secession by an almost two-to-one majority. Even after Sumter, when the upper South states did secede, it is clear that loyalty to the Union was still a powerful sentiment.

Throughout the war southern Unionists were active in opposition to the Confederacy. Areas of strong Unionist feeling, like eastern Tennessee, western Virginia, northern Alabama, and the mountain counties of Arkansas, quickly come to mind. In eastern Tennessee, for example, Unionist sentiment was so widespread and deep-felt that for a large part of the war, the courts of the Confederacy in that area could not function without military support and not always even then. After the war broke out, Charles Galloway, a staunch Unionist who had opposed secession in Arkansas, led two companies of his fellow southerners to Springfield, Missouri, where they were mustered into the Union Army. Galloway then led his men back to Arkansas to fight the Confederates. Some 48,000 white southern Unionists, it has been estimated, served voluntarily in the Army of the United States. In northern Alabama and Georgia in 1863 and after, peace societies, replete with secret grips, passwords and elaborate security precautions, worked to encourage desertion from the Confederate Army.

A recent study of the Southern Claims Commission provides the most explicit and detailed evidence of the character of southern Unionism during the war. The commission was set up by the United States government at the end of hostilities in order to reimburse those southerners who had sustained certain kinds of property losses because of their loyalty to the Union. (Only actual material losses incurred by loyal southerners in behalf of the Union armies were to be honored; acts of charity or mercy, or losses occasioned by Confederate action, for example, were not included.) Since all claimants first had to offer ironclad proof of loyalty before their losses could even be considered, those who did file claims may well be taken as the hard core of southern Unionism. There must have been thousands more who, because they lacked the opportunity or the substance to help the Union armies, went uncounted. Still others may not have been able to meet the high standards set for proof of loyalty, though their devotion to the Union was unquestioned. Under these circumstances, 22,298 claimants is an impressive number.

One of the striking facts that emerges from a study of the records of the commission is the great number of southern Unionists who were people of substance. The total amount of the claims was $22.5 million, and 701 claims were for losses of $10,000 or more—a very substantial sum in the 1860's. The wealthy claimants were mainly planters, owners of great plantations and large numbers of slaves. Despite their wealth, or perhaps because of it, they stood with the Union when the storm of secession broke upon them—though to do so often meant obloquy and harassment at the very least, and not infrequently confiscation of property and personal danger.

Southern Unionism also played its part in the complicated history of Reconstruction. Tennessee, for example, probably escaped radical congressional Reconstruction because of the large number of Unionists in the state. William "Parson" Brownlow, an old Whig and Unionist turned Republican, was able to gain control of the state after the war, and under his leadership Tennessee managed to avoid the military occupation that was the retribution visited upon its more recalcitrant neighbors.

In Louisiana, the first Republican governor, Michael Hahn, was also a lifelong Unionist; though originally a Democrat, he had opposed secession and during the war had refused to take a pledge of loyalty to the Confederacy. About a third of the members of the Mississippi legislature during Reconstruction were so-called scalawags; but far from being the disreputable persons usually associated with that label, most of them were actually respectable former Whig Unionists turned Republican.

This shift in allegiance from Whig to Republican—by no means a rarity in the Reconstruction South—is not so strange when it is recalled that Lincoln, the first Republican President, was once a confirmed Whig. Indeed, to many former southern Whigs it must have seemed that the Republican party—the party of business, national authority, sound money, and internal improvements—was a most fortunate reincarnation of Henry Clay's old organization. And now that slavery was no more, it seemed that southerners could once again divide politically as their interests dictated.

The opportunity, however, proved to be short-lived, for to resist effectively the excesses of the Radicals during Reconstruction, all southerners of consequence became Democrats as a matter of necessity. But though they may have been Democrats in name, in principles they were Whigs, and as such worked quite easily with northern Republicans to end Reconstruction and to bring new railroads and industry to the South in the 1880's.

Most Americans assume that between 1830 and 1860 all southerners favored slavery. This is not so. In the earlier years of the Republic, the great Virginians had not defended the institution but only excused it as an undeniable evil that was exceptionally difficult to eradicate. It was not until the 1830's that it began to be widely upheld as something to be proud of, a positive good. Here too, as in the nullification controversy, Calhoun's thought dominated the southern mind. He had been among the first prominent southerners to shake off the sense of guilt over slavery and to proclaim it a "great moral revolution." At the same time, however, many men and women in the South continued to doubt the utility, the wisdom, and the justice of slavery. These, too, constituted another South.

Although there were some southerners who opposed slavery for reasons of Christian ethics, many more decried it for economic and political reasons. Cassius Marcellus Clay of Kentucky, a cousin of the more famous Henry, was prominent among those who abominated slavery because it retarded the economic growth of the South. The son of a wealthy slaveholder, Clay was educated at Yale, where his future is supposed to have been decided by hearing William Lloyd Garrison present an abolitionist lecture. Regardless of the cause for Clay's subsequent antislavery views, he emancipated his slaves in 1833, soon after his graduation, and devoted himself to ridding his state of slavery. Despite his proclaimed hostile sentiments on the subject, Clay gained a large following in state and national politics.

The nature of Clay's objections to slavery were made clear in a speech he delivered before the Kentucky legislature in 1841:

> Gentlemen would import slaves "to clear up the forests of the Green River country." Take one day's ride from this capital and then go and tell them what you have seen. Tell them that you have looked upon the once most lovely and fertile lands that nature ever formed; and have seen it in fifty years worn to the rock . . . tell them of the depopulation of the country and the consequent ruin of the towns and villages; tell them that the white Kentuckian has been driven out by slaves, by the unequal competition of unpaid labor; tell them that the mass of our people are uneducated; tell them that you have heard the children of white Kentuckians crying for bread, whilst the children of the African was [sic] clothed, and fed, and laughed! And then ask them if they will have blacks to fell their forests.

The troublesome race question effectively prevented some antislavery southerners from taking any concrete steps to end slavery; others saw a threat in the possibility of a large free Negro population. To many, the return of former slaves to Africa seemed the necessary first step in any movement toward emancipation. Cassius Clay was both more radical and more realistic. He recognized that colonization was as illusory a solution to the evils of slavery and the Negro problem as it actually proved to be; many more Negroes were born each year than could possibly be sent to Liberia in a generation. Instead, Clay boldly advocated gradual emancipation, with the owners of the slaves being compensated by the state.

Hinton Rowan Helper is better known today as an antislavery southerner than Clay, though the latter was certainly the more prominent at the time. Helper was the son of a poor North Carolina farmer; with the publication of his book, *The Impending Crisis of the South*, in 1857, he became a nationally known figure. In an effort to demonstrate the material and cultural backwardness of the slave states, Helper brought together statistics from the Census of 1850—compiled by that most indefatigable southern publicist, J. D. B. De Bow, and therefore unimpeachable in southern eyes—to show that in number of libraries, newspapers, and schools, as well as in wealth, manufactures, population, and commerce, the North far outdistanced the South. Helper pointed out that even in agriculture, the vaunted specialty of Dixie, northern production exceeded southern. Almost contemptuously, he observed that the value of the Cotton Kingdom's chief staple was surpassed by that of the North's lowly hay crop. The cause for all these discrepancies, Helper contended, was slavery.

Helper's indictment of slavery was sufficiently telling to arouse violent southern attacks. He also serves to illustrate the variety of motives underlying the southern antislavery movement. He was more disturbed about what slavery did to the poor white man than about what it did to the Negro. Many antislavery men felt the same, but Helper went further; his concern for the white man was coupled with an almost pathological hatred of the black.

Not its economic disadvantages, but its essential incompatibility with the genius of America, was the more compelling argument against slavery for some southerners. The great Virginians of the eighteenth century—men like Washington, Marshall, Patrick Henry, Madison, Jefferson, and Monroe—all felt that it somehow contradicted their ideal of a new republic of freemen. Echoes of this view were heard by Frederick Law Olmsted when he traveled through the back country of the South in the 1850's. One mountain dweller told Olmsted that he "was afraid that there was many a man who had gone to the bad world, who wouldn't have gone if he hadn't had any slaves."

Though less moralistic in his conclusions, Henry Clay was of much the same opinion. "I am no friend to slavery," he wrote to an Alabaman in 1838. "I think it is an evil; but I believe it better that slaves should remain slaves than to be set loose as free men among us. . . ." For Clay, as for many antislavery southerners, it was difficult to believe that emancipated Negroes and whites could live together peacefully in the same country. This deep-seated belief in the incompatibility of the two races constituted the great dilemma in the minds of antislavery southerners; often it paralyzed all action.

The effects of this dilemma were certainly evident in the course of the remarkable debate on slavery in the Virginia legislature in 1832.

The event which precipitated it was a brief but violent uprising of slaves in Southampton County on August 21, 1831. Led by Nat Turner, a slave preacher given to visions and prophecies, the insurrectionists deliberately killed some sixty white people, mainly women and children. But even the rapidity and efficiency with which the might of the white man had been mobilized against the runaway slaves did not assuage the fear that surged through the minds of southerners everywhere. And so it was that on January 11, 1832, there began one of the most searching debates on slavery ever held by the elected representatives of a slaveholding people. For two weeks the venerable institution was subjected to the frankest kind of criticism.

Three quarters of the members of the House of Delegates held slaves, yet more than half of that body spoke out against the institution in one fashion or another. In analyzing the statements and the notes of the members, one historian concluded that 60 of the 134 delegates were consistently antislavery, working for legislation that would eventually terminate Negro bondage in Virginia. Twelve more, whom he calls the compromisers, were antislavery in belief, but were not prepared to vote for any measure which would, at that time, commit the state to emancipation. It was this latter group, in league with the sixty or so defenders of the *status quo*, who defeated the efforts to initiate gradual emancipation in 1832.

Though individual opponents of slavery remained in the South right up to the Civil War, it is impossible to ascertain their numbers. However, a glimpse into the mind of one such southerner has been afforded by the publication of the diary of Mary Minor Blackford. Mrs. Blackford lived in Fredericksburg, Virginia, across the street from a slave trader's house, a location which permitted her to see slavery at its worst. And it was slavery as a moral evil rather than as an economic fallacy which troubled her: how could people otherwise good and humane, kind and Christian, hold fellow human beings in bondage? For unlike some northern abolitionists, she knew slave owners too well to think them innately evil. Her answer was not surprising: material self-interest morally blinded them.

The tragedy of the South's history was woven into the fabric of Mary Minor Blackford's life. Despite her long opposition to slavery, she proudly saw five of her sons serve in the Confederate Army. Yet with its defeat, she could still write early in 1866: "A New Era has dawned since I last wrote in this book. Slavery has been abolished!!!"

Other individual opponents of slavery in the South could be cited, but perhaps it would be best to close by mentioning an antislavery organization. The American Colonization Society, founded in 1817 by southern and northern antislavery men, always included prominent southerners among its leaders. In the course of its half century of operations, the society managed to send more than six thousand Negroes to its African colony in Liberia.

The society was strongest in the South; indeed, it was anathema to the New England and middle western abolitionists. Though it is true that antislavery was never a popular cause in the South, it was never a dead one, either, so long as thousands of southerners refused to view slavery as anything but an evil for their region.

As we have seen, the South was even less united on nullification and secession than it was on the question of slavery. In fact, it is now clear that if a majority of southerners ever did support secession—and there is real doubt on this—it was never a big majority, and it was not achieved until the very eve of the Civil War. In short, the South, rather than being a monolith of undivided opinion, was not even of one mind on the two most vital issues of the thirty years that led up to the war.

Of Time and Frontiers: The Myth of "Cavalier" Confederate Leadership

Wilbur J. Cash

Of those myths peculiar to the pre–Civil War South, none has proved more enduring than the belief in a historically continuous southern aristocracy. According to the romantic myth of the Old South, country gentlemen of courtliness and stately hospitality presided over southern society during the antebellum period. The late Wilbur Cash, freelance writer and former associate editor of the Charlotte (North Carolina) *News,* seeks to counter this image by forwarding arguments against such a legendary sociology. In pursuing the social reality of the antebellum South, Mr. Cash notes that two critical factors were perpetually at odds with the idea of an all-pervasive cavalier society—the element of time and the ever present frontier environment. In addition, the proven incidence of social mobility among earlier southerners scarcely suggests a full-blown, closed aristocracy in the making. To the degree that subtle notions of class did begin to manifest themselves in the Old South, such social distinctions were linked, as is invariably the case in most Western societies, not to lineage but rather to property ownership. The southern "aristocracy" of the Old Regime was at best one of rank rather than caste—a creation of the mind of the South.

Though . . . nobody any longer holds to the Cavalier thesis in its overt form, it remains true that the popular mind still clings to it in essence. Explicit or implicit in most considerations of the land, and despite a gathering tendency on the part of the more advanced among the professional historians, and lately even on the part of popular writers, to cast doubt on it, the assumption persists that the great South of the first half of the nineteenth century—the South which fought the Civil War—was the home of a genuine and fully realized aristocracy, coextensive and identical with the ruling class, the planters; and sharply set apart from the common people, still pretty often lumped indiscriminately together as the poor whites, not only by economic condition but also by the far vaster gulf of a different blood and a different (and long and solidly established) heritage.

To suppose this, however, is to ignore the frontier and that *sine qua non* of aristocracy everywhere—the dimension of time. And to ignore the frontier and time in setting up a conception of the social state of the Old South is to abandon reality. For the history of this South throughout a very great part of the period from the opening of the nineteenth century to the Civil War (in the South beyond the Mississippi until long after that war) is mainly the history of the roll of frontier upon frontier—and on to the frontier beyond.

Prior to the close of the Revolutionary period the great South, as such, has little history. Two hundred years had run since John Smith had saved Jamestown, but the land which was to become the cotton kingdom was still more wilderness than not. In Virginia—in the Northern Neck, all along the tidewater, spreading inland along the banks of the James, the York, the Rappahannock, flinging thinly across the redlands to the valley of the Shenandoah, echoing remotely about the dangerous water of Albemarle—in South Carolina and Georgia—along a sliver of swamp country running from Charleston to Georgetown and Savannah—and in and around Hispano-Gallic New Orleans, there was something which could be called effective settlement and societal organization.

Here, indeed, there was a genuine, if small, aristocracy. Here was all that in aftertime was to give color to the legend of the Old South. Here were silver and carriages and courtliness and manner. Here were great houses—not as great as we are sometimes told, but still great houses: the Shirleys, the Westovers, the Stratfords. Here were the names that were some time to flash with swords and grow tall in thunder—the Lees, the Stuarts, and the Beauregards. Charleston, called the most brilliant of American cities by Crèvecoeur, played a miniature London, with overtones of La Rochelle, to a small squirarchy of the rice plantations. In Virginia great earls played at Lord Bountiful, dispensing stately hospitality to every passer-by—to the barge captain on his way down the river, to the slaver who had this morning put into the inlet with a cargo of likely Fulah boys, to the wandering Yankee peddling his platitudinous wooden nutmeg, and to other great earls, who came, with their ladies, in canopied boats or in coach and six with liveried outriders. New Orleans was a pageant of dandies and coxcombs, and all the swamplands could show a social life of a considerable pretension.

It is well, however, to remember a thing or two about even these Virginians. (For brevity's sake, I shall treat only of the typical case of the Virginians, and shall hereafter generally apply the term as embracing all these little clumps of colonial aristocracy in the lowlands.) It is well to remember not only that they were not generally Cavaliers in their origin but also that they did not spring up to be aristocrats in a day. The two hundred years since Jamestown must not be forgotten. It is necessary to conceive Virginia as beginning very much as New England began—as emerging by slow stages from a primitive backwoods community, made up primarily of farmers and laborers. Undoubtedly there was a sprinkling of gentlemen of a sort—minor squires, younger sons of minor squires, or adventurers who had got themselves a crest, a fine coat, and title to huge slices of the country. And probably some considerable part of the aristocrats at the end of the Revolution are to be explained as stemming from these bright-plumed birds. It is certain that the great body of them cannot be so explained.

The odds were heavy against such gentlemen—against any gentlemen at all, for that matter. The land had to be wrested from the forest and the intractable red man. It was a harsh and bloody task, wholly unsuited to the talents which won applause in the neighborhood of Rotten Row and Covent Garden, or even in Hants or the West Riding. Leadership, for the great part, passed inevitably to rough and ready hands. While milord tarried at dice or languidly directed his even more languid workmen, his horny-palmed neighbors increasingly wrung profits from the earth, got themselves into position to extend their holdings, to send to England for redemptioners and convict servants in order to extend them still further, rose steadily toward equality with him, attained it, passed him, were presently buying up his bankrupt remains.

The very redemptioners and convict servants were apt to fare better than the gentleman. These are the people, of course, who are commonly said to explain the poor whites of the Old South, and so of our own time. It is generally held of them that they were uniformly shiftless or criminal, and that these characters, being inherent in the germ plasm, were handed on to their progeny, with the result that the whole body of them continually sank lower and lower in the social scale. The notion has the support of practically all the standard histories of the United States, as for example those of John Bach McMaster and James Ford Rhodes. But, as Professor G. W. Dyer, of Vanderbilt University, has pointed out in his monograph, *Democracy in the South Before the Civil War*, it has little support in the known facts.

In the first place, there is no convincing evidence that, as a body, they came of congenitally inferior stock. If some of the convicts were thieves or cutthroats or prostitutes, then some of them were also mere political prisoners, and so, ironically, may very well have represented as good blood as there was in Virginia. Perhaps the majority were simply debtors. As for the redemptioners, the greater number of them seem to have been mere children or adolescents, lured from home by professional crimps or outright kidnapped. It is likely enough, to be sure, that most of them were still to be classed as laborers or the children of laborers; but it is an open question whether this involves any actual inferiority, and certainly it involved no practical inferiority in this frontier society.

On the contrary. Most of them were freed while still in their twenties. Every freeman was entitled to a headright of fifty acres. Unclaimed lands remained plentiful in even the earliest-settled areas until long after the importation of bound servants had died out before slavery. And to cap it all, tobacco prices rose steadily. Thus, given precisely those qualities of physical energy and dogged application which, in the absence of degeneracy, are pre-eminently the heritage of the laborer, the former redemptioner (or convict, for that matter) was very likely to do what so many other men of his same general stamp were doing all about him: steadily to build up his capital and become a man of substance and respect. There is abundant evidence that the thing did so happen. Adam Thoroughgood, who got to be the greatest planter in Norfolk, entered the colony as an indentured servant. Dozens of others who began in the same status are known to have become justices of the peace, vestrymen, and officers of the militia—positions reserved, of course, for gentlemen. And more than one established instance bears out *Moll Flanders.*

In sum, it is clear that distinctions were immensely supple, and that the test of a gentleman in seventeenth-century Virginia was what the test of a gentleman is likely to be in any rough young society—the possession of a sufficient property.

Aristocracy in any real sense did not develop until after the passage of a hundred years—until after 1700. From the foundations carefully built up by his father and grandfather, a Carter, a Page, a Shirley began to tower decisively above the ruck of farmers, pyramided his holdings in land and slaves, squeezed out his smaller neighbors and relegated them to the remote Shenandoah, abandoned his story-and-a-half house for his new "hall," sent his sons to William and Mary and afterward to the English universities or the law schools in London. These sons brought back the manners of the Georges and more developed and subtle notions of class. And the sons of these in turn began to think of themselves as true aristocrats and to be accepted as such by those about them—to set themselves consciously to the elaboration and propagation of a tradition.

But even here the matter must not be conceived too rigidly, or as having taken place very extensively. The number of those who had moved the whole way into aristocracy even by the time of the Revolution was small. Most of the Virginians who counted themselves gentlemen were still, in reality, hardly more than superior farmers. Many great property-holders were still almost, if not quite, illiterate. Life in the greater part of the country was still more crude than not. The frontier still lent its tang to the manners of even the most advanced, all the young men who were presently to rule the Republic having been more or less shaped by it. And, as the emergence of Jeffersonian democracy from exactly this milieu testifies, rank had not generally hardened into caste.

But this Virginia was not the great South. By paradox, it was not even all of Virginia. It was a narrow world, confined to the areas where tobacco, rice, and indigo could profitably be grown on a large scale—to a relatively negligible fraction, that is, of the Southern country. All the rest, at the close of the Revolution, was still in the frontier or semi-frontier stage. Here were no baronies, no plantations, and no manors. And here was no aristocracy nor any fully established distinction save that eternal one between man and man.

In the vast backcountry of the seaboard states, there lived unchanged the pioneer breed—the unsuccessful and the restless from the older regions; the homespun Scotch-Irish, dogged out of Pennsylvania and Maryland by poverty and the love of freedom; pious Moravian brothers, as poor as they were pious; stolid Lutheran peasants from northern Germany; ragged, throat-slitting Highlanders, lusting for elbow-room and still singing hotly of Bonnie Prince Charlie; all that generally unpretentious and often hard-bitten crew which, from about 1740, had been slowly filling up the region. Houses, almost without exception, were cabins of logs. Farms were clearings, on which was grown enough corn to meet the grower's needs, and perhaps a little tobacco which once a year was "rolled" down to a landing on a navigable stream. Roads and trade hardly yet existed. Life had but ceased to be a business of Indian fighting. It was still largely a matter of coon-hunting, of "painter" tales and hard drinking.

Westward, Boone had barely yesterday blazed his trail. Kentucky and Tennessee were just opening up. And southward of the Nashville basin, the great Mississippi Valley, all that country which was to be Alabama, Mississippi, western Georgia, and northern Louisiana, was still mainly a wasteland, given over to the noble savage and peripatetic traders with an itch for adventure and a taste for squaw seraglios.

Then the Yankee, Eli Whitney, interested himself in the problem of extracting the seed from a recalcitrant fiber, and cotton was on its way to be king. The despised backcountry was coming into its own—but slowly at first. Cotton would release the plantation from the narrow confines of the coast-lands and the tobacco belt, and stamp it as the reigning pattern on all the country. Cotton would end stagnation, beat back the wilderness, mow the forest, pour black men and plows and mules along the Yazoo and the Arkansas, spin out the railroad, freight the yellow waters of the Mississippi with panting stern-wheelers—in brief, create the great South. But not in a day. It was necessary to wait until the gin could be proved a success, until experience had shown that the uplands of Carolina and Georgia were pregnant with wealth, until the rumor was abroad in the world that the blacklands of the valley constituted a new El Dorado.

It was 1800 before the advance of the plantation was really under way, and even then the pace was not too swift. The physical difficulties to be overcome were enormous. And beyond the mountains the first American was still a dismaying problem. It was necessary to wait until Andrew Jackson and the men of Tennessee could finally crush him. 1810 came and went, the battle of New Orleans was fought and won, and it was actually 1820 before the plantation was fully on the march, striding over the hills of Carolina to Mississippi—1820 before the tide of immigration was in full sweep about the base of the Appalachians.

From 1820 to 1860 is but forty years—a little more than the span of a single generation. The whole period from the invention of the cotton gin to the outbreak of the Civil War is less than seventy years—the lifetime of a single man. Yet it was wholly within the longer of these periods, and mainly within the shorter, that the development and growth of the great South took place. Men who, as children, had heard the war-whoop of the Cherokee in the Carolina backwoods lived to hear the guns at Vicksburg. And thousands of other men who had looked upon Alabama when it was still a wilderness and upon Mississippi when it was still a stubborn jungle, lived to fight—and to fight well, too—in the ranks of the Confederate armies.

The inference is plain. It is impossible to conceive the great South as being, on the whole, more than a few steps removed from the frontier stage at the beginning of the Civil War. It is imperative, indeed, to conceive it as having remained more or less fully in the frontier stage for a great part—maybe the greater part—of its antebellum history. However rapidly the plantation might advance, however much the slave might smooth the way, it is obvious that the mere physical process of subduing the vast territory which was involved, the essential frontier process of wresting a stable foothold from a hostile environment, must have consumed most of the years down to 1840. . . .

How account for the ruling class, then? Manifestly, for the great part, by the strong, the pushing, the ambitious, among the old coon-hunting population of the backcountry. The frontier was their predestined inheritance. They possessed precisely the qualities necessary to the taming of the land and the building of the cotton kingdom. The process of their rise to power was simplicity itself. Take a concrete case.

A stout young Irishman brought his bride into the Carolina up-country about 1800. He cleared a bit of land, built a log cabin of two rooms, and sat down to the pioneer life. One winter, with several of his neighbors, he loaded a boat with whisky and the coarse woolen cloth woven by the women and drifted down to Charleston to trade. There, remembering the fondness of his woman for a bit of beauty, he bought a handful of cotton seed, which she planted about the cabin with the wild rose and the honeysuckle—as a flower. Afterward she learned, under the tutelage of a new neighbor, to pick the seed from the fiber with her fingers and to spin it into yarn. Another winter the man drifted down the river, this time to find the halfway station of Columbia in a strange ferment. There was a new wonder in the world—the cotton gin— and the forest which had lined the banks of the stream for a thousand centuries was beginning to go down. Fires flared red and portentous in the night—to set off an answering fire in the breast of the Irishman.

Land in his neighborhood was to be had for fifty cents an acre. With twenty dollars, the savings of his lifetime, he bought forty acres and set himself to clear it. Rising long before day, he toiled deep into the night, with his wife holding a pine torch for him to see by. Aided by his neighbors, he piled the trunks of the trees into great heaps and burned them, grubbed up the stumps, hacked away the tangle of underbrush and vine, stamped out the poison ivy and the snakes. A wandering trader sold him a horse, bony and half-starved, for a knife, a dollar, and a gallon of whisky. Every day now—Sundays not excepted—when the heavens allowed, and every night that the moon came, he drove the plow into the earth, with uptorn roots bruising his shanks at every step. Behind him came his wife with a hoe. In a few years the land was beginning to yield cotton—richly, for the soil was fecund with the accumulated mold of centuries. Another trip down the river, and he brought home a mangy black slave—an old and lazy fellow reckoned of no account in the ricelands, but with plenty of life in him still if you knew how to get it out. Next year the Irishman bought fifty acres more, and the year after another black. Five years more and he had two hundred acres and ten Negroes. Cotton prices swung up and down sharply, but always, whatever the return, it was almost pure velvet. For the fertility of the soil seemed inexhaustible.

When he was forty-five, he quit work, abandoned the log house, which had grown to six rooms, and built himself a wide-spreading frame cottage. When he was fifty, he became a magistrate, acquired a carriage, and built a cotton gin and a third house—a "big house" this time. It was not, to be truthful, a very grand house really. Built of lumber sawn on the place, it was a little crude and had not cost above a thousand dollars, even when the marble mantel was counted in. Essentially, it was just a box, with four rooms, bisected by a hallway, set on four more rooms bisected by another hallway, and a detached kitchen at the back. Wind-swept in winter, it was difficult to keep clean of vermin in summer. But it was huge, it had great columns in front, and it was eventually painted white, and so, in this land of wide fields and pinewoods it seemed very imposing.

Meantime the country around had been growing up. Other "big houses" had been built. There was a county seat now, a cluster of frame houses, stores, and "doggeries" about a red brick courthouse. A Presbyterian parson had drifted in and started an academy, as Presbyterian parsons had a habit of doing everywhere in the South—and Pompeys and Caesars and Ciceros and Platos were multiplying both among the pickaninnies in the slave quarters and among the white children of the "big houses." The Irishman had a piano in his house, on which his daughters, taught by a vagabond German, played as well as young ladies could be expected to. One of the Irishman's sons went to the College of South Carolina, came back to grow into the chief lawyer in the county, got to be a judge, and would have been Governor if he had not died at the head of his regiment at Chancellorsville.

As a crown on his career, the old man went to the Legislature, where he was accepted by the Charleston gentlemen tolerantly and with genuine liking. He grew extremely mellow in age and liked to pass his time in company, arguing about predestination and infant damnation, proving conclusively that cotton was king and that the damyankee didn't dare do anything about it, and developing a notable taste in the local liquors. Tall and well made, he grew whiskers after the Galway fashion—the well-kept whiteness of which contrasted very agreeably with the brick red of his complexion—donned the long-tailed coat, stove-pipe hat, and string tie of the statesmen of his period, waxed innocently pompous, and, in short, became a really striking figure of a man.

Once, going down to Columbia for the inauguration of a new Governor, he took his youngest daughter along. There she met a Charleston gentleman who was pestering her father for a loan. Her manner, formed by the Presbyterian parson, was plain but not bad, and she was very pretty. Moreover, the Charleston gentleman was decidedly in hard lines. So he married her.

When the old man finally died in 1854, he left two thousand acres, a hundred and fourteen slaves, and four cotton gins. The little newspaper which had recently set up in the county seat spoke of him as "a gentleman of the old school" and "a noble specimen of the chivalry at its best"; the Charleston papers each gave him a column; and a lordly Legaré introduced resolutions of respect into the Legislature. His wife outlived him by ten years—by her portrait a beautifully fragile old woman, and, as I have heard it said, with lovely hands, knotted and twisted just enough to give them character, and a finely transparent skin through which the blue veins showed most aristocratically.

American Slavery

Gerald N. Grob and George Athan Billias

A great measure of the South's mythology not only results from the undeniable strength of the region's collective beliefs, social codes, and cultural rituals but also emanates from its racially based mythology as well. Compounding the matter still further, the peculiar nature of the institution of slavery has generated significant points of debate and interpretation—a contributing influence in its own right to the ambiguities that plague one's clear understanding of the region. Drawing special attention to the historiography of slavery—the perpetual interplay of historical facts and the theoretical frames of interpretation historians have drawn in an attempt to explain an elusive past—Gerald N. Grob of Rutgers and George Athan Billias of Clark University dramatize the point that the usual image of slavery as rather exclusively a southern phenomenon must be adjusted in favor of a national perspective. The patterns of "American slavery" not only implicitly obliterate what has been called the "myth of the Mason-Dixon line"—the guilt-relieving assumption most often made by northerners that their responsibility in relation to slavery was peripheral at best—but also emphasize the many points of theoretical and practical debate with which historians have still to contend. The "politics of interpretation," the manner in which set assumptions as to the nature and meaning of slavery almost always reflect contemporary preoccupations, itself is a contributing influence to the creation of myth. Moreover, the black experience must be seen as central to the southern experience—blacks, if you will, are southerners too. Resting solidly at the center, for those seeking to explain the black experience in some detail, are recurring questions regarding slavery's morality, legitimacy, and profitability; its relationship to paternalism and capitalism; and its effects upon black culture, identity, community, and social institutions.

Although Americans of the mid-nineteenth century were prone to glorify their nation and its institutions, they were also aware that millions of blacks remained enslaved and possessed none of the legal rights and privileges promised to citizens by the Declaration of Independence. Paradoxically, a people who prided themselves on having created one of the freest societies in the world also sanctioned slavery—an institution that many other nations less free had long since abolished.

The existence of the "peculiar institution," of course, played a crucial

role in American history. In the Constitutional Convention of 1787 the founding fathers were forced to deal with its presence. Despite subsequent efforts at
suppression the slavery controversy would not remain quiescent. The presumed compromise settlements of 1820 and 1850 proved transitory. Ultimately it took a long and bloody civil war to end the legal existence of the
"peculiar institution." Even after that war the problems posed by the presence
of a black minority in a predominantly white society continued to plague generations of Americans from the Civil War to the present.

Just as northerners and southerners debated the morality and legitimacy
of slavery in antebellum decades, so too have later historians disagreed over
the nature of the "peculiar institution." Controversy rather than consensus
characterizes the debates among historians. Scholars cannot agree on the origins of slavery; they debate why it was that only blacks were enslaved and
Indians and indentured servants were not. They disagree as to whether racism
preceded slavery or if racial prejudice developed as a rationalization of an already established institution.[1] Similarly, historians continue to debate the nature of slavery and its immediate and enduring impact upon black Americans.

The framework for the historical debate over slavery was first established
by the participants in the controversy in the decades preceding the Civil War.
Northerners bent on making a strong case against slavery were prone to seek
out those facts that buttressed their positions. Southerners, on the other hand,
were equally determined to show the beneficence of their "peculiar institution." Similarly, the large number of eyewitness accounts of travelers in the
South tended to reflect personal views regarding the morality or immorality
of slavery. From the very beginning, therefore, questions about the nature of
slavery tended to be discussed within a predominantly moral framework.

The first serious scholarly effort to delineate the nature of slavery came
from a group of historians who came to the fore in the 1880s and 1890s. Being
a generation removed from the Civil War they were less involved emotionally
in the issue. These scholars tended to view the end of slavery as a blessing to
both North and South. The Civil War, once and for all, had sealed the bonds
of unity in blood and had created a single nation rather than a collection of
sovereign states. Nationalistic in their orientation, these historians developed
an interpretation of slavery similar in many respects to the one held by some
prewar antislavery partisans.

James Ford Rhodes, a businessman turned historian who published a major multivolume history of the United States covering the period from 1850 to
1877, was perhaps typical of this nationalist school of scholars. His first volume began with an unequivocal statement of his position: slavery was an immoral institution. Rhodes's treatment of slavery was little more than a restatement of Henry Clay's famous dictum that "slavery is a curse to the master
and a wrong to the slave." He cited evidence that blacks were often over-
worked and underfed. The institution was brutalizing; the slave and slave family lacked any legal right to afford a measure of protection against the arbitrary
and often cruel behavior by white masters. Pointing to the sexual exploitation
of black women, Rhodes insisted that slavery had debased the entire nation.[2]

His study established the pattern for much of the subsequent treatment of American slavery by historians.

Surprisingly enough Rhodes's work gained general acceptance not only among northern historians but among southern scholars as well. Southerners were willing to condemn slavery as a reactionary institution that inhibited the economic development of their section. They now welcomed its abolition and looked forward to a new era of prosperity in which the South would share in the nation's industrial progress. Rhodes's hostility toward the Radical Reconstruction program after 1865 and his willingness to acquiesce in the right of southern whites to deal with the race question as they saw fit made his views acceptable in that part of the country.

For nearly a quarter of a century, the historical view of slavery followed the pattern set forth by Rhodes and other nationalist scholars. In 1918, however, Ulrich Bonnell Phillips—undoubtedly the most important historian of the antebellum South—published his *American Negro Slavery*. From that moment the debate over slavery assumed a somewhat different form. Subsequent historians, whatever their views, had to take Phillips's work into account. Indeed, it may not be too much to claim that the vitality of the historiographical debate over slavery was due in large measure to Phillips's pioneering contributions.

Born in Georgia in 1877, Phillips attended the state university and then went on to receive his doctorate at Columbia University. Rather than return to the South he accepted an offer from the University of Wisconsin, then a center of American Progressivism. Phillips adopted many of the tenets of Progressivism; as a scholar he attempted to break with the emphasis on political and legal events and to study the underlying social and economic factors responsible for shaping the nation's history. Aside from his commitment to much of the ideology of Progressivism, Phillips was an indefatigable researcher; his work was marked by deep and intensive study of original sources drawn from plantation records.

Phillips's view of slavery grew out of his general interpretation of antebellum Southern society. Focusing on the plantation system he sought to demonstrate that it was more than a system of landholding or of racial exploitation. The plantation was rather a complete social system in which paternalism and capitalism went hand in hand. Indeed, his commentaries on the new postwar South tended to be highly critical because he believed that industrial capitalism without any redeeming humane and paternalistic features was cruel and harsh. His sympathetic portrayal of the Old South, as Eugene Genovese remarked, was "an appeal for the incorporation of the more humane and rational values of pre-bourgeois culture into modern industrial life."

Slavery, according to Phillips, was above all a system of education. Sharing the racial views held by many southerners and northerners (particularly those who believed in the Progressive ideology), Phillips viewed blacks as a docile, childlike people who required the care and guidance of paternalistic whites. In this sense he rejected another stereotype held by many of his contemporaries who feared and hated blacks. Bringing together massive evidence from original sources Phillips painted a subtle and complex portrait of slavery that repudiated the older allegations that the system was inhumane and cruel. Indeed, he emphasized over and over again the profound human relationship that existed between paternal white masters and faithful and childlike black slaves. Yet Phillips, despite the sharp differences in interpretation, owed a significant debt to earlier scholars like Rhodes, for his categories in studying slavery—labor, food, clothing, shelter, care, and the profitability of the system—were precisely the same as those of his predecessor. *American Negro Slavery*, then, was both a sympathetic portrait of the past and commentary on a harsh and impersonal present.[3] For nearly a generation Phillips's view of slavery remained the dominant one. Scholars who followed in his footsteps made a few revisions, but none altered the general picture he had so skillfully sketched. One of the few exceptions was Herbert Aptheker's study of slave revolts in 1943. Aptheker challenged Phillips's portrait of docile slaves and insisted that "discontent and rebelliousness" was more characteristic.[4]

At the same time that Phillips's interpretation of slavery was becoming dominant, a reaction began setting in against the prevailing theories of race. The work of figures like Franz Boas and others had begun to undermine racial interpretations of culture; an emphasis on environment slowly began to replace the earlier belief in the primacy of race. The experiences of the 1930s and 1940s further discredited racist theories, particularly after the ramifications of this doctrine were revealed by events in Nazi Germany. The political ideologies of these decades, moreover, involved a rejection of race theory on both scientific and philosophical grounds. In view of these developments, it was not surprising that the interpretation espoused by Phillips began to be challenged by critics who did not share his historical, racial, or political ideas.

The attack on Phillips and the efforts to discredit *American Negro Slavery*, oddly enough, did not alter the framework within which the debate over slavery took place. Indeed, critics accepted the same categories of analysis employed by Phillips and his predecessors. Their differences with him were largely moral in character. Where Phillips painted a portrait of a harmonious, interdependent, and humane system, his detractors emphasized the cruel and arbitrary nature of slavery, its economic and sexual exploitation, and the degree to which blacks resisted the abominations practiced by their masters. Moreover, Phillips's research methodology came under careful scrutiny. Richard Hofstadter, in an article published in 1944, argued that *American Negro Slavery* was flawed because its thesis rested on a faulty sampling of plantation records. Most slaves lived on smaller plantations or farms, Hofstadter noted, whereas Phillips used records of large plantations.[5]

The attack on Phillips culminated in 1956 when Kenneth M. Stampp published *The Peculiar Institution*. Stampp, some years earlier, had become convinced that the time was ripe for a complete reappraisal of the subject. Besides the problems of a biased sample of plantation records and a reluctance to use unfavorable contemporary travel accounts, Stampp charged, Phillips had accepted without question assumptions about the supposed inferiority of blacks.[6] *The Peculiar Institution*, then, was written specifically to revise

American Negro Slavery. In place of a harmonious antebellum South, Stampp pictured a system of labor that rested upon the simple element of force. In a chapter entitled "To Make Them Stand in Fear," he argued that, without the power to punish, the system of bondage could not have been sustained.

Yet Stampp was unable to break out of the mold within which the debate over slavery had taken place; his analytical categories were virtually identical to those of Rhodes and Phillips. The difference—which was by no means insignificant—was that Stampp's view of slavery was quite similar to that held by northern abolitionists.

The Peculiar Institution summed up nearly a century of historical controversy. Its author, as a matter of fact, was forced by his own evidence to qualify any sweeping generalization about slavery. He conceded that the "only generalization that can be made with relative confidence is that some masters were harsh and frugal, others were mild and generous, and the rest ran the whole gamut in between." Moreover, Stampp's egalitarian commitment led him to see slavery not through the eyes of slaves (an admittedly difficult task) but through the eyes of whites. "Negroes," he wrote in his introduction, *"are,* after all, only white men with black skins, nothing more, nothing less."[7]

Shortly after Stampp published his book the debate over slavery took a new shape. There were a number of reasons for this transformation. No doubt the diminishing returns within the traditional conceptual framework played a role. More important, historians and social scientists were beginning to raise certain kinds of issues about the nature of the black experience in America that resulted in some radical rethinking about slavery. Computer technology also made it possible for the first time to use data in ways that were previously impracticable. But perhaps the most significant factor was the changes in the intellectual milieu of the late 1950s and the period thereafter. During the civil rights movement, blacks and whites alike challenged the prevailing patterns of social and economic relations between the races. The ensuing reorientation of social and political thought quickly influenced the writing of American history. Slavery became one of the most vital and controversial subjects in American history, and the evidence is strong that the subject will continue to be of great interest to future scholars.

The first major challenge to traditional historiography came in 1959 when Stanley Elkins published a brief study entitled *Slavery: A Problem in American Institutional and Intellectual Life.* Elkins's book was not based on new data. Indeed, when compared with Stampp's *The Peculiar Institution,* it was evident that *Slavery* was written without significant research in existing primary sources. What Elkins did—and herein lay the significance of his work—was to pose a series of questions that moved the debate over the nature of slavery to a totally new plane.

Elkins began his study by noting that the abolition of slavery in Latin America had not left the severe race problem faced by the United States. Intrigued by this observation, Elkins concluded that it was the absence of countervailing institutions in the United States such as a strong national church that permitted slavery to develop without any obstructions that might mitigate its power. Second, Elkins stressed the harshness of American slavery and argued that it had a devastating impact on the black personality. He insisted that the Black Sambo stereotype—the shuffling, happy-go-lucky, not very intelligent black—had a basis in fact. Elkins used the analogy of the Nazi concentration camps to demonstrate that total, or totalitarian, institutions could reduce their inmates to perpetual childlike dependency. Hence the all-encompassing institution of slavery had given rise to the Sambo personality type. Implicit in Elkins's work was the belief that slavery victimized blacks by stripping them of their African heritage, making them dependent on whites, and preventing them from forming any cohesive family structure.

Elkins's thesis seemed acceptable to historians and other Americans, at first, partly because it undermined still further a racial ideology that had assumed the innate inferiority of blacks. By stressing that blacks were victims of slavery, Elkins repudiated the more benign view of that institution and even made Stampp's unflattering description far less potent. Moreover, Elkins appeared to provide intellectual support for compensatory social and economic programs in the 1960s designed to help blacks overcome residual effects of slavery. Elkins implicitly placed the responsibility for the nation's racial dilemmas squarely upon whites by picturing blacks as unwilling victims of white transgressions.

Elkins's book had (and still has) a profound influence. First, it raised questions heretofore neglected, such as the relationship between slavery and subsequent racial conflict. Second, it inspired a group of scholars to undertake studies of comparative slave systems in order to answer some questions posed by Elkins. Third, it placed the slavery debate within a new conceptual framework, for Elkins had focused less on slavery as an institution and more upon blacks themselves. Finally, Elkins—more than his colleagues—had linked history with other social science disciplines.[8]

Yet within a few years after the appearance of his book, Elkins found himself under attack from both within and outside his discipline. Some historians were concerned about the book's facile use of hypotheses taken from the other social sciences and its relative neglect of data from primary sources. Others felt that Elkins had made too much of the Sambo stereotype; evidence of slave resistance seemed to disprove the thesis that blacks had been reduced to childlike dependency. Still others, though not explicitly contradicting Elkins, produced studies that demonstrated that slavery was a far more complex institution than Elkins implied. Richard C. Wade's study of urban slavery, for example, showed that there were behavioral differences between urban black slaves and those who labored on plantations and farms. Conceding that urban slavery was in a state of decline before the Civil War because of the difficulties in maintaining social control, Wade's portrait of urban slaves was not always in agreement with Elkins's Sambo stereotype.[9]

The major assault on Elkins, however, came from outside the ranks of historians. By the mid-1960s a number of ideologies had emerged within the black community. Although integration was still the dominant goal for most blacks, a significant number of them turned inward and articulated black nationalist or other separatist points of view. Bitter at continued white resistance to black demands for full equality, they rejected the goal of integration and assimilation as inappropriate and unattainable. To such spokesmen Elkins's Sambo stereotype undermined the search for a usable past that emphasized instead black achievement and black pride in the face of unremitting white oppression. Moreover, some blacks (and whites) did not care for a thesis that emphasized deprivation. They felt it was simply a sophisticated restatement of racism because it placed part of the responsibility or blame upon the deprived group. Finally, some radicals were hostile to the Sambo image. They posited the idea of perpetual conflict between the oppressors and oppressed, and acceptance of the concept of a docile and nonresisting slave would contradict their own ideological position.

Disagreement with Elkins's view of slave personality and his emphasis on the absence of resistance to white pressure soon led some scholars to study anew the actual life of slaves on plantations. Previous scholarship dealing with slavery, of course, was largely dependent on predominantly *white* sources, including plantation records, newspapers, manuscripts, court records, and travel accounts. The newer scholarship, however, was based on hitherto neglected sources, including a significant number of slave narratives published both before and after the Civil War. During the depression of the 1930s, moreover, the Federal Writers' Project of the Works Progress Administration had subsidized an oral history project in which more than two thousand ex-slaves who were still alive were interviewed. Using these and other sources, historians began to raise some new questions. If, for example, the control of whites was so complete, why did some slaves run away and others engage in all kinds of covert resistance? What kind of institutional structures developed within the slave community? To what degree were these black institutions partly or fully autonomous? Influenced by the "new social history," scholars began to study slave society not as one created by whites but as one that represented to some degree the hopes, aspirations, and thoughts of blacks.

Indicative of the newer approach was the publication in 1972 of two works. The first, *From Sundown to Sunup: The Making of the Black Community*, was based upon the interviews with ex-slaves during the 1930s. Its author, George P. Rawick, also edited eighteen additional volumes printing the text of the interviews. Rawick emphasized that slaves were not passive; he insisted that plantation life showed considerable interaction between whites and blacks. Forcibly removed from Africa, blacks created a way of life that fused their African heritage with the "social forms and behavior patterns" of southern society. The slave personality, Rawick emphasized, was ambivalent. On the one hand slaves were submissive and accepted the belief that one deserved to be a slave. On the other hand they demonstrated the kind of anger that served as a protection against infantilization and dependency. Blacks, concluded Rawick, "developed an independent community and culture which molded the slave personality" and permitted a measure of autonomy.[10]

In a similar vein, John Blassingame's *The Slave Community: Plantation Life in the Ante-Bellum South* described a social setting in which slaves employed a variety of means to circumscribe and inhibit white authority. Family ties among slaves persisted, thus creating a partial protective shield. Blacks also developed and retained religious and mythological beliefs that enabled them to maintain a high degree of autonomy. Slowly but surely the focus of the debate over slavery began a shift of emphasis away from white slaveowners and toward the slaves themselves.[11]

The works of Rawick and Blassingame were received without fanfare or extended debate. Although some criticisms were raised, their contributions were relatively noncontroversial. The same was not true of a book by Robert Fogel and Stanley L. Engerman, *Time on the Cross: The Economics of American Negro Slavery*, which appeared in 1974. Based on quantified data, computer-based analysis, and modern economic theory, Fogel and Engerman presented an interpretation of slavery that set off a fierce and heated debate. Purportedly rejecting virtually every previous work on slavery, the two "new economic historians" presented what seemed to be a series of novel findings about the institution.

Slavery, the two authors emphasized, was not an economically backward system kept in existence by plantation owners unaware of their true interest. On the contrary, southern slave agriculture was highly efficient on the eve of the Civil War. "Economies of large-scale operation, effective management, and intensive utilization of labor and capital made southern slave agriculture 35 percent more efficient than the northern system of family farming." Nor were slaves Sambo-like caricatures; they were hardworking individuals who within the limitations of bondage were able to pursue their own self-interest precisely because they internalized the capitalist values of their masters. Slaveowners encouraged stable black families, rejected the idea of indiscriminate force, did not sexually abuse black women, and provided—by the standards of that era—adequate food, clothing, and shelter. Slavery, therefore, was a model of capitalist efficiency. Within its framework blacks learned and accepted the tenets of the "Protestant ethic" of work. They received, in return, incentives in the form of material rewards, opportunities for upward mobility within the plantation hierarchy, and a chance to create their own stable families. Although Fogel and Engerman in no way diminished the moral evil of slavery, they claimed their goal was "to strike down the view that black Americans were without culture, without achievement, and without development for their first two hundred and fifty years on American soil." A major corollary to their view of slavery was their conclusion that in the century following its abolition white Americans systematically attacked and degraded black citizens. Whites drove freed blacks out of skilled occupations, paid them minimal wages, limited their access to education, and imposed a rigid system of segregation that deprived them of many of the opportunities available to whites.[12]

Time on the Cross immediately became the object of an acrimonious debate. Some condemned the hypothesis that slaves willingly accepted white-imposed values. Others attacked the way in which the two authors used historical data to reach flawed conclusions. Still others were unwilling to accept many of the underlying assumptions of the two authors. Indeed, within a short period of time the literature criticizing *Time on the Cross* was enormous.[13]

At precisely the same time that *Time on the Cross* appeared Eugene D.

Genovese published *Roll, Jordan, Roll: The World the Slaves Made.* Genovese, who had already written some distinguished works on the antebellum South, denied in his book that slavery was to be understood within the context of modern capitalism. The key to an understanding of the peculiar institution, he insisted, was to be found in the crucial concept of *paternalism.* The destinies of masters and slaves were linked by a set of mutual duties and responsibilities comparable in many ways to the arrangements between lords and serfs under the feudal system. Whites exploited and controlled the labor of socially inferior blacks and, in return, provided them with the basic necessities of life. To blacks slavery meant a recognition of their basic humanity, and this gave them a claim upon their masters. This claim could be manipulated by slaves who accepted the concessions offered to them by their masters and molded them to suit themselves. Within the limitations of the legal system of bondage, therefore, blacks were able to create their own culture. Genovese particularly emphasized slave religion because its affirmation of life served as a weapon for "personal and community survival." The price the blacks paid for this partial autonomy was the development of a nonrevolutionary and prepolitical consciousness.[14]

In keeping with the newer focus upon the autonomy of slave society as contrasted with the earlier emphasis on dependency, Herbert G. Gutman in 1976 published his study of the black family. Gutman had been one of the most severe critics of *Time on the Cross,* and he wrote a book-length critique which attacked Fogel and Engerman precisely because of their claims of "black achievement under adversity." In *The Black Family in Slavery and Freedom, 1750–1925,* Gutman offered his own views, which, surprisingly enough, were not at all at variance with Fogel and Engerman or, for that matter, with Rawick, Blassingame, or Genovese.

Like many recent "new social historians" Gutman stressed the ability of blacks to adapt themselves to oppression in their own unique ways. In this respect he rejected the claims of Elkins and others about the debilitating impact of slavery upon its unwilling victims. Yet Gutman at the some time denied that plantation capitalism (Fogel and Engerman) and paternalism (Genovese) were necessary components in the process of adaptation. Slaves were able to create their own society, not by reacting to white offers of rewards or by molding the concessions granted them by their masters, but rather by developing a sophisticated family and kinship network that transmitted the Afro-American heritage from generation to generation. The black family, in effect, served to cushion the shock of being uprooted from Africa. If parents were separated from their children by being sold, other relatives became surrogate parents to the remaining children. The stability of the black family rested upon a closely knit nuclear arrangement. Adultery after wedlock, for example, was infrequent. These family values were not imposed by white masters, according to Gutman, for they were rooted in the African cultural inheritance. Blacks were more loyal to each other than were whites, moreover, because the community was the basic means of survival.[15]

The debate over the nature of slavery took a somewhat different turn with the publication in 1977 of Lawrence Levine's *Black Culture and Black Consciousness: Afro-American Folk Thought from Slavery to Freedom.* Rather than utilizing standard plantation and demographic records, Levine uncovered and studied thousands of black songs, folktales, jokes, and games in an effort to penetrate the minds and personalities of individuals who left few written records. Levine emphatically rejected Elkins's claim that slavery destroyed black culture and thus helped to create a dependent childlike individual. On the contrary, Levine insisted the evidence suggested that blacks preserved communal values amid the harsh restrictions of a slave environment.

The newer emphasis on slave society and culture has had several curious results. One has been the subtle transformation of slavery from an ugly and malignant system to an institution that is somewhat more benign in its character. This is not to imply that scholars like Fogel, Engerman, Genovese, and Gutman are in any way sympathetic to slavery, for all of them concede without reservation its immorality. But by focusing on the ability of black slaves to create a partially autonomous culture and society they implicitly diminish the authority of dominant white masters whose control was less than complete. Ironically, the emphasis on an indigenous black culture moved contemporary scholarship closer to Ulrich Bonnell Phillips, who had emphasized the contentment of blacks under slavery. Recent scholars, of course, take a quite different approach, but there is a distinct implication in their work that whites did not control many major elements in the lives of their slaves, who exercised considerable authority in determining their personal and familial relations. Compared with the Stampp and Elkins interpretation of slavery, these more recent works diminish, in part, the tragic view of slavery as an institution.

There is little doubt also that the parameters of the lively debate over the nature of slavery have been defined by a strong intellectual current that emphasizes the autonomy rather than the dependence of the American black experience. White scholars have been extremely sensitive to charges (particularly by blacks) that they have made the history of blacks a mere appendage of white actions and behavior. Consequently the emphasis on a unique and separate black identity and culture has had the effect of diminishing the importance of the white man's oppression as a major determinant in black history. By way of contrast, the Stampp-Elkins approach emphasized white responsibility for black problems.[16]

Virtually all of the interpretations of slavery since the 1950s tended to treat the "peculiar institution" as a single unit; with only an occasional exception historians did not distinguish between time and place. In 1980, however, Ira Berlin threw down an explicit challenge to his colleagues. In a significant article in the *American Historical Review* he noted that "time and space"— the "traditional boundaries of historical inquiry"—had been largely ignored by American historians, most of whom had produced a "static vision of slave culture." In a detailed examination of seventeenth- and eighteenth-century slavery Berlin went on to identify three distinct slave systems: a northern nonplantation system; and two southern plantation systems, one in the Chesapeake Bay region and the other in the Carolina and Georgia low country. In each of these areas slavery developed in a unique manner; the differences had important consequences for black culture and society.

In the North, according to Berlin, acculturation incorporated blacks into American society while at the same time making them acutely conscious of their African past. Whites, who outnumbered blacks by a wide margin, allowed their slaves considerable autonomy. In the Southern low country, on the other hand, blacks were deeply divided; urban blacks pressed for incorporation into white society while plantation blacks remained physically separated and estranged from the Anglo-American world and closer to their African roots. In the Chesapeake region a single unified Afro-American culture emerged. Because of the impress of white paternalism, Afro-American culture paralleled Anglo-American culture; the African heritage was submerged. Berlin's analysis constituted an explicit and clear challenge to the parameters of the debate over slavery from the 1950s through the 1970s. "If slave society during the colonial era can be comprehended only through a careful delineation of temporal and spatial differences among Northern, Chesapeake, and low-country colonies," Berlin observed, "a similar division will be necessary for a full understanding of black life in nineteenth-century America. The actions of black people during the American Revolution, the Civil War, and the long years of bondage between these two cataclysmic events cannot be understood merely as a function of the dynamics of slavery or the possibilities of liberty, but must be viewed within the specific social circumstances and cultural traditions of black people. These varied from time to time and from place to place. Thus no matter how complete recent studies of black life appear, they are limited to the extent that they provide a static and singular vision of a dynamic and complex society."[17]

In evaluating the competing interpretations of American slavery it is important to understand that more than historical considerations are involved. Any judgment upon the nature of slavery implicitly offers a judgment of the present and a prescription for the future. To emphasize the harshness of slavery and the dependence of its victims is to maximize the white man's responsibility. On the other hand to downplay the effectiveness of white authority is to move toward a position that concedes black autonomy and hence accepts the view that responsibility for post–Civil War developments rests in part with blacks.

Which of the various viewpoints of slavery are correct? Were slaves contented or discontented under slavery? In what ways were they successful in resisting the efforts of their masters to make them totally dependent human beings? To what degree did an autonomous black culture and social order develop during slavery? Was slavery a prebourgeois feudal system or a modern version of rational capitalism? What was the nature of the master-slave relationship? Is it possible to generalize about the lives of several millions of individuals under slavery? Must historians begin to distinguish between the common and the unique elements of the institution of slavery in terms of time and space? The answers to these questions undoubtedly will rest upon the continued analysis of surviving sources. But to a considerable degree they will rest also upon the attitudes and values of historians, whose own personal commitments play a role in shaping their perceptions of the past and their view of the present and future.

Notes

1. Cf. Oscar and Mary F. Handlin, "Origins of the Southern Labor System," *William and Mary Quarterly,* 3d ser. 7 (1950): 199–222; Winthrop D. Jordan, *White over Black: American Attitudes toward the Negro, 1550–1812* (Chapel Hill, 1968); and Edmund S. Morgan, *American Slavery, American Freedom: The Ordeal of Colonial Virginia* (New York, 1975).
2. James Ford Rhodes, *History of the United States from the Compromise of 1850 to the Final Restoration of Home Rule in the South in 1877,* 7 vols. (New York, 1893–1906), 1.
3. For sympathetic evaluations of Phillips's achievements see Eugene D. Genovese, "Race and Class in Southern History: An Appraisal of the Work of Ulrich Bonnell Phillips," *Agricultural History* 41 (October 1967): 345–358; and Daniel J. Singal, "Ulrich Bonnell Phillips: The Old South as the New," *Journal of American History* 63 (March 1977): 871–891.
4. Herbert Aptheker, *American Negro Slave Revolts* (New York, 1943).
5. Richard Hofstadter, "U.B. Phillips and the Plantation Legend," *Journal of Negro History* 29 (April 1944): 109–124. The criticisms of Phillips can be followed in the pages of the *Journal of Negro History.*
6. Kenneth M. Stampp, "The Historian and Southern Negro Slavery," *American Historical Review* 57 (April 1952): 613–624.
7. Kenneth M. Stampp, *The Peculiar Institution: Slavery in the Ante-Bellum South* (New York, 1956), pp. vii, 616.
8. See Ann. J. Lane, ed., *The Debate over Slavery: Stanley Elkins and His Critics* (Urbana, Ill. 1971); and Kenneth M. Stampp, "Rebels and Sambos: The Search for the Negro's Personality in Slavery," *Journal of Southern History* 27 (August 1971): 367–392. For examples of the recent concern with comparative slave systems see Herbert S. Klein, *Slavery in the Americas: A Comparative Study of Cuba and Virginia* (Chicago, 1967); Carl N. Degler, *Neither Black nor White: Slavery and Race Relations in Brazil and the United States* (New York, 1971); and David Brion Davis, *The Problem of Slavery in Western Culture* (Ithaca, 1966), and *The Problem of Slavery in the Age of Revolution* (Ithaca, 1975).
9. Richard C. Wade, *Slavery in the Cities: The South 1820–1860* (New York, 1964).
10. George P. Rawick, *From Sundown to Sunup: The Making of the Black Community* (Westport, Conn., 1972), and *The American Slave: A Composite Autobiography,* 18 vols. (Westport, Conn., 1972).
11. John W. Blassingame, *The Slave Community: Plantation Life in the Ante-Bellum South* (New York, 1972).
12. Robert W. Fogel and Stanley L. Engerman, *Time on the Cross: The Economics of American Negro Slavery,* 2 vols. (Boston, 1974). The second volume was subtitled *Evidence and Methods.*
13. See Herbert G. Gutman, *Slavery and the Numbers Game: A Critique of* Time on the Cross (Urbana, Ill., 1975); and Paul A. David *et al., Reckoning with Slavery: A Critical Study in the Quantitative History of American Negro Slavery* (New York, 1976).

14. Genovese's major works include *The Political Economy of Slavery: Studies in the Economy and Society of the Slave South* (New York, 1965), *The World the Slave-holders Made: Two Essays in Interpretation* (New York, 1969), and *Roll, Jordan, Roll: The World the Slaves Made* (New York, 1974).

15. Herbert G. Gutman, *The Black Family in Slavery and Freedom, 1750–1925* (New York, 1976).

16. For some recent discussions of this point see Stanley M. Elkins, *Slavery: A Problem in American Institutional and Intellectual Life* (3rd ed., Chicago, 1976), pp. 223–302; and George M. Fredrickson, "The Gutman Report," *New York Review of Books* 23 (September 30, 1976): 18–23.

17. Ira Berlin, "Time, Space, and the Evolution of Afro-American Society on British Mainland North America," *American Historical Review* 85 (February 1980): 44–78.

Southern Women and the Indispensable Myth

Shirley Abbott

The plantation legend, that most cherished, sunny "stage piece" of the nineteenth-century South—wherein the allegedly gentlemanly "massa," the supposedly sinister overseeer, the happy darky testifying that "de ole times was the bestis times ole Sam evah seed," the general courtly ambiance of the plantation itself, and of course the exquisitely lovely southern belle all coalesced to form a world of luxuriant splendor—has come fundamentally to be reexamined. The "ole" image of the Old South has been significantly readjusted. Perhaps no greater reformulation of this once-fashionable historical myth has recently appeared than that of the place and condition of women—both black and white. In a personal retrospective born of her childhood in Arkansas, Shirley Abbott, former editor of *Horizon* magazine, here closely examines the "ominous assumptions" as to both race and gender that worked to sustain the myth of the Old South, both then and beyond its own century. Southern myths about race and gender not only served to structure the social life of the southern past, but their historical power still affects a contemporary South that continues to live its history.

"We're used to living around 'em. You Northerners aren't. You don't know anything about 'em." This is or was the all-purpose utterance of white Southerners about blacks. Everybody from Jefferson Davis to Strom Thurmond has said it, in some version, at one time or another. Turned on its obverse, the old saw means, "You can't know how bad they are." Or conversely, "You can't imagine how deeply we understand them." This racial intimacy has served as the explanation of everything from lynch mobs to the recent and comparatively peaceful integration of Southern schools, accomplished while Boston and Detroit sometimes literally went up in flames.

In the small town in Arkansas where I grew up, I heard about this interracial coziness, or read about it in novels, and for years I believed in it. But in fact it simply did not exist, at least not for me. With one exception, the only people I ever knew were white.

Several thousand black people lived in Hot Springs, of course, in three or four different tumbledown sections that butted right up against equally tumbledown white neighborhoods. I always saw more black men than black women. Black men ran the elevators in the three or four buildings where doctors and dentists had offices. They swept the floors and emptied the spittoons in the casino where my father worked. (Gambling—illegal—was the major local industry. I was not allowed inside a gambling house, even to visit my dad, but he used to tell me about the high rollers from New York who would tip the black porter twenty dollars.) Black men worked as garbage collectors, as waiters, as kitchen help—sometimes as yardmen, though elderly white men most often claimed such jobs.

Besides the kitchen help and porters, there existed, according to my father, an utterly terrifying class of Negroes who got drunk and went after each other with razors on Saturday nights. Their names and crimes would be listed in the newspapers in the "Colored" column on Mondays.

I never saw hide or hair of these bad men with their razors. But I knew a few of the well-behaved black men by name. For example, I knew Crip, who ran the elevator in the Medical Arts Building, a twelve-story skyscraper where all the dentists had offices. My teeth rotted continuously, so Mother and I got quite familiar with Crip, white-haired, bent forward at the middle, his joints twisted by arthritis into grotesque knots of agony. He always put on the most astonishing act. My father's nickname in the gambling world was "Hat," as Crip knew, since his son worked as a casino porter, so Crip called my mother "Miz Hat." "Why, mornin', Miz Hat," and he would hand her in and out of the creaky old elevator cage as though she were some plantation queen mounting and dismounting her blooded steed. I was "Little Miz Hat," and he would bow and scrape and somehow make me feverishly aware of my adorable blonde curls. He never would sit down in the presence of whites and would set me on the operator's jump seat instead. I don't know how my mother felt about all this, but I loved it. It made me feel that my mother and I were ladies. Why else would this poor old man act so silly?

Black women were a complete mystery to me. In those days, surely, most black women earned their living as domestics, and yet I scarcely knew a family who kept a maid. Then, when I was about seven, my father got a raise and decided to hire one for my mother—over her objections, for she was quite capable of keeping the house clean by herself and would rather have banked the money. But Daddy wanted his wife to have some leisure, and so one morning, very early, he brought Emma to our back door. For the two or three years that we were able to afford her, he would go and fetch her in the car six mornings a week, and then Mother would drive her home again in the afternoon. Emma earned ten dollars a week and Daddy sixty-five dollars (he too worked six days out of seven). He forbade me to tell any of the neighbor children what Emma's salary was, since the going rate was a dollar a day and sometimes less. But Mother had said she would be ashamed to work anybody for a dollar a day.

Thus commenced my only childhood association with a black woman. Emma was five feet tall, round but not fat, and so black that her facial features, quite delicate and small, seemed indistinct. Her eyes were blacker than her skin and seemed to have no whites to them. Though she looked like a girl, she

was already a grandmother. Watching her as she expertly thrust the point of
the iron into ruffles and pleats, I used to beg to touch the palms of her hands,
which were the color of cream slipper satin, and when I asked her how she got
her palms so light, she would laugh and say it was from washing on a rub-
board.

I was already corrupted, perhaps by books, or perhaps by Emma's shy deference
toward me. I wanted to play the daughter of the manor. How wonderful to
have a maid to order around. But Mother quickly set me straight. The first
time she heard me bragging to the neighborhood children that we had a maid,
she gave me a switching. And worse than that, my dream of becoming a pam-
pered child of the leisure class vanished as Mother proceeded to work side by
side with Emma.

Together on a Monday morning they would set the white linens boiling
on the stove and then heft the caldron to the washing machine on the back
porch—it was an "automatic" that had to be filled and emptied by hose. Together they fished the steaming sheets out of the soapsuds and fed them
through the wringer. Two black arms and two sunburned, freckled ones
pumped up and down in the rinse tubs. Mother and Emma hung everything
on the line just so—right side out and hems down. Before the days of Emma,
lunch on washdays had been a piece of bread, and supper bacon and eggs—the
wages of exhaustion. But now the laundry was finished at noon and by three
o'clock the clean, sweet fragrance of freshly ironed cotton pervaded the house.
While one of the women ironed, the other would peel the vegetables for the
pot roast and cut up a salad, maybe even stir up a cake or pudding. Instead of
saving labor for my mother, having a housemaid simply empowered her to do
more work.

I don't claim that her way of managing her black maid was typical. Nor
do I have any idea what Emma really thought of this hard-driving woman who
insisted on equality in a basically unequal situation. Nor, even yet, do I wholly
understand why my mother did what she did. Compulsive housewifery had
some part in it. So did her upbringing: her people had been subsistence farmers
since they migrated from Ulster in the eighteenth century. If she wanted
Emma to be her sister rather than her servant, it was because the work made
them sisters, and because, out on the farm, nobody but a parasite or an invalid
or a baby sat still while other people worked.

There was another motive too. As I went my way in this small Southern
town, I began gradually to perceive that in the relationship between white
women and black people lay an ominous political assumption that cut in two
directions. Had she used Emma in just the right way, Mother could have become a lady. But Mother didn't want to be a lady. Something in her was against
it—she couldn't explain what frightened her, which was why she cried when
my father ridiculed her about her refusal to leave the house to Emma even for
an afternoon. Siding with my father, as I invariably did at that epoch, I thought
Mother was foolish and countrified. A bumpkin. Why would anybody refuse
to be a lady? I sure intended to be a lady when I grew up.

Small girls these days don't worry anymore, I hope, about whether to grow up and be ladies, but the questions tormented me, even before I understood the political implications. That the daughter of a bookmaker and a farm woman in the middle of Arkansas in the 1940s should fret about such a thing is illogical if not ludicrous—but the obsession came quite naturally. At the age of eight or nine I had turned into a terminally addicted bookworm, and the book I loved was *Gone With the Wind*. I read it all the time. I still read it. What draws me, besides the drive of the plot, is the power and clarity of the female characters. The women in the book function as the electrical charge that holds the South together. All the men are flawed—Gerald O'Hara is a baby, Ashley Wilkes passive and helpless, and Rhett Butler, for all his elegant machismo, is cold and mean and sarcastic. The women fight the battles and get along a lot better than the men. Not just Scarlett or the saintly Melanie, who both grow predictable and cloying even to the most devoted reader. But the minor characters—Beatrice Tarleton with fiery red hair and eight children, who wears not hoopskirts but a riding habit and understands horses better than any man in the county. Dolly Merriwether, the dowager queen of Atlanta, and Grandma Fontaine, the bony old lady who has lived through the Indian wars of an earlier generation. And there are a dozen others too, vivid and tough. Nowhere before in American fiction had there been women of this caliber. Plucky heroines maybe. Brave or independent. Strong-minded, like Jo March. But not tough.

I always took these women literally, as portraits of real people the author had known personally or had heard stories about in the Georgia uplands. Margaret Mitchell, as everyone knows, worked ten years on her one masterwork, and so far as I know, has never been caught in the smallest technical inaccuracy. The book may or may not be stuffed with truth but it is stuffed with facts—information about food, fabric, furnishings (if she says that Scarlett carried a cambric handkerchief, you can be sure that's what ladies' handkerchiefs were made of then). What I did not realize was that the author had read a lot of historical novels, too, and that some of her characters came not from life but from books. That is, they were stereotypes.

One of the most important of the women characters falls into that category. This is Ellen O'Hara, archetype of the Southern lady, an authoritative definition of the species, and the first honest-to-God Southern lady I had ever met, in or out of a book. Ellen simply enraptured me. I did not know, nor would I have cared, that plantation mistresses like Ellen had been stock characters on the literary landscape for a hundred years and that plantation novels had periodically been best sellers in America since an opus called *Swallow Barn* came out in 1832.

Ellen is the high-born wife of Gerald O'Hara, an Irishman on the make who wins his Georgia plantation in a card game. Then he catches Ellen, a Savannah beauty suffering from a misbegotten attachment to a rakehell cousin who gets killed in a brawl. Ellen never loves Gerald, but she represses her grief and walks the earth in a halo of piety and wifely loyalty. Practical and ethereal all at once, she is the mainstay of Tara's economy, which she regulates with the combined powers of queen and prime minister. Naturally she contrives to cover up her executive abilities so as not to embarrass her husband or startle the servants. But whether she is supervising the poultry yard or merely suppressing her feelings, her forte is management.

But Ellen's essential role is not with Gerald or even their three daughters. The slaves at Tara work all day in the field or the great house, but when night comes and they have an opportunity to live their own lives, they are helpless as babies. The only black women at Tara with a grain of sense are the two ponderous housemaids, Mammy and Dilcey. But instead of sending them down to the quarters to oversee life's crucial events, Ellen herself goes.

Nighttime finds her down at the cabins, ministering over sickbeds and presiding at deathbeds. But wherever her nightly exertions may have taken her, Ellen is always at breakfast the next morning, catering to her husband's notions and settling her daughters' spats.

This is the Southern lady at her height—not a woman but a mode—"the magnolia grandiflora of a race of Cavaliers," as a piece of 1920s rhetoric had it.

In 1897, thirty-five years before Ellen O'Hara was set down on paper, a Virginia literary man wrote a kind of idyll about the Southern goddess and her duties in life. This was Thomas Nelson Page, one of the best-known writers of his day. He specialized in dialect stories about good darkies ("O massa," his people went around saying, "de ole times was the bestis times ole Sam evah seed"). He also was an eloquent defender of the white man's right to lynch. (Page was by no means some regional joke. He served for many years as Woodrow Wilson's ambassador to Italy, and the President, who was a Virginian himself, referred to him as a "national ornament.") Here, according to Page, is Dixie's queen mother:

"The plantation mistress was the most important personage about the home, the presence which pervaded the mansion, the centre of all that life, the queen of that realm; the master willingly and proudly yielding her entire management of all household matters and simply carrying out all her directions . . . because he knew her and acknowledged her infallibility. She was indeed a surprising creature—often delicate in frame and of a nervous organization so sensitive as to be a great sufferer; but her force and character pervaded and directed everything, as unseen yet as unmistakable as the power of gravity controls the particles that constitute the earth. . . . She was mistress, manager, doctor, nurse, counsellor, seamstress, teacher, housekeeper, slave, all at once. . . . Her life was one long act of devotion to God, devotion to her husband, devotion to her children, devotion to her servants, to her friends, to the poor, to humanity. . . . She managed her family, regulated her servants, fed the poor, nursed the sick, consoled the bereaved. Who knew of the visits she paid to the cabins of her sick and suffering servants?"

The only catch is that the lady was in part hallucinatory. Sometimes she did not act like Ellen O'Hara at all.

Political image-making is no novelty in the South. If the production of self-serving folklore qualified as an industry, the South would have been an industrial power since colonial times. The first heroes to emerge were the Tidewater aristocrats. These most distinguished of all immigrants to our shores were described if not actually invented by a mid-nineteenth-century lawyer and scribbler from Alabama named Daniel Hundley. They were, he said, "English courtiers of aristocratic mien and faultless manner . . . French Huguenots and Scotch Jacobites, the retainers and associates of Lord Baltimore . . . Spanish dons and French Catholics, a race of heroes and patriots." Hundley's *Social Relations in Our Southern States,* which appeared in 1860, as prewar propaganda went into full swing, was a sort of dictionary of received wisdom. His key figure was the cavalier. Whether Hundley had ever seen any cavaliers or not, he and his contemporaries firmly believed that somewhere, if not in the immediate vicinity, had lived a band of Southern noblemen who divided their time between riding their acres and reading philosophy in the well-stocked libraries of their stately homes.

Before the Revolutionary War there were a few great families in the coastal South—Virginia's celebrated Randolphs, Carters, and Byrds—who lived more or less like English gentry and even had books in the house. And yet a whole generation of scholars proved that virtually no English or French aristocrats settled in the Southern colonies. The overwhelming majority of immigrants to Virginia and Maryland and South Carolina in colonial times were poor people. Half of them were actually indentured servants and convicts. The real American aristocrats, when there were any, built their fortunes after they got here, and they had little time for the pursuits and trappings of high culture. In the newly settled land, even the rich people worked. Charming and hospitable they may or may not have been, but they were not the aristocracy of Europe transplanted—no matter what their latter-day descendants wanted to believe.

Even if they had been aristocrats, the old Tidewater culture based on rice, tobacco, and indigo was largely bankrupt and stagnant by the end of the eighteenth century. The cavalier myth would certainly have died, and the Southern lady would never even have been heard of, had not a Massachusetts Yankee named Eli Whitney invented the cotton gin in 1793. Suddenly cotton was transformed from a time-consuming nuisance to a highly profitable crop. It provided a whole new rationale for slavery, for cotton required almost year-round labor. The market for it already existed in the mills of England. As the gin made cotton profitable, cotton made slavery profitable.

The number of Southern slave owners was always relatively small. At any given moment the majority of people did not own slaves. In 1790 the 658,000 Southern slaves were held by about 79,000 families (only 23 percent of all Southern families). In 1850 only two men owned as many as 1,000 slaves; only nine owned as many as 500. The typical holding was 5 slaves. Of the 350,000 owners, 310,000 had fewer than 20 slaves.

What this meant for the slaves might vary from house to house, but what it meant for white Southern women was that in every generation, greater numbers found themselves in managerial roles with black servants. With fifty slaves on a rice plantation in South Carolina in 1780, a man would hire an overseer. With ten slaves on a cotton farm in Alabama in 1830, the man's wife would be the overseer.

Willing or not, thousands of Southern women in the first half of the nineteenth century were cast in this role. "Ladies" were no longer a luxury of upper-class life in the Tidewater. They were a necessity—a psychological and moral one. For if slavery is to be the foundation of economic life, and if one important crop on any large farm includes healthy black babies, a plantation becomes a complex mechanism that can hardly be expected to function without a white woman around to figure out the endless domestic details. Not only that, but without her supposedly softening and mitigating influence around the place— or her mere cosmetic value—the whole operation quickly turns too rotten for a Christian to contemplate.

Thoughtful people north and south had a bad conscience about what the nation was permitting: even if you accepted the idea that the slave was a savage in need of redemption, did that justify owning him? The first answer to be devised by the Southern apologists was that the self-interest of the owner would make him merciful. After all, only a fool would spend fifteen hundred dollars for a worker and then starve him to death. But it is hardly a watertight case. Men sometimes are fools.

A better answer held that slavery was merely part of a universal scheme, the proper reflection, here below, of the divine order of things. God the Father ruled the universe, delegating some powers to man, who ruled the world as well as the women, children, and slaves who depended on him. How else had society ever been held together? And if this still were not sufficient justification, there was an ace in the hole. That was the Southern lady.

In theory, anyhow, the lady would naturally stand between the victim and his tormentor. She would be the civilizing force. If the master tried to whip his slave, the lady would stay his hand. If he tried to sell a black man away from his black wife, the lady would of course intercede with her lord. (Could he refuse her?) She would apportion the food and give extra rations to the sick. She would see that black bodies were clothed and black souls saved. And if the master showed any desire to seduce the housemaid, the very sight of the beautiful and virtuous woman who carried the keys to his household and mothered his fine white sons would certainly cause him to change his mind. The lady, in short, would function as the mother of the black race.

When Harriet Beecher Stowe set out to deliver the most killing blow she could muster against the Southern apologia for slavery (she was not a very perceptive critic of slavery itself, and she knew nothing about slaves), she loaded the dice as follows: She created a black man named Tom, a pious de-sexed old toady if ever there was one. She takes Tom out of his old Kentucky home and transports him, step by step, to a hellish place in Louisiana. The reason it is hellish is that it has no Southern lady. Simon Legree is not married. He is a vile old man with no idea how to run a home. In the end he beats poor Tom to death. If Legree had had a proper Southern lady for a wife, Mrs. Stowe could never have made things turn out that way. Mrs. Legree would have cleaned up the mess and made some curtains. She would have read the Bible before every meal, and if Legree had tried to beat anybody to death, she would have joshed him out of the notion. Harriet Beecher Stowe may not have known much about black men, but she obviously knew what Southern ladies were put on earth for. No lady, no apologia. It was simple as that.

As to whether, from the slaves' point of view, the Southern lady actually did mitigate their bondage, the answer, not surprisingly, is no. The flesh-and-blood Southern ladies did not measure up to their heavenly image. Of course, white women lived on most plantations and farms and did their share of the work. A number of them must have been intelligent, capable, and kind-hearted. Many of them took on the role of family doctor for both white and black. But ministering angels? Looking over newly published slave testimonials, I conclude that angels were as scarce then as now: I have never come across so much as one reference to a white angel in female form. Once in a while a slave does speak of his mistress as a good woman, a merciful woman, a Christian. But if I had to characterize white mistresses from the memoirs I have read, I should have to say that as a group they were demanding, harsh, impatient, capricious, and quick to call for the laying on of the lash. Some were even sadists, with no redeeming qualities whatever.

Roving through a massive recent collection called *Slave Testimony, Two Centuries of Letters, Speeches, Interviews, and Autobiographies*, edited by John W. Blassingame, I uncovered a few white ladies:

"What did ole missus look like? Well, I tell yer, honey, she looked like a witch. She'd set dere an' dat look 'ud come unto her eyes an' she'd study an' study what to whip me about."

"While I worked in the house and waited upon my mistress, she always treated me kindly, but to other slaves, who were as faithful as I was, she was very cruel." The speaker then describes how this woman once beat a black child to death.

"There was a woman slave who persisted in running away. Whippings did not frighten her, and so her mistress had her belled. An iron hoop was welded across her waist, another about her neck and attached to these a long rod went up her back to which, up over her head and beyond her reach, a bell was hung. It rang as she moved, and when she lay down at night the least motion started the clapper."

The records are full of other kinds of cruelty too. Seven-day workweeks, maidservants required to sleep on the floor every night at the foot of their mistress's bed, slaves deprived of sleep and decent food or sent out to die in their old age—all this the work of white ladies. And running like a fine seam through the slave testimonials is the contempt of the servant for the mistress. What else could any reasonable intelligent able-bodied person have felt for a woman who might refuse to care for her own babies or mend her own clothing or even get out of bed in the middle of the night to fetch a glass of water?

Yet besides the sadist and tyrants and monsters of indolence, there were great numbers of white women who lived with their servants in harmony, women who did the best they could to remain human, even as the slaves remained human under adverse circumstances. In 1970 Anne Firor Scott, professor of history at Duke University, published *The Southern Lady*, which has become a classic among students of women's history. Anne Scott was the first to perceive that the notion of "lady" in the South was an invention of a slaveholding society, which far from pampering its upper-class white women, demanded a great deal of them. Under slavery, of course, it was not only the slaves who must know their place and keep it, but everybody. The role played by the women of the ruling class was critical, for it was up to them to enforce the system. A woman's job was to marry early, please her husband in all ways, be a model of Christian piety, and as the kindly overseer of the slaves and the children, carefully train the young of both races to play the roles expected of them and thus perpetuate the social system.

Though they may have been collaborators in the institution of slavery, Southern women often turn up as closet abolitionists. "I hate slavery," wrote the most famous of all Southern diarists, Mary Chesnut. "All Southern women are abolitionists at heart." Some women hated the system, some hated the slaves, and some both. Others saw well enough what the crimes of slavery were. Ellen Glasgow, the Virginia novelist, wrote of hearing her mother say, many years after the Civil War was over, "Even in the midst of the horrors, a wave of thankfulness rushed over me when I heard that the slaves were freed." This same leitmotif runs through the hundred or more diaries published by Southern women after the war. These women hated Yankees but they had hated slavery, too—Judith McGuire, Frances Fearne, Carnelia McDonald, Caroline Merrick, Constance Harrison. Their names are long since forgotten, and no one reads their diaries but scholars. These few dared, at least, to write down treasonous views. Even if they did not condemn slavery itself, women often complained of the burdens it laid on then. They knew it was evil and unChristian and that it deprived white women of the very ease it was supposed to provide them with. And though few of them have much to say about it, they also knew that white men loved black women, had children by them, and frequently treated their mulatto sons and daughters as well as their white ones. The hatred Southern women felt for slavery mingles with their hatred of slave women.

Mary Chesnut, the most extraordinary of all Southern ladies, would have found Ellen O'Hara unbelievably tiresome. Mary Chesnut was as great a lady as any to be found—a citified aristocrat who could have held her own with any English duchess of the day. The old South had an urban upper crust of predictably small size, perhaps three hundred families in all. This was the world where Mary Chesnut moved, and she understood the limitations it placed on women. But within the limits, Mary did as she pleased.

She was as different from the white angel as anyone could have been. For one thing, she hated the country and preferred the relative discomfort of a small townhouse in Charleston or Richmond to the spacious luxury of the Chesnut country home.

Whereas most women of her class were toiling many hours each day to keep their households running, Mary was truly at leisure: that was the appeal of town life. Whereas most women were bearing and rearing a dozen children each, she was childless. Whereas most women thought or said that black people were incompetent juveniles, she looked upon them as servants and was honest in her expectations that they should take care of her. Whereas most women kept their opinions, if any, to themselves, Mary had a shrewd political mind and—if only in her diary—said what she thought.

Crowded as her diary is with a thousand names and happenings, Mary could not let the subject of slavery alone. She took it as a personal affront. "I wonder if it be a sin to think slavery a curse to any land," she wrote in March 1861. She pitied black women but hated them, too. Most of all she hated white male hypocrisy and the casual bonds that white men made with black women.

"We live surrounded by prostitutes. An abandoned woman is sent out of any decent house. . . . God forgive us, but ours is a monstrous system, a wrong and an iniquity. . . . Like the patriarchs of old, our men live all in one house with their wives and their concubines; and the mulattoes one sees in every family exactly resemble the white children—and every lady tells you who is the father of all the mulatto children in everybody's household, but those in her own she seems to think drop from the clouds. . . ."

She spent a great deal of her time arguing, at a distance, with Harriet Beecher Stowe about *Uncle Tom's Cabin.* She knew Stowe was talking through her hat and she was particularly contemptuous that she missed "the sorest spot," which is the exploitation of black women by white men—at the emotional and material expense of white women. "Oh I knew half a Legree, a man said to be as cruel as Legree. But the other half of him did not correspond. He was a man of polished manners. And the best husband and father and member of the church in the world. . . . He was high and mighty. But the kindest creature to his slaves—and the unfortunate results of his bad ways were not sold, had not to jump over ice blocks. They were kept in full view, and were provided for handsomely in his will. His wife and daughters, in the might of their purity and innocence, are supposed never to dream of what is as plain . . . as the sunlight. . . ."

Mary Chesnut's rage is a cry of sexual as well as social desperation. How could white women compete with black ones? Slave women were readily available, obliged in the circumstances to keep silent, legally and possibly physically helpless against the white men who wanted them. And since the Southern lady, at least according to what her menfolk said of her, matched the Virgin Mary for reticence and purity, how willing a sexual partner could she be?

It is pointless to try to generalize about the sexual behavior of a whole class of women over a whole century. Who can know such secrets? But the Georgia novelist Lillian Smith, whose most famous work, *Strange Fruit,* published in 1944, was about a white man who took a lovely black woman as his mistress, truly believed that Southern white women had been forced into frigidity and that such female sexuality and tenderness as still survived in the South survived in the hearts and bodies of its black women. "The more trails the white man made to back yard cabins," wrote Smith in *Killers of the Dream* in 1949, "the higher he raised his white wife on her pedestal when he returned to the big house. The higher the pedestal, the less he enjoyed her whom he had put there, for statues after all are only nice things to look at."

Feminist historians these days like to blame the "patriarchy" for a whole spectrum of evils, from poverty to child abuse to warfare to defense spending. Men thought up these things, apparently, and keep them going, and so long as men are running the world, nothing will much improve. And yet women are superb collaborators, none more so than the good old-fashioned Southern lady.

In March 1865, Mary Chesnut wrote these words: "So we whimper and whine, do we? Always we speak in a deprecating voice, do we? . . . Does a man ever speak to his wife and children except to find fault? Does a woman ever address any remark to her husband that does not begin with an excuse? . . . Now if a man drinks too much and his wife shows that she sees it, what a storm she brings about her ears. She is disrespectful, unwifelike. Does she set up for strong-minded? So unwomanly—*so unlike his mother.* . . . And yet they say our voices are the softest, sweetest in the world."

Growing up in Arkansas, I had never heard of Mary or her diary and believed Ellen O'Hara to be "the truth." But in the end the idea of woman as collaborator was what I couldn't tolerate about the Southern mystique. One day, as an adult, I realized in horror that the little charade between the elevator man and me had been truly evil. Poor Crip had been broken for sure, and he needed to bend me to the same wheel. Uncle Tom must have his little Eva. Harriet Beecher Stowe was wiser than I thought. But unlike Crip, I had the choice of saying no.

And my mother, what of her refusal to have a maid when clearly she had one? Here were two women, with much in common, innocent as lambs concerning the potent forces of history that had placed each one where she was. Neither posed any sort of threat to the other. If Mother had dressed up and gone out six days a week or had simply sat around and let Emma do the dirty work, it would hardly have been a crime. That was what my father had intended to accomplish with his hard-earned ten dollars a week. Emma needed the ten dollars. She didn't mind hard work. But Mother wouldn't do it. Some querulous old voice from her Scotch-Irish past told her that if you enslave somebody, you do it at the expense of your own identity. The mistress is the slave of the slave. So she and Emma fished the sheets out of the washer and laughed as they pinned them on the line, ironed the shirts, and stewed the parsnips. Meanwhile, behind the rose trellis, I dressed paper dolls or harassed the dog or read romances. It was an edifying childhood. I hope my daughters will learn something half as useful from theirs.

The Confederate Myth

Frank E. Vandiver

Looking backward with fondness and nostalgia, the American South has succeeded in manufacturing an elaborate "Confederate Myth." It is the product of every person's appetite for historical romance. The Confederate Myth has been fed by a social psychology receptive to such patterns of thought, both North and South; it is here challenged by Frank E. Vandiver, former professor of history at Rice University and now president of Texas A&M University. Vandiver, a student of the southern mind and its mystique, systematically destroys, each in turn, the major pillars of the Confederate mythic edifice. Created in the antebellum period, nurtured during the War Between the States, and fashioned in "marble images" during the postwar era, the myth of the Confederacy, Vandiver claims, has withstood the test of time but has burdened the South with a "pseudo-past."

In the states of the old Confederacy the Centennial celebration of the Civil War is to be largely a refurbishing of the Confederate myth. The Confederate myth is a vital part of life in the South. According to this legend, sanctified southern ancestors fought valiantly against virtually hopeless odds to sustain a "way of life" peculiar to the section of long, hot summers, and Negro field hands. This "way of life" never seemed to be wholly understood, but it found description in various paeans of nostalgia and in the self-image of all southerners. Key elements in the southern mode of living were tradition, dedication to the protocols of lineage, land, cotton, sun, and vast hordes of blacks. Tending southern life were a special breed represented by the planters. Not everybody by any means was a planter, but the myth holds that everybody wanted to be and that all had the same chance to rise to that pinnacle of grace—all save the noncitizens with dark skin. The planters came to hoard their status with a certain grim zeal. Under increasing pressure throughout the 1830's, 40's, and 50's, they turned to all types of protection—censorship, intimidation, propaganda, open hostility to fellow-Americans.

But their tactics were glossed by myth into a creditable struggle for self-determination against a tide of urban nationalism which threatened extinction of the "way of life" so happy and so alien to the time.

The crusade of the planters spread to a campaign for Southern Rights, and hence the small farmer, the town merchant, the southern clergy found themselves sharing the planter's war. What was good for the planter was good for the South.

War, according to the myth, may not have been the only way to save the social and economic order, but it showed how deeply dedicated were the southerners to their inarticulated "rights." Against forces most formidable the southerner pitted himself, his small fortune, his Lilliputian industry, his life, and his girded honor. He lost, but lost magnificently. He lost wholly, utterly, but out of the ashes of his homes, his cities, his broken generation, he salvaged his sacred honor. And with this scrap of victory he could build the myth that has sustained him, has shackled him to a false image, and has convinced him of a lasting difference between himself and the rest of the United States.

Marshall Fishwick, in a brave and controversial essay, "Robert E. Lee: The Guardian Angel Myth" (*Saturday Review*, March 4, 1961), points out that Lee's noble virtues, peerless leadership, and heroic acceptance of defeat fixed in the southern mind the meaning of the Lost Cause. That cause represented the true acme of southern achievement; for with it died the flower of the South, and those who yielded up their blood were such southerners as all those who came since would like to be. They were the shining model, the marble image, the men above men who lived a brief moment as destiny's chosen. They were the South.

They still are the South, for they stand above, around, and beyond what the South now is, and loom as silent prophets to lesser men in troubled times. And so they are God and curse, inspiration and death. Their stone faces look from countless shafts to the past, and their sons, grandsons, and great-grandsons look with them. They are different from the present; they were alien to their time. So, too, the modern southerner who points to difference, to his ageless "white man's burden" and his genteel poverty. His ancestors lurking from musty picture frames stood against the leviathan state and its leveling tendencies. He, too, stands with his own perception of past obligations and future duties. If the rest of the nation has lost its agrarian innocence, the southerner remembers. He, at least, is faithful to a dim Jeffersonian image and to a Greek democracy ideal which came, was fleetingly touched by life and sustained by blood, and faded to the pantheon of lost glories. But the brief bloodbath lent a strange endurance and gave hope to generations held tight in inertia, fear, poverty, and the horror of a lost dream and a shattered mirror. The broken image had to be conjured again, and when it came it was twisted into a grotesque sort of plaster beauty which satisfied its designers and doomed the past it seemed to limn to a hundred years of distortion.

Distorting Civil War southerners was not easy. They lived larger than most, fought, raged, cowed, bled, spoke, and died with the nobility of desperation. They were, like their northern brethren, touched with timeless animation. They were unique and so should have been immune to the myth-makers and falsifiers of history. But myth-makers are determined and their works often approved by necessity. So the Confederate changed from a human, striving, erring being to something much different. All Confederates automatically became virtuous, all were defenders of the rights of states and individuals, all were segregationists, all steadfast, all patriotic.

Like all lasting myths, this one had enough validity to sound good. The Lost Cause came on to the present as the last American resistance against the Organization State, against racial indistinction, against mass and motor.

And while post–Civil War southerners were pushing as fast as they could into the New South, were grasping Yankee dollars with enthusiasm, they purified their motives in the well of Lost Causism. Politicians found it a bottomless source of bombast and ballots, preachers found it balm and solace to somewhat reluctant middle-class morals, writers found it a noble and salable theme. What the South had been could be the touchstone for the future, could be the fundament of a section going into the industrial age with part of its heart and holding firm to the past with the other.

Lost Causism came to fulfill a role similar to that of the pro-slavery argument in antebellum times. It offered justification for resistance to the leveling tendencies continued by harsh Reconstruction measures. It cloaked the lawless Klansman and lent license to the segregating Christian. It was, finally, the cornerstone of the New South.

The tragedy is that the Confederate myth is so wrong. That the Confederacy could come to represent in the present things it never represented in its lifetime is an irony of the present southern dilemma.

What, then, are some of the axioms of the Confederate myth?

First: The Confederate States represented the unified nationalistic yearning of all the states' rights advocates in the South.

Wrong. States' righters were not unified and there is considerable doubt that they were in the majority when the Confederacy took form in February, 1861. Certain it is that they failed to gain control of the government under Jefferson Davis, and although they did much to impede the Confederate war effort, they did not dominate the high councils.

Second: The Confederacy was defended to the last by gaunt gray heroes who went with Lee and Johnson and others to the bitterest end.

Wrong again. There was probably more per capita desertion from Confederate ranks than from the ranks of the Union. Far more Rebel troops were absent from roll call at the end of the war than were with the colors. Much bravery, even shining, incredible heroism the southern men did display, but that they were all blind patriots is demonstrably untrue.

Third: Any Confederate could lick ten Yankees.

Possibly, but in the end the Rebels were "overwhelmed."

Fourth: Everyone behind the Confederate lines showed the same dauntless dedication to oblivion as the soldiery. Men, women, and children all served the cause to the last shred of cloth, the last window weight, the last crust of bread.

Not so. While there were many magnificent examples of fate-defying loyalty by southern civilians, there were also many examples of petty speculation, wanton brigandage, Unionism, criminal selfishness, and treason. Defection behind the lines, open resistance to Confederate laws, became a matter of national scandal before the conflict ended.

Fifth: All Confederate leaders were unswervingly dedicated to the cause and would have preferred to perish rather than survive under a despised and crushing victor.

Still wrong. Many Confederate leaders, including Davis, Stephens, Lee, and Stonewall Jackson, looked on secession with a jaundiced eye. Legal they thought it to be, but they doubted its practicality. And when the war ended only a few of the leaders who survived buried themselves in the past. Davis did, and so did lasting disservice to the section he strove to defend. Lee, on the other hand, put the war behind him and worked unsparingly for a prosperous New South sharing fully the destiny of a re-United States. His example set the tone for most veterans. Numbers of former generals, to be sure, used their combat records to gain some personal advantage, but most wanted the advantage to further a career in business or politics and hence partook of the new industrial age.

Sixth: The Confederacy fought not only for states' rights, but also and especially to preserve racial integrity. The government and the people of the embattled southern states were solidly against letting down racial barriers and understood that a northern victory would mean abolition. The Negro was kept in his place in the Confederacy, was used only for agricultural and menial tasks, and what was good enough for the Confederates is good enough for us.

False, and this is false on two levels. During the war the South did attempt for a time to shore up the bonds of servitude, but when the pressure of defeat grew grim, various southern leaders, including Lee and Davis, came to advocate the use of slaves in the army; some even suggested freedom in return for service. And after the war, on the level of special pleading, the South engaged in a long paper conflict with northern historians about the causes of the fighting. A point which the southerners strove staunchly to sustain was that the war had not been fought to preserve slavery, but to preserve the "Southern Way of Life," of which slavery was only an aspect. Finally some argued that the war had been fought solely to gain independence, and cited the offer to England in March, 1865, of total freedom in exchange for recognition as proof.

Seventh: The Confederate government was a supreme, unsullied example of a states' rights organization that remained loyal to the principles of Calhoun, even in face of defeat.

This is the wrongest of all assumptions. Davis and his administration tried for a while to do what seemed constitutional under the narrow southern view of law, but war and a curiously unnoticed strain of mind in the South changed the course of governmental conduct.

Union sentiment, long-standing in many parts of the South, united with conservative Democratic sentiment and with latent Whiggery to introduce a new element in southern politics. Men who looked on violent change with repugnance banded together to prevent the secessionists from carrying the Confederacy to revolutionary excesses. These men, including Davis himself, kept the Montgomery Convention in hand, saw to it that the trend toward vast, ruinous upheaval was halted by moderate counsel. The result of moderate control at Montgomery was a Confederate constitution much like that of the Union, and a government based on established and familiar federal principles, and a president who had not camped with the fire-eaters. Many with these cautious views were elected to the various Confederate congresses and so held some authority through the war.

Caution and the natural conservatism of some Democrats and Whigs did not mean that these members of the Confederate Congress were unwilling to fight a hard war. Most of these southern moderates were men dedicated to strong central government as the main bulwark of law and order. They hated disturbance and resisted disruption of the Union. But when it came, they "went with their state," they stayed with family and land. They stayed, too, with principles of steady government, strong law, and established order. Consequently they stood for power in the hands of the executive, power in the federal government and a stern war effort.

It was these Whiggish moderates who came to represent the Confederate "left" and to urge big government to fight a big war. They knew something of the corporate state, saw that it had virtues for organization, and urged Davis and his cabinet to centralize and command. These neo-organization men supported the growth of a large army, strict taxation (in keeping with sound Whig monetary views), conscription, impressment of private property, and finally the use of Negro slaves in the ranks—even to the point of manumission in return for service. When the war ended, these same "leftists" of the Confederacy moved into the New South.

Many became leaders in new southern industries, some went into politics and supported the coming of northern capital, most stood for sound finances, restoration of order, and the onward march of business. These moderates, these quiet men who abhorred revolution but used it when they had to, were the ones who brought about the greatest revolution of the South. They changed the Confederacy right under the eyes of the rabid secessionists from a localistic community into a small industrial power run along centralized lines. They aroused resistance from the Confederate "right"—states' righters and fire-eaters—but kept control and forced their opponents to adopt modern centralist measures to resist them. When their attempt to remake the wartime South ended in defeat, they continued their efforts with the aid of Radical Republicans and ultimately achieved their goal. The Old South disappeared in the smoke of Chattanooga's and Birmingham's iron furnaces, in the dust of Alabama's coal pits, in the busy marts of Atlanta, Houston, Memphis, and New Orleans. These quiet, soft action men were the ones who set the base for the rise of a new industrial giant south of Mason and Dixon's Line, a giant whose future, according to Professor Walter Prescott Webb, is limitless because of its natural resources.

But in one salient respect these Whiggish gentlemen failed to remold their native section: this boundless potential painted by Webb and many chambers of commerce is sharply restricted by the Confederate myth. Although the moderate businessmen of the Confederate and New South were willing and partially able to set the black man free, and did break the bonds of southern agriculture, they could not unshackle the mind of the South—the Negro became a symbol of all troubles, and the Confederacy lingered as the herald of the South's greatness. The myth holds that the South was so great when it fought with piteous ardor for a twisted past and for principles aged and vestigial, that there was no future left for it. Its future lay buried with its gray dead.

This stultifying acceptance of decline is the wages of the Confederate myth. What was, was pure and better than what is, and in what was lies a sort of self-realization. While the South was transformed by Confederates into a moderately modern, progressive nation, the myth twists the achievement of the rebellious generation and dooms descendants to cheating themselves. Acceptance of the illusion of rabid Confederate racism, for instance, leads the modern Confederate to waste a vast source of manpower—a source which could be of inestimable value if the South is to move into the rosy future that some have predicted for it.

The Centennial years could best be devoted to revising the Confederate myth and bringing it up to date. Instead of standing for a pseudo-past, for false traditions and sham virtues, it should be repaired by the reality of perspective into what it has always been. Lee, Davis, members of the Confederate Congress, many soldiers who fell gallantly on scores of fields, were alert, forward-looking southerners. They were willing, for the sake of their cause, to abandon old shibboleths, to change the very nature of their body politic and body social. Instead of looking back and making war with weapons withered by age, they looked at the new ones their enemies used and copied, improved, progressed. The Confederate States of America did not have America in the name for nothing. Confederates were Americans, too, and so had no fear of challenge. The Rebels accepted challenge and also met it. Most of them surely would regard with scorn their descendants who look backward in frustration.

The Northern Origins of Southern Mythology

Patrick Gerster and Nicholas Cords

While many explanations for the rise of southern mythology have been offered—ranging from the South's physical landscape to the distorted passions aroused by sectionalism, race relations, and civil conflict—the subject of its northern origins has seldom been given more than passing attention. Indeed, a fairly complete canvassing of relevant historical literature on the question of southern mythology's northern origins discloses some rather interesting results. As argued by the editors of this volume, Patrick Gerster and Nicholas Cords, northerners such as Harriet Beecher Stowe, Stephen C. Foster, Daniel Decatur Emmett, Winslow Homer, Charles Francis Adams, Edgar Lee Masters, and F. Scott Fitzgerald all contributed to creating a romantic and mythical image of Dixie in the American consciousness. The South according to its own devices enjoyed sufficient materials and surely the imagination to shape fictitious mental constructs of its history and thereby fashion a usable past to which southerners could relate as if it were true. But, in addition, regions to the north of the Mason-Dixon line had an important hand in these legendary creations. The formulation and execution of southern mythology are clearly national as well as regional in character. Any view that continues to see the origins of southern legend as a strictly regional prerogative must overlook the attraction of southern mythology for northern artists and writers, the North's romantic fascination with aristocracy and lost causes, and the national appeal of the agrarian myth and the South's supposed personification of that ideal, as well as the persistent use of the South in the peregrinations of northern racial mythology. Southern mythology stands as testimony to the durable value of seeing the "southerner as American," even as it bears an indelible regional birthmark.

Though America long has been a haven for myth, the American South, more than any other region of the country, has taken hold of the nation's mythic imagination. In fact, it seems scarcely necessary to argue any longer the relevance of myth to the study of the southern past. Most have come to share David M. Potter's view that "southern history, more than most branches of historical study, seems to point up the anomalous relationships between the past, or our image or legend of the past, and the present, or our image of the

From the *Journal of Southern History*, 43 (November 1977), pp. 567–82. Copyright 1977 by the Southern Historical Association. Reprinted by permission of the Managing Editor, with minor editorial changes. Notes have been omitted.

present." It is therefore appropriate to ask, What are those historical factors which explain the penchant of southerners and "other Americans" for romance and myth in their view of southern history?

Particularly since George B. Tindall's seminal essay . . . "Mythology: A New Frontier in Southern History," various studies utilizing mythology as a focal point have offered new levels of insight into topics such as the southern lady, the plantation overseer, the Underground Railroad, the Lost Cause, and the New South creed. These, in conjunction with earlier published efforts, have informed us that southern mythology is the product of many forces. It seems possible to argue, for example, that a psychological frame of reference for myth was provided the South through the utopia-saturated age of its discovery, colonization, and settlement. Or perhaps, as Wilbur Cash has suggested, it was the South's physical landscape which helped to shape "a sort of cosmic conspiracy against reality in favor of romance." It is plausible as well that the growth of southern mythology is related to the passions aroused by sectionalism, race relations and civil conflict. And finally, one must not forget the role played by southern literature in transcribing and perpetuating the region's mythology.

While additional explanations for the rise of southern mythology have been offered, the subject of its northern origins and acceptance has seldom been given more than passing attention. Though widely noted, it has never been given the focused study it deserves. Perhaps because of a long-standing desire to discover a "central theme" for southern history, historians have not cultivated enough of a national perspective on the role the Yankee has played in both the original creation and the tenacious adherence to the South's legendary past. One recent review of a relatively new attempt to explain "The Myth of the Lost Cause," for example, offers the critique that it fails to "throw any new light on how a regional myth attracted such a national audience." Any fairly thorough canvassing of historical literature on the question of southern mythology's northern origins discloses some rather interesting results. Many students of the South have already seen this subject as a rich and worthy challenge for their talents, and their findings, collectively, deserve greater emphasis.

The South enjoyed sufficient sources and imagination to shape fictitious images of its history and thereby fashion a usable past to which southerners could relate as if it were true. But it is worth recalling with Henry Steele Commager that "the most familiar of southern symbols came from the North: Harriet Beecher Stowe of New England gave us Uncle Tom and Little Eva and Topsy and Eliza, while it was Stephen Foster of Pittsburgh who sentimentalized the Old South, and even 'Dixie' had northern origins." Indeed, the efforts of northern artists—literary, musical, and pictorial—have contributed substantially to the national credibility of southern mythology.

Connecticut Yankee Mrs. Stowe, for example, basing her impressions of the South on extremely limited firsthand experience, worked to implant the "faithful darky" (Sambo) image of blacks. She also graphically portrayed a stereotyped version of the plantation overseer, who, interestingly enough, uniquely symbolized the acquiescence of the North in southern myth by his Yankee origin: Simon Legree was a Vermonter. And in the process she obliquely gave vitality to the complementary images of semifeudal Cavaliers and virtuous belles. While these distorted characterizations no doubt contributed to the book's emotional appeal and phenomenal sales, they also contributed their share of myth to the nation's understanding of slave conditions in the Old South.

Three years after the appearance of Harriet Beecher Stowe's faithful old Tom, suffering Eliza, and sadistic Simon Legree, another northerner gave additional weight to the developing myth of southern antebellum luxury. In 1855 David Christy of Ohio published his book *Cotton Is King* and in the process touched off a great deal of discussion both in America and Europe about the industrial world's dependence upon the raw cotton of the South. The effect of the book was to obscure the realities of the South's diversified economy and create the impression that Dixie was an empire of plantations and slaveholders. Less than a decade later, the South itself came to rely much too heavily on the fetching idea of King Cotton in formulating its Civil War foreign policy. The literary efforts of Christy in the years before the conflict had helped to instill the idea nationally that the large cotton plantation, caressed by the fragrance of magnolia blossoms, was the principal habitat of the "typical" southerner.

Stephen C. Foster reinforced synthetic southern stereotypes in "Susanna" (1847) and "Old Folks at Home" (1851), composed prior to a one-month excursion into the South in 1852, after which he published "Massa's in de Cold Ground" (1852), "My Old Kentucky Home" (1852), and "Old Black Joe" (1860). These songs, as one scholar has suggested, "nostalgically describe a 'longing for the old plantation'" and along with the novels of John Pendleton Kennedy and William Alexander Caruthers helped to fix the "Plantation Illusion" in the American mind. For decades they continued to feed the nation's romantic imagination trite and charming renditions of antebellum splendor.

Another fact about Foster's myth-building concerns one of the tourist showplaces of Kentucky—Federal Hill near Bardstown—where the composer purportedly wrote "My Old Kentucky Home." Local Kentuckians' efforts to feed the nation's nostalgic taste for the Old South notwithstanding, no evidence exists that Foster ever visited the estate, much less that he wrote his famous song there. According to a letter of Stephen's brother, Morrison Foster, "lyrics and songs including 'My Old Kentucky Home' were composed at Stephen's home in Allegheny County, Pennsylvania." Undeniably, his plantation songs and the notoriety they have received through the efforts of Bardstown residents have had a legend-creating impact on the popular mind of both the North and South as they offer succeeding generations easily evoked versions of an ideal life in the sunny South before the war.

Even considering the influence of Harriet Beecher Stowe, David Christy, and Stephen C. Foster, however, perhaps nothing has captured the flavor of southernism with greater emotional impact than the song "Dixie." Symbolic of the southern way of life, it was written in New York City by an Ohioan,

Daniel Decatur Emmett, in 1859. Though used as a marching tune by both Union and Confederate forces during the Civil War, it soon became the unofficial national anthem of the South and has remained one of the most important sentimental expressions of southern regional feeling ever since. As Jefferson Davis and Alexander H. Stephens assumed the leadership of the Confederate States of America, the Emmett-inspired romance had already begun to work its magic. Clement Eaton has described the scene in this fashion: "On February 18, 1861, they were inaugurated in the state capitol at Montgomery, and at the ceremonies a band played the new song 'Dixie,' with its pervading nostalgia. Like the cradles, coffins, patent medicines, tall silk hats, plow—indeed, most manufactured articles used in the South—the song that was destined to become the unofficial anthem of the Confederacy was also an import from the Yankees. . . ."

For succeeding generations the pervading nostalgia of "Dixie" has carried an emotional impact described by the northern novelist F. Scott Fitzgerald in "The Ice Palace" (1920). On a visit to the North, Fitzgerald's heroine, the Georgia belle Sally Carrol Happer, attends a vaudeville performance which concludes with the playing of "Dixie." Fitzgerald describes her as immediately responding to its strong and enduring strains. "To the spirited throb of the violins and the inspiring beat of the kettledrums her own ghosts were marching by and on into the darkness, and as fifes whistled and sighed in the low encore they seemed so nearly out of sight that she could have waved good-by."

The efforts of northern artists to romanticize the South are of course not limited to Stowe, Christy, Foster, and Emmett. Francis Pendleton Gaines reveals that northern drama and northern minstrelsy, as well as northern paintings of the South such as Eastman Johnson's *My Old Kentucky Home* (1859) and Winslow Homer's *Sunday Morning in Virginia* (ca. 1870), gave important consideration to mythical plantation materials. William R. Taylor argues that it was the literary energies of the North as well as the South, the work of James Kirke Paulding of New York, for example, that seeded the fictional southern plantation in literature. And not to be forgotten are the numerous sentimental lithographs of Nathaniel Currier of Roxbury, Massachusetts, and James Merritt Ives of New York City, which offered a national audience unblemished images of Americana, both North and South. Collectively, northern works of art from Stowe and Foster to Currier and Ives did much to effect a national unity of emotion and belief concerning southern history whose verisimilitude was seldom examined by their avid audience. Their creations evoked southern images which were sometimes at odds with fact but of critical importance, nonetheless, to the development of a nationally created regional mythology.

But the questions remain: Why did the North find the myths of the Old South so very comfortable and comforting? What caused this fusion of southern and northern sentiment? How was it that so many northerners were so distinctly of the southern persuasion? Francis Pendleton Gaines was perhaps the first historian to address himself to these questions in a systematic way and to explain the process whereby the South and the North became copartners in the creation of a pseudo-past—what the poet Stephen Vincent Benét called "the sick magnolias of the false romance." A form of mythical reciprocity evolved, says Gaines, in that "two opposing sides of the fiercest controversy that ever shook national thought agreed concerning certain picturesque elements of plantation life and joined hands to set the conception unforgettably in public consciousness." In attempting to explain further this sectional compromise which allowed southern mythmakers to forge an entente with the North, Gaines cited America's latent "love of feudalism" and a "romantic hunger" for "some allegory of aristocracy." The southern plantation, Gaines concludes, "alone among native institutions, satisfies this craving for a system of caste." While a titled aristocracy had long since been declared at odds with the American Creed, the idea of an American aristocracy has never lost its fascination. The Yankee, despite his stated though often superficial differences, liked to fancy himself a Cavalier at heart.

The testimony of the Swedish sociologist Gunnar Myrdal, in his classic study *An American Dilemma* (1944), adds further evidence to the thesis that northern support for southern mythology was a result of "Yankee class romanticism." Noting that the nation has long had a severely distorted mythology about the rank and privilege of European aristocrats, Myrdal maintains that the North was led to fantasize when it came to understanding the "aristocracy" which they thought they knew best—that of the antebellum South. Myrdal could thus explain why southern mythmakers found ready allies in the North for their notions of caste and class: "The North has so few vestiges of feudalism and aristocracy of its own that, even though it dislikes them fundamentally and is happy not to have them, Yankees are thrilled by them. Northerners apparently cherish the idea of having had an aristocracy and of still having a real class society—in the South. So it manufactures the myth of the 'Old South' or has it manufactured by Southern writers working for the Northern market." Myrdal's point must be understood to be that it was not only "Southern writers working for the Northern market" who portrayed an essentially legendary South, but northern writers joining hands with their southern brethren in allowing myth to parade as history. In line with the earlier findings of Gaines, Myrdal sees that northern regional disaffection and subliminal cravings for the imagined benefits of aristocracy made the province of southern myth a dual domain.

A similar argument about the sustained vitality of the plantation legend in the North has ben offered by William R. Taylor. The acceptance of the southern legend among Yankees, claims Taylor, relates to the "age of anxiety," the decade of the 1830s. The so-called Age of the Common Man, based as it was on the ideas of participatory democracy and egalitarianism—though in some ways more imaginary than real—proved threatening to those who wished to salvage remnants of their status which they perceived to be endangered. This crosscurrent of antidemocratic sentiment, says Taylor, produced a "hankering after aristocracy in the North [which] took the form of eulogizing the social system of the South." In short, the social structure of the South came to symbolize for many northerners—James Fenimore Cooper, for example—an important counterpoint, an enviable brand of social stability, when crisis, flux, and anxiety were the order of the day on northern fronts. The strictures and standards of an older order were under fire—or were thought to be—as the nation sought to sustain former republican virtues while also seeking to accommodate itself to far-reaching social and economic change.

Confronted with ambivalence and contradiction growing out of swift change and the social mobility of a new class of expectant capitalists, the North displayed a flirtatious attitude toward stable mythical images then emerging in the South. Many northerners began to cast their eyes southward because it appeared that an Old World aristocracy there had somehow discovered a way of assuring stability and cultivating a sense of gentility and decorum while maintaining a commitment to the public good under a republican form of government. As northern politicians, writers, and social critics attempted to come to terms with the variant and elusive aspects of Jacksonian democracy, conditions precipitated a social imagination in the North conducive to the emergence of a mythmaking frame of mind. And since southerners had already begun to stabilize their own social system through mythology, it was to them that the North turned for guidance and inspiration. C. Vann Woodward has recently summarized this point. The northern zest for southern myth, he observes, owes much to the North's "compensatory dream of aristocracy, the airs of grace and decorum left behind, secretly yearned for but never realized."

According to Wilbur J. Cash, the North's passion for the myth of the Old South was indeed fed by the "imaginary glory" of a mythical aristocracy, but it was also being stirred by a pristine nostalgia for a "purely agricultural past" which the South had come flawlessly to symbolize during the antebellum age. In the Age of Jackson the country was in many ways enamored of the promise of an urbanized and industrialized America, but the United States, according to Richard Hofstadter, had been "born in the country" before it "moved to the city." It was thus being drawn by a memory of things past to the imagined glory of its agricultural beginnings and was continuing to view the tillers of the soil as both ideal men and ideal citizens. Accordingly, as the antebellum North seemed to be moving ideologically further and further away from the nation's agricultural origins, the South had taken its stand with the solid values of agrarianism. In the words of Cash, the North "was not only ready but eager to believe in the Southern legend . . . it fell with a certain distinct gladness on this last purely agricultural land of the West as a sort of projection ground for its own dreams of a vanished golden time." As America came to cherish the notion that agriculture was the most basic of industries and the agriculturist the most virtuous of men, both the North and the South could mutually agree to the plantation legend because of their mutual admiration for the agrarian myth.

While the efforts of artists and a fixation with both aristocracy and the agrarian myth were important contributors to the ready acceptance of Old South mythology, the North seems also to have conspired in southern mythmaking because of its guilt over slavery and its repressed attitudes on race relations. Though it is fairly clear that the South came to defend its "peculiar institution" for reasons of guilt and political survival, it is too easily forgotten that many northerners more than indirectly supported the plantation legend by assuming a posture *opposed* to slavery. C. Vann Woodward has explained that "the North . . . had deeply felt needs of its own to be served by an antislavery myth, needs that were sufficient at all times to keep the legend vital and growing to meet altered demands."

As layers of fantasy and romance came to cloud the historical reality of the northern position on the slavery issue before the Civil War, the revered notion that racial inhumanity was a condition to be found only in the prewar South became a northern exercise in atonement for its own social guilt. Woodward states, "The South has long served the nation in ways still in great demand. It has been a moral lightning rod, a deflector of national guilt, a scapegoat for stricken conscience. It has served the country much as the Negro has served the white supremacist—as a floor under self-esteem." The resultant idea that the Mason-Dixon line divided slavery from freedom in antebellum America was, of course, a historical lie, but "it sprang from . . . [the abolitionists'] laudable impulse to be identified with noble deeds." The antislavery myth did not square with the latent commitment to white supremacy which was a national, not simply a regional, credo. In addition, it fit badly with the subtle forms of de facto segregation encouraging discrimination against northern blacks, and with later forms of social control and subordination when the South after Reconstruction "resorted to many of the devices originally developed in the North to keep the Negro in his 'place.' " Only to the degree to which the South could be seen as morally inferior could the North establish its claim to moral superiority. The major props of the myths of antebellum southern society, at least as they related to the question of slavery, demanded political and psychological efforts national in scope. Woodward wryly concludes, "As yet . . . the Yankee remains to be fully emancipated from his own legends of emancipation. Confront him with a given set of symbols and he will set his sense of humor aside, snap to attention and come to a full salute. In the ensuing rigidities of that situation, conversation tends to lag."

The practical impact of this kind of duplicity, of course, was that one brand of mythology energized another. By endorsing the traditional picture of plantation life, northerners were able to hide their own mistreatment of the black man behind the facade of an "antislavery myth." By creating the impression that all Negroes would at last be free if only the institutions and traditions of the South were changed, the North would not have to face up to its own forms of racial inhumanity. The revered notion that race prejudice was a condition to be found exclusively in the prewar South allowed the North to escape its social guilt over the continued existence of discrimination. At its grossest extreme it allowed even some abolitionist organizations to rationalize the exclusion of Negroes. The northern endorsement of the plantation legend in a backhanded way, then, helped support the myth that ideas of white supremacy were to be found only in the Cotton Kingdom. In this way the North found southern mythology useful as a means of stabilizing and perpetuating its own racial mythology well beyond antebellum days. One scholar has concluded that the American South "is a distillation of those traits which are the worst (and a few which are the best) in the national character. . . . And the nation reacts emotionally to the South precisely because it subconsciously recognizes itself there."

The North's racial attitudes seem also to have been a force leading to that region's complicity in the creation of "the tragic legend of Reconstruction." Kenneth M. Stampp has argued that the North functioned as a co-conspirator in the developing mythology of the South following the Civil War:

> Southerners, of course, have contributed much to the legend of Reconstruction, but most northerners have found the legend quite acceptable. Many of the historians who helped to create it were northerners, among them James Ford Rhodes, William A. Dunning, Claude Bowers, and James G. Randall. Thus the legend cannot be explained simply in terms of a southern literary or historiographical conspiracy, satisfying as the legend has been to most white southerners. What we need to know is why it also satisfies northerners—how it became part of the intellectual baggage of so many northern historians. Why, in short, was there for so many years a kind of national, or inter-sectional, consensus that the Civil War was America's glory and reconstruction her disgrace?

Having posed the question of northern involvement in Reconstruction's "tragic legend" and mythology, Stampp demonstrates that feelings of accommodation affected modifications of wartime passions. "Northerners were willing to concede that southerners had fought bravely for a cause that they believed to be just," says Stampp; and "both northerners and southerners agreed that the preservation of the federal Union was essential to the future power of the American people." In even more important ways, however, both North and South could judge Reconstruction to be a "horrid nightmare." Latent and basic racial antipathy toward enfranchised blacks began to find expression after the demise of the Radical Republicans as a reforming force. And outside of Congress changes were occurring which would have the same effect. Northern writers were becoming increasingly "indifferent" to the problems of the freedman, the country began to meet the "threat" of the new immigration with the construction of racial stereotypes, and social scientists supplied national racist thinking with an academic rationale supportive of its prejudiced position. As a result, Stampp concludes, "the old middle classes of the North looked with new understanding upon the problems of the beleaguered white men of the South." Just as it had developed the antislavery myth of the antebellum era, the North found it both emotionally and practically convenient after the War for the Union to subscribe for racial reasons to the legend that Reconstruction had been a "tragic era" and a "dreadful decade."

Along with the myths of Reconstruction, the various myths of the Old South continued to enjoy both emotional and strategic appeal in the North after the War for Southern Independence. Indeed, this was true even for those who in other ways saw through the nation's shams and illusions. Particularly during the period that Mark Twain critically labeled the "Gilded Age"—when the smell of scandal and corruption reeked from government offices and the boardrooms of industrial corporations—some northern writers began to argue that the social, political, and economic system of the Old South had been in many ways better than the allegedly golden age they saw before them. Thus, in the process of criticizing the shortcomings of Yankee civilization in the 1870s and 1880s, northern writers such as Herman Melville, Henry James, and Henry Adams sought to compare the progress and optimism of the early South with the stagnation and despair of America's "age of excess." The antebellum South, it seemed, had been neither as hypocritical about equality nor as materialistic as the America of Ulysses Simpson Grant, Jay Gould, and "Boss" William Marcy Tweed.

The shortcomings of American Yankee culture in the declining years of the nineteenth century seemed all the more obvious when measured against the seemingly vibrant and charming days when things were different in the South. Post–Civil War America seemed somehow much more vulgar and vain than the South of the Old Regime. The South's long-standing commitments to family, leisured living, honorable conduct, and chivalry seemed to be precisely the values and virtues which America most lacked. In the words of the transplanted southerner Basil Ransom, the leading character of Henry James's novel *The Bostonians* (1886), the "gilded age" which the North had pasted together after the Civil War was "a nervous, hysterical, chattering, canting age, an age of hollow phrases and false delicacy." Though James later admitted to knowing "terribly little" of the kind of life he had attempted to describe, or of the supposed superiority of the South which he offered as an alternative, he felt comfortable in suggesting that the South's heroic age had much to commend it. Now that slavery had been purged from the southern utopia, one could more easily imagine, through a hindsight conditioned by illusion, that the South of an earlier day had been something very close to the most perfect society America had yet produced. For this reason the North's developing alliance with the South in the creative enterprise of southern mythology worked to unite the sections; for "to the North it offered a way in which to apologize without sacrificing the fruits of victory." Together with forces already at work in Dixie, supporting a legendary view of the southern past, the result could only be "a national love feast for the Old South." The kinship which had eluded the sections through the Civil War period was to be more successfully achieved by means of mythology. On this level they could well communicate, for they were Americans and mythmakers all. They could join hands in a post-war setting for a mutual reacceptance of a southern mythology which had been born decades before, had survived the war years, and was only now at the point of maturing.

In this spirit Henry Adams symbolically suggested the northern fixation for a mythical South in his *Education* (1918). Therein he describes how before the Civil War he (a Boston Yankee) had been a classmate of William Henry Fitzhugh "Roony" Lee at Harvard. In a retrospective on his experiences and his exposure to the symbolic South, Adams writes: "For the first time Adams's education brought him in contact with new types and taught him their values. He saw the New England type measure itself with another, and he was part of the process. . . . This momentary contact with Southern character was a sort of education for its own sake. . . ." Adams's feelings of affinity for the South, personified in his dealings with the son of Robert E. Lee, implied a common ground developing between the regions which would eventually help to effect a concert of interests between the sections.

As the future became the past and southern mythology moved from a nineteenth- to a twentieth-century phenomenon, the North continued to sustain distorted perceptions of the South. The mirage for some continued in the manner of the old romantic school. Thomas Dixon, Jr.'s *The Leopard's Spots*, for example, fed northern audiences his mythical version of Reconstruction history from a New York stage in 1903. Not only did Broadway accept his version of the southern past, but the production was the hit of the theatrical season. Twelve years later David Wark Griffith's cinema classic, *The Birth of a Nation* (1915), adapted Dixon's novel *The Clansman* for the nation's fastest-developing new medium and in the process synthesized the images of the Old South and Reconstruction in "epic" proportions for national consumption. The formidable combination of Dixon's bigotry, Griffith's emotional memories, and the nation's already well developed appetite for the legendary South assured the film monetary success. In this instance at least, as Gunnar Myrdal observed, southerners had discovered the salability of southern mythology in the northern market.

The North's attention to the heroic character of the South also found interesting expression early in the twentieth century through the efforts of a northern-dominated cult of Robert E. Lee. In 1900 General Lee was elected by a nationwide board of electors to the American Hall of Fame. Although he received only 68 votes to General Grant's 93, it was nonetheless a clear prelude to his national canonization. In the succeeding years a northerner, Charles Francis Adams, Jr., became the nation's foremost spokesman in defense of Lee's nobility. Addressing the American Antiquarian Society in 1901 on the topic of "Lee at Appomattox," Adams did his part to assure the acceptance of an entirely positive image for the Confederate leader in northern minds. A high-water mark in Lee's rise from mortal man to an ethereal and heroic ideal, however, came in January 1907 when Adams delivered the Lee Centennial Address at Washington and Lee University. Adams's efforts, in the opinion of one historian, represented the acceptance of Lee as a national symbol and marked "a transition which almost entailed his capture from the South." In the view of the scholar of American heroes, Dixon Wecter, this new stage of Lee hero worship proved "the age of big business felt . . . that it could use a great gentleman in its national pantheon, like a buffalo in a museum of vanishing Americana." The exaggeration and distortion which led to Robert E. Lee's apotheosis may have peaked with the publication in 1926 of Edgar Lee Masters's massive effort, "Lee: A Dramatic Poem." Even as this Chicago lawyer-turned-poet was adding his dash of drama to the burgeoning Lee legend, however, the good general was already suffering the kind of inflation which haunts the memory of most men of historical importance.

Americans of the 1920s were also exposed to a sympathetic treatment of the imagined glory of the Old South through the literary efforts of Minnesota-born F. Scott Fitzgerald. His southern sensibilities seem to have been garnered in the first place from his father, Edward Fitzgerald, a descendant of old and aristocratic Maryland families, the Scotts and the Keys. "He . . . came from another America," Fitzgerald noted on the occasion of his father's death. Indeed, the elder Fitzgerald "instilled in his son not only beautiful manners, but a sense of honor, an almost eighteenth-century code of decorum. . . . And it was from his father that he 'acquired an extended and showy, if very superficial, knowledge of the Civil War (with an intense southern bias . . .).' It is not surprising, then, to discover that his son saw in that conflict the 'broken link in the continuity of American life.' " Given Fitzgerald's personal testimony, it seems clear that the northern writer firmly believed in the synthetic stereotypes of Cavalier and Yankee and was also willing to accept other features of the Plantation Legend—such as the Southern Belle.

Fitzgerald's romantic attachment to the legendary South was of course stimulated by his personal relationship with Zelda Sayre of Montgomery. She was, in his fanciful imagination at least, "the last of the belles." In her he seems to have found a kindred spirit, as captivated as he with dreams of aristocratic grandeur. Nancy Milford quotes Edmund Wilson to the effect that "if ever there was a pair whose fantasies matched . . . it was Zelda Sayre and Scott Fitzgerald." It was through her, then, that Fitzgerald, in stories such as "The Ice Palace" (1920), drew the nation's attention to what he called the "strange courtliness and chivalry" of "the most beautiful thing in the world—the dead South." Though the setting for the short story is the 1920s, the characters reflect historic sentiments drawn from an earlier day. Neither the Southern Lady nor the Sunny South had changed, apparently, since the golden and legendary days of the Old Regime. His heroine, Sally Carrol, is one of those "gracious, soft-voiced girls, who were brought up on memories instead of money." And the background for her romantic intrigues are "lazy cotton-fields, where even the workers seemed intangible shadows lent by the sun to the earth, not for toil, but to while away some age-old tradition in the golden September fields. And round the drowsy picturesqueness, over the trees and shacks, and muddy rivers, flowed the heat, never hostile, only comforting, like a great warm nourishing bosom for the infant earth." In his personal affairs and in his fiction—in many ways inseparable—Fitzgerald subscribed to the myth of the Old South. The myth-conditioned South provided him both artistic inspiration and an idyllic mental sanctuary.

It was left to a southerner, however, a contemporary of Fitzgerald's, to most directly capture the flavor of the emotional and strategic appeal which the various myths of the South have had for the North. Nobel laureate William Faulkner, through his character Gavin Stevens in *Intruder in the Dust* (1948), points succinctly to the manner in which northerners have been willing captives of a developing southern mythology. The North, Stevens declares, has displayed a "gullibility: a volitionless, almost helpless capacity and eagerness to believe anything about the South not even provided it be derogatory but merely bizarre enough and strange enough."

The strange career of southern mythology, not unlike that of Jim Crow, saw Dixie "look away" to tap important reservoirs of precedent and support in the nation at large. It would be a mythology forged in the spirit of union, an "all-American" effort to be sure. David M. Potter was surely speaking with measured understatement and pointing only to the most obvious evidence of the South's success at capturing the imagination of its northern neighbor when he observed, "Today, the predilection of Yankee children for caps, flags, and toys displaying the Rebel insignia bears further witness to the enduring truth that lost causes have a fascination even for those who did not lose them. Indeed, it is important to notice that the myths of the South—Old and New— were cultivated by those—North and South—who never owned a slave or planted an acre of cotton. We have heard much of the importance of seeing the "southerner as American"; perhaps we should hear more of the many ways in which "the American" has been distinctly of the southern persuasion, especially when it comes to mythology. For any view which continues to see the creation and perpetuation of southern legend as a regional prerogative would be forced to ignore the attention of northern artists to southern mythology, the North's fascination with aristocracy and lost causes, the national appeal of the agrarian myth, and the South's personification of that ideal, to say nothing of the persistent use of the South in the manipulation of northern racial mythology. All this considered, one trusts that the North and the South will continue to explore the new frontiers of mythology with the same spirit of union they have displayed in the past.

VI

Myths of the Civil War and Reconstruction

A great literature will yet arise out of the era of those four [Civil War] years, those scenes—era compressing centuries of native passion, first-class pictures, tempests of life and death—an inexhaustible mine for the histories, drama, romance, and even philosophy, of peoples to come—indeed the verteber of poetry and art (of personal character too) for all future America—far more grand, in my opinion, to the hands capable of it, than Homer's siege of Troy, or the French wars to Shakespeare.
Walt Whitman *(1879)*

There they are, cutting each other's throats, because one half of them prefer hiring their servants for life, and the other by the hour.
Thomas Carlyle

David M. Potter,
"The Causes of the Civil War"

Richard Hofstadter,
**"Abraham Lincoln and the
Self-made Myth"**

Allan Nevins,
"The Glorious and the Terrible"

Stephen B. Oates,
**"Abraham Lincoln:
The Man Behind the Myths"**

Eric Foner,
"The New View of Reconstruction"

Thomas C. Cochran,
**"Did the Civil War Retard
Industrialization?"**

Richard White,
**"The Winning of the West:
The Expansion of the Western Sioux"**

The Glorious: John A. Logan in action. [Virginia State Library and Archives.]

The Terrible: Union dead after Gettysburg. [Reproduced from the collections of the Library of Congress.]

*T*oday the Civil War remains central to America's historical experience. For many Americans, the War Between the States represents the greatest single event in their history. From the epic struggle emerges a gallery of heroic figures and memorable episodes— Lincoln and Lee, Shiloh and Gettysburg. "The War" enjoys the status of an American *Iliad*. As novelist and poet Robert Penn Warren suggests, the Civil War marked America's "Homeric Age." To Warren, the War Between the States quickly became the great synthesis of the American experience and the inexhaustible reservoir of American symbol and myth:

> *From the first, Americans had a strong tendency to think of their land as the Galahad among nations, and the Civil War, with its happy marriage of victory and virtue, has converted this tendency into an article of faith nearly as sacrosanct as the Declaration of Independence.*

As Warren implies, ideas concerning the past often combine with emotion. Because of this, time, which is supposed to bring detachment and objectivity to one's historical understanding, very often has the opposite effect. The American Civil War proves an interesting case in point. Images of either the heroic (the war itself) or the tragic (the period of Reconstruction that followed) have supplanted a proportioned view. Civil War and Reconstruction history has been an exceptionally fertile breeding ground for distortion and myth.

Recognizing what people think happened as against what actually happened—the discrepancy between history as perceived and history as actuality—is particularly significant, then, in our historical judgments concerning the war and its aftermath. A proper view of our "Homeric Age" requires that the American penchant for overemphasizing both the heroic and the tragic elements of history be challenged. A proper understanding of the era of the Civil War must yield much more than the pageantry and legend of the martyred and the Christ-like Lee. It must supply more than the tragic legend of the war's aftermath. One can begin to appreciate the entire era in its proper historical perspective only by noting the war's multiple causes, the complexity of Lincoln both as politician and as cultural hero, the conflict in both its glorious and its terrible aspects, Reconstruction's importance to the course of American race relations, the war's importance to American industrial development, and the encounter between the Plains Indians and white America. In the end, the Civil War and its heritage can indeed remain central to our national historical experience, but for reasons other than those we might previously have imagined.

The Causes of the Civil War

David M. Potter

In what he describes as a "historiographical foray," David Potter, late Coe Professor of History at Stanford University, describes the dimensions of historical research into the causes of the Civil War. Clearly reflecting the span of his academic experience, Potter speaks to both the causes of the Civil War *per se* and those topics that bear directly on the growing sectionalism between North and South. Following a discussion of the "revisionists" and the counterattack that has been directed against their views, Potter concludes by redefining the question in terms of the problem of race—indeed the fulcrum on which the delicate balance of the sections rested.

The last three decades have witnessed considerable advances in the historical understanding of many of the developments which preceded the Civil War, but it can hardly be said that they have brought us visibly closer to the point at which a jury of historians seems likely to arrive at a verdict which will settle the controversy as to causes. Indeed some of the most fundamental issues in the controversy, namely those turning upon the significance of the slavery question, have been reactivated and seem now to have given new dimensions to the whole dispute.

By 1940, the literature on the Civil War had already been accumulating for eighty years. During these eight decades, interpretation of the war had passed through three major phases. First, during the immediate postwar era, there had been a literature by participants and partisans, designed to justify their own course of conduct and therefore striving either to vindicate or indict. Both sides had appealed to absolute values: if they were partisans of the Union, they had explained the war in terms of slavery and disunion, appealing to the moral absolutes of human freedom and national unity; if they were partisans of the South, they had explained it in terms of the secession issue, appealing to the legal absolute inherent in the theory of state sovereignty and to the moral absolute of the right of self-government.

Second, in the period after the wounds of war began to heal, there had been a nationalistic interpretation, well exemplified in the seven-volume history by James Ford Rhodes (1893–1906), which avoided the attribution of blame and emphasized the sincerity and high motive of both the Blue and the Gray. Rhodes himself argued unequivocally that slavery was the cause of the war, but he held the nation rather than the South responsible for slavery, and if he blamed the South for secession, he blamed the North for Reconstruction. In such an interpretation the concept of an inevitable or "irrepressible" conflict fitted well, for if the war could not possibly have been prevented, then no one could be blamed for failing to prevent it, and thus no one was guilty. Charles Francis Adams pushed this view to its logical limit in 1902 by declaring that "Everybody, in short, was right; no one wrong."

Third, in the 1920's, after ideas of economic determinism began to prevail widely in American intellectual circles, Charles and Mary Beard had published an immensely influential interpretation of the war in their *The Rise of American Civilization* (1927). Seeing the great contests of history as struggles for power, rather than for principle, and regarding moral and legal arguments as mere rationalizations, the Beards had denied that the South really cared about states' rights or the North about slavery. The South had simply used states' rights as a tactical device in defending a minority position. The Republicans had simply used the slavery issue to turn public opinion against the South, but in fact the Republicans had not been abolitionists and had done nothing to help the slaves, but had sought only to "contain" the power of the slaveholders by excluding them from the new territories. The war, therefore, had not been a contest over principles but a struggle for power—a clash of economic sections in which freedom did not necessarily combat slavery but industrialism most assuredly combated the planter interests.

These three were, in brief, the major interpretations which had held sway up to 1940. Since 1940, the major tendencies have been : (1) the development of a so-called "revisionist" interpretation which minimized the importance of slavery or any other fundamental factor as a cause of the war and also argued that the war could have been and should have been averted; (2) a counterattack upon the revisionists by writers who reassert the causative importance of the slavery question; and (3) a shifting of the question away from a sharp focus upon the "causes" of the hostilities as such, together with a more generalized concern with the relation between the war and the pattern of race relations in the United States.

The Revisionists

Although sometimes mentioned as if they were a "school," the so-called revisionists have in fact been a number of distinctively independent scholars, working separately, disagreeing on occasion, and united only by their skepticism about the role of slavery as the heart of the sectional issue and by their doubt that the conflict was irrepressible.

These doubts are as old as the war itself, but modern revisionism possibly begins with Albert J. Beveridge, Republican Senator from Indiana and biographer of John Marshall. About 1920, Beveridge set out to write a biography of Lincoln. He approached this undertaking with the traditional Republican reverence for an almost superhuman being—the inevitable protagonist of the antislavery drama in which there had to be an antagonist or villain, and in which Stephen A. Douglas was inevitably stereotyped for the latter role. But when Beveridge began his research, he found the facts far more complex than the tradition, and when he came to the Lincoln-Douglas debates, he concluded that Douglas had acted with integrity and had represented a very respectable point of view—namely that the question of slavery in the territories was a fictitious issue, not worth a crisis which would endanger the nation. Because the abolitionists had "agitated" this issue in such a way as to precipitate the crisis, Beveridge formed an unfavorable opinion of them and began to think that, without them, there might have been no war—indeed that slavery might in time have disappeared peaceably under the pressure of economic forces.

In 1927, Beveridge died. His life of Lincoln, published in the following year, had been completed only to the year 1858, and we can never know what broad, overall interpretation he would have advanced. But certain of the ideas which he had foreshadowed continued to develop in the decade of the thirties. In 1933, Gilbert H. Barnes published an account of the early abolitionist movement (*The Anti-Slavery Impulse, 1830–1844*) in which he emphasized the neglected figure of Theodore Dwight Weld, and de-emphasized the importance of William Lloyd Garrison, at the same time condemning the fanaticism of the abolitionists in general. During the same year, Gerald W. Johnson of the Baltimore *Sun* published a small interpretive volume on *The Secession of the Southern States*, which stated brilliantly the argument that dogmatic, rigid adherence to "principle" on the part of both antislavery zealots like Charles Sumner of Massachusetts and doctrinaire legalists like John C. Calhoun of South Carolina had caused an unnecessary war in which "everybody was wrong and no one was right." Johnson's little book has been neglected, perhaps because he was not a professional historian, but it remains to this day one of the most vigorous and effective statements of a major thesis of revisionism. In 1934, George Fort Milton, editor of the Chattanooga *News*, brought out a full-scale biography of Douglas, based on extensive new manuscripts and bearing the significant title *The Eve of Conflict: Stephen A. Douglas and the Needless War.* Like Beveridge, Milton considered Douglas statesmanlike in his effort to play down the territorial issue, and believed that unwise political leadership was responsible for the war.

After these preliminaries, the full tide of the revisionist reaction struck in the late thirties and early forties, primarily as the result of the work of two men—James G. Randall and Avery O. Craven—advancing independently along somewhat parallel lines.

Craven first enunciated his views clearly in an article, "Coming of the War Between the States: An Interpretation," in 1936. He followed this with a brief interpretive volume, *The Repressible Conflict,* in 1939, and with a full-scale history of the years from 1830 to 1861 in *The Coming of the Civil War* in 1942. Since then he has continued to develop and to modify his ideas in a number of writings, including notably a volume in the History of the South series, *The Growth of Southern Nationalism, 1848–1861* (1953), a set of interpretive lectures, *Civil War in the Making, 1815–1860* (1959), and a volume of essays, *An Historian and the Civil War* (1964).

Perhaps the crucial feature of Craven's interpretation is his belief that the basic and essential differences between North and South were not great enough to make war necessary. The dissimilarities between the agrarian society of the South and the industrial society of the Northeast were, to be sure, a fertile seedbed for friction and for misunderstandings, but these misunderstandings were not, on the whole, realistic. The great difference traditionally emphasized is that of slavery, but Craven argued that the economic condition of the Negro as an unskilled laborer engaged in the cotton culture was much more important in controlling the conditions of his life than his legal status as a chattel. Because of these economic factors the condition of the Negro after emancipation changed very little until the cotton economy itself changed in the 1930's. Craven also emphasized the fact that three-quarters of the Southern whites were not slaveholders and were not directly involved in the slavery complex. North and South did not, in fact, present polar extremes.

But if sectional antagonisms did not arise out of fundamental differences, what did they arise from? Craven believed that they resulted from the creation of false images of each section by the other, and from the charging of these images with a high, unreasoning emotional content. He believed that these stereotypes were to some extent manufactured by irresponsible political agitators, both North and South—that is by the "fire-eating" secessionists and by the abolitionists. In other words, the explanation lies more in psychological attitudes than in objective conditions. From this conclusion, it follows that we should beware of any arbitrary assumption that the conflict was irrepressible (though Craven later concluded that the opposite assumption should also be avoided, since the question really cannot be determined). It follows, too, that slavery should be played down: Craven suggested "the possibility that behind the determination to put slavery on the road to ultimate extinction there may have lain drives that had little to do with Negro slavery or the American South, as well as others that were the direct product of slavery itself and of the so-called 'Slave Power.' " Since, in his opinion, "the great body of Americans were moderate and conservative in their attitudes [and] . . . came to the brink of Civil War reluctantly," a heavy burden of what may really be called war guilt rests with the political leaders ("extremists") like Charles Sumner and Barnwell Rhett who played upon public emotions until they brought about a conflict which the circumstances did not require and which neither the Northern nor the Southern majority wanted.

While Craven was developing these themes at the University of Chicago, James G. Randall at the University of Illinois was concurrently working out an interpretation to which he himself applied the term "revisionist." His first clear-cut statement of this interpretation appeared, but was not heavily emphasized, in his *The Civil War and Reconstruction* in 1937. It was more fully elaborated in three important articles, "The Blundering Generation," "The Civil War Restudied," and "When War Came in 1861," all published in 1940. Finally, in *Lincoln, the President: Springfield to Gettysburg* (1945), he set forth his views in their fully matured form.

Critics sometimes discuss Craven and Randall as if their views were identical. It is easy to see why this happens, for both men held a number of major ideas in common: that sectional differences were not great enough to necessitate a war; that the crisis resulted more from the whipping-up of emotions than from the impact of realistic issues; that extremists on both sides were responsible for this emotional jag, but that the responsibility of the extremists of the North (i.e., the abolitionists), which had been disregarded by many historians, needed to be emphasized rather more than the responsibility of the extremists of the South (i.e., the fire-eating secessionists), whom historians had blamed excessively; and above all, that the war was both avoidable and unnecessary and that it occurred as the result of a failure of leadership. But within this broad framework of agreement, Craven and Randall each developed distinctive points of emphasis. Where Craven argued that the Civil War in particular ought not to have occurred, Randall showed greater concern with the problem of war as such, and writing at a time when the world was rapidly losing the international peace which World War I and the League of Nations were supposed to have won, he argued that war as such should be prevented, that it is a "fallacy" to believe that "fundamental motives produce war." Indeed, he contended that analysis of the causes of war must fail unless it takes into consideration psychopathic factors.

Because of his greater concern with the general problem of the causation of war, Randall was also more concerned than was Craven to refute the idea of economic determinism, in the Beardian sense, as an explanation of war. In some of his best analysis, Randall pointed out that economic determinists have a kind of "heads, I win—tails, you lose" formula. If a people who lack economic diversity make war, their belligerence can be explained in terms of the need for economic self-sufficiency. But if a people with diversity have an internal war, their conflict can be explained in terms of the clash of diverse interests. In either case, the explanation for war stands ready-made. As Randall argued, features of diversity may lead to mutual interdependence rather than to war, and the existence of economic differences creates no presumption that antagonism need follow. Where antagonism exists, it must be explained on specific grounds.

A second respect in which Randall's emphasis differed from Craven's is that where Craven discounted the significance of slavery as an institution, Randall minimized its significance as an issue. One of his most effective arguments was his contention that, while the broad issue of freedom versus slavery may be worth a war, the issue as defined by the opposing forces in 1861 was not that broad, and was not worth a war in the form in which they defined it. For the Republicans in 1861 did not propose to emancipate the slaves; they even agreed in 1861 to guarantee slavery in the existing slave states and to return fugitives to slavery. The one point on which they stuck was that they would not sanction slavery in any of the new territories. But since the climate and the economy of these new regions made them inhospitable to slavery anyway, the territorial question could be viewed as an abstraction—a contest over "an imaginary Negro in an impossible place," and a very inadequate cause for a war. The idea that the territorial issue was a fictitious one was not new—it had been vigorously expressed by James K. Polk—but Randall gave it a new application in his treatment of the causes of the war.

A third major expression of revisionism appeared in 1948, when Roy F. Nichols of the University of Pennsylvania published his *The Disruption of American Democracy*. Unlike Craven and Randall, Nichols did not undertake a general interpretation of the sectional crisis as a whole. Instead he set himself to the more specialized study of the impact of sectional antagonisms in shattering a national political party—the Democratic Party. His work, which won the Pulitzer Prize, was, therefore, an institutional study of the impact of sectional pressures upon American political machinery. But the findings fitted well with the revisionist thesis, for Nichols showed how the defects of the political system (excessive localism, the need for agitation in order to stimulate voters in the frequent elections, etc.) contributed to the breakdown of a national political organization under the weight of sectional pressures. Moreover, Nichols asserted in clear-cut terms his belief that the "hyperemotionalism" of the times made it possible for "irresponsible and blind operators of local political machinery" to exploit the inflammable issues which led to war.

Toward the end of the forties, revisionism had very largely swept the field of Civil War literature. With the partial exception of Allan Nevins' *Ordeal of the Union* (1947), all the major works on the Civil War for a decade had reflected a revisionist view. Revisionism had made its way into the textbooks and had been taken up by popular writers. It is perhaps symptomatic that, in 1951, William E. Woodward's posthumous history of the war, tentatively entitled *The Civil War: A National Blunder*, was finally issued under the title *Years of Madness*.

The Counterattack on Revisionism

About nine years after Craven and Randall had sounded the first trumpets of a broad revisionism, Arthur Schlesinger, Jr., in his *The Age of Jackson* (1945) entered a dissenting opinion. In a brief discussion, made in passing, Schlesinger affirmed his belief that "the emotion which moved the North finally to battlefield and bloodshed was moral disgust with slavery." He also denied the Beardian thesis that slavery was resisted because it constituted an obstacle to industrial capitalism; on the contrary, he said, "the aspirations which were first felt to be menaced by the slave power were in actuality democratic aspirations." Four years later, in an article on Randall's contention, he returned to the subject for a more extended treatment. Attacking the revisionists for using the claim of objectivity and the concept of automatic progress as devices for avoiding consideration of the moral issue of slavery, Schlesinger argued that the focus of the slavery contest had fallen on the territories, not because industrialists on-the-make were covetous of power in new regions and indifferent to slave hardships in old ones, but because Americans found their moral scruples about slavery in conflict with their civic scruples to obey the Constitution, which protected slavery in the slave states. Therefore, their powerful impulse against human bondage was deflected from its natural target, slavery in the states, and was sublimated, as it were, into an attack on the peripheral question of slavery in the territories. But despite this displacement of the objective, Schlesinger felt no doubt that the moral question of slavery was basic in precipitating conflict between the sections.

During the same year when Schlesinger published this latter article, Pieter Geyl, an eminent Dutch historian of major stature, also published, in Dutch, a critique of Randall's idea that the war could have been avoided. (A part of this was published in English translation in 1951.) Geyl focused his attention especially on Randall's contention that because the majority did not want conflict, war should have been avoidable. He argued that the historical process is not as rational as Randall assumed, and that the issues of sectional disagreement could not be neatly separated from the emotions which they generated, and which ultimately got out of control. His criticism must rank with Schlesinger's as one of the two major rebuttals to the revisionist argument, but other voices have been raised as well. Bernard DeVoto assailed the revisionists in two influential articles in *Harper's* which were notable for their early date (1946) as well as for their vigorous, hard-hitting tone. In 1950, Oscar Handlin, in a review of Nevins, deplored the practice of equating the abolitionists and the secessionists because both groups were fanatics: "There is surely a difference," he said, "between being a fanatic for freedom and being a fanatic for slavery."

Harry V. Jaffa has provided an important full-scale criticism of much of the revisionist position. Jaffa denied that slavery had reached the geographical limits of its expansion and that the political restriction was redundant. He denied also that Douglas' popular sovereignty and Lincoln's restrictionism would both have come to the same thing, that is, freedom in the territories, and that the two men's views did not conflict in any basic way. Instead, he argued, Douglas was willing to sacrifice the principles of freedom and equality to the principle of majority rule, while Lincoln, though not a doctrinaire equalitarian, wanted "the highest degree of equality for which general [majority] consent could be obtained." Emphasizing this distinction as he did, he dismissed the idea that emotions of the crisis period were "whipped up" or unrealistic.

By the time Jaffa published his refutation, revisionism had reached the end of its active phase. James G. Randall's voice had been stilled by death in 1953, and Avery Craven had greatly modified his earlier arguments as to the irrepressibility of the conflict. In certain respects, revisionism, like many other historical correctives, had served its purpose—not by winning adoption of its own doctrinal views, but by forcing a correction of previous stereotypes and oversimplifications. Never again could well-trained historians explain the Civil War purely in terms of economic determinism or as a moral crusade against slavery. Nor could they dismiss questions of responsibility and the failure of leadership with an unsupported assertion that the conflict was irrepressible.

But much of the revisionist position remained under attack. One of the most protracted and intensive controversies that had ever occurred among

American historians had not terminated in agreement. This was true despite the fact that revisionism was woven into such major historical studies as those of Randall, Craven, and Nichols, while most of the critics of revisionism had been essayists making their forays from other fields: Jaffa from political science, Geyl from Dutch history, and Schlesinger from the New Deals of Andrew Jackson and Franklin Roosevelt. Perhaps the dispute remained unresolved because, although it purported to be disagreement of an analytical sort about the nature of historical forces, it was also, in cryptic and indirect form, a disagreement of a philosophical sort about the relative importance of three moral objectives: the avoidance of war, the abolition of slavery, and the preservation of the American union. In each case there was an issue not only as to the relative moral priority of the objective (e.g., Was it more important to avoid war than to free slaves?), but also as to whether there were acceptable alternative ways of attaining the objectives (e.g., Could the slaves have been freed without waging a war? Could the Union have been preserved without sacrificing the objectives of ultimate emancipation? Could war have been averted without destroying the Union or leaving the blacks permanently enslaved?). The shifting emphases on first one moral objective and then another, without a corresponding shift in attitudes toward the contingent alternatives, had resulted in constant alterations of the questions which historians were trying to answer. For instance, Randall was so deeply preoccupied with the evil of war that he concentrated primarily on why it was not avoided, without giving full consideration to the evil of slavery, even as a secondary thought. Schlesinger and Kenneth Stampp have given primacy to the evil of slavery and have at least implied that while war is, in most situations, worse than the alternatives, there are cases such as that of Hitlerite Germany where war is preferable, and that the confrontation with slavery was such a case. In the historical writing of today, the Union is usually taken for granted, and historians no longer ask to what extent union has enough intrinsic worth to justify either a resort to the evil of war or a compromise with the evil of slavery. But in the 1860's, this was the crucial question for many. Paul C. Nagel's *One Nation Indivisible: The Union in American Thought, 1776–1861* furnishes striking evidence of the intensity with which the union was regarded, in the mid-nineteenth century, as an absolute value.

In short, while the revisionists and their critics systematically conducted their discourse in the terminology of causation, they were usually bent upon defending the moral priority of one objective over another. Insofar as this was true, they were engaged more in justification than in explanation. Disputes on points of moral justification cannot be settled by objective means. That is one reason why the results of the great revisionist controversy remained inconclusive despite the vast barrage of factual data that was thrown into the campaign by both the revisionists and their critics.

Redefining the Question: The Problem of Race Adjustment

While much of the literature of revisionism and of the counterattack upon it was almost ostentatiously focused upon what purported to be systematic analysis, the shifting fortunes of the revisionist view were illuminated in an especially revealing way in a major work which scarcely attempted such analytical interpretation at all, but which undertook instead to provide the first modern, full-scale narrative of the period from 1850 to 1861. This was the work of Allan Nevins. Many years ago, Nevins began a study of the vast array of source materials that had accumulated in repositories throughout the country, and he set himself to write such a comprehensive and at the same time detailed history as no one had even attempted since James Ford Rhodes. The triumphant results of this enterprise began to appear in 1947 when Nevins published two volumes, *Ordeal of the Union*, covering the period 1850–57. Two more in 1950, *The Emergence of Lincoln*, carried the narrative to 1860, and a fifth and sixth, *The War for the Union*, in 1959 and 1960, have covered the outbreak of war and major aspects of the war itself.

The primary importance of Nevins' work, as I have tried to emphasize, is that it stands today as the only great overall narrative based upon modern research. But for the examination of historiographical trends, it is pertinent here to concentrate upon the rather brief and infrequent passages in which Nevins offers observations on the causative aspects of his theme. At times, especially in the earlier volumes, he seemed to some extent to share the ideas of the revisionists. He spoke of "the unrealities of passion" and of "the failure of American leadership" and he even stated a conviction that "the war should have been avoidable." It is worth noting, however, that this is by no means the same thing as saying that it could have been avoided. But in *The Emergence of Lincoln*, he struck at the chief weakness of revisionism by observing that "while hysteria was important, we have always to ask what basic reasons made possible the propaganda which aroused it." Also in 1950, he rejected the older simplistic idea that slavery in the strict sense of the chattel servitude of Negroes, was the crux of the controversy, and he offered instead the hypothesis that "the main root of the conflict (and there were minor roots) was the problem of slavery *with its complementary problem of race-adjustment*. . . . It was a war over slavery *and* the future position of the Negro race in North America."

Nevins' striking observation is valid or not, according to the level of meaning at which one reads it. If it is read to mean that the men who fought each other did so because they held opposing views about the future position of the Negro race in America, it is not tenable, for the evidence is abundant that North and South, in 1860, both regarded the subordination of the Negro as axiomatic. In this sense, it may be argued that although the war perhaps ought to have been about the future position of the Negro, in fact that is not what it was about, since American whites did not recognize that question as an issue. Just as Randall sought to refute the assertion that slavery was the cause of the war by showing that the Republicans, during the slavery controversy, disavowed any purpose to tamper with slavery, and declared their intention only to monopolize the territories for white settlers, so a critic of Nevins might even more persuasively refute the assertion that the future position of the Negro race was the main root of the conflict by showing that hardly anyone at that time contemplated raising the Negro from his position of inferiority, much less fighting a war for such a purpose. From this view, the tragedy of the war is that Americans sacrificed so much without tackling or even perceiving the ultimate question—without even recognizing what was really at stake.

But it is by no means certain historically that the participants in a war necessarily understand why they fight, nor that the conscious objectives of belligerents are an adequate measure of the historical meaning of a war. If Nevins' statement is read to mean that in the crisis leading to the Civil War the blind forces of history were working toward a long-protracted and agonizing readjustment of the future position of the Negro, it is entirely tenable, and may also be regarded as having a broad significance which previous explanations had lacked. In fact, coming as it did, four years before *Brown* vs. *Board of Education*, and five years before Martin Luther King's Montgomery Improvement Association, Nevins' statement was historiographically prophetic in foreseeing the viewpoints of historians for at least the next two decades.

Even if historians between 1950 and 1968 had not been plying their trade in a society whose foremost development was the Negro Revolution, probably they would have corrected some of the excesses of the revisionist position simply because the revisionists had carried some of their claims to an extreme. For instance, from the time of Albert J. Beveridge through that of J. G. Randall, the prevailing treatment of Lincoln had insisted that his only greatness appeared after he became President, that there was little to choose between him and Stephen A. Douglas (except that Douglas was more straightforward), and that morally, Lincoln was an opportunist who skillfully contrived to win the votes of both antislavery men and Negrophobes.

The first serious refutation of this view in almost a generation appeared in Don E. Fehrenbacher's *Prelude to Greatness: Lincoln in the 1850's* (1962). Fehrenbacher shunned all the legendary melodrama which pictured Lincoln as a foreordained Emancipator, but he showed very accurately and specifically that Lincoln's position was fundamentally incompatible with that of Douglas, and that he was eager to emphasize the divergence. Fehrenbacher's Lincoln was politically ambitious, but not opportunistic, and his ambition "was leavened by moral conviction."

This emphasis upon Lincoln's moral stature and responsibility was a reaffirmation, at a more subtle and more scholarly level, of a view that had prevailed widely before the revisionist onslaught. But when the focus shifted from Lincoln to the abolitionists, there was very little in the way of accepted legend to build upon. Ever since the Civil War, every historian who sympathized with the South or gave a priority to peace or to Union over emancipation held the abolitionists answerable for driving the South into secession, and thus responsible for both disunion and war. Partly in consequence of these reactions and also perhaps because they did manifest more than the average amount of self-righteousness and moral absolutism, the abolitionists were customarily portrayed as "fanatics" or "extremists." But by 1960, a widespread sense of guilt about American racial attitudes had reached such a degree of intensity that many people, both inside and outside the historical profession, had lost all interest in the complexities of the relationship between the slavery issue and the war, and had come to regard emancipation and equality for the Negro as the only meaningful aspects of the conflict. In short, the problem of justification had replaced the closely related problem of explanation. As it did so, there was a compulsion to understand the war once more not as a clash of interests but as a crusade against slavery. The shift is well indicated by the titles of the two principal books in the last thirty years which have covered the whole period from the Mexican War through the Civil War. The first of these, by Roy F. Nichols, published in 1961, was entitled *The Stakes of Power, 1845–1877*; the second, by Elbert B. Smith, published in 1967, was *The Death of Slavery, 1837–1865.*

To validate the crusade against slavery, it was, of course, necessary to legitimize the crusaders (just as it had been necessary, in discrediting the crusade, to disparage the crusaders). David Donald discovered this historical correlation in 1960 when he published the first volume of his biography of the foremost political adversary of slavery, *Charles Sumner and the Coming of the Civil War.* Donald had researched his subject superbly, and in many respects it seems that he appreciated Sumner's qualities of conviction and devotion to all worthy causes. But he portrayed quite explicitly Sumner's rigid self-righteousness, his arrogance and tendency to quarrel even with his close friends, and his humorless egoism. Although he won a Pulitzer Prize for his work, Donald was assailed in at least three articles or lengthy reviews for dealing so harshly with an antislavery leader. He had unwittingly violated an axiom which has served many writers, not all of them outside the historical profession: a man's character is to be inferred from the cause with which he is or was identified and not from the evidence of his personal behavior. Although the slavery question was certainly an ethical one, it does not follow that the vice or virtue of any given individual is a direct coefficient of his position on that question. But nonetheless, true believers will never doubt that if Sumner was sound on slavery, he was one of the good guys, and therefore must, by definition, have had a sense of humor.

This comment should not be read as a covert attack on the abolitionists. They may well have been maligned more indiscriminately in the past than they were lauded indiscriminately in the 1960's. But it is unfortunate that one school, which admires "moderation," tends to denounce the abolitionists as unmitigated bigots, while another school, which admires morality, cannot admit that moral absolutism leads to excessive self-righteousness. All parties tend to avoid facing the fact that every value has its cost. The cost of deep commitment is a certain measure, more or less, of intolerance, and the cost of tolerance is a certain measure, more or less, of moral apathy.

In a larger sense, the vital question concerning the abolitionists is not whether they were "fanatics," but first whether they were humanitarians in a broad sense—that is whether the dynamic of their antislavery was an outgoing concern for the welfare of others or a neurotic impulse to find outlets for psychological problems of their own—and second, whether they really perceived the problem of race adjustment in America, to which Nevins alludes, and which was the essence of the problem of slavery.

The literature of antislavery began to treat its theme somewhat more broadly beginning about 1930. Perhaps the first scholarly modern treatment appeared in 1933 when Gilbert H. Barnes published *The Anti-Slavery Impulse, 1830–1844.* This work broke the monopolistic focus upon William Lloyd Garrison as the one standard symbol of abolitionism by showing the great importance of Theodore Dwight Weld and others. At the same time, it shifted attention from New England to the Middle West. It also began to link antislavery with other forces by demonstrating the integral relationship of abolitionism with the fervent evangelical religion of which Weld was apostle. With the Garrisonian mold thus broken, other writers did much more to explore the social and intellectual origins and relationships of the antislavery movement. Illustrative of this tendency are: Alice Felt Tyler, *Freedom's Ferment* (1944), which deals comprehensively with the many-faceted movement of humanitarian reform, within the context of which the antislavery movement developed; Thomas E. Drake, *Quakers and Slavery in America* (1950), which focused attention again on some of the less sensational, less militant aspects of the resistance to slavery; Samuel Flagg Bemis, *John Quincy Adams and the Union* (1956), which told the story of Adams' career as an antislavery leader in Congress, and thus showed how broad the antislavery movement was in comparison with the abolitionists' campaign for immediate emancipation; and Philip S. Foner, *The Life and Writings of Frederick Douglass* (1950–55), which emphasized the role of free Negroes in the abolition movement.

Identification of the antislavery movement with the humanitarian movement usually implies a measure of approbation for the abolitionists. But, while this approval has certainly been prominent in part of the literature, there also remained a marked tendency to question the basic motivation of abolitionists, sometimes in modern psychological terms. The abolitionists have, of course, always been condemned by writers who attribute the disruption of the Union to the fanaticism of the antislavery crusade. But some of the recent criticism, coming from quite an opposite direction, reflects a belief that the abolitionists were motivated less by a concern for Negro welfare than by other objectives and even by a drive to fulfill certain peculiar psychological needs of their own.

This theme was implied in 1949, in Russel B. Nye's *Fettered Freedom*, which argued that the slave system, both in itself and in its zealous defensiveness, constituted a threat to civil liberties and thus provoked the opposition of men who opposed the slave power without necessarily caring about the slave. At almost the same time, Richard Hofstadter, in his *The American Political Tradition*, described Lincoln as one who owed his success to his skill in finding a way "to win the support of both Negrophobes and antislavery men." Hofstadter did not picture the antislavery men as being Negrophobes themselves, but Joseph C. Furnas has actually carried the argument to this position in *Goodbye to Uncle Tom* (1956). Furnas castigates the abolitionists for paving the way to the later system of segregation by their acceptance of the idea of the inferiority of the Negro, and he shows very clearly that many abolitionists, although rejecting slavery, nevertheless did "type" the Negro as an inferior. Since his book appeared, Robert F. Durden's *James Shepherd Pike* (1957) has shown how the strands of antislavery and Negrophobia were strikingly united in the person of one of the editors of the New York *Tribune*, the most important journalistic organ of the antislavery cause.

More recently, biographies of Cassius M. Clay by David Smiley (1962), of George W. Julian by Patrick Riddleberger (1966), and of Hinton R. Helper by Hugh C. Bailey (1965) have illustrated other striking cases of men who hated slavery but had no love for the Negro.

Meanwhile, David Donald has advanced some generalizations about the abolitionists, based upon a study of the backgrounds of 106 prominent anti-slavery men. He found them, in general, conservative, indifferent to the exploi-tation of industrial labor, and hostile to Jacksonian democracy. He also sug-gested that many of them were descendants of New England clerical families who found their leadership challenged by the new industrialism and who turned to reform as a medium through which "their own class" could reassert "its former social dominance . . . an attack upon slavery was their best, if quite unconscious, attack upon the new industrial system."

In short, Donald applied to the abolitionists the same concept of status anxiety and status politics which Richard Hofstadter and the authors of *The New American Right* (1955) were applying, at about the same time, to the Progressives and to the McCarthy Era—and with the same disparaging results.

The treatment of individual abolitionists was usually more favorable than in the generalized accounts. This is true, for instance, of biographies of Gerrit Smith, by Ralph V. Harlow (1939), Harriet Beecher Stowe, by Forrest Wilson (1941), William Lloyd Garrison and Wendell Phillips, by Ralph Korn-gold (1950), Theodore Weld, by Benjamin P. Thomas (1950), William Lloyd Garrison, by Russel B. Nye (1955), James G. Birney, by Betty Fladeland (1955), and Wendell Phillips, by Oscar Sherwin (1958).

But the real watershed in antislavery histories came with the publication of Louis Filler's *The Crusade Against Slavery, 1830–1860* and Clifford S. Grif-fin's *Their Brothers' Keepers, Moral Stewardship in the United States, 1800–1865*, both in 1960, and Dwight L. Dumond's *Antislavery*, in 1961. Filler pro-vided the first modern, general, scholarly account of the antislavery movement and one sympathetic to the cause whose history it recorded. Griffin identified antislavery with a reform tradition that was somewhat self-righteous, pater-nalistic, and given to the use of compulsory methods, but which was neverthe-less high-minded, public-spirited, and civically responsible. Dumond, who ap-proached his subject with immense erudition (only partly reflected in his editing of the Weld and Grimke papers [2 vols., 1934] and the Birney papers [2 vols., 1938]), launched the most learned, most extensive, and most uncritical history of antislavery since Pillsbury Parker had published *The Acts of the Antislavery Apostles* in 1883. This work, a kind of fifth gospel according to Dumond, asserted that the antislavery movement was "the greatest concentra-tion of moral and intellectual power ever assembled in support of any cause before or since."

Dumond's hyperbole was such as to make his book, with all its learning, something of a curiosity, but any reader who compared his panegyric with previous acerbic treatments of the abolitionists could easily tell that "the times they are a-changing." Four years later, Martin Duberman, as editor of a collection of essays by various hands, *The Antislavery Vanguard*, made the same point with vastly more restraint and with strong effect. Duberman specifically rejected the stereotype of the abolitionist as a crank and a fanatic, and claimed for the antislavery movement an immense constructive value. No longer were abolitionists the irresponsible and bigoted men who brought disunion and civil war upon the country. Rather they were the defenders of freedom when none else would defend it.

This account of the literature of antislavery might be extended to include a discussion of biographies of Wendell Phillips by Irving H. Bartlett (1961—the best treatment), of Elijah P. Lovejoy by Merton L. Dillon (1961), of Thomas Wentworth Higginson by Mary Ann Wells (1963), of Lydia Maria Child by Helene G. Baer (1964—with some shortcomings), of John P. Hale by Richard H. Sewell (1965), of James Russell Lowell by Martin Duberman (1966), of Benjamin Lundy by Merton L. Dillon (1966), of Owen Lovejoy by Edward Magdol (1967), of Sarah and Angelina Grimke by Gerda Lerner (1967), and two 1963 biographies of William Lloyd Garrison, one by John L. Thomas, the other by Walter M. Merrill. Larry Gara's history of the fact and legend of the Underground Railroad, *The Liberty Line* (1961), should also be mentioned. Finally, it is important to note James M. MacPherson's *The Struggle for Equality* (1964), for MacPherson followed the careers of the antislavery men into the era of Reconstruction and argued with considerable force that many of the leading abolitionists were not racists, did not hold the unrealistic view that all the slaves needed was to be set legally free, did not abandon the freedman to his fate, and were motivated by concern for the welfare of the blacks and not by neurotic anxiety concerning their own status.

Since MacPherson's book deals with Reconstruction, it may seem completely misguided of me to include it in a discussion of the literature concerning the background of the Civil War. But it is pertinent because MacPherson is one of the first writers who applied Nevins' idea that the main root of the conflict—whether the participants knew it or not—was the problem of "slavery *and* of the future position of the Negro race in North America." For almost a century, the histories of slavery had treated it as something unique, and either did not consider its relation to the broader practice of the subordination of the blacks, or even treated the subordination as one result of the stigma of slavery. So long as slavery was conceived to be central, the two main questions were: what did slavery have to do with causing the Civil War and how necessary was the war to the ending of slavery? But by the 1960's, it was beginning to be recognized that slavery was only a special form of racial subordination, and not everyone would even agree that it was the severest of all forms, though it was certainly one of the most complete. But if racial subordination was the essence, and slavery was only an overt form, then the question had to be restated: what did racial subordination have to do with causing the Civil War and how did the war impinge on racial subordination? Unless the war played a vital part in these connections, perhaps it was really not as important as people had imagined, and not worth all the controversy that had raged for a century.

To express this in another way, the war was certainly vital in the history of slavery, but it was not necessarily significant in the history of racism, except insofar as the end of slavery transformed the real social position of the blacks, which clearly it did not do. Perhaps as a result, the focus on the war began to be diffused. In a somewhat anomalous way, a more pervasive influence was attributed to slavery as social subordination, while at the same time it was recognized that, as chattel bondage, it constituted only one dimension of the more enduring problem of racial caste.

Thus, Thomas Jefferson came under fire. Jefferson had always been the South's symbol of its own intrinsic liberalism, and in the eyes of Southern liberals, Calhoun had only been an unfortunate aberration. But Leonard Levy in 1963, in a study of *Jefferson and Civil Liberties: The Darker Side,* pictured the great Democrat as repressive and illiberal in many important respects. A year later, Robert McColley, in *Slavery in Jeffersonian Virginia,* made the most sustained assault ever launched upon the long-standing legend that Jefferson and Virginia would have abolished slavery if they had only gotten around to it. Similarly, for a century, the nullification crisis was believed to have turned upon the tariff issue, but in 1966, William W. Freehling approached the question in a new way. In *Prelude to Civil War: The Nullification Controversy in South Carolina, 1816–1836* he advanced the theory that slavery underlay nullification.

Slavery is now being emphasized more than ever before, to the exclusion of economic and other sectional factors which received major stress. However, it is not slavery as chattel servitude, but slavery as racial subordination. Leon Litwack's *North of Slavery: The Negro in the Free States, 1790–1860* (1964) showed conclusively that complete segregation, formalized discrimination, and belief in Negro inferiority prevailed throughout the states that fought for the Union in the Civil War. How could the Union victory mean a defeat for racism, when both of the antagonists were racists? William Stanton, *The Leopard's Spots: Scientific Attitudes Toward Race in America,* shows how ideas of Negro biological inferiority were supported by a widely accepted doctrine that the races of men were actually distinct species. Philip J. Stadenraus, *The African Colonization Movement, 1816–1865* (1961), showed to what a great extent the idea of sending freed slaves to Liberia meant in fact deporting Negroes to Africa. Eugene F. Berwanger's *The Frontier Against Slavery: Western Anti-Negro Prejudice and the Slavery Extension Controversy* (1967) documented the antipathy toward Negroes which made so many Northern whites eager to keep them out of the territories. Finally, and perhaps most significant of all, David Brion Davis' ground-breaking *The Problem of Slavery in Western Culture* (1967) has shown the depth of the roots of ideological belief in slavery, and Winthrop Jordan's massive study, *White over Black: American Attitudes Toward the Negro, 1550–1812* (1968), has noted the protracted duration and the pervasiveness of the rejection of the Negro by American whites. On this long road, the Civil War scarcely seemed more than a jog.

Increasingly in recent years, the period preceding the Civil War has been discussed in terms of racism and the subordination of the Negro, rather than in terms of slavery alone, or of the territorial issue. Ironically, this emphasis leaves the explanation of the war even more remote than ever before. The work of men like Litwack, Stanton, Stadenraus, Berwanger, and Jordan shows that the dominant forces in both sections spurned and oppressed the Negro. Since this was true, it is difficult to understand why the particular form which this oppression took in the South should have caused acute tension, as it did, between the sections. Was it because Northerners hated and envied the aristocratic pretensions of the slaveholders, but at the same time stood aloof from the slaves? Was the South needlessly frightened into breaking up the Union, and was the issue of union really much more vital than we are now psychologically prepared to believe?

The overwhelming preoccupation with racial questions during the 1960's has to some extent diverted attention from analytical explanations of war. Despite this general shift in focus away from what was for a time *the* central question in American historiography, a few genuinely analytical approaches are still being taken. Two especially may be mentioned here. First, Barrington Moore's chapter "The American Civil War: The Last Capitalist Revolution" in his *Social Origins of Dictatorship and Democracy* (1966) has been written with remarkable cogency and decisiveness. Moore argues that "the strictly economic issues were very probably negotiable"; he also accepts the view that the Northern public did not care enough about slavery to fight for its overthrow. As to conflict of interests, he regards the "tugging and hauling and quarreling and grabbing" by diverse interest groups as chronic in any society, and therefore useless for diagnostic purposes in explaining a civil war. Generally, slavery was a form of capitalism, not inherently incompatible with industrial capitalism: "There is no abstract general reason why the North and South had to fight. Special historical circumstances, in other words, had to be present." The special historical circumstance which brought on a war, as Moore sees it, was the fact that the slave system was an obstacle "to a *particular kind* of capitalism at a specific historical stage." The South wanted a capitalism with fixed hierarchical status; the North wanted "a competitive democratic capitalism" and "was still committed to notions of equal opportunity," deriving from "the Puritan, American, and French Revolutions." It was impossible "to establish political and social institutions that would satisfy both" North and South. The Civil War was the last of several major nineteenth-century conflicts waged by the bourgeois against the landed classes.

In Moore, old ideas are echoed in a new, somewhat Marxian context. A second important interpretation, also Marxist, but not at all literal-minded in its Marxism, has appeared in Eugene D. Genovese, "Marxian Interpretations of the Slave South," in *Towards a New Past: Dissenting Essays in American History* (Barton J. Bernstein, editor, 1968). The heart of Genovese's argument is to be found in his critique of Moore. The fallacy in Moore, he contends, is the view that since both slavery and industry were forms of capitalism, there was therefore no necessary ground for conflict between them, in general terms, and that specific circumstances had to be invoked. But, says Genovese, while slavery may have partaken of the nature of capital, it "simultaneously extruded a ruling class with strong pre-bourgeois qualities and economic interests." In short, if industrialists and slaveholders were both capitalists, the resemblance was purely semantic and at an abstract level. Concretely, they clashed partly because one group was bourgeois while the other, although not feudal (the distinction is brilliantly made), was pre-bourgeois.

Today, historians seem to have agreed on a good many points: that the North did not hate slavery enough to go to war about it; that slavery was too close to capitalism to justify the old antithesis of industrialism versus agrarianism; that the conflict of economic interests was negotiable and the conflict of civilizations was, to some extent, trumped up; that the power of the planters was real; that slavery was not a dying institution; and that the South was not a land primarily of Jeffersonian yeomen. Thus the "causes of the Civil War" remain moot.

Nevertheless, in every aspect, slavery was important. Economically, it was an immensely powerful property interest, somewhat inimical to the interests of free farming, because the independent farmer could not compete with the slave. Socially, it was the keystone of a static society of social hierarchy which challenged the dynamic, mobile, and equalitarian modes of life and labor that prevailed in the free states. Ideologically, it was a negation of the basic American principles of freedom and equality. It is futile to draw analytical distinctions between the slavery issue and (a) economic conflict of interest, (b) cultural incompatibilities, and (c) ideals as a social force. For the slavery issue was not, for explanatory purposes, an alternative to any of the others. It was part of the essence of all of them.

Abraham Lincoln and the Self-made Myth

Richard Hofstadter

Rather than attempt to destroy the immense body of myth that surrounds Abraham Lincoln, Richard Hofstadter, late De Witt Clinton Professor of American History at Columbia University, looks to the myth's origin, development, and final effect on its subject. Accepting the fact that elements of the myth are true, Professor Hofstadter finds that it was Lincoln himself who was the "first author of the Lincoln legend" and then continued to be its chief exponent. The "self-made myth" was propelled by Lincoln's political ambition for the presidency. The effects of the myth's fulfillment on the sensitive Lincoln were tragic; instead of glory, "he had found only ashes and blood."

I happen, temporarily, to occupy this White House. I am a living witness that any one of your children may look to come here as my father's child has.
Abraham Lincoln to the 166th Ohio Regiment

His ambition was a little engine that knew no rest.
William H. Herndon

The Lincoln legend has come to have a hold on the American imagination that defies comparison with anything else in political mythology. Here is a drama in which a great man shoulders the torment and moral burdens of a blundering and sinful people, suffers for them, and redeems them with hallowed Christian virtues—"malice toward none and charity for all"—and is destroyed at the pitch of his success. The worldly-wise John Hay, who knew him about as well as he permitted himself to be known, called him "the greatest character since Christ," a comparison one cannot imagine being made of any other political figure of modern times.

If the Lincoln legend gathers strength from its similarity to the Christian theme of vicarious atonement and redemption, there is still another strain in American experience that it represents equally well. Although his métier was politics and not business, Lincoln was a pre-eminent example of that self-help which Americans have always so admired. He was not, of course, the first eminent American politician who could claim humble origins, nor the first to exploit them. But few have been able to point to such a sudden ascent from relative obscurity to high eminence; none has maintained so completely while scaling the heights the aspect of extreme simplicity; and none has combined with the attainment of success and power such an intense awareness of humanity and moral responsibility. It was precisely in his attainments as a common man that Lincoln felt himself to be remarkable, and in this light that he interpreted to the world the significance of his career. Keenly aware of his role as the exemplar of the self-made man, he played the part with an intense and poignant consistency that gives his performance the quality of a high art. The first author of the Lincoln legend and the greatest of the Lincoln dramatists was Lincoln himself.

Lincoln's simplicity was very real. He called his wife "mother," received distinguished guests in shirtsleeves, and once during his presidency hailed a soldier out of the ranks with the cry: "Bub! Bub!" But he was also a complex man, easily complex enough to know the value of his own simplicity. With his morbid compulsion for honesty he was too modest to pose coarsely and blatantly as a Henry Clay or James G. Blaine might pose. (When an 1860 campaign document announced that he was a reader of Plutarch, he sat down at once to validate the claim by reading the *Lives*.) But he did develop a political personality by intensifying qualities he actually possessed.

Even during his early days in politics, when his speeches were full of conventional platform bombast, Lincoln seldom failed to strike the humble manner that was peculiarly his. "I was born and have ever remained," he said in his first extended campaign speech, "in the most humble walks of life. I have no popular relations or friends to recommend me." Thereafter he always sounded the theme. "I presume you all know who I am—I am humble Abraham Lincoln. . . . If elected I shall be thankful; if not it will be all the same." Opponents at times grew impatient with his self-derogation ("my poor, lean, lank face") and a Democratic journal once called him a Uriah Heep. But self-conscious as the device was, and coupled even as it was with a secret confidence that Hay called "intellectual arrogance," there was still no imposture in it. It corresponded to Lincoln's own image of himself, which placed him with the poor, the aged, and the forgotten. In a letter to Herndon that was certainly not meant to impress any constituency, Lincoln, near his thirty-ninth birthday, referred to "my old , withered, dry eyes."

There was always this pathos in his plainness, his lack of external grace. "He is," said one of Mrs. Lincoln's friends, "the *ungodliest* man you ever saw." His colleagues, however, recognized in this a possible political asset and transmuted it into one of the most successful of all political symbols—the hard-fisted rail-splitter. At a Republican meeting in 1860 John Hanks and another old pioneer appeared carrying fence rails labeled: "Two rails from a lot made by Abraham Lincoln and John Hanks in the Sangamon Bottom in the year 1830." And Lincoln, with his usual candor, confessed that he had no idea whether these were the same rails, but he was sure he had actually split rails every bit as good. The time was to come when little Tad could say: "Everybody in this world knows Pa used to split rails."

402 MYTHS OF THE CIVIL WAR AND RECONSTRUCTION

Humility belongs with mercy among the cardinal Christian virtues. "Blessed are the meek, for they shall inherit the earth." But the demands of Christianity and the success myth are incompatible. The competitive society out of which the success myth and the self-made man have grown may accept the Christian virtues in principle but can hardly observe them in practice. The motivating force in the mythology of success is ambition, which is closely akin to the cardinal Christian sin of pride. In a world that works through ambition and self-help, while inculcating an ethic that looks upon their results with disdain, how can an earnest man, a public figure living in a time of crisis, gratify his aspirations and yet remain morally whole? If he is, like Lincoln, a man of private religious intensity, the stage is set for high tragedy.

The clue to much that is vital in Lincoln's thought and character lies in the fact that he was thoroughly and completely the politician, by preference and by training. It is difficult to think of any man of comparable stature whose life was so fully absorbed into his political being. Lincoln plunged into politics almost at the beginning of his adult life and was never occupied in any other career except for a brief period when an unfavorable turn in the political situation forced him back to his law practice. His life was one of caucuses and conventions, party circulars and speeches, requests, recommendations, stratagems, schemes, and ambitions. "It was in the world of politics that he lived," wrote Herndon after his death. "Politics were his life, newspapers his food, and his great ambition his motive power."

Like his father, Lincoln was physically lazy even as a youth, but unlike him had an active forensic mind. When only fifteen he was often on stumps and fences making political speeches, from which his father had to haul him back to his chores. He was fond of listening to lawyers' arguments and occupying his mind with them. Herndon testifies that "he read specially for a special object and thought things useless unless they could be of utility, use, practice, etc."[1] When Lincoln read he preferred to read aloud. Once when Herndon asked him about it he answered: "I catch the idea by two senses, for when I read aloud I *hear* what is read and I see it . . . and I remember it better, if I do not understand it better." These are the reading habits of a man who is preparing for the platform.

For a youth with such mental habits—and one who had no business talents in the narrower sense—the greatest opportunities on the Illinois prairies were in the ministry, law, or politics. Lincoln, who had read Paine and Volney, was too unorthodox in theology for the ministry, and law and politics it proved to be. But politics was first: at twenty-three, only seven months after coming to the little Illinois community of New Salem, he was running for office. Previously he had worked only at odd jobs as ferryman, surveyor, postmaster, storekeeper, rail-splitter, farm hand, and the like; and now, without any other preparation, he was looking for election to the state legislature. He was not chosen, but two years later, in 1834, Sangamon County sent him to the lower house. Not until his first term had almost ended was he sufficiently qualified as a lawyer to be admitted to the state bar.

From this time to the end of his life—except for the years between 1849 and 1854, when his political prospects were discouraging—Lincoln was busy either as officeholder or office-seeker. In the summer of 1860, for a friend who wanted to prepare a campaign biography, he wrote in the third person a short sketch of his political life up to that time: 1832—defeated in an attempt to be elected to the legislature; 1834—elected to the legislature "by the highest vote cast for any candidate"; 1836, 1838, 1840—re-elected; 1838 and 1840—chosen by his party as its candidate for Speaker of the Illinois House of Representatives, but not elected; 1840 and 1844—placed on Harrison and Clay electoral tickets "and spent much time and labor in both those canvasses"; 1846—elected to Congress; 1848—campaign worker for Zachary Taylor, speaking in Maryland and Massachusetts, and "canvassing quite fully his own district in Illinois, which was followed by a majority in the district of over 1500 for General Taylor"; 1852—placed on Winfield Scott's electoral ticket, "but owing to the hopelessness of the cause in Illinois he did less than in previous presidential canvasses"; 1854—" . . . his profession had almost superseded the thought of politics in his mind, when the repeal of the Missouri Compromise aroused him as he had never been before"; 1856—"made over fifty speeches" in the campaign for Frémont; prominently mentioned in the Republican national convention for the vice-presidential nomination. . . .

The rest of the story is familiar enough. . . .

As an economic thinker, Lincoln had a passion for the great average. Thoroughly middle-class in his ideas, he spoke for those millions of Americans who had begun their lives as hired workers—as farm hands, clerks, teachers, mechanics, flatboatmen, and rail-splitters—and had passed into the ranks of landed farmers, prosperous grocers, lawyers, merchants, physicians, and politicians. Theirs were the traditional ideals of the Protestant ethic: hard work, frugality, temperance, and a touch of ability applied long and hard enough would lift a man into the propertied or professional class and give him independence and respect if not wealth and prestige. Failure to rise in the economic scale was generally viewed as a fault in the individual, not in society. It was the outward sign of an inward lack of grace—of idleness, indulgence, waste, or incapacity.

This conception of the competitive world was by no means so inaccurate in Lincoln's day as it has long since become; neither was it so conservative as time has made it. It was the legitimate inheritance of Jacksonian democracy. It was the belief not only of those who had arrived but also of those who were pushing their way to the top. If it was intensely and at times inhumanly individualistic, it also defied aristocracy and class distinction. Lincoln's life was a dramatization of it in the sphere of politics as, say, Carnegie's was in business. His own rather conventional version of the self-help ideology[2] is expressed with some charm in a letter written to his feckless stepbrother, John D. Johnston, in 1851:

> Your request for eighty dollars I do not think it best to comply with now. At the various times when I have helped you a little you have said to me, "We can get

along very well now"; but in a very short time I find you in the same difficulty again. Now, this can only happen by some defect in your conduct. What that defect is, I think I know. You are not lazy, and still you are an idler. I doubt whether, since I saw you, you have done a good whole day's work in any one day. You do not very much dislike to work, and still you do not work much, merely because it does not seem to you that you could get much for it. This habit of uselessly wasting time is the whole difficulty.

Lincoln advised Johnston to leave his farm in charge of his family and go to work for wages.

I now promise you, that for every dollar you will, between this and the first of May, get for your own labor . . . I will then give you one other dollar. . . . Now if you will do this, you will soon be out of debt, and, what is better, you will have a habit that will keep you from getting in debt again. . . . You have always been kind to me, and I do not mean to be unkind to you. On the contrary, if you will but follow my advice, you will find it worth more than eighty times eighty dollars to you.

Given the chance for the frugal, the industrious, and the able—for the Abraham Lincolns if not the John D. Johnstons—to assert themselves, society would never be divided along fixed lines. There would be no eternal mud-sill class. "There is no permanent class of hired laborers among us," Lincoln declared in a public address. "Twenty-five years ago I was a hired laborer. The hired laborer of yesterday labors on his own account today, and will hire others to labor for him tomorrow. Advancement—improvement in condition—is the order of things in a society of equals." For Lincoln the vital test of a democracy was economic—its ability to provide opportunities for social ascent to those born in its lower ranks. The belief in opportunity for the self-made man is the key to his entire career; it explains his public appeal; it is the core of his criticism of slavery.

There is a strong pro-labor strain in all of Lincoln's utterances from the beginning to the end of his career. Perhaps the most sweeping of his words, and certainly the least equivocal, were penned in 1847. "Inasmuch as most good things are produced by labor," be began,

it follows that all such things of right belong to those whose labor has produced them. But it has so happened, in all ages of the world, that some have labored, and others have without labor enjoyed a large proportion of the fruits. This is wrong and should not continue. To secure to each laborer the whole product of his labor, or as nearly as possible, is a worthy object of any good government.

This reads like a passage from a socialist argument. But its context is significant; the statement was neither a preface to an attack upon private property nor an argument for redistributing the world's goods—it was part of a firm defense of the protective tariff!

In Lincoln's day, especially in the more primitive communities of his formative years, the laborer had not yet been fully separated from his tools. The rights of labor still were closely associated in the fashion of Locke and Jefferson with the right of the laborer to retain his own product; when men talked about the sacredness of labor, they were often talking in veiled terms about the right to own. These ideas, which belonged to the age of craftsmanship rather than industrialism, Lincoln carried into the modern industrial scene. The result is a quaint equivocation, worth observing carefully because it pictures the state of mind of a man living half in one economy and half in another and wishing to do justice to every interest. In 1860, when Lincoln was stumping about the country before the Republican convention, he turned up at New Haven, where shoemakers were on strike. The Democrats had charged Republican agitators with responsibility for the strike, and Lincoln met them head-on:

> . . . I am glad to see that a system of labor prevails in New England under which laborers can strike when they want to, where they are not obliged to work under all circumstances, and are not tied down and obliged to labor whether you pay them or not! I like the system which lets a man quit when he wants to, and wish it might prevail everywhere. One of the reasons why I am opposed to slavery is just here. What is the true condition of the laborer? I take it that it is best for all to leave each man free to acquire property as fast as he can. Some will get wealthy. I don't believe in a law to prevent a man from getting rich; it would do more harm than good. So while we do not propose any war upon capital, we do wish to allow the humblest man an equal chance to get rich with everybody else. When one starts poor, as most do in the race of life, free society is such that he knows he can better his condition; he knows that there is no fixed condition of labor for his whole life. . . . That is the true system.

If there was a flaw in all this, it was one that Lincoln was never forced to meet. Had he lived to seventy, he would have seen the generation brought up on self-help come into its own, build oppressive business corporations, and begin to close off those treasured opportunities for the little man. Further, he would have seen his own party become the jackal of the vested interests, placing the dollar far, far ahead of the man. He himself presided over the social revolution that destroyed the simple equalitarian order of the 1840's, corrupted what remained of its values, and caricatured its ideals. Booth's bullet, indeed, saved him from something worse than embroilment with the radicals over Reconstruction. It confined his life to the happier age that Lincoln understood—which unwittingly he helped to destroy—the age that gave sanction to the honest compromises of his thought.

A story about Abraham Lincoln's second trip to New Orleans when he was twenty-one holds an important place in the Lincoln legend. According to John Hanks, when Lincoln went with his companions to a slave market they saw a handsome mulatto girl being sold on the block, and "the iron entered his soul"; he swore that if he ever got a chance he would hit slavery "and hit it hard." The implication is clear: Lincoln was half abolitionist and the Emancipation Proclamation was a fulfillment of that young promise. But the authenticity of the tale is suspect among Lincoln scholars. John Hanks recalled it thirty-five years afterward as a personal witness, whereas, according to Lincoln, Hanks had not gone beyond St. Louis on the journey. Beveridge observes that Lincoln himself apparently never spoke of the alleged incident publicly or privately,[3] and that for twenty years afterward he showed little concern over slavery. We know that he refused to denounce the Fugitive Slave Law, viciously unfair though it was, even to free Negroes charged as runaways. ("I confess I hate to see the poor creatures hunted down," he wrote to Speed, ". . . but I bite my lips and keep quiet.")

His later career as an opponent of slavery extension must be interpreted in the light of his earlier public indifference to the question. Always moderately hostile to the South's "peculiar institution," he quieted himself with the comfortable thought that it was destined very gradually to disappear. Only after the Kansas-Nebraska Act breathed political life into the slavery issue did he seize upon it as a subject for agitation; only then did he attack it openly. His attitude was based on justice tempered by expediency—or perhaps more accurately, expediency tempered by justice.

Lincoln was by birth a Southerner, a Kentuckian; both his parents were Virginians. His father had served on the slave patrol of Hardin County. The Lincoln family was one of thousands that in the early decades of the nineteenth century had moved from the Southern states, particularly Virginia, Kentucky, and Tennessee, into the Valley of Democracy, and peopled the southern parts of Ohio, Indiana, and Illinois.

During his boyhood days in Indiana and Illinois Lincoln lived in communities where slaves were rare or unknown, and the problem was not thrust upon him. The prevailing attitude toward Negroes in Illinois was intensely hostile. Severe laws against free Negroes and runaway slaves were in force when Lincoln went to the Springfield legislature, and there is no evidence of any popular movement to liberalize them. Lincoln's experiences with slavery on his journeys to New Orleans in 1828 and 1831 do not seem to have made an impression vivid enough to change his conduct. Always privately compassionate, in his public career and his legal practice he never made himself the advocate of unpopular reform movements.

While Lincoln was serving his second term in the Illinois legislature the slavery question was discussed throughout the country. Garrison had begun his agitation and petitions to abolish slavery in the District of Columbia had begun to pour in upon Congress. State legislatures began to express themselves upon the matter. The Illinois legislature turned the subject over to a joint committee, of which Lincoln and his Sangamon County colleague, Dan Stone, were members. At twenty-eight Lincoln thus had occasion to review the whole slavery question on both sides. The committee reported proslavery resolutions, presently adopted, which praised the beneficent effects of white civilization upon African natives, cited the wretchedness of emancipated Negroes as proof of the folly of freedom, and denounced abolitionists.

Lincoln voted against these resolutions. Six weeks later—the delay resulted from a desire to alienate no one from the cause that then stood closest to his heart, the removal of the state capital from Vandalia to Springfield—he and Stone embodied their own opinions in a resolution that was entered in the Journal of the House and promptly forgotten. It read in part: "They [Lincoln and Stone] believe that the institution of slavery is founded on injustice and bad policy, but that the promulgation of abolition doctrines tends to increase rather than abate its evils." (Which means, the later Lincoln might have said, that slavery is wrong but that proposing to do away with it is also wrong because it makes slavery worse.) They went on to say that while the Constitution does not permit Congress to abolish slavery in the states, Congress can do so in the District of Columbia—*but* this power should not be exercised unless at "the request of the people of the District." This statement breathes the fire of an uncompromising insistence upon moderation. Let it be noted, however, that it did represent a point of view faintly to the left of prevailing opinion. Lincoln had gone on record as saying not merely that slavery was "bad policy" but even that it was unjust; but he had done so without jeopardizing his all-important project to transfer the state capital to Springfield.

In 1845, not long before he entered Congress, Lincoln again had occasion to express himself on slavery; this time in a carefully phrased private letter to a political supporter who happened to be an abolitionist.

> I hold it a paramount duty of us in the free States, due to the Union of the States, and perhaps to liberty itself (paradox though it may seem), to let the slavery of the other states alone; while, on the other hand, I hold it to be equally clear that we should never knowingly lend ourselves, directly or indirectly, to prevent that slavery from dying a natural death—to find new places for it to live in, when it can not longer exist in the old.

Throughout his political career he consistently held to this position.

After he had become a lame-duck Congressman, Lincoln introduced into Congress in January 1849 a resolution to instruct the Committee on the District of Columbia to report a bill abolishing slavery in the District. The bill provided that children born of slave mothers after January 1, 1850, should be freed and supported by their mothers' owners until of a certain age. District slaveholders who wanted to emancipate their slaves were to be compensated from the federal Treasury. Lincoln himself added a section requiring the municipal authorities of Washington and Georgetown to provide "active and efficient means" of arresting and restoring to their owners all fugitive slaves escaping into the District. (This was six years before he confessed that he hated "to see the poor creatures hunted down.") Years later, recalling this fugitive-slave provision, Wendell Phillips referred to Lincoln somewhat unfairly as "that slavehound from Illinois." The bill itself, although not passed, gave rise to a spirited debate on the morality of slavery, in which Lincoln took no part.

When Lincoln returned to active politics the slavery issue had come to occupy the central position on the American scene. Stephen Douglas and some of his colleagues in Congress had secured the passage of the Kansas-Nebraska Act, which, by opening some new territory, formally at least, to slavery, repealed the part of the thirty-four-year-old Missouri Compromise that barred slavery from territory north of 36° 30'. The measure provoked a howl of opposition in the North and split Douglas's party. The Republican Party, built on opposition to the extension of slavery, began to emerge in small communities in the

Northwest. Lincoln's ambitions and interests were aroused, and he proceeded to rehabilitate his political fortunes.

His strategy was simple and forceful. He carefully avoided issues like the tariff, internal improvements, the Know-Nothing mania, or prohibitionism, each of which would alienate important groups of voters. He took pains in all his speeches to stress that he was not an abolitionist and at the same time to stand on the sole program of opposing the extension of slavery. On October 4, 1854, at the age of forty-five, Lincoln *for the first time in his life* denounced slavery in public. In his speech delivered in the Hall of Representatives at Springfield (and later repeated at Peoria) he declared that he hated the current zeal for the spread of slavery: "I hate it because of the monstrous injustice of slavery itself." He went on to say that the had no prejudice against the people of the South. He appreciated their argument that it would be difficult to get rid of the institution "in any satisfactory way." "I surely will not blame them for not doing what I should not know how to do myself. If all earthly power were given me, I should not know what to do as to the existing institution. My first impulse would be to free all the slaves and send them to Liberia, to their own native land." But immediate colonization, he added, is manifestly impossible. The slaves might be freed and kept "among us as underlings." Would this really better their condition?

> What next? Free them, and make them politically and socially our equals. *My own feelings will not admit of this,* and if mine would, we well know that those of the great mass of whites will not. Whether this feeling accords with justice and sound judgment is not the sole question, if indeed it is any part of it. A universal feeling, whether well or ill founded, cannot be safely disregarded.[4]

And yet nothing could justify an attempt to carry slavery into territories now free, Lincoln emphasized. For slavery is unquestionably wrong. "The great mass of mankind," he said at Peoria, "consider slavery a great moral wrong. [This feeling] lies at the very foundation of their sense of justice, and it cannot be trifled with. . . . No statesman can safely disregard it." The last sentence was the key to Lincoln's growing radicalism. As a practical politician he was naturally very much concerned about those public sentiments which no statesman can safely disregard. It was impossible, he had learned, safely to disregard either the feeling that slavery is a moral wrong or the feeling—held by an even larger portion of the public—that Negroes must not be given political and social equality.

He had now struck the core of the Republican problem in the Northwest: how to find a formula to reconcile the two opposing points of view held by great numbers of white people in the North. Lincoln's success in 1860 was due in no small part to his ability to bridge the gap, a performance that entitles him to a place among the world's great political propagandists.

To comprehend Lincoln's strategy we must keep one salient fact in mind: the abolitionists and their humanitarian sympathizers in the nation at large and particularly in the Northwest, the seat of Lincoln's strength, although numerous enough to hold the balance of power, were far too few to make a successful political party. Most of the white people of the Northwest, moreover, were in fact not only not abolitionists, but actually—and here is the core of the matter—Negrophobes. They feared and detested the very thought of living side by side with large numbers of Negroes in their own states, to say nothing of competing with their labor. Hence the severe laws against free Negroes, for example in Lincoln's Illinois.[5] Amid all the agitation in Kansas over making the territory a free state, the conduct of the majority of Republicans there was colored far more by self-interest than by moral principle. In their so-called Topeka Constitution the Kansas Republicans *forbade free Negroes even to come into the state,* and gave only to whites and Indians the right to vote. It was not bondage that troubled them—it was the Negro, free or slave. Again and again the Republican press of the Northwest referred to the Republican Party as the "White Man's Party." The motto of the leading Republican paper of Missouri, Frank Blair's *Daily Missouri Democrat,* was "White Men for Missouri and Missouri for White Men." Nothing could be more devastating to the contention that the early Republican Party in the Northwest was built upon moral principle. At the party convention of 1860 a plank endorsing the Declaration of Independence was almost hissed down and was saved only by the threat of a bolt by the antislavery element.

If the Republicans were to succeed in the strategic Northwest, how were they to win the support of both Negrophobes and antislavery men? Merely to insist that slavery was an evil would sound like abolitionism and offend the Negrophobes. Yet pitching their opposition to slavery extension on too low a moral level might lose the valued support of the humanitarians. Lincoln, perhaps borrowing from the old free-soil ideology, had the right formula and exploited it. He first hinted at it in the Peoria speech:

> The whole nation is interested that the best use shall be made of these Territories. *We want them for homes of free white people. This they cannot be, to any considerable extent, if slavery shall be planted within them.* Slave States are places for poor white people to remove from, not to remove to. New free States are the places for poor people to go to, and better their condition. For this use the nation needs these Territories.

The full possibilities of this line first became clear in Lincoln's "lost" Bloomington speech, delivered at a Republican state convention in May 1856. There, according to the report of one of his colleagues at the Illinois bar, Lincoln warned that Douglas and his followers would frighten men away from the very idea of freedom with their incessant mouthing of the red-herring epithet: "Abolitionist!" "If that trick should succeed," he is reported to have said,[6] "if free negroes should be made *things,* how long, think you, before they will begin to make *things* out of poor white men?"

Here was the answer to the Republican problem. Negrophobes and abolitionists alike could understand this threat; if freedom should be broken down they might themselves have to compete with the labor of slaves in the then free states—or might even be reduced to bondage along with the blacks! Here was an argument that could strike a responsive chord in the nervous system of every Northern man, farmer or worker, abolitionist or racist: *if a stop was not put somewhere upon the spread of slavery, the institution would become nation-wide.*[7] Here, too, is the practical significance of the repeated statements Lincoln made in favor of labor at this time. Lincoln took the slavery question out of the realm of moral and legal dispute and, by dramatizing it in terms of free labor's self-interest, gave it a universal appeal. To please the abolitionists he kept saying that slavery was an evil thing; but for the material benefit of all Northern white men he opposed its further extension.

The importance of this argument becomes increasingly clear when it is realized that Lincoln used it in every one of his recorded speeches from 1854 until he became the President-elect. He once declared in Kansas that preventing slavery from becoming a nation-wide institution "is *the purpose* of this organization [the Republican Party]." The argument had a great allure too for the immigrants who were moving in such great numbers into the Northwest. Speaking at Alton, in the heart of a county where more than fifty percent of the population was foreign-born, Lincoln went out of his way to make it clear that he favored keeping the territories open not only for native Americans, "but as an outlet for *free white people* everywhere, the world over—in which Hans, and Baptiste, and Patrick, and all other men from all the world, may find new homes and better their condition in life."

During the debates with Douglas, Lincoln dwelt on the theme again and again, and added the charge that Douglas himself was involved in a Democratic "conspiracy . . . for the sole purpose of nationalizing slavery."[8] Douglas and the Supreme Court (which a year before had handed down the Dred Scott decision) would soon have the American people "working in the traces that tend to make this one universal slave nation." Chief Justice Taney had declared that Congress did not have the constitutional power to exclude slavery from the territories. The next step, said Lincoln, would be

> another Supreme Court decision, declaring that the Constitution of the United States does not permit a *State* to exclude slavery from its limits. . . . We shall lie down pleasantly, dreaming that the people of Missouri are on the verge of making their State free; and we shall awake to the reality instead, that the Supreme Court has made Illinois a slave State.

So also the theme of the "House Divided" speech:

> I do not expect the Union to be dissolved—I do not expect the House to fall—but I do expect it to cease to be divided. It will become all one thing or all the other. Either the opponents of slavery will arrest the further spread of it, and place it where the public mind shall rest in the belief that it is in the course of ultimate extinction; or its advocates will push it forward, till it shall become alike lawful in all the States, old as well as new, North as well as South.
> Have we no tendency to the latter condition?[9]

The last sentence is invariably omitted when this passage is quoted, perhaps because from a literary standpoint it is anticlimactic. But in Lincoln's mind—and, one may guess, in the minds of those who heard him—it was not anticlimactic, but essential. Lincoln was *not* emphasizing the necessity for abolition of slavery in the near future; he was emphasizing the immediate "danger" that slavery would become a nation-wide American institution if its geographical spread were not severely restricted at once.

Once this "House Divided" speech had been made, Lincoln had to spend a great deal of time explaining it, proving that he was not an abolitionist. These efforts, together with his strategy of appealing to abolitionists and Negrophobes at once, involved him in embarrassing contradictions. In northern Illinois he spoke in one vein before abolition-minded audiences, but farther south, where settlers of Southern extraction were dominant, he spoke in another. It is instructive to compare what he said about the Negro in Chicago with what he said in Charleston.

> Chicago, July 10, 1858:
>
> Let us discard all this quibbling about this man and the other man, this race and that race and the other race being inferior, and therefore they must be placed in an inferior position. Let us discard all these things and unite as one people throughout this land, until we shall once more stand up declaring that all men are created equal.

> Charleston, September 18, 1858:
>
> I will say, then, that I am not, nor ever have been, in favor of bringing about in any way the social and political equality of the white and black races [applause]: that I am not, nor ever have been, in favor of making voters or jurors of negroes, nor of qualifying them to hold office, nor to intermarry with white people. . . .
>
> And inasmuch as they cannot so live, while they do remain together there must be the position of superior and inferior, and I as much as any other man am in favor of having the superior position assigned to the white race.

It is not easy to decide whether the true Lincoln is the one who spoke in Chicago or the one who spoke in Charleston. Possibly the man devoutly believed each of the utterances at the time he delivered it; possibly his mind too was a house divided against itself. In any case it is easy to see in all this the behavior of a professional politician looking for votes.[10]

Douglas did what he could to use Lincoln's inconsistency against him. At Galesburg, with his opponent sitting on the platform behind him, he proclaimed: "I would despise myself if I thought that I was procuring your votes by concealing my opinions, and by avowing one set of principles in one part of the state, and a different set in another." Confronted by Douglas with these clashing utterances from his Chicago and Charleston speeches, Lincoln replied: "I have not supposed and do not now suppose, that there is any conflict whatever between them."

But this was politics—the premium was on strategy, not intellectual consistency—and the effectiveness of Lincoln's campaign is beyond dispute. In the ensuing elections the Republican candidates carried a majority of the voters and elected their state officers for the first time. Douglas returned to the Senate only because the Democrats, who had skillfully gerrymandered the election districts, still held their majority in the state legislature. Lincoln had contributed greatly to welding old-line Whigs and antislavery men into an effective party, and his reputation was growing by leaps and bounds. What he had done was to pick out an issue—the alleged plan to extend slavery, the alleged danger that it would spread throughout the nation—which would turn attention from the disintegrating forces in the Republican Party to the great integrating force. He was keenly aware that the party was built out of extremely heterogeneous elements, frankly speaking of it in his "House Divided" speech as composed of "strange, discordant, and even hostile elements." In addition to abolitionists and Negrophobes, it united high- and low-tariff men, hard- and soft-money men, former Whigs and former Democrats embittered by old political fights, Maine-law prohibitionists and German tipplers, Know-Nothings and immigrants. Lincoln's was the masterful diplomacy to hold such a coalition together, carry it into power, and with it win a war. . . .

Lincoln was shaken by the presidency. Back in Springfield, politics had been a sort of exhilarating game; but in the White House, politics was power, and power was responsibility. Never before had Lincoln held executive office. In public life he had always been an insignificant legislator whose votes were cast in concert with others and whose decisions in themselves had neither finality nor importance. As President he might consult others, but innumerable grave decisions were in the end his own, and with them came a burden of responsibility terrifying in its dimensions.

Lincoln's rage for personal success, his external and worldly ambition, was quieted when he entered the White House, and he was at last left alone to reckon with himself. To be confronted with the fruits of his victory only to find that it meant choosing between life and death for others was immensely sobering. That Lincoln should have shouldered the moral burden of the war was characteristic of the high seriousness into which he had grown since 1854; and it may be true, as Professor Charles W. Ramsdell suggested, that he was stricken by an awareness of his own part in whipping up the crisis. This would go far to explain the desperation with which he issued pardons and the charity that he wanted to extend to the conquered South at the war's close. In one of his rare moments of self-revelation he is reported to have said: "Now I don't know what the soul is, but whatever it is, I know that it can humble itself." The great prose of the presidential years came from a soul that had been humbled. Lincoln's utter lack of personal malice during these years, his humane detachment, his tragic sense of life, have no parallel in political history.

"Lincoln," said Herndon, "is a man of heart—aye, as gentle as a woman's and as tender. . . ." Lincoln was moved by the wounded and dying men, moved as no one in a place of power can afford to be. He had won high office by means sometimes rugged, but once there, he found he could not quite carry it off. For him it was impossible to drift into the habitual callousness of the sort of officialdom that sees men only as pawns to be shifted here and there and "expended" at the will of others. It was a symbolic thing that his office was so constantly open, that he made himself more accessible than any other chief executive in our history. "Men moving only in an official circle," he told Carpenter," are apt to become merely official—not to say arbitrary—in their ideas, and are apter and apter with each passing day to forget that they only hold power in a representative capacity." Is it possible to recall anyone else in modern history who could exercise so much power and yet feel so slightly the private corruption that goes with it? Here, perhaps, is the best measure of Lincoln's personal eminence in the human calendar—that he was chastened and not intoxicated by power. It was almost apologetically that he remarked in response to a White House serenade after his re-election that "So long as I have been here, I have not willingly planted a thorn in any man's bosom."

There were many thorns planted in *his* bosom. The criticism was hard to bear (perhaps hardest of all that from the abolitionists, which he knew had truth in it). There was still in him a sensitivity that the years of knock-about politics had not killed, the remarkable depths of which are suddenly illumined by a casual sentence written during one of the crueler outbursts of the opposition press. Reassuring the apologetic actor James Hackett, who had unwittingly aroused a storm of hostile laughter by publishing a confidential letter, Lincoln added that he was quite used to it: "I have received a great deal of ridicule without much malice; and have received a great deal of kindness, not quite free from ridicule."

The presidency was not something that could be enjoyed. Remembering its barrenness for him, one can believe that the life of Lincoln's soul was almost entirely without consummation. Sandburg remarks that there were thirty-one rooms in the White House and that Lincoln was not at home in any of them. This was the house for which he had sacrificed so much!

As the months passed, a deathly weariness settled over him. Once when Noah Brooks suggested that he rest, he replied: "I suppose it is good for the body. But the tired part of me is *inside* and out of reach." There had always been a part of him, inside and out of reach, that had looked upon his ambition with detachment and wondered if the game was worth the candle. Now he could see the truth of what he had long dimly known and perhaps hopefully suppressed—that for a man of sensitivity and compassion to exercise great powers in a time of crisis is a grim and agonizing thing. Instead of glory, he once said, he had found only "ashes and blood." This was, for him, the end product of that success myth by which he had lived and for which he had been so persuasive a spokesman. He had had his ambitions and fulfilled them, and met heartache in his triumph.

Notes

1. For years Herndon kept on their office table the *Westminster Review*, the *Edinburgh Review*, other English periodicals, the works of Darwin, Spencer, and other English writers. He had little success in interesting Lincoln. "Occasionally he would snatch one up and peruse it for a little while, but he soon threw it down with the suggestion that it was entirely too heavy for an ordinary mind to digest."
2. William C. Howells, father of the novelist, wrote in an Ohio newspaper shortly before Lincoln's inauguration as President that he and his wife represented "the western type of Americans." "The White House," he said, "has never been occupied by better representatives of the bourgoise [sic] or citizen class of people, than it will be after the 4th proximo. If the idea represented by these people can only be

allowed to prevail in this government, all will be well. Under such a rule, the practical individual man, who respects himself and regards the rights of others, will grow to just proportions.''

3. Herndon, however, attested that he heard Lincoln refer to having seen slaves on sale. *Herndon's Life of Lincoln* (Angle ed., 1930), p. 64. In a letter to Alexander H. Stephens, January 19, 1860, Lincoln wrote: "When a boy I went to New Orleans in a flat boat and there I saw slavery and slave markets as I have never seen them in Kentucky, and I heard worse of the Red River plantations."

4. Later, in the debate at Ottawa, Illinois, Lincoln repeated a larger passage containing this statement, and added: "this is the true complexion of all I have said in regard to the institution of slavery and the black race."

5. The Illinois constitutional convention of 1847 had adopted and submitted to a popular referendum a provision that instructed the legislature to pass laws prohibiting the immigration of colored persons. It was ratified by a vote of 50,261 to 21,297. If this vote can be taken as an index, the Negrophobes outnumbered their opponents by more than two to one. In 1853 the state was in effect legally closed to Negro immigration, free or slave. A Negro who entered in violation of the law was to be fined exorbitantly, and if unable to pay the fine could be sold into service. None of the states of the Northwest allowed Negro suffrage.

6. The only existing version of this speech is not a verbatim report.

7. Stephen A. Douglas's appeal to this fear was as strong as Lincoln's: "Do you desire to turn this beautiful State into a free Negro colony in order that when Missouri abolishes slavery she can send one hundred thousand emancipated slaves into Illinois to become citizens and voters, on an equality with yourselves?" But Douglas had no comparable appeal to antislavery sentiment, and Lincoln was able to exploit the fact.

The conception that slavery was a menace to free labor throughout the nation was by no means new, nor peculiar to Lincoln. At the time of the Mexican War, Lowell had made Hosea Biglow say:

> Wy, it's jest ez clear ez figgers,
>   Clear ez one an' one make two.
> Chaps that make black slaves o' niggers
>   Want to make white slaves o' you.

Seward, in his "Irrepressible Conflict" speech, delivered four months after Lincoln's "House Divided" speech, declared: "The United States must, and will sooner or later, become either entirely a slaveholding nation or entirely a free-labor nation. Either the cotton and rice-fields of South Carolina and the sugar plantations of Louisiana will ultimately be tilled by free labor, and Charleston and New Orleans become marts for legitimate merchandise alone, or else the rye-fields and wheat-fields of Massachusetts and New York must again be surrendered by their farmers to slave culture and to the production of slaves, and Boston and New York become once more markets for trade in the bodies and souls of men." But largely because Lincoln was considered more *conservative* than Seward on the slavery question he was chosen for the party nomination in 1860.

8. Historians have dismissed these charges as untrue. Lincoln admitted that they were based on circumstantial evidence.

9. Lincoln is reported to have said to political friends of the "house divided" utterance: "I would rather be defeated with this expression in my speech, and uphold it and discuss it before the people, than be victorious without it." (Herndon refused to believe it would harm him politically, assuring: "It will make you President.")

It would probably be truer to say that Lincoln was making the great gamble of his career at this point than to say that he was sacrificing his political prospects for a principle. He had had his experience with pettifogging politics of the timid sort during his Congressional phase, and it had led only to disaster.

When Joseph Medill asked Lincoln in 1862 why he had delivered "that radical speech," Lincoln answered: "Well, after you fellows had got me into that mess and begun tempting me with offers of the Presidency, I began to think and I made up my mind that the next President of the United States would need to have a stronger anti-slavery platform than mine. So I concluded to say something." Then Lincoln asked Medill to promise not to repeat his answer to others.

10. Lincoln was fond of asserting that the Declaration of Independence, when it said that all men are created equal, included the Negro. He believed the Negro was probably inferior to the white man, he kept repeating, but in his right to eat, without anyone's leave, the bread he earned by his own labor, the Negro was the equal of any white man. Still he was opposed to citizenship for the Negro. How any man could be expected to defend his right to enjoy the fruits of his labor without having the power to defend it through his vote, Lincoln did not say. In his Peoria speech he had himself said: "No man is good enough to govern another man, without that man's consent." In one of his magnificent private memoranda on slavery Lincoln argued that anyone who defends the moral right of slavery creates an ethic by which his own enslavement may be justified. ("Fragment on Slavery," 1854.) But the same reasoning applies to anyone who would deny the Negro citizenship. It is impossible to avoid the conclusion that so far as the Negro was concerned, Lincoln could not escape the moral insensitivity that is characteristic of the average white American.

The Glorious and the Terrible

Allan Nevins

It was the American Civil War General William Tecumseh Sherman who was purported to have said "War is Hell"; yet it seems that few have truly taken his words to heart. War's pageantry and splendor, the fascination of its drama, have most often resulted in historical myopia. The slaughter and destruction that all know to be the deserts of warfare are buried as quickly as its casualties. Perhaps in no instance is this truer than in the classic confrontation between the Blue and the Gray. But the lustrous veneer, says the late Allan Nevins of the Huntington Library in San Marino, California, must be stripped away for sound historical judgment to proceed. The Civil War was not, in the words of the military historian Bruce Catton, "Glory Road." Rather, it was the testing of the character of an entire civilization. Though we are inclined to remember the glorious and forget the terrible, historical integrity requires we recognize both in order to understand the mythology of the American Civil War.

Every great war has two sides, the glorious and the terrible. The glorious is perpetuated in multitudinous pictures, poems, novels, statues: in Meissonier's canvases of Friedland and Austerlitz, Byron's stanzas on Waterloo and Tennyson's on the Light and Heavy brigades, Saint-Gaudens's Sherman riding forward victory-crowned, Freeman's "Lee." The terrible is given us in a much slighter body of memorabilia: Jacques Callot's gruesome etchings of the Thirty Years War, Goya's paintings of French atrocities in Spain, Zola's "The Debacle," Walt Whitman's hospital sketches, and the thousand-page novels that drearily emerged from the Second World War.

The two aspects do exist side by side. Every student of war comes upon hundreds of veracious descriptions of its pomp and pageantry, innumerable tales of devotion and heroism. They exalt the spirit. Yet every such student falls back from this exaltation upon a somber remembrance of the butchery, the bereavement, and the long bequest of poverty, exhaustion, and despair. In observing the centenary of the Civil War, every sensible man should keep in mind that the conflict was a terrible reproach to American civilization and a source of poison and debilities still to be felt.

If it were not true that its debits far outweighed its credits, we might conclude that the republic would profit by a civil war in every generation, and that we should have commemorated Bull Run . . . by again setting Yankee boys and Southern boys to killing each other. The mind recoils from the thought. But as the Civil War histories, novels, and motion pictures continue to pour forth, we shall be fortunate if we escape two very erroneous views.

The first view is that the war can somehow be detached from its context and studied as if it stood alone, without reference to causes or effects. War in fact, as Clausewitz long ago insisted, does not stand apart from and opposed to peace. It is simply a transfer of the normal inescapable conflicts of men from the realm of adjustment to that of violence. It represents not a complete transformation of national policy, but a continuance of policy by sanguinary means. That is, it cannot be understood without regarding both its causes and its results. Our Civil War, as Walt Whitman insisted, grew peculiarly out of national character. The other erroneous view is that the Civil War was, in the phrase of that graphic military historian Bruce Catton, a "Glory Road."

"Consider it not so deeply," Lady Macbeth says to her husband, stricken by the thought of red-handed murder; and "Consider it not so deeply," people instinctively say to those who remind them of war's inhuman massacre. Who wishes to while away an idle hour by looking at the harrowing pictures in the "Medical and Surgical History" of the war? It is a trick of human memories to forget, little by little, what is painful, and remember what is pleasant, and that tendency appertains to the folk memory as well. One of the finest descriptive pieces of the war was written by the true-hearted Theodore Winthrop, novelist and poet, just after his regiment crossed the Potomac on a spring night in 1861 to encamp on the Virginia side. It is rapturous in its depiction of the golden moon lighting a path over the river, the merry files of soldiers, the white tents being pitched in the dewy dawn. But ere long Winthrop was slain at Big Bethel in an engagement too blundering, shabby and piteous for any pen. We remember the happy march but forget the death.

Or take two contrasting scenes later in the war, of the same day—the day of Malvern Hill, July 1, 1862. That battle of Lee and McClellan reached its climax in the gathering dusk of a lustrous summer evening, no breath of wind stirring the air. The Union army had placed its ranks and its artillery on the slope of a great hill, a natural amphitheatre, which the Southerners assaulted. Participants never forgot the magnificence of the spectacle. From the Confederate and Union guns stately columns of black smoke towered high in the blue sky. The crash of musketry and deeper thud of artillery; the thunder of gunboat mortars from the James River, their shells curving in fiery golden lines; the cavalry on either flank, galloping to attack; the foaming horses flying from point to point with aides carrying dispatches; the steady advance of the Confederate columns and the unyielding resistance of the dense Union lines; then as darkness gathered, the varicolored signal lights flashing back and forth their messages—all this made an unforgettable panorama.

But the sequel! The troops on both sides sank exhausted on their arms. From the field the shrieking and moaning of the wounded were heart-rending, yet nothing could be done to succor them. The sky grew overcast; intense darkness shut down; and at dawn came a fierce downpour. "Such rain, and such howling set up by the wounded," wrote one Southern soldier; "such ugly wounds, sickening to the sight even of the most hardened as the rain beat upon them, washing them to a pale purple; such long-fingered corpses, and in piles, too, like cordwood—may I never see the like again!"

Both novelist and poet almost instinctively turn to the heroic aspects and picturesque incidents of war. Lowell's "Commemoration Ode," one of the half-dozen finest pieces of literature born from the conflict, necessarily eulogizes the heroes; Mary Johnston's "The Long Roll," perhaps the best Southern war novel, celebrates the ardors, not the anguishes, of Stonewall Jackson's foot-cavalry; Saint-Gaudens's monument on Boston Common to Robert Gould Shaw and his black infantry—the men whose dauntless hearts beat a charge right up the red rampart's slippery swell—shows the fighters, not the fallen. The historian assists in falsifying the picture. Cold, objective, he assumes that both the glorious and horrible sides exist, and need no special emphasis. He thus tends to equate the two, although the pains and penalties of war far outweigh its gleams of grandeur.

Then, too, a problem of expression impedes the realistic writer. It is not difficult to describe the pageantry of Pickett's charge. But when we come to the costs, what can we say except that the casualties were 3,000 killed, 5,000 wounded? It is impossible to describe the agony of even one soldier dying of a gangrened wound, or the heartache of one mother losing her firstborn; what of 10,000 such soldiers and mothers? Moreover, most historians, like the novelists and poets, have an instinctive preference for the bright side of the coin. Henry Steele Commager's otherwise fine introduction to his valuable compilation "The Blue and The Gray" has much to say about gallantry and bravery, but nothing about the squalor, the stench, and the agony.

If we protest against the prettification of the Civil War, the thoughtless glorification of what was essentially a temporary breakdown of American civilization, we must do so with an acknowledgement that it did call forth many manifestations of an admirable spirit. The pomp and circumstance, the parade and pageantry, we may dismiss as essentially empty. The valor of the host of young men who streamed to the colors we may deeply admire, but as valor we may fortunately take it for granted, for most men are brave. The patriotic ardor displayed in the first months of the war may also be taken for granted. What was highly impressive was the serious, sustained conviction, the long-enduring dedication, of countless thousands on both sides for their chosen cause. This went far beyond the transient enthusiasms of Sumter and Bull Run; far beyond ordinary battlefield courage. Lecky was correct in writing: "That which invests war with a certain grandeur is the heroic self-sacrifice which it elicits." All life is in a real sense a conflict between good and evil, in which every man or woman plays a part. A host of young Americans felt that they were enlisted in this larger struggle, and regarded their service to the North or South as part of a lifetime service to the right.

Those who seek examples of this dedication can find them scattered throughout the war records. Lincoln specially admired his young friend Elmer Ellsworth, who had endured poverty and hardship with monastic devotion to train himself for service; Lee specially admired John Pelham, the daring artillerist. Both gave their lives. Some fine illustrations of the consecrated spirit can be found in the two volumes of the "Harvard Memorial Biographies" edited by Thomas Wentworth Higginson just after the war. The ninety-eight Harvard dead were no better than the farm lads from Iowa or Alabama, the clerks from New Orleans or New York, but some of them had special gifts of self-expression. Hearken, for example, to Colonel Peter A. Porter, who wrote in his last will and testament:

> I can say, with truth, that I have entered on the course of danger with no ambitious aspirations, nor with the idea that I am fitted, by nature, or experience, to be of any important service to the government; but in obedience to the call of duty, demanding every citizen to contribute what he could, in means, labor, or life, to sustain the government of his country—a sacrifice made the more willingly by me when I consider how singularly benefitted I have been, by the institutions of the land. . . .

As we distinguish between the shining glory of the war—this readiness of countless thousands to die for an enduring moral conviction—and the false or unimportant glories, so we must distinguish between the major and the lesser debits of the conflict. Some evils and mischiefs which seemed tremendous at the time have grown less in the perspective of years; some which at first appeared small now loom large.

It was one of the bloodiest of all wars; the total deaths in the Union and Confederate armies have been computed at about 620,000; and one of the facts which appalls any careful student is the enormous amount of suffering on the field and in the hospitals. The evidence of this, while not within the view of general readers, is incontrovertible. Armies the world over in 1860 were *worse* provided with medical and surgical facilities than in Napoleon's day. The United States, after its long peace, began the war with practically no medical service whatever. Surgical application of the ideas of Pasteur and Lister lay in the future. Almost every abdominal wound meant death. Any severe laceration of a limb entailed amputation, with a good chance of mortal gangrene or erysipelas. The North systematically prevented shipments of drugs and surgical instruments to the South, a measure which did not shorten the conflict by a day, but cost the Southern troops untold agony. Had it not been for the Sanitary Commission, a body privately organized and supported, Northern armies would have duplicated the experience of British forces in the Crimea; yet Secretary of War Stanton at first deliberately impeded the Commission's work.

The story of battle after battle was the same. Night descended on a field ringing with cries of agony: Water! Water! Help!—if in winter, Blankets! Cover!

All too frequently no help whatever was forthcoming. After some great conflicts the wounded lay for days, and sometimes a week, without rescue. Shiloh was fought on a Sunday and Monday. Rain set in on Sunday night, and the cold April drizzle continued through Tuesday night. On Tuesday morning nine-tenths of the wounded still lay where they fell; many had been there forty-eight hours without attention; numbers had died of shock or exhaustion; some had even drowned as the rain filled depressions from which they could not crawl. Every house in the area was converted into a hospital, where floors were covered with wretches heavily wounded, sometimes with arms or legs torn off, who, after the first bandages, got no nursing, medical care, or even nourishment. "The first day or two," wrote a newspaper reporter, "the air was filled with groans, sobs, and frenzied curses, but now the sufferers are quiet; not from cessation of pain, but mere exhaustion." Yet at this time the war was a year old.

Still more poignant versions of the same story might be given. Lee and Pope fought Second Manassas on the last Friday and Saturday in August, 1862, so near Washington that groups standing on housetops in the capital heard the rumble of artillery. The battleground, five miles long and three wide, was thickly strewn with dead and wounded. Pope retreated in confusion; many in Washington feared the city might be taken. In these circumstances, as late as the following Wednesday one member of the inadequate body of surgeons estimated that 2,000 wounded had received no attention. Many had not tasted food for four days; some were dying of hunger and thirst. A reporter for the Washington *Republican* wrote on Thursday that some dying men could yet be saved by prompt help. And on Friday, a week after the battle began, a correspondent of the New York *Tribune* told of heart-rending scenes as the doctors searched among heaps of putrefying dead men for men yet clinging to life— men who, when anyone approached, would cry, "Doctor, come to *me*; you look like a kind man; for God's sake come to *me*."

Anyone who is tempted to think of Gettysburg only in terms of its heroic episodes, its color and drama, should turn to the pages in "Battles and Leaders" in which General John D. Imboden describes the transport of the Confederate wounded, after their defeat, back into Maryland. He was ordered to ride to the head of the long wagon column as, in darkness and storm, it moved south:

> For four hours I hurried forward on my way to the front, and in all that time I was never out of hearing of the groans and cries of the wounded and dying. Scarcely one in a hundred had received adequate surgical aid, owing to the demands on the hard-working surgeons from still worse cases that had to be left behind. Many of the wounded in their wagons had been without food for thirty-six hours. Their torn and bloody clothing, matted and hardened, was rasping the tender, inflamed, and still oozing wounds. Very few of the wagons had even a layer of straw in them, and all were without springs. The road was rough and rocky from the heavy washings of the preceding day. The jolting was enough to have killed strong men, if long exposed to it. From nearly every wagon as the teams trotted on, urged by whip and shout, came such cries and shrieks as these:

"My God! Why can't I die?"

"My God! Will no one have mercy and kill me?"

"Stop! Oh, for God's sake stop just for one minute; take me out and leave me to die on the roadside."

Occasionally a wagon would be passed from which only low, deep moans could be heard. No help could be rendered to any of the sufferers. No heed could be given to any of their appeals. Mercy and duty to the many forbade the loss of a moment in the vain effort then and there to comply with the prayers of the few. On! On! We must move on. The storm continued and the darkness was appalling. There was no time even to fill a canteen with water for a dying man; for, except the drivers and the guards, all were wounded and utterly helpless in that vast procession of misery. During this one night I realized more of the horrors of war than I had in all the preceding two years.

After such a description, we can understand why a radical Northern Senator, looking across the battlefield of the Wilderness as fighting ended, told Hugh McCulloch that if in 1861 he had been given one glimpse of the agonies he there beheld, he would have said to the South: "Erring sisters, go in peace." John Esten Cooke was right in his elegy for Pelham; the living were brave and noble, but the dead were the bravest of all.

Yet *this* was far from being the ugliest side of war. Nor was the suffering in the huge prison camps, South and North, part of the worst side of war; the suffering which MacKinlay Kantor describes in his novel to which Benét briefly adverts in "John Brown's Body":

The triple stockade of Andersonville the damned,
Where men corrupted like flies in their own dung
And the gangrened sick were black with smoke and their filth.

What maims the bodies of men is less significant than what maims their spirit.

One ugly aspect of the Civil War too generally ignored is the devastation, more and more systematic, that accompanied it. For three reasons too little has been said of this devastation: the facts were kept out of official reports, the tale is too painful, and the recital easily becomes monotonous. Yet by 1862 the war in the South had become one of general depredation; by 1863, of wanton destruction; and by 1864, of an organized devastation which in terms of property anticipated the worst chapters of the two world wars. Georgia and the Shenandoah suffered in 1864 almost precisely as Belgium and Serbia suffered in 1914—the executions omitted. It was barbaric, and the only excuse to be made is that war is barbarism.

The turning point in the attitude of Northern military men was reached when General John Pope on July 18, 1862, issued from Washington headquarters a set of Draconian general orders. Order No. 5 directed that the army should subsist as far as practicable upon the country, giving vouchers for supplies seized. Order No. 7 decreed the summary execution of persons caught firing upon Union troops from houses. Order No. 11 (five days later) required officers to arrest immediately all disloyal males within reach, to make them take the oath of allegiance or go South, and to shoot all who violated their oath or who returned from the Confederacy. The order for living on the country, widely publicized East and West, changed the attitude of troops, and inspired private looting as well as public seizures of property. Pope was soon ousted, but the moral effect of his orders persisted.

Though most of the facts were excluded from official reports, their sum total, insofar as one shrewd observer could arrive at it, may be found in John T. Trowbridge's graphic volume written in 1866, "A Picture of the Desolated States." In his preface Trowbridge speaks of the Union forces not as our heroic armies but our destroying armies. Even this practiced reporter is less graphic, however, than the people who suffered under the onslaught and wrote while their emotions, like their property, still burned. Hear a lady of Louisiana tell what occurred when N.P. Banks's army passed:

> I was watching from my window the apparently orderly march of the first Yankees that appeared in view and passed up the road, when, suddenly, as if by magic, the whole plantation was covered with men, like bees from an overthrown hive; and, as far as my vision extended, an inextricable medley of men and animals met my eye. In one place, excited troopers were firing into the flock of sheep; in another, officers and men were in pursuit of the boys' ponies, and in another, a crowd were in excited chase of the work animals. The kitchen was soon filled with some, carrying off the cooking utensils and the provisions of the day; the yard with others, pursuing the poultry. . . . They penetrated under the house, into the outbuildings, and into the garden, stripping it in a moment of all its vegetables. . . . This continued during the day . . . and amid a bewildering sound of oaths and imprecations. . . . When the army had passed, we were left destitute.

Sherman believed in total war; that is, in waging war not only against the Southern armies, but the Southern people. His theory was that every man, woman, and child was "armed and at war." He wrote his wife in the summer of 1862 that the North might fall into bankruptcy, "but if they can hold on the war will soon assume a turn to extermination, not of soldiers alone, but the people." He denied, in effect, that Southerners had a right to resist invasion. When Union steamers were fired on near Randolph, Mississippi, in the fall of 1862, he destroyed Randolph, and a little later had all houses, farms, and cornfields devastated for fifteen miles along the banks.

When he drove his red plowshare across Georgia and the Carolinas, his object was to leave only scorched earth behind. He had already written of his Western operations: "Not a man is to be seen; nothing but women with houses plundered, fields open to the cattle and horses, pickets lounging on every porch, and desolation sown broadcast; servants all gone, and women and children bred in luxury . . . begging . . . for soldiers' rations." His aim was that which Phil Sheridan avowed: to leave them nothing but their eyes to weep with.

The final devastation of half the South was horrible to behold, and it was distressing to think that these savage losses had been inflicted by Americans upon fellow Americans. Yet this was far from being the worst aspect of the conflict, or the least easily reparable. Damages on which we can fix the dollar sign are important not in themselves, but as they become translated into cultural and spiritual losses; into the intellectual retardation caused by poverty, for example. The physical recovery of the South was rapid. As it was primarily an agricultural section, a few good crops at fair prices did much to restore it; and the swiftness with which housing, railroads, bridges, and public facilities were rebuilt astonished observers of the 1870s just as the swift postwar recovery of Germany and Poland has astonished observers of our day.

Infinitely worse were the biological losses—the radical hurts—inflicted by the Civil War. The killing of between 600,000 and 700,000 young men in a nation of 33,000,000 and the maiming or permanent debilitation of as many more had evil consequences projected into the far-distant future. We lost not only these men, but their children, and their children's children. Here, indeed, was a loss that proved highly cumulative. During the First World War, Lord Dunsany wrote a slender volume called "Tales of War." One of his apologues showed the Kaiser, as the embodiment of German militarism, commanded by a spirit to come on a tour. They crossed the German plain to a neat garden. Look, said the spirit:

> The Kaiser looked; and saw a window shining and a neat room in a cottage; there was nothing dreadful there, thank the good German God for that; it was all right, after all. The Kaiser had had a fright, but it was all right; there was only a woman with a baby sitting before a fire, and two small children and a man. And it was quite a jolly room. And the man was a young soldier; and, why he was a Prussian Guardsman—there was a helmet hanging on the wall—so everything was all right. They were jolly German children; that was well. How nice and homely the room was. . . . The firelight flickered, and the lamp shone on, and the children played on the floor, and the man was smoking out of a china pipe; he was strong and able and young, one of the wealth-winners of Germany.
>
> "Have you seen?" asked the phantom.
>
> "Yes," said the Kaiser. . . .
>
> At once the fire went out and the lamp faded away, the room fell sombrely into neglect and squalor, and the soldier and the children faded away with the room; all disappeared phantasmally, and nothing remained but the helmet in a kind of glow on the wall, and the woman sitting all by herself in the darkness.
>
> "It has all gone," said the Kaiser.
>
> "It has never been," said the phantom.
>
> The Kaiser looked again. Yes, there was nothing there, it was just a vision. . . .
>
> "It might have been," said the phantom.

Just so, we can say the multitude of Civil War dead represent hundreds of thousands of homes, and hundreds of thousands of families, that might have been, and never were. They represent millions of people who might have been part of our population today and are not. We have lost the books they might have written, the scientific discoveries they might have made, the inventions they might have perfected. Such a loss defies measurement.

The only noteworthy attempt to measure the biological losses was made by David Starr Jordan and his son Harvey in a volume called "War's Aftermath" (1914). The authors circulated carefully drawn questionnaires in Spottsylvania and Rockbridge Counties in Virginia, and in Cobb County in Georgia,

inquiring particularly into the eugenic effects of the conflict. One of their que-
ries brought out evidence that by no means all casualties were among the men;
numerous girls and women succumbed to the hardships and anxieties of the
conflict in the South. Another question elicited unanimous agreement that
"the flower of the people" went into the war at the beginning, and of these a
large part died before the end. [Stanford University] President Jordan, weighing
all the responses, reached two conclusions: first, that the evidence "leaves a
decided evidence in favor of grave racial hurt," and second, that "the war has
seriously impoverished this country of its best human values."

Even the terrible loss of young, productive lives, the grave biological injury to the nation, however, did not constitute the worst side of the war. One
aspect of the conflict was still more serious. It was the aspect to which Lowell
referred in lines written a few years after Appomattox:

> I looked to see an ampler atmosphere
> By that electric passion-gust blown clear
> I looked for this; consider what I hear. . . .
> Murmur of many voices in the air
> Denounces us degenerate,
> Unfaithful guardians of a noble fate. . . .

The war, as Walt Whitman truly said, had grown out of defects in the
American character; of American faults it cured few, accentuated a number,
and gave some a violently dangerous trend. Far behind the lines, it added to the
already discreditable total of violence in American life. Applying to industry a
great forcing-draft, the bellows of huge wartime appropriations, it strengthened the materialistic forces in our civilization. Its state and federal contracts,
its bounty system, its innumerable opportunities for battening on the nation's
woes, made speculation fashionable, and corruption almost too common for
comment. Its inflation bred extravagance and dissipation.

Every month heightened the intolerance of war; it began with mobs in New
York threatening newspaper offices, a mob in Philadelphia trying to lynch Senator James A. Bayard, and mobs in the South flogging and exiling Union men;
as it went on, freedom of speech almost disappeared over broad areas. The
atmosphere of war fostered immorality; Richmond and Washington alike became filled with saloons, brothels, and gambling dens, and such occupied
cities as Memphis and Nashville were sinks of iniquity. For every knightly
martyr like James Wadsworth or Albert Sidney Johnston there arose two such
coarse, aggressive, selfish careerists as Ben Butler and Dan Sickles. Wadsworth
and Johnston died in battle, but Butler and Sickles remained to follow postwar
political careers. Seen in perspective, the war was a gigantic engine for coarsen-
ing and lowering the American character even while it quickened certain of
our energies.

Parson Brownlow, a Tennessee Unionist, went from city to city in the
North in 1862 demanding "grape for the Rebel masses, and hemp for their
leaders"; saying that he himself would tie the rope about the necks of some

rebel generals; calling for the confiscation of all Southern property; proclaiming that he would be glad to arm every wolf, bear, catamount, and crocodile, every devil in hell, to defeat the South; and declaring he would put down the rebellion "if it exterminates from God's green earth every man, woman, and child south of Mason and Dixon's Line."

In the South two famous leaders, Robert Toombs and Howell Cobb, united that year in an address to their people just as virtriolic. "The foot of the oppressor is on the soil of Georgia," it began. "He comes with lust in his eye, poverty in his purse, and hell in his heart. How shall you meet him? . . . With death for him or for yourself!" Better the charnel house for every Southerner, they continued, than "loathsome vassalage to a nation already sunk below the contempt of the civilized world." Thaddeus Stevens nursed his hatred until he spoke of "exterminating" or driving into exile *all* Southerners, just as Sherman declared he would "slay millions" to assure the safety of the Mississippi. Women of the South meanwhile expressed the most vindictive detestation of all Yankees. "I hate them," wrote one Mississippi woman after a raid on her community, "more now than I did the evening I saw them sneaking off with all we cared for, and so it will be every day I live."

Hatred was seen in its most naked form in those communities divided against themselves and racked by guerrilla war; in Missouri, Arkansas, parts of Kentucky, and east Tennessee. Writes Charles D. Drake, a distinguished Missouri leader, of his state: "Falsehood, treachery, and perjury pervaded the whole social fabric." He went on: "Could there be written a full account of all the crimes of the rebels of Missouri, and the outrages and wrongs inflicted by them upon her loyal inhabitants, during the four years of the rebellion, the world would shrink aghast from a picture which has no parallel in the previous history of any portion of the Anglo-Saxon race." Confederate sympathizers in Missouri would have said the same of Union irregulars. One atrocity provoked another. These hatreds long survived the conflict, and indeed in some spots the embers still smolder. Typifying the whole range of spiritual injuries wrought by the war, they justify the poet Blake's cry:

> The soldier, armed with sword and gun,
> Palsied strikes the summer sun.

The historian Mendelssohn Bartholdy, in his volume entitled "War and German Society," written as part of the Carnegie Endowment's huge economic history of World War I, concluded that the moral effects of war are much worse than the material effects. He also concluded that they are radically bad, for they strike at the very heart of a country's character: "modern war, with its robot-like disregard of individual values, is bound to make the peculiar virtue of a nation an object of attack." As respects the Civil War, we can agree. If it was necessary for preserving the Union and extinguishing slavery, it was of course worth more than it cost; but should it have been necessary? Could not better leadership from 1830 to 1860 have averted it? This is a bootless question. But it is certain that the conflict, so much the greatest convulsion in our history, so tremendous in its impact on our national life, so fascinating in its drama, was in spite of all compensating elements, all the heroism, all the high example we find in Lee's character and Lincoln's wisdom, materially a disaster and morally a tragedy.

It is unfortunate that of the flood of books on the war ninety-nine in a hundred are on military topics and leaders, and that a great majority fasten attention on the floating banners, the high-ringing cheers, the humors of the camp, the ardors of the charge; the whole undeniable fascination and romance of the first true *Volkskrieg* in history. It is right, within measure, to let them lift our hearts. But the long commemoration will pass essentially unimproved if it does not give us a deeper, sterner, more scientific study of the collision of two creeds and two ways of life as related to an examination of war in general.

We should probe more deeply into its roots, a process that will expose some of the weaknesses of our social fabric and governmental system. We should pay fuller attention to its darker aspects, and examine more honestly such misrepresentations as the statement that it was distinguished by its generosity of spirit, the magnanimity with which the combatants treated each other; a statement absurd on its face, for no war which lasts four years and costs 600,000 lives leaves much magnanimity in its later phases. We should above all examine more closely the effects of the great and terrible war not on the nation's politics—we know that; not on its economy—we also know that; but on its character, the vital element of national life.

This examination will lead into unpleasant paths, and bring us to unhappy conclusions; but it will profit us far more than stirring battle canvases. All nations must be schooled in such studies if the world is ever to find an answer to a question uttered just after World War I by William E. Borah, a question that still rings in men's ears: "When shall we escape from war? When shall we loosen the grip of the monster?"

Abraham Lincoln: The Man Behind the Myths

Stephen B. Oates

As the Richard Hofstadter selection earlier noted, important elements of the "Lincoln myth" are attributable to and were rather consciously sustained by Abraham Lincoln himself. Beyond this, however, it is necessary to take account as well of associated myths—and mythmakers—after Lincoln. For ever since his tragic assassination, both his accomplishments and his memory have strongly affected the emotional and political life of the nation. The Lincoln who *was* largely remains the Lincoln who *is*, so strongly has his mythic reputation persisted—for poets (Walt Whitman), for sculptors (Gutzon Borglum, who fashioned Mount Rushmore), for foreign novelists (Leo Tolstoy), and for the American people at large. Finding the myths of Lincoln essentially benign—if taken as myths, not history—Professor Stephen B. Oates of the University of Massachusetts at Amherst tries to sustain a careful distinction between the two as he notes how "democracy's mythic hero" came to succeeding generations of Americans as the Man of the People, the Great Commoner, and Father Abraham. The poet Carl Sandburg, especially, had the greatest hand in crafting these images, emotionally shaping the contours of Lincoln's memory for a nation eager to reconstruct itself and carry on the traditions of democracy.

In 1858, against a backdrop of heightening sectional tensions over slavery, Abraham Lincoln stood in the Great Hall of the Illinois House of Representatives, warning his countrymen that a house divided against itself could not stand. Across Illinois that year, in a series of forensic duels with Stephen A. Douglas, this tall and melancholy man addressed himself boldly to the difficult problems of his day: to the haunting moral contradiction of slavery in a nation based on the Declaration of Independence . . . to the combustible issue of Negro social and political rights . . . to the meaning and historic mission of America's experiment in popular government. This same man went on to the presidency, charged with the awesome task of saving the Union—and its experiment in popular government—in the holocaust of civil war. In the end, after enduring four unendurable years, he himself became a casualty of that conflict, gunned down by John Wilkes Booth just when the war was won and popular government preserved for humankind the world over.

The man who died that dark and dismal day had flaws as well as

Excerpt from *Abraham Lincoln: The Man Behind the Myths* by Stephen B. Oates. Copyright © 1984 by Stephen B. Oates. Reprinted by permission of Harper & Row, Publishers, Inc.

strengths, made mistakes and suffered reversals just as surely as he enjoyed his remarkable achievements. But in the days that followed his assassination, the man became obscured in an outpouring of flowery orations and tear-filled eulogies. As the seasons passed, Lincoln went on to legend and martyrdom, inflated by the myth makers into a godly Emancipator who personified America's ideal Everyman.

Before proceeding, I had best try to define myth as I am using it here. Above all, I do not mean some preposterous story. Nor do I mean a story that is uncontaminated by life. Myth, as I am using the term, is a grandiose projection of a people's experience. As X. J. Kennedy has put it, "Myths tell us of the exploits of the gods—their battles, the ways in which they live, love, and perhaps suffer—all on a scale of magnificence larger than our life. We envy their freedom and power; they enact our wishes and dreams." In other words, the grandiose dimensions and symbol-building power of the myths we create reveal our deepest longings as a people. And this is especially true of the myths we Americans have fashioned about the powerful figure who presided over the Civil War, our greatest trial as a nation. Our extravagant projections of Lincoln in myth suggest a great deal about the spiritual and psychological needs of our culture ever since.

As historian David Donald has noted, two traditions of Lincoln mythology developed after the war. The first began on "Black Easter," April 16, 1865, when ministers across the North portrayed the slain President as an American Christ who died to expiate the sins of his guilty land. For them, it was no coincidence that he had fallen on Good Friday. Did not the times of his shooting and death—just after ten in the evening and just after seven-twenty the next morning—make on the clock an outline of the crucifix? "Oh, friends," cried the Reverend C. B. Crane from the pulpit of Broadway Tabernacle, "it was meet that the martyrdom should occur on Good Friday. It is no blasphemy against the Son of God and the Saviour of men that we declare the fitness of the slaying of the second Father of our Republic on the anniversary of the day on which He was slain. Jesus Christ died for the world, Abraham Lincoln died for his country."

Blacks, too, viewed Lincoln with uninhibited reverence. "We mourn for the loss of our great and good President," a Negro soldier wrote his fiancée. "Humanity has lost a firm advocate, our race its Patron Saint, and the good of all the world a fitting object to emulate. . . . The name Abraham Lincoln will ever be cherished in our hearts, and none will more delight to lisp his name in reverence than the future generations of our people." In truth, black Americans came to regard Lincoln as a perfect, personal emancipator and kept pictures of him pasted on the walls above their mantelpieces. "To the deeply emotional and religious slave," as one man explained, "Lincoln was an earthly incarnation of the Saviour of mankind."

And so one body of writings depicted him in the ensuing decades. Typical of this school was Josiah Gilbert Holland's *The Life of Abraham Lincoln*, which appeared in 1866 and sold more than 100,000 copies. Holland's Lincoln is a model youth and an impeccable Christian gentleman. When war clouds gather in 1860, he supposedly tells an Illinois associate: "I know there is a God and that he hates injustice and slavery. I see the storm coming, and I know that His hand is in it. If he has a place for and work for me—and I think he has—I believe I am ready. I am nothing, but truth is everything. I know I am right, because I know that liberty is right, for Christ teaches it and Christ is God." For Holland and other writers, ministers, and orators of this tradition, Lincoln was a martyr-saint, as pure and perfect a spirit as the Almighty ever created. He was "savior of the republic, emancipator of a race, true Christian, true man."

Sheer nonsense! thundered William H. Herndon, Lincoln's nervous, besotted law partner, when he read Holland's book. This prettified character was not the Lincoln he had known in Illinois. That Lincoln had never belonged to a church. He was *"an infidel,"* a prairie lawyer who told stories that made the pious wince. Determined to correct Holland's portrait, Herndon set out "to write the life of Lincoln as I saw him—honestly—truthfully—co[u]rageously—fearlessly cut whom it may." He jotted down his own impressions and interviewed old settlers in Indiana and Illinois who remembered Lincoln. They spun yarns about "Old Abe" that made Herndon's eyes hang out on his shirt front. Their Lincoln was an Illinois Paul Bunyan who could hoist a whiskey barrel overhead, a prairie Davy Crockett who roared that he was "the big buck of the lick." No historian, Herndon embraced such tales as zealously as he did actual fact. As a consequence, *Herndon's Lincoln: The True Story of a Great Life,* which came out in 1889, brimmed with gossip, hearsay, and legend, all mixed in with Herndon's own authentic observations of Lincoln in their law office, in Springfield's muddy streets, in courthouses and on the platform.

In sharp contrast to Holland's Christian gentleman, Herndon's Lincoln is a Western folk hero, funny, ambitious, irreverent, and sorrowful by turns. He is born in a "stagnant, putrid pool," the son of a shiftless poor white and "the illegitimate daughter" of a prominent Virginia planter. Though he rises above his impoverished origins, Herndon's Lincoln still has the stamp of the frontier on him: he plays practical jokes and performs legendary feats of strength. Still, he fears that he is illegitimate, too, and that and other woes often make him depressed. In New Salem, Herndon's Lincoln has the only love affair of his life. This is the Ann Rutledge story, a chimerical story which Herndon popularized and which subsequent biographies shamelessly repeated. In Herndon's telling, Lincoln falls deeply in love with Ann and almost goes mad when she dies. As she lies in her grave, he moans miserably, "My heart is buried there." If his heart is buried there, then he cannot possibly love Mary Todd. Herndon certainly bears her no love; in fact, he detests the woman; she is *"the female wildcat of the age."* What follows about Lincoln and Mary is mostly malicious gossip. In Springfield, Herndon's Lincoln does promise to wed Mary, only to plummet into despair. How can he marry this nasty little woman? Still, his sense of honor torments him. He has given his word. Sacrificing domestic happiness, Herndon's Lincoln goes ahead with the marriage, and Mary, a "tigress," "soured," "insolent," "haughty," and "gross," devotes herself to making Lincoln miserable. For him, life with Mary is "worse punishment . . . than burning by the stake." He finds escape in law and politics, and through adversity rises to "the topmost rung of the ladder." No haloed saint, Herndon's Lincoln in sum is a product of the great Western prairies, a religious skeptic, open, candid, energetic, trusting, and brave.

Herndon had promised that his *Lincoln* would "cause a squirm," and he was right. From across American Christendom came a fierce and unrelenting cry, "Atheist! Atheist! Herndon's an atheist!" With that, Herndon's partisans took on those of the Holland school in what David Donald has termed "a religious war." And so the two mythical conceptions—one portraying Lincoln as a frontier hero, the other as a martyr-saint—battled one another into the twentieth century.

By 1909, the centennial year of Lincoln's birth, the two traditions had begun to blend into "a composite American ideal," as Donald has said. But it remained for Carl Sandburg, in his epochal *Abraham Lincoln,* to combine the saint and folklore Lincoln and capture the mythic figure more vividly and consistently than any other folk biographer. In truth, Sandburg's became the most popular Lincoln work ever written, as a procession of plays, motion pictures, novels, children's books, school texts, and television shows purveyed Sandburg's Lincoln to a vast American public, until that Lincoln became for most Americans the real historical figure.

Yet, ironically enough, Sandburg did not set out to write an enduring epic. When he began his project in 1923, he intended only to do a Lincoln book for teenagers. He had collected Lincoln materials since his days at Lombard College in Galesburg, Illinois. Now he read voraciously in the sources, particularly in *Herndon's Lincoln.* And he retraced Lincoln's path across Illinois, chatting with plain folk as Herndon had done, looking for the Lincoln who lived in their imaginations and memories. As he worked, Sandburg strongly identified with "Abe" and even dressed, acted, and physically resembled the figure taking shape in his mind. "Like him," Sandburg said, "I am a son of the prairie, a poor boy who wandered over the land to find himself and his mission in life." Both were commoners from Illinois, both champions of the underdog, both great storytellers, and "both poets withal," as Stuart Sherman said.

As it happened, another poet had the most influence on Sandburg as a Lincoln biographer. This was Walt Whitman, who before the Civil War had actually anticipated the kind of mythic Lincoln who subsequently emerged. In the rollicking preface to *Leaves of Grass,* first published in 1855, Whitman's Poet Hero was "the equable man," simple, generous, and large, who spoke for the common people and for national union. In 1856, with uncanny foresight, Whitman asserted that "I would be much pleased to see some heroic, shrewd, fully-informed, healthy bodied, middle-aged, beard-faced American blacksmith come down from the West across the Alleghanies, and walk into the Presidency, dressed in a clean suit of working attire, and with the tan all over his face, breast, and arms." Four years later, Republican campaign propaganda depicted the rail-splitter candidate as almost exactly such a man.

In February, 1861, Whitman saw the President-elect as he passed through New York City on his way to Washington. Lincoln's "look and gait" captivated Whitman—"his dark-brown complexion, seam'd and wrinkled yet canny-looking face, his black, bushy head of hair, disproportionately long neck, and his hands held behind him as he stood observing the people." Here was a hero fit for the author of *Leaves of Grass*. From that moment on, Whitman idolized Lincoln and insisted that only the combined genius of Plutarch, Aeschylus, and Michelangelo—"assisted by Rabelais"—could have captured Lincoln's likeness. A true portrait, in other words, must have the dimensions and powerful symbols of myth.

"He has a face like a hoosier Michel Angelo," Whitman wrote three years later, "so awful ugly it becomes beautiful, with its strange mouth, its deep cut, criss-cross lines, and its doughnut complexion." Then he wrote something that was to affect Carl Sandburg enormously: "My notion is, too, that underneath his outside smutched mannerism, and stories from third-class country bar-rooms (it is his humor,) Mr. Lincoln keeps a fountain of first-class practical telling wisdom. I do not dwell on the supposed failures of his government; he has shown, I sometimes think, an almost supernatural tact in keeping the ship afloat at all, with head steady, not only not going down, and now certain not to, but with proud and resolute spirit, and flag flying in sight of the world, menacing and high as ever." Here was the mythic "equalizer of his age and land" who inhabited Whitman's *Leaves of Grass*, a poet leader who in peace "speaks in the spirit of peace," but in war "is the most deadly force of the war."

In Lincoln, Whitman saw the archetypical Captain who was destined to lie "fallen cold and dead." And after Lincoln did fall, the poet poured out his grief in "When Lilacs Last in the Dooryard Bloom'd," a melodic farewell to the leader he loved, "O powerful western fallen star!" "the sweetest, wisest soul of all my days and lands." In 1886, broken down from a stroke, this "tender mother-man" with whiskered face and luminous blue-gray eyes, smelling of soap and cologne, wearing his gray felt hat tilted straight back, gave a memorial lecture about Lincoln which he repeated almost every year until his death in 1892. It was a ritual reenactment of Lincoln's assassination, a poet's celebration of a "sane and sacred death" that filtered "into the nation and race" and gave "a cement to the whole People, subtler, more underlying, than anything in written Constitution, or courts or armies."

In Whitman's writings, Sandburg found the central themes of the life he wanted to tell. He was already publishing verse that reflected Whitman's influence and would soon be known as his heir, describing him as "the only distinguished epic poet in America." But it was Whitman's mythic vision of Lincoln that most captured Sandburg's imagination, setting many of the expectations in treatment, mood, and archetype, as Justin Kaplan has pointed out, which Sandburg would try to satisfy in his biography. "In Lincoln," Sandburg himself wrote, "the people of the United States could finally see themselves, each for himself and all together." And he intended, Sandburg said, "to take Lincoln away from the religious bigots and the professional politicians and restore him to the common people."

Sandburg became completely absorbed in his Lincoln enterprise, so much so that at times he "felt as if in a trance, saw automobiles as horses and wagons, and saw cities of brick and stone dissolve into lumber cottages and shanties." What began as a teenagers' book swelled into a massive "life and times" that took fifteen years to complete and ran to 3,765 pages in six published volumes: the two-volume *Prairie Years*, which appeared in 1928, and the four-volume *War Years*, which followed in 1939. Sandburg's was a sprawling panorama, the literary equivalent of a Cecil B. DeMille motion-picture spectacular, with Lincoln himself alternately disappearing and reappearing in a rush of crowded scenes and events. And the Lincoln that emerges is not only a composite of the patron saint and Western hero; he is democracy's mythic hero, a great commoner who rises to the White House from utter obscurity, an "All-American" President who personifies the American ideal that "a democracy can choose a man," as Sandburg writes, "set him up with power and honor, and the very act does something to the man himself, raises up new gifts, modulations, controls, outlooks, wisdoms, inside the man, so that he is something else again than he was before they sifted him out and anointed him . . . Head of the Nation."

Sandburg's *Lincoln* captured the hearts of an entire generation of Americans, a generation that came of age in the cynical twenties, with its gang wars and brassy speakeasies, unbridled speculation and declining moral values, and that struggled through the Great Depression of the thirties, the worst crisis of American democracy since the Civil War. Small wonder that Sandburg won near universal acclaim. For poet Stephen Vincent Benét, Sandburg's "mountain range of biography" was "a good purge for our own troubled time and for its wild-eyed fears. For here we see the thing working, clumsily, erratically, often unfairly, attacked and reviled by extremists of left and right, yet working and surviving nevertheless." For Henry Bertram Hill of the Kansas City *Star*, Sandburg's Lincoln was "an apotheosis of the American people as well as of Lincoln as the greatest exemplar of their essential worth and goodness." For historian Henry Steele Commager, poets had always understood Lincoln best, and so it was "fitting that from the pen of a poet should come the greatest of all Lincoln biographies." For playwright Robert E. Sherwood, it was "a monument that would live forever."

Yet, as some critics pointed out, Sandburg's Lincoln could not be regarded as authentic biography, as an approximation of the real-life Lincoln based on accurate detail. No, Sandburg was not after that Lincoln. He was after the mythic figure—the Man of the People who had always fascinated him the most. And proven fact and sound documentation did not impede the poet in his search. "He suggests," as one critic said, "a bard sitting before a rude fireplace, chanting his hero tale with a poet's repetitions and refrains."

As *The Prairie Years* opens, we find the future Head of the Nation born of ordinary pioneer stock on the cutting edge of the Kentucky frontier. What follows is a gripping story, a poetic story, and it abounds in fictional scenes and lyrical apocrypha. As a boy, Sandburg's Lincoln shucks corn from early dawn till sundown and then reads books all night by the flickering fire. He kisses Green Taylor's girl. He once fights William Grigsby and cries out (as did Herndon's Lincoln), "I'm the big buck of this lick." He lifts barefoot boys so they can leave muddy footprints on the ceiling of the Lincoln cabin. Later, as a New Salem clerk, he walks six miles to return a few cents a customer has overpaid on her bill. And of course, he loves Ann Rutledge with an aching heart. "After the first evening in which Lincoln had sat next to her and found that bashful words tumbling from his tongue's end really spelled themselves out into sensible talk, her face, as he went away, kept coming back. So often all else would fade out of his mind and there would be only this riddle of a pink-fair face, a mouth and eyes in a frame of light corn-silk hair. He could ask himself what it meant and search his heart for an answer and no answer would come. A trembling took his body and dark waves ran through him sometimes when she spoke so simple a thing as, 'The corn is getting high, isn't it?' " Which prompted Edmund Wilson to remark, "The corn is getting high indeed!"

When Ann dies, Sandburg's Lincoln, like Herndon's, is stricken with a lover's grief: he wanders absently in the forest; he makes his way to the burying ground outside New Salem and lies with an arm across Ann's grave. "In the evenings it was useless to try to talk with him," Sandburg writes. "He sat by the fire one night as the flames licked up the cordwood and swept up the chimney to pass out into a driving storm-wind. The blowing weather woke some sort of lights in him and he went to the door and looked out into a night of fierce stumbling wind and black horizons. And he came back saying, 'I can't bear to think of her out there alone.' And he clenched his hands, mumbling, 'The rain and the storm shan't beat on her grave.' "

Though he eventually recovers from Ann's death, Sandburg's Lincoln never forgets the love he felt for her.*

As he grows to maturity, Sandburg's Lincoln is indigenously American, utterly shaped by the sprawling, unruly, pungent democracy of his day. He is simple, honest and ambitious, practical and wise. Professionally he is a homespun village lawyer and politician, always dressed in a rumpled suit and an old stovepipe hat. It is noticed among men that he has "two shifting moods," one when he lapses into "a gravity beyond any bystander to penetrate," the other when he recounts a "rollicking, droll story," usually to illustrate some point about people or politics. In the company of his male friends, he can tell off-color jokes, too, and indulge in an expletive like "son-of-a-bitch." He is a colorful and yet mystic man, a kind of prairie Socrates brimming with wilderness wit and prairie sagacity. Above all, his heart beats with the pulse of rural, working-class America, and he loves the common folk and revels in daily contact with them.

But behind his bucolic plainness is a profound and mystical spirit awaiting its call to greatness. And that call comes in the grim and terrible years that

---

*There is not a scintilla of evidence for Sandburg's scenes about Lincoln and Ann. In fairness, though, Sandburg did delete a lot of this material in a one-volume condensation of the *Prairie* and *War Years*. But even there he persists in suggesting a romance between Lincoln and Ann and even quotes Edgar Lee Masters's ridiculous poem about how Ann Rutledge, "beloved in life of Abraham Lincoln," was wedded to him in her grave. Later Sandburg was sorry that he had fallen for the legend. He should have known it was out of character for Lincoln, he said.

follow the Kansas-Nebraska Act of 1854. Now Sandburg's Lincoln is a ghost on the platform, explaining to the people that the Revolution and freedom really mean something and reminding them of forgotten oaths and wasted sacrifices. In his great debates with Stephen A. Douglas, Sandburg's Lincoln is always one with the people, thrilling them with his "stubby, homely words." For the folk masses, he is both "the Strange Friend and Friendly Stranger." He is "something out of a picture book for children"—tall, bony, comical, haunted-looking, and sad. Already stories about him are spreading among the plain folk, and many sit brooding and talking about this "fabulous human figure of their own time." By 1861, history has called him to his tragic destiny: his is "a mind, a spirit, a tongue, and a voice" for an American democracy caught in its greatest trial. As he leaves Illinois for Washington, the presidency, and the war years, voices cry out on the wind, "Good-bye, Abe."

When he wrote *The War Years*, Sandburg abandoned poetical imaginings and produced a kind of symphonic documentary of the war and the man at its center. Though marred by a plethora of unauthenticated scenes and stories, the four volumes are full of the blood and stench—the sound and fury—of Civil War. And they capture all the immense tumult and confusion through which Lincoln day by day had to make his way. When we see the President, in between extensive passages on military and political developments in North and South alike, he is entirely an external Lincoln, an observed hero filtered to us through the vision and sensibilities of hundreds of witnesses who called at his White House office, from generals and politicians and office seekers to the infirm, the destitute, and the ordinary. By revealing Lincoln through the observations of others and relating him to almost everything that happened in his shell-torn land, Sandburg is trying to demonstrate that "the hopes and apprehensions of millions, their loves and hates, their exultation and despair, were reflected truthfully in the deep waters of Lincoln's being," as Robert Sherwood said.

In the "tornado years" of civil war, Sandburg's Lincoln is both the hero and the instrument of the people. He is the umpire of an embattled Union, patiently sticking to the cherished middle way. When it comes to emancipation, he always follows the pulse of the people: with a genius for timing, he issues his proclamation only when that is what they want. Now "a piece of historic drama" has been played, and across the world, among the masses of people who create folk gods out of slender fact, there runs the story of "the Strong Man who arose in his might and delivered an edict, spoke a few words fitly chosen, and thereupon the shackles and chains fell from the arms and ankles of men, women, and children born to be chattels for toil and bondage."

As the war rages on, Lincoln's "skilled referee hand" guides the ship of state through cross winds of passion and cross plays of hate. Throughout he has the folk masses behind him. He is still their Friendly Stranger in a storm of death and destruction. Even during his lowest ebb in 1864, he remains the people's President: he retains their love and loyalty even as Republican leaders raise a howl against his renomination and reelection. And he wins in 1864 because the wisdom of the people prevails.

Moreover, in the last long year of the war, Sandburg's Lincoln does battle with the so-called radicals of the party—vindictive cynics like Charles Sumner and old Thad Stevens, who in Sandburg's view want to exterminate the South's ruling class and convert Dixie into "a vast graveyard of slaughtered whites, with Negro State governments established and upheld by Northern white bayonets." But a mild and moderate Lincoln refuses to go along with them. He is now in his grandest hour, this Lincoln of *The War Years*, as he plans to reconstruct the South with tender magnanimity. He is the only man in the entire country who can peaceably reunite the sections. But, as in a Greek tragedy, Lincoln is murdered before he can bind up the nation's wounds and heal the antagonisms of his divided countrymen. In North and South, common people weep aloud, realizing the painful truth of the old folk adage that a tree is measured best when it is down.

"To a deep river," writes Sandburg, "to a far country, to a by-and-by whence no man returns, had gone the child of Nancy Hanks and Tom Lincoln, the wilderness boy who found far lights and tall rainbows to live by, whose name even before he died had become a legend inwoven with men's struggle for freedom the world over." There was the story of how Count Leo Tolstoy, traveling into the Caucasus of czarist Russia, encountered tribesmen demanding to know about Lincoln, the "greatest general and greatest ruler of the world." Says Sandburg: "To Tolstoy the incident proved that in far places over the earth the name of Lincoln was worshipped and the personality of Lincoln had become a world folk legend."

Sandburg ended his narrative with Lincoln's funeral in Springfield. But others have added an epilogue implied by Sandburg's story. Without Father Abraham, the epilogue goes, the nation foundered in the harsh years of reconstruction, as an all-too-mortal President succumbed to "vengeful radicals" on Capitol Hill. Alas, how much better reconstruction would have been had Father Abraham only lived. How much more easily a divided nation would have set aside the war years and come together again in a spirit of mutual respect and harmony. There would never have been an impeachment trial, never a radical reconstruction, never an army of occupation, never a Ku Klux Klan, never all those racial troubles to haunt later generations, if only Father Abraham had not died that terrible day in 1865.

And so Lincoln comes to us in the mists of mythology. Still, I have no quarrel with this Lincoln, so long as we make a careful distinction between myth and history. Myth, after all, is not an untrue story to be avoided like some dread disease. On the contrary, myth carries a special truth of its own—a truth, however, that is different from historical truth, from what actually happened. In the case of Lincoln, the myth is what Americans wish the man had been, not necessarily the way he was in real life. That is why Sandburg's Lincoln has such irresistible appeal to us. He is a "baffling and completely inexplicable" hero who embodies the mystical genius of our nation. He possesses what Americans have always considered their most noble traits—honesty, unpretentiousness, tolerance, hard work, a capacity to forgive, a compassion for the underdog, a clear-sighted vision of right and wrong, a dedication to God and country, and an abiding concern for all. As I have said elsewhere, no real-life person has ever risen to such mythic proportions, to epitomize all that we have longed to be since 1776. No real-life person can ever rise to such proportions. So we have invented a Lincoln who fulfills our deepest needs as a people—a Father Abraham who in the stormy present still provides an example and show us the way. The Lincoln of mythology carries the torch of the American dream, a dream of noble idealism, of self-sacrifice and common humanity, of liberty and equality for all.

Our folly as a nation, though, is that we too often confuse myth with history, mistake our mythologized heroes for their real-life counterparts, regard the deified frontiersman as the actual frontiersman. As a consequence, we too often try to emulate our mythical forebears, to be as glorious, as powerful, as incapable of error, as incessantly right, as we have made them. As journalist Ronnie Dugger has reminded us, those who live by the lessons of mythology rather than the lessons of history—as Lyndon Johnson did in the Vietnam era—are apt to trap themselves in catastrophe.

This is not to say that myths have no function in our cultural life. On the contrary, if we Americans can accept our myths as inspiring tales rather than as authentic history, then surely myths can serve us as they have traditional myth-bound societies. Like fiction and poetry, they can give us insight into ourselves, help us understand the spiritual needs of our country, as we cope with the complex realities of our own time. In that event, the Lincoln of mythology—the Plain and Humble Man of the People who emerged from the toiling millions to guide us through our greatest national ordeal—can have profound spiritual meaning for us.

The New View of Reconstruction

Eric Foner

Generations of American college students, at least those schooled prior to the 1960s, were rather comfortably conveyed the impression that Reconstruction—the era after the Civil War involved with "binding up the nation's wounds" opened by civil conflict—was an era of America's past simply portrayed in shades of black and white. It was said to offer a tale of black rule (the "Africanization" of southern politics), resultant corruption, political subordination of southern whites, military despotism, and radical congressional control of Reconstruction policy. Offering a summary of new research findings, Columbia University professor Eric Foner demonstrates how almost every previous assumption regarding Reconstruction has been overturned. Black supremacy was a myth, the era was far more conservative than radical, southern whites were not categorically disenfranchised, and military despotism was hardly the rule. Moreover, recent scholarship has formulated a new agenda for Reconstruction study, emphasizing social rather than political issues, noting the continuing relevance of Reconstruction issues to American society, and, most important, conceding the role of blacks as active agents in the profound changes of the time.

In the past twenty years, no period of American history has been the subject of a more thoroughgoing reevaluation than Reconstruction—the violent, dramatic, and still controversial era following the Civil War. Race relations, politics, social life, and economic change during Reconstruction have all been reinterpreted in the light of changed attitudes toward the place of blacks within American society. If historians have not yet forged a fully satisfying portrait of Reconstruction as a whole, the traditional interpretation that dominated historical writing for much of this century has irrevocably been laid to rest.

Anyone who attended high school before 1960 learned that Reconstruction was an era of unrelieved sordidness in American political and social life. The martyred Lincoln, according to this view, had planned a quick and painless readmission of the Southern states as equal members of the national family. President Andrew Johnson, his successor, attempted to carry out Lincoln's policies but was foiled by the Radical Republicans (also known as Vindictives or Jacobins). Motivated by an irrational hatred of Rebels or by ties with North-

From "The New View of Reconstruction" by Eric Foner. Reprinted with permission from *American Heritage*, Volume 34, No. 6. Copyright 1983 by American Heritage Publishing Co. Inc.

ern capitalists out to plunder the South, the Radicals swept aside Johnson's lenient program and fastened black supremacy upon the defeated Confederacy. An orgy of corruption followed, presided over by unscrupulous carpetbaggers (Northerners who ventured south to reap the spoils of office), traitorous scalawags (Southern whites who cooperated with the new governments for personal gain), and the ignorant and childlike freedmen, who were incapable of properly exercising the political power that had been thrust upon them. After much needless suffering, the white community of the South banded together to overthrow these "black" governments and restore home rule (their euphemism for white supremacy). All told, Reconstruction was just about the darkest page in the American saga.

Originating in anti-Reconstruction propaganda of Southern Democrats during the 1870s, this traditional interpretation achieved scholarly legitimacy around the turn of the century through the work of William Dunning and his students at Columbia University. It reached the larger public through films like *Birth of a Nation* and *Gone With the Wind* and that best-selling work of myth-making masquerading as history, *The Tragic Era* by Claude G. Bowers. In language as exaggerated as it was colorful, Bowers told how Andrew Johnson "fought the bravest battle for constitutional liberty and for the preservation of our institutions ever waged by an Executive" but was overwhelmed by the "poisonous propaganda" of the Radicals. Southern whites, as a result, "literally were put to the torture" by "emissaries of hate" who manipulated the "simple-minded" freedmen, "inflaming the negroes' egotism" and even inspiring "lustful assaults" by blacks upon white womanhood.

In a discipline that sometimes seems to pride itself on the rapid rise and fall of historical interpretations, this traditional portrait of Reconstruction enjoyed remarkable staying power. The long reign of the old interpretation is not difficult to explain. It presented a set of easily identifiable heroes and villains. It enjoyed the imprimatur of the nation's leading scholars. And it accorded with the political and social realities of the first half of this century. This image of Reconstruction helped freeze the mind of the white South in unalterable opposition to any movement for breaching the ascendancy of the Democratic party, eliminating segregation, or readmitting disfranchised blacks to the vote.

Nevertheless, the demise of the traditional interpretation was inevitable, for it ignored the testimony of the central participant in the drama of Reconstruction—the black freedman. Furthermore, it was grounded in the conviction that blacks were unfit to share in political power. As Dunning's Columbia colleague John W. Burgess put it, "A black skin means membership in a race of men which has never of itself succeeded in subjecting passion to reason, has never, therefore, created any civilization of any kind." Once objective scholarship and modern experience rendered that assumption untenable, the entire edifice was bound to fall.

The work of "revising" the history of Reconstruction began with the writings of a handful of survivors of the era, such as John R. Lynch, who had served as a black congressman from Mississippi after the Civil War. In the

1930s white scholars like Francis Simkins and Robert Woody carried the task forward. Then, in 1935, the black historian and activist W. E. B. Du Bois produced *Black Reconstruction in America*, a monumental reevaluation that closed with an irrefutable indictment of a historical profession that had sacrificed scholarly objectivity on the altar of racial bias. "One fact and one alone," he wrote, "explains the attitude of most recent writers toward Reconstruction; they cannot conceive of Negroes as men." Du Bois's work, however, was ignored by most historians.

It was not until the 1960s that the full force of the revisionist wave broke over the field. Then, in rapid succession, virtually every assumption of the traditional viewpoint was systematically dismantled. A drastically different portrait emerged to take its place. President Lincoln did not have a coherent "plan" for Reconstruction, but at the time of his assassination he had been cautiously contemplating black suffrage. Andrew Johnson was a stubborn, racist politician who lacked the ability to compromise. By isolating himself from the broad currents of public opinion that had nourished Lincoln's career, Johnson created an impasse with Congress that Lincoln would certainly have avoided, thus throwing away his political power and destroying his own plans for reconstructing the South.

The Radicals in Congress were acquitted of both vindictive motives and the charge of serving as the stalking-horses of Northern capitalism. They emerged instead as idealists in the best nineteenth-century reform tradition. Radical leaders like Charles Sumner and Thaddeus Stevens had worked for the rights of blacks long before any conceivable political advantage flowed from such a commitment. Stevens refused to sign the Pennsylvania Constitution of 1838 because it disfranchised the state's black citizens; Sumner led a fight in the 1850s to integrate Boston's public schools. Their Reconstruction policies were based on principle, not petty political advantage, for the central issue dividing Johnson and these Radical Republicans was the civil rights of freedmen. Studies of congressional policy-making, such as Eric L. McKitrick's *Andrew Johnson and Reconstruction*, also revealed that Reconstruction legislation, ranging from the Civil Rights Act of 1866 to the Fourteenth and Fifteenth Amendments, enjoyed broad support from moderate and conservative Republicans. It was not simply the work of a narrow Radical faction.

Even more startling was the revised portrait of Reconstruction in the South itself. Imbued with the spirit of the civil rights movement and rejecting entirely the racial assumptions that had underpinned the traditional interpretation, these historians evaluated Reconstruction from the black point of view. Works like Joel Williamson's *After Slavery* portrayed the period as a time of extraordinary political, social, and economic progress for blacks. The establishment of public school systems, the granting of equal citizenship to blacks, the effort to restore the devastated Southern economy, the attempt to construct an interracial political democracy from the ashes of slavery, all these were commendable achievements, not the elements of Bowers's "tragic era."

Unlike earlier writers, the revisionists stressed the active role of the freedmen in shaping Reconstruction. Black initiative established as many schools as did Northern religious societies and the Freedmen's Bureau. The right to vote was not simply thrust upon them by meddling outsiders, since blacks began agitating for the suffrage as soon as they were freed. In 1865 black conventions throughout the South issued eloquent, though unheeded, appeals for equal civil and political rights.

With the advent of Radical Reconstruction in 1867, the freedmen did enjoy a real measure of political power. But black supremacy never existed. In most states blacks held only a small fraction of political offices, and even in South Carolina, where they comprised a majority of the state legislature's lower house, effective power remained in white hands. As for corruption, moral standards in both government and private enterprise were at low ebb throughout the nation in the postwar years—the era of Boss Tweed, the Credit Mobilier scandal, and the Whiskey Ring. Southern corruption could hardly be blamed on former slaves.

Other actors in the Reconstruction drama also came in for reevaluation. Most carpetbaggers were former Union soldiers seeking economic opportunity in the postwar South, not unscrupulous adventurers. Their motives, a typically American amalgam of humanitarianism and the pursuit of profit, were no more insidious than those of Western pioneers. Scalawags, previously seen as traitors to the white race, now emerged as "Old Line" Whig Unionists who had opposed secession in the first place or as poor whites who had long resented planters' domination of Southern life and who saw in Reconstruction a chance to recast Southern society along more democratic lines. Strongholds of Southern white Republicanism like east Tennessee and western North Carolina had been the scene of resistance to Confederate rule throughout the Civil War; now, as one scalawag newspaper put it, the choice was "between salvation at the hand of the Negro or destruction at the hand of the rebels."

At the same time, the Ku Klux Klan and kindred groups, whose campaign of violence against black and white Republicans had been minimized or excused in older writings, were portrayed as they really were. Earlier scholars had conveyed the impression that the Klan intimidated blacks mainly by dressing as ghosts and playing on the freedmen's superstitions. In fact, black fears were all too real: the Klan was a terrorist organization that beat and killed its political opponents to deprive blacks of their newly won rights. The complicity of the Democratic party and the silence of prominent whites in the face of such outrages stood as an indictment of the moral code the South had inherited from the days of slavery.

By the end of the 1960s, then, the old interpretation had been completely reversed. Southern freedmen were the heroes, the "Redeemers" who overthrew Reconstruction were the villains, and if the era was "tragic," it was because change did not go far enough. Reconstruction had been a time of real progress and its failure a lost opportunity for the South and the nation. But the legacy of Reconstruction—the Fourteenth and Fifteenth Amendments—endured to inspire future efforts for civil rights. As Kenneth Stampp wrote in *The Era of Reconstruction*, a superb summary of revisionist findings published in 1965, "if it was worth four years of civil war to save the Union, it was worth a few years of radical reconstruction to give the American Negro the ultimate promise of equal civil and political rights."

As Stampp's statement suggests, the reevaluation of the first Reconstruction was inspired in large measure by the impact of the second—the modern civil rights movement. And with the waning of that movement in recent years, writing on Reconstruction has undergone still another transformation. Instead of seeing the Civil War and its aftermath as a second American Revolution (as Charles Beard had), a regression into barbarism (as Bowers argued), or a golden opportunity squandered (as the revisionists saw it), recent writers argue that Radical Reconstruction was not really very radical. Since land was not distributed to the former slaves, they remained economically dependent upon their former owners. The planter class survived both the war and Reconstruction with its property (apart from slaves) and prestige more or less intact.

Not only changing times but also the changing concerns of historians have contributed to this latest reassessment of Reconstruction. The hallmark of the past decade's historical writing has been an emphasis upon "social history"—the evocation of the past lives of ordinary Americans—and the downplaying of strictly political events. When applied to Reconstruction, this concern with the "social" suggested that black suffrage and officeholding, once seen as the most radical departures of the Reconstruction era, were relatively insignificant.

Recent historians have focused their investigations not upon the politics of Reconstruction but upon the social and economic aspects of the transition from slavery to freedom. Herbert Gutman's influential study of the black family during and after slavery found little change in family structure or relations between men and women resulting from emancipation. Under slavery most blacks had lived in nuclear family units, although they faced the constant threat of separation from loved ones by sale. Reconstruction provided the opportunity for blacks to solidify their preexisting family ties. Conflicts over whether black women should work in the cotton fields (planters said yes, many black families said no) and over white attempts to "apprentice" black children revealed that the autonomy of family life was a major preoccupation of the freedmen. Indeed, whether manifested in their withdrawal from churches controlled by whites, in the blossoming of black fraternal, benevolent, and self-improvement organizations, or in the demise of the slave quarters and their replacement by small tenant farms occupied by individual families, the quest for independence from white authority and control over their own day-to-day lives shaped the black response to emancipation.

In the post–Civil War South the surest guarantee of economic autonomy, blacks believed, was land. To the freedmen the justice of a claim to land based on their years of unrequited labor appeared self-evident. As an Alabama black convention put it, "The property which they [the planters] hold was nearly all earned by the sweat of *our* brows." As Leon Litwack showed in *Been in the*

Storm So Long, a Pulitzer Prize–winning account of the black response to emancipation, many freedmen in 1865 and 1866 refused to sign labor contracts, expecting the federal government to give them land. In some localities, as one Alabama overseer reported, they "set up claims to the plantation and all on it."

In the end, of course, the vast majority of Southern blacks remained propertyless and poor. But exactly why the South, and especially its black population, suffered from dire poverty and economic retardation in the decades following the Civil War is a matter of much dispute. In *One Kind of Freedom,* economists Roger Ransom and Richard Sutch indicted country merchants for monopolizing credit and charging usurious interest rates, forcing black tenants into debt and locking the South into a dependence on cotton production that impoverished the entire region. But Jonathan Wiener, in his study of postwar Alabama, argued that planters used their political power to compel blacks to remain on the plantations. Planters succeeded in stabilizing the plantation system, but only by blocking the growth of alternative enterprises, like factories, that might draw off black laborers, thus locking the region into a pattern of economic backwardness.

If the thrust of recent writing has emphasized the social and economic aspects of Reconstruction, politics has not been entirely neglected. But political studies have also reflected the postrevisionist mood summarized by C. Vann Woodward when he observed "how essentially nonrevolutionary and conservative Reconstruction really was." Recent writers, unlike their revisionist predecessors, have found little to praise in federal policy toward the emancipated blacks.

A new sensitivity to the strength of prejudice and laissez-faire ideas in the nineteenth-century North has led many historians to doubt whether the Republican party ever made a genuine commitment to racial justice in the South. The granting of black suffrage was an alternative to a long-term federal responsibility for protecting the rights of the former slaves. Once enfranchised, blacks could be left to fend for themselves. With the exception of a few Radicals like Thaddeus Stevens, nearly all Northern policy-makers and educators are criticized today for assuming that, so long as the unfettered operations of the marketplace afforded blacks the opportunity to advance through diligent labor, federal efforts to assist them in acquiring land were unnecessary.

Probably the most innovative recent writing on Reconstruction politics has centered on a broad reassessment of black Republicanism, largely undertaken by a new generation of black historians. Scholars like Thomas Holt and Nell Painter insist that Reconstruction was not simply a matter of black and white. Conflicts within the black community, no less than divisions among whites, shaped Reconstruction politics. Where revisionist scholars, both black and white, had celebrated the accomplishments of black political leaders, Holt, Painter, and others charge that they failed to address the economic plight of the black masses. Painter criticized "representative colored men," as national black leaders were called, for failing to provide ordinary freedmen with effective political leadership. Holt found that black officeholders in South Carolina mostly emerged from the old free mulatto class of Charleston, which shared many assumptions with prominent whites. "Basically bourgeois in their origins and orientation," he wrote, they "failed to act in the interest of black peasants."

In emphasizing the persistence from slavery of divisions between free blacks and slaves, these writers reflect the increasing concern with continuity and conservatism in Reconstruction. Their work reflects a startling extension of revisionist premises. If, as has been argued for the past twenty years, blacks were active agents rather than mere victims of manipulation, then they could not be absolved of blame for the ultimate failure of Reconstruction.

Despite the excellence of recent writing and the continual expansion of our knowledge of the period, historians of Reconstruction today face a unique dilemma. An old interpretation has been overthrown, but a coherent new synthesis has yet to take its place. The revisionists of the 1960s effectively established a series of negative points: the Reconstruction governments were not as bad as had been portrayed, black supremacy was a myth, the Radicals were not cynical manipulators of the freedmen. Yet no convincing overall portrait of the quality of political and social life emerged from their writings. More recent historians have rightly pointed to elements of continuity that spanned the nineteenth-century Southern experience, especially the survival, in modified form, of the plantation system. Nevertheless, by denying the real changes that did occur, they have failed to provide a convincing portrait of an era characterized above all by drama, turmoil, and social change.

Building upon the findings of the past twenty years of scholarship, a new portrait of Reconstruction ought to begin by viewing it not as a specific time period, bounded by the years 1865 and 1877, but as an episode in a prolonged historical process—American society's adjustment to the consequences of the Civil War and emancipation. The Civil War, of course, raised the decisive questions of America's national existence: the relations between local and national authority, the definition of citizenship, the balance between force and consent in generating obedience to authority. The war and Reconstruction, as Allan Nevins observed over fifty years ago, marked the "emergence of modern America." This was the era of the completion of the national railroad network, the creation of the modern steel industry, the conquest of the West and final subduing of the Indians, and the expansion of the mining frontier. Lincoln's America—the world of the small farm and artisan shop—gave way to a rapidly industrializing economy. The issues that galvanized postwar Northern politics—from the question of the greenback currency to the mode of paying holders of the national debt—arose from the economic changes unleashed by the Civil War.

Above all, the war irrevocably abolished slavery. Since 1619, when "twenty negars" disembarked from a Dutch ship in Virginia, racial injustice had haunted American life, mocking its professed ideals even as tobacco and cotton, the products of slave labor, helped finance the nation's economic development. Now the implications of the black presence could no longer be ignored. The Civil War resolved the problem of slavery but, as the Philadelphia diarist Sydney George Fisher observed in June 1865, it opened an even more intractable problem: "What shall we do with the Negro?" Indeed, he went on, this was a problem "*incapable* of any solution that will satisfy both North and South."

As Fisher realized, the focal point of Reconstruction was the social revolution known as emancipation. Plantation slavery was simultaneously a system of labor, a form of racial domination, and the foundation upon which arose a distinctive ruling class within the South. Its demise threw open the most fundamental questions of economy, society, and politics. A new system of labor, social, racial, and political relations had to be created to replace slavery.

The United States was not the only nation to experience emancipation in the nineteenth century. Neither plantation slavery nor abolition were unique to the United States. But Reconstruction was. In a comparative perspective Radical Reconstruction stands as a remarkable experiment, the only effort of a society experiencing abolition to bring the former slaves within the umbrella of equal citizenship. Because the Radicals did not achieve everything they wanted, historians have lately tended to play down the stunning departure represented by black suffrage and officeholding. Former slaves, most fewer than two years removed from bondage, debated the fundamental questions of the polity: What is a republican form of government? Should the state provide equal education for all? How could political equality be reconciled with a society in which property was so unequally distributed? There was something inspiring in the way such men met the challenge of Reconstruction. "I knew nothing more than to obey my master," James K. Greene, an Alabama black politician later recalled. "But the tocsin of freedom sounded and knocked at the door and we walked out like free men and we met the exigencies as they grew up, and shouldered responsibilities."

"You never saw a people more excited on the subject of politics than are the negroes of the south," one planter observed in 1867. And there were more than a few Southern whites as well who in these years shook off the prejudices of the past to embrace the vision of a new South dedicated to the principles of equal citizenship and social justice. One ordinary South Carolinian expressed the new sense of possibility in 1868 to the Republican governor of the state: "I am sorry that I cannot write an elegant stiled letter to your excellency. But I rejoice to think that God almighty has given to the poor of S. C. a Gov. to hear to feel to protect the humble poor without distinction to race or color. . . . I am a native borned S. C. a poor man never owned a Negro in my life nor my father before me. . . . Remember the true and loyal are the poor of the whites and blacks, outside of these you can find none loyal."

Few modern scholars believe the Reconstruction governments established in the South in 1867 and 1868 fulfilled the aspirations of their humble constituents. While their achievements in such realms as education, civil rights, and the economic rebuilding of the South are now widely appreciated, historians today believe they failed to affect either the economic plight of the

emancipated slave or the ongoing transformation of independent white farmers into cotton tenants. Yet their opponents did perceive the Reconstruction
governments in precisely this way—as representatives of a revolution that had
put the bottom rail, both racial and economic, on top. This perception helps
explain the ferocity of the attacks leveled against them and the pervasiveness
of violence in the postemancipation South.

The spectacle of black men voting and holding office was anathema to
large numbers of Southern whites. Even more disturbing, at least in the view
of those who still controlled the plantation regions of the South, was the emergence of local officials, black and white, who sympathized with the plight of
the black laborer. Alabama's vagrancy law was a "dead letter" in 1870, "because those who are charged with its enforcement are indebted to the vagrant
vote for their offices and emoluments." Political debates over the level and
incidence of taxation, the control of crops, and the resolution of contract disputes revealed that a primary issue of Reconstruction was the role of government in a plantation society. During presidential Reconstruction, and after
"Redemption," with planters and their allies in control of politics, the law
emerged as a means of stabilizing and promoting the plantation system. If Radical Reconstruction failed to redistribute the land of the South, the ouster of
the planter class from control of politics at least ensured that the sanctions of
the criminal law would not be employed to discipline the black labor force.

An understanding of this fundamental conflict over the relation between government and society helps explain the pervasive complaints concerning corruption and "extravagance" during Radical Reconstruction. Corruption there
was aplenty; tax rates did rise sharply. More significant than the rate of taxation, however, was the change in its incidence. For the first time, planters and
white farmers had to pay a significant portion of their income to the government, while propertyless blacks often escaped scot-free. Several states, moreover, enacted heavy taxes on uncultivated land to discourage land speculation
and force land onto the market, benefiting, it was hoped, the freedmen.

As time passed, complaints about the "extravagance" and corruption of
Southern governments found a sympathetic audience among influential
Northerners. The Democratic charge that universal suffrage in the South was
responsible for high taxes and governmental extravagance coincided with a
rising conviction among the urban middle classes of the North that city government had to be taken out of the hands of the immigrant poor and returned
to the "best men"—the educated, professional, financially independent citizens unable to exert much political influence at a time of mass parties and
machine politics. Increasingly the "respectable" middle classes began to retreat from the very notion of universal suffrage. The poor were no longer perceived as honest producers, the backbone of the social order; now they became
the "dangerous classes," the "mob." As the historian Francis Parkman put it,
too much power rested with "masses of imported ignorance and hereditary
ineptitude." To Parkman the Irish of the Northern cities and the blacks of the

South were equally incapable of utilizing the ballot: "Witness the municipal corruptions of New York, and the monstrosities of negro rule in South Carolina." Such attitudes helped to justify Northern inaction as, one by one, the Reconstruction regimes of the South were overthrown by political violence.

In the end, then, neither the abolition of slavery nor Reconstruction succeeded in resolving the debate over the meaning of freedom in American life. Twenty years before the American Civil War, writing about the prospect of abolition in France's colonies, Alexis de Tocqueville had written, "If the Negroes have the right to become free, the [planters] have the incontestable right not to be ruined by the Negroes' freedom." And in the United States, as in nearly every plantation society that experienced the end of slavery, a rigid social and political dichotomy between former master and former slave, an ideology of racism, and a dependent labor force with limited economic opportunities all survived abolition. Unless one means by freedom the simple fact of not being a slave, emancipation thrust blacks into a kind of no-man's land, a partial freedom that made a mockery of the American ideal of equal citizenship.

Yet by the same token the ultimate outcome underscores the uniqueness of Reconstruction itself. Alone among the societies that abolished slavery in the nineteenth century, the United States, for a moment, offered the freedmen a measure of political control over their own destinies. However brief its sway, Reconstruction allowed scope for a remarkable political and social mobilization of the black community. It opened doors of opportunity that could never be completely closed. Reconstruction transformed the lives of Southern blacks in ways unmeasurable by statistics and unreachable by law. It raised their expectations and aspirations, redefined their status in relation to the larger society, and allowed space for the creation of institutions that enabled them to survive the repression that followed. And it established constitutional principles of civil and political equality that, while flagrantly violated after Redemption, planted the seeds of future struggle.

Certainly, in terms of the sense of possibility with which it opened, Reconstruction failed. But as Du Bois observed, it was a "splendid failure." For its animating vision—a society in which social advancement would be open to all on the basis of individual merit, not inherited caste distinctions—is as old as America itself and remains relevant to a nation still grappling with the unresolved legacy of emancipation.

Did the Civil War Retard Industrialization?

Thomas C. Cochran

Nations in the twentieth century tend to define their existence largely in economic terms. We as Americans see our economic strength and fate invariably linked to "capitalism" as both an economic and a political way of life. Thus it is not surprising that, historically speaking, the nation has come to attach considerable importance to the development of the American economy. In the traditional view, the Civil War was always considered basic to American economic development. It served as the convenient dividing line between limited economic growth and massive industrial expansion. In the selection here reprinted, however, Thomas C. Cochran, Professor of Economic History at the University of Pennsylvania, posits that the Civil War, rather than generating economic growth, actually retarded its development.

In most textbooks and interpretative histories of the United States the Civil War has been assigned a major role in bringing about the American Industrial Revolution. Colorful business developments in the North—adoption of new machines, the quick spread of war contracting, the boost given to profits by inflation, and the creation of a group of war millionaires—make the war years seem not only a period of rapid economic change but also one that created important forces for future growth. The superficial qualitative evidence is so persuasive that apparently few writers have examined the available long-run statistical series before adding their endorsement to the conventional interpretation. The following quotations taken from the books of two generations of leading scholars illustrate the popular view.

"The so-called Civil War," wrote Charles A. and Mary R. Beard in 1927, "... was a social war ... making *vast changes* in the arrangement of classes, in the accumulation and distribution of wealth, *in the course of industrial development.*" Midway between 1927 and the present, Arthur M. Schlesinger, Sr., wrote: "On these tender industrial growths the Civil War *had the effect of a hothouse.* For reasons already clear ... nearly every branch of industry grew lustily." Harold U. Faulkner, whose textbook sales have ranked near or at the top, said in 1954: "In the economic history of the United States the Civil War was extremely important. . . . In the North *it speeded the Industrial*

From "Did the Civil War Retard Industrialization?" by Thomas C. Cochran, in *Mississippi Valley Historical Review*, September 1961. Reprinted by permission of the *Journal of American History*.

Revolution and the development of capitalism by the prosperity which it brought to industry." The leading new text of 1957, by Richard Hofstadter, William Miller, and Daniel Aaron, showed no weakening of this interpretation: "The growing demand for farm machinery as well as for the 'sinews of war' led to American industrial expansion. . . . Of necessity, *iron, coal, and copper* production boomed during the war years." A sophisticated but still essentially misleading view is presented by Gilbert C. Fite and Jim E. Reese in a text of 1959: "The Civil War proved to be a boon to Northern economic development. . . . Industry, for example, was not created by the war, but wartime demands *greatly stimulated and encouraged industrial development* which already had a good start." In a reappraisal of the Civil War, in *Harper's Magazine* for April, 1960, Denis W. Brogan, a specialist in American institutions, wrote: "It may have been only a catalyst but the War *precipitated the entry* of the United States *into the modern industrial world,* made 'the take-off' (to use Professor W. W. Rostow's brilliant metaphor) come sooner."

In all of these reiterations of the effect of the Civil War on industrialism, statistical series seem to have been largely neglected. None of the authors cited reinforce their interpretations by setting the war period in the context of important long-run indexes of industrial growth. Since 1949, series of the period 1840 to 1890 that would cast doubt on the conventional generalizations have been available in *Historical Statistics of the United States, 1789–1945.* In 1960 a new edition of *Historical Statistics* and the report of the Conference on Research in Income and Wealth in *Trends in the American Economy in the Nineteenth Century* have provided additional material to support the argument that the Civil War retarded American industrial development. These volumes give data for many growth curves for the two decades before and after the war decade—in other words, the long-run trends before and after the event in question. The pattern of these trends is a mixed one which shows no uniform type of change during the Civil War decade, but on balance for the more important series the trend is toward retardation in *rates* of growth rather than toward acceleration. The fact is evident in many series which economists would regard as basic to economic growth, but in order to keep the discussion within reasonable limits only a few can be considered here.

Robert E. Gallman has compiled new and more accurate series for both "total commodity output," including agriculture, and "value added by manufacture," the two most general measures of economic growth available for this period. He writes: "Between 1839 and 1899 total commodity output increased elevenfold, or at an average decade rate of slightly less than 50 percent. . . . Actual rates varied fairly widely, high rates appearing during the decades ending with 1854 and 1884, and a very low rate during the decade ending with 1869." From the over all standpoint this statement indicates the immediately retarding effect of the Civil War on American economic growth, but since most of the misleading statements are made in regard to industrial growth, or particular elements in industrial growth, it is necessary to look in more detail at "value added by manufacture" and some special series. Gallman's series for value added in constant dollars of the purchasing power of 1879 shows a rise of 157 percent from 1839 to 1849; 76 percent from 1849 to 1859; and only 25 percent from 1859 to 1869. By the 1870's the more favorable prewar rates were resumed, with an increase of 82 percent for 1869–1879, and 112 percent for 1879–1889. Thus two decades of very rapid advance, the 1840's and the 1880's, are separated by thirty years of slower growth which falls to the lowest level in the decade that embraces the Civil War.

Pig-iron production in tons, perhaps the most significant commodity index of nineteenth-century American industrial growth, is available year-by-year from 1854 on. Taking total production for five-year periods, output increased 9 percent between the block of years from 1856 to 1860 and the block from 1861 to 1865. That even this slight increase might not have been registered except for the fact that 1857 to 1860 were years of intermittent depression is indicated by an 81 percent increase over the war years in the block of years from 1866 to 1870. If annual production is taken at five-year intervals, starting in 1850, the increase is 24 percent from 1850 to 1855; 17 percent from 1855 to 1860; 1 percent from 1860 to 1865; and 100 percent from 1865 to 1870. While there is no figure available for 1845, the period from 1840 to 1850 shows 97 percent increase in shipments, while for the period 1870 to 1880 the increase was 130 percent. To sum up, depression and war appear to have retarded a curve of production that was tending to rise at a high rate.

Bituminous coal production may be regarded as the next most essential commodity series. After a gain of 199 percent from 1840 to 1850 this series shows a rather steady pattern of increase at rates varying from 119 to 148 percent each decade from 1850 to 1890. The war does not appear to have markedly affected the rate of growth.

In the mid-nineteenth century copper production was not a basic series for recording American growth, but since three distinguished authors have singled it out as one of the indexes of the effect of the war on industry it is best to cite the statistics. Before 1845 production of domestic copper was negligible. By 1850 the "annual recoverable content" of copper from United States mines was 728 tons, by 1860 it was 8,064 tons, by 1865 it was 9,520 tons, and by 1870 it was 14,112 tons. In this series of very small quantities, therefore, the increase from 1850 to 1860 was just over 1,000 percent, from 1860 to 1865 it was 18 percent, and from 1865 to 1870 it was 48 percent.

Railroad track, particularly in the United States, was an essential for industrialization. Here both the depression and the war retarded the rate of growth. From 1851 through 1855 a total of 11,627 miles of new track was laid, from 1856 through 1860, only 8,721 miles, and from 1861 through 1865, only 4,076 miles. After the war the rate of growth of the early 1850's was resumed, with 16,174 miles constructed from 1866 through 1870. Looked at by decades, a rate of over 200 percent increase per decade in the twenty years before the war was slowed to 70 percent for the period from 1860 to 1870, with only a 15 percent increase during the war years. In the next two decades the rate averaged about 75 percent.

Next to food, cotton textiles may be taken as the most representative consumer-goods industry in the nineteenth century. Interference with the flow of southern cotton had a depressing effect. The number of bales of cotton consumed in United States manufacturing rose 143 percent from 1840 to 1850 and 47 percent from 1850 to 1860, but *fell* by 6 percent from 1860 to 1870. From then on consumption increased at a little higher rate than in the 1850's.

While woolen textile production is not an important series in the overall picture of industrial growth, it should be noted that, helped by protection and military needs, consumption of wool for manufacturing more than doubled during the war, and then *fell* somewhat from 1865 to 1870. But Arthur H. Cole, the historian of the woolen industry, characterizes the years from 1830 to 1870 as a period of growth "not so striking as in the decades before or afterwards."

Immigration to a nation essentially short of labor was unquestionably a stimulant to economic growth. Another country had paid for the immigrant's unproductive youthful years, and he came to the United States ready to contribute his labor at a low cost. The pattern of the curve for annual immigration shows the retarding effect of both depression and war. In the first five years of the 1850's an average of 349,685 immigrants a year came to the United States. From 1856 through 1860 the annual average fell to 169,958, and for the war years of 1861 to 1865 it fell further to 160,345. In the first five postwar years the average rose to 302,620, but not until the first half of the 1870's did the rate equal that of the early 1850's. Had there been a return to prosperity instead of war in 1861, it seems reasonable to suppose that several hundred thousand additional immigrants would have arrived before 1865.

In the case of farm mechanization the same type of error occurs as in the annual series on copper production. "Random" statistics such as the manufacture of 90,000 reapers in 1864 are frequently cited without putting them in the proper perspective of the total number in use and the continuing trends. Reaper and mower sales started upward in the early 1850's and were large from 1856 on, in spite of the depression. William T. Hutchinson estimates that most of the 125,000 reapers and mowers in use in 1861 had been sold during the previous five years. While the business, without regard to the accidental coming of the war, was obviously in a stage of very rapid growth, the war years presented many difficulties and may actually have retarded the rate of increase. Total sales of reapers for the period 1861–1865 are estimated at 250,000—a quite ordinary increase for a young industry—but the 90,000 figure for 1864, if it is correct, reinforces the evidence from the McCormick correspondence that this was the one particularly good year of the period. During these years William S. McCormick was often of the opinion that the "uncertainties of the times" made advisable a suspension of manufacturing until the close of the war.

For a broader view of agricultural mechanization the series "value of farm implements and machinery" has special interest. Here the census gives a picture which, if correct, is explicable only on the basis of wartime destruction. Based on constant dollars the dollar value of all loans was more than 15 percent lower than just before the war. If instead of examining loans one looks at total assets of all banks the decline in constant dollars from 1860 to 1870 is reduced to 10 percent, the difference arising from a larger cash position and more investment in government bonds.

Net capital formation would be a more proper index of economic growth than bank loans or assets. Unfortunately, neither the teams of the National Bureau of Economic Research nor those of the Census Bureau have been able to carry any reliable series back of 1868. From colonial times to 1960, however, the chief single form of American capital formation has undoubtedly been building construction. Farm houses, city homes, public buildings, stores, warehouses, and factories have year-by-year constituted, in monetary value, the leading type of capital growth. Gallman has drawn up series for such construction based on estimating the flow of construction materials and adding what appear to be appropriate markups. Admittedly the process is inexact, but because of the importance of construction in reflecting general trends in capital formation it is interesting to see the results. The rate of change for the ten-year period ending in 1854 is about 140 percent; for the one ending in 1859 it is 90 percent; for 1869 it is 40 percent; and for 1879 it is 46 percent. Taking a long view, from 1839 to 1859 the average decennial rate of increase was about 70 percent, and from 1869 to 1899 it was about 40 percent. The *rate* of advance in construction was declining and the war decade added a further dip to the decline.

Since the decline in rate is for the decade, the exact effect of the war years can only be estimated, but the logic of the situation, reinforced by the record of sharp cut-backs in railroad building, seems inescapable: the Civil War, like all modern wars, checked civilian construction. The first year of war was a period of depression and tight credit in the Middle West, which checked residential and farm construction in the area that grew most rapidly before and after the war. In both the East and the West the last two years of the war were a period of rapid inflation which was regarded by businessmen as a temporary wartime phenomenon. The logical result would be to postpone construction for long-term use until after the anticipated deflation. The decline in private railroad construction to a small fraction of the normal rate exemplifies the situation.

Lavish expenditure and speculation by a small group of war contractors and market operators gambling on the inflation seem to have created a legend of high prosperity during the war years. But the general series on fluctuations in the volume of business do not bear this out. Leonard P. Ayres's estimates of business activity place the average for 1861 through 1865 below normal, and Norman J. Silberling's business index is below its normal line for all years of the war. Silberling also has an intermediate trend line for business, which smooths out annual fluctuations. This line falls steadily from 1860 to 1869. Much of Silberling's discussion in his chapter "Business Activity, Prices, and Wars" is in answer to his question: "Why does it seem to be true that despite a temporary stimulating effect of war upon some industries, wars are generally associated with a long-term retarding of business growth . . .?" He puts the Civil War in this general category.

Collectively these statistical estimates support a conclusion that the Civil War retarded American industrial growth. Presentation of this view has been the chief purpose of this article. To try to judge the non-measurable or indirect effects of the war is extremely difficult. But since further discussion of the conventional qualitative factors may help to explain the prevailing evaluation in American texts, it seems appropriate to add some conjectural obiter dicta.

Experience with the apparently stimulating effects of twentieth-century wars on production makes the conclusion that victorious war may retard the growth of an industrial state seem paradoxical, and no doubt accounts in part for the use of detached bits of quantitative data to emphasize the Civil War's industrial importance. The resolution of the paradox may be found in contemporary conditions in the United States and in the nature of the wartime demand. The essential wastefulness of war from the standpoint of economic growth was obscured by the accident that both of the great European wars of the twentieth century began when the United States had a high level of unemployment. The immediate effect of each, therefore, was to put men to work, to increase the national product, and to create an aura of prosperity. Presumably, the United States of the mid-nineteenth century tended to operate close enough to full employment in average years that any wasteful labor-consuming activities were a burden rather than a stimulant.

By modern standards the Civil War was still unmechanized. It was fought with rifles, bayonets, and sabers by men on foot or horseback. Artillery was more used than in previous wars, but was still a relatively minor consumer of iron and steel. The railroad was also brought into use, but the building of military lines offset only a small percentage of the overall drop from the prewar level of civilian railroad construction. Had all of these things not been true, the Confederacy with its small industrial development could never have fought through four years of increasingly effective blockade.

In spite of the failure of direct quantitative evidence to show accelerating effects of the war on rates of economic growth, there could be long-run effects of a qualitative type that would gradually foster a more rapid rate of economic growth. The most obvious place to look for such indirect effects would be in the results of freeing the slaves. Marxists contended that elimination of slavery was a necessary precursor of the bourgeois industrialism which would lead to the socialist revolution. The creation of a free Negro labor force was, of course, of great long-run importance. In the twentieth century it has led to readjustment of Negro population between the deep South and the northern industrial areas, and to changes in the use of southern land.

But economically the effects of war and emancipation over the period 1840 to 1880 were negative. Richard A. Easterlin writes: "In every southern state, the 1880 level of per capita income originating in commodity production and distribution was below, or at best only slightly above that of 1840. . . . [This] attests strikingly to the impact of that war and the subsequent disruption on the southern economy." In general the Negroes became sharecroppers or wage laborers, often cultivating the same land and the same crops as before the war. In qualification of the argument that free Negro labor led to more rapid industrialization it should be noted that the South did not keep up with the national pace in the growth of non-agricultural wealth until after 1900.

Two indirect effects of the war aided industrial growth to degrees that cannot accurately be measured. These were, first, a more satisfactory money market, and, secondly, more security for entrepreneurial activity than in the prewar period. The sharp wartime inflation had the usual effect of transferring income from wage, salary, and interest receivers to those making profits. This meant concentration of savings in the hands of entrepreneurs who would invest in new activities; and this no doubt helps to explain the speculative booms of the last half of the 1860's and first two years of the 1870's which have been treated as the prosperity resulting from the war. Inflation also eased the burdens of those railroads which had excessive mortgage debts. But a great deal of new research would be needed to establish causal connections between the inflationary reallocation of wealth, 1863 to 1865, and the high rate of industrial progress in the late 1870's and the 1880's.

The National Banking Act, providing a more reliable currency for interstate operations, has been hailed as a great aid to business expansion although it would be hard to demonstrate, aside from a few weeks during panics, that plentiful but occasionally unsound currency had seriously interfered with earlier industrial growth. The existence of two and a half billion dollars in federal bonds also provided a basis for credit that was larger than before the war. This led to broader and more active security markets as well as to easier personal borrowing. But two qualifications must be kept in mind. First, local bank lending to favored borrowers had probably tended to be too liberal before the war and was now put on a somewhat firmer basis. In other words, since 1800 a multiplication of banks had made credit relatively easy to obtain in the United States, and in the North this continued to be the situation. Second, the southern banking system was largely destroyed by the war and had to be rebuilt in the subsequent decades. It should also be remembered that by 1875 some 40 percent of the banks were outside the national banking system.

Because of a few colorful speculators like Jay Gould, Daniel Drew, and Jim Fisk, and the immortality conferred on them, initially by the literary ability of the Adams brothers, the New York stock exchange in the postwar decade appears to have mirrored a new era of predatory wealth. But one has only to study the scandals of the London and New York stock exchanges in 1854 to see that there was little growth in the sophistication or boldness of stock operators during these fifteen years. In any case, the exploits of market operators were seldom related in a positive way to economic growth. Even a record of new issues of securities, which is lacking for this period, would chiefly reflect the flow of capital into railroads, banks, and public utilities rather than into manufacturing. Very few "industrial" shares were publicly marketed before the decade of the 1880's; such enterprises grew chiefly from the reinvestment of earnings.

There was strong government encouragement to entrepreneurial activity during the Civil War, but to ascribe to it unusual importance for economic growth requires both analysis of the results and comparison with other periods. Government in the United States has almost always encouraged entrepreneurs. The federal and state administrations preceding the Civil War could certainly be regarded as friendly to business. They subsidized railroads by land grants, subscribed to corporate bond issues, and remitted taxes on new enterprise. Tariffs were low, but railroad men and many bankers were happy with the situation. Whether or not American industrialism was significantly accelerated by the high protection that commenced with the war is a question that economists will probably never settle.

The building of a subsidized transcontinental railroad, held back by sectional controversies in the 1850's, was authorized along a northern route with the help of federal loans and land grants when the southerners excluded themselves from Congress. Putting more than a hundred million dollars into this project in the latter half of the 1860's, however, may have had an adverse effect on industrial growth. In general, the far western roads were built for speculative and strategic purposes uneconomically ahead of demand. They may for a decade, or even two, have consumed more capital than their transportation services were then worth to the economy.

To sum up this part of the obiter dictum, those who write of the war creating a national market tied together by railroads underestimate both the achievements of the two decades before the war and the ongoing trends of the economy. The nation's business in 1855 was nearly as intersectional as in 1870. Regional animosities did not interfere with trade, nor did these feelings diminish after the war. By the late 1850's the United States was a rapidly maturing industrial state with its major cities connected by rail, its major industries selling in a national market, and blessed or cursed with financiers, security flotations, stock markets, and all the other appurtenances of industrial capitalism.

But when all specific factors of change attributable to the war have been deflated, there is still the possibility that northern victory had enhanced the capitalist spirit, that as a consequence the atmosphere of government in Washington among members of both parties was more friendly to industrial enterprise and to northern-based national business operations than had formerly been the rule. It can be argued that in spite of Greenbackers and discontented farmers legislation presumably favorable to industry could be more readily enacted. The Fourteenth Amendment, for example, had as a by-product greater security for interstate business against state regulation, although it was to be almost two decades before the Supreme Court would give force to this protection. By 1876, a year of deep depression, the two major parties were trying to outdo each other in promises of stimulating economic growth. This highly generalized type of argument is difficult to evaluate, but in qualification of any theory of a sharp change in attitude we should remember that industrialism was growing rapidly from general causes and that by the 1870's it was to be expected that major-party politics would be conforming to this change in American life.

Massive changes in physical environment such as those accompanying the rise of trade at the close of the Middle Ages or the gradual growth of industrialism from the seventeenth century on do not lend themselves readily to exact or brief periodization. If factory industry and mechanized transportation be taken as the chief indexes of early industrialism, its spread in the United

States was continuous and rapid during the entire nineteenth century, but in general, advance was greater during periods of prosperity than in depression. The first long period without a major depression, after railroads, canals, and steamboats had opened a national market, was from 1834 to 1857. Many economic historians interested in quantitative calculations would regard these years as marking the appearance of an integrated industrial society. Walter W. Rostow, incidentally, starts his "take-off" period in the 1840's and calls it completed by 1860. Others might prefer to avoid any narrow span of years. Few, however, would see a major stimulation to economic growth in the events of the Civil War.

Finally, one may speculate as to why this exaggerated conception of the role of the Civil War in industrialization gained so firm a place in American historiography. The idea fits, of course, into the Marxian frame of revolutionary changes, but it seems initially to have gained acceptance quite independently of Marxian influences. More concentrated study of the war years than of any other four-year span in the nineteenth century called attention to technological and business events usually overlooked. Isolated facts were seized upon without comparing them with similar data for other decades. The desire of teachers for neat periodization was probably a strong factor in quickly placing the interpretation in textbooks; thus, up to 1860 the nation was agricultural, after 1865 it was industrial. Recent study of American cultural themes suggests still another reason. From most standpoints the Civil War was a national disaster, but Americans like to see their history in terms of optimism and progress. Perhaps the war was put in a perspective suited to the culture by seeing it as good because in addition to achieving freedom for the Negro it brought about industrial progress.

The Winning of the West:
The Expansion of the
Western Sioux

Richard White

The image of the fierce mounted warrior astride his fleet pony—silhouetted against an austere western landscape, surveying the inexorable advance of white civilization's "manifest destiny"—is surely the most enduring stereotype of the American Indian, thanks especially to nineteenth-century pulp fiction and the twentieth-century media. The "winning of the West," however, involves a set of historical complexities that fit the strictures of the stereotype scarcely at all. The process whereby the Plains Indians came to be dispossessed of their lands and cultures during and by virtue of the Plains Wars, argues Professor Richard White of the University of Utah, needs to be more methodically scrutinized and reassessed. Violent episodes between Indians and whites—often bred by cultural misunderstandings—were both a symptom and a foreshadowing of the false beliefs that continued to haunt white-Indian relations. Most needed as a historical corrective, White concludes, is a proper understanding of intertribal relations, especially the rise of the western Sioux to imperial supremacy. Although we have been inclined to view Indian resistance to the whites' "winning of the West" as a short story with a simple plot—the Indian stoically suffering tragic retreat, the inevitable consequence of white territorial ambition—the true story is rather more complex. Close scrutiny of the historical facts yields a different picture, for the western Sioux had already "won the West" by intertribal warfare before the period of white advancement. In fact, traders, and then settlers, *followed* the Sioux, who had largely subdued other Indian tribes militarily prior to the whites' arrival. The "winning of the West" was in great measure, then, a conflict between the two remaining major expanding powers in the area— the Sioux and the white Americans.

The mounted warrior of the Great Plains has proved to be the most enduring stereotype of the American Indian, but like most stereotypes this one conceals more than it reveals. Both popularizers and scholars have been fascinated with the individual warrior to the neglect of plains warfare itself. Harry Turney-

From "The Winning of the West: The Expansion of the Western Sioux in the Eighteenth and Nineteenth Centuries," by Richard White, in *Journal of American History*, 65 (September 1978), pp. 319–343. Copyright © 1985 Organization of American Historians. Reprinted by permission. The author wishes to acknowledge the financial assistance of the Center for the History of the American Indian, Newberry Library.

High, in his classic *Primitive Warfare,* provided the most cogent justification of this neglect. The plains tribes, he contended, were so loosely organized that they remained below the "military horizon"; there really was no warfare on the plains, only battles that were little more than "a mildly dangerous game" fought for largely individual reasons. In much of the literature, intertribal warfare has remained just this: an individual enterprise fought for individualistic reasons—glory, revenge, prestige, and booty. Robert Lowie's statement on warfare, in what is still the standard work on the Plains Indians, can be taken as typical of much anthropological thought: "The objective was never to acquire new lands. Revenge, horse lifting, and lust for glory were the chief motives. . . ."

There is, however, a second group of anthropologists, W. W. Newcomb, Oscar Lewis, Frank Secoy, and more recently Symmes Oliver, who have found this explanation of intertribal warfare unconvincing. These scholars, making much more thorough use of historical sources than is common among anthropologists, have examined warfare in light of economic and technological change. They have presented intertribal warfare as dynamic, changing over time; wars were not interminable contests with traditional enemies, but real struggles in which defeat was often catastrophic. Tribes fought largely for the potential economic and social benefits to be derived from furs, slaves, better hunting grounds, and horses. According to these scholars, plains tribes went to war because their survival as a people depended on securing and defending essential resources.

Historians have by and large neglected this social and economic interpretation of plains warfare and have been content to borrow uncritically from the individualistic school. Western historians usually present intertribal warfare as a chaotic series of raids and counter-raids; an almost irrelevant prelude to the real story: Indian resistance to white invasion. The exaggerated focus on the heroic resistance of certain plains tribes to white incursions has recently prompted John Ewers, an ethnologist, to stress that Indians on the plains had fought each other long before whites came and that intertribal warfare remained very significant into the late nineteenth century.

The neglect by historians of intertribal warfare and the reasons behind it has fundamentally distorted the historical position of the Plains Indians. As Ewers has noted, the heroic resistance approach to plains history reduces these tribes who did not offer organized armed resistance to the white American invaders, and who indeed often aided them against other tribes, to the position of either foolish dupes of the whites or of traitors to their race. Why tribes such as the Pawnee, Mandan, Hidatsa, Oto, Missouri, Crow, and Omaha never took up arms against white Americans has never been subject to much historical scrutiny. The failure of Indians to unite has been much easier to deplore than to examine.

The history of the northern and central American Great Plains in the eighteenth and nineteenth centuries is far more complicated than the tragic retreat of the Indians in the face of an inexorable white advance. From the perspective of most northern and central plains tribes the crucial invasion of the plains during this period was not necessarily that of the whites at all. These tribes had few illusions about American whites and the danger they presented, but the Sioux remained their most feared enemy.

The Teton and Yanktonai Sioux appeared on the edges of the Great Plains early in the eighteenth century. Although unmounted, they were already culturally differentiated from their woodland brothers, the Santee Sioux. The western Sioux were never united under any central government and never developed any concerted policy of conquest. By the mid-nineteenth century the Plains Sioux comprised three broad divisions, the Tetons, Yanktons, and Yanktonais, with the Tetons subdivided into seven component tribes—the Oglala, Brulé, Hunkpapa, Miniconjou, Sans Arc, Two Kettles, and Sihaspas, the last five tribes having evolved from an earlier Sioux group—the Saones. Although linked by common language, culture, interest, and intermarriage, these tribes operated independently. At no time did all the western Sioux tribes unite against any enemy, but alliances of several tribes against a common foe were not unusual. Only rarely did any Teton tribe join an alien tribe in an attack on another group of Sioux.

Between approximately 1685 and 1876 the western Sioux conquered and controlled an area from the Minnesota River in Minnesota, west to the head of the Yellowstone, and south from the Yellowstone to the drainage of the upper Republican River. This advance westward took place in three identifiable stages: initially a movement during the late seventeenth and early eighteenth centuries onto the prairies east of the Missouri, then a conquest of the middle Missouri River region during the late eighteenth and nineteenth centuries, and, finally, a sweep west and south from the Missouri during the early and mid-nineteenth century. Each of these stages possessed its own impetus and rationale. Taken together they comprised a sustained movement by the Sioux that resulted in the dispossession or subjugation of numerous tribes and made the Sioux a major Indian power on the Great Plains during the nineteenth century. . . .

The conquests of the western Sioux during the nineteenth century were politically united in only the loosest sense. The various Sioux tribes expanded for similar demographic, economic, and social reasons, however, and these underlying causes give a unity to the various wars of the Sioux.

Unlike every other tribe on the Great Plains during the nineteenth century, the Sioux appear to have increased in numbers. They were not immune to the epidemics that decimated the other tribes, but most of the Tetons and Yanktonais successfully avoided the disastrous results of the great epidemics, especially the epidemic of 1837 that probably halved the Indian population of the plains. Through historical accident the very conquests of the Sioux protected them from disease. This occurred in two opposite ways. The advance of Oglalas and Brulés to the southwest simply put them out of reach of the main epidemic corridor along the Missouri. Furthermore, Pilcher, the Indian agent on the Missouri, succeeded in giving them advance warning of the danger in 1837, and, unlike the Blackfeet and other nomadic tribes that suffered heavily from the epidemic, they did not come in to trade. The Tetons were infected, and individual tribes lost heavily, but the losses of the Sioux as a whole were comparatively slight. The Yanktons, Yanktonais, and portions of the Saone Tetons, however, dominated the Missouri trade route, but paradoxically this probably helped to save them. In 1832 the Office of Indian Affairs sent doctors up the river to vaccinate the Indians. Many of the Sioux refused to cooperate, but well over a thousand people, mostly Yanktonais, received vaccinations. Only enough money was appropriated to send the doctors as far upriver as the Sioux; so the Mandans and Hidatsas further upriver remained unvaccinated. As a result, when smallpox came, the Yanktonais were partially protected while their enemies in the villages once again died miserably in great numbers. The renewed American efforts at mass vaccination that followed the epidemic came too late for the Mandans, but in the 1840s thousands more Sioux were given immunity from smallpox.

The combination of freedom from disease, a high birth rate (in 1875 estimated as capable of doubling the population every twenty years), and continued migration from the Sioux tribes further east produced a steadily growing population for the western Sioux. Although the various censuses taken by the whites were often little more than rough estimates, the western Sioux appear to have increased from a very low estimate of 5,000 people in 1804 to approximately 25,000 in the 1850s. This population increase, itself partly a result of the new abundance the Sioux derived from the buffalo herds, in turn fueled an increased need for buffalo. The Sioux used the animals not only to feed their expanding population, but also to trade for necessary European goods. Since pemmican, buffalo robes, hides, and tongues had replaced beaver pelts as the main Indian trade item on the Missouri, the Sioux needed secure and profitable hunting grounds during a period when the buffalo were steadily moving west and north in response to hunting pressure on the Missouri.

Increased Indian hunting for trade contributed to the pressure on the buffalo herds, but the great bulk of the destruction was the direct work of white hunters and traders. The number of buffalo robes annually shipped down the Missouri increased from an average of 2,600 between 1815 and 1830 to 40,000 to 50,000 in 1833, a figure that did not include the numbers slaughtered by whites for pleasure. In 1848 Father Pierre-Jean De Smet reported the annual figure shipped downriver to St. Louis to be 25,000 tongues and 110,000 robes.

Despite what the most thorough student of the subject has seen as the Indians' own prudent use of the buffalo, the various tribes competed for an increasingly scarce resource. By the late 1820s the buffalo had disappeared from the Missouri below the Omaha villages, and the border tribes were already in desperate condition from lack of game. The Indians quickly realized the danger further up the Missouri, and upper Missouri tribes voiced complaints about white hunters as early as 1833. By the 1840s observations on the diminishing number of buffalo and increased Indian competition had become commonplace. Between 1833 and 1844 buffalo could be found in large numbers on the headwaters of the Little Cheyenne, but by the mid-1840s they were receding rapidly toward the mountains. The Sioux to a great extent simply had to follow, or move north and south, to find new hunting grounds. Their survival and prosperity depended on their success.

But buffalo hunting demanded more than territory; it also required horses, and in the 1820s, the Sioux were hardly noted for either the abundance or the quality of their herds. Raids and harsh winters on the plains frequently depleted Sioux horse herds, and the Sioux had to replenish them by raiding or trading farther to the south. In this sense the economy of the Sioux depended on warfare to secure the horses needed for the hunt. As Oscar Lewis has pointed out in connection with the Blackfeet, war and horse raiding became important economic activities for the Plains Indians.

The Yanktonais, Yanktons, and Saone Tetons had a third incentive for expansion. Power over the sedentary villagers secured them what Tabeau had called their serfs. Under Sioux domination these villages could be raided or traded with as the occasion demanded, their corn and beans serving as sources of supplementary food supplies when the buffalo failed. A favorite tactic of the Sioux was to restrict, as far as possible, the access of these tribes to both European goods and the hunting grounds, thus forcing the village peoples to rely on the Sioux for trade goods, meat, and robes. To escape this exploitation, the villagers, in alliance with the nomadic tribes who traded with them, waged a nearly constant, if often desultory, war.

It is in this context of increasing population, increasing demand for buffalos and horses, the declining and retreating bison populations, and attempted domination of the sedentary villagers that the final phase of Sioux expansion during the nineteenth century took place. And, as the Omahas had found out, the loose structural organization of the western Sioux worked to make the impetus of their advance even more irresistible. Accommodation with one band or tribe often only served to increase inroads from others. There was no way for a tribe to deal with the whole Sioux nation.

On the Missouri the Sioux had long feared the logical alliance of all the village tribes against them, and they worked actively to prevent it. After 1810, the Arikaras sporadically attempted to break away from Sioux domination by allying themselves with the Mandans and Hidatsas. In response, the Sioux blockaded the villages, cutting them off from the buffalo and stopping the white traders who came up the Missouri from supplying them. The Mandan-Arikara alliance, in turn, sent out war parties to keep the river open. But these alliances inevitably fell apart from internal strains, and the old pattern of oscillating periods of trade and warfare was renewed.

But if the Sioux feared an alliance of the sedentary village tribes, these tribes had an even greater fear of a Sioux-American partnership on the Missouri. The Arikaras, by attacking and defeating an American fur trading party under William Ashley in 1823, precipitated exactly the combination from which they had most to fear. When 1,500 Sioux warriors appeared before their village that year, they were accompanied by United States troops under Colonel Henry Leavenworth. This joint expedition took the Arikara village and sacked it, but the Sioux were disgusted with the performance of their American auxiliaries. They blamed American cautiousness for allowing the Arikaras to escape further upstream. Although they remained friendly to the United States, the whole affair gave them a low estimation of the ability of white soldiers that would last for years. They finished the removal of the Arikaras themselves, forcing them by 1832 to abandon both their sedentary villages and the Missouri River and to move south to live first with, and then just above, the Skidi Pawnees. The Yanktonais, 450 lodges strong, moved in from the Minnesota River to take over the old Arikara territory.

With the departure of the Arikaras, the Mandans and Hidatsas alone remained to contest Sioux domination of the Missouri. In 1836 the Yanktonais, nearly starving after a season of poor hunts, began petty raids on the Mandans and Hidatsas. In retaliation, a Mandan-Hidatsa war party destroyed a Yanktonai village of forty-five lodges, killing more than 150 people and taking fifty prisoners. The Sioux counterattacks cost the Mandans dearly. During the next year they lost over sixty warriors, but what was worse, when the smallpox hit in 1837, the villagers could not disperse for fear of the hostile Yanktonais who still occupied the plains around the villages. The Mandans were very nearly destroyed; the Hidatsas, who attempted a quarantine, lost over half their people, and even the luckless Arikaras returned in time to be ravaged by the epidemic. The villages that survived continued to suffer from Yanktonai attacks and could use the plains hunting grounds only on sufferance of the Sioux.

The Oglala-Brulé advance onto the buffalo plains southwest of the Missouri was contemporaneous with the push up the Missouri and much more significant. Here horse raids and occasional hunts by the Sioux gave way to a concerted attempt to wrest the plains between the Black Hills and the Missouri from the Arapahos, Crows, Kiowas, and Cheyennes. By 1825, the Oglalas, advancing up the drainage of the Teton River, and the Brulés, moving up the drainage of the White River, had dispossessed the Kiowas and driven them south, pushed the Crows west to Powder River, and formed with the Cheyennes and Arapahos an alliance which would dominate the north and central plains for the next half century.

Historians have attributed the movement of the Sioux beyond the Black Hills into the Platte drainage to manipulations of the Rocky Mountain Fur Company, which sought to capture the Sioux trade from the American Fur Company. But, in fact, traders followed the Sioux; the Sioux did not follow the traders. William Sublette of the Rocky Mountain Fur Company did not lure the Sioux to the Platte. He merely took advantage of their obvious advance toward it. He was the first to realize that by the 1830s Brulé and Oglala hunting grounds lay closer to the Platte than to the Missouri, and he took advantage of the situation to get their trade. The arrival of the Sioux on the Platte was not sudden; it had been preceded by the usual period of horse raids. Nor did it break some long accepted balance of power. Their push beyond the Black Hills was merely another phase in the long Sioux advance from the edge of the Great Plains.

What probably lured the Sioux toward the Platte was an ecological phenomenon that did not require the total depletion of game in the area they already held and that was not peculiar to the plains. Borders dividing contending tribes were never firm; between the established hunting territory of each people lay an indeterminate zone, variously described as war grounds or neutral grounds. In this area only war parties dared to venture; it was too dangerous for any band to travel into these regions to hunt. Because little pressure was put on the animal populations of these contested areas by hunters, they provided a refuge for the hard-pressed herds of adjacent tribal hunting grounds. Since buffalo migrations were unpredictable, a sudden loss of game in a large part of one's tribe's territory could prompt an invasion of these neutral grounds. Thus, throughout the nineteenth century, there usually lay at the edges of the Sioux-controlled lands a lucrative area that held an understandable attraction for them. In the contest for these rich disputed areas lay the key not only to many of the Sioux wars, but also to many other aboriginal wars on the continent.

These areas were, of course, never static. They shifted as tribes were able to wrest total control of them from other contending peoples, and so often created, in turn, a new disputed area beyond. Between 1830 and 1860, travelers on the plains described various neutral or war grounds ranging from the Sand Hills north of the Loup River in Nebraska down to the Pawnee Fork of the Arkansas. But for the Sioux four areas stand out: the region below Fort Laramie between the forks of the Platte in dispute during the 1830s; the Medicine Bow–Laramie plains country above Fort Laramie, fought over in the 1840s; the Yellowstone drainage of the Powder, Rosebud, and Big Horn rivers initially held by the Crows but reduced to a neutral ground in the 1840s and 1850s; and portions of the Republican River country contested from the 1840s to the 1870s. Two things stand out in travelers' accounts of these areas: they were disputed by two or more tribes and they were rich in game.

Francis Parkman vividly described and completely misinterpreted an episode of the Sioux conquest of one of these areas, the Medicine Bow Valley, in 1846. He attributed the mustering of the large expedition that went, according to his account, against the Shoshones, and according to others against the Crows, to a desire for revenge for the loss of a son of Whirlwind, an important Sioux chief, during a horse raid on the Shoshones. But in Parkman's account, Whirlwind, who supposedly organized the expedition, decided not to accompany it, and the Oglalas and Saones who went ended up fighting neither the Crows nor the Shoshones. What they did, however, is significant. They moved into disputed Medicine Bow country west of Fort Laramie, land which all of these tribes contested.

The Sioux entered the area warily, took great precautions to avoid, not seek out, Crow and Shoshone war parties, and were much relieved to escape unscathed after a successful hunt. Parkman was disgusted, but the Sioux were immensely pleased with the whole affair. They had achieved the main goal of their warfare, the invasion and safe hunting of disputed buffalo grounds without any cost to themselves. White Shield, the slain man's brother, made another, apparently token, attempt to organize a war party to avenge his loss, but he never departed. The whole episode—from the whites' confusion over what tribe was the target of the expedition, to their misinterpretation of Indian motives, to Parkman's failure to see why the eventual outcome pleased the Sioux—reveals why, in so many accounts, the logic of Indian warfare is lost and wars are reduced to outbursts of random bloodletting. For the Sioux, the disputed area and its buffalo, more that the Shoshones or Crows, were the targets of the expedition; revenge was subordinate to the hunt. Their ability to hunt in safety, without striking a blow, comprised a strategic victory that more than satisfied them. To Parkman, intent on observing savage warriors lusting for blood revenge, all this was unfathomable.

Not all expeditions ended so peacefully, however. Bloodier probes preceded the summer expedition of 1846, and others followed it. When the Sioux arrived in strength on the Platte in the mid-1830s, their raiding parties were already familiar to peoples from the Pawnee south to the Arkansas and the Santa Fe Trail. As early as the 1820s, their allies, the Cheyennes and Arapahos, had unsuccessfully contested hunting grounds with the Skidi Pawnees. But by 1835, these tribes had agreed to make peace.

The arrival of the Oglalas and Brulés at the Laramie River presented both the Pawnees and the Crows with more powerful rivals. The Crows were by now old enemies of the Tetons. Initially as allies of the Mandans and Hidatsas, and later as contestants for the hunting grounds of the plains, they had fought the Sioux for at least fifty years. By the 1840s, however, the once formidable Crows were a much weakened people. As late as the 1830s they had possessed more horses than any other tribe on the upper Missouri and estimates of their armed strength had ranged from 1,000 to 2,500 mounted men, but the years that followed brought them little but disaster. Smallpox and cholera reduced their numbers from 800 to 460 lodges, and rival groups pressed into their remaining hunting grounds. The Blackfeet attacked them from the north while the Saones, Oglalas, and Brulés closed in on the east and south. Threatened and desperate, the Crows sought aid west of the Rockies and increasingly allied themselves with the Shoshones and Flatheads.

The Pawnees, the last powerful horticultural tribe left on the plains, did not have a long tradition of warfare with the Sioux. The four Pawnee tribes—the Republicans, Skidis, Tapages, and Grands—lived in permanent earth-lodge villages on the Platte and Loup rivers, but twice a year they went on extended hunts in an area that stretched from between the forks of the Platte in the north to the Republican, Kansas, and Arkansas rivers in the south. Sioux horse raids had originally worried them very little, but, after the wars with Arapahos and Cheyennes, the growing proximity of the Sioux and their advantage in firearms had begun to concern the Pawnees enough to ask Americans to act as intermediaries in establishing peace. In the 1830s they remained, in the words of their white agent, along with the Sioux, one of the "two master tribes in the Upper Indian Country . . . who govern nearly all the smaller ones."

Under BullBear the Oglalas spearheaded the conquest of the Platte River hunting grounds of the Skidi Pawnees. By 1838, the Pawnee agent reported that the Skidis, fearing the Sioux would soon dominate the entire buffalo country, were contesting "every inch of ground," and, he added, "they are right for the day is not far off when the Sioux will possess the whole buffalo region, unless they are checked." In 1838, smallpox struck both the Oglalas and the Pawnees, but, as happened further north, the populous horticultural villages of the Pawnees suffered far more than the nomadic Sioux bands. The next year the intertribal struggle culminated in a pitched battle that cost the Pawnees between eighty and one-hundred warriors and led to the *de facto* surrender of the Platte hunting grounds by the Skidis.

The murder of BullBear in 1841 during a factional quarrel prompted a split in the Oglalas. One band, the Kiyuskas, BullBear's old supporters, continued to push into the Pawnee lands along the Platte and Smoky Hill rivers, while the other faction, the Bad Faces, moved west and north often joining with the Saone bands who were pushing out from the Missouri in attacks on the Crows. During these advances the Utes and Shoshones would be added to the ranks of Teton enemies, and further north the Yanktonais and Hunkpapas pushed into Canada, fighting the Metis, Plains Crees, and Assiniboines.

The Oregon, California, and Utah migrations of the 1840s made the Platte River Valley an American road across the plains. Like the traders on the Missouri before them, these migrants drove away game and created a new avenue for epidemic diseases, culminating in the cholera epidemic of 1849–1850. For the first time, the whites presented a significant threat to Sioux interests, and this conflict bore as fruit the first signs of overt Teton hostility since Chouteau's and Pryor's expeditions. But on the whole whites suffered little from the initial Teton reaction to the Oregon trail. The Crows and Pawnees bore the consequences of the decline of the Platte hunting grounds.

The Brulé and Kiyuska Oglalas attacked the Pawnee on the South Platte and the Republican. The Tetons did not restrict their attacks to the buffalo grounds; along with the Yanktons and Yanktonais from the Missouri, they attacked the Pawnees in their villages and disrupted the whole Pawnee economy. While small war parties stole horses and killed women working in the fields, large expeditions with as many as 700 men attacked the villages themselves. This dual assault threatened to reduce the Pawnees to starvation, greatly weakening their ability to resist.

The Sioux struck one of their most devastating blows in 1843, destroying a new village the Pawnees had built on the Loup at the urging of the whites. They killed sixty-seven people and forced the Pawnees back to the Platte, where they were threatened with retribution by whites for their failure to remove as agreed. The Pawnees vainly cited American obligations under the treaty of 1833 to help defend them from attacks by other tribes; and they also repeatedly sought peace. Neither availed. Unlike the Otos, Omahas, and Poncas, who eventually gave up all attempts to hunt on the western plains, the Pawnees persisted in their semiannual expeditions. The tribal census taken in 1859 reveals the price the Pawnees paid. When Zebulon Pike had visited the Pawnees in 1806 he found a roughly equivalent number of men and women in each village. In his partial census, he gave a population of 1,973 men and 2,170 women, exclusive of children. In 1859, agent William Dennison listed 820 men and 1,505 women; largely because of war, women now outnumbered men by nearly two to one.

The final blow came in 1873, three years before the Battle of the Little Bighorn, when the Sioux surprised a Pawnee hunting party on the Republican River, killing about 100 people. The Pawnees, now virtually prisoners in their reservation villages, gave in. They abandoned their Nebraska homeland and, over the protests of their agents, moved to Indian Territory. White settlers may have rejoiced at their removal, but it was the Sioux who had driven the Pawnees from Nebraska.

The experience of the Crows was much the same. Attacked along a front that ran from the Yellowstone to the Laramie Plains, they were never routed, but their power declined steadily. The Sioux drove them from the Laramie Plains and then during the 1850s and 1860s pushed them farther and farther up the Yellowstone. In the mid-1850s, Edwin Denig, a trapper familiar with the plains, predicted their total destruction, and by 1862 they had apparently been driven from the plains and into the mountains. They, too, would join the Americans against the Sioux.

In a very real sense the Americans, because of their destruction of game along the Missouri and Platte, had stimulated this warfare for years, but their first significant intervention in intertribal politics since the Leavenworth expedition came with the celebrated Laramie Peace Conference of 1851. Although scholars have recognized the importance of both intertribal warfare and the decline of the buffalo in prompting this conference, they have, probably because they accepted without question the individualistic interpretation of Indian wars, neglected the Indian political situation at the time of the treaty. They have failed to appreciate the predominance of the Sioux-Cheyenne-Arapaho alliance on the northern and central plains.

By 1851, American Indian officials has recognized that white travel and trade on the Great Plains had reduced the number of buffalo and helped precipitate intertribal wars. They proposed to restore peace by compensating the Indians for the loss of game. Their motives for this were hardly selfless, since intertribal wars endangered American travelers and commerce. Once they had established peace and drawn firm boundaries between the tribes, they could hold a tribe responsible for any depredations committed within its allotted area. Furthermore, by granting compensation for the destruction of game, the government gave itself an entrée into tribal politics: by allowing or withholding payments, they could directly influence the conduct of the Indians.

Although American negotiators certainly did not seek tribal unity in 1851, it is ethnocentric history to contend that the Fort Laramie Treaty allowed the Americans to "divide and conquer." Fundamentally divided at the time of the treaty, the plains tribes continued so afterward. The treaty itself was irrelevant; both the boundaries it created and its prohibition of intertribal warfare were ignored from the beginning by the only tribal participants who finally mattered, the Sioux.

Indeed the whole conference can be interpreted as a major triumph for the Tetons. In a sense, the Fort Laramie Treaty marked the height of Sioux political power. Of the 10,000 Indians who attended the conference, the great majority of them were Sioux, Cheyennes, and Arapahos. Sioux threats kept the Pawnees and all but small groups of Crows, Arikaras, Hidatsas, and Assiniboines from coming to Fort Laramie. The Shoshones came, but the Cheyennes attacked their party and part turned back. With the Sioux and their allies so thoroughly dominating the conference, the treaty itself amounted to both a recognition of Sioux power and an attempt to curb it. But when American negotiators tried to restrict the Sioux to an area north of the Platte, Black Hawk, an Oglala, protested that they held the lands to the south by the same right the Americans held their lands, the right of conquest: "These lands once belonged to the Kiowas and the Crows, but we whipped those nations out of them, and in this we did what the white men do when they want the lands of the Indians." The Americans conceded, granting the Sioux hunting rights, which, in Indian eyes, confirmed title. The Sioux gladly accepted American presents and their tacit recognition of Sioux conquests, but, as their actions proved, they never saw the treaty as a prohibition of future gains. After an American war with the Sioux and another attempt to stop intertribal warfare in 1855, Bear's Rib, a Hunkpapa chief, explained to Lieutenant G. K. Warren that the Tetons found it difficult to take the American prohibition of warfare seriously when the Americans themselves left these conferences only to engage in wars with other Indians or with the Mormons.

After the treaty, the lines of conflict on the plains were clearly drawn. The two major powers in the area, the Sioux and the Americans, had both advanced steadily and with relatively little mutual conflict. Following the treaty they became avowed and recognized rivals. Within four years of the treaty, the first American war with the Tetons would break out; and by the mid-1850s, American officers frankly saw further war as inevitable. The Sioux, in turn, recognized the American threat to their interests, and the tribes, in a rare display of concerted action, agreed as a matter of policy to prohibit all land cessions and to close their remaining productive hunting grounds to American intrusions. These attempts consistently led to war with the Americans. After a century of conquest the Sioux had very definite conceptions of the boundaries of their tribal territory. Recent historians and some earlier anthropologists contended that Indians never fought for territory, but if this is so, it is hard to explain the documented outrage of the Saones, Oglalas, and Brulés at the cession of land along the Missouri by the Yanktons in 1858. The Tetons had moved from this land decades before and had been replaced by the Yanktons, but from the Teton point of view the whole western Sioux nation still held title to the territory and the Yanktons had no authority to sell it. Fearing that acceptance of annuities would connote recognition of the sale, the Saone tribes refused them, and the cession provoked a crisis on the western plains and hardened Teton ranks against the Americans.

The warfare between the northern plains tribes and the United States that followed the Fort Laramie Treaty of 1851 was not the armed resistance of a people driven to the wall by American expansion. In reality these wars arose from the clash of two expanding powers—the United States, and the Sioux and their allies. If, from a distance, it appears that the vast preponderance of strength rested with the whites, it should be remembered that the ability of the United States to bring this power to bear was limited. The series of defeats the Sioux inflicted on American troops during these years reveals how real the power of the Tetons was.

Even as they fought the Americans, the Sioux continued to expand their domination of plains hunting grounds, as they had to in order to survive. Logically enough, the tribes the Sioux threatened—the Crows, Pawnees, and Arikaras especially—sided with the Americans, providing them with soldiers and scouts. For white historians to cast these people as mere dupes or traitors is too simplistic. They fought for their tribal interests and loyalties as did the Sioux.

It is ironic that historians, far more than anthropologists, have been guilty of viewing intertribal history as essentially ahistoric and static, of refusing to examine critically the conditions that prompted Indian actions. In too much Indian history, tribes fight only "ancient" enemies, as if each group were doled out an allotted number of adversaries at creation with whom they battled mindlessly through eternity. Historians have been too easily mystified by intertribal warfare, too willing to see it as the result of some ingrained cultural pugnacity. This is not to argue that the plains tribes did not offer individual warriors incentives of wealth and prestige that encouraged warfare, but, as Newcomb pointed out, the real question is why the tribe placed such a premium on encouraging warriors. This is essentially a historical question. Without an understanding of tribal and intertribal histories, and an appreciation that, like all history, they are dynamic, not static, the actions of Indians when they come into conflict with whites can be easily and fatally distorted.